1500mc
01

SAMUEL BECKETT

His Works and
His Critics

Raymond Federman
and John Fletcher

SAMUEL BECKETT

His Works and His Critics

An Essay in Bibliography

UNIVERSITY OF CALIFORNIA PRESS
BERKELEY / LOS ANGELES / LONDON   1970

University of California Press
Berkeley and Los Angeles, California
University of California Press, Ltd.
London, England
Copyright © 1970 by The Regents of the University of California
ISBN: 0-520-01475-8
Library of Congress Catalog Card Number: 68-23782
Designed by W. H. Snyder
Printed in the United States of America

Acknowledgments

It is not possible to compile a bibliography such as this without drawing heavily on the work of others, and we have consulted freely the sources listed in chapter 14. In this connection, we offer special thanks to Joan L. Ensink, who in a spirit of true scholarly generosity gave us a free hand to mine the riches of her M.A. thesis, "Samuel Beckett: An Annotated Bibliography of Criticism, 1934-1965" (Columbia University, 1966). As a result, we have been able to include several items first listed by her. Moreover, we were able to consult Robin J. Davis' excellent University of London Diploma in Librarianship bibliography of Samuel Beckett's works, and to check all discrepancies between his data and our own, thereby reducing in this compilation, it is hoped, the chances of error in the chapters devoted to Samuel Beckett's works. In addition to the sources listed in chapter 14, we have also been able to consult the files of clippings relating to Beckett's literary activities held at the offices of the Éditions de Minuit, Paris, by kind permission of Jérôme Lindon and with the indulgence of his staff, who gladly tolerated the presence of researchers and willingly answered questions, as did Mr. Lindon himself. Similar generosity and forbearance were shown by Geneviève Serreau whenever we called at the *Lettres Nouvelles* office in Paris to ask questions and to examine her collection of clippings relating to the first production of *En attendant Godot* in her husband's Théâtre Babylone. More recently, Dr. A. J. Leventhal, formerly of Trinity College, Dublin, handed over to us his valuable set of index cards relating to articles and reviews devoted to Beckett's work; the bibliography as a whole has benefited from the information generously supplied by this old friend of Samuel Beckett.

Others who unstintingly gave help, information, and advice can only be listed briefly, but we extend our grateful thanks to them all: Louis Allen, Yoram Bar-David, Professor Jacques Benay, Theodore Besterman, Roger Blin, Konrad Blumenstock, Claude Bonnefoy of Roussillon, Vaucluse, Pierre Bordas, Marion Boyars, James Campbell, J. Cazemajou, Professor Ross Chambers, Chatto and Windus Ltd., London, Claude Clergé, H. Alan Clodd, Professor Richard N. Coe, Professor Ruby Cohn, Professor Yves Courteville, Pierre Coustillas, Professor K. G. W. Cross, the late Nancy Cunard, the late Leslie Daiken, Professor V. Dupont, Professor Richard Ellmann, Martin Esslin, Faber and Faber Ltd., London, Peter Faulkner, Professor Brian T. Fitch, David Fletcher, Professor Hugh Ford, Norman Franklin of Routledge and Kegan Paul Ltd., London, Lois Friedberg-Dobry, Professor Melvin J. Friedman, Dr. Niklaus Gessner, Stuart Gilbert, Peggy Guggenheim, Sandra K. Harlan of Indiana

University Press, Bloomington, Indiana, W. Harrison, Josette Hayden, the staff of Heugel et Cie, Paris, John Hewitt, Mary M. Hirth and the Committee on the Use of Literary and Historical Manuscripts at the University of Texas Library, Austin, Texas, Peter C. Hoy, Professor A. N. Jeffares, Roger Joulain, Fernand Lagarde, F. N. Lees, Professor J. W. McFarlane, Luís Carlos Maciel, Elisabeth Maltzahn of Suhrkamp Verlag, Frankfort on the Main, Nicole Mangin of Galerie Maeght, Paris, Christian Marc, Dr. J. H. Marshall, Professor Jean-Jacques Mayoux, Oliver and Boyd Ltd., Edinburgh, Scotland, John Pilling, Jacques Putnam, Hilary Pyle and F. J. E. Hurst of the Library, Trinity College, Dublin, Owen Rackleff, Professor Bodo Richter, Professor Christopher Ricks, Milton Rosenthal, Professor B. A. Rowley, Professor Michel Rybalka, Victor Sage, Judith Schmidt of Grove Press, Inc., New York City, Dr. J. Schwartz, John B. Simon, the editor of the *Times Literary Supplement*, Arthur Uphill, Professor Eugene Webb, Webb Son and Co., Ltd., London, and Hugh Ross Williamson.

These institutions have generously cooperated in our research: the Bibliothèque Nationale, the British Broadcasting Corp. (BBC), the British Museum, the University of California at Santa Barbara Library, the Cambridge University Library, the University of Chicago Library, the Columbia University Library, the Library of Congress, the Durham University Library, the University of East Anglia Library, the State University of New York at Buffalo Library, the Ohio State University Library, the National Theatre at the Old Vic, London, the Library of Princeton University, the Radiodiffusion-Télévision française (ORTF), the Sterling Library, University of London, the Bibliothèque municipale de Toulouse, the Bibliothèque de l'Université de Toulouse, and the Waddington Galleries, London.

Finally, we acknowledge the constant forbearance and help of our wives, the patient and careful editing of the final manuscript by Mrs. Teresa Joseph, and the vigilant attention paid to the proofs by Mrs. Grace H. Stimson, both of the University of California Press, and the financial assistance of the Research Funds of the State University of New York at Buffalo and of the University of Durham. Our warmest thanks of all, however, must go to Samuel Beckett himself, without whose ready answers to our questions, patient help, and constant generosity this bibliography would have been far more incomplete and imperfect than it is. With all its defects we would like, nevertheless, to dedicate this book to him, offering it as the expression of our deep admiration for his genius and in modest recognition of one of the most profoundly original and creative talents at work in the literature of today.

R. F.

J. F.

Contents

Introduction

As this book goes to press, Samuel Beckett, at the age of sixty, is still writing, and we give in an appendix ten different drafts and the English translation from the French of his most recent text, *Bing*. It may therefore seem premature to compile a bibliography of his works and of the critical reaction to them. It is partly for this reason that we have chosen to give this volume a slightly different title than is usual in such instances. Although we have made every effort to compile an accurate, up-to-date, and reasonably complete (to 1966) bibliography, we are fully aware of the provisional nature of our work and feel no obligation to apologize for this. Later on, a possible second edition might correct errors, add further material, and generally attempt to round off an enterprise that in the nature of things we must consider *inachevé* at the present time. [At the last moment we were able to update (to 1968) the sections on Beckett's works and books devoted entirely to his work. It was, however, impossible to do so for the other sections.]

The other reason for our somewhat unorthodox title is the somewhat unorthodox nature of our book, which is not organized on lines usual for bibliographies. We therefore see the necessity of explaining our procedure in this introduction.

First of all, we should perhaps attempt to answer the question, "Why a bibliography?" To this we can only say that we have long been aware of the need for a full, detailed, and accurate list of Samuel Beckett's published and unpublished writings and of the reactions of his critics, and that this need has been echoed by other scholars, both in their published utterances and in their kind private expressions of encouragement to us to persevere in our task. There can be little doubt that Beckett is now receiving the sort of attention given only to great writers; the response to him is not only reflected in this book but will also be sharpened, we hope, as a result of our labors in correcting errors, clearing away misunderstandings, and exploding certain myths that have inevitably accumulated around Beckett's difficult and challenging *œuvre*. Arduous as the task has sometimes been, it was worthwhile, and we can only hope that others will come to share our view when they see the sheer bulk of the data already available and increasing every month around the works of Samuel Beckett. Some order had to be imposed on this chaos, and this is what we have sought to do.

Our methods may disconcert, and so we should attempt to clarify them. For quick reference, every entry has been numbered; to allow for eventual addition or revisions, we have jumped to the next 100 number at the beginning of each new chapter. For instance, chapter 5, "Books Devoted Entirely to Samuel Beckett," begins with number **700** and ends with number **731**; therefore, chapter 6, "Dissertations and Theses on Samuel Beckett," begins with number **800**. To simplify cross-reference, the number scheme adopted throughout is according to a decimal system. The importance of an item is indicated by the decimal (major independent items are assigned whole numbers such as **377**; minor dependent items are assigned a number like **377.001** or **377.1**). The original edition or the first publication of a text receives a whole number, **377**. The publication of the same text by a different publisher, or the reprinting of a poem, a story, or an excerpt in a different journal, is numbered **377.1**. The second edition of a volume by the same publisher is numbered **377.101**, third edition, **377.102**, and so on. A further advantage of this system lies in the possibility of grouping "families" of items (e.g., **376.1**, the British edition of *Endgame,* and **376.11**, the paperback reprint of the same), thus avoiding confusion and clearly establishing priorities.

In chapter 5, "Books Devoted Entirely to Samuel Beckett," where reviews of these books are listed, we used such numbers as **1a**, **1b**, and so on, for listing reviews. Otherwise, all other entries for criticism receive a whole number.

Our classification throughout is mainly chronological: Beckett's English works, for example, run from **1** (*Dante . . . Bruno . Vico . . Joyce*) straight through, irrespective of the importance of any given item, to **46** (*Come and Go*), taking en route everything from whole volume to minor poem, each in its approximate chronological position, as far as this can be ascertained. A similar procedure governs the classification of material in the sections devoted to Beckett criticism, where the principle of alphabetical grouping within the year is adopted.

We were of the opinion that such a method of classification was best suited to show the growth of Beckett's *œuvre* in Part One and the evolution of critical attitudes to it in Part Two. In the first instance, no other grouping would have revealed the development from early dilettantism and preciosity to the vital experimentation of recent years, just as in the second instance no other classification would have brought out the movement from early journalistic superficiality distinguished by some perceptive criticism to today's exact and penetrating scholarship which takes for granted Beckett's importance.

Turning now to individual chapters of the bibliography, we feel the necessity to make certain observations to help the user find his way. In Part One, Beckett's works are grouped by language of composition, because it is such a crucial matter in his case; English works are placed first, not only because Beckett's mother tongue is English, but because he began writing in that language. Immediately after this come the translations into French of the English works that have been translated (it should be emphasized at this point that in most cases Beckett has taken a hand in his own translating), listed as usual in chronological order. Next come the works in French, followed by their translations into English, and after that Beckett's translations of works other than his own and various miscellaneous items such as manifestos and notes. Finally, all known unpublished works by Samuel Beckett, whether extant or not, are listed in chronological order of supposed composition. It will be noticed that much detail is given in the chapters on Beckett's works; this is because we have directed those chapters to such categories of users as literary critics, scholars, librarians, and bibliophiles, and we have tried to keep the interests of each in mind. The only way of ensuring that all needs are met is to give as much detail as possible short of pedantry.

Throughout the bibliography, all items have been carefully checked for accuracy, but it will be appreciated that we were to some extent dependent on such sources of information as publishers' records, so that our data cannot be guaranteed. Furthermore, those who are accustomed to consulting bibliographies and who find our practice different in some ways, should recognize that we have adapted the rules, such as they are, to suit the case of a living writer and to meet the difficulties of identifying, distinguishing, and tracing divergent editions in the field of modern book production. Finally, certain items are omitted from the Works chapters, such as book blurbs (for Alexander Trocchi's *Cain's Book* and Henry Miller's *Tropic of Cancer*) lifted without the author's express permission from private letters, and by the same token unpublished letters (as opposed to published letters) are not listed, because we felt that to catalogue these would be an unjustified violation of Mr. Beckett's privacy.

Nevertheless, we hope that the section devoted to Beckett's works, with all its possible oversights and errors, will show not only how many-sided is his creative talent, but also how popular some of his books, such as *En attendant Godot,* have been, each edition of which has run into several reprints.

The chapters devoted to Samuel Beckett criticism are arranged in order of diminishing importance. First come books written exclusively about Beckett. They already make an impressive total and range from German and Portuguese to English and French; not all are of equal value by any means, but we have sought to treat each one impartially, following every book by a selection of the most relevant reviews devoted to it on publication. Next we list unpublished dissertations and theses devoted exclusively or in part to Samuel Beckett, followed by the special Beckett issues of journals, in which articles are often reprinted or translated from other sources, and not infrequently taken up again elsewhere (our cross-references should make this clear). Where a journal or a book is devoted exclusively to Beckett we reproduce the table of contents, because we feel it supplies the nature of the works in question. Next are listed books containing a chapter or a substantial section on Beckett. This is followed by a selection of the many books that refer to him briefly or merely in passing. Here our choice was determined primarily by what we were able to consult ourselves and found worthy of mention.

In the substantial section on articles devoted to Samuel Beckett, we have supplied summaries and critical comments, as we have done with books, on as many as possible, especially those written in English or French, unless the title itself indicated the content. All material that did not legitimately fall within this section has been grouped in chapter 11: book reviews, play notices, letters to editors, passing comments, allusions, and notes of various kinds are listed but not abstracted, and only a selection of the massive quantity of material extant could be given.

Our geographical coverage, though fairly wide, does not extend to the Far East or to South Africa, and one should not be disappointed if he fails to find entered a clipping he once took from a Tokyo newspaper, which reveals religious overtones in *Waiting for Godot*. We could not hope to list everything, and so we have adopted the uneasy compromise of listing a little of most things, short of omitting chapter 11 altogether. We can only beg indulgence of anyone who feels that we should have concentrated less, say, on Swedish newspaper items and more on Hungarian. It may be of some interest to many scholars to know that a Polish bibliography lists more than fifty items on *En attendant Godot* even before the play was translated into English.

Certain points need to be made about the sections devoted to criticism before we leave them. First, "anonymous" means either that the article or review is unsigned or simply that we have no information about its author. Second, all such anonymous pieces are grouped at the beginning of their respective years as being outside normal alphabetical sequence. Third, anyone interested in theater and in Beckett as playwright would wish to consult regularly such journals as *Tulane Drama Review, Modern Drama, Drama Survey, Cahiers de la Compagnie Madeleine Renaud – Jean-Louis Barrault, Plays and Players,* and so on, where Beckett is often mentioned: we have only abstracted the articles that deal specifically with his work. Fourth, certain patterns should emerge of themselves, but we briefly outline them here. The user will note, for instance, that the British reviews of the thirties give way to the French notices of the early fifties, with a natural gap during the war years; soon other countries (Germany, Switzerland, and others) take over, only to be rapidly outstripped by the United States, and by Great Britain again: a fairly accurate notion of the spread and nature of Beckett's fame over the years should therefore emerge from our work. A further aspect of note is the exploitation by many writers of their own work: a review is reprinted almost without alteration in another journal and then reproduced in a book, even when the value of the particular critical point being made was long since surpassed. Similarly, a critical idea put forward by one writer will be taken by others and echoed for several years. This can be almost comic at times: far too many pieces are entitled "Waiting for Beckett" or play on the notion of arrivals or noncomings; and, as Joan Ensink points out in the introduction to her thesis, critics flagrantly contradict each other, with frequent if unconscious humor.

The importance of the British Broadcasting Corporation in championing Beckett's work emerges from the large number of items in the BBC's journal *The Listener,* not to mention the many broadcasts devoted to Beckett on the BBC. Chapter 12 lists some of the criticism of Samuel Beckett on the BBC.

In chapter 13 we have gathered items of a primarily biographical interest for the convenience of those especially concerned with that aspect of the bibliography, but ample cross-references link material here with that in other chapters. In chapter 14 are listed the principal bibliographical sources used; these should be consulted to bring our bibliography up-to-date in coming years. *French VII Bibliography* should prove especially valuable in this connection.

Appendix I lists, by kind permission of the institutions concerned, the priceless manuscripts and other material held at the Ohio State University and University of Texas libraries, and Appendix II presents the ten drafts of *Bing* followed by the author's English translation *Ping;* these should convince the skeptics that Beckett is neither a hoax nor a careless writer, since it is doubtful if many pages written by more prolific authors have required more labor than the few that make up *Bing.* Our main purpose, however, in including these texts is to show variants in a specific Beckett work, as explained in the brief introduction we offer with the texts.

Appendix III consists of an alphabetical list of titles of Beckett's main works, with reference numbers as used in this bibliography. It serves as a quick guide to the works of Beckett. Appendix IV comprises two lists, one for periodicals and journals, another for newspapers, in which criticism of Beckett's works has been published and which appear in the body of this bibliography, both lists showing places of publication. Shortened or abbreviated forms of titles employed in the bibliography are also listed. These two lists also serve as a quick reference to where most Beckett criticism has been or is likely to be published.

Finally, the Index will guide the user to any author, title, periodical, or printer with comparative ease and speed by means of its reference number.

We wish to conclude by saying that this book could not have been produced without the closest collaboration between the two compilers working in complete harmony over several years. Nevertheless, it was clear from the outset that a rough division of labor was necessary if wasteful duplication was to be avoided. Thus John Fletcher was primarily responsible for establishing the sections dealing with Samuel Beckett's works, book reviews, odd notes, biographical items, and the first two appendixes, while Raymond Federman was concerned with setting up the serious Beckett criticism: books, dissertations, special issues, and articles, and abstracting the items in these sections. Within this broad pattern, and for obvious geographical reasons, John Fletcher has taken general responsibility for the continent of Europe, and Raymond Federman for the Western Hemisphere.

We will be most grateful to anyone who notices an error or an omission for communicating with either of us.

Raymond Federman

John Fletcher

April 1969

Part One
The Works of Samuel Beckett

1.
Published Works in English

1929

Dante . . . Bruno.Vico . . Joyce

Critical essay on *Work in Progress,* by James Joyce.
About 6,000 words.

1 First published in *Our Exagmination* by Shakespeare and Company, Paris, 1929 [May 27].
[i-ii] *blank* [iii] *half title* [iv] *blank* [v] OUR EXAGMINATION | ROUND HIS FACTIFICATION | FOR INCAMINATION | OF WORK IN PROGRESS | BY | SAMUEL BECKETT, MARCEL BRION, FRANK BUDGEN, | STUART GILBERT, EUGENE JOLAS, VICTOR LLONA, | ROBERT McALMON, THOMAS McGREEVY, | ELLIOT PAUL, JOHN ROD-KER, ROBERT SAGE, | WILLIAM CARLOS WILLIAMS. | *with* | *LETTERS OF PROTEST* | BY | G.V.L. SLINGSBY AND VLADIMIR DIXON. | SHAKESPEARE AND COMPANY | SYLVIA BEACH | 12, RUE DE L'ODÉON — PARIS | [short rule] | M CM XX IX [vi] Tous droits de reproduction, de traduction | et d'adaptation réservés pour tous pays. | *Copyright by Sylvia Beach, 1929.* [vii] TABLE OF CONTENTS | [short rule] | DANTE . . . BRUNO.VICO . . JOYCE, by Samuel Beckett [etc.] [viii] *blank* [1] DANTE . . . BRUNO.VICO . . JOYCE | BY | *SAMUEL BECKETT* [2] *blank* [3]-22[text of Beckett's article] [23]-194[rest of text] [195] 96 COPIES OF THIS BOOK | HAVE BEEN PRINTED ON | VERGÉ D'ARCHES NUMBERED | 1-96 [196] [rule] | CHARTRES. — IM-PRIMERIE DURAND, RUE FULBERT (5-1929). | [rule]. [Endpaper] *blank.* 19 cm; Arches copies, 20 cm. Soft cover, cream; front cover, wheel device, title on circle with alphabetically and clockwise the twelve names as spokes, over publisher's imprint and date: SHAKESPEARE AND COMPANY | 12, RUE DE L'ODÉON, PARIS | M CM XX IX. Back cover, list of works by James Joyce; title in vertical caps. on spine. (Some copies rubber-stamped at foot of title page MADE IN | GREAT BRITAIN.)

1929

1.01   Reprinted in *Transition*, 16-17 (June, 1929), 242-253. [Published, with **2**, under general heading "British Isles."]

1.1   Second (British) edition [1936]. Printed from the same type as above, but for imprint, p. [v]: FABER AND FABER LIMITED | 24, RUSSELL SQUARE | LONDON, W.C.1., and p. [vi], which merely reads: PRINTED IN FRANCE | ALL RIGHTS RE- SERVED. 18¾ cm. Hardbound, turquoise cloth; title in vertical gold caps. on spine.

1.11   Reissued Feb. 23, 1962. Photographic reprint.
            [i] *half title* [ii] *blank* [iii] as [v] above, but for imprint: FABER AND FABER | 24 Russell Square | London [iv] *First published in mcmxxix* | [...] | *Second impression mcmlxi* | *Printed in Great Britain* | *by Bradford and Dickens, London, W.C.1.* | [...] [v] TABLE OF CON- TENTS [...] [vi] *blank* [vii-viii] INTRODUCTION (1961) [signed] Sylvia Beach. [195-196] *blank*. 21 cm. Hardbound, blue cloth; title etc. in vertical and horizontal gold italics on spine. Note on p. [iv] incorrect date and false impression conveyed that 1929 and 1936 eds. were simultaneous in 1929.

1.2   Third edition (American). *An Exagmination of James Joyce: An- alyses of the "Work in Progress,"* by Samuel Beckett, [etc.] (Norfolk, Conn.: New Directions, 1939); identical with **1** except for overstamp on title page and information concerning printer and copyright verso.

1.21   Reprinted in 1962 by John Dickens and Conner, Northampton, England (similar to **1.11**).

NOTE. It seems fairly certain that the essay was issued in volume form before it appeared in *Transition;* Stuart Gilbert in a letter of July 3, 1964, "vaguely remembers" that this was the case, but Professor Richard Ellmann (letter of Oct. 5, 1964) says he "really can't tell" which came first. See Gilbert, ed., **3058**, pp. 279-280, for the letter of May 27, 1929, to Harriet Shaw Weaver in which Joyce makes it fairly clear that the volume preceded the review in date.

See also *ibid.*, p. 265, for a letter from Joyce to Adrienne Monnier of Sep- tember 3, 1928, in which eleven articles are mentioned, together with Stuart Gil- bert's, making twelve in all. But at this time Joyce did not know Beckett, who only arrived in Paris to take up his École Normale Supérieure post in October, 1928. Thus it is possible that Joyce had someone else in mind who later dropped out, to be replaced by Beckett, but it has not been possible to confirm this. Perhaps, as Richard Ellmann says in his letter referred to above, "it seems likely that Joyce projected 12 essays without having them all assigned until later."

Mr. Beckett has explained the punctuation of the title as follows: from Dante to Bruno is a jump of about three centuries, from Bruno to Vico about one, and from Vico to Joyce about two.

1929

Assumption

Short story. About 1,500 words. Signed Samuel Beckett.

2   *Transition* (Paris), 16-17 (June, 1929), 268-271.

2.1   Reprinted in *Transition Workshop,* ed. Eugene Jolas (New York: The Vanguard Press, 1949; 413 pp., 24 cm.), pp. 41-44 (in section 1, headed "Paramyths"; Beckett mentioned in editor's introduction and in "Selected Bibliography" on p. 400 [see also **22.02**]).

NOTE. This early story, pregnant with future Beckettian themes, tells how a sensitive young man, unable in speech to give an outlet to the words welling up within him, "afraid of that wild rebellious surge that aspired violently towards realization in sound," is visited by "the Woman." "When at last she went away he felt that something had gone out from him, something he could not spare, but still less could grudge, something of the desire to live, something of the unreasonable tenacity with which he shrank from dissolution." Finally, she is instrumental in releasing him: "She was swept aside by a great storm of sound . . . until, dispersed, it fused into the breath of the forest and the throbbing cry of the sea. They found her caressing his wild dead hair." A phrase from this story, "one with the birdless cloudless colourless skies" is, in accordance with a frequent habit of Beckett's, used again, in this case in a poem in **611** inscribed by the hero Belacqua to "his darling blue flower," the Smeraldina.

Che Sciagura

Satire in dialogue form. About 420 words. Not signed, but Mr. Beckett affirms that he is the author.

3   *T.C.D.: A College Miscellany,* XXXVI (Nov. 14, 1929), 42, on two columns.

NOTE. Mr. Beckett says that the satire, published in the Trinity College undergraduate weekly newspaper, was inspired by the embargo on the import of contraceptives into the Republic of Ireland. Instead of a signature the letters D.E.S.C. figure at the bottom of the piece. Together with the title (which recurs in the short story "What a Misfortune" [in **16**] and in Malone's lament on losing his stick, "quel malheur" [**258**, p. 88]) they refer to the words spoken by the eunuch in Voltaire's *Candide* (chap. 11, *ad fin.*), "Che sciagura d'essere senza coglioni." The Report of the Editorial Sub-Committee for Michaelmas Term 1929 (ed. G. S. Power) has this to say. "*Che Sciagura,* by D.E.S.C., was extremely clever, though fortunately a trifle obscure for those who do not know their JOYCE and their VOLTAIRE" (XXXVI [March 6, 1930], 137).

1930

For Future Reference

Poem of seventy-four lines. Signed Samuel Beckett.

4   *Transition,* 19-20 (Spring-Summer, June, 1930), 342-343. (In the
         glossary, p. 395: "Samuel Beckett, an Irish poet and essayist, is instruc-
         tor at the *Ecole Normale* in Paris.")

NOTE. Published under the heading "Reality and Beyond," this obscure and
immature poem, written in the vein of *Che Sciagura,* has never been reprinted.

Whoroscope

Poem of ninety-eight lines, numbered in tens, followed by notes.

5   Paris: The Hours Press, 1930 [Midsummer].
         [i] 300 *copies of this Poem* | *have been printed, of* | *which* 100 *copies
         are* | *signed by the author.* | *This is No* [copy in British Museum num-
         bered 66 in ink and signed in ink Samuel Beckett; copy in Bibliothèque
         nationale numbered 252 in ink, unsigned] [ii] *blank* 1-4 [text of poem]
         [5-6] [text of notes]. No printer indicated. Hand-set in 11 pt. Caslon
         Old Face, notes in 10 pt., on Vergé de Rives paper. 22½ cm. Scarlet
         stiff-paper cover, sewn (some copies stapled), front cover printed in
         black: *WHOROSCOPE* | *by* | SAMUEL BECKETT | [THE HOURS
         PRESS in form of clock dial] | [printed in an arc:] 15, *Rue
         Guénégaud, Paris*-6ᵉ | 1930. Some copies (e.g., Bibliothèque na-
         tionale) have a printed white slip gummed on front cover which
         reads: *This Poem was awarded the* £10 *prize for the* | *best poem on
         TIME in the competition judged by* | *Richard Aldington and Nancy
         Cunard at* | *THE HOURS PRESS, and is published in an* | *edition
         of* 100 *signed copies at* 5s. | *and* 200 *unsigned at* 1s. | [   ] *This is also
         Mr. Samuel Beckett's first separately published work.*

5.1   Reprinted in **40**, pp. 7-14;

5.2   and in **40.1**, pp. 9-17;

5.3   and in **704**, Appendix, pp. 303-307;

5.4   and in Nancy Cunard, *These Were the Hours* (Carbondale: Southern
         Illinois University Press, 1969).

NOTE. The poem, based according to Beckett on Adrien Baillet's late seven-
teenth-century life of Descartes, was written very quickly and at the last moment
submitted for the Nancy Cunard competition, for which poems on the subject
of time of not more than 100 lines in length were eligible. Beckett added the
notes later to clarify some of the allusions at the suggestion of Richard Aldington. Nancy Cunard gives full details about the competition and the printing
and publishing of the poem in **5.4** and in **1781**. The information in *The Hours
Press Booklet: Being a List of Books Published by Nancy Cunard at the Hours
Press during 1929 & 1930, with a Detailed Description of Each* (Paris: The

1930

5

Hours Press, n.d.), p. [18], is less reliable, since Miss Cunard did not draft it herself.

From the Only Poet to a Shining Whore (For Henry Crowder to Sing)

Poem of seventeen lines, to a musical score by Henry Crowder.

6   In *Henry-Music,* by Henry Crowder. Paris: The Hours Press, 1930 [Dec.], pp. [vi], 12-14.
[i] HENRY-MUSIC | by | *Henry Crowder* | POEMS | by | Equatorial Way [   ] *Nancy Cunard* | Madrigal [   ] *Richard Aldington* | Creed [   ] *Walter Lowenfels* | From the only Poet to a shining Whore [.] *Samuel Beckett* | From Tiresias [   ] *Harold Acton* | Memory Blues [   ] *Nancy Cunard* | HOURS PRESS | 15 Rue Guénégaud Paris | 1930 [ii] This edition is limited to 100 | signed copies, privately printed. | This is no. [52, in Sterling Library, University of London]. [iii] EQUA-TORIAL WAY | *For Henry* [iv] MADRIGAL [v] CREED [vi] FROM THE ONLY POET | TO A SHINING WHORE | *For Henry Crowder to sing.* | [. . .] | *Samuel Beckett* [vii] FROM "TIRESIAS" [viii] MEMORY BLUES [1]-20[scores], 12-14 FROM THE ONLY POET [etc.]. 32 cm. Music printed by Imprimerie française de musique [bottom of p. 20]; copyright by Henry Crowder, 1930; recorded on Sonabel Records by the composer. Hardbound, paper; illus. front and back with black and white pho-tomontages incorporating title, etc.

NOTE. Copies of the folio are rare. It is mentioned briefly in **5.4**, and described in **1781** as having 20 pages, issued in 150 [*sic*] copies signed by the composer, with "hard board covers, front and back different, specially designed photomon-tages by Man Ray, of African sculptures belonging to me. When opened out, back and front covers run admirably into one composition. Published Decem-ber 1930 at 10s.6d." Henry Crowder is described as a "professional Afro-American pianist" to whom Beckett "dedicated his poem . . . it was often sung in Paris cabarets by Henry, with mine." In *The Hours Press Booklet* (see **5**, Note), the folio is described as "bound in photographic covers on boards from a series of photographs by MAN RAY. . . . The reproductions on the cover were made from African sculptures and ivories in a famous private col-lection" (p. [7]). Among illus. on cover is a photograph of Henry Crowder incorporated into the general design. In Beckett's title, the "shining whore" is Rahab of Jericho, and the "only poet" is Dante.

1931

Proust

Critical study of *A la recherche du temps perdu,* by Marcel Proust. Seventy-two pages.

7   London: Chatto and Windus, 1931 [March 5]. Published at 2s. as the seventh volume in the Dolphin Books series.

1931

7   [i-ii] *blank* [iii] THE DOLPHIN BOOKS | PROUST [iv] [list of Dol-
phin Books] [v] PROUST | *By* | SAMUEL BECKETT | 'E fango è
il mondo' | LEOPARDI | [dolphin device] | LONDON | *CHATTO
& WINDUS* | 1931 [vi] PRINTED IN GREAT BRITAIN | BY T.
AND A. CONSTABLE LTD. | AT THE UNIVERSITY PRESS |
EDINBURGH | ALL RIGHTS RESERVED | FIRST PUBLISHED
| 1931 [vii] FOREWORD | [text of Foreword] | [viii] *blank* [1]-72
[text]. 18½ cm. Hardbound, paper imitation cloth. Cover, cream,
illus. front and back with brown dolphin device, title etc. in brown
lettering front and spine, spine lettered vertically. Dust jacket buff,
printed blue design with dolphin device (uniform with rest of series),
no blurb.

7.1/101   Reprinted photographically by Grove Press, New York, and Evergreen Books, London [March 15, 1957] (Evergreen Book E-50). 20
cm. Soft cover. First issue: front cover Felsenthal black and white
abstract design lettered in black and mauve. Second issue: front
cover black, illus. with a portrait of Proust in black and white, and
lettered white.

7.11   Hardbound edition.

7.12   Specially bound, limited edition of 250 copies, signed by the author.
All references to the original publisher and printer have been removed
from **7.1**, **7.11**, and **7.12** and replaced by the Grove Press imprint; no
[i-ii], [iii] *half title* only, [iv] *blank,* [73-74] *blank* added.

7.2   Third edition. London: John Calder, 1965 [Nov. 4], followed by **31.2**.
[1] *half title* [2] *Other Works by Samuel Beckett:* | [list] [3] SAMUEL
BECKETT | PROUST | [swell rule] | THREE DIALOGUES |
SAMUEL BECKETT & GEORGES DUTHUIT | [tree device] |
LONDON | JOHN CALDER [4] FIRST PUBLISHED IN GREAT
BRITAIN IN 1965 BY | JOHN CALDER (PUBLISHERS) LIM-
ITED | 18, BREWER STREET, LONDON, W. I. | ALL RIGHTS
RESERVED | PROUST © COPYRIGHT SAMUEL BECKETT
1931 | THREE DIALOGUES © SAMUEL BECKETT | AND
GEORGES DUTHUIT 1949 | MADE AND PRINTED IN THE
REPUBLIC OF IRELAND | BY HELY THOM LIMITED, DUB-
LIN [5] CONTENTS | [list] [6] *blank* [7] PROUST [half title]
[8] *blank* [9] FOREWORD [to *Proust*] [10] *blank* 11-93 [text of
Proust] [94] *blank* [95] THREE DIALOGUES* | SAMUEL BECK-
ETT AND GEORGES DUTHUIT | *From *Transition* '49, no. 5.
Georges Duthuit, | Editor. [96] *blank* [97] I [98] *blank* [99] TAL
COAT [half title] [100] *blank* 101-103 [text of *Tal Coat*] [104] *blank*
[105] II [106] *blank* [107] MASSON [half title] [108] *blank* 109-113
[text of *Masson*] [114] *blank* [115] III [116] *blank* [117] BRAM
VAN VELDE [half title] [118] *blank* 119-126 [text of *Bram van*

1931

7.2   *Velde*] [127-128] *blank.* 20 cm. Hardbound, mauve paper imitation
cloth, gold vertical italic l.c. and horizontal caps. on spine. Dust
jacket design orange, red, and brown on white, incorporating full-
length portrait of Proust; back blurb, and flaps catalogue lists, brown
lettering on white ground.

NOTE. Mr. Beckett says he found the book a "hard job," and that he "didn't
enjoy it." He worked on it conscientiously, however, rereading the sixteen
volumes of Proust's novel twice in order to do so. He owed the commission
from Chatto and Windus to Richard Aldington. In all 3,000 copies were
printed of which 2,600 were sold by 1937. The balance of 400 was remaindered
in 1941. There is a misprint on p. 70 of **7**, **7.1**, **7.11**, **7.12**, "hölder" which should
read "holder," and which is corrected in **7.2**, p. 91. **2849** notes the mistake, still
uncorrected in **7.2**, that Gilberte Swann becomes Duchesse de Guermantes.

The Possessed

Dramatic parody. About 380 words. Unsigned.

8   *T.C.D.: A College Miscellany,* XXXVII (March 12, 1931), 138, on
two columns.

NOTE. The anonymous piece is preceded by the following note: *"We are given
to understand that the following is a reply to our reporter's criticism of the
M.L.S. Plays; as such we publish it.*—Ed., *T.C.D."* The anonymous review here
referred to was published in *T.C.D.,* XXXVII (Feb. 26, 1931), 116, under
the title "The M.L.S. Players" (M.L.S. = Modern Language Society). It was
sympathetic to the two other plays presented, but hostile to the parody of
Corneille's *Le Cid* entitled *Le Kid,* in which Beckett played Don Diègue, and
had this to say of the cast: "None of the actors was outstanding, but all were
capable." The French plays were produced by Georges Pelorson, exchange
lecturer from the École Normale Supérieure, and contributor to *Transition.* He
and Beckett were coauthors of *Le Kid* (see **609**), the text of which does not
seem to have survived.

The Report of the Editorial Sub-Committee for Hilary Term, 1931 (ed., H.
G. Yates, B.A.), in *T.C.D.,* XXXVII (June 4, 1931), 185, has this to say
about *The Possessed:* "In the Joycian medley *The Possessed* its anonymous
author performs some diverting verbal acrobatics but, in the manner of a number of *Transition*'s offspring, is too allusive to be generally comprehensible.
This contribution lost some of its topical appeal by the unnecessary postponing
of its publication."

There is no doubt about the authorship of the piece; not only has Mr.
Beckett acknowledged it, it is also recognizably written in the style he used at
the time.

1931

Hell Crane to Starling

9A   Poem of twenty-five lines. Pp. 475-476.

Note. The title is based on the fifth canto of Dante's *Inferno,* one of the most quoted in Beckett's writings, containing as it does the famous Paolo and Francesca episode. The souls of the Lustful are compared to wheeling flocks of starlings and to "cranes chanting their lay" (ll. 40-48). In Beckett's poem, however, there is scant reference to Dante, beyond the title.

Casket of Pralinen for a Daughter of a Dissipated Mandarin

9B   Poem of seventy-five lines. Pp. 476-478.

Note. The "daughter" in the title is the Smeraldina, and the poem is based on an espisode in **611**, a disastrous New Year's Eve party which seals the failure of Belacqua's liaison with the Smeraldina in Vienna.

Text

9C   Poem of sixty-nine lines. Pp. 478-480 (see also **9.01**).

Note. The poem contains a meditation on the story of Tiresias and Manto, as told in the twentieth canto of *Inferno.*

Yoke of Liberty

9D   Poem of thirteen lines. P. 480.

Note. The title is based on Dante's *giogo della libertà;* cf. **1**, p. 7.

The four poems published on the pages indicated in:

9   THE EUROPEAN | CARAVAN | AN ANTHOLOGY OF THE NEW SPIRIT IN | EUROPEAN LITERATURE | Compiled and Edited by | SAMUEL PUTNAM | MAIDA CASTELHUN DARNTON, GEORGE REAVEY | and | J. BRONOWSKI | With Special Introductions by | ANDRÉ BERGE, MASSIMO BONTEMPELLI, JEAN CASSOU | and | E. GIMÉNEZ CABALLERO | PART I | FRANCE, SPAIN, ENGLAND and IRELAND | BREWER, WARREN & PUTNAM | NEW YORK, 1931. xviii + 577 pp., 22 cm.

Note. The poems are published by "Courtesy of the Author," who is named as Samuel B. Beckett. The following editorial note heads the poems on p. 475: "S. B. Beckett is the most interesting of the younger Irish writers. He is a graduate of Trinity College, Dublin, and has lectured at the *Ecole Normale Supérieure* in Paris. He has a great knowledge of Romance literature, is a friend of Rudmose-Brown and of Joyce, and has adapted the Joyce method to his poetry with original results. His impulse is lyric, but has been deepened through this influence and the influence of Proust and of the historic method. He has recently won the Hours Press prize with a poem *Whoroscope;* and has contributed to *Transition* and *This Quarter,* and to the examination of Joyce's *Work in Progress.*"

Part I of *The European Caravan* was the only part ever issued.

1931

9.01 **9C** was reprinted in *New Review,* I (Winter, 1931-32), 338-339, *"Courtesy* of *THE EUROPEAN CARAVAN."*

NOTE. The word "by" has been added to l. 57, to make "as they slouch by unnamed," but this may be a printer's slip, occasioned by the next line, which reads, in both versions, "scorned by the black ferry."

Return to the Vestry

Poem of forty-six lines.

10 *New Review,* I (Aug.-Sept.-Oct., 1931), [98]-99.

NOTE. The author of the poem, which is very like **4** in form and tone, is named as Samuel BECKETT. The credits of *New Review* run as follows: "The New Review | 'SEMPER AFRICA NOVI ALIQUID APPORTAT' | An International Notebook for the Arts | Published from Paris | 15 Francs — 60 Cents — 2 Shillings 6 Pence | Edited by Samuel Putnam | American distributors: The Gotham Book Mart | 51 West 47th Street, New York."

Alba

Poem of seventeen lines, early version of **22D**. Signed Samuel Beckett.

11 *Dublin Magazine,* VI, n.s. (Oct.-Dec., 1931), 4.

11.1 Reprinted with variants in **22**;

11.11 and in **266**, p. 20;

11.12 and in **40**, p. 23;

11.13 and in **40.1**, p. 28.

NOTE. The poem, later to be placed fourth in the *Echo's Bones* cycle, was written while Beckett was lecturer at Trinity College, Dublin. It is based largely on Dante, like most of the poems dating from this period, but the title is Provencal, an alba being an aubade. This fact explains the first line, "before morning you shall be here." One of the women characters in **611** and **16** is also called the Alba. The variants in the version given in **22** are as follows:
l. 1: "before" for "Before";
ll. 6-8: commas suppressed after "silk," "areca," "bamboos," "smoke";
l. 9: "with" for "like";
l. 10: "endorse" for "sign";
l. 11: "shall not" for "cannot," and comma suppressed after "bounty";
ll. 12-15: commas suppressed after "me," "emblems," and "host."

1932

Sedendo et Quiescendo

Short story. About 2,800 words. Signed Samuel Beckett.

1932

12   *Transition; An International Workshop for Orphic Creation, edited by Eugene Jolas* (Servire Press, Rietzangerlaan 15, The Hague, Holland), 21 (March, 1932), 13-20.

NOTE. The piece is an extract, showing variants, from **611**, and is classified by the editor Eugene Jolas as an "anamyth" or "psychograph," the first being a fantastic narrative reflecting preconscious relationships, the second a prose text expressing hallucinations and phantoms. Three stories by Kafka also come under this heading. Owing to a misprint, the story is persistently entitled *Sedendo et Quiesciendo.*

Text

Prose fragment. About 210 words.

13   *New Review,* II (April, 1932), 57.

13.1   Reprinted in **704**, Appendix, p. 308.

NOTE. The piece is also an extract, with variants and misprints, from **611**. Some of the misprints in **13** have been corrected in **13.1**, but fresh ones have crept in. Like **12**, the piece is imitative of Joyce's style in *Work in Progress.*

Home Olga

Poem of ten lines.

14   *Contempo* (Chapel Hill, N.C.), III, no. 13 (Feb. 15, 1934), 3.

14.1   Reprinted in **3061**, p. 714;

14.2   and in **704**, p. 235 (one variant).

NOTE. The obscure acrostic poem based on the letters of James Joyce's name was shown to members of the Joyce circle before July 22, 1932, which would therefore be the correct publication date. Joyce refers to it in a letter of July 22, 1932, to Stuart Gilbert (see **3058**, p. 323). According to Cohn (**704**, p. 235), Beckett composed the acrostic "on the occasion of Joyce's fiftieth birthday, in 1934." Apart from the fact that Joyce was fifty not in 1934 but, of course, in 1932, his birthday was February 2, several months before the acrostic is known to have circulated, so that it seems unlikely that it was composed in honor of that birthday. If anything, Bloomsday is the more probable anniversary (June 16, 1932). Mr. Beckett has said that the acrostic was unsolicited, and that is all we know. Joyce's remarks in the letter show that the acrostic was received with some coolness by Eugene Jolas, who thought it "acid and not funny." The subject himself, however, thought it "all right."

Dante and the Lobster

Short story. Signed Samuel Beckett.

1932

15   *This Quarter,* V (Dec., 1932), 222-236 (ed. and pub. Edward W. Titus, 4 and 8 rue Delambre, Paris.)

15.1   Reprinted (with variants) in **16**, pp. 1-20;

15.11   and in **16.03**;

15.12/14 and in **16.031/33**.

NOTE. The story was submitted for a *This Quarter* short-story competition, but it did not win the fifty-guinea prize offered by William Heinemann Ltd., the publishing firm. It was thoroughly revised before being incorporated into **16** as the first story of that collection.

1934

More Pricks Than Kicks

Collection of ten short stories. 278 pages.

16   London: Chatto and Windus, 1934 [May 24]. Published at 7s. 6d.
        [i] *half title* [ii] *By the same Author* | PROUST | *Chatto and Windus*
        [iii] SAMUEL BECKETT | [swell rule] | MORE PRICKS | THAN
        KICKS | [swell rule] | CHATTO AND WINDUS | 1934 | LONDON
        [iv] PRINTED IN GREAT BRITAIN | BY R. & R. CLARK, LTD.
        | EDINBURGH | ALL RIGHTS RESERVED [v] DANTE AND
        THE LOBSTER [   ] p. 1 | FINGAL [   ] 21 | DING-DONG [   ]
        41 | A WET NIGHT [   ] 59 | LOVE AND LETHE [   ] 115 |
        WALKING OUT [   ] 139 | WHAT A MISFORTUNE [   ] 159 |
        THE SMERALDINA'S BILLET DOUX [   ] 215 | YELLOW
        [   ] 227 | DRAFF [   ] 253 [vi] *blank* [vii] DANTE AND THE
        LOBSTER [viii] *blank* 1-[278] [text]. [279-280] *blank*. 18¾ cm. Hard-
        bound, ocher cloth; title, author, and publisher in blue horizontal caps.
        on spine; dust jacket, buff, title etc. in blue caps. printed over brown
        semiabstract device of a head. Blurb: "Here is a new independent
        spirit at work, one that employs the intellect to illumine the comicality
        and poetic beauty which permeate ordinary vulgar feelings and events.
        These close-ups from the life of a young man Belacqua deal with
        his domestic vagaries and such incidents as a party, making love, an
        abortive suicide-pact. Mr. Beckett's humour proceeds by the mock-
        heroic as much as by the emphasis of crass poignant fact; it is brusque
        and defiant — that rare humour, the last weapon against despair.
        His dazzling moments are won with a strong punch. *More Pricks
        Than Kicks* is a piece of literature, memorable, exceptional, the utter-
        ance of a very modern voice."

16.01   "The Smeraldina's Billet Doux" was reprinted in *Zero Anthology of
        Literature and Art,* no. 8, ed. Themistocles Hoetis (New York: Zero
        Press, 1956), pp. 56-61.

1934

16.02   "Yellow" was reprinted in *New World Writing,* 10 (Nov., 1956), 108-119 [slight variants].

16.03   "Dante and the Lobster" was reprinted in *Evergreen Review,* I, no. 1 (1957), 24-36, and in

16.031   1221, pp. 297-308, and in

16.032   *A Samuel Beckett Reader,* ed. John Calder (London: Calder and Boyars, and New English Library, 1967). pp. 23-33, followed by extracts from **25, 32, 374, 375, 377, 373, 376A,** by **24, 370.1, 255Aa, 255Bb, 255Cc,** by an extract from **384,** by **385,** and in

16.033   *Evergreen Review Reader* (New York: Grove Press, 1968), pp. 3-8 [see also **382.22**].

NOTE. The volume published by Chatto and Windus sold only 500 copies out of 1,500 printed, and is now rare. Mr. Beckett has so far not been willing to authorize its republication, but, on the last page of the November, 1966, issue of the *London Magazine,* a Calder and Boyars limited reedition was advertised. **16.1** This "Special edition Hors Commerce for Scholars" was released in December, 1966. It consists of a mimeographed typescript copy of iv + 107 recto pages stapled between white shiny paper covers.

There is an error in **16,** p. 134, l. 7: the name "Lucy" should read "Ruby."

Review of *Poems,* by Rainer Maria Rilke, trans. J. B. Leishmann [*sic*]. About 500 words.

[RAINER MARIA RILKE | POEMS | TRANSLATED FROM | THE GERMAN BY | J. B. LEISHMAN | [device] | LONDON . 1934 | PUBLISHED BY LEONARD & VIRGINIA WOOLF | AT THE HOGARTH PRESS, TAVISTOCK SQUARE. 51 pp., 21 cm.]

17   *The Criterion,* XIII (July, 1934), 705-707.

NOTE. Signed "S.B.," the piece has no title. That S.B. stands for Samuel Beckett is confirmed on p. 5 of the index to the volume, where the name is given in full. The review appears under the section "Books of the Quarter," subsection "Shorter Notices." This is all Beckett ever published in T. S. Eliot's *The Criterion;* it is the first of a series of book reviews he wrote when he was trying to build a career in literary journalism, to which end he had met Desmond MacCarthy. It came to nothing, perhaps because Beckett's reviews were either too obscure or too honest to be acceptable to editors, and it does not seem likely that he could have been versatile or prolific enough to read innumerable ephemeral productions and write cleverly on them. The Rilke review judges Leishmann [*sic*] harshly as an inept translator ("the numerous deviations are unwarrantable, that is to say, ineffective") and is not indulgent toward Rilke himself ("Turmoil of self-deception and naif discontent. . . . There is no position here, . . . no faculty for one . . ."). Beckett is, however, guilty

1934

17

of a certain arch flippancy, and betrays an oddly defensive manner in this as in other pieces of journalism.

Gnome

Poem of four lines. Signed "Sam Beckett."

18   *Dublin Magazine,* IX, n.s. (July-Sept., 1934), 8.

NOTE. The form of this gnomic poem was inspired, according to the author, by Goethe's *Xenien*. Like all Beckett's work in the *Dublin Magazine,* it was published during Seumas O'Sullivan's editorship.

Humanistic Quietism

Review of *Poems,* by Thomas McGreevy. About 480 words.
[POEMS | BY | THOMAS McGREEVY | [ornament] | [windmill device] | [rule] | LONDON: WILLIAM HEINEMANN LTD | 1934. viii + 60 pp., 18 cm.]

19   *Dublin Magazine,* IX, n.s. (July-Sept., 1934), 79-80.

NOTE. Signed "S.B.," the review is very favorable to McGreevy, a fellow member of Joyce's circle and fellow contributor to *Our Exagmination* and to *Transition.* It is not possible to ascertain whether Beckett or the editor chose "Humanistic Quietism" as the title. Apart from its enthusiastic appraisal of McGreevy, supported by quotations, the piece is notable for the following definition: "All poetry, as discriminated from the various paradigms of prosody, is prayer."

A Case in a Thousand

Short story. About 2,000 words (one and a half pages of text, on two columns).

20   *The Bookman,* LXXXVI (Aug., 1934), 241-242.

A CASE IN A THOUSAND | A SHORT STORY | by Samuel Beckett.

NOTE. Apparently the story was accepted by *The Bookman* (a literary monthly that was to be incorporated from January, 1935, with the *London Mercury* and to lose its separate identity) on the strength of *More Pricks Than Kicks,* which received a favorable review in the July number (see **1916**). The August number was a special one devoted to Irish writing. With this publication Beckett was exposed to a wider public than he ever again would be, at least until the staging of *Waiting for Godot.* The story itself is curiously out of key with the rest of Beckett's fiction; in particular, it has little in common with the *More Pricks Than Kicks* cycle. One element, however, seems to have been recalled in **263A**, as mentioned by Fletcher in **708**, pp. 101-102. The

1934

20

story tells of Dr. Nye's trauma, rooted in some unexplained erotic involvement with his nurse as a child. He meets her again, on the occasion of the fatal illness of her own son, and is thus able to exorcize his trauma.

21A   *Ex Cathezra*

Review of *Make It New,* by Ezra Pound. About 750 words. [MAKE IT NEW | *ESSAYS BY* | EZRA POUND | [four Chinese characters] | *LONDON* | FABER AND FABER LIMITED | *24 RUSSELL SQUARE* (1934). 407 pp., 22 cm.]

21B   *Papini's Dante*

Review of *Dante Vivo,* by Giovanni Papini. About 750 words. [GIOVANNI PAPINI | Dante Vivo | Translated from the Italian by | ELEANOR HAMMOND BROADUS | and ANNA BENEDETTI | [device] | LOVAT DICKSON LIMITED | *PUBLISHERS* | LONDON (1934). 340 pp., 21 cm.]

21C   *The Essential and the Incidental*

Review of *Windfalls,* by Sean O'Casey. About 550 words. [WINDFALLS | STORIES, POEMS AND PLAYS | BY | SEAN O'CASEY | MACMILLAN AND CO., LIMITED | ST. MARTIN'S STREET, LONDON | 1934. x + 201 pp., 19 cm.]

21   *The Bookman,* LXXXVII (Christmas 1934), 10, 14, and 111, respectively; the first two reviews in the "Art, Poetry and Criticism" section, the last in the "Miscellaneous" section. The Christmas number, the last to appear, was a supplement to the December, 1934, number.

NOTE. Beckett chose the titles of these reviews, all signed Samuel Beckett. *Ex Cathezra,* an unawed but quite appreciative review of Pound's essays, is notable mainly for an enthusiastic comment on Apollinaire's *Chanson du mal-aimé,* considered worth as much as all the works of the late Symbolists put together. *Papini's Dante* takes Giovanni Papini somewhat unjustly to task for misrepresenting Dante, revealing once more how much Beckett owes to the Florentine poet. Finally, Sean O'Casey's stories and verse in the volume are tactfully dismissed in favor of two farces that show him to be a "master of knockabout" and possibly the precursor of much that is *clownerie* in Beckett's own drama.

1935

Echo's Bones and Other Precipitates

Cycle of thirteen poems.

22A   *The Vulture,* six lines.

Based on Goethe, *Harzreise im Winter,* in *Vermischte Gedichte,* of which the first line reads: "Dem Geier gleich."

22B   *Enueg I,* seventy-six lines.

1935

22C   *Enueg II,* twenty-nine lines.
        The title means "complaint" in Provençal, the poems being dirges
        and expressions of disgust and revolt. There is extant an "Enueg"
        by Peire de Vic, monk of Montaudon, which itemizes things and
        people who displease or disgust him, such as "dompna grassa ab magre
        con," "a tiny c . . . in a fat woman." It seems likely that Beckett
        knew this poem. He may even have read it in André Berry's *Florilège
        des Troubadours* (Paris: Firmin-Didot, 1930).

22D   *Alba,* seventeen lines.
        First published as **11**, this poem was written at the same time as
        Enueg I, that is, when Beckett was a lecturer at Trinity College
        Dublin. Cf. the "Alba" of Guiraut de Borneil and its refrain "Et
        ades sera l'alba," "And the dawn will soon break," or the "Alba" or
        "aube mystique" of Folquet de Marseille, which has a refrain of
        four lines similar in form to the tercet here, or several other albas in
        Berry's *Florilège* treating of lovers' laments at imminent separation or
        the *gaita*'s (watchman's) warning of dawn.

22E   *Dortmunder,* fourteen lines.
        Written, according to Mr. Beckett, in "Kassel when drunk," the poem
        seems to relate a visit paid by Belacqua to a prostitute; the title is,
        of course, based on the famous beer.

22F   *Sanies I,* fifty-two lines.

22G   *Sanies II,* forty-three lines.
        The title is the Latin word for diseased and corrupted blood, similar
        to pus. The first poem is set in Dublin, the second in Paris.

22H   *Serena I,* fifty-three lines.

22J   *Serena II,* fifty-three lines.

22K   *Serena III,* twenty-seven lines.
        The only extant Provençal "Serena," by Guiraut Riquier, tells of a
        lover's impatient longing for evening and a promised consummation.
        The *Serena* poems in this cycle are on the whole characterized by a
        more resigned tone than *Enueg* and *Sanies.*

22L   *Malacoda,* twenty-nine lines.
        Malacoda in Dante is a deceitful demon (*Inf.* XXI. 76) and in
        Beckett (cf. "Draff," in **16**) an undertaker; he is both in this poem.

22M   *Da tagte es,* four lines.
        The title is based on the Minnesinger Walther von der Vogelweide's
        Nemt, frowe, disen kranz, of which the last line reads: "dô taget ez
        und muose ich wachen," "it dawned and I had to awake." The link
        with **22D** is obvious.

22N   *Echo's Bones,* five lines.
        Based on Ovid's *Metamorphoses iii.* 341-401.

1935

22   Paris: Europa Press, 1935 (Europa Poets, no. 3). Ordinary edition
                3s. 6d., signed copies 6s.
                [1-4] *blank* [5] *half title* [6] By the same Author | [*em block*] |
                WHOROSCOPE — *The Hours Press* | *Paris* 1930 | PROUST —
                Chatto and Windus | *London* 1932 | MORE PRICKS THAN
                KICKS — *Chatto* | *and Windus* *London* 1934 | COPYRIGHT BY
                AUTHOR AND EUROPA PRESS | ALL RIGHTS RESERVED
                1935 [7] *ECHO'S BONES* | *AND OTHER PRECIPITATES* | BY
                [   ] SAMUEL BECKETT | EUROPA PRESS [   ] 1935 | 13,
                RUE BONAPARTE [   ] PARIS [8] *blank* [9] CONTENTS |
                THE VULTURE | ENUEG 1 | ENUEG 2 | ALBA | DORTMUN-
                DER | SANIES 1 | SANIES 2 | SERENA 1 | SERENA 2 | SERENA
                3 | MALACODA | DA TAGTE ES | ECHO'S BONES [10] *blank*
                [11] *THE VULTURE* [etc.] [37] *blank* [38] THIS EDITION IS
                LIMITED TO 327 COPIES OF | WHICH 25 ON NORMANDY
                VELLUM SIGNED BY | THE AUTHOR ARE NUMBERED I
                TO XXV; | 250 ON ALFA PAPER NUMBERED 1 TO 250; |
                AND 50 COPIES MARKED HORS COMMERCE. | 2 COPIES
                ON NORMANDY VELLUM MARKED | A AND B ARE RE-
                SERVED FOR THE AUTHOR | AND PUBLISHER RESPEC-
                TIVELY. PRINTED BY | THE G. L. M. PRESS. PARIS. NO-
                VEMBER 1935. | No . . . [XI in British Museum, signed Samuel
                Beckett in ink, 90 in Bibliothèque nationale] [39] *blank* [40] [list of
                titles in Europa Poets series] [41-44] *blank*. 22¼ cm. Stiff buff paper
                covers, with flaps over pp. [1-2] and [43-44], front printed in black:
                ECHO'S BONES | *AND OTHER PRECIPITATES* | BY [.]
                SAMUEL BECKETT [from same type as upper half of title page].

22.01   **22L, 22C,** and **22E** reprinted in *Transition: A Quarterly Review,* 24
                (June, 1936), 8-10 [see **1919**]. (Published under the general heading
                of "Vertigral," the poems are sometimes divided into more stanzas
                than in **22.** "Contributors," p. 5, includes a note on Beckett, mention-
                ing his publications *More Pricks Than Kicks* and *Echo's Bones and
                Other Precipitates.*)

22.02   **22L** reprinted in *Transition Workshop,* ed. Eugene Jolas (New York:
                Vanguard Press, 1949), p. 204, in sec. 3, headed "Intercontinental
                Poets" (see also **2.1**).

22.03   **22A, 22B, 22C, 22F, 22G, 22H, 22J, 22K, 22M, 22N** reprinted pho-
                tographically in *Evergreen Review,* I, no. 1 (1957), 179-192. (The
                stanza divisions show variants, but they seem to be imputable to the
                reproduction process.)

22.1   Reprinted in entirety in **266**, dated 1933-1935, with slight variants
                of punctuation, and with facing German translations by Eva Hesse,
                pp. 7-47;

22.2   and in **40**, pp. 15-38;

1935

22.21 and in **40.1**, pp. 19-46.

NOTE. The pagination in **22** is that of the Alfa paper Bibliothèque nationale copy, which was preferred as being untouched by binders. The British Museum copy, although on better paper, was bound between stiff boards. It has six blank pages ([1-6]) at the beginning, and only two at the end ([43-44]). Both copies, of course, have in all forty-four unnumbered pages, and on balance it seems more likely that the present British Museum pagination is not imputable to the library's binders but survives from the original Normandy Vellum copy deposited there. Of note also is the fact that for *Enueg* (etc.), Arabic numerals are used on p. [9], but Roman numerals in the text.

For a variant introduced by Beckett into a radio broadcast of an anthology of his poems selected and introduced by John Fletcher and concerning **22J**, see **255**, note.

1936

An Imaginative Work!

Review of *The Amaranthers*, by Jack B. Yeats. About 600 words. [THE AMARANTHERS | *by* | JACK B. YEATS | [ornament] | [windmill device] | [rule] | WILLIAM HEINEMANN LTD | LONDON : : TORONTO [1936]. 273 pp., 19 cm.]

23 *Dublin Magazine*, XI, n.s. (July-Sept., 1936), 80-81.

NOTE. The review, signed S.B., is very favorable to Yeats's novel, and is notable largely for a comparison between Yeats and Ariosto. The title is probably not Beckett's.

Cascando

Poem in three sections.
I (eleven lines, of which the first is separated by a small gap from the other ten in **24**, and fourteen lines in three separate stanzas in **24.1/2/3**)
II (twenty-two lines in three separate stanzas in **24**, in four stanzas in **24.1/2/3**)
III (one line)

24 *Dublin Magazine*, XI, n.s. (Oct.-Dec., 1936), 3-4.

24.1 Reprinted in **266**, pp. 48 and 50;

24.2 and in **40**, pp. 41-42 (dated 1936, first of "Two Poems," the second being **29**, *Saint-Lô*) ;

24.3 and in **40.1**, pp. 49-50.

1936

24.4   See **16.032**, pp. 167-168 (no stanza division in Section I).

NOTE. Signed Samuel Beckett, this poem bears the same title as **271**, the French radio play of 1963. There are interesting variants between the first and later printings, e.g.: "is it better abort than be barren" (l. 1 in **24**), and "why not merely the despaired of | occasion of | wordshed | . . . | is it not better abort than be barren" (first four lines of **24.1/2/3**).

1938

Murphy

Novel. Thirteen chapters.

25   London: Routledge, 1938 [March 7]. Published at 7s. 6d.
[i] *half title* [ii] *By the Same Author* | *[rule]* | PROUST | MORE PRICKS THAN KICKS | WHOROSCOPE | ECHO'S BONES [iii] Samuel Beckett | MURPHY | LONDON | GEORGE ROUT-LEDGE & SONS, LTD. | BROADWAY HOUSE: 68-74 CARTER LANE, E.C. [iv] *First published 1938* | Printed in Great Britain by Butler & Tanner Ltd., Frome and London [v] *half title* [vi] *blank* 1-282 *text* [283-286] NEW ROUTLEDGE | FICTION | *A selection from the Spring List, 1938* [catalogue includes advertisement, p. [285], for MURPHY | SAM BECKETT. *Author of "More Pricks than Kicks," "Whoroscope," etc.,* followed by a blurb]. 19 cm. Hardbound, green cloth; title, author, and publisher in horizontal gold italics and italic caps. on spine. Bound by Webb Son and Co., London E.C.1, in three batches, Feb., 1938, Nov., 1941, April, 1942 (war shortages may have resulted in later bindings in different cloth); dust jacket, yellow, with large orange R (for "Routledge"), title etc. in green. Blurb: ". . . Its meaning is implicit and symbolic, never concrete. . . . What spirit! What gusto! What hilarity! The reader is carried along on the wave of an abundant creative imagination expressing itself in scene after scene of superlative comedy, ironic situations that only the Irish genius could conceive. Murphy is a character for whom the unseen is the real and the seen a necessary obstacle to reality. To get beyond that obstacle is his aim in life, and he neglects or despises the criteria of the substantial world. Hence he moves in the lowest strata of society; all the efforts of the other characters fail to nail him more securely to life. From the reader's point of view it is a good thing, for the bottom rung of the ladder seems to be a most entertaining vantage-point for observing people and places. . ."

25.1   Reprinted photographically by Grove Press, New York, n.d. [March 15, 1957] (Evergreen Book E-104), [iv] + 282 pages, 20 cm. Soft cover, white, illus. with red and black design by Roy Kuhlman based on letters of title, with vertical caps. on spine and blurb on back;

1938

25.11 Also a specially bound, limited edition of 100 copies, signed by the author. Hardbound, natural linen, title etc. in vertical brown caps. on spine; dust jacket, white with design on front by Felsenthal, of rocking chair in gray, lettered black, vertical black caps. on spine, press comments on **375** on back. All references to original publisher and printer removed from **25.1/11** and replaced by Grove Press imprint, [iv] overstamped in **25.11**: Copyright 1957 Grove Press, Inc.

25.2 Third edition. London: John Calder, 1963 (Oct., Jupiter Books, J. 1; uniform with **32.3**).
[1] *half title* [2] WORKS BY SAMUEL BECKETT [list] [3] MURPHY | SAMUEL BECKETT | *A Jupiter Book* | LONDON | JOHN CALDER [4] FIRST PUBLISHED IN GREAT BRITAIN IN 1938 | BY G. ROUTLEDGE AND CO., LONDON | PUBLISHED AS A JUPITER BOOK IN 1963 | BY JOHN CALDER (PUBLISHERS) LIMITED | [. . .] | PRINTED IN GREAT BRITAIN BY | LATIMER, TREND AND CO. LTD., PLYMOUTH | 5-192 [text]. 18 cm. Both soft cover (front illus. with photograph of the author; back, blurb and catalogue list; title in vertical black and brown caps. and l.c. on spine) and hardbound (brown cloth, title and author in vertical gold italics on spine, dust jacket front illus. with photograph of the author) editions.

25.21 See **16.032**, pp. 34-40.

NOTE. According to Mr. Norman Franklin of Routledge and Kegan Paul, there is no truth in the story that *Murphy* was a failure and that the bulk of the edition, unsold, was destroyed in the blitz. No copies were lost through enemy action, and sales were good if not brilliant (in the first year, about 568 copies were sold; in the second year, 23, in the third, 20, in the fourth, 7; the balance of a total printing of 1,500, 782 copies, was sold as a cheap edition at 4*s*. 0*d*. in 1942). According to Mr. Beckett, the book, written about 1935, was accepted for publication on the recommendation of George Reavey and Herbert Read (the latter was one of Routledge's readers). It was favorably reviewed on publication, and at least one writer, Iris Murdoch, has recorded the lasting impression it made on her at the time (see **1104** and **2606**).

The question of possible binding variants of **25** is somewhat obscure. **3139** (p. 63) refers to "a second issue [London] in rough green cloth," but does not offer one for sale or produce any evidence for its existence, and neither Routledge and Kegan Paul nor Webb Son and Co. can throw any light on the matter so many years after the event. All copies examined were bound in smooth green cloth.

Ooftish

Poem. Nineteen lines.

26 *Transition: Tenth Anniversary,* 27 (April-May, 1938), 33.

1938

26.1   Reprinted in **704**, Appendix, p. 309.

NOTE. The title is a Yiddish expression meaning "put your money down on the table," hence the first line "offer it up plank it down."

Denis Devlin

Review of *Intercessions,* by Denis Devlin. About 1,500 words.
[INTERCESSIONS | POEMS | BY | DENIS DEVLIN | LONDON | EUROPA PRESS | 30 Red Lion Square, W.C.1. (1937, Europa Poets V). 64 pp., 22 cm.]

27   *Transition: Tenth Anniversary,* 27 (April-May, 1938), 289-294.

NOTE. Published under the general heading "Commentaries," the review springs ably to Devlin's defense against the attacks of the *Times Literary Supplement* reviewer, and is notable for its assertion that "art has nothing to do with clarity, does not dabble in the clear and does not make clear." The following note appears in the glossary, p. 381: *"Samuel Beckett, an Irish writer, who has appeared in Transition* with poems, essays and stories since 1928 [*sic*], has now settled in Paris."

The anonymous review that Beckett attacks was published in the *Times Literary Supplement,* Oct. 23, 1937, p. 786, and uses terms like "more intoxicated than intelligible," and "gulf of tangid [*sic*] incoherence," in referring especially to the poem "Gradual," which earns particular praise in Beckett's review. Beckett paraphrases rather than cites the exact wording of the review when he quotes its author as condemning "mental confusion and technical ineptitude."

1945

MacGreevy on Yeats

Review of *Jack B. Yeats* by Thomas MacGreevy. About 700 words exclusive of quotations.
[JACK B. YEATS | *An Appreciation and an Interpretation* | BY | THOMAS MACGREEVY | VICTOR WADDINGTON PUBLICATIONS | LIMITED DUBLIN (June 1945). 39 pp. + plates, 18 cm.]

28   *Irish Times,* Aug. 4, 1945, p. 2, cols. 6, 7.

NOTE. A nuanced review of MacGreevy's study, this piece "by Samuel Beckett" is notable for its expression of deep admiration for Yeats, not so much as the national painter presented by MacGreevy, but as one who "brings light, as only the great dare bring light, to the issueless predicament of existence. . . ." On p. 14 of his study, MacGreevy quotes Beckett's comment on Jack B. Yeats: "He grows Watteauer and Watteauer."

1946

Saint-Lô

Poem of five lines in **29**, four lines in **29.1/2**.

29   *Irish Times,* June 24, 1946, p. 5, cols. 5, 6.

29.1   Reprinted in **40**, p. 43 (dated 1946) ;

29.2   and in **40.1**, p. 51.

NOTE. In **29**, the poem reads :

Vire will wind in other shadows
unborn through the bright ways tremble
and the old mind
ghost-abandoned
sink into its havoc

In **29.1/2**, line 4 is modified to "ghost-forsaken" and attached to line 3, making only four lines in all.

Poem. Untitled. Five lines.

30   Attributed to "Oblomov" [Samuel Beckett] by Peggy Guggenheim in **3057**, p. 205 n. The fact that Miss Guggenheim first met Beckett the day after Christmas, 1937, would seem to date this poem *ca.* 1937.

30.1   In a slightly different French version, **253A**, it is to be found in **253**.

30.11   Reprinted in **266**, p. 54.

NOTE. Mr. Beckett believes he originally wrote this poem in English, which would make this version the original one. In a letter of April 10, 1965, Miss Guggenheim writes : "I do not know how I got it but I believe Beckett must have written it out for me as I quoted it. I can't remember how many versions there were. Possibly two. Probably two. . . . The punctuation would be from my memory and therefore nonexistent." The use of capitals at the beginnings of lines, and the fact that the first two lines are indented, may or may not owe to Miss Guggenheim's transcription. The variant "life" for "amour" in the last line, on the other hand, is almost certainly a genuine Beckettian variant.

1949

Three Dialogues

Three conversations between Samuel Beckett and Georges Duthuit, referred to as B. and D. in the text, on the painters :

31A   Tal Coat (dialogue numbered I),

31B   André Masson (II), and

31C   Bram van Velde (III).

1949

31   *Transition Forty-Nine,* 5 ([Dec.], 1949), 97-103 (I, 97-98; II, 98-100;
            III, 100-103).

31.1   Reprinted in **711**, pp. 16-22;

31.2   and in **7.2**, pp. 95-126.

31.01   Extract from **31C** (translated into French by Samuel Beckett) pub-
            lished by Galerie Michel Warren (Paris, 10 rue des Beaux-Arts, 6e)
            in the form of a large brochure on one sheet of stiff paper folded
            down the middle, in honor of the Bram van Velde exhibition held
            at the gallery May 7-June 1, 1957. White art paper, 32 x 50 cm.,
            printed dark green; outside cover has brief details about Bram van
            Velde; inside cover has brief details about the composition and trans-
            lation of the text, which is set out in two columns, with the contri-
            butions by B. in roman intercalated with those by D. in italic.

31.011   Abridged extract from **31.01** reprinted in *Nouvelle Revue Française,*
            V (June 1, 1957), Notes: Les Revues, pp. 1125-1126, under the
            title "Samuel Beckett et la peinture."

31.012   Extract from long paragraph near the end of **31.01** reprinted in **500**,
            pp. 9-[15] (variants).

31.0121 **31.012** (translated back into English) reprinted in **500.2/21**, pp. 9-10,
            13.

NOTE. In **31**, **31.1/2**, the text, being complete, is signed "Samuel Beckett and
Georges Duthuit," but the extracts **31.011/2/21** are ascribed to Beckett only.
Georges Duthuit, a leading French critic and art historian, was editor of post-
war *Transition*. Beckett wrote up their informal conversations on contemporary
painters at Duthuit's suggestion but says, "I do not think he approved them;
they merely reflect, very freely, the many conversations we had at that time
about painters and painting." D. acts largely as prompter to B., who humor-
ously presents himself as something of an intellectual clown. The joint signature is misleading since it implies that the dialogues were written in collaboration, which was not the case, and its maintenance owes to Mr. Beckett's usual
scrupulous generosity in such matters.

1953

Watt

Novel in four parts or long chapters, followed by a section of Addenda, dated on bottom of last page "Paris, 1945."

32   Paris: Olympia Press, 1953.
            [1-2] *blank* [3] *half title* [4] THERE HAVE BEEN PRINTED OF
            THIS WORK ONE | THOUSAND ONE HUNDRED TWENTY-
            FIVE COPIES, OF | WHICH TWENTY-FIVE ARE ON FINE

1953

32   PAPER, LETTERED | FROM A TO Y AND SIGNED BY THE
          AUTHOR, AND ELEVEN | HUNDRED, INTENDED FOR
          GENERAL CIRCULATION, | NUMBERED FROM 1 TO 1100.
          | *THIS PRINTING CONSTITUTES* | *THE FIRST EDITION*
          OF | *WATT* | *NUMBER* . . . [837 in private copy] [5] SAMUEL
          BECKETT | *WATT* | COLLECTION MERLIN [bird device in
          black] | *THE OLYMPIA PRESS* [6, bottom of page] *Printed in*
          France | *All world rights reserved* | *Copyright 1953* [7]-65 [text of
          part one] [66] *blank* [67]-149 [text of part two] [150] *blank* [151]-213
          [text of part three] [214] *blank* [215]-246 [text of part four] [247]-254
          [text of Addenda] [255] ACHEVÉ D'IMPRIMER | LE 31 AOUT
          1953 | SUR LES PRESSES DE | L'IMPRIMERIE RICHARD |
          24, RUE STEPHENSON | P A R I S - X V I I I e | *Dépôt légal:* |
          3e trimestre 1953. [256] *blank.* 18 cm. Soft cover, crimson. Front
          cover, within border of white stars, in black lettering with white rules:
          SAMUEL BECKETT | [double rule] | *WATT* | [double rule] | COL-
          LECTION MERLIN [bird device in black] | *THE OLYMPIA*
          PRESS; back cover blank except for bottom right: PRINTED IN
          FRANCE; on spine, author and title in vertical caps. and l.c., pub-
          lisher in horizontal caps.

32.001   Fine paper edition. Soft cover, off-white, lettered in black *WATT* |
          [device] | Collection | Merlin. 19 cm.

32.01   Extract from pp. 16-24 published in *Envoy,* I (Jan., 1950), 11-19.
          Variants, e.g., Mr. Hackett does not understand Mr. Nixon when he
          gives Watt's name, but thinks he says "what?" and so repeats his
          statement, "I say you haven't told us his name." Presumably in the
          definitive text (p. 18) Beckett thought it unnecessary to emphasize
          the pun implicit in the name of his hero.

32.02   Extract from pp. 151-162 and p. 213 published in *Irish Writing,* 17
          (Dec., 1951), 11-16. Variants; also shortened to enable the extract
          to stand on its own. According to Biographical Notes (p. 68), Beckett
          was "recently a runner-up for the Renaudot Prize."

32.03   Extract from pp. 199-213 published in *Merlin,* I (Winter, 1952-53),
          118-126. Variants.

32.04   Extract from pp. 71-85 (shortened) published in *Irish Writing,* 22
          (March 1953), 16-24. A note says "an unexpurgated edition of *Watt*
          will be published in the late spring by Collection Merlin."

32.05   Extract from pp. [7]-15 published in **1079**, pp. 213-220.

32.1   Second edition, 1958.
          [1-2] *blank* [3] *half title* [4] *blank* [5] [within green tassels border]
          SAMUEL BECKETT | WATT | THE TRAVELLER'S COMPAN-
          ION | *SERIES* | published by | THE OLYMPIA PRESS | *7, rue St-*

1953

32.1   *Séverin, Paris 5* [6] PRINTED IN FRANCE | [rule] | *All rights reserved by The Olympia Press, Paris* | COPYRIGHT 1958 | 7-272 [text] 273-[279] ADDENDA [280] PRINTED IN FRANCE | [rule] | Printed January 1958 by S. I. P., Montreuil, France | *Dépôt légal: 1ᵉʳ trimestre 1958* | 17 cm. Hardbound, green paper (imitation cloth), gold and black labels on front and spine with title etc. in gold and white caps; scarlet endpapers; colored dust jacket, mainly dark-blue design. Also issued in standard green soft cover, uniform with **377.11.**

32.2   Third edition. New York: Grove Press, 1959 (Evergreen Original E-152).
[i-ii] *blank* [1] *half title* [2] *blank* [3] WATT | By | Samuel Beckett | GROVE PRESS, INC. / NEW YORK | John Calder Ltd. / London [4] [. . .] | Originally published by The Olympia Press, Paris, 1953 | First American edition published 1959 | *Watt* is published in four editions: | An Evergreen Book (E-152) | A cloth bound edition | A specially bound limited edition | of 100 numbered copies | A specially bound and signed edition | of 26 copies lettered A through Z | and 4 copies, *hors commerce,* numbered | 1 through 4 | [. . .] [5] *half title* [6] *blank* [7]-246 [text in four parts, beginning [67], [151], [215] respectively] [247]-254 ADDENDA [pagination identical with **32**] [255-258] *blank.* 20 cm. Hardbound, gray cloth; title etc. in vertical gold caps. on spine; dust jacket, black and green; title white on black above author and design of broken circle black on green; back photograph and biographical comments on author; front and back flap blurb etc. and price $3.50.

32.21   Also in a specially bound and signed edition of 26 lettered copies.
[iii] [page inserted, verso blank, between [2] and [3], giving special information, letter, author's signature]. Hardbound, beige and brown, vertical gold letters on spine.

32.22   Paperback edition (n.d.).
[No i, ii] [2] Other Works by Samuel Beckett [*list*] [3] [. . .] EVER-GREEN BOOKS LTD. / LONDON [4] [shortened but with "Fourth printing" inserted] [255-256] [catalogue extract]. 20 cm. Soft cover, like **32.2** dust jacket except for back blurb, press comments.

32.3   Fourth edition. London: John Calder, 1963 (Oct., Jupiter Books, J. 2; uniform with **25.2**).
[1] *half title* [2] WORKS BY SAMUEL BECKETT [list] [3] WATT | SAMUEL BECKETT | *A Jupiter Book* | *by arrangement with* | *the OLYMPIA PRESS* | LONDON | JOHN CALDER [4] FIRST PUBLISHED BY OLYMPIA PRESS, PARIS, 1953 | FIRST PUBLISHED IN GREAT BRITAIN AS A CALDER JUPITER BOOK IN 1963 | [. . .] | PRINTED IN GREAT BRITAIN BY | LATIMER, TREND AND CO. LTD., PLYMOUTH 5-246 [text] 247-

1953

32.3 255 ADDENDA [256] *blank.* 18 cm. Both soft cover (illus. with
photograph of the author) and hardbound (brown cloth, title and
author in vertical gold italics on spine, dust jacket front illus. with
photograph of the author) editions.

32.31 See **16.032**, pp. 41-57.

NOTE. All editions (including the French translation, **155**) contain a curious
mistake in Martin Ignatius MacKenzie's letter written from *Lourdes | Basses-
Pyrénées | France* (**32**, p. 28; **32.1**, p. 30). Mr. Beckett says that the displace-
ment of Lourdes from the department of the Hautes-Pyrénées was accidental
and not intentional. In **32.3**, after "It is the end of the penny fare, said Mrs.
Nixon" (p. 17), a sentence is added, evidently omitted in error from earlier
editions: "That depends where he got on, said Mr. Nixon." On the other
hand, the score is omitted in error from **32.3**, p. 255, and there are other slips.

1956

From an Abandoned Work

Fragment of an unfinished novel, written *ca.* 1955.

33 *Trinity News; A Dublin University Weekly,* III (June 7, 1956), 4.
(Printed on five columns, with a photograph of the author. Variants.)

33.1 Reprinted in *Evergreen Review,* I, no. 3 (n.d., [1957]), 83-91;

33.2 and by Faber and Faber, London, 1958.
[3] *half title* [4] by the same author | [. . .] [5] FROM AN | ABAN-
DONED WORK | by | SAMUEL BECKETT | FABER **AND**
FABER | 24 Russell Square | London [6] *First published in mcmlviii* |
by Faber and Faber Limited | [. . .] | *Printed in Great Britain by* |
Latimer Trend & Co Ltd Plymouth | [. . .] | © *Samuel Beckett* | 1958
[7] [details of first broadcast] [8] *blank* 9-22 *text.* 22 cm. Soft cover,
with flaps over stiff paper counting as [1-2] and [23-24]. Front cover
illus. with red, pale-blue, and black design, title etc. in black quasi-
handwritten lettering; back cover plain blue.

33.21 Reprinted in **386.1**, pp. [137]-149.

33.22 Reprinted with **154** by Manus Presse, Stuttgart, 1967.
[1-2] *blank* [3] Samuel Beckett | Aus einem | aufgegebenen Werk |
FROM AN ABANDONED WORK | D'UN OUVRAGE ABAN-
DONNÉ | Original-Radierungen von | Max Ernst | manus presse
1967 [4] *blank* 5-10 [text in English] 11-16 [text in French] 17-23
[text in German] [24] [details of printing (55 copies) and copyright;
lithographs printed by Visat, Paris]. 39 cm. Unbound, with three
lithographs inserted loose before each text. Soft cover with flaps,
printed on front, dust jacket of transparent paper, boxed (black,
title etc. in vertical caps. on spine, line drawing on white square on
front).

1956

33

Broadcast in BBC Third Programme, Dec. 14, 1957; reader Patrick Magee, produced by Donald McWhinnie. American premiere Campbell Hall, University of California at Santa Barbara, Feb. 24, 1965, played by James Maguire of Theatre Group 20.

NOTE. According to Mr. Beckett, the fragment results from an attempt to return to fiction in English, in 1954 or 1955. Asked why it ends abruptly, he has replied that "there was just no more to be said" [see **2808**]. *Trinity News* seems to owe the honor of being the first publisher of the fragment to the fact that it is the student newspaper of his university. It also ran a short feature on Beckett entitled "The Man Himself" [see **3077**], but treated the contribution from him with little regard for accuracy of punctuation.

1957

All That Fall

Radio play in one act for eleven voices.

34   New York: Grove Press, 1957.
[i] A | L | L | | T | H | A | T | | F | A | L | L | *By* | SAMUEL BECKETT | GROVE PRESS, INC. | New York [ii] [. . .] | *All That Fall* is published in three editions: | A hard bound edition | A specially bound Limited Edition of 100 numbered copies | A Special Edition of 25 numbered copies, signed by the author | [. . .] | *Manufactured in the United States of America* [iii] *blank* [iv] [cast list] 1-59 [text] [60] *blank*. 20 cm. Hardbound.

34.01   Limited edition of 25 numbered and signed copies has extra loose sheet gummed to [iii] which reads: *This is a* | *SPECIALLY BOUND, LIMITED EDITION* | *of*   *Numbered copies,* | *of which this is copy number* [numbers filled in in ink, signature below]. Hardbound, half brown cloth, half gray paper; title etc. in vertical gilt caps. on cloth front and spine, small two-tone circle mark on bottom right paper front. Cover 21 cm.

34.02   Limited edition of 100 numbered copies, hardbound.

34.03   Christmas edition. Soft cover, white; spine and back blank; front printed green: [row of four Christmas trees] | ALL THAT FALL | a play by | Samuel Beckett | [Christmas tree] | *With Best Wishes for the Holiday Season* | *from* | GROVE PRESS | [row of six Christmas trees].

34.1   London: Faber and Faber, 1957 [Aug. 30].
[i-iv] *blank* [1] *half title* [2] by the same author | * | WAITING FOR GODOT [3] All That Fall | *A Play for Radio* | *by* | SAMUEL BECKETT | FABER AND FABER | 24 Russell Square | London [4] *First published in mcmlvii* | [. . .] | *Printed in Great Britain by* |

1957

34.1 *Ebenezer Baylis and Son, Ltd., Worcester and London* | [. . .] [5] CAST [list] [6] [details of first broadcast] 7-[37] [text] [38-44] *blank.* 20 cm. Soft cover, with flaps over stiff paper, design in pale blue, black, and red; red l.c. for title etc.; title etc. in vertical l.c. on spine; catalogue items on pale blue back cover.

34.101 Second impression, 1959.

34.11 Reissued in 1965 in a Faber Paper Covered Edition, same text expanded over more pages (7-41), shorter (18 cm.), pp. [42-48] blank. No preliminary blank pages. [2] other works by the same author | [includes to *Happy Days*] [4] [. . .] | *First published in this edition mcmlxv* | *Printed in Great Britain* | *by Ebenezer Baylis and Son, Ltd.* | *The Trinity Press, Worcester, and London* | [. . .] Front cover, glossy surface common to series, design in red, white, and black based on title etc; back cover, press comments; title etc. in vertical caps. and l.c. on spine.

34.2 Reprinted in *Krapp's Last Tape and Other Dramatic Pieces* (New York: Grove Press, 1960 [E-226]), pp. [29]-91.
[1] *half title* [2] *blank* [3] [on the left a vertical oblong panel of black rule] SAMUEL | BECKETT | Krapp's | Last | Tape | AND OTHER | DRAMATIC PIECES | GROVE PRESS, INC. | NEW YORK [4] [copyright details] [5] CONTENTS [list] [6] *blank* [7] [panel, as above] Krapp's | Last | Tape | A PLAY IN | ONE ACT [8] [first performance details] 9-28 [text] [29] [panel, as above] All | That | Fall | A PLAY | FOR RADIO [30] [first broadcast details] [31] [cast list] [32] *blank* 33-91 [text] [92] *blank* [93] [panel, as above] Embers | A PLAY | FOR RADIO [94] [first broadcast details] 95-121 [text] [122] *blank* [123] [panel, as above] Act | Without | Words I | A MIME FOR | ONE PLAYER | Translated from the | French by the author [124] [first performance details] 125-133 [text] [134] *blank* [135] [panel, as above] Act | Without | Words II | A MIME FOR | TWO PLAYERS | Translated from the | French by the author [136] *blank* 137-141 [text] [142-144] *blank.* 20 cm. Soft cover, typographical design in red, brown, and black on front; title etc. vertical caps. on spine; blurb, and "Cover design by Roy Kuhlman," on back.

34.21 Reprinted in **1075**, pp. 487-502.

34.3 Reprinted in *Dramatische Dichtungen*, Band 2 (Frankfort on the Main: Suhrkamp Verlag, 1964), pp. [6]-[81], with facing German translation by Erika and Elmar Tophoven. [See also **270.**]
[1] Samuel Beckett [2] *blank* [3] Samuel Beckett | Dramatische Dichtungen | Band 2 | Englische Originalfassungen | Deutsche Übertragung von Erika und Elmar Tophoven | Französische Übertragung von Samuel Beckett | Suhrkamp Verlag [4] Erstes bis drittes Tausend 1964 | © Suhrkamp Verlag Frankfurt am Main 1964. [. . .] [5] *half*

1957

34.3   *title* [6] All That Fall | [and characters list] [7] Alle, die da fallen |
[*idem*] 8-[81] text in two languages [p. 8 is headed "Act one" and
p. 9 "Erster Akt" in error] [82] Krapp's Last Tape [83] Das letzte
Band 84-[109] [text in two languages] [110] Embers | *A play for
radio* | [cast] [111] Aschenglut | *Ein Hörspiel* | [*idem*] 112-[145] [text
in two languages] [146] Happy Days | [cast] [147] Glückliche Tage |
[*idem*] 148-[233] [text in two languages] [234] Play | [cast] [235]
Spiel | [*idem*] 236-[269] [text in two languages] [270] Words and
Music [271] Worte und Musik 272-[291] [text in two languages]
[292] *blank* [293] Tous ceux qui tombent | [cast] [294] *blank* 295-
[328] [text, with pages of English original indicated at foot of each
page, from here to end of volume] [329] La dernière bande [330]
blank 331-[343] [text] [344] *blank* [345] Cendres | [details and cast]
[346] *blank* 347-362 [text] [363] Oh les beaux jours | [cast] [364]
blank 365-[405] [text] [406] *blank* [407] Comédie | [cast] [408] *blank*
409-[424] [text] [425-426] *blank* [427] Inhalt | [list] [428-429] [copy-
right details] [430-432] *blank.* 20 cm. Hardbound, gray cloth; title
etc. in horizontal caps. and l.c. (white on black panel) on spine; two
white tape bookmarks; dust jacket, shiny gray-green, attractively lettered in black within black line panels on front; vertical letters on
spine; blurb on inside flaps; gray cardboard slipcase.

First broadcast on BBC Third Programme, Jan. 13, 1957, 9.30 (to 10.30)
P.M. Largely Irish cast, including Mary O'Farrell, J. G. Devlin, Patrick
Magee, and Jack MacGowran. Production by Donald McWhinnie.

NOTE. The play, not truly "commissioned" as often stated but rather "suggested" by the BBC after the London success of *Waiting for Godot,* was entered
for the 1957 Italia Prize, without success. The original broadcast has been
repeated at least six times by the BBC. The broadcast version shows slight
variants from the text in **34.1**; for the BBC mimeographed Italia Prize submission text, see Appendix I.

Lettercard to "Mr. Joyce" from "Sam Beckett." Undated.

35   Reproduced in facsimile in **3059,** p. 169.

NOTE. The original of the short lettercard, which supplies Joyce with some
Greek and supporting grammatical comments, is preserved in the Lockwood
Memorial Library, State University of New York at Buffalo.

1958

Beckett's Letters on Endgame

Fourteen letters, "extracts from his correspondence with director Alan
Schneider," dated December 27, 1955, through March 4, 1958.

1958

36   *Village Voice,* March 19, 1958, pp. 8 and 15, accompanied by drawings of *Endgame* by Roy Colonna.

36.1   Reprinted in **1054** (Doubleday), pp. 182-186.

36.11   Second edition. New York: Grove Press, 1963, pp. 166-169.

NOTE. The letters not only deal with the genesis of *Endgame* but are interesting in a more general way about Beckett's attitudes toward his work and
toward his audiences.

Krapp's Last Tape

Play in one act for one character and tape recorder.

37   *Evergreen Review,* II (Summer, 1958), 13-24.

37.1   London: Faber and Faber, 1959 (Dec. 18; with **38**).
[1-2] [stiff endpaper] *blank* [3] *half title* [4] by the same author | * |
WAITING FOR GODOT | ALL THAT FALL | END GAME |
FROM AN ABANDONED WORK [5] KRAPP'S LAST TAPE |
and | EMBERS | * | SAMUEL BECKETT | FABER AND FABER
| 24 Russell Square | London [6] *First published in mcmlix* | [. . .]
| *Printed in Great Britain by* | *Latimer Trend & Co Ltd Plymouth* |
[. . .] [7] details and cast lists of first performances of *Krapp's
Last Tape* and **38** [8] *blank* 9-19 [text of *Krapp's Last Tape*]
20-36 [text of **38**] [37-40] *blank* [limp and stiff endpapers]. 20 cm.
Paper wrappers, green, over endpapers; title etc. in red and black
l.c. and italics on wrappers and spine.

37.11   Later impression issued in Faber Paper Covered Editions in [April],
1965. Type identical but pages shorter (18 cm.), fewer lines on
more pages. Thus: 9-20 [text of *Krapp's Last Tape*], 21-39 [text of **38**].
Also, [i-iv, 1-2] and [40-44] *blank.* Soft cover, glossy surface common
to series, red and white; title etc. in black italic caps., l.c. and italics
on cover and spine.

37.2   Reprinted in **34.2**, pp. [7]-28;

37.3   and in **34.3**, pp. [82]-[109].

First performance in Great Britain at Royal Court Theatre, London, Oct. 28,
1958, with Patrick Magee (for whom the play was written), directed by Donald McWhinnie (with **376A**, directed by George Devine). First performance
in United States at Provincetown Playhouse, New York, Jan. 14, 1960, with
Donald Davis, directed by Alan Schneider.

37.31   Recorded on Argo (Spoken Arts) Records, RG 220 (33⅓ rpm, 12
inches), by Donald Davis, directed by Alan Schneider, presented by
Arthur Luce Klein. Recording first issued in 1960.

1959

Embers

Radio play in one act for five voices.

38   *Evergreen Review,* III (Nov.-Dec., 1959), 28-41.

38.1   Reprinted in **37.1**, pp. 20-36;

38.11 and in **37.11**, pp. 21-39;

38.2   and in **34.2**, pp. [93]-121;

38.3   and in **34.3**, pp. [110]-[145].

First broadcast on BBC Third Programme, June 24, 1959, 8.00 (to 9.00) P.M. Cast included Jack MacGowran and Patrick Magee.. Produced by Donald McWhinnie.

NOTE. *Embers* won the 1959 Italia Prize for literary or dramatic works, with or without music. For the BBC mimeographed Italia Prize submission text, see Appendix I.

1961

Happy Days

Play in two acts for two characters.

39   New York: Grove Press, 1961 (E-318).
      [1] [vertical oblong panel of black rule, half title on the right] [2]
      blank [3] [panel, as above] SAMUEL | BECKETT | HAPPY DAYS
      | A PLAY IN | TWO ACTS | GROVE PRESS, INC. | NEW YORK
      [4] Copyright © 1961 by Grove Press, Inc. | [. . .] | First Printing |
      Manufactured in the United States of America [5] CHARACTERS
      [list] [6] *blank* 7-48 [text of Act I] 49-64 [text of Act II]. 20 cm.
      Soft cover, green, black, and white front designed by Roy Kuhlman;
      spine, title etc. vertical black and green caps.; back cover, blurb and
      E-318 and price $1.45.

39.01 Second edition (n.d.).
      [2] Other Works by Samuel Beckett [list] [4] [. . .] Fourth printing
      [. . .] [5] [details of premiere cast, etc.] 20 cm. Soft cover; front,
      photograph of first production by Alix Jeffry, lettered orange and
      black; spine, lettered orange; back blurb, as above, on orange ground.

39.1   London: Faber and Faber, 1962 [June 15].
      [1] *half title* [2] *by the same author* | * | WAITING FOR GODOT |
      ALL THAT FALL | FROM AN ABANDONED WORK | KRAPP'S
      LAST TAPE *and* EMBERS | ENDGAME *and* ACT WITHOUT
      WORDS [3] HAPPY DAYS | *A Play in Two Acts* | *by* | SAMUEL
      BECKETT | FABER AND FABER | 24 Russell Square | London
      [4] [. . .] | *Printed in Great Britain by* | *Latimer Trend & Co Ltd*
      Plymouth | [. . .] 5 [details and cast list of first peformance] [6]

1961

39.1   *blank* 7 CHARACTERS [list] [8] *blank* 9-36 [text of Act One] 37-
48 [text of Act Two]. 20 cm. Hardbound, red cloth; title etc. in
vertical gold caps. on spine; dust jacket illus. with photograph of
the New York production by Alix Jeffry.

39.101 Offprint of p. 35 in *Sample*, 1 (Spring, 1962), 6. [*Sample* is Faber's
publicity brochure, and this is evidently an offprint of page proof and
not of the definitive text, for the penultimate line shows the variant
(*Pause.*) for *Pause.*]

39.11 Also issued in Faber Paper Covered Editions, uniform with **34.11**,
dated 1966, cover design like dust jacket of **39.1**.

39.2 Reprinted in *Plays and Players*, X (Nov., 1962), 34-42, on two cols.,
illus. with photographs of the New York production by Alix Jeffry;

39.3 and in **34.3**, pp. [146]-[233].

First performance at Cherry Lane Theatre, New York, Sept. 17, 1961, with
Ruth White as Winnie and John C. Becher as Willie, directed by Alan
Schneider. First performance in Great Britain at Royal Court Theatre, Lon-
don, Nov. 1, 1962, with Brenda Bruce as Winnie, directed by George Devine.

Poems in English

40 London: John Calder, 1961 [late Aug.].
[i-ii] *blank* [endpapers incorporated in sewn gatherings] [1] *half title*
[2] By SAMUEL BECKETT [list] [3] POEMS IN ENGLISH |
SAMUEL BECKETT | [heavy rule] | [short rule] | LONDON |
JOHN CALDER [4] FIRST EDITION | PUBLISHED 1961 IN
GREAT BRITAIN | BY JOHN CALDER (PUBLISHERS) LTD |
[. . .] | A LIMITED EDITION OF ONE HUNDRED COPIES
ON HAND- | MADE PAPER AND SIGNED BY THE AUTHOR
HAS BEEN PRINTED | (HORS COMMERCE) IN ADVANCE
OF THE FIRST EDITION | ACKNOWLEDGMENTS | *Whoro-
scope* was first published by Nancy | Cunard, The Hours Press, 1930,
and *Echo's* | *Bones* by George Reavey, Europa Press, 1935 | PRINTED
IN GREAT BRITAIN BY | A WHEATON AND CO LTD EX-
ETER [5] CONTENTS [list] [6] *blank* [7] I Whoroscope [8] *blank*
9-14 [text and notes of *Whoroscope*] [15] II Echo's Bones [16] *blank*
17-38 [text of *Echo's Bones* cycle] [39] III Two Poems [40] *blank*
41-42 [text of *Cascando*] 43 [text of *Saint-Lô*] [44] *blank* [45] IV
Quatre Poèmes 46 [*Dieppe*, French text] 47 [*Dieppe*, English text]
48 je suis ce cours de sable qui glisse | [. . .] 49 my way is in the
sand flowing | [. . .] 50 que ferais-je sans ce monde sans visage
sans questions | [. . .] 51 what would I do without this world face-
less incurious | [. . .] 52 je voudrais que mon amour meure | [. . .]
53 I would like my love to die | [. . .] | (translated from the French
by the author) [54-58] *blank*. 20 cm. Hardbound, blue cloth; title
etc. in vertical gold caps., italic caps. and l.c. on spine; dust jacket,
plain blue paper, title etc. in black caps., blurb.

1961

40.01   Handmade paper edition (published after first edition) numbered
and signed by author on p. [4] (no. 42 in British Museum) in ink;
23 cm.; hardbound, buff cloth (imitation grained leather); gold
caps. on spine; top edge gilt, rest untrimmed.

40.1   Second edition. New York: Grove Press, 1963.
[1] *half title* [2] *blank* [3] Poems In English | *by* | *Samuel Beckett* |
GROVE PRESS, INC. [   ] NEW YORK [4] [Acknowledgments,
date (1963), etc.] [5] *half title* [6] Other Works by Samuel Beckett |
Published by Grove Press [list] [7] Contents [list] [8] *blank* [9] I
Whoroscope [10] *blank* 11-17 [text and notes of *Whoroscope*] [18]
blank [19] II Echo's Bones [20] *blank* 21-46 [text of *Echo's Bones*
cycle] [47] III Two Poems [48] *blank* 49-50 1. Cascando 51 2.
Saint-Lô [52] *blank* [53] IV Quatre Poèmes 54 1. Dieppe [French
text] 55 1. Dieppe [English text] 56 2. je suis ce cours de sable [. . .]
57 2. my way [. . .] 58 3. que ferais-je [. . .] 59 3. what would I do
[. . .] 60 4. je voudrais [. . .] 61 4. I would like [. . .] | (*translated
from the French* | *by the author*) [62-64] *blank*. 20 cm. Hardbound,
green cloth; title in vertical black caps. and l.c. on spine.

40.101 Paperback edition. Evergreen Books, E-379, issued in 1964, at $1.45.

NOTE. According to H. Alan Clodd, there seem to be binding variants in **40**,
some copies having been bound in green cloth.

1962

Words and Music

Radio play in one act for two voices, to a musical score by John
Beckett, the author's cousin.

41   *Evergreen Review,* VI (Nov.-Dec., 1962), 34-43.

41.1   Reprinted in **34.3**, pp. [270]-[291];

41.2   and in **42**, pp. [25]-36.

First broadcast on BBC Third Programme, Nov. 13, 1962, at 9.35 P.M. (to
10.05), produced by Michael Bakewell, with Felix Felton and Patrick Magee.

1964

Play

Play in one act for three characters.

42   London: Faber and Faber, 1964 (March 26; with **41.2** and **383.2**).
[1] PLAY | and two short pieces | for radio [2] by the same author |
* | WAITING FOR GODOT | ALL THAT FALL | FROM AN
ABANDONED WORK | KRAPP'S LAST TAPE *and* EMBERS |
ENDGAME *and* ACT WITHOUT WORDS | HAPPY DAYS

1964

42   [3] PLAY | and two short pieces | for radio | * | SAMUEL |
        BECKETT | FABER & FABER | 24 Russell Square | London [4]
        First published in mcmlxiv | [. . .] *Printed in Great Britain by* |
        Latimer Trend & Co Ltd Plymouth | [. . .] [5] CONTENTS [list]
        [6] *blank* [7] PLAY | A Play in One Act [8] [details and cast list of
        first performance of *Play*] 9-22 [text of *Play*] 23-24 [notes to director
        on light, chorus, and urns] [25] WORDS AND MUSIC [26] [details
        and cast list of first broadcast of *Words and Music*] 27-36 [text of
        Words and Music] [37] CASCANDO | A Radio Piece for Music
        and Voice [38] [details and cast list of French broadcast of *Cascando*]
        39-48 [text of *Cascando*]. 20 cm. Hardbound, red cloth; title etc. in
        vertical gold caps. on spine; dust jacket, illus. with photograph by
        Jack Nisberg taken during first production of *Play*.

42.1   Reprinted in **34.3**, pp. [234]-[269];

42.2   and in *Evergreen Review,* VIII (April, 1965), 42-47, 92.

First performance (in German translation, subsequently published in *Theater
Heute,* July, 1963, being the first appearance of the play in any language)
at Ulmer Theater, Ulm-Donau, June 14, 1963, with Nancy Illig, Sigrid Pfeiffer,
and Gerhard Winter, directed by Deryk Mendel, who on the same occasion
acted in the two *Acts Without Words* [see **265B**, **270A**]. First performance in
the United States at Cherry Lane Theatre, New York, Jan. 4, 1964, with
Frances Sternhagen, Marian Reardon, and Michael Lipton, directed by Alan
Schneider. First performance in Great Britain at National Theatre (The Old
Vic), London, April 7, 1964, with Rosemary Harris, Billie Whitelaw, and
Robert Stephens, directed by George Davis.

NOTE. According to H. Alan Clodd, there are binding variants in **42**, "one
a dull red and the other a much brighter, almost geranium red."

1965

Jem Higgins' Love-Letter to the Alba

Excerpt from *Dream of Fair to Middling Women*. About 600 words.
Signed SAMUEL BECKETT. (One misprint, "respecful" for "re-
spectful," p. [11].)

43   *New Durham,* n.v., n.d. [June, 1965], pp. [10-11].

NOTE. The fragment, published in the Durham University magazine (ed.
Peter Mew), is followed by this note: "This excerpt from his unpublished novel
Dream of Fair to Middling Women (*ca.* 1932) is printed here for the first
time by kind permission of Samuel Beckett. © Samuel Beckett, 1965." In his
letter, the rugby man Jem Higgins declares his love for the Alba in characteristically uncouth and cliché-ridden terms, while she chuckles cynically to
herself over his invitations and promises. The love letter is referred to by
John Fletcher in **708**, p. 15.

1965

A Tribute to Richard Aldington.

44   Published in *Richard Aldington: An Intimate Portrait,* ed. Alister
Kershaw and Frédéric-Jacques Temple (Carbondale and Edwards-
ville: Southern Illinois University Press, 1965), p. 3 [see **2869**].

NOTE. Under Samuel Beckett's name in large print appears the following
passage: *"J'ai moins de souvenirs que si j'avais six mois.* Among the ghostly
few is that of the great kindness shown me, in Paris, in the late twenties and
early thirties, by Richard Aldington. My first two publications, by Hours
Press and Chatto and Windus, I owe in part to his good offices. I think of
him with affection and gratitude."

"Notes on the Contributors" states: "Samuel Beckett, author and playwright, was born in Dublin in 1906. He was educated at Portora Royal
School and Trinity College in Dublin. He has lived mostly in France since
1947 [*sic*]. He has written many poems, short stories, novels, and plays. Among
them are the well-known plays *Waiting for Godot* and *Krapp's Last Tape.*"

1967

45A   *Eh Joe,* "a piece for television," for male actor and female voice.

[379]   *Act Without Words II,* "a mime for two players."

45B   *Film,* a screenplay.

45   *Eh Joe and Other Writings.* London: Faber and Faber, 1967.
[1-2] *blank* [3] *half title* [4] Books by Samuel Beckett [list] [5] EH
JOE | and Other Writings | by | SAMUEL | BECKETT | FABER
AND FABER | 24 Russell Square | London [6] *First published in
mcmlxvii | by Faber and Faber Limited | 24 Russell Square London
WC1 | Printed in Great Britain by | Robert MacLehose and Co. Ltd
| The University Press, Glasgow* | [copyright data] 7 NOTE [on first
productions] [8] *blank* 9 ACKNOWLEDGEMENT [to **379**] [10]
blank 11 CONTENTS [list] [12] *blank* [13] *half title* (**45A**) [14]
blank 15-21 [text, **45A**] [22] *blank* [23] *half title* (**379**) [24] *blank*
25-28 [text, **379**] [29] *half title* (**45B**) [30] [author's note on **45B**]
31-44 [text, **45B**] [45-46] *blank, serving as endpaper.* 20 cm. Hardbound, red cloth; title etc. in vertical gold caps. and l.c. on spine;
dust jacket, illus. with photograph of Jack MacGowran as Joe in
the BBC production of **45A**.

45.1   **45A** and **45B** reprinted in **151.2**.

45.2   **45A** reprinted in *Evergreen Review,* XIII (Jan., 1969), 43-46.

NOTE. **45B** was written in May 1963 and produced in 1964 by Evergreen
Theatre, Inc. directed by Alan Schneider and starring Buster Keaton (other
parts played by Nell Harrison, James Karen, and Susan Reed). Shown at the
Venice Film Festival on Sept. 4, 1965, it was awarded the Prix Filmcritica, and

1967

45

the Special Jury Prize at the International Film Festival of Short Subjects at Tours in January, 1966. Its running time is 24 minutes. **45A** was produced by BBC Television (BBC-2) on July 4, 1966, 10.20 (to 10.40) P.M., with Jack MacGowran playing Joe and Sian Phillips the Voice; direction was by Alan Gibson and production by Michael Bakewell, assisted by the author.

1967

Come and Go

"A dramaticule" for three female characters.

46   London: Calder and Boyars, 1967.
[i] *half title* [ii] *blank* [iii] COME AND GO | *Dramaticule* | *by* | SAMUEL BECKETT | CALDER AND BOYARS | LONDON | [iv] *First published in Great Britain 1967 by* | *Calder and Boyars Limited* | *18 Brewer Street, London, W.1.* | © Samuel Beckett 1967 | for John Calder | A limited edition of 100 numbered copies, signed | by the author and bound in full buckram have | been printed in advance of the first edition and may | be obtained (hors commerce) on application to the | publisher. | *Printed and bound in Great Britain by* | *Unwin Brothers Limited, The Gresham Press, Woking* [v] CHARACTERS [list] [vi] [plate] 1-10 [text] (plates [2], [4], [6], Notes, 9-10). 19½ cm. Soft cover, flaps over stiff paper; front incorporating plate on p. [6]; title etc. in vertical caps. on spine; back blank; inside flaps, blurb and catalogue list.

46.1   Reprinted with **152** and German trans. by Manus Presse, Stuttgart, in deluxe edition similar to **265.4**.

NOTE. The photographs were taken by Ilse Buhs of Deryk Mendel's Berlin production with Lieselotte Rau, Charlotte Foeres, and Sibylle Gilles at the Schiller Theater, Jan., 1966.

Translations into French of the English Works

1938

Alba [11]

"Traduit de l'anglais par A. R. Peron [*sic*]."

144   *Soutes: Revue de Culture Révolutionnaire Internationale,* 9 (1938), 41 [Bibliothèque nationale date stamp: 2 V 1938].

1938

144

Note. Published in the last issue of *Soutes* (founded by Luc Decaunes), this translation by his close friend was not checked by Beckett, who thinks it "not very good." It has seventeen lines and sticks closely to the original. It is signed: Samuel BECKETT.

1947

Murphy [25]

145   Translated by the author. Paris: Bordas, 1947.
[1-2] *blank* [3] *half title* [4] Paru en anglais, sous le même titre, | aux éditions Routledge, en 1938. [5] SAMUEL BECKETT | MURPHY | BORDAS | 1947 [6] *à Alfred Péron* | Tous droits réservés pour tous pays. Copyright BORDAS 1947. Dépôt légal: | 2me trimestre 1947. — N^o d'Éditeur: 220 — N^o d'Imprimeur: 12 [7]-201 *text* [202] *blank* [203] TABLE [list] [204] *blank* [205] Achevé d'imprimer le présent | ouvrage le 15 Avril 1947, | sur les presses de l'imprimerie | de la PRESSE JURASSIENNE | — à DOLE-du-JURA — [206-208] *blank.* 20½ cm. Soft cover, white; front cover, title etc. in yellow and black caps., number in collection (yellow) and device (black), all within border formed of "COLLECTION LES IMAGINAIRES" in yellow and black caps., and of yellow and black stars; back cover, catalogue items within yellow line border.

145.01   Reissued in soft cover, white, with blue and black lettering on front: SAMUEL BECKETT | MURPHY | *roman* | [star and m device] | *LES ÉDITIONS DE MINUIT* [within blue line border]. Back cover, press comments on *Molloy, Malone meurt, L'Innommable, En attendant Godot,* with Éditions de Minuit address, within blue line border; title etc. in blue and black horizontal caps. on spine.

145.1   Reprinted photographically by Éditions de Minuit, Paris, 1965. First printing: 2,799.
[1-2] *blank* [3] *half title* [4] DU MÊME AUTEUR [includes to *Comment c'est* and *Oh les beaux jours*] [5] SAMUEL BECKETT | MURPHY | [star and m device] | LES EDITIONS DE MINUIT | [6] *à Alfred Péron* | © 1965, by Les Editions de Minuit | 7, rue Bernard-Palissy, Paris (6e) | *Tous droits réservés pour tous pays* | [7]-201 [text] [202] *blank* [203] TABLE [204] *blank* [205] CET OUVRAGE A ETE ACHEVE D'IMPRIMER | LE 22 JUIN MIL NEUF CENT SOIXANTE CINQ | SUR LES PRESSES DE JOSEPH FLOCH A MAYENNE | ET INSCRIT DANS LES REGISTRES DE L'EDITEUR | SOUS LE NUMERO 555 | Imprimé en France [206-208] *blank.* 18½ cm. Soft cover, white, with flaps, with list of works by Beckett (to *Oh les beaux jours*) and other authors on inside of flaps; price, Fr. 12; back cover blank except for blue star and m device. Title etc. horizontal caps. on spine; all edges trimmed.

1947

145.001   Extract from **145**, pp. 63-65, reprinted in *Advanced Level French Course, Book I*, by W. T. John, M.A., and G. W. Crowther, M. A. (London, etc., Thomas Nelson and Sons, Ltd., 1962; printed in Great Britain) p. 94, under the title "Getting One's Money's Worth." Extract shortened, slightly adapted; begins " 'Apportez-moi une tasse de thé . . .' " and ends "1,83 tasse approximativement"; figures as no. 21 among "Prose Passages for Translation into English." Volume has 132 pages. 20 cm. [See **257.002**.]

NOTE. According to Mr. Beckett he had completed this translation by the outbreak of World War II, with the occasional informal assistance of Alfred Péron, to whom it is dedicated. Péron was exchange lecturer in French at Trinity College, Dublin, from 1926 to 1928; there is an anonymous valedictory note on him in *T.C.D.*, XXXIV (June 14, 1928), 206, "College Notes." Deported by the Gestapo, he was to die soon after his liberation from a concentration camp. He had been a brilliant *agrégé d'anglais* of great promise. It was probably his example that led Beckett to join the Resistance early in the war, before Péron's arrest forced him to flee to the Vaucluse. Published by Bordas in the series "Les Imaginaires" (no. 5), *Murphy* in four years sold only about 95 of the 3,000 copies printed. M. Jérôme Lindon took over the contract and unsold stock for the Éditions de Minuit at the end of 1951, since Bordas had refused *Molloy* and *Malone meurt*. According to the Éditions de Minuit catalogue (Autumn, 1958), p. 3, no reviews of the novel appeared in the press at the time of publication.

1957

Tous ceux qui tombent [**34**]

Translated by Robert Pinget and the author.

146   "Texte radiophonique." *Lettres Nouvelles*, V (March, 1957), 321-351 ("Traduit de l'anglais par Robert Pinget avec la collaboration de l'auteur").

146.1   Paris: Éditions de Minuit, 1957. First printing: 3,000. [1-2] *blank* [3] *half title* [4] DU MÊME AUTEUR [list to *Nouvelles et Textes pour rien, Fin de partie*] [5] SAMUEL BECKETT | Tous ceux | qui tombent | PIÈCE RADIOPHONIQUE | *Traduit de l'anglais par Robert Pinget* | [star and m device] | LES EDITIONS DE MINUIT [6] IL A ÉTÉ TIRÉ DE CET OUVRAGE | SOIXANTE-DIX EXEMPLAIRES SUR PUR | FIL MARAIS NUMÉROTÉS DE 1 A 70 | PLUS DIX EXEMPLAIRES HORS-COMMERCE | NUMÉROTÉS DE H.C. 1 A   H.C. 10 | © 1957 by Les Editions de Minuit | 7, rue Bernard-Palissy, Paris-6ᵉ. | Tous droits réservés pous tous pays 7 [cast list] 7-77 *text* [78] *blank* [79] CET OUVRAGE A ÉTÉ ACHEVÉ D'IMPRIMER | LE 18 OCTOBRE 1957 SUR LES PRESSES | DE L'IMPRIMERIE VICTOR-HUGO, A | POITIERS, SOUS LE NUMÉRO 162, |

1957

146.1   DÉPOT LÉGAL 4ᵉ TRIMESTRE 1957, | ET INSCRIT DANS
LES REGISTRES DE | L'ÉDITEUR SOUS LE Nº 332 [80] *blank*.
18 cm. Soft cover, white; title etc. in blue and black caps., italic caps.
and l.c. on front within blue line border; back cover, biographical
summary within blue line border.

146.11   Reprinted photographically, 1964. 3,000 copies.
[4] *DU MÊME AUTEUR* [includes to *Oh les beaux jours,* but not to
Comment c'est] [79] CET OUVRAGE A ÉTÉ ACHEVÉ D'IM-
PRIMER | LE 1ᵉʳ AVRIL 1964 SUR LES PRESSES DE | JOSEPH
FLOCH, MAITRE-IMPRIMEUR A | MAYENNE ET INSCRIT
DANS LES REGISTRES | DE L'ÉDITEUR SOUS LE Nº 515
[otherwise identical, except for back cover (catalogue list)].

146.2   Reprinted in **34.3**, pp. [293]-[328].

NOTE. Although Pinget is named as the sole translator in the Éditions de
Minuit edition, Beckett, as usual, thoroughly revised the text. A televised version of the play was first broadcast (against the author's better judgment, for
he considers it unsuitable for television) by R.T.F. on Jan. 25, 1963, produced
by Michel Mitrani.

1959

La Dernière Bande [**37**]

Translated by Pierre Leyris and the author.

147   *Lettres Nouvelles,* 1 (March 4, 1959), 5-13.

147.1   Reprinted with **148** in *La Dernière Bande, suivi de Cendres* (Paris:
Éditions de Minuit, 1960).
[1-2] *blank* [3] *half title* [4] DU MEME AUTEUR [list to *Fin de
partie, Tous ceux qui tombent*] [5] SAMUEL BECKETT | La
dernière bande | Traduit de l'anglais par Pierre Leyris et l'auteur |
[star and m device] | LES EDITIONS DE MINUIT [6] IL A ÉTÉ
TIRÉ DE CET OUVRAGE QUA- | RANTE EXEMPLAIRES
SUR PUR FIL DU | MARAIS NUMÉROTÉS DE 1 A 40 PLUS |
SEPT EXEMPLAIRES HORS-COMMERCE | NUMÉROTÉS DE
H-C I A H-C VII | © 1959, by Les Editions de Minuit | 7, rue
Bernard-Palissy, Paris (6ᵉ) | *Tous droits réservés pour tous pays*
7-33 [text of **147**] [34] *blank* [35] Cendres | Traduit de l'anglais par
Robert Pinget et l'auteur [36] *blank* 37-[72] text of **148** [73] CET
OUVRAGE A ÉTÉ ACHEVÉ D'IMPRIMER | LE 5 JANVIER
1960 SUR LES PRESSES | DE LA PREMIÈRE IMPRIMERIE
UKRAI- | NIENNE EN FRANCE, 3, RUE DU SABOT, | A
PARIS ET INSCRIT DANS LES REGIS- | TRES DE L'ÉDITEUR
SOUS LE NUMÉRO 403 [74-76] *blank*. 18½ cm. Soft cover;
front reads: La dernière bande [blue] | *suivi de* | Cendres [blue];

1959

147.1 printed white slip, inserted loose into volume, reads: Par suite d'une erreur, on a omis d'indiquer | que la seconde pièce de ce volume, CENDRES, | est une pièce radiophonique. First printing: 2,302 (Jan. 5); second impression: 2,121 (March 13).

147.11 Reprinted photographically, 1965. 3,000 copies.
[4] *DU MÊME AUTEUR* [to *Comment c'est, Oh les beaux jours*] [5] SAMUEL BECKETT | La dernière bande | Traduit de l'anglais par l'auteur | [star and m device] | LES EDITIONS DE MINUIT [35] Cendres | PIECE RADIOPHONIQUE | Traduit de l'anglais par Robert Pinget et l'auteur [73] ACHEVÉ D'IMPRIMER | LE 2 FÉVRIER 1965 | PAR JOSEPH FLOCH | MAITRE-IMPRIMEUR | A MAYENNE | nº 2277 [otherwise identical, except for back cover, catalogue list to *Oh les beaux jours*].

147.2 Reprinted with *Lettre morte* by Robert Pinget as no. 42 in *Collection du Répertoire* (Paris: Éditions de Minuit and Théâtre national populaire, 1960), pp. [65]-77. "Achevé d'imprimer" dated March 21, 1960. Copyright 1959 by Éditions de Minuit. Printed by Laboureur et Cie, Paris. 80 pp., illus. 18 cm. Soft cover, white, red and black lettering. (The credit in **147.2** records "Traduit de l'anglais par l'auteur.")

147.3 Reprinted with *Lettre morte* by Robert Pinget in *L'Avant-Scène/ Femina-Théâtre*, 222 (June 15, 1960), 25-28. (The translator is again specified as the author.)

147.4 Reprinted in **34.3**, pp. [329]-[343];

147.5 and in **1078**, pp. 15-26 (see also **263.04**);

147.6 and in **1246**, pp. 113-124.

First performed at the Théâtre national populaire's Théâtre Récamier in Paris on March 22, 1960, with R.-J. Chauffard as Krapp, directed by Roger Blin. *Lettre morte* by Robert Pinget, directed by Jean Martin, was included in the program.

147.7 Also set to music by Marcel Mihalovici.
[i] KRAPP | ou | La dernière bande | *Opéra* | Samuel BECKETT [ ] Marcel MIHALOVICI | The last tape | opera | Krapp | oder | Das letzte Band | *Oper* | (*Deutsch von Elmar Tophoven*) | Couverture de Jacques DUPONT | AU MÉNESTREL, 2 bis, Rue Vivienne, Paris (2e), HEUGEL & Cie | ÉDITEURS-PROPRIÉTAIRES POUR TOUS PAYS | Tous droits de reproduction, de traduction, d'arrangement, d'adaptation | et d'exécution réservés en tous pays. | Imprimé en France [ii] [details for performance ("Durée: musique seule, 50' environ, avec jeux de scène, 60' environ")] [1] pour Monique HAAS | KRAPP | ou | LA DERNIÈRE BANDE | OPÉRA | SAMUEL BECKETT [ ] MARCEL MIHALOVICI | op. 81 | [score and libretto follows, bottom p. [1]: © HEUGEL & Cie, 1961] [1]-146 [score with libretto in French, English, German;

1959

147.7 stage directions in French only] 146 [bottom] *Dépôt légal N° 658* [ ] H. 31716 [ ] Paris, du 25 mai au 30 décembre 1959. | IMP. ROLLAND Père et Fils — PARIS | Printed in France. 31 cm. by 23 cm. Soft cover, back and spine blank, front design in black, green, turquoise, and ocher, signed at bottom in black "Dupont," "KRAPP" in vertical black letters down left-hand side against spine, "Heugel et Cie" in horizontal ocher letters along bottom. [Bibliothèque nationale date stamp (dépôt légal) : 23 1 61.]

First broadcast by R.T.F. (France III) on May 15, 1961 (repeated May 2, 1965); conductor, Serge Baudo; performed at the Théâtre des Nations (Paris) by the Bielefeld Opera on July 3, 1961; director, Joachim Klaiber, conductor Bernhard Konz. [See **719**, pp. 20-22.]

NOTE. Although Pierre Leyris' name appears in several places, M. Jérôme Lindon has said that Beckett entirely reworked his translation but nevertheless insisted on Leyris receiving royalty payments for it.

Cendres [**38**]

Translated by Robert Pinget and the author.

148 *Lettres Nouvelles,* 36 (Dec. 30, 1959), 3-14.

148.1/11 See **147.1** and **147.11**.

148.2 Reprinted in *L'Avant-Scène du Théâtre,* 313 (June 15, 1964), 21-25, as a "pièce radiophonique en un acte de Samuel Beckett" with no mention of translator (see **149.1**);

148.3 and in **34.3**, pp. [345]-362.

1963

Oh les beaux jours [**39**]

149 Translated by the author. Paris: Éditions de Minuit, 1963 [First printing: 4,000].
[1-2] *blank* [3] *half title* [4] DU MÊME AUTEUR [includes to *Comment c'est* and *La Dernière Bande*] [5] SAMUEL BECKETT | Oh | les beaux jours | PIÈCE EN DEUX ACTES | [star and m device] | LES ÉDITIONS DE MINUIT [6] IL A ÉTÉ TIRÉ DE CET OUVRAGE QUATRE-VINGTS | EXEMPLAIRES SUR PUR FIL, NUMÉROTÉS DE 1 A | 80, PLUS SEPT EXEM-PLAIRES HORS-COMMERCE, | NUMÉROTÉS DE H.-C. I A H.-C. VII | IL A ÉTÉ TIRÉ EN OUTRE QUATRE CENT DOUZE | EXEMPLAIRES SUR VELIN MARQUÉS «412», NU- | MÉROTÉS DE 1 A 412 ET RÉSERVÉS A LA LIBRAIRIE | DES ÉDITIONS DE MINUIT | © 1963 by LES ÉDITIONS DE MINUIT | 7, rue Bernard-Palissy — PARIS-VIe | *Tous droits réservés pour tous pays* [7] PERSONNAGES [list] [8] *blank* 9-65 [Act I] [66] *blank* 67-89 [Act II] [90] CET OUVRAGE A ÉTÉ

1963

149   ACHEVÉ | D'IMPRIMER LE 23 FÉVRIER 1963 | SUR LES PRESSES DE L'IMPRI- | MERIE CORBIÈRE ET JUGAIN | A ALENÇON ET INSCRIT DANS | LES REGISTRES DE L'ÉDI-TEUR | — SOUS LE NUMÉRO 488 — | *Imprimé en France* [91-92] *blank.* 18 x 10 cm., narrow format. Soft cover; title etc. in blue and black caps., italic caps. and l.c. within blue-line border; on back cover: list of *"COLLECTION IN-16"* and price: 4,95 F; title etc. in blue and black horizontal caps. on spine. Back cover of numbered copies blank except for ÉDITION ORIGINALE.

149.01   Reprinted Nov. 15, 1963 (3,000) ;

149.02   and Jan. 11, 1965 (5,000).

149.1   Reprinted in *L'Avant-Scène du Théâtre,* 313 (June 15, 1964), 10-19. [See also **148.2**.]

149.11   Extracts recorded by Madeleine Renaud and Jean-Louis Barrault on a Disque L'Avant-Scène 33 rpm, 12 inches (Collection "Théâtre" dirigée par Paul-Louis Mignon, no. 3) on Feb. 5 and 6, 1964, with linking passages read by Roger Blin. Disques Adès, TS30LA568.

149.2   Reprinted in **34.3**, pp. [363]-[405].

First performed at Twenty-second International Festival of Prose Drama, Venice (Teatro del Ridotto) on Sept. 28, 1963, and in Paris at Odéon-Théâtre de France, Nov. 15, 1963, with Madeleine Renaud as Winnie and Jean-Louis Barrault as Willie, directed by Roger Blin.

NOTE. No translator is mentioned in the Éditions de Minuit text, but "Traduite de l'anglais par l'auteur" figures among the credits in *L'Avant-Scène,* p. 7, where Roger Blin's direction is called "présentation."

1964

Comédie [**42**]

Translated by the author.

150   *Lettres Nouvelles,* XII (June-July-Aug., 1964), 10-31. [Subtitled "Un acte de Samuel Beckett," and followed by the note *"traduit de l'anglais par l'auteur"* and "© Editions de Minuit."]

150.1   Reprinted in **34.3**, pp. [407]-[424];

150.2   and in **151.1**, pp. [7]-35;

150.21   and in *Panorama du théâtre nouveau,* ed. Jacques Benay and Reinhard Kuhn (New York: Appleton-Century-Crofts, 1967), I, 17-34.

First performed at Pavillon de Marsan, Paris, June 11, 1964, with Delphine Seyrig, Eléonore Hirt, and Michael Lonsdale, directed by Jean-Marie Serreau.

1964

150

Filmed by Mariu Karmitz, Jean Ravel, and Jean-Marie Serreau with the same cast in Jan., 1966.

See also **152**, Note.

NOTE. In **150** on p. 2 of the review, under *"NOS COLLABORATEURS"*: "La pièce de SAMUEL BECKETT, montée à New York et à Londres, le sera prochainement à Paris, par Jean-Marie Serreau."

1966

Dis Joe [**45A**]

Translated by the author.

151   *Arts: l'Hebdomadaire Complet de la Vie Culturelle,* 15 (Jan. 5-11, 1966), 3 (on 4 cols.), subtitled *UN* | *INÉDIT* | *DE* | BECKETT. (In an introductory note the imminent publication of **151.1** is announced.)

151.1   Reprinted in *Comédie et actes divers* (Paris: Éditions de Minuit, 1966), pp. [79]-91.
[1-2] *blank* [3] *half title* [4] DU MÊME AUTEUR [list to **272**] [5] SAMUEL BECKETT | Comédie | et | actes divers | [star and m device] | LES EDITIONS DE MINUIT [6] IL A ÉTÉ TIRÉ DE CET OUVRAGE | QUATRE-VINGTS EXEMPLAIRES SUR | PUR FIL LAFUMA, NUMÉROTÉS DE | 1 A 80 PLUS SEPT EXEMPLAIRES | HORS-COMMERCE NUMÉROTÉS DE | H.-C. I A H.-C. VII | IL A ÉTÉ TIRÉ EN OUTRE CENT | DOUZE EXEMPLAIRES SUR BOUFFANT | SÉLECT MARQUÉS «112» NUMÉRO- | TÉS DE 1 A 112 ET RÉSERVÉS A LA | LIBRAIRIE DES ÉDITIONS DE MINUIT | © 1966 by LES EDITIONS DE MINUIT | 7, rue Bernard-Palissy — PARIS-VIe | *Tous droits réservés pour tous pays* [7] COMÉDIE | PIÈCE EN UN ACTE | *Traduit de l'anglais par l'auteur* [8] *blank* 9-35 [text of **150**] [36] *blank* [37] VA ET VIENT | DRAMATICULE | *Traduit de l'anglais par l'auteur* [38] *pour John Calder* 39-44 [text of **152**] [45] CASCANDO | PIÈCE RADIOPHONIQUE | POUR MUSIQUE ET VOIX | Musique: Marcel Mihalovici [46] *blank* 47-60 [text of **271**] [61] PAROLES ET MUSIQUE | PIÈCE RADIOPHONIQUE | Musique: John Beckett | *Traduit de l'anglais par l'auteur* [62] *blank* 63-78 [text of **153**] [79] DIS JOE | PIÈCE POUR LA TÉLÉVISION | *Traduit de l'anglais par l'auteur* [80] *blank* 81-91 [text of **151**] | [92] *blank* [93] ACTE SANS PAROLE [*sic*] II | POUR DEUX PERSONNAGES ET UN AIGUILLON [94] *blank* 95-99 [text of **270A**] [100] *blank* [101] TABLE DES MATIERES [list] [102] *blank* [103] CET OUVRAGE A ÉTÉ ACHEVÉ D'IM- | PRIMER LE DIX JANVIER MIL NEUF | CENT SOIXANTE-SIX SUR LES | PRESSES DE L'IMPRIMERIE CORBIÈRE | ET

1966

151.1 JUGAIN A ALENÇON ET INSCRIT | DANS LES REGISTRES DE L'ÉDITEUR | SOUS LE NUMÉRO 570 | *Imprimé en France* [104] *blank*. 18 cm. Soft cover, with flaps, very similar to **145.1**; all edges trimmed.

151.2 Reprinted with **45A**, **45B**, and Beckett's French trans. of **45B** in *Film, He Joe, in drei Sprachen* (Frankfort on the Main: Suhrkamp Verlag, 1968).

NOTE. Production for ORTF was by Michel Mitrani assisted by the author, who himself directed the German television production at Stuttgart, assisted only by technicians.

> *Va et vient* [46]
>
> "Dramaticule," translated by the author.

152 Published in **151.1**, pp. [37]-44.

152.1 See **46.1**.

Produced in Paris at Odéon-Théâtre de France in March, 1966, with Madeleine Renaud, Simone Valère, and Annie Bertin in a "Spectacle Beckett, Pinget, Ionesco" grouping plays by these authors and including **150**, *Comédie*, in Jean-Marie Serreau's production with Delphine Seyrig's part taken by Danielle van Bercheycke.

> *Paroles et musique* [41]
>
> Translated by the author.

153 Published in **151.1**, pp. [61]-78.

NOTE. This play does not appear in **34.3**, *Dramatische Dichtungen*, Band II; a note on p. 427 explains that no French translation existed at the time of going to press.

1967

> *D'un ouvrage abandonné* [33]
>
> Translated by Ludovic and Agnès Janvier in collaboration with the author.

154 Paris: Éditions de Minuit, 1967.

[1-4] *blank* [5] *half title* [6] *blank* [7] SAMUEL BECKETT | d'un ouvrage | abandonné | *Traduit de l'anglais par Ludovic et Agnès Janvier* | *en collaboration avec l'auteur* | [star and m device] | LES ÉDITIONS DE MINUIT [8] L'ÉDITION ORIGINALE DE CET | OUVRAGE A ÉTÉ TIRÉE A DEUX | CENT VINGT-DEUX EXEMPLAI- | RES SUR VELIN CUVE B. F. K. | RIVES, DONT QUATRE-VINGT- | DIX EXEMPLAIRES NUMÉROTÉS | DE 1 A 90, CENT DOUZE EXEM- | PLAIRES MARQUÉS «112» |

1967

NUMÉROTÉS DE 1 A 112 ET | RÉSERVÉS A LA LIBRAIRIE | DES ÉDITIONS DE MINUIT ET | VINGT EXEMPLAIRES HORS- | COMMERCE NUMÉROTÉS DE | H.-C. I A H.-C. XX | H.-C. XVI [Bibliothèque nationale copy] | © 1967 by Les Éditions de Minuit | [...] 9-30 [text, dated at end (1957)] [31] *blank* [32] CET OUVRAGE A ÉTÉ ACHEVÉ D'IM- | PRIMER LE VINGT FÉVRIER MIL | NEUF CENT SOIXANTE-SEPT SUR LES | PRESSES DE L'IMPRIMERIE CORBIÈRE | ET JUGAIN A ALENÇON ET INSCRIT | DANS LES REGISTRES DE L'ÉDITEUR | SOUS LE NUMÉRO 608 | *Imprimé en France* Narrow format like **149**. Soft cover, white, printed black.

154.1 Reprinted in *Têtes-mortes* (Paris: Éditions de Minuit, 1967), pp. 7-30.

[1-2] *blank* [3] *half title* [4] DU MÊME AUTEUR [list to *Bing*] [5] SAMUEL BECKETT | TÊTES-MORTES | [star and m device] | LES ÉDITIONS DE MINUIT [6] © 1967 by Les Éditions de Minuit | 7, rue Bernard-Palissy — Paris 6e | *Tous droits réservés pour tous pays* [7] d'un ouvrage abandonné [8] *Ce texte a été traduit de l'anglais | par Ludovic et Agnès Janvier | en collaboration avec l'auteur.* 9-30 [text, dated at end (1957)] [31] assez [32] *blank* 33-47 [text of **275**, undated] [48] *blank* [49] imagination morte | imaginez [50] *blank* 51-57 [text of **272**, undated] [58] *blank* [59] bing [60] *blank* 61-66 [text of **276**, undated] [67] CET OUVRAGE A ÉTÉ ACHEVÉ D'IM- | PRIMER LE VINGT FÉVRIER MIL | NEUF CENT SOIXANTE-SEPT SUR LES | PRESSES DE L'IM-PRIMERIE CORBIÈRE | ET JUGAIN A ALENÇON ET IN-SCRIT | DANS LES REGISTRES DE L'ÉDITEUR | SOUS LE NUMÉRO 609 | *Imprimé en France* [68] blank. 18 x 9 cm., narrow format, similar in presentation to **149**, except for vertical lettering on spine.

154.2 Reprinted in **33.22**.

1968

Watt [**32**]

Translated by Ludovic and Agnès Janvier in collaboration with the author.

155 Paris: Éditions de Minuit, 1968.
[1-2] *blank* [3] *half title* [4] DU MEME AUTEUR [list to **151.1** and **154.1**] [5] SAMUEL BECKETT | WATT | [star and m device] | LES ÉDITIONS DE MINUIT [6] IL A ÉTÉ TIRÉ DE CET OUVRAGE | QUATRE-VINGT-DIX EXEMPLAIRES | SUR

1968

ALFAMOUSSE, NUMÉROTÉS DE | 1 A 90 PLUS SEPT EXEM-
PLAIRES | HORS-COMMERCE NUMÉROTÉS DE | H.-C. I A
H.-C. VII | IL A ÉTÉ TIRÉ EN OUTRE QUATRE- | VINGT-
DOUZE EXEMPLAIRES SUR | BOUFFANT SÉLECT MAR-
QUÉS | «92» NUMÉROTÉS DE 1 A 92 ET | RÉSERVÉS A LA
LIBRAIRIE DES | ÉDITIONS DE MINUIT | © 1968 [etc.]
7-268 [text with Addenda] [269-270] *blank* [271] CET OUVRAGE
A ÉTÉ ACHEVÉ D'IM- | PRIMER LE VINGT-SIX DÉCEMBRE
| MIL NEUF CENT SOIXANTE-HUIT SUR | LES PRESSES
DE L'IMPRIMERIE | CORBIÈRE ET JUGAIN, A ALENÇON,
| ORNE, ET INSCRIT DANS LES | REGISTRES DE L'ÉDITEUR
SOUS LE | NUMÉRO 702 | *Imprimé en France* [272] *blank*.
18½ cm. Soft cover, with flaps, similar to **145.1** in design, except
that front flap has biographical, and back flap bibliographical, notes.

155.01 Extract from the beginning of Part IV entitled "L'Histoire de Watt"
printed prior to publication in *Les Lettres Nouvelles* (Sept.-Oct.,
1968), pp. 11-16.

2.

Published Works in French

1945

La Peinture des van Velde, ou: le monde et le pantalon

Critical article "écrit au début de 1945, peu de temps après les expositions de A. et G. van Velde respectivement aux Galeries Mai et Maeght."

251   *Cahiers d'Art*, 20-21 (1945-46), 349-354 and 356, with six black and white reproductions of Abraham van Velde and nine of Geer van Velde, six of which cover the whole of p. 355. Dépôt légal 4e trimestre 1946. Imprimerie Kapp, Vanves (Seine).

NOTE. According to Mr. Beckett, this article, which is closely printed and of some length, was solicited. He has not wished it to be reprinted. Its tone is an odd combination of naïvety and aggressiveness, but it is not without either humor or shrewdness (the title comes from the joke used also in **265A**, p. 38).

1946

Suite

Short story. Early version of **263C**, *La Fin*.

252   *Temps Modernes*, I (July 1, 1946), 107-119.

252.1   Reprinted in **263**. [Extensive variants; see Appendix II, below.]

NOTE. In reply to the question, "Why did you submit *L'Expulsé* to *Fontaine* and *Suite* to *Temps Modernes* in 1946? Had you any contacts with the editors?" Mr. Beckett writes: "I knew Sartre but not Max-Pol Fouchet [editor of *Fontaine*, see **254**] at the time. They must have seemed to me the most likely reviews." Only a truncated version of *Suite* was printed, ending at "stupide espoir de repos ou de moindre peine" (**263**, p. 105). Mr. Beckett explains this as follows: "A misunderstanding with the rédaction who thought 1st half, sent separately I forget why, was the whole story, and declined to

1946

252

publish second half in next issue — for reasons I could not understand, something to do, according to S. de Beauvoir, with the 'tenue de la revue.' "

Poèmes 38-39

Cycle of twelve poems numbered I through XIII.

253A   I "elles viennent" (five lines) ; French version of **30**.

253B   II "à elle l'acte calme" (eleven lines in two stanzas).

253C   III "être là sans mâchoires sans dents" (twenty lines).

253D   IV *Ascension* (eighteen lines in five stanzas).

253E   [V] *La Mouche* (ten lines in two stanzas).

253F   VI "musique de l'indifférence" (six lines).

253G   VII "bois seul" (seven lines).

253H   VIII "ainsi a-t-on beau" (fourteen lines).

253J   IX "encore le dernier reflux" [*Dieppe*] (four lines).

253K   X *Rue de Vaugirard* (five lines).

253L   XII *Arènes de Lutèce* (twenty-three lines).

253M   XIII "jusque dans la caverne ciel et sol" (twelve lines).

253   *Temps Modernes*, II (Nov., 1946), 288-293.

253.1   Reprinted in **266**, pp. 53-77, with facing German translations by Elmar
            Tophoven, under the general heading *1937-1939*. [Principal variants:
            253H, l. 11, *bon* replaces *gentil*; **253J**, given title, *Dieppe*; **253K**, l. 2,
            me dropped from *je me débraye*; **253L**, l. 21, *nous* replaces *vous*;
            poems unnumbered.]

253.11 **253J** reprinted in **255.1**, p. 3;

253.12 and in **40**, p. 46;

253.13 and in **40.1**, p. 54, with facing English translation by the author (a
            revised version of **370**), pp. 2, 47, and 55, respectively.

253.2   Reprinted in **279**, pp. 9-20.

NOTE. The eccentric numbering in **253**, including the omission of any number at all for **253E**, was, according to Mr. Beckett, a mere error. According to the author, also, **253J** is based on Hölderlin's lines from *Der Spaziergang:*

Ihr lieblichen Bilder im Tale,
Zum Beispiel Gärten und Baum,
Und dann der Steg, der schmale,
Der Bach zu sehen kaum . . .

1946

L'Expulsé

Short story. Early version of **263A**.

254   *Fontaine,* X (Dec., 1946-Jan., 1947), 685-708.

254.1   Reprinted in **263** [extensive variants; see Appendix II];

254.2   and in **257.2**, pp. [235]-253.

1948

Trois poèmes

255A   "je suis ce cours de sable qui glisse" (ten lines in two stanzas of five).

255Aa   "my way is in the sand flowing" (nine lines in two stanzas of five and four).

255B   "que ferais-je sans ce monde sans visages sans questions"

255Bb   "what would I do without this world faceless incurious" (both fifteen lines in two stanzas and nine and six).

255C   "je voudrais que mon amour meure"

255Cc   "I would like my love to die" (both four lines).

255   *Transition Forty-Eight,* 2 ([June], 1968), 96-97. (French text on left, English text on right, "translated by the author.")

255.01   **255Aa, 255Bb, 255Cc** reprinted in *Poetry Ireland,* II (April, 1949), 8.

255.02   **255A, 255B, 255C** reprinted in **266**, pp. 86-91, with facing German translations by Elmar Tophoven, with **262A/B/C** under the general heading *Six Poèmes (1947-1949)*. [Principal variants: **255B**, l. 1, *visage* for *visages*; l. 10, *aujourd'hui* replaces *avant-hier*; **255C**,ll. 3-4, read *et les ruelles où je vais | pleurant celle qui crut m'aimer* instead of *et dans les rues où je vais | pleurent la seule qui m'ait aimé*.]

255.021 Reprinted in **279**, pp. 24-26.

255.1   **370.1, 255Aa, 255Bb, 255Cc, 253J, 255A, 255B, 255C** reprinted in *Stand,* V, no. 1 [1961], 2-3, English texts on left numbered 1 through 4, French texts on right numbered 1 through 4; in both texts, 1 titled DIEPPE and dated 1937, 2, 3, and 4 each dated individually 1948. Note at foot of p. 3 states, "These are the first poems of Beckett's to be published in this country. First published by permission of John Calder (Publishers) Ltd., whose edition of Beckett's poems under the title *Poems in English* is due to be published in May." Note at foot of p. 2 (English texts) states within brackets "translated from the French by the author."

255.11   **253J, 370.1, 255A, 255Aa, 255B, 255Bb, 255C, 255Cc,** reprinted in **40**, pp. 46-53;

1948

255.12   and in **40.1**, pp. 54-61, French texts on left numbered 1 through 4, English texts on right *idem*, 1 titled *DIEPPE* in both texts but dated 1937 only in French text, 2, 3, 4 dated 1948 only in French texts, "translated from the French by the author" noted at end of **255Cc**. Both **255.1** and **255.11/12** under general heading "Four Poems," **255.11/12** adding "Quatre Poèmes." The French texts reproduce the variants in **255.02**, and the English texts conform to those in **255**.

255.13   **370.1**, **255Aa**, **255Bb**, **255Cc**, reprinted in *The Guinness Book of Poetry 1960/61* (London: Putnam, 1962; 21 cm., 120 pp.), as *"FOUR POEMS | Translated from the French by the author,"* numbered 1 through 4 and dated 1937, 1948, 1948, 1948, respectively, pp. 40-41. **370.1** alone with title: *DIEPPE*. Acknowledgments, p. 7, fourth item: "SAMUEL BECKETT: Four Poems: *"Poems in English"* John Calder | (Publishers) Ltd. THE CONTRIBUTORS, p. 113, third item, biographical note. [This volume was the fifth and last in the series of *Guinness Books of Poetry*.]

255.14   See **16.032**, pp. 169-170.

NOTE. Mr. Beckett confirms that these poems were written as dated, after World War II, and in French first. In a broadcast anthology, *Poems by Samuel Beckett*, selected and introduced by John Fletcher on BBC Third Programme, March 8, 1966, the following variants (italicized) were introduced into **255Cc** by the author at studio rehearsals at which he was present:
   I would *love* my love to die
   and the rain to be *raining* on the graveyard
   and on me walking the streets
   mourning *her who thought she loved me*
thereby bringing the poem into closer conformity with its original, **255C**. At the same time a variant was introduced into the text of **22J**, "packet of Churchman *sodden*." Other poems read in the program were **5**, **22B**, **22L**, **22D**, **24**, **29**, **255Aa**, and **255Bb**. Readers were Jack MacGowran and Denys Hawthorne; production was by Martin Esslin. See also **506**, the second broadcast anthology, selected this time by the author himself.

Peintres de l'empêchement

Critical article on Bram and Geer van Velde.

256   *Derrière le Miroir* (Galerie Maeght; Paris: Éditions Pierre à Feu), 11 and 12 (June, 1948), 3, 4, and 7.

256.01   Short extract (about seventy-five words) reprinted in **500**, p. [7];

256.02   and in **500.1**, p. [16];

256.03   and translated into English by an anonymous translator (not the author), in **500.11**, p. [16].

1948

256

NOTE. There are slight variants between **256** and **256.01** ("d'impénétrables proximités" becomes "d'impénétrable proximité") and between **256.01** and **256.02** (a section of thirteen words is omitted and the punctuation modified in consequence). In **256.01** the text is signed and dated SAMUEL BECKETT, 1948, but in **256.02/03**: Samuel Beckett 1949.

On p. 13 of **256** are several "Paroles de Bram van Velde," some of which are translated by Beckett in **495**.

On p. 11 of **256** there is an allusion to Beckett.

1951

Molloy

Novel in two chapters or parts.

257   Paris: Éditions de Minuit, 1951 [March 10; 3,000 copies, 50 deluxe].
[1-2] *blank* [3] *half title* [4] DU MEME AUTEUR | [short rule] |
A paraître chez le même éditeur: | MALONE MEURT (roman) |
L'INNOMMABLE (roman) | ELEUTHERIA (pièce en 3 actes)
| EN ATTENDANT GODOT (pièce en 2 actes) | *Aux Editions Bordas:* | MURPHY (roman) 1947 [5] SAMUEL BECKETT |
MOLLOY | [star and m device] | LES EDITIONS DE MINUIT |
PARIS [6] Copyright 1951 by les Editions de Minuit | 22, boulevard
St-Michel, Paris | *Tous droits réservés* 7-141 [text of I] 142-272 [text
of II] [273-274] *blank* [275] L'EDITION ORIGINALE DE CET
OUVRAGE | COMPORTE CINQUANTE EXEMPLAIRES SUR |
VELIN SUPERIEUR ALBELIO DES PAPETERIES | DE CON-
DAT, NUMEROTES DE 1 A 50 ET | COMPORTANT LA
MENTION | «EDITION ORIGINALE» | IL A ETE TIRE EN
OUTRE, POUR LE COMPTE | DES AMIS DES EDITIONS
DE MINUIT | CINQ CENTS EXEMPLAIRES SUR ALFA | DES
PAPETERIES NAVARRE, NUMEROTES | DE 1 A 500 ET
COMPORTANT LA MENTION | «LES AMIS DES EDITIONS
DE MINUIT» [276] CET OUVRAGE A ETE ACHEVE | D'IM-
PRIMER LE 10 MARS | MIL NEUF CENT CINQUANTE | ET
UN SUR LES PRESSES DE | L'IMPRIMERIE SPECIALE DES |
EDITIONS DE MINUIT ET A | ETE INSCRIT DANS LES |
REGISTRES DE L'EDITEUR SOUS | LE NUMERO 164. 19 cm.
Soft cover; front, title etc. in blue and black caps. and italic caps.
within blue line border; back, "Extrait du catalogue" also within
blue line border.

257.01   Reprinted photographically in 1953 [May; 3,000 copies].
[4] DU MEME AUTEUR | [star and m device] | MALONE MEURT

1951

257.01   (roman) | EN ATTENDANT GODOT (pièce en 2 actes) | *A paraître:* | L'INNOMMABLE (roman) | ELEUTHERIA (pièce en 3 actes) [6] Copyright 1951 by les Editions de Minuit | 7, rue Bernard-Palissy, Paris 6ᵉ | *Tous droits réservés* 7-141 I 142-[272] II [272, bottom] I.F.M.R.P., 4, rue Camille-Tahan, PARIS-18ᵉ. 1953. [273-276] *blank*.

257.011   Reprinted photographically on Feb. 19, 1960 [3,000 copies, marked "8ᵉ mille"].
[272, bottom, under rule] Joseph FLOCH, Maître-Imprimeur à Mayenne. 19-2-1960.

257.02   Reprinted photographically in 1965 [3,000 copies].
[1-2] *missing* [3] *half title* [4] *DU MÊME AUTEUR* [list to **268** and **149**] [273] CET OUVRAGE A ETE ACHEVE D'IMPRIMER | LE 11 JUIN MIL NEUF CENT SOIXANTE CINQ | SUR LES PRESSES DE JOSEPH FLOCH, MAÎTRE- | IMPRIMEUR A MAYENNE ET INSCRIT DANS | LES REGISTRES DE L'EDI- TEUR SOUS LE | NUMERO 554 | Imprimé en France [274] *blank*. 18 cm. Soft cover, with flaps, pages trimmed, as in **145.1**.

257.03   Reprinted photographically in 1967 [20ᵉ mille].
[4] DU MÊME AUTEUR [list to **154.1** and **151.1**] [5] [reset in new type] SAMUEL BECKETT | MOLLOY | [star and m device] | LES ÉDITIONS DE MINUIT [6] © 1951 by Les Editions de Minuit | 7, rue Bernard-Palissy — Paris 6ᵉ | *Tous droits réservés pour tous pays* [273] CET OUVRAGE A ÉTÉ ACHEVÉ D'IM- | PRIMER LE SEPT NOVEMBRE MIL | NEUF CENT SOI- XANTE SEPT SUR LES | PRESSES DE L'IMPRIMERIE DE LA | MANUTENTION A MAYENNE ET INSCRIT | DANS LES REGISTRES DE L'ÉDITEUR | SOUS LE NUMÉRO | 636 | Imprimé en France [274] *blank*. Otherwise as **257.02**, except for "20 mille" bottom, rear flap.

257.1   Second edition. Paris: Club français du livre, 1959.
[i] *blank* [ii] *vol* | ♡ 243 | *romans* [iii] le club français du livre 1959 [iv] *blank* [v] Samuel Beckett Molloy [title in gray] [vi] *blank* [vii] Molloy [viii] © 1951 by les Editions de Minuit 1-186 [text of 1] 187-[367] [text of 2] [368] [photograph of author, full face] [369- 370] [biographical and bibliographical summary] [371-372] *blank* [373] CET OUVRAGE, composé d'après les | maquettes de Jacques Daniel en carac- | tère compacte corps 12 plein, a été | achevé d'imprimer le 27 août mil neuf | cent cinquante neuf sur les presses des | imprimeries Lang, Grandemange S.A. | à Paris et relié par Engel à Malakoff. | CETTE EDITION, HORS COM- | MERCE, est réservée exclusivement | aux membres du club français du | livre. Elle comprend vingt-six exem- | plaires marqués A à Z,

1951

257.1   cent exem- | plaires numérotés de I à C destinés | aux animateurs
du club et six mille | exemplaires numérotés de 1 à 6.000. | No. 3448
[*Bibliothèque nationale copy*] [374] le club français du livre, 8, rue
de la Paix, Paris (2ᵉ) [375-376] *blank.* 20½ cm., all edges trimmed.
Hardbound, gray and white cloth, with black dot on front and on
back; title and author in horizontal black caps. on spine; endpapers
pale gray and white with one off-white dot on each; black tape
bookmark, 35 cm.

257.2   Third edition. Paris: Union générale d'éditions, 1963 [with **254.2**],
no. 81/82 in the collection "Le Monde en 10 x 18."
[1] UNION GÉNÉRALE D'ÉDITIONS | 8, rue Garancière —
PARIS [2] *blank* [3] MOLLOY | L'EXPULSÉ | PAR | Samuel
BECKETT | *suivis de* | BECKETT | LE PRÉCURSEUR | PAR |
Bernard PINGAUD | *et du* | *Dossier de presse* | *de Molloy* | le monde
en | 10 18 [figures within squares] [4] [catalogue extract, credits for
cover, copyright, etc.] [5] *half title* [6] *blank* [7]-234 [text of *Molloy*]
[235] *half title* [236] *blank* [237]-253 [text of *L'Expulsé*] [254] *blank*
[255] LE DOSSIER DE PRESSE | DE MOLLOY [256] *blank*
[257]-286 [text of *Dossier*] [287] BECKETT | LE PRÉCURSEUR
[288] *blank* [289]-311 [text of Pingaud's essay, dated "Novembre
1962" (see **1061**)] [312] *blank* [313] TABLE DES MATIÈRES [list]
[314] *blank* [315] ACHEVÉ D'IMPRIMER LE | 21 JANVIER
1963 SUR LES | PRESSES DE L'IMPRIMERIE | BUSSIÈRE,
SAINT-AMAND (CHER) | — Nº d'édit. 58 — Nº d'imp. : 286 |
Dépôt légal: 1ᵉʳ trimestre 1963 | *Imprimé en France* [316-320] cata-
logue and publicity. 18 cm. Soft cover, glossy surface; front illus.
with "dessin à l'encre de Chine de Arikha (Collection Samuel Beckett)" [see p. 4]; back cover, blurb; title etc. in vertical lettering on
spine. Pocketbook gummed binding, inexpensive edition [Fr. 4,50;
25,000 copies].

257.001 Extract printed in **1022** (see also **260.03**).

257.002 Extract from **257**, pp. 104-105, reprinted in *Advanced Level French
Course, Book II*, by W. T. John and G. W. Crowther (London:
Thomas Nelson and Sons, 1963; printed in Great Britain), p. 137,
under the title "A Seaside Reminiscence." Extract shortened, and
incorrectly copied in one place; adopts, however, correct spelling
pagaie given in **257.2** (**257** has *pagäie*). Extract begins "Il y a des
gens a qui la mer ne réussit pas . . ." and ends ". . . je n'entends pas
grincer sur la grève la frêle carène." The passage figures among those
proposed for "Translation into English," and is no. 9. The volume
has 164 pages. 20 cm. Hardbound. [See **145.001**.]

NOTE. The *Dossier de presse* in **257.2** contains extracts from the most important
articles devoted to *Molloy* on first publication, about which see **719**, pp. 17-19.

1951

Malone meurt

Novel.

258   Paris: Éditions de Minuit, 1951 [Oct. 8; 3,000 copies].
[1-2] *blank* [3] *half title* [4] *DU MEME AUTEUR* | [star and m
device] | MOLLOY, roman. | *A paraître:* | L'INNOMMABLE,
roman. | ELEUTHÉRIA (pièce en 3 Actes). | EN ATTENDANT
GODOT (pièce en 2 Actes). [5] SAMUEL BECKETT | MALONE
| *meurt* | [star and m device] | LES ÉDITIONS DE MINUIT
[6] *Copyright 1951 by* Les Editions de Minuit. | *Tous droits réservés
pour tous pays.* [7]-217 [text] [218] *blank* [219] L'ÉDITION ORI-
GINALE DE CET OUVRAGE | A ÉTÉ TIRÉE A 50 EXEM-
PLAIRES DONT | 3 EXEMPLAIRES SUR PAPIER VELIN MA- |
DAGASCAR DES PAPETERIES DE NAVARRE | NUMÉROTÉS
DE 1 A 3 ET 47 EXEM- | PLAIRES SUR PAPIER VELIN DU
GHALD- | WILL NUMÉROTÉS DE 4 A 50. | TOUS CES
EXEMPLAIRES COMPORTENT | LA MENTION «ÉDITION
ORIGINALE». [220] *blank* [221] CET OUVRAGE A ÉTÉ
ACHEVÉ | D'IMPRIMER EN NOVEMBRE 1951 | SUR LES
PRESSES DE L'IMPRIME- | RIE HÉRISSEY, A EVREUX, ET
A | ÉTÉ INSCRIT SUR LES REGISTRES DE | L'ÉDITEUR
SOUS LE NUMÉRO 176. [222-224] *blank.* 19 cm. Soft cover; front
title etc. in blue and black caps., italic caps. and l.c.; back photograph and biographical summary of the author and press comments
on *Molloy,* all within blue line borders, on both covers.

258.01 Reprinted photographically in 1959 [2,000 copies];

258.011 and in 1963 [March 21; 5,100 copies], both by J. Floch.
[4] [works list to *Nouvelles et Textes pour rien* and *Tous ceux qui
tombent,* omitting mention of *Éleuthéria*] [221] ACHEVÉ D'IM-
PRIMER | PAR JOSEPH FLOCH | MAITRE IMPRIMEUR |
MAYENNE 25 — 2 — 1959. 18 cm. Soft cover; back, catalogue
list only within blue line border [otherwise identical] (**258.011** [221]:
ACHEVÉ *dated* LE 25 MARS 1963).

258.1   Extract, entitled "Malone s'en conte," published in *84* (Paris: Éditions
de Minuit), 16 (Dec., 1950 [*Dépôt légal,* Dec. 21, 1950]), 3-10.
The extract is taken from **258**, pp. 45-58. The variants are extensive,
comprising both omissions and additions. "Brandissait," given incorrectly as "brandissais" in **258**, p. 50, l. 24, figures correctly in **258.1**.

258.2   Extract, entitled "Quel malheur . . ." published in *Temps Modernes,*
VII (Sept., 1951), 385-416. There are variants in this passage taken
from **258**, pp. 88-151.

NOTE. The MS of *Malone meurt* in the University of Texas library shows that
the novel was originally entitled "L'Absent" [see Appendix I].

1952

En attendant Godot

Play in two acts for five male characters.

259   Paris: Éditions de Minuit, 1952 [Oct. 17; 2,500 copies].
       [1-2] *blank* [3] *half title* [4] DU MÊME AUTEUR | [star and m
       device] | MOLLOY, *roman.* | MALONE MEURT, *roman.* | L'IN-
       NOMMABLE, *roman (à paraître).* [5] SAMUEL BECKETT | En
       attendant | Godot | PIÈCE EN DEUX ACTES | [star and m device]
       | *LES ÉDITIONS DE MINUIT* | 1952 [6] Copyright 1952 by les
       Editions de Minuit, 7, rue | Bernard-Palissv Paris 6e. | Tous droits
       réservés. [7] PERSONNAGES | ESTRAGON | VLADIMIR |
       LUCKY | POZZO | UN JEUNE GARÇON [8] *blank* [9] ACTE
       PREMIER [10] *blank* [11]-91 [text of Act I] [92] *blank* [93] ACTE
       DEUXIÈME [94] *blank* [95]-163 [text of Act II] [164] *blank* [165]
       IL A ÉTÉ TIRÉ DE CET OUVRAGE | TRENTE-CINQ EXEM-
       PLAIRES SUR | VÉLIN SUPÉRIEUR NUMÉROTÉS | DE 1 A
       35 ET CONSTITUANT | L'ÉDITION ORIGINALE. [166] *blank*
       [167] ACHEVÉ D'IMPRIMER SUR LES | PRESSES DE L'IM-
       PRIMERIE HABAUZIT | A AUBENAS (ARDÈCHE), EN SEP-
       TEMBRE | MIL NEUF CENT CINQUANTE DEUX. | Dépôt
       légal 3e trimestre 1952 [168] *blank.* 18 cm. Soft cover; front, title
       etc. in blue and black caps., italic caps. and l.c.; back, photograph
       and biographical summary of the author and press comments on
       Molloy and *Malone meurt,* all within blue-line border, both covers.

259.01 Reprinted with corrections by Fayat in Sept., 1953 [2,000 copies].

259.1   Second edition (illustrated with four plates), April, 1954 [3,000
        copies].
        [4] [as above, except that "à paraître" is missing after L'INNOM-
        MABLE, *roman.*] [7] *"En attendant Godot" a été créé le 5 jan-* |
        vier 1953 au Théâtre Babylone, dans une mise | *en scène de Roger*
        Blin et avec la distribution | *suivante:* | Estragon. . . . Pierre
        LATOUR. | Vladimir. . . . Lucien RAIMBOURG. | Lucky. . . .
        Jean MARTIN. | Pozzo. . . . Roger BLIN. | Un jeune garçon. . . .
        Serge LECOINTE. [164] REPRODUCTION PHOTOGRAPHI-
        QUE | PAR L'I.F.M.R.P. 4, RUE CAMILLE TAHAN | 1er TRIM.
        1954 [   ] PARIS - 18e. Soft cover; back: press comments on
        Murphy, Molloy, Malone meurt, L'Innommable, En attendant Godot
        within blue-line border, marked "15e Edition." Plates: one photo-
        graph facing p. 48, two facing p. 49, two facing p. 144, one facing
        p. 145, six photographs in all taken during tour of Germany by
        Babylone troupe: Vladimir, Jean-Marie Serreau; Estragon, Pierre
        Latour; Lucky, Jean Martin; Pozzo, Albert Rémy; Jeune garçon,
        Albert Duby; photographs in black and white, by Donitz.

1952

259.2   Third edition (with and without plates), Sept. 17, 1956 [4,500 copies, 30 deluxe, 12 H.C.]. Printed by I.F.M.R.P., 4, rue Camille-Tahan, Paris.

[6] Il a été tiré de cette édition | 30 exemplaires sur alfama | numérotés de 1 à 30 et 5 | exemplaires hors commerce | marqués H.C. [164] ACHEVÉ D'IMPRIMER EN JUILLET 1956 | [. . .].

259.21   Reprinted photographically without plates Dec. 3, 1958 [4,000 copies] by J. Grou-Radenez, 11, rue de Sèvres, Paris.
[5] [as in **259**, except that date "1952" is missing at foot of page] [164] OFF-SET J. GROU RADENEZ.

259.22   Reprinted photographically by J. Grou-Radenez, Dec. 28, 1960 [8,000 copies].
[5] [as in **259**, "1952" restored].

259.221 Reprinted photographically by J. Grou-Radenez, Feb. 15, 1963 [8,250 copies].
[4] [list extends to *Comment c'est* and *La Dernière Bande*].

259.222 Reprinted photographically by J. Grou-Radenez, Nov. 17, 1964 [15,000 copies].
Back cover reads "45ᵉ mille."

259.3   School edition, ed. Germaine Brée and Eric Schoenfeld, published in Macmillan Modern French Literature Series (New York: Macmillan, 1963; 120 pp., 21 cm.), with introduction, notes, and vocabulary.

259.31   College edition, ed. Colin Duckworth, with a foreword by Harold Hobson, preceded by a long introduction and followed by detailed notes with variant material (London: George G. Harrap and Co. Ltd., cxxxvi + 101 pp.; 19½ cm., hardbound). [See **714**.]

259.4   Reprinted in **270**, pp. [6]-[205].

259.001 Facsimile of **259**, p. 158, with author's autograph corrections adding a fragment of dialogue between Vladimir and the boy, reproduced in the Éditions de Minuit catalogue, Oct., 1954, p. 4, and Autumn, 1958, p. 5.

259.011 Excerpt published in **1072**, pp. 323-330, taken from **259.01**, pp. 30-43. Excerpt followed by two excerpts (**265.31/32**) from *Fin de partie* and vocabulary notes (p. 336; these contain an odd error of interpretation: "il ne fait pas la liaison" (**259.01**, p. 32) is misread as "he doesn't get the connection" instead of "he doesn't make the *liaison* [between *pas* and *encore*]"). Excerpt preceded by introductory matter, pp. 316-323.

259.012 Excerpt from end of Act I published in **1225**, pp. 439-445.

1952

259.013   Excerpt published in Edith Kern and Agnès G. Raymond, eds., *La Joie de lire: Premières Lectures littéraires* (New York: Macmillan; London: Collier-Macmillan, 1966), pp. 57-65 (right-hand pages only, notes on left-hand pages), preceded by a note on Beckett, p. 56.

For details of first performance at Théâtre Babylone, see **259.1**, p. [7]. There have been important subsequent stagings in Paris, notably at the Théâtre Hébertot in 1956 and Odéon-Théâtre de France in 1961, and in the provinces, notably by Le Grenier de Toulouse in 1964; all directed by Roger Blin [see **1866**].

NOTE. There are variants between **259** and **259.01**, since Beckett corrected his text in the light of performance, largely, though not entirely, at Roger Blin's suggestion. For details, see **1864**; also **259.001**. For many details concerning variants between the various MSS and printed states of the text, see **714**.

1953

L'Innommable

Novel.

260   Paris: Éditions de Minuit, 1953 [July 18; 3,000 copies, 50 deluxe].
[1-2] *blank* [3] *half title* [4] DU MÊME AUTEUR | [star and m device] | MOLLOY, roman | MALONE MEURT, roman | EN ATTENDANT GODOT, pièce en deux actes [5] SAMUEL BECKETT | L'INNOMMABLE | [star and m device] | LES EDITIONS DE MINUIT [6] L'ÉDITION ORIGINALE DE CET OUVRAGE | A ÉTÉ TIRÉE A CINQUANTE EXEMPLAIRES | SUR VÉLIN SUPÉRIEUR NUMÉROTÉS DE 1 A 50 | Copyrigth [*sic*] 1953 by Les Editions de Minuit | 7, rue Bernard Palissy, Paris. | *Tous droits réservés* 7-262 [text] [263] CET OUVRAGE A ÉTÉ | ACHEVÉ D'IMPRIMER | LE 20 MAI 1953 | SUR LES PRESSES DE LA | SOCIÉTÉ NOUVELLE | D'IMPRESSION | MUH - LE ROUX | A STRASBOURG | ET A ÉTÉ INSCRIT | DANS LES REGISTRES | DE L'EDITEUR SOUS | LE NUMÉRO 184 | Dépôt légal: 2e trimestre 1953 [264] *blank*. 19 cm. Soft cover; front, title etc. in blue and black caps. and italic caps.; back, press comments on *Molloy, Malone meurt, En attendant Godot,* all within blue line borders, both covers.

260.1   Reprinted Feb. 6, 1961 [2,000 copies].
[1-2] *blank* [4] *DU MÊME AUTEUR* [includes to *Nouvelles et Textes pour rien* and *La Dernière Bande*] [6] [...] | © 1953 [etc., as above] [263] ACHEVÉ D'IMPRIMER | PAR JOSEPH FLOCH | MAITRE-IMPRIMEUR | MAYENNE 30 — 1 — 1961 | N° D'ÉDITEUR : 432 | Imprimé en France. 18½ cm. Soft cover; back lists works to *Comment c'est* and is marked "4e mille" (later copies "5e mille"); pages untrimmed.

260.01   Extract, entitled "Mahood," published in *Nouvelle Revue Française,* I (Feb. 1, 1953), 214-234. Taken from **260**, pp. 80-113; variants.

1953

260.02   Facsimile photograph of "Une page du MS de l'*Innommable,* écrit
sur un grand registre" published in *Arts-Spectacles,* 418 (July 3-9,
1953), 5. Shows pp. 58 and 59 of register, with autograph text on
left-hand side and right-hand side left blank for corrections (and
doodles). [See also **263.02.**]

260.03   Extract printed in **1022** [see also **257.001**].

1954

Hommage à Jack B. Yeats

Critical comments on Yeats's paintings. About 200 words.

261   *Lettres Nouvelles,* II (April, 1954), 619-620.

NOTE. The short piece appears in the review under the general heading
"Variétés" and is followed by texts devoted to Yeats by Pierre Schneider and
Jacques Putman. An editorial footnote reads: "A propos de l'exposition des
peintures de Jack B. Yeats qui eut lieu le mois dernier à la Galerie Beaux-Arts.
Rappelons que le peintre Jack B. Yeats est le frère du poète et dramaturge
William B. Yeats." Beckett's piece is characterized by an oracular tone and
marked by utterances like "L'artiste qui joue son être est de nulle part,"
which link it with **28.** The piece is very favorable to Yeats, ending "s'incliner
simplement, émerveillé."

1955

Trois poèmes

262A   1 *Accul* ["bon bon il est un pays"] (twenty lines in three stanzas of
eight, six, and six lines).

262B   2 *Mort de A. D.* (fifteen lines).

262C   3 "vive morte ma seule saison" (five lines).

262   *Cahiers des Saisons,* 2 (Oct., 1955), 115-116.

262.1   Reprinted in **266,** pp. 80-85, with facing German translations by
Elmar Tophoven, and with **255A/B/C,** under the general heading
"Six Poèmes (1947-1949)."

262.11   Reprinted in **279,** pp. 21-23.

262.2   **262A** reprinted in a catalogue of works by Avigdor Arikha, the illus-
trator of **263.1** (London: Matthiessen Gallery, 1959).
[i] AVIGDOR ARIKHA | PAINTINGS • GOUACHES • DRAW-
INGS | THE MATTHIESSEN GALLERY 142 NEW BOND
STREET LONDON W1 | APRIL 8 TO MAY 2 1959 [ii] [list of
previous exhibitions and of book illustrations, last of which is **263.1**]
[iii] [**262A,** signed] SAMUEL BECKETT [iv] *blank* [v-vi] [titles and

1955

262.2   dimensions of exhibited works] [vii] *blank* [viii] [in very small type, inner corner foot of page] PRINTED IN ENGLAND BY | GEORGE PITMAN AND SON, LTD | LONDON, W.1. 24 cm. White art paper covers, front bearing color reproduction of painting (untitled) by Arikha, back cover NEXT EXHIBITION: ODILON REDON.

NOTE. Variants in **266**: **262A**, l. 18, "qu'est-ce que c'est" replaces "Qu'est-ce que c'est" and title dropped; **262B**, l. 14, "grêlé" omitted after "vieux bois." Mr. Beckett has confirmed the dating of these poems (**262B** was written in memory of a colleague at the Irish Hospital in Saint-Lô). The *Cahiers des Saisons,* in which the poems are not dated, is *84* renamed (see **258.1**).

    Beckett's friendship with Arikha has led him to contribute to other items by the artist, on the lines of **262.2**. These include: *Avigdor Arikha Drawings 1965-1966* (Jerusalem and Tel-Aviv: Tarshish Books and Dvir, 1967), and the exhibit announcement *Pour Avigdor Arikha* (Paris: Galerie Claude Bernard, 1967).

Nouvelles et Textes pour rien

263A   *L'Expulsé.*
    Short story [see **254**].

263B   *Le Calmant.*
    Short story previously unpublished.

263C   *La Fin.*
    Short story previously partially published as **252**, *Suite.*

263D/E/F/G/H/J/K/L/M/N/P/Q/R
    Textes pour rien.

    Thirteen short prose texts, numbered I through XIII.

263   Paris: Editions de Minuit, 1955 [Nov. 18; 1,110 copies, plus 30 deluxe, 5 deluxe H.C., 50 H.C.].
    [1-2] *blank* [3] *half title* [4] *DU MEME AUTEUR* | [star and m device] | MURPHY, *roman.* | MOLLOY, *roman.* | MALONE MEURT, *roman.* | L'INNOMMABLE, *roman.* | EN ATTENDANT GODOT, *pièce en 2 actes.* [5] SAMUEL BECKETT | NOUVELLES | ET | TEXTES POUR RIEN | [star and m device] | LES EDITIONS DE MINUIT [6] IL A ÉTÉ TIRÉ DE CET OUVRAGE | TRENTE EXEMPLAIRES SUR PUR | FIL NUMÉROTÉS DE 1 A 30, MILLE | CENT EXEMPLAIRES SUR VÉLIN | NUMÉROTÉS DE 31 A 1130. | [para., indented] PLUS CINQ EXEMPLAIRES HORS | COMMERCE SUR PUR FIL | NUMÉROTÉS DE H. C. 1 A H C. 5 | ET CINQUANTE EXEMPLAIRES | HORS-COMMERCE SUR VÉLIN | NUMÉROTÉS DE H.C. 6 A H.C. 55 | EXEMPLAIRE Nº [880 in British Museum copy] | *Copyright 1955 by les Editions de Minuit* | *7, rue Bernard-Palissy, Paris VIe* | *Tous droits réservés pour tous pays* [7] *Note de l'Editeur* | Les

1955

263   *Nouvelles* sont de 1945, les *Textes pour rien* de 1950. [8] *blank* [9]
Nouvelles [10] *blank* [11]-40 [text of *L'Expulsé*] [41]-75 [text of *Le
Calmant*] [76] *blank* [77]-123 [text of *La Fin*] [124] *blank* [125]
Textes pour Rien [126] *blank* [127]-135 [text of I (**263D**)] [136]
blank [137]-142 [text of II (**263E**)] [143]-152 [text of III (**263F**)]
[153]-158 [text of IV (**263G**)] [159]-166 [text of V (**263H**)] [167]-174
[text of VI (**263J**)] [175]-180 [text of VII (**263K**)] [181]-188 [text of
VIII (**263L**)] [189]-196 [text of IX (**263M**)] [197]-201 [text of X
(**263N**)] [202] *blank* [203]-210 [text of XI (**263P**)] [211]-214 [text
of XII (**263Q**)] [215]-220 [text of XIII (**263R**)] [221] TABLE DES
MATIÈRES [list] [222] *blank* [223] CET OUVRAGE A ÉTÉ
ACHEVÉ D'IMPRIMER | LE 15 NOVEMBRE 1955, SUR LES
PRESSES | DE L'IMPRIMERIE VICTOR-HUGO A POITIERS
| ET A ÉTÉ INSCRIT DANS LES REGISTRES | DE L'ÉDITEUR
SOUS LE NUMERO 289 [224] *blank*. 18 cm. Soft cover, blue-line
border, and usual Editions de Minuit style; all edges untrimmed.

263.1   Second edition, illus. with six ink line drawings by Avigdor Arikha,
text reprinted photographically, 1958 [July 16; 2,110 copies].
[4] *DU MÊME AUTEUR* [list includes *Fin de partie, Tous ceux qui
tombent*] [5] SAMUEL BECKETT | NOUVELLES | ET | TEXTES
POUR RIEN | avec 6 illustrations d'Avigdor Arikha | [etc., as in
263] [6] IL A ÉTÉ TIRÉ DE CET OUVRAGE | DEUX MILLE
EXEMPLAIRES SUR | VELIN AVEC 6 ILLUSTRATIONS |
D'AVIGDOR ARIKHA NUMÉROTÉS | DE 1 A 2.000 | EXEM-
PLAIRE Nº [000814 in private copy] | *Copyright 1958 by les Editions
de Minuit* | [etc., as in **263**] [223] CET OUVRAGE A ÉTÉ ACHEVÉ
D'IMPRIMER | LE 20 JUIN 1958 SUR LES PRESSES DE |
JOSEPH FLOCH, MAITRE-IMPRIMEUR A | MAYENNE ET
A ÉTÉ INSCRIT SUR LES | REGISTRES DE L'ÉDITEUR SOUS
LE Nº 368 [otherwise identical]. Soft cover; front, illus. with ink
line drawing by Arikha, top and bottom title etc. in horizontal caps.
as on spine; back blank except star and m device; dust jacket of
transparent paper. Illus. face pp. [5], 14 [identical with front cover],
80, 96, 176, 192. These do not merely illustrate the *Nouvelles et
Textes pour rien*, but other works as well, e.g., Estragon struggling
with his boot in *En attendant Godot* [f.p. 80], Molloy riding his
bicycle with crutches [f.p. 96] and Malone using his stick in bed
[f.p. 176]. Each illustration, blank verso, is *hors-texte*, i.e., gummed
to the page opposite the page it faces. The process is phototype;
"pap. de la Moselle" named in publisher's ledgers as having carried
it out.

263.2   Third edition, without illustrations, reprinted photographically in
1965 [Feb. 27; 3,050 copies].
[4] [list extends to *Comment c'est, Oh les beaux jours*] [5] [as in **263**]
[6] © 1958 by Les Editions de Minuit | 7, rue Bernard-Palissy —

1955

263.2   Paris 6ᵉ | *Tous droits réservés pour tous pays* [223] CET OUVRAGE
A ETE ACHEVE D'IMPRIMER | LE 27 FEVRIER 1965 SUR
LES PRESSES DE | JOSEPH FLOCH, MAITRE-IMPRIMEUR
A | MAYENNE ET INSCRIT DANS LES REGISTRES | DE
L'EDITEUR SOUS LE Nᵒ 543 | Imprimé en France. 18½ cm.
Soft cover, blue-line border and usual Éditions de Minuit style;
catalogue items on back; pages untrimmed.

263.01   **263F**, **263J**, and **263N** [III, VI, and X, numbered I, II, III] first
published as *Trois Textes pour rien* in *Lettres Nouvelles,* I (May,
1953), 267-277. (Variants, e.g., in **263N** [263, p. 198, ll. 8-9] "entre
bonnes mains" for "en bonnes mains" in definitive text.)

263.02   **263P** [XI] first published as *Encore un pour rien: Texte inédit de
Samuel Beckett,* in *Arts-Spectacles,* 418 (July 3-9, 1953), 5; extensive
variants [see also **260.02**].

263.03   **263D** and **263Q** [I, XII] first published as *Deux Textes pour rien* in
Monde Nouveau/Paru, X (May-June, 1955), 144-149; variants
in **263D** only.

263.04   **263G**, **263L**, and **263R** [IV, VIII, XIII] reprinted in **1078**, pp. 121-
132, with **147** [see **147.5**].

NOTE. It is well known that the *Textes pour rien* brought Beckett to a tem-
porary impasse in his work. It is possible, in the light of the author's testimony and that of the MSS in the University of Texas library, to place in
approximate order and to roughly date the principal French works listed
above and written in what has been called "the great creative period,"
1945-1950:
La Fin; L'Expulsé [Oct. 6-14, 1946]; *Premier Amour* (unpublished) [Oct. 28–
Nov. 12, 1946]; *Le Calmant* [Dec. 23, 1946 (started)]; *Mercier et Camier* (unpublished); *Molloy* [1947]; *Éleuthéria* (unpublished); *Malone meurt* [1947-
1948]; *En attendant Godot* [1949]; *L'Innommable* [1949-1950]; *Textes pour
rien* [1950, perhaps extending to 1952].
    Mr. Beckett writes: "This is the correct order to the best of my recollec-
tion. I have no means of checking it. *Godot* is without any doubt between
Malone and *L'Innommable. Mercier et Camier* was first attempt at novel in
French and cannot have preceded *Nouvelles.* It is possible *Éleuthéria* preceded
Molloy, but I think not." See also Appendix I, and **500**, Note.

Henri Hayden, homme-peintre

Short critical text, dated "Janvier 1952."

264   First published in *Les Cahiers d'Art—Documents,* 22 (Nov., 1955), [?]
[Soft cover, white, front] NOVEMBRE 1955 [   ] *ÉCOLE DE
PARIS Nᵒ 4* | [rule] | [decorative title] documents ART | [rule] |
ENCYCLOPÉDIE GÉNÉRALE DES BEAUX-ARTS AUX XIXᵉ

1955

264   et XXe SIÈCLES | PEINTRES, SCULPTEURS, GRAVEURS, ARCHITECTES, DÉCORATEURS, ETC. | HENRI | HAYDEN | 1883 | Documentation réunie | par Jean-Albert Cartier | LES CAHIERS D'ART — DOCUMENTS — NUMÉRO 22 — 1955 | *ÉDITIONS PIERRE CAILLER — GENÈVE — SUISSE* [1] [signatures and photograph of Hayden] [2] Henri Hayden, homme-peintre [dated] *Janvier 1952* [signed] Samuel Beckett 3-16 [biography, bibliography, reproductions in black and white, press comments, gallery advertisements, etc.] [Back cover: recto, book advertisement; verso, gallery and other advertisements and details of **264**, including:] Directeur et éditeur responsable: Pierre Cailler | Clichés de la Photogravure Dupuis et Cie, Cheneau-de-Bourg, Lausanne. | Imprimerie de la Plaine du Rhône S.A., Aigle (Suisse). | Fr.s. 2, — [   ] Fr.f. 160, — [Verso front cover] Tous droits de reproduction, même partielle, rigoureusement réservés. | IMPRIMÉ EN SUISSE | Copyright 1955 by Éditions Pierre Cailler, Genève. 24 cm. 16 pp., partially numbered.

264.1   Reprinted in Waddington Galleries catalogue, 1959.
[1] HENRI HAYDEN | RECENT PAINTINGS | 12th February — 7th March 1959 | The Waddington Galleries [in decorative script] | 2 Cork Street, London W1. REGent 1719 [2] HENRI HAYDEN [signed] *Samuel Beckett* [n.d.] [3-4] [black and white reproductions on shiny paper] [5-6] [exhibition list on *idem*] [7] HENRI HAYDEN [chronology] [8] FORTHCOMING | EXHIBITIONS | [list] [. . .] | Printed by Graphis Press Ltd., London. 23 cm. Soft blue cover; front, bottom, in decorative script: The Waddington Galleries; otherwise blank.

264.2   Reprinted in *Hayden*, by Jean Selz (Geneva: Éditions Pierre Cailler, 1962), pp. 40-41 (in section "Extraits de Presse") [variants].
[Collection "Peintres et sculpteurs d'hier et d'aujourd'hui," no. 57 (no. 35 in small format), printed April 19, 1962, by Imprimerie de la Plaine du Rhône S.A., Aigle; 100 deluxe and unspecified number ordinary copies; illus. color and black and white reproductions. 18½ cm. Soft cover; front, illus., color reproduction; back, catalogue list; spine, title vertical caps. 48 pp. + 103 plates.]

NOTE. On the genesis of this text, Mme. Josette Hayden writes: "Le texte de Samuel Beckett a été écrit en janvier 1952 pour une collection particulière — c'est un amateur de peinture de mon mari qui a fait un album: un peintre — un écrivain — peinture à l'huile du peintre — texte manuscrit de l'écrivain — le texte n'a jamais été publié [Mme. Hayden is unaware of **264**], c'est avec la permission de S. Beckett qu'il a été reproduit dans le catalogue Waddington — et dans le livre sur Hayden — le manuscript est toujours en possession de l'amateur qui l'avait commandé." The variants in **264.2** are stylistic improvements, no doubt the work of Selz, such as the insertion of two commas in the sixth paragraph, and the correction, in the seventh, of "notre cher vieux

1955

264

bon temps" to "notre cher bon vieux temps." The Selz volume is of interest
also for two reproductions (p. 38, in color, p. 39, in black and white) of
Roussillon landscapes, painted in 1944 when Beckett and Hayden were both
living in the Vaucluse village (see p. 33). Revealing also is the first sentence
of Beckett's text, written after the *Textes pour rien:* "On me demande des
mots, à moi qui n'en ai plus, même pas, plus guère, sur une chose qui les récuse."

1957

Fin de partie, suivi de Acte sans paroles

265A   *Fin de partie.*
            Play in one act for four characters.

265B   *Acte sans paroles* [I].
            Mime for one player, to music by John Beckett (see **376B**, Note).

265   Paris: Éditions de Minuit, 1957 [Feb. 1; 3,000 copies + 65 deluxe].
            [1-2] *blank* [3] Fin de partie [4] DU MÊME AUTEUR [list to
            Nouvelles et Textes pour rien] [5] SAMUEL BECKETT | Fin de
            partie | *suivi de* | Acte sans paroles | [star and m device] | LES
            ÉDITIONS DE MINUIT [6] © 1957 by Les Editions de Minuit |
            7, rue Bernard-Palissy, Paris 6e. | Tous droits réservés pour tous pays.
            [7] Pour Roger Blin [8] *blank* [9] Fin de partie [10] *blank* [11] PER-
            SONNAGES | NAGG | NELL | HAMM | CLOV [12] *blank* [13]-
            112 [text of *Fin de partie*] [113] Acte sans paroles | *Cet acte comporte
            une partie | musicale de JOHN BECKETT.* [114] *blank* [115]-122
            [text of *Acte sans paroles*] [123] TABLE DES MATIÈRES [list]
            [124] *blank* [125] IL A ÉTÉ TIRÉ DE CET | OUVRAGE QUATRE
            EXEMPLAI- | RES SUR VELIN D'ARCHES | NUMÉROTÉS
            DE 1 A 4 ET SIX | EXEMPLAIRES HORS COMMERCE |
            NUMÉROTÉS DE H.C. 1 A H.C. 6, | CINQUANTE EXEMPLAI-
            RES SUR | VELIN PUR FIL DU MARAIS | NUMÉROTÉS DE
            5 A 54 ET | CINQ EXEMPLAIRES HORS | COMMERCE
            NUMÉROTÉS DE | H.C. 7 A H.C. 11 [126] *blank* [127] CET
            OUVRAGE A ÉTÉ ACHEVÉ | D'IMPRIMER LE 30 JANVIER |
            1957 SUR LES PRESSES DE | L'IMPRIMERIE VICTOR-HUGO,
            | A POITIERS, ET INSCRIT DANS | LES REGISTRES DE
            L'ÉDITEUR | SOUS LE NUMÉRO 308 [128] *blank*. 18½ cm.
            Soft cover; front, title etc. in blue and black lettering; back, bio-
            graphical summary and catalogue extract, all within blue-line bor-
            ders, both covers; spine, horizontal lettering.

265.001 Reprinted on same presses May 18, 1957 [4,500 copies].
            [11] [form of words on corresponding p. [11] in **265** replaced by
            details and cast lists of first London and Paris performances] [115]
            [details of Deryk Mendel in first London and Paris performances]
            [116] *blank* [117]-124 [text of *Acte sans paroles*] [125] TABLE DES

1957

265.001   MATIÈRES [list] [127] [as in 265, except for LE 18 MAI in second line, and 322 in last line].

265.01   Reprinted photographically in 1961 [July 6; 5,000 copies].
          [4] *DU MÊME AUTEUR* [list to *Comment c'est, La Dernière Bande*] [11] «Fin de partie» a été créée en fran- | çais le 1er avril [*sic*] 1957 au *Royal Court* | *Theatre*, à Londres, avec la distribution | suivante: | [etc., cast list, details of Paris staging] [115] [details of first stagings of *Acte sans paroles*, London (also misdated April 1, 1957) and Paris] [116] *blank* [117]-124 [text of *Acte sans paroles*] [125] TABLE DES MATIÈRES [identical with 265, p. 123] [126] *blank* [127] CET OUVRAGE A ÉTÉ ACHEVÉ | D'IMPRIMER LE 30 JUIN 1961 | PAR JOSEPH FLOCH | MAITRE-IMPRIMEUR A MAYENNE | No ÉDITEUR 450 [128] *blank* [as in 265]. 18½ cm. Soft cover; front, as in 265; back, catalogue list within blue-line border, bottom dated 6-61; spine similar.

265.02   Reprinted photographically in 1965 [June 2; over 6,000 copies].
          [4] DU MEME AUTEUR [list to *Oh les beaux jours*] [127] ACHEVE D'IMPRIMER | LE 2 JUIN 1965 | PAR JOSEPH FLOCH | MAITRE-IMPRIMEUR | A MAYENNE | No D'EDITEUR: 553. 18 cm. Soft cover, as for 145.1, with flaps; pages trimmed; spine, horizontal caps.

265.03   Reprinted photographically in 1967 [35e mille].
          [4] DU MÊME AUTEUR [list to 154.1 and 151.1] [5] [265B is cited as:] Acte sans paroles I [113], [125] [likewise:] Acte sans paroles I [127] CET OUVRAGE A ÉTÉ ACHEVÉ D'IM- | PRIMER LE DOUZE OCTOBRE MIL | NEUF CENT SOIXANTE SEPT SUR LES | PRESSES DE L'IMPRIMERIE DE LA | MANUTENTION A MAYENNE ET INSCRIT | DANS LES REGISTRES DE L'ÉDI-TEUR | SOUS LE NUMÉRO | 634 | Imprimé en France [otherwise similar to 265.02, except for "35 mille" on bottom of back flap].

265.1   265A reprinted in *L'Avant-Scène/Fémina-Théâtre*, 156 [Aug., 1957], 7-22.

265.2   265A reprinted in *Vingt Pièces en un acte choisies dans le théâtre contemporain: Textes choisis et présentés par Odette ASLAN* (Paris: Éditions Seghers, 1959), introduction, pp. 65-66; text, pp. 67-104.

265.21   265B adapted as a "film de marionnettes des Bettiol" and presented at the "Journées internationales du cinéma d'animation" at Annecy (France), June 17-22, 1965, as one of the French entries [see 2847 and 2867].

265.3   265A and 265B reprinted in 270, pp. [206]-[317] and [318]-[329], respectively.

265.31   Two excerpts from 265A (265, pp. 33-38 and 106-112)

1957

265.32 reprinted in **1072**, pp. 330-333 and 333-335, respectively [see also
259.011].

265.4 **265B** reprinted with **270A**, **376B**, and **379** by Manus Presse, Stuttgart,
1965.

[1] manus presse 1965 [2] *Acte sans paroles 1* | *Acte sans paroles 2* |
Gravures sur linoléum par | *H M Erhardt* | *Le jeu de Deryk Mendel
a conduit H M Erhardt aux Pantomimes* | *de Beckett. Les natures
mortes imprimées dans ce livre sont dédiées à D. M.* [3] Beckett [in
handwritten script] | Akt ohne Worte 1 Act Without Words 1 | Akt
ohne Worte 2 Act Without Words 2 | Linolschnitte von Lino cuts
by | H M Erhardt H M Erhardt | [etc., in German and English]
[4] *blank* [5] [linocut] [6-7] *half titles* 8-[15] [text of **265B** in three
languages, even pages only numbered] [16-33] [linocuts (odd-
numbered pages) and line drawings (even-numbered pages)] [34-35]
half titles 36-[41] [text of **270A** in three languages, as above] [42-57]
[linocuts and line drawings, as above] [58] *blank* [59] [details of
printing (200 copies) and copyright, signatures] [60] *blank*. Endpapers, linocut and blank. 42 cm. Hardbound, gray jute, author and
artist in vertical caps. and l.c. on label gummed top end spine. Boxed
(black, linocut bottom front).

First performance of both works at Royal Court Theatre, London, April 3,
1957. **265A** performed in French, with Roger Blin as Hamm, Jean Martin as
Clov, Christine Tsingos as Nell and Georges Adet as Nagg, directed by Roger
Blin. Recorded studio performance broadcast in French by the BBC on Third
Programme on May 2, 1957, 8.50-10.20 p.m. **265B** performed and directed by
Deryk Mendel. Both plays first performed in France at Studio des Champs-
Élysées, Paris, April 26, 1957, with the same cast and direction, except that
Nell was played by Germaine de France.

1959

Gedichte

Collected poems, with facing German translations.

266 Wiesbaden: Limes Verlag, 1959 [June 26; 2,000 copies].
[1] [device, top right-hand corner] [2] *blank* [3] SAMUEL BECKETT
| GEDICHTE | LIMES VERLAG WIESBADEN [4] Die Ausgabe
enthält die Gedichte des Bandes Echo's Bones | and other precipitates,
© by author and Europa Press, Paris, 1935, | sowie bisher nur in
Zeitschriften publizierte französische Gedichte. | Die Übertragungen
aus dem Englischen sind von Eva Hesse, | die aus dem Französischen
von Elmar Tophoven | © für die deutsche Ausgabe Limes Verlag,
Wiesbaden, 1959 | Alle Rechte vorbehalten | Druck: Rud. Bechtold
& Comp., Wiesbaden | Einband: Karl Hanke, Düsseldorf | Ein-
bandentwurf: Hannes Jähn, Köln | Printed in Germany [5] INHALT
[list, continued over] [7] ECHO'S BONES | ECHOS GEBEIN |
1933-1935 8-47 [text of *Echo's Bones* with translations facing on

1959

266

right-hand pages] 48-51 [text of *Cascando* with facing translation, grouped with *Echo's Bones* cycle in this edition] [52] *blank* [53] 1937-1939   54-77 [text of 1937-1939 poems] [78] *blank* [79] SIX POEMES | SECHS GEDICHTE | 1947-1949   80-91 [text of 1947-1949 poems] [92] *blank.* 19½ cm. Hardbound, pink paper covered with cellophane, design continuous over back, spine, and front incorporating title etc. in orange and (front only) black typescript lettering, with photograph of author (lower front only); vertical caps. on lower spine.

266.01

Translation of **22A** [*Der Geier*] reprinted from **266**, p. 9, in *Lyrik im Limes Verlag* [1961], p. 6, followed by press comments and bibliographical summary. *Lyrik im Limes Verlag* is a publicity booklet, similar to **39.101**.

L'Image

Prose fragment, early version of **268**, p. 33, l. 28, to p. 38, l. 18.

267

X: A Quarterly Review, I (Nov., 1959), 35-37.

NOTE. There are numerous variants between the two versions, most significantly in the layout of the text, which is presented as an unbroken block in **267**, without the "verse" divisions of **268**.

1961

Comment c'est

Novel in three parts.

268

Paris: Éditions de Minuit, 1961 [Jan. 9; printing, 3,000 copies + 80 deluxe + 7 H.C. + 100 club + 10 H.C. club].
[1-2] *blank* [3] *half title* [4] *DU MÊME AUTEUR* [list to *La Dernière Bande*] [5] SAMUEL BECKETT | COMMENT C'EST | [star and m device] | LES ÉDITIONS DE MINUIT [6] L'ÉDITION ORIGINALE DE CET OUVRAGE A ÉTÉ TIRÉE | A QUATRE-VINGT HUIT EXEMPLAIRES SUR ALFA | MOUSSE NAVARRE DONT QUATRE-VINGT EXEMPLAIRES | NUMÉROTÉS DE 1 A 80 ET HUIT EXEMPLAIRES HORS- | COMMERCE NUMÉROTÉS DE H.-C. I A H.C. VII. [*sic*] | IL A ÉTÉ TIRÉ EN OUTRE CENT DIX EXEMPLAIRES | SUR ALFA MOUSSE NAVARRE RÉSERVÉS AU CLUB DE | L'ÉDITION ORIGINALE DONT CENT EXEMPLAIRES | NUMÉROTÉS DE C. 1 A C. 100 ET DIX EXEMPLAIRES | HORS-COMMERCE MARQUÉS H.-C. CLUB. | © 1961 by Les Editions de Minuit | 7. rue Bernard-Palissy — Paris 6e | Tous droits réservés pour tous pays [7] 1 [8] *blank* 9-59 [text of first part] [60]

1961

268   *blank* [61] 2 [62] *blank* 63-121 [text of second part] [122] *blank*
[123] 3 [124] *blank* 125-177 [text of third part] [178] *blank* [179]
CET OUVRAGE A ETE ACHEVE D'IMPRIMER | LE 6 JAN-
VIER 1961 SUR LES PRESSES DE | L'IMPRIMERIE JACQUES
ET DEMONTROND, A | BESANÇON ET INSCRIT DANS LES
REGISTRES | DE L'EDITEUR SOUS LE NUMERO 433. |
Imprimé en France [180] *blank*. 18½ cm. Soft cover, white; title
etc. in blue and black lettering on front and spine (horizontal);
catalogue list on back, within blue-line borders front and back,
bottom back dated 1-61. (Club copies, back cover blank except for
ÉDITION ORIGINALE).

268.001   Reprinted March 9, 1961 [3,000 copies].

268.1   Reprinted photographically in 1964 [Jan. 31; 3,000 copies].
[4] [list to **149**] [179] ACHEVÉ D'IMPRIMER | LE 31 JANVIER
1964 | PAR JOSEPH FLOCH | MAITRE IMPRIMEUR | A
MAYENNE | n° 2078 | *Imprimé en France*. 18½ cm. Pages un-
trimmed, price Fr. 9, as in **268**.

268.01   Extract from Part II published under the title "Découverte de Pim"
in *L'VII* [i.e., *Le Sept*], 1 [Dec. 1959], 9-13 (variants; see also **267**).

NOTE. About 1,100 copies of **268.001** were destroyed in a fire at the publisher's,
together with copies of other Beckett books; the print order does not therefore correctly reflect sales. There are several misprints in **268** which remain
uncorrected in **268.1**, e.g., p. 64, 1. 10: *l'ordre* for *d'ordre*; p. 71, 1. 3: *existais*
for *existait*; and p. 170, 1. 22: *voyages* for *couples*.

Letter to Albert Reps.

269   *Die Drei: Zeitschrift für Anthroposophie und Dreigliederung,* 4 (July-
Aug., 1961), 251.

NOTE. The letter, published with the author's permission, was a reply to
one from Albert Reps accompanying the latter's article on **259** in **1569**.

1963

270A   *Acte sans paroles II*

Mime for two male players.

270   First published in *Dramatische Dichtungen,* Band 1 (Frankfort on
the Main: Suhrkamp Verlag, 1963), pp. [330]-[337], with facing
German translation by Elmar Tophoven [see also **34.3**].
[1] Samuel Beckett [2] *blank* [3] Samuel Beckett | Dramatische
Dichtungen | Band I | Französische Originalfassungen | Deutsche
Übertragung von Elmar Tophoven | Englische Übertragung von
Samuel Beckett | Suhrkamp Verlag [4] Erstes bis drittes Tausend
1963 | © Suhrkamp Verlag Frankfurt am Main 1963. [. . .] [5] *half
title* [6] En attendant Godot | [cast] [7] Warten auf Godot | [cast]

1963

270   8-[205] [text in two languages] [206] Fin de partie | [cast] [207]
           Endspiel | [cast] 208-[317] [text in two languages] [318] Acte sans
           paroles I [319] Spiel ohne Worte I 320-[329] [text in two languages]
           [330] Acte sans paroles 2 | *Pour deux Personnages* | *et un Aiguillon*
           [331] Spiel ohne Worte 2 | *Für zwei Personen* | *und einen Stachel* 332-
           [337] [text in two languages] [338] Cascando [339] Cascando 340-
           [361] [text in two languages] [362] *blank* [363] Waiting for Godot |
           [cast] [364] *blank* 365-[452] [text (from here to end of volume, pages
           of French original are indicated at foot of each page, as in **34.3**, pp.
           295 ff.)] [453] Endgame | [cast] [454] *blank* 455-[503] [text] [504]
           blank [505] Act Without Words I [506] *blank* 507-[511] [text]
           [512] *blank* [513] Act Without Words 2 | A mime for two players
           and a sting [514] *blank* 515-[517] [text] [518] *blank* [519] Cascando
           [520] *blank* 521-[530] [text in English] [531-532] *blank* [533] Inhalt
           [list] [534] [copyright details] [535] [manufacturing details] [536]
           blank. Binding uniform with **34.3**, *q.v.*

270.1   Reprinted in **151.1**, pp. [93]-99; and in

270.11   **265.4**.

           Cascando

           Radio play for music and voice.

271   First published in **270**, pp. [338]-[361], with facing German transla-
           tion by Elmar Tophoven.

271.1   Reprinted in **151.1**, pp. [45]-60.

First performed on RTF-France Culture, Oct. 13, 1963, at 10.30 P.M. (duration 22 min.), to music by Marcel Mihalovici and with Roger Blin as Opener
and Jean Martin as Voice. Production by Roger Blin.

NOTE. Contract specifies that this play may not be performed without
Mihalovici's music, which exists in a few multigraphed copies published and
loaned by Heugel et Cie., Paris, copyright 1963, under the title *Cascando,
invention pour musique et voix, Op. 86.* 35 x 27 cm. (approx.), 38 pp., dated
"Paris, 30-XII-1962."

     Perhaps to avoid confusion with **24**, Beckett's first title was *Calando*, a
musical term meaning "diminishing in tone" (equivalent to *diminuendo* or
decrescendo). It was changed when it was pointed out by RTF officials
that *calendos* was slang for "cheese" in French. The name translated as
"Woburn" in **383** is "Maunu" in **271** ("Mißler" in the German text).

           1965

           Imagination morte imaginez

           Prose text.

272   Paris: Éditions de Minuit, 1965 (edition limited to 612 copies).
           [1-4] *blank* [5] *half title* [6] *blank* [7] SAMUEL BECKETT | imagi-

1965

272   nation morte | imaginez | [star and m device] | LES ÉDITIONS DE
       MINUIT [8] L'ÉDITION ORIGINALE DE CET | OUVRAGE
       A ÉTÉ TIRÉE A SIX | CENT DOUZE EXEMPLAIRES SUR |
       VELIN CUVE B. F. K. RIVES, | DONT QUATRE CENT
       CINQUANTE | EXEMPLAIRES NUMÉROTÉS DE | 1 A 450,
       CENT DOUZE EXEM- | PLAIRES MARQUÉS «112» | NU-
       MÉROTÉS DE 1 A 112 ET | RÉSERVÉS A LA LIBRAIRIE |
       DES ÉDITIONS DE MINUIT | ET CINQUANTE EXEM-
       PLAIRES | HORS-COMMERCE NUMÉROTÉS | DE H.-C. I A
       H.-C. L | Nº . . . | © 1965 by LES EDITIONS DE MINUIT |
       7, rue Bernard-Palissy — PARIS-VIᵉ | *Tous droits réservés pour tous
       pays* 9-18 *text* [19-20] *blank* [21] CET OUVRAGE A ÉTÉ
       ACHEVÉ | D'IMPRIMER LE PREMIER | OCTOBRE MIL
       NEUF CENT | SOIXANTE-CINQ SUR LES | PRESSES DE
       L'IMPRIMERIE | CORBIÈRE ET JUGAIN A | ALENÇON ET
       INSCRIT DANS | LES REGISTRES DE L'ÉDITEUR | SOUS
       LE NUMÉRO 559 | *Imprimé en France* [22-24] *blank.* 19 cm. Soft
       cover with flaps folded over [1-2] and [23-24], white; front printed
       black SAMUEL BECKETT | imagination morte | imaginez | [star
       and m device at foot, right], rest blank; dust jacket of transparent
       paper, but provided on copies in the "112" series only (see also **275**).

272.1 Reprinted to coincide with publication in *Lettres Nouvelles,* [XIII]
       (Oct.-Nov., 1965), 13-16.

272.2 Reprinted in **154.1**, pp. [49]-57.

Mercier et Camier (Extrait)

273   *Annales publiées trimestriellement par la Faculté des Lettres et
       Sciences Humaines de Toulouse* (n.s.), I, fasc. 3 (Nov., 1965),
       Littératures XII: Études et Documents, XIXᵉ-XXᵉ siècles, pp. 153-
       154.

NOTE. The extract, the first to be published in the original French, taken from
the eleventh and penultimate chapter of **615**, is appended as an annex to
1846, which contains long quotations in the original French from other parts
of the novel. The publication was authorized by Mr. Beckett; the fragment
concerns the visit made by Watt, Mercier, and Camier to a bar. [Another
extract appeared in *Le Monde, Supplément au Numéro 7157,* Jan. 17, 1968,
p. V; see also **380**.]

Letter to Madeleine Renaud

274   *Cahiers de la Compagnie Madeleine Renaud–Jean-Louis Barrault,*
       52 [Marguerite Duras number] (Dec., 1965), 6. [Published by Galli-
       mard, Paris.]

NOTE. The short letter, dated "Paris, 9 novembre 1965," addressed "Chère
Madeleine" and signed "Affectueusement, Samuel Beckett," wishes Madeleine

1965

274

Renaud good luck with the production of *Des Journées entières dans les arbres* by Marguerite Duras.

1966

Assez

Prose text.

275   Paris: Éditions de Minuit, 1966 (edition limited to 662 copies).
[1-4] *blank* [5] *half title* [6] *blank* [7] SAMUEL BECKETT | assez |
[star and m device] | LES ÉDITIONS DE MINUIT [8] L'ÉDITION
ORIGINALE DE CET | OUVRAGE A ÉTÉ TIRÉE A SIX |
CENT SOIXANTE-DEUX EXEM- | PLAIRES SUR VELIN
CUVE | B. F. K. RIVES, DONT QUATRE | CENT CINQUANTE
EXEMPLAIRES | NUMÉROTÉS DE 1 A 450, CENT | DOUZE
EXEMPLAIRES MARQUÉS | «112» NUMÉROTÉS DE 1 A | 112
ET RÉSERVÉS A LA LI- | BRAIRIE DES ÉDITIONS DE
MI- | NUIT ET CENT EXEMPLAIRES | HORS-COMMERCE
NUMÉROTÉS | DE H.-C. I A H.-C. C | N° . . . | © 1966 by
LES EDITIONS DE MINUIT | 7, rue Bernard-Palissy — PARIS-
VIᵉ | *Tous droits réservés pour tous pays* 9-29 *text* [30] CET
OUVRAGE A ÉTÉ ACHEVÉ | D'IMPRIMER LE DIX-NEUF |
FÉVRIER MIL NEUF CENT | SOIXANTE-SIX SUR LES |
PRESSES DE L'IMPRIMERIE | CORBIÈRE ET JUGAIN A |
ALENÇON ET INSCRIT DANS | LES REGISTRES DE
L'ÉDITEUR | SOUS LE NUMÉRO 575 | *Imprimé en France*
[31-32] *blank*. 19 cm. Cover very similar in material and design to
272, except for added features of title etc. in vertical caps. and italic
caps. on spine, and no dust jacket on copy purchased in the publisher's bookshop (according to the publishers, dust jackets are provided only on copies in the "112" series).

275.1   Reprinted to coincide with publication in *Quinzaine Littéraire,* 1
(March 15, 1966), 4-5 (on 5 cols.), subtitled UN TEXTE INÉDIT
| DE | SAMUEL BECKETT. (This new literary review is edited
by François Erval and Maurice Nadeau.)

275.2   Reprinted in **154.1**, pp. [31]-47.

NOTE. See **386.1**, pp. 153-159, and *Catalogue No. 2* (London: Carters and
Landry, n.d. [1966?]), covers and p. 1.

Bing

Prose text.

276   Paris: Éditions de Minuit, 1966 (edition limited to 762 copies).
[1-4] *blank* [5] *half title* [6] *blank* [7] SAMUEL BECKETT | bing |

1966

276   [star and m device] | LES ÉDITIONS DE MINUIT [8] L'ÉDITION ORIGINALE DE CET | OUVRAGE A ÉTÉ TIRÉE A SEPT | CENT SOIXANTE-DEUX EXEM- | PLAIRES SUR VELIN CUVE | B. F. K. RIVES, DONT CINQ | CENT CINQUANTE EXEMPLAI- | RES NUMÉROTÉS DE 1 A 550, | CENT DOUZE EXEMPLAIRES | MARQUÉS «112» NUMÉROTÉS | DE 1 A 112 ET RÉSERVÉS A | LA LIBRAIRIE DES ÉDITIONS | DE MINUIT ET CENT EXEM- | PLAIRES HORS-COMMERCE NU- | MÉROTÉS DE H.-C. I A H.-C. C | H.-C. LXIV [in private copy] | © 1966 by LES EDITIONS DE MINUIT | 7, rue Bernard-Palissy — PARIS-VIᵉ | *Tous droits réservés pour tous pays* 9-17 *text* [18] CET OUVRAGE A ÉTÉ ACHEVÉ | D'IMPRIMER LE TRENTE ET | UN OCTOBRE MIL NEUF CENT | SOIXANTE-SIX SUR LES | PRESSES DE L'IMPRIMERIE | CORBIÈRE ET JUGAIN A | ALENÇON ET INSCRIT DANS | LES REGISTRES DE L'ÉDITEUR | SOUS LE NUMÉRO 597 | *Imprimé en France* [19-20] *blank.* 19 cm. Cover very similar in design to **275**.

276.1   Reprinted in **154.1**, pp. [59]-66.

NOTE. See also **386.1**, pp. 165-168; **386.11**; and Appendix II.

1967

Dans le cylindre

Prose text.

277   *Livres de France,* XVIII [Samuel Beckett issue] (Jan., 1967), 23-24 [see also **618** and **905**].

Letter in Defense of Fernando Arrabal.

278   Quoted in *Le Monde,* Sept. 28, 1967, p. 5.

NOTE. The letter is quoted in the anonymous article entitled "Devant le tribunal d'ordre public de Madrid, le dramaturge Fernando Arrabal s'est défendu de l'accusation d' 'injure à la patrie' et de 'blasphème'." Beckett's letter was one of several protests sent to the Spanish authorities in Madrid. Arrabal was subsequently acquitted.

1968

Poèmes

Collected French poetry.

279   Paris: Éditions de Minuit, 1968 [edition limited to 762 copies]. [1-4] *blank* [5] *half title* [6] *blank* [7] SAMUEL BECKETT | poèmes | [star and m device] | LES ÉDITIONS DE MINUIT [8] L'ÉDITION ORIGINALE DE CET | OUVRAGE A ÉTÉ TIRÉE A SEPT | CENT SOIXANTE-DEUX EXEM- | PLAIRES SUR VELIN CUVE | B. F. K. RIVES, DONT CINQ | CENT CINQUANTE EXEMPLAI- | RES, NUMÉROTÉS DE 1 A 550,

1968

279 | CENT DOUZE EXEMPLAIRES | MARQUÉS «112» NU-
MÉROTÉS | DE 1 A 112 ET RÉSERVÉS A | LA LIBRAIRIE
DES ÉDITIONS | DE MINUIT ET CENT EXEM- | PLAIRES
HORS-COMMERCE NU- | MÉROTÉS DE H.-C. I A H.-C. C |
[serial number] | © 1968 by LES EDITIONS DE MINUIT | 7, rue
Bernard-Palissy — Paris 6ᵉ | *Tous droits réservés pour tous pays*
9 [253A] 10 [253B] 11 [253C] 12 [253D] 13 [253E] 14 [253F]
15 [253G] 16 [253H] 17 [253J] 18 [253K] 19 [253L] 20 [253M]
21 [262A] 22 [262B] 23 [262C] 24 [255A] 25 [255B] 26 [255C]
[27] *blank* 28-30 NOTES ET VARIANTES [signed (p. 30) John
FLETCHER] [31] CET OUVRAGE A ÉTÉ ACHEVÉ | D'IM-
PRIMER LE PREMIER MARS | MIL NEUF CENT SOIXANTE-
HUIT | SUR LES PRESSES DE L'IMPRI- | MERIE CORBIÈRE
ET JUGAIN A | ALENÇON ET INSCRIT DANS LES |
REGISTRES DE L'ÉDITEUR SOUS | LE NUMÉRO 656 |
Imprimé en France [32] *blank*. Watermark: B F K RIVES. Edges
untrimmed. 19 cm. Soft cover with flaps folded in, white, front
right (printed black) SAMUEL BECKETT | poèmes | [star and
m device], spine lettered black (vertical caps. and italic caps.), no
dust jacket on copy serial number H.-C. XXXIII.

NOTE. This first collection of Beckett's verse to be published in France adopts
the text of **266** except for the correction of two misprints (**266**, p. 62, l. 9,
"inpuissant," and p. 74, l. 9, "disparait").

L'Issue

Prose text.

280   Paris: Éditions Georges Visat, 1968 (edition limited to 154 copies).
[i-iv] *blank* [1] *half title* [2] © Les Éditions de Minuit 1968 [3] *blank*
[4] [engraving] [5] SAMUEL BECKETT | L'ISSUE | Six gravures
originales | de | ARIKHA | LES ÉDITIONS GEORGES VISAT
PARIS [6] *blank* 7-10 [text] [11] [engraving] [12] *blank* 13-14 [text,
cont.] [15] [engraving] [16] *blank* 17-18 [text, cont.] [19] [engrav-
ing] [20] *blank* 21-22 [text, cont.] [23] [engraving] [24] *blank* 25-[26]
[text ends] [27] [engraving] [28] *blank* [29] Il a été tiré 139 exem-
plaires sur grand vélin de | Rives, numérotés de 1 à 139, et 15
exemplaires | H. C. numérotés de I à XV. Toutes les gravures | sont
signées par l'artiste. | Le texte inédit de Samuel Beckett a été composé
| à la main en Elzévir Caslon corps 28, et imprimé | par Fequet et
Baudier, typographes. | Les six eaux-fortes originales de Avigdor
Arikha, | ont été tirées sur les presses de Georges Visat. | Achevé à
Paris, le 28 mai 1968. | Exemplaire | VI [author's private copy]
[30-36] *blank*. 28 cm. Unbound. Soft cover, white, with flaps, em-
bossed dry-stamped title on front. Enclosed loose within stiff boards
and boxed (brown cloth, title in white horizontal caps. on spine).

NOTE. This text comes from the same stable as **276**, **277**, and **618**.

Translations into English of the French Works

1945

Dieppe 193?

Poem of five lines, translation of **253J**.

370   *Irish Times,* June 9, 1945, p. 2, cols. 5-6.

370.1   A revised version of four lines printed in **255.1**, p. 2;

370.11   reprinted in **40**, p. 47,

370.12   and in **40.1**, p. 55 (see also **253.11/13, 255.11/12**) ;

370.13   and in **255.13**;

370.14   and in **16.032**, p. 169.

NOTE. Mr. Beckett confirms that this poem was first written in French. The poem reads as follows in the *Irish Times:*
     again
     the last ebb
     the dead shingle
     the turning then the steps
     to the lighted town.
In the definitive version, ll. 1-2 run together and "to" in l. 5 reads "towards." The title is simply "Dieppe" but the poem is dated "1937" (see also **253**, Note).

1950

Two Fragments

371A   1. An extract from *Molloy,* translated by the author [taken from **257**, pp. 97-100].

371B   2. An extract from *Malone meurt,* translated by the author [taken from **258**, pp. 7-9].

371   *Transition Fifty,* 6 ([Oct.], 1950), pp. 103-105 and 105-106, respectively.

NOTE. The translations, published before the French originals, show variants from the definitive texts (**374** and **375**); curiously, **371A** is closer to the definitive text translated in collaboration with Patrick Bowles than is **371B** to **375** translated alone (see Appendix II).

1954

The End [252, 263C]

Short story, "translated from the French by Richard Seaver in collaboration with the author."

372   *Merlin* (ed. Alexander Trocchi), II (Summer-Autumn, 1954), 144-159.

372.1   Reprinted in *Evergreen Review*, IV (Nov.-Dec., 1960), 22-41 [extensive variants; see Appendix II];

372.11   and in **1198**, pp. 350-366;

372.2   and in **386**, pp. 47-72;

372.21   and in **386.1**, pp. 43-67.

Waiting for Godot [259]

"Tragicomedy in two acts," translated by the author.

373   New York: Grove Press, 1954 [Sept. 8] (Evergreen Book E-33).
          [i] *blank* [ii] [letters staggered across pages] W | A | I | T | I | N |
          G [iii] F | O | R | G | O | D | O | T | *tragicomedy in 2 acts* | *by*
          samuel beckett | *grove press* | *new york* [iv] *Copyright 1954* | *by*
          Grove Press [. . .] | *Manufactured in the United States of America* |
          by H. Wolff Book Manufacturing Company | DESIGN: *Marshall*
          Lee | *Translated from his original French text* | *by the author* [v-viii]
          plates [ix] [cast] [x] *blank* [xi] [staggered as above] A | C | T | I |
          A country road. A tree. | *Evening.* [xii ff.] [text; pagination begins,
          left side only paginated, two facing pages counting as one, 7 to 60;
          final pages [61-63a] include note on first French production and
          biographical note]. 21 cm. Hardbound, black cloth, dry-stamped
          title; spine, silver and gold horizontal italics; scarlet endpapers.
          Plates: photographs of production preceded by portrait of author.

373.001   Reprinted in **1364**, pp. 36-61, illus.

373.002   Gramophone record of first New York production, New York: Columbia, 1956 (Columbia O2L-238 [OL5015-5016], 33⅓ rpm, 12 inches, 4 sides).

373.003   Long extracts published in *The Best Plays of 1955-1956*, ed. Louis Kronenberger (New York and Toronto: Dodd, Mead, 1956), pp. 295-317.

373.004   Reprinted in **1164**, pp. 1-83.

373.1   Faber and Faber, London, 1956 [Feb. 10].
          [1] *half title* [2] *blank* [3] WAITING | FOR | GODOT | a tragicomedy in two acts | by Samuel Beckett | Faber and Faber Limited |
          24 Russell Square London [4] *First published in England in mcmlvi* |
          by Faber and Faber Limited | *24 Russell Square, London, W.C.1* |
          Printed in Great Britain by | *Western Printing Services Limited,*

1954

373.1 *Bristol | All rights reserved* [5] *Note | This play is copyright in* 1955. | [details of performing rights, first British production, etc.] [White slip attached to [5] reads:] PUBLISHER'S NOTE | [details of textual deletions "made to satisfy the requirements of the Lord Chamberlain. The text printed here is that used in the Criterion Theatre production."] [6] *Characters* | ESTRAGON | VLADIMIR | POZZO | LUCKY | A BOY [7] ACT I | *A country road. A tree | Evening* [8] *blank* 9-53 [text of Act I] [54] *blank* [55] ACT II | *Next Day. Same Time. Same Place* [56] *blank* 57-94 [text of Act II] [95-96] *blank.* 20 cm. Hardbound, ocher cloth; vertical crimson caps. and l.c. on spine.

373.101 Second impression, Feb. 1956.
[4] *First published in England in February mcmlvi* | [. . .] | *Second impression February mcmlvi* | [. . .] [5] [slip suppressed; data now printed on page].

373.102/103 Reprinted 1957, 1961.

373.1001 Exchanges from **373.1** text ("All the dead voices . . ." and "we are incapable of keeping silent," pp. 62-63) set to music by Marc Wilkinson as "Voices," for contralto, flute, E♭ clarinet, bass clarinet, violoncello (10 mins. duration). Score published by Universal Edition (UE 12912), London, 1960; 24 pp., 24 cm. (text in English and German).

373.1002 Extract from last half of Act II published in *An Introduction to Drama,* 2d ed., by George Joshua Newbold Whitfield (London: Oxford University Press, 1963), under section "The Modern Stage II," pp. 192-206.

373.1003 See **16.032**, pp. 153-159.

373.11 Reprinted in Faber Paper Covered Editions in 1959 [June 5; British Museum date stamp, May 15]. Same pagination, same printer. [2] *Also by Samuel Beckett | ALL THAT FALL* [4] *First published in this edition mcmlix* | [. . .]. 18 cm. Soft cover, glossy, white and brown, lettered black.

373.111/112 Reprinted 1962; March, 1964;

373.2 and in **270**, pp. [363]-[452].

373.3 Second British edition, unexpurgated, revised. London: Faber and Faber, 1965 [May 6]. Same printer.
[2] *By the same author* [list to *Play*] [4] [. . .] | *This revised and unexpurgated edition first published mcmlxv* [. . .] [5] *Note | Copyright* © *Samuel Beckett* 1955 *and* 1965 | [then as **373.1** omitting mention of textual deletions] [6] *Characters* | ESTRAGON | VLADIMIR | LUCKY | POZZO | A BOY 9-54 [text of Act I] [pagination

1954

373.3   identical for Act II, except that p. 94 is not entirely filled as in
              373.1]. Binding identical, cloth paler in tone, and about 1 mm
              shorter (the pages are 2 mm shorter than in **373.1**); dust jacket (as
              in **373.1**) illus. front photograph of British production, but left-hand
              inner flap speaks of "A NEW EDITION, . . . authorized by Mr.
              Beckett as definitive."

373.31   **373.112** text subsequently brought into line with **373.3**.

373.4   French's Acting Edition, No. 510. London: Samuel French, 1957
              [illus.].
              [i] WAITING FOR GODOT | A Tragicomedy in Two Acts | by |
              SAMUEL BECKETT | [device] | LONDON | SAMUEL FRENCH
              LIMITED [ii] [. . .] | MADE AND PRINTED IN GREAT BRIT-
              AIN BY | LATIMER, TREND AND CO., LTD, PLYMOUTH |
              [. . .] [iii] [cast list and synopsis of scenes] [iv] [fee details] Facing p.
              [1] [photograph of set] [1]-38 [text of Act I] [39]-70 [text of Act II]
              [71]-72 FURNITURE AND PROPERTY LIST [73] LIGHTING
              PLOT [74-76] *blank*. 21½ cm. Soft cover, blue; title etc., red and
              darker blue.

First performance in Great Britain at the Arts Theatre Club, London, on
Aug. 3, 1955, with Peter Woodthorpe as Estragon, Paul Daneman as Vladimir,
Timothy Bateson as Lucky, Peter Bull as Pozzo, and Michael Walker as the
Boy, directed by Peter Hall, decor by Peter Snow. Later transferred to the
Criterion Theatre after a small number of textual deletions had been made.
The complete and unexpurgated text first performed publicly in Great
Britain at the Royal Court Theatre, London, on Dec. 30, 1964, directed by
Anthony Page, assisted by the author.

    First performance in the United States on Jan. 3, 1956, at the Coconut
Grove Playhouse, Miami, Florida, with Bert Lahr as Estragon and Tom Ewell
as Vladimir, directed by Michael Myerberg. First performance in New York
on April 19, 1956, at the John Golden Theatre, with Bert Lahr as Estragon
and E. G. Marshall as Vladimir, directed by Herbert Berghof.

NOTE. Apart from the expurgated passages in **373.1** (the chief of these
concerns hanging and erection, p. 17), there are one or two curious discrepancies between the texts in **373** and **373.1**: e.g., "depuis la mort de Voltaire,"
259.01, p. 73, becomes in **373.1**, p. 43, "since the death of Samuel Johnson."
In **373.3**, p. 44, this is altered to "since the death of Bishop Berkeley," thus
conforming to the phrase used in **373**. As for the text in **373.4**, it must be
recorded that the adapters have tampered extensively and naïvely with both
dialogue and stage directions. The fact that **270** reprints the expurgated Faber
text and not the Grove text mars the usefulness of the collection.

1955

Molloy [**257**]

Novel translated by Patrick Bowles in collaboration with the author.

1955

374   Paris: Olympia Press, 1955.
             [1-2] *blank* [3] *half title* [4] ALL RIGHTS RESERVED IN ALL
             COUNTRIES | BY THE OLYMPIA PRESS, PARIS | AND
             GROVE PRESS, NEW YORK [5] SAMUEL BECKETT | MOL-
             LOY | a novel | *translated from the French* | *by Patrick Bowles* | *in
             collaboration with the Author* | COLLECTION MERLIN | *THE
             OLYMPIA PRESS* | 8 rue de Nesle, Paris, 6ᵉ [6] *blank* [7]-124 [text
             of I] [125]-241 [text of II] [242] *blank* [243] PRINTED MARCH
             1955 BY | IMPRIMERIE MAZARINE | PARIS | Printed in France
             | [rule at foot of page] | Dépôt légal: 1ᵉʳ trimestre 1955 [244-248]
             blank. 18 cm. Soft cover, with flaps over stiff paper; design in yel-
             low, blue, and black running over back and spine to front; title etc.
             in black (caps., l.c. and italics) incorporated on front only. Front of
             some copies for distribution in Great Britain overstamped FRANCE
             FEATURES, and [5] FRANCE FEATURES | 15, NEW ROW, ST.
             MARTIN'S LANE, | LONDON, W.C.2 | [. . .], from ink pad.

374.01   Extract published in *Merlin,* II (Autumn, 1953), 88-103 [variants].

374.02   Extract (**374**, pp. 92-106, i.e., "Stones" passage) published in *Paris
             Review,* 5 (Spring, 1954), 124-135 [variants, and notes on contribu-
             tors, Beckett entry, p. 136].

374.021   **374.02** reprinted as "Stones" in *Best Short Stories from the Paris
             Review,* introduced by William Styron (New York: E. P. Dutton,
             1959; also a Dutton Paperback Everyman, 1961), pp. 49-59.

374.03   Extract (opening section of **374**) published in *New World Writing,*
             5 [April, 1954], 316-323 [variants].

374.04   Extract from **374**, pp. 93-100, entitled "Stones," published in **1235**,
             pp. 200-204.

374.1   New York: Grove Press, 1955 [Fall] (Evergreen Book E-18) [photo-
             graphic reprint of **374**].
             [5] [at foot of page] GROVE PRESS, INC. | NEW YORK [6] ALL
             RIGHTS RESERVED IN ALL COUNTRIES | BY THE OLYM-
             PIA PRESS, PARIS | AND GROVE PRESS, NEW YORK | *Library
             of Congress Catalog Card* | *Number 55-5113* | First Grove Press Edi-
             tion 1955 | MANUFACTURED IN THE UNITED STATES OF
             AMERICA [242-246] Evergreen Books [catalogue]. 20 cm. Soft
             cover; front design in white, blue, and black incorporating title etc.;
             back, blurb and press comments; spine, vertical caps.

374.11/19   Reprinted at least nine times.

374.2   Reprinted in **377.1, 377.11, 377.12**.

374.3   London: Calder and Boyars, 1966 (Jupiter Book J-13). [Printed in
             Great Britain by Philips Park Press, 189 pp. Similar in format to
             25.2 and **32.3**.]

1955

374.31   See **16.032**, pp. 62-114.

NOTE. Some copies of **374** carry the following legend at the top of the flap of the back wrapper: "Special Printing for Sale in the U.K. and Commonwealth," underneath which a price (in sterling) has been deleted. Other copies simply carry the price [FRS 1.200] centered about ⅛ in. below the top edge of the wrapper. This would seem to indicate, writes H. Alan Clodd, "that Olympia intended to issue two editions, one for France and one for the U.K., right from the initial publication of the book. Otherwise they would surely have overprinted the price in francs and then added the legend 'Special Printing, etc.' and the price in £."

1956

Malone Dies [258]

Novel translated by the author.

375   New York: Grove Press, 1956 (Evergreen Book E-39).
            [i] *half title* [ii] *blank* [iii] SAMUEL | BECKETT | MALONE | DIES | *a novel translated from the French* | *by the author* | Grove Press | New York [iv] Copyright ©, 1956, by Grove Press | Library of Congress Catalogue Card Number: 56-8440 | [. . .] | *Malone Dies* is published in two editions: | An Evergreen Book (E-39) | A hard bound limited edition of 500 copies | *Manufactured in the United States of America* [v] *half title* [vi] *blank* 1-120 [text] [121-122] *blank*. 20¼ cm. Soft cover, abstract design in orange, white, and black with lettering in same colors; press comments on back.

375.01   Also issued in a hardbound limited edition of 500 copies; bound in natural linen; front cover, title etc. in black caps. and l.c.; spine, vertical black caps. and l.c.; glassine dust wrapper stamped black $3.75.

375.02   Reprinted in **377.1**, **377.11**, and **377.12**.

375.1   British edition. London: John Calder, 1958 [March 7] (photographic reprint of **375**).
            [iii] SAMUEL | BECKETT | MALONE | DIES | *a novel translated from the French* | *by the author* | John Calder | London [iv] First published in Great Britain in 1958 by | John Calder (Publishers) Ltd., | 17 Sackville Street, London, W.1 | *All Rights Reserved* | *Printed in Great Britain by* | *Taylor Garnett Evans & Co. Ltd.,* | *Watford.* 19½ cm. Hardbound, black paper (imitation cloth); title and author in vertical gold italic caps. on spine; dust jacket design in black, yellow, and white.

375.2   Paperback edition. Harmondsworth, Middlesex: Penguin Books, 1962 (Penguin Books 1691) [20,000 copies].
            [1] *half title* [. . .] [2] *blank* [3] *Samuel Beckett* | MALONE DIES |

1956

375.2 A novel translated from the French | by the author | PENGUIN
BOOKS [4] [...] | Published in Penguin Books 1962 | [...] | Made
and printed in Great Britain | by Butler & Tanner Ltd, | Frome
and London | Set in Monotype Baskerville | [...] 5-144 [text]. 18 cm.
Soft cover, red and white, lettered in black, with front illus. with
drawing by Virgil Burnett representing Malone writing in bed;
back, blurb; title and author in vertical l.c. on spine; inside front
cover, photograph of author by Brassaï and biographical summary.

375.21 Reprint dated 1965 has slightly modified front-cover design.

375.22 Later reissued with a new cover as a "Penguin Modern Classic."

375.001 Extract published in *Irish Writing*, 34 (Spring, 1956), 29-35.

375.002 See **16.032**, pp. 115-132.

1958

Endgame, Followed by Act Without Words [**265A, 265B**]

376A *Endgame.*
Play in one act, translated by the author.

376B *Act Without Words* [I].
Mime for one player, translated by the author.

376 New York: Grove Press, 1958 (Evergreen Book E-96).
[i] ENDGAME | A Play in One Act | *followed by* | ACT WITH-
OUT WORDS | A Mime for One Player | by | Samuel Beckett |
translated from the French | *by the author* | [rule] | Grove Press,
Inc. [...] New York [ii] Copyright ©, 1958, by Grove Press, Inc. |
[...] | *Endgame* and *Act Without Words* is published in four editions:
| An Evergreen Book (E-96) | A hard bound edition | A specially
bound, Limited Edition of | 100 numbered copies | A special edition
of 26 copies signed | by the author | [...] | MANUFACTURED IN
THE UNITED STATES OF AMERICA [iii] *For Roger Blin* |
ENDGAME | A Play in One Act | NAGG | NELL | HAMM |
CLOV [iv] [details and cast lists of first performances] 1-84 [text of
Endgame] [85] ACT WITHOUT WORDS | A Mime for One
Player [86] *blank* 87-91 [text of *Act without Words*] [92] *blank*.
20 cm. Hardbound, off-white cloth; front, title etc. in horizontal
caps.; spine, vertical caps.; both brown.

376.01 Also soft cover, as indicated p. [ii].

376.02 **376B** reprinted in **34.2**, pp. [123]-133; and in

376.021 **265.4**.

376.03 **376A** reprinted in **1033**.

1958

376.04   **376A** and **376B** reprinted in **270**, pp. [453]-[503] and [505]-[511], respectively.

376.05   See **16.032**, pp. 161-163.

376.1   London: Faber and Faber, 1958 [April 25].
[1] *blank* [2] by the same author: | * | WAITING FOR GODOT | ALL THAT FALL [3] ENDGAME | *A Play in one Act* | *followed by* | ACT WITHOUT WORDS | A Mime for one Player | by | SAMUEL BECKETT | *Translated* | *from the original French* | *by the author* | FABER AND FABER | 24 Russell Square | London [4] *First published in mcmlviii* | [. . .] | *Printed in Great Britain by* | *Ebenezer Baylis and Son Ltd., Worcester and London* | [. . .] | © 1958 *by Grove Press* 5 [note on performing rights, first performances, etc.] [6] *blank* [7] ENDGAME | For Roger Blin [8] *blank* [9] THE CHARACTERS | HAMM | CLOV | NAGG | NELL [10] *blank* 11-53 [text of *Endgame*] [54] *blank* [55] ACT WITHOUT WORDS | *A Mime for one Player* | To Music by JOHN BECKETT [56] *blank* 57-60 [text of *Act Without Words*] [61-62] *blank,* serving as endpaper, there being a different endpaper before [1]. 20 cm. Hardbound, reddish-brown cloth; title etc. in vertical blue caps. on spine; dust jacket, front, photograph of Roger Blin in the role of Hamm; back, catalogue list; blurbs and press comments on inside flaps.

376.11   Reissued in Faber Paper Covered Editions, 1964 [April 10; British Museum date stamp, March 13].
[2] [list includes to *Play*] [4] [. . .] | *First published in this edition mcmlxiv* | *Printed in Great Britain by* | *Latimer Trend & Co Ltd, Whitstable* | [. . .] [61-64] *blank.* 18 cm. Pagination identical, but in process of photoreprinting the text has been reduced, so that it is shorter (15.2 cm as against 15.9 cm in **376.1**) and the characters are smaller. Soft cover, glossy surface common to series, red, black, and white, lettered in black and white.

First performed in the United States at the Cherry Lane Theater, New York, directed by Alan Schneider, on Jan. 28, 1958 (**376A** only; **376B** first performed in New York at the YMHA in 1960).

First performed (**376A** only, with *Krapp's Last Tape*) in Great Britain at the Royal Court Theatre, London, on Oct. 28, 1958, with George Devine and Jack MacGowran, directed by George Devine.

NOTE. Contract specifies that **265B/376B** may not be performed without John Beckett's music, the existence of which is not mentioned in the American edition.

The Unnamable [260]

Novel translated by the author.

377   New York: Grove Press, 1958 (Evergreen Book E-117).
[i] *half title* [ii] *blank* [iii] SAMUEL BECKETT | THE UN-

1958

377   NAMABLE | TRANSLATED FROM THE FRENCH BY THE
        AUTHOR | GROVE PRESS INC. [   ] NEW YORK [iv] COPY-
        RIGHT © 1958 BY GROVE PRESS INC. | [. . .] | TYPE SET BY
        THE POLYGLOT PRESS, NEW YORK | MANUFACTURED
        IN THE UNITED STATES OF AMERICA [v] *The Unnamable*
        is published in five editions: | An Evergreen Book (E-117) | A cloth
        bound edition | A specially bound limited edition of | 100 numbered
        copies | A specially bound and signed edition | of 26 copies, num-
        bered A through Z | A specially bound and signed edition | of 4
        copies, *hors commerce,* numbered | 1 through 4 [vi] *blank* [vii]
        [Beckett works published by Grove Press listed] [viii] *blank* [1] *half
        title* [2] *blank* 3-179 [text] [180-184] *blank.* 20 cm. Soft cover; red,
        turquoise, blue, and black abstract design by Roy Kuhlman on front;
        top front, title etc. in black caps. on white; spine, vertical white caps.
        on black; back, blurb and press comments.

377.01   Hardbound edition of 100 copies.

377.02   Specially bound, limited edition of 26 numbered signed copies.

377.001 Extract published in *Spectrum,* II (Winter, 1958), 3-7 [from opening
         paragraphs; variants].

377.002 Extract published in *Texas Quarterly,* 2 (Spring, 1958), 127-131
         (with an introduction by David Hayman [see **1450**]) [variants].

377.003 Extract published in *Chicago Review,* XII (Summer, 1958), 82-86
         [variants].

377.004 See **16.032**, pp. 133-151.

377.1   Reprinted with **374** and **375** in one volume by Grove Press, New
         York, 1959; hardbound.

377.101 Paperback edition, 1965.
         [1] *half title* [2] *blank* [3] THREE NOVELS | BY SAMUEL
         BECKETT | [rule] | MOLLOY | MALONE DIES | THE UN-
         NAMABLE | *An Evergreen Black Cat* [cat device] *Book* | GROVE
         PRESS, INC.   NEW YORK [4] Copyright © 1955, 1956, 1958 by
         Grove Press, Inc. | All Rights Reserved | First Evergreen Black Cat
         Edition 1965 | MANUFACTURED IN THE UNITED STATES
         OF AMERICA [5] MOLLOY | Translated from the French by |
         Patrick Bowles | in collaboration with the author [6] *blank* 7-176
         [text of *Molloy*] [177] MALONE DIES | Translated from the French
         by the author [178] *blank* 179-288 [text of *Malone Dies*] [289] THE
         UNNAMABLE | Translated from the French by the author [290]
         blank 291-414 [text of *The Unnamable*] [415 416] *blank.* 18 cm.
         Soft cover; front, lettered black, blue, and green on white; black,
         blue and green vertical and horizontal caps. on spine; back, blurb
         and press comments and price $1.45.

1958

377.11   Reprinted by Olympia Press, Paris, 1959 (Traveller's Companion Series no. 71).
[i] SAMUEL BECKETT | MOLLOY | MALONE DIES | THE UNNAMABLE | *A TRILOGY* | THE TRAVELLER'S COMPANION | *SERIES* | published by | THE OLYMPIA PRESS | 7 *rue Saint-Séverin, Paris 5* [within border of green tassles] [ii] PRINTED IN FRANCE | October 1959 | by Imprimerie du Lion, Paris | In the same series | and by the same author: | WATT | Copyright © 1956, 1958 by Grove Press, Inc. | *Copyright © 1959 by The Olympia Press, Paris* | Library of Congress Catalog Card Number: 59-13886 | [rule] | *Dépôt légal: 4ᵉ trimestre 1959* [1] MOLLOY | Translated from the French by | PATRICK BOWLES | in collaboration with the author [2] *blank* [3]-240 [text of *Molloy*] [241] MALONE DIES | Translated from the French | by the author [242] *blank* [243]-398 [text of *Malone Dies*] [399] THE | UNNAMABLE | Translated from the French by the author [400] *blank* [401-402] [lacking] 403-579 [text of *The Unnamable*] [580] *blank*. 17 cm. Thin paper. Soft cover, green; front, lettered black within black and white borders; spine, vertical italic caps., black on white; back cover, note forbidding sale in U.S.A. or U.K.

377.12   Reprinted by John Calder, London, 1960 [late March].
[i] *half title* [ii] *blank* [1] SAMUEL BECKETT | *Molloy* | *Malone Dies* | *The Unnamable* | [tree device] | LONDON | JOHN CALDER [2] THIS TRILOGY FIRST PUBLISHED IN ONE VOLUME IN 1959 [*sic*] BY JOHN | CALDER (PUBLISHERS) LTD., 17 SACKVILLE STREET, LONDON, W.1 | © JOHN CALDER (PUBLISHERS) LTD., 1959 | PRINTED IN GREAT BRITAIN BY | WODDERSPOON & CO. LTD. | ASHFORD, MIDDLESEX [3] CONTENTS [list] [4] *Other works by Samuel Beckett | in the Evergreen Books series:* | [list] [5] PART I | [star] | MOLLOY [6] *blank* [7]-176 [text of *Molloy*] [177] PART II | [star] | MALONE DIES [178] *blank* [179]-289 [text of *Malone Dies*] [290] *blank* [291] PART III | [star] | THE UNNAMABLE [292] *blank* [293]-418 [text of *The Unnamable*]. 19 cm. Hardbound, dark-blue paper, imitation cloth; title etc. in horizontal gold caps. and italic caps. on spine.

377.121   Reprinted 1966 by Lowe and Brydone, London, with modifications taking account of publishers' new name, Calder and Boyars.

1959

Text for Nothing I [**263D**]

Text translated by the author.

378   *Evergreen Review,* III (Summer, 1959), 21-24.

378.1   Reprinted with variants in **386**, pp. 75-79;

378.11   and in **386.1**, pp. 71-75.

1959

Act Without Words II [**270A**]

Mime for two players, translated by the author.

379   *New Departures,* 1 (Summer, 1959), 89-90.

379.1   Reprinted in **34.2,** pp. [135]-141 [slight variants; description "Translated from the French by the author"];

379.2   and in **270,** pp. [513]-[517];

379.3   and in **45,** pp. [23]-28 ("Translated from the original French by the author");

379.4   and in **265.4.**

First performed in Great Britain at Institute of Contemporary Arts, London, Jan. 25, 1960; performed a second time at In-Stage, London, in July 1962, directed by Charles Marowitz. First performance in United States probably at Living Theatre, New York, in 1959.

NOTE. Mr. Beckett writes that this mime was written in French at about the same time as *Acte sans paroles I* (**265B**), that is, in 1956.

1960

Mercier and Camier

Two extracts from **615,** entitled "Madden" and "The Umbrella," translated by Hugh Kenner assisted by Raymond Federman, with the permission of the author.

380   *Spectrum,* IV (Winter, 1960), 3-11 ["Madden," taken from beginning of chap. 4, on pp. 3-6; "The Umbrella," taken from middle of chap. 7, on pp. 6-11].

Extract broadcast by KPFK, Los Angeles, in the framework of **504** (q.v.), presented by Michael Harvey, on Dec. 28, 1962, 10.15 to 10.30 P.M.

NOTE. Apart from quotations in books and articles, these are the only fragments of the unpublished novel *Mercier et Camier* to have appeared in English. The translation was not seen by the author before publication [see also **273**].

Stories and Texts for Nothing, III [**263F**]

Translated by Anthony Bonner and the author.

381   Published in **1130,** pp. 313-317.

381.1   Reprinted (with variants), newly translated by the author, in **386,** pp. 85-90;

381.11   and in **386.1,** pp. 81-86.

NOTE. The title in **381** is evidently an error, being a literal translation of the whole compilation **263,** which groups, of course, three texts dating from 1945, and thirteen, one of which is given here, dating from 1950; it can hardly, therefore, have been chosen by the author.

1962

The Expelled [**254, 263A**]

Short story [dated 1946], "translated by Richard Seaver in collaboration with the author."

382   *Evergreen Review,* VI (Jan.-Feb., 1962), 8-20.

382.1   Reprinted in *The Existential Imagination,* ed. Frederick R. Karl and Leo Hamalian (Greenwich, Conn.: Fawcett Publications, 1963), pp. 217-229, preceded by short note on Beckett, p. 217.

382.2   Reprinted in **386**, pp. 9-25;

382.21 and in **386.1**, pp. 9-24;

382.22 and in **16.033**, pp. 448-454.

1963

Cascando [**271**]

Play for radio, translated by the author.

383   *Evergreen Review,* VII (May-June, 1963), 47-57. [Footnote, p. 47, reads: "Samuel Beckett wrote *Cascando* in French for the composer Marcel Mihalovici. It will shortly be produced by RTF. The English translation is by the author."]

383.1   Reprinted in **270**, pp. [519]-[530];

383.2   and in **42**, pp. [37]-48 [variants], where it is described as "A Radio Piece for Music and Voice."

First broadcast on BBC Third Programme on Oct. 6, 1964, at 10.33 P.M. (duration 23 mins.), with Patrick Magee as Voice and Denys Hawthorne as Opener, music by Marcel Mihalovici, produced by Donald McWhinnie.

NOTE. The BBC broadcast of this play (described by the announcer as "a meditation written for radio by Samuel Beckett") followed the **383** text. The variants in **383.2**, especially p. 40, l. 8, "I open the door," seem to be misprints; this particular sentence reads "I open the other" in **383**, p. 48. (Mr. Beckett has confirmed that this particular reading is a mistake.)

1964

How It Is [**268**]

Novel translated by the author.

384   New York: Grove Press, 1964.
            [i-ii] *blank* [1] *half title* [2] *blank* [3] HOW IT IS | by | Samuel Beckett | Translated from the French | by the author | GROVE PRESS, INC. / NEW YORK [4] Copyright © 1964 by Grove Press, Inc. | [. . .] | First Printing | MANUFACTURED IN THE

1964

384   UNITED STATES OF AMERICA [5] 1 [6] *blank* 7-48 [text of
          Part I] [49] 2 [50] *blank* 51-99 [text of Part II] [100] *blank* [101] 3
          [102] *blank* 103-147 [text of Part III] [148-150] *blank*. 20 cm. Hard-
          bound, black cloth; title etc. in vertical and horizontal gold caps. on
          spine; dust jacket, white; front typographical design in red and
          black; back, press comments; back flap, photograph; front flap,
          blurb and price $3.95.

384.01   Extract published under the title "From an Unabandoned Work"
          in *Evergreen Review*, IV (Sept.-Oct., 1960), 58-65 [taken from the
          opening pages of the novel; extensive variants in this extract pub-
          lished before the French original].

384.02   Extract published in *Paris Review*, 28 ([Summer-Fall], 1962), 113-
          116 [beginning of Part III; variants].

384.03   Extract published in *Arna*, n.v. (1962), 32-35 [*idem*] [see **1336**].

384.04   Extract published in *Transatlantic Review*, 13 (Summer, 1963), 5-15
          [end of Part III].

384.1   London: John Calder, 1964 [April 30].
          [1] *half title* [2] *By the same author:* | [list] [3] HOW | IT | IS | by |
          SAMUEL BECKETT | Translated from the French by the Author |
          [tree device] | JOHN CALDER | LONDON [4] FIRST PUB-
          LISHED IN GREAT BRITAIN | BY JOHN CALDER (PUB-
          LISHERS) LTD | [. . .] | FIRST EDITIONS OF *How It Is* HAVE
          BEEN PRINTED AS FOLLOWS: | 100 COPIES ON HAND
          MADE PAPER BOUND IN VELLUM MARKED | A 1 TO A 100
          SIGNED BY THE AUTHOR (HORS COMMERCE). | 100
          COPIES ON HAND MADE PAPER BOUND IN MOROCCO
          MARKED | B 1 TO B 100 SIGNED BY THE AUTHOR (HORS
          COMMERCE). | 4,000 COPIES OF A HARDBOUND TRADE
          EDITION. | PRINTED IN GREAT BRITAIN BY | BLACKIE
          & SON LTD, BISHOPBRIGGS, GLASGOW [5] PART I
          [6] *blank* 7-54 [text of Part I] [55] PART II [56] *blank* 57-108
          [text of Part II] [109] PART III [110] *blank* 111-160 [text of Part
          III]. 20 cm. Hardbound, gray paper imitation cloth; title etc. in
          vertical gold italics on spine; dust jacket front, design in black, white
          and brown; blurb on back.

384.101   Series B edition. 21 cm. Hardbound, full fawn morocco binding;
          title and author in gold caps. within three gold rules on spine; top
          edge gilt, others untrimmed; fawn paper slipcase.

384.102   Series A similar except for full vellum binding.

384.11   See **16.032**, pp. 173-185.

NOTE. Contrary to the declaration on p. [4] of **384.101** (A LIMITED EDI-
TION OF ONE HUNDRED COPIES ON HAND- | MADE PAPER,

1964

384

SERIES B BOUND MOROCCO, AND SIGNED BY | THE AUTHOR,
HAS BEEN PRINTED (HORS COMMERCE) IN | ADVANCE OF THE
FIRST EDITION), these copies were, in fact, issued after **384.1**. Number
and author's signature follow immediately after this declaration.

1965

Imagination Dead Imagine [**272**]

385   *Sunday Times,* Nov. 7, 1965, p. 48, cols. 2-3, headed "SAMUEL
BECKETT: An unpublished text."

385.1   London: Calder and Boyars, 1965.
[1] *half title* [2] *Other Works by Samuel Beckett* [list] [3] IMAGI-
NATION | DEAD | IMAGINE | by Samuel Beckett | *translated
from the French | by the author* | LONDON | CALDER AND
BOYARS [4] FIRST PUBLISHED IN GREAT BRITAIN 1965 |
BY CALDER AND BOYARS LTD. | [. . .] | A LIMITED EDI-
TION OF ONE HUNDRED COPIES ON | HAND-MADE PAPER
AND SIGNED BY THE AUTHOR | HAS BEEN PRINTED
(HORS COMMERCE) IN ADVANCE | OF THE FIRST EDI-
TION | SET IN 14pt. MONOTYPE GARAMOND | PRINTED
AT THE BAYNARD PRESS, LONDON, S.W.9 [5] *half title* [6]
blank 7-14 [text] [15-16] *blank.* 19½ cm. Soft cover, flaps over stiff
paper; front, design by Brian Paine incorporating "Head on a
Stalk" by Giacometti; title etc. in vertical caps. on spine; back
blank; inside flaps, blurb and biographical matter.

385.101 Limited edition, hardbound, cloth, in slipcase.

385.11   Reprinted in *Evergreen Review,* X (Feb., 1966), 48-49;

385.2   and in **386.1**, pp. 161-164;

385.21   and in **16.032**, pp. 187-189.

Read on BBC Third Programme on March 18, 1967, reader Jack MacGowran,
produced by Martin Esslin, and introduced by Barbara Bray.

1967

Stories and Texts for Nothing [**263**]

386A   *The Expelled* [**382**].

386B   *The Calmative* [**263B**], "translated by the author."

386C   *The End* [**372**].

386D/E/F/G/H/J/K/L/M/N/P/Q/R
    Texts for Nothing [**378, 263E, 381, 263G/H/J/K/L/M/N/P/Q/R**].

1967

386   New York: Grove Press, 1967 (GP-394), illus. with six ink line drawings by Avigdor Arikha (as **263.1**).
[1] *half title* [2] [drawing] [3] *STORIES* | *&* | *TEXTS FOR NOTH-ING* | by Samuel Beckett | GROVE PRESS, INC. / NEW YORK [4] [copyright details] [5] *CONTENTS* [list] [6] *blank* [7] *STORIES* [8] *blank* 9-25 [text of **386A**] [26] *blank* 27-46 [text of **386B**] 47-72 [text of **386C**] 73 *TEXTS FOR NOTHING* [74] *Translated by the author* 75-79 [text of **386D**] [80] *blank* 81-84 [text of **386E**] 85-90 [text of **386F**] 91-94 [text of **386G**] 95-99 [text of **386H**] [100] *blank* 101-105 [text of **386J**] [106] *blank* 107-110 [text of **386K**] 111-115 [text of **386L**] [116] *blank* 117-121 [text of **386M**] [122] *blank* 123-125 [text of **386N**] [126] *blank* 127-131 [text of **386P**] [132] *blank* 133-135 [text of **386Q**] [136] *blank* 137-140 [text of **386R**] [141-142] *blank*. 20 cm. Hardbound, black cloth, gold vertical italic caps. and horizontal caps. on spine; dust jacket design by Kuhlman Associates with drawing of the author on back by Avigdor Arikha; blurb and press comments on flaps.

386.01   **386B** printed prior to book publication in *Evergreen Review,* XI (June, 1967), 46-49, 93-95, with two drawings by Avigdor Arikha.

386.1   Reprinted in *No's Knife* (London: Calder and Boyars, 1967).
[1] *half title* [2] *By the Same Author* [list] [3] NO'S KNIFE | Collected Shorter Prose | 1945-1966 | SAMUEL BECKETT | CALDER AND BOYARS | LONDON [4] [copyright information, then:] A LIMITED EDITION OF 100 NUMBERED COPIES PRINTED A AND SIGNED BY | THE AUTHOR HAVE BEEN PRINTED (HORS COMMERCE) BOUND IN QUARTER | CALF AND BUCKRAM, AND A SECOND SERIES OF 100 NUMBERED COPIES | PRINTED B AND SIGNED BY THE AUTHOR (HORS COMMERCE) BOUND IN FULL | BUCKRAM HAVE BEEN PRINTED IN ADVANCE OF THE FIRST EDITION | PRINTED IN GREAT BRITAIN | BY UNWIN BROTHERS LIMITED | WOKING AND LONDON [5] CONTENTS [list] [6] PREFACE [signed] The Publishers. [7] STORIES [8] *blank* 9-24 [text of **386A**] 25-42 [text of **386B**] 43-67 [text of **386C**] [68] *blank* [69] TEXTS FOR NOTHING | *Translated from the French* | *by the author* [70] *blank* 71-75 [text of **386D**] [76] *blank* 77-80 [text of **386E**] 81-86 [text of **386F**] 87-90 [text of **386G**] 91-95 [text of **386H**] [96] *blank* 97-101 [text of **386J**] [102] *blank* 103-106 [text of **386K**] 107-111 [text of **386L**] [112] *blank* 113-117 [text of **386M**] [118] *blank* 119-121 [text of **386N**] [122] *blank* 123-127 [text of **386P**] [128] *blank* 129-131 [text of **386Q**] [132] *blank* 133-136 [text of **386R**] [137] FROM AN ABANDONED WORK [138] *blank* 139-149 [text of **33**] [150] *blank* [151] RESIDUA [152] *blank* 153-159 [text of **275** translated as *Enough* by the author] [160] *blank* 161-164 [text of **385**] 165-168 [text of **276** translated as *Ping* by the author]. 20 cm. Hard-

1967

386.1   bound, red paper, imitation cloth, gold vertical and horizontal caps.
             on spine; dust jacket red and white, lettered black.

386.101   Limited edition, as detailed on p. [4] of **386.1**.

386.11   *Ping* [**276**] printed prior to book publication in *Encounter*, XXVIII
             (Feb., 1967), 25-26. [See also Appendix II.]

386.12   **386J** printed prior to book publication in *London Magazine*, VII
             (Aug., 1967), 47-50.

3.

Translations, Manifestos, and Miscellaneous

Translations of the works of Samuel Beckett into and from languages other than English or French are not listed in this bibliography, but it should be noted that the German translations by Elmar Tophoven were checked by Beckett himself, and are therefore of some interest to the scholar (the same does not apply to Italian and other translations). With the exception of **25** (published in Germany by Rowohlt) and **266**, all German translations are published by Suhrkamp Verlag, Frankfort on the Main (for details, see **716**, p. 149, and **864**, pp. 112-125).

1930

485A   *Delta*
Poem by Eugenio Montale.

485B   *Landscape*
Text by Raffaello Franchi.

485C   *The Home-Coming*
Text by Giovanni Comisso.
These texts, "translated from the Italian by S. B. Beckett," published on pp. 630, 672, and 675-683, respectively, of

485   *This Quarter*, II (April-May-June, 1930), in the context of a "Miniature Anthology of Contemporary Italian Literature," compiled by *This Quarter*'s associate editor, Samuel Putnam.

NOTE. It was evidently these translations that opened the doors of both *This Quarter* and *The European Caravan* to the young Irishman, who soon abandoned the practice of signing himself by his initials. The original of *Delta* figures in "Ossi di Seppia 1920-1927," and can be read, for example, in the volume published by A. Mondadori (Milan, 1948), p. 131. Beckett translates it in a style closely resembling that of his own poems of the same period, without, however, being unfaithful to Montale's *Delta*.

1931

Anna Livia Plurabelle, by James Joyce.

"Traduit de l'anglais par Samuel Beckett, Alfred Perron [*sic*], Ivan Goll, Eugène Jolas, Paul-L. Léon, Adrienne Monnier et Philippe Soupault, en collaboration avec l'auteur."

486   *Nouvelle Revue Française,* XIX (May, 1931), 633-646, introduced by Philippe Soupault ("A propos de la traduction d'*Anna Livia Plurabelle*").

486.1   Reprinted in *Souvenirs de James Joyce,* by Philippe Soupault, "Collection *Fontaine*" (Algiers: Éditions E. Charlot, 1943), pp. 71-90 [Soupault's introduction shows some variants];

486.2   and in *Finnegans Wake: Fragments adaptés par André du Bouchet, suivis de Anna Livia Plurabelle,* by James Joyce (Paris: Gallimard, 1962), pp. 87-102 [Bouchet reproduces Soupault's introduction as in **486**, and corrects some manifest misprints in both **486** and **486.1** texts of the translation].

NOTE. In his introduction, Soupault says "un premier essai a été tenté par Samuel Beckett, irlandais, lecteur à l'École Normale. Il a été aidé dans cette tâche par Alfred Perron [*sic*], agrégé de l'Université, qui avait séjourné pendant un an à Dublin." Soupault gives the impression that the part played by Beckett was minimal. But in **3063**, p. 19, Adrienne Monnier maintains that the work reached the galley-proof stage, but not the *bon à tirer,* since Joyce wished to have other opinions. As a result of the lengthy discussions described by Soupault, the text was considerably modified. Mr. Beckett merely says that he and Péron had done "three-quarters," and that it was afterward transformed.

1932

Poetry Is Vertical

Manifesto, signed by Hans Arp, Samuel Beckett, Carl Einstein, Eugene Jolas, Thomas McGreevy, Georges Pelorson, Theo Rutra, James J. Sweeney, Ronald Symond.

487   *Transition,* 21 (March, 1932), 148-149.

NOTE. The title of this manifesto, which bears the stamp of Eugene Jolas' style, is explained by the epigraph from Léon-Paul Fargue, "On a été trop horizontal, j'ai envie d'être vertical." It is difficult to decide how far it represents Beckett's opinions at the time, but we may assume that he does not sign anything lightly. The manifesto proclaims, among other things, "the autonomy of the poetic vision, the hegemony of the inner life over the outer life. . . ."

Translations of Surrealist Writings

By André Breton:

488A   "The Free Union" (pp. 72-73).

1932

488B   "Lethal Relief" (pp. 74-75).

488C   "Factory" (p. 75).

488D   Extract from *Soluble Fish*, 1924 (pp. 75-76).

By Paul Éluard:

488E   "Lady Love" (p. 86).

488F   "Out of Sight in the Direction of My Body" (pp. 86-87).

488G   "Scarcely Disfigured" (p. 87).

488H   "The Invention" (pp. 87-88).

488J   "Definition" (p. 89).

488K   "A Life Uncovered or The Human Pyramid" (p. 89).

488L   "The Queen of Diamonds" (pp. 89-90).

488M   "Do Thou Sleep" (pp. 90-91).

488N   "Second Nature" (p. 92).

488P   "Scene" (pp. 92-93).

488Q   "All-Proof: Universe-Solitude" (pp. 94-95) [and]

488R   "Confections" (pp. 96-98).

By André Breton and Paul Éluard:

488S   "The Possessions" (pp. 119-120).

488T   "Simulation of Mental Debility Essayed" (pp. 121-122).

488U   "Simulation of General Paralysis Essayed" (pp. 123-125).

488V   "Simulation of the Delirium of Interpretation Essayed" (pp. 126-128).

By René Crevel:

488W   "Every One Thinks Himself Phoenix . . ." (pp. 158-165).

488   All "rendered into English by Samuel Beckett" and published on the pages indicated in *This Quarter*, V (Surrealist Number, guest ed., André Breton, Sept., 1932).

488E [p. 1], **488H** [p. 8], **488N** [p. 23], **488G** [p. 36], **488P** [pp. 37-38], **488Q** [pp. 40-41], and **488F** [p. 42], reprinted in July, 1936, in:

488.1   PAUL ELUARD | THORNS | OF THUNDER | SELECTED POEMS | With a Drawing by Pablo Picasso | * | Edited by George Reavey | * | *Translated from French by* | Samuel Beckett, Denis Devlin, David | Gascoyne, Eugene Jolas, Man Ray, | George Reavey and Ruthven Todd | * | LONDON | EUROPA PRESS & STANLEY NOTT. xii + 67 pp. 22 cm. Hardbound, light-blue

1932

488.1   cloth; title etc. in white caps. on spine. [Printed in England by
Henderson and Spalding at the Sylvan Press, Sylvan Grove, S.E. 15,
for Stanley Nott, 69 Grafton Street, Fitzroy Square, W.1. Limited
edition, 600 copies: no. 1, printed on handmade paper, containing
an original drawing by Pablo Picasso and an original MS by Paul
Éluard, and signed by the author, artist, and the translators; nos. 2
to 51 signed by the author, nos. 52 to 575, ordinary edition, and 25
copies reserved for author and publishers. Illus.; frontispiece drawing
of Paul Éluard by Pablo Picasso.]

488.101 **488E**, **488H**, **488N** reprinted in Willis Barnstone, ed., *Modern European Poetry* (New York: Bantam Books, 1966), pp. 29-30, together
with other translations of Paul Éluard (some from **488.1**) in the
section "French Poetry." George Reavey is named as one of the sub-
editors of this volume in the Bantam Classics series.

488.102 **488G** and **488F** reprinted in George Steiner, ed., *The Penguin Book
of Modern Verse Translation* (Harmondsworth, Middlesex: Penguin
Books, 1966), p. 203, under the heading SAMUEL BECKETT |
(b. 1906), numbered 1 and 2, respectively. Samuel Beckett and **488.1**
acknowledged in acknowledgments, p. 37. [The only variant is a full
stop added in error at the end of the antepenultimate line of **488F**.]

NOTE. Beckett's translations in the collected volume (**488.1**) are all signed
"S. B." The "Surrealist Number" of *This Quarter* was not produced
without some friction between Edward Titus, the regular editor, and André
Breton, who showed characteristic intransigence and insisted on his group
being entirely responsible for and having a completely free hand in the issue,
as their condition for cooperating at all (see **854**). In his preface to the issue,
p. 6, Titus says: "We cannot refrain from singling out Mr. Samuel Beckett's
work for special acknowledgement. His rendering of the Éluard and Breton
poems in particular is characterizable only in superlatives" [see also **610**].

1934

Negro

Texts "translated from the French by SAMUEL BECKETT":

489A   "The Best Negro Jazz Orchestras," by Robert Goffin (pp. 291-293).

489B   "Louis Armstrong," poem by Ernst Moerman (p. 295).

489C   "Hot Jazz," by Robert Goffin (pp. 378-379).

489D   "Summary of the History of Hayti," by Jenner Bastien (pp. 459-464).

489E   "A Note on Haytian Culture," by Ludovic Morin Lacombe (pp. 470-
471).

489F   "The King of Gonaives," by Jacques Boulenger (pp. 471-473).

1934

489G   "The Child in Guadeloupe," by E. Flavia-Léopold (pp. 497-500).

489H   "Black and White in Brazil," by Benjamin Péret (pp. 510-514).

489J   "Sambo without Tears," by Georges Sadoul (pp. 570-573).

489K   "Murderous Humanitarianism," by the Surrealist Group in Paris: André Breton, Roger Caillois, René Char, René Crevel, Paul Éluard, J.-M. Monnerot, Benjamin Péret, Yves Tanguy, André Thirion, Pierre Unik, Pierre Yoyotte (pp. 574-575).

489L   "Races and Nations," by Léon Pierre-Quint (pp. 575-580).

489M   "The Negress in the Brothel," by René Crevel (I-III, i.e., pp. [581-583]).

489N   "A Short Historical Survey of Madagascar," by J.-J. Rabearivelo (pp. 618-622).

489P   "The Ancient Bronzes of Black Africa," by Charles Ratton (pp. 684-686).

489Q   "Essay on Styles in the Statuary of the Congo," by Henri Lavachery (pp. 687-693).

489R   "Magic and Initiation among the Peoples of Ubanghi-Shari," by B. P. Feuilloley (pp. 734-738).

489S   " 'Primitive' Life and Mentality," by Raymond Michelet (pp. 739-761).

489T   "A Negro Empire: Belgium," by E. Stiers (pp. 795-801).

489U   "French Imperialism at Work in Madagascar," by Georges Citerne and Francis Jourdain (pp. 801-802).

Published on the pages indicated in:

489   NEGRO | ANTHOLOGY MADE BY | NANCY CUNARD | 1931-1933 | Published by | Nancy Cunard at Wishart & Co | 9 John Street • London • W • C • 2 | 1934. 856 pp. 31 cm. Hardbound, brown cloth, lettered red. [Published Feb. 16, 1934; 1,000 copies; printed at The Ballantyne Press by Spottiswoode, Ballantyne & Co., Colchester, London & Eton.   Blocks by Leonardson & Co., 1 Slingsby Place, W.C.2.]

1937

Contribution to a Pamphlet

490   [1] AUTHORS TAKE SIDES | ON THE SPANISH WAR | LEFT REVIEW | 2 Parton Street | London | W. C. 1. [6] [. . .] | Samuel Beckett | ¡ UPTHEREPUBLIC ! | [. . .]. 32 unnumbered pages. 25

1937

490   cm. Soft cover, yellow; title etc. in red. Price 6*d*. Late 1937 (British Museum date stamp, 20 Jan. 38). Printed by Purnell and Sons, Paulton (Somerset) and London.

NOTE. Beckett's lapidary contribution appears under the section FOR THE GOVERNMENT as the last entry but one on p. [6]. It is in reply to the questionnaire "Are you for, or against, the legal Government and the People of Republican Spain? Are you for, or against, Franco and Fascism?" sent out from Paris in June, 1937, by Aragon, W. H. Auden, Nancy Cunard, Stephen Spender, Tristan Tzara, and others. The pamphlet contains in all 148 contributions, the overwhelming majority "For the Government." *Left Review,* organ of the Writers' International, British Section, sponsored and published the pamphlet, which, as may be seen from the advertisements appearing in the review in late 1937 and early 1938, provoked considerable and diverse reactions in the press of the time.

1938

Translation of a Preface by Cocteau

491   Catalogue for an exhibition of drawings, and of furniture designed for *Les Chevaliers de la table ronde,* by Jean Cocteau, at Guggenheim Jeune, 30 Cork Street, Burlington Gardens, Bond Street, London W.1., Jan. 24-Feb. 12, 1938.

NOTE. This is the text of the preface, translated (unsigned) by Samuel Beckett, reproduced by kind permission of Peggy Guggenheim:

"The time has come to do no longer what I do do, the time has come to go on doing what I do do, the time has come never again to do what I have done and undone. Tighten my hand on the hand of the arrogant horse, tighten my hand on the pen, the pen in my rampant hand in the million drawers of the girdle of the earth. Marcel Duchamp has prescribed the diet. We must eat, we must eat, stones, so long as they come from the finest shop in London. The time has come to give him thanks and to undo what I have done. The procedure consists in being eaten (with a smile) by the obscure designs of providence, all this, entre nous. I open an exhibition, I open it like a pomegranate, for it to be eaten and for it to eat me and for the visitors to the exhibition to eat the succulent stones of vest pocket death. Ladies and Gentlemen, it is a mad thing to exhibit oneself in vain.

JEAN COCTEAU"

Miss Guggenheim, who kindly supplied this text, doubts whether many copies of this catalogue have survived.

1938-39

Contributions to the *London Bulletin*

492A   "Geer van Velde"
Biographical sketch, signed Samuel BECKETT. About 120 words.

1938-39

492   *London Bulletin,* 2 (May, 1938), 15 (under heading GUGGEN-
          HEIM JEUNE, 30 Cork Street, London W.1., following a catalogue
          list).

492B   "Wolfgang Paalen," by André Breton, "translated by S. B."

492.1   *London Bulletin,* 10 (Feb., 1939), 16-[17] (French original, pp. 13-
          15).

492C   Exhibition "Abstract and Concrete Art," preface by Kandinsky
          dated "Paris, en avril 1939." Text in French, *London Bulletin,* 14
          (May 1, 1939), 2. Unsigned translation of this on p. 44 of:

492.2   Peggy Guggenheim, ed., *Art of This Century: Objects — Drawings —
          Photographs — Sculpture — Collages, 1910 to 1942.* Art of This
          Century, 30 West Fifty-seventh Street, New York [1942]. 26 cm., 157
          pp. Hardbound, yellow cloth. 2,500 copies, printed in the United
          States.

NOTE. The *London Bulletin,* formerly the *London Gallery Bulletin,* was edited
by E. L. T. Mesens and published by the London Gallery, 28 Cork Street,
London W.1. It was closely associated with the surrealist movement and with
Miss Guggenheim's neighboring gallery, hence Beckett's brief association
with it.

492A is written in a curt, rather flippant tone, reminiscent of 251; it
contains material to be found also in the unsigned short biography (pp. 53-55)
in 500, which may indicate Beckett's authorship of the latter.

492B was "very likely translated by me, but can't assure," writes Mr.
Beckett. The initials make this highly probable, but not certain. Paalen also
was being exhibited at Guggenheim Jeune at the time of publication.

492C is a much more problematical piece as far as Beckett's authorship
is concerned, for he can remember nothing about it. In her memoirs (3057,
p. 241), Peggy Guggenheim writes: "[Beckett] had translated the preface to
the catalogue for Kandinsky's exhibition," and in a note of July, 1965, she
confirms that the extract in 492.2 is the same preface and that its anonymous
translator is Samuel Beckett. 492C is a preface by Kandinsky to a Guggenheim
Jeune exhibition of May, 1939, under the general title of "Abstract and Concrete Art," grouping works by Arp, Calder, Gabo, Hartung, Hepworth, Kandinsky, Mondrian, Nicholson, and others; it cannot, therefore, be strictly called
"Kandinsky's exhibition." Whether this slight inaccuracy is enough in itself
to throw doubt on Miss Guggenheim's testimony is a matter for conjecture.

1948

Apoem 4, by Henri Pichette

Translated by Samuel Beckett.

493   *Transition Forty-Eight,* 2 ([June], 1948), 24-43 [French text on left,
          English text (unsigned) on right].

1949

F——, by Suzanne Dumesnil

Translated by Samuel Beckett, unsigned.

494   *Transition Forty-Eight,* 4 ([Jan., 1949]), 19-21.

Some Sayings of Bram van Velde

Translated by Samuel Beckett, unsigned; see **256**, Note.

495   *Transition Forty-Nine,* 5 ([Dec.], 1949), 104.

Translation of a Poem by Gabriela Mistral

We are grateful to Milton Rosenthal, Literature Division, United Nations Educational, Scientific and Cultural Organization, Paris, for the following information, contained in his letter of Oct. 6, 1964:

496   "The poem by Gabriela Mistral was included in a collection of essays called *GOETHE: Unesco's Homage on the Occasion of the Two Hundredth Anniversary of His Birth.* This book has the following details on the back of the title page: Unesco Publication 411, Copyright 1949 by Unesco Paris, Printed in Switzerland by Berichthaus, Zurich. A 1950 letter from Mr. Beckett states that 'last summer, at the request of Unesco, I revised the English translation of a group of texts on Goethe, including a poem by Gabriela Mistral. I was obliged to retranslate this poem, with the help of a scholar specialized in Spanish, and some friends.'

"The poem is found on pages 75-81 of the book mentioned above. Its title is given as *Message from the Earth.* There is no way I can determine whether this was Mr. Beckett's title, that of the original translator, or of Miss Mistral. ["Recado terrestre" is the original title.] The poem has fifty-eight lines in English, and fifty-eight in Spanish (on facing pages). Evidently Mr. Beckett also had a hand in revising much of the English prose in the volume."

1950

Armand, Last Chapter, by Emmanuel Bove

Translated by Samuel Beckett, unsigned.

497   *Transition Fifty,* 6 ([Oct.], 1950), 99-102.

Zone, by Guillaume Apollinaire

Translated by Samuel Beckett, unsigned.

498   *Transition Fifty,* 6 ([Oct.], 1950), 126-131.

NOTE. Postwar *Transition,* edited by Georges Duthuit, did not attempt to continue the work of prewar *Transition* edited by Eugene Jolas, but sought merely to offer, in English translation, "the best of French art and thought" [no. 1, p. 6] to an English-speaking audience. Beckett did many translations for Duthuit ("pure pot-boiling . . ."), including parts of Duthuit's long article "Sartre's

1950

498
Last Class" [nos. 1-4 and 6], but he cannot remember which parts he was responsible for. Beckett's work, all unsigned, may have included some of the "Notes about Contributors," notably those devoted to his wife Suzanne Dumesnil [no. 4, p. 151], and to Bram van Velde [no. 5, p. 129]. Mr. Beckett is certain, however, of having translated **493, 494, 495, 497**, and **498**. He thinks he may have checked "The Revenge of a Russian Orphan" (*La Vengeance d'une orpheline russe*) by Henri Rousseau, trans. Jack T. Nile and Bernard Frechtman, *Transition Forty-Eight*, 3 ([Oct.], 1948), 41-46.

1956

The Word Is Graven [L'Écriture est gravure]

Poems by Jean Wahl. "The poems have been translated from the french [*sic*] original by the author with the kind assistance of Samuel BECKET [*sic*]."

499   Published in "Illustrations for the Bible by Marc Chagall," *Verve*, IX, nos. 33-34 (1956). [English-language edition, printed in France. One hundred and five etchings by Chagall to illustrate the Old Testament, made between 1930 and 1956, with an introduction by Meyer Schapiro and poems by Jean Wahl. The originals of Wahl's poems, covering six pages of text, can be found in the French-language edition, *Verve*, VIII, nos. 33-34 (1956), also printed in France. The poems cover seven pages of text in the English-language edition.]

1958

Bram van Velde

By Samuel Beckett, Georges Duthuit, and Jacques Putman.

500   Paris: Georges Fall, 1958.
[1-2] *blank* [3] *half title* [4] *Collection dirigée par Jean-Clarence Lambert | Photographies de Luc Joubert |* © 1958, tous droits de reproduction réservés, LE MUSÉE DE POCHE, | Georges Fall, éditeur, 58, rue du Montparnasse, Paris-14e. [5] SAMUEL BECKETT | GEORGES DUTHUIT | JACQUES PUTMAN | Bram Van Velde | *Douze reproductions* | [device] | LE MUSÉE DE POCHE [6] *blank* [7] [**256.01**] [8] *blank* 9-10, 12, 14-[15] [**31.012**] [16] *blank* 17-18, 20, 22, 24-[25] [text of Georges Duthuit's contribution] [26] *blank* 27-28, 30-32, 34-36, 38-40, 42-44, 46-[48] [text of Jacques Putman's contribution] [50] *blank* [51] BIOGRAPHIE [52] *blank* 53-[55] [biography] [56] *blank* [57] BIBLIOGRAPHIE [58] *blank* 59-[60] [bibliography] [61] [contents] [62] *blank* [63] *ACHEVÉ D'IMPRIMER | en octobre 1958, sur les Presses de | l'Imprimerie Letouzey et Ané, Paris, | pour le compte de Georges Fall, éditeur. | Les reproductions en couleurs ont été | tirées par l'Im-*

1958

500   *primerie Blanchard, Paris.* [64] *blank.* 18 cm. Soft cover, flaps oveɪ
stiff paper; front, illus., color reproduction; back, catalogue list;
title, vertical caps. spine [Putman only author mentioned on front
cover]. Color reproductions attached to pp. [11], [13 (from the collection of Samuel Beckett)], [19], [21], [23], [29], [33], [37], [41], [45],
[49].

500.1   Deluxe edition. Turin: Fratelli Pozzo, 1961.
[1] BRAM VAN VELDE [brown] | P [brown] | EDIZIONI D'ARTE
FRATELLI POZZO — TORINO | ET EN FRANCE, CHEZ
GUY LE PRAT, ÉDITEUR A PARIS [2] *Le portrait de Bram Van
Velde a été pris par Alechinsky* [3] *half title* [4] *blank* [5] [photo-
graph of Bram van Velde] [6] COLLECTION DIRIGÉE PAR
EZIO GRIBAUDO | © COPYRIGHT BY EDIZIONI D'ARTE
FRATELLI POZZO — TORINO (ITALY). [7] *"La vie — écrit
Pierre Schneider, dans son bel essai sur | Corbière — est une faute
d'orthographe dans le texte de la mort." | Il en est heureusement de
plus sérieuses. | Celles dont voici les laves. | Balayés les repentirs. |
Peinture de vie et de mort. | Amateurs de natron, abstenez.* | SAM-
UEL BECKETT [16] [**256.02**] [18] BIBLIOGRAPHIE [see **500**,
p. 59] [Last page (unnumbered) of reproductions:] *"Le calmant,"
nouvelle de Samuel Beckett, 1941 | trois illustrations de Bram Van
Velde (inédit).* [Last page (unnumbered):] *Le tirage de l'édition
française a été limité a 1500 exemplaires numérotés, | les cinquante
premiers comportant deux lithographies originales signées par l'artiste.
| Quelques exemplaires hors-commerce sont réservés aux collabora-
teurs de l'ouvrage.* | 321 [Bibliothèque nationale copy]. 27 x 29
cm. Hardbound, buff cloth; title etc. vertical brown caps. and l.c.
on spine; artist's signature in brown on front. All edges trimmed.
Printed in Italy. The total *œuvre* of Bram van Velde reproduced,
including Samuel Beckett's collection.

500.11   American edition. New York: Harry N. Abrams, [1962].
[3] BRAM VAN VELDE | [device] | HARRY N. ABRAMS, INC.,
PUBLISHERS, NEW YORK [6] Library of Congress Catalog Card
Number: 62-12840 [. . .] Printed in Italy. © Copyright in Italy by
Edizioni d'Arte Fratelli Pozzo, Turin. [7] [text as in **500.1**, p. [7],
translated into English by anonymous translator, not Beckett] [16]
[**256.03**] [Otherwise as **500.1**, except for, on dust jacket left flap,
extract from **31C** signed SAMUEL BECKETT (1949).]

500.2   New York: Grove Press, 1960 (Evergreen Gallery Book, no. 5, E-174,

500.21   and hardbound edition).
[3] BRAM | VAN VELDE | by | Samuel Beckett | Georges Duthuit |
Jacques Putman | Translated from the French by Olive Classe | and
Samuel Beckett | *Color Photographs by Luc Joubert • Black | and
White Photographs by Georges Garcin | Twelve Color Plates | Nine*

1958

500.21   *Black and White Illustrations* | GROVE PRESS, INC. • NEW
YORK | Evergreen Books, Ltd. • London [4] Copyright © 1958 by
Georges Fall, Paris | First Grove Press Edition 1960 | Library of
Congress Catalog Card Number: | 59-14401 | *BRAM VAN VELDE*
is published in two editions: | An Evergreen Gallery Book | A cloth
bound edition | [. . .] | Color Plates Printed in France | MANU-
FACTURED IN THE UNITED STATES OF AMERICA [5] *half
title* [6] *blank* [7] Bram van Velde | by SAMUEL BECKETT [8]
blank 9-10 [text of **31.0121**] [11-12] [plates in black and white]
13 [text of **31.0121** continued, dated 1949] [14] [blank, followed by
Duthuit's and Putman's contributions] 63 [bibliography, with Beckett's
three items]. 64 pp. 20 cm. Cover illus., photographs of Bram van
Velde, and with Beckett's name in gray. **500.21** bound blue cloth,
vertical gold lettering on spine.

NOTE. For details concerning variants in the texts published in the **500** series,
see **31** and **256**. The text published in **500.1**, p. [7], "a figuré, pour la première
fois, sur la carte d'invitation de la Galerie Maeght, exposition Bram van Velde
de février 1952," writes Jacques Putman in a letter dated May 28, 1965. On
the puzzling dating of **263B** in **500.1** [last page of reproductions] as "1941,"
Mr. Beckett writes in a letter of May 7, 1965: "It is possible there was a rough
draft of *Le Calmant* as early as 41 though it seems to be unlikely, and that
I showed it to Bram. It remains correct to say that the three stories were not
ready in their published form before 45." Finally, it should be noted that
although all these editions of *Bram van Velde* follow the same lines (essays
by Beckett, Duthuit, and Putman, with reproductions), they differ considerably. **500** is a small book, as its title implies; **500.1** and **500.11** are large, luxur-
ious, and exhaustive volumes, differing only in the language of composition;
and **500.2** drops the shorter of the Beckett texts but has black and white photographs not provided in **500** which it most closely resembles. The deluxe volumes, of course, drop the text from **31C** but print a short text not found elsewhere.

Anthology of Mexican Poetry

Translated by Samuel Beckett.

501   Bloomington: Indiana University Press, 1958 (Unesco Collection of
Representative Works: Latin American Series) [214 pp., 21 cm.,
printed in the U.S.A.].
[3] Anthology | of | Mexican Poetry | *translated by* SAMUEL
BECKETT | *compiled by Octavio Paz* | *preface by C. M. Bowra*
[4] TRANSLATOR'S NOTE: I SHOULD LIKE TO THANK
MR. GERALD BRENAN | FOR KINDLY READING THE
ENTIRE MANUSCRIPT AND FOR MAKING | A NUMBER
OF USEFUL SUGGESTIONS. S. B.

501.01   Paperback edition identical to **501**, 1965.

1958

501.1   British edition (reprinted photographically from **501**). London: Thames and Hudson, 1959 [Jan.].

501.02   Two sonnets by Miguel de Guevara, "I am not moved to love thee, my lord God," and "Time and account" [**501**, pp. 61-62 and 63-64, respectively], first published on p. 81 (with Spanish originals facing on p. 80) in *Hermathena: A Series of Papers by Members of Trinity College, Dublin,* LXXXIII (May, 1954), under section "Kottabistae," signed "Samuel Beckett" [extensive variants].

NOTE. Unesco commissioned this translation in 1950, and urged Beckett to complete it as quickly as possible, which he did in 1951. To his annoyance Unesco then failed to publish it for seven years. It was the last commercial translation he did and he has said that he "loathed" the work. Nevertheless, there is no doubt he did it very well. By the time it appeared his fame was considerable, which explains why the publishers, especially Thames and Hudson, give his name such prominence on their dust jacket. It was Beckett's friend Dr. A. J. Leventhal of Dublin, assistant editor of *Hermathena,* who was responsible for inserting the early versions of the Guevara sonnets into the journal. The anthology, which contains over a hundred poems by thirty-five poets, has also been issued in France in a French translation, prefaced by Paul Claudel.

1960

The Old Tune [La manivelle]

Radio play by Robert Pinget translated into English by Samuel Beckett.

502   Paris: Éditions de Minuit, 1960.
            [5] ROBERT PINGET | La manivelle | *pièce radiophonique* | texte anglais | de | SAMUEL BECKETT | [star and m device] | LES ÉDITIONS DE MINUIT [1960]. 64 pp. 18½ cm. Soft cover; front reads in blue and black lettering: ROBERT PINGET | *texte anglais de* | SAMUEL BECKETT | LA MANIVELLE | THE | OLD TUNE | [device] | *LES ÉDITIONS DE MINUIT.* Printed in France on Sept. 19, 1960, by Imprimerie Corbière et Jugain, Alençon. Pinget's text on left (even-numbered pages), Beckett's facing on right (odd-numbered pages).

502.1   Reprinted in *New Writers II* (London: John Calder, 1962; 127 pp., 20 cm.) pp. 95-127, "English adaptation by Samuel Beckett" on right facing French text on left.

502.01 Beckett's text alone reprinted in *Evergreen Review,* V (March-April, 1961), 47-60.

502.02 Beckett's text alone reprinted in *Plays,* by Robert Pinget (London: John Calder, 1963; 131 pp., 20 cm.) I, 1-17, described as "adaptation."

1960

502.021   Reprinted in paperback as Calderbook CB101, n.d. (1966?).

502.03   Beckett's text alone reprinted in *Traverse Plays,* ed. Jim Haynes (Harmondsworth, Middlesex: Penguin Books, 1966), pp. 45-60.
First broadcast (English text only) on BBC Third Programme, Aug. 23, 1960, from 9.55 P.M. to 10.25 P.M., with Jack MacGowran as Cream and Patrick Magee as Gorman, produced by Barbara Bray.

NOTE. Beckett has skillfully transposed into pure Dublin the colloquial French of Pinget, whose Toupin becomes Gorman and whose Pommard becomes Cream. The play, called "a conversation piece for radio" by the BBC, was written specially for the Third Programme by Robert Pinget.

1962

End of Day

"An entertainment from the works of Samuel Beckett."

503   Selections from **373**, **376A**, **37**, **34**, **374**, **33**, **32**, and **377** set within the framework of **376B** and performed by Jack MacGowran at the Gaiety Theatre as part of the program of the Dublin Theatre Festival in 1962, and in Oct., 1962, at the New Arts Theatre, London; based on an idea by Donald McWhinnie.

503.1   Version of **503** revised and supervised by the author broadcast on BBC Television program *Monitor* on Feb. 23, 1965, performed by Jack MacGowran, edited and introduced by Jonathan Miller and produced by Nancy Thomas and Christopher Burstall, under the title *Beginning to End: A Television Exploration of the World of Samuel Beckett.* The program, which consisted of extracts from **375**, **33**, **38**, **374**, **37**, **32**, **377**, **373**, **384**, set within the framework of **383**, ran for about 40 mins. from 10.15 P.M.

503.11   A similar program, but not using **383** as framework, was prepared for Irish Television (Telefís Éireann) in Sept., 1965, under the same title, *Beginning to End* (repeated on BBC Television, Aug. 8, 1967).

NOTE. Discussing **503.1** in *Radio Times* at the time of broadcast, Patrick Garland described how the program developed from **503**, which the author did not approve: "he found our version correct in its content [but] he disapproved of the shape, and . . . set about reconstructing an entirely different one. . . . And so what appears on tonight's *Monitor* is basically under the direct supervision of the author." On the subject of certain variants in the texts read, Mr. Beckett wrote in a letter of March 11, 1965: "I was informed of the textual changes in the Monitor programme and accepted them."
    Such series of read selections are popular with performers. To the accompaniment of music by John Beckett, Patrick Magee read selections from **374**, **375**, and **377** on the BBC Third Programme between 1957 and 1959. In 1965 the Traverse Theatre Club presented, on the "fringe" of the Edinburgh

1962

503

Festival, another series of selections read from the works of Samuel Beckett [see **2848**]. In August, 1967, Jack Emery gave a Beckett recital at the YWCA Hall in Edinburgh (recorded on Saga/Psyche PSY 30003, entitled *"A Remnant,* Selected from the Works of Samuel Beckett by Frank Doherty").

1962-63

L'ooneyverse de Samuel Beckett

504

Series of selections from **16, 25, 32, 380, 382, 374, 375, 377**, together with **373, 38, 376A, 37**, and **34**, broadcast between Dec. 24, 1962, and Jan. 5, 1963, by KPFK (Los Angeles) radio station. Series endorsed by the author and coordinated by Raymond Federman. [See *KPFK Program Folio* (Los Angeles), IV, no. 12 (1962).]

1963

Second Testament [Deuxième testament]

Poems by Alain Bosquet, translated by Samuel Beckett.

505

New York: New Directions [1963], pp. 60-63.
[3] *ALAIN BOSQUET* | SELECTED POEMS | *Translations by Samuel Beckett,* | *Charles Guenther, Edouard Roditi* | *and Ruth Whitman* | THE WORLD POETS SERIES [no. 4]. 64 pp., 18 cm. Printed in Great Britain. Soft cover. French texts on left, English texts facing on right.

505.1

Beckett's translations alone reprinted in *Marginales,* XXIV (April, 1969), 44-45.

NOTE. These three short poems were translated about 1960 at Bosquet's request.

1966

More Poems by Samuel Beckett

506

Anthology selected by the author and introduced by John Fletcher, BBC Third Programme, Nov. 24, 1966, 10.40 (to 11.00) P.M., comprising **22A, 22H, 22K, 22N**, "Watt will not" (**32**, pp. 249-250), **22M, 22F**, "who may tell the tale" (**32**, p. 247), "Age is when to a man" (**41**, p. 39), and **18**.

NOTE. Beckett was present in the BBC studio on Jan. 27, 1966, during the recording of the first program of his poems, selected and introduced by John Fletcher (see **255**, Note). The author suggested, and producer Martin Esslin accepted, his selections for a second program also to be introduced by John Fletcher. This was recorded on Feb. 9, 1966, in the author's absence, but readers Jack MacGowran and Denys Hawthorne had worked with Beckett on both programs.

Unclassified

1934?

A Review of a Work by W. B. Yeats

600

NOTE. Mr. Beckett remembers having published about 1934, presumably in a London or a Dublin periodical, a review of a "late work by W. B. Yeats." He can remember no more than that, and thus far all efforts to trace it in the periodical literature of the time have been unsuccessful. It may have appeared unsigned, but to date no anonymous review of a late work by W. B. Yeats has been found bearing any resemblance to Beckett's style. Neither Allan Wade's *Bibliography of the Writings of W. B. Yeats* (2d ed.; London: Hart-Davis, 1958), nor Professor K. G. W. Cross of Newcastle University, Australia, who is an expert on the bibliography of Yeats criticism, has yielded any light. It is conceivable that the review was commissioned for a literary journal but never published; at a time when the failure rate of such periodicals was high (even the long-established *Bookman* succumbed), this is not improbable. (See "Information, Please," *Times Literary Supplement,* March 25, 1965, p. 240.)

4.

Known
Unpublished Works

LATE TWENTIES

Le Convergisme

606   Paper read to the Modern Language Society, Trinity College, Dublin, on the "Convergistes," an imaginary literary movement in France. Probably lost [see **1769**].

1928

Research Essay on the *Unanimistes* (Jouve, Duhamel, etc.)

607   Submitted at Trinity College, Dublin, in accordance with the conditions attending the award of the Moderatorship Prize in 1927 for an outstanding performance in the B.A. final examinations. [See *Dublin University Calendar* (1928-1929), p. 454.] Mr. Beckett describes the dissertation as "frivolous." The prize was worth £50. No copy has been preserved at Trinity College, Dublin. The essay was written in English.

1930?

Unpublished Sonnet

608   On verso last page of MS of *Whoroscope* held in University of Texas Library (See Appendix I).

1931

Le Kid

609   Parody of *Le Cid* by Pierre Corneille, written in collaboration with Georges Pelorson, and performed by the Modern Language Society at Peacock Theatre, Dublin, in Feb., 1931 [**8**, Note]. Written in French. Probably lost.

1932

Translation of *Le Bateau ivre* by Arthur Rimbaud

610   Commissioned by Edward Titus for *This Quarter* but never published. Beckett was paid Fr. 800 for it. Probably lost.

ca. 1932

Dream of Fair to Middling Women

611   Novel in English, early version of **16**. Unfinished. 214 pp. Typescript. (For published fragments, see **12**, **13**, and **43**.) Contains Beckett's first extant writings in French, a letter from Lucien to the hero Belacqua (typescript, pp. 17-19), which also includes a poem in French, p. 18. Other lines of French verse on p. 127.

ca. 1938

Les Deux Besoins

612   Critical article in French, "written," says Mr. Beckett, "1938 or early 1939 at latest"; referred to by Lawrence E. Harvey in **1849**, pp. 548 ff.

ca. 1945

Les Bosquets de Bondy

613   "One of first writings in French . . . unpublished, jettisoned," says Mr. Beckett. MS held in University of Texas Library [see Appendix I].

Premier Amour

614   Short story in French, of the 1945 *Nouvelles* group. 32 pp. Typescript. 38 pp. MS [see Appendix I and **263**, Note].

ca. 1946

Mercier et Camier

615   Novel in French in twelve chapters. 150 pp. Typescript. [See **273** and **380**.] "First attempt at novel in French," says Mr. Beckett [see **263**, Note].

ca. 1947

Éleuthéria

616   Play in French in three acts for seventeen characters. 133 pp. Typescript. Beckett's first play.

1950-52

Unpublished Material with MS of **263D-R**.

617   Held in University of Texas Library (see Appendix I).

ca. 1966

Chacun son dépeupleur

618   Prose text in MS. In typescript entitled "Le Dépeupleur" (15 **pp., of**
          which **277** forms pp. 14-15).

Part Two
Criticism of Samuel Beckett's Work

5.

Books Devoted Entirely to Samuel Beckett

1957

700   GESSNER, Niklaus. *Die Unzulänglichkeit der Sprache: Eine Untersuchung über Formzerfall und Beziehungslosigkeit bei Samuel Beckett.* Zurich: Juris, 1957. 127 pp. Originally a Ph.D. dissertation for the First Faculty of Philosophy, University of Zurich.
Contents:
A. Anzeichen von Formzerfall bei Marcel Proust
B. Formzerfall und Beziehungslosigkeit bei Samuel Beckett
1. Das Verkümmern des Gestalteten
2. Die formlose Fabel
3. Der Untergang des sprachlichen Ausdrucks
   Der Stil Becketts
   Beckett über die Sprache
   Konsequenzen der Unzulänglichkeit der Sprache
4. Die Beziehungslosigkeit
5. Das Ende der Literatur
C. Die neue Formalierung der Welt durch Antoine de Saint-Exupéry
Bibliographie (p. 123; briefly lists Beckett's major works, mostly in French, to 1957, and a handful of critical articles)
Nachtrag
Curriculum Vitae

A penetrating study of Beckett's use of language and how it reflects the disintegration of form. The comparison between Proust and Beckett on a stylistic level reveals interesting relationships between these two authors and their vision of decadence.

Review:
700a   Weinrich, H. *Archiv für das Studium der neueren Sprachen,* 196 (1960), 235-236.

1959

701   MACIEL, Luís Carlos. *Samuel Beckett e a solidão humana.* Pôrto
Alegre: Secretaria de Educação e Cultura, Divisão de Cultura,
Instituto Estadual do Livro, Rio Grande do Sul, 1959. 111 pp.
Contents:
Explicação
Um testemunho de nosso tempo
Os filhos do espanto
A espera por Godot
Mundo sem promessa

Primarily an analysis of *Waiting for Godot* as seen from an existentialist point
of view. The first three chapters consist mostly of a discussion of existentialism
and its approach to the question of absurdity and of human loneliness.

1960

702   DELYE, Huguette. *Samuel Beckett, ou la philosophie de l'absurde.*
Aix-en-Provence: La Pensée Universitaire, 1960. iv + 132 + III
pp. Publications des Annales de la Faculté des Lettres, série
Travaux et Mémoires, No. XVI. Typescript text, roneograph
reproduction, recto and verso.
Contents:
Bibliographie (pp. 1-6; contains a few errors)
I. Sources biographiques et influences
   1. L'Irlandais
   2. "The last of the Left Bank Mohicans of the Twenties"
   3. La nouvelle jeunesse ou l'auteur à succès
   4. Le premier des Jeunes Hommes en Colère
II. Analyse du message beckettien
   A. La condition humaine
      1. Le péché
      2. L'impuissance
      3. Le temps
      4. La souffrance
   B. Les évasions hors de la condition humaine
      1. Dieu
      2. La science et le procès de la réalité
      3. La société — L'abdication de la personnalité dans
         l'altruisme
         a) La femme
         b) L'enfant
         c) Le refuge du moi
         d) Dissolution de la personnalité dans le cosmos
      4. La mort et la résignation à la vie
III. L'esthétique beckettienne
   1. La création absurde
   2. L'humour de Beckett

1960

702 3. Le style de Beckett
4. La poésie
5. Le symbolisme
6. L'art dramatique de Beckett
   a) La tarte à la crème au service de la philosophie
   b) La technique expressionniste
   c) Le tragique beckettien
7. Le roman beckettien
Conclusion
Notes

A somewhat arid and perhaps misguided attempt to place Beckett among the existentialists, but not without useful insights. Marred by an oversystematic presentation.

Review:
702a Fletcher, John. "Le Cas Samuel Beckett," *Bulletin de l'Université de Toulouse,* LXXII (Jan., 1963), 405-406.

1961

703 KENNER, Hugh. *Samuel Beckett: A Critical Study.* New York: Grove Press, 1961; London: John Calder, 1962. 208 pp. New revised edition, University of California Press, 1968.
Contents:
Preface
The Man in the Room (contains a chronology, pp. 26-28, giving "Biographical Data" and "Work" with dates of composition and publication of works)
The Rational Domain
The Cartesian Centaur [see **711, 900,** and **1499**]
Life in the Box
Voices in the Dark

A brilliantly written study of all the works placing emphasis on philosophic sources, particularly Cartesianism. Has been called an impressionistic approach, each chapter examining a specific topic or theme. First to point out the existence of unpublished manuscripts.

Reviews:
703a Anonymous. "Waiting for What?" *Times of London,* Nov. 8, 1962, p. 15*d*.

703b _____. *Times Literary Supplement,* Dec. 21, 1962, p. 988.

703c _____. *Modern Fiction Studies,* VIII (Winter, 1962-63), 427-428.

703d Chambers, Ross. *Nation,* June 29, 1963, p. 6.

703e Davenport, Guy. "Beckett and Kenner, Tandem," *National Review,* XII (May 8, 1962), 330-332.

1961

703*f*   Davie, Donald. *The Guardian,* Oct. 26, 1962, p. 6.
703*g*   Esslin, Martin. *The Listener,* LXVIII (Nov. 29, 1962), 923.
703*h*   Fletcher, John. "Le Cas Samuel Beckett," *Bulletin de l'Université de Toulouse,* LXXII (Jan., 1963), 405-406.
703*i*   Friedman, Melvin J. "Book Reviews," *Wisconsin Studies in Contemporary Literature,* III (Fall, 1962), 100-106.
703*j*   Harvey, J. R. *Cambridge Quarterly,* I (Autumn, 1966), 384-395 [see 1869].
703*k*   Hesla, David H. *Critique: Studies in Modern Fiction,* VI (Fall, 1963), 103-106.
703*l*   Johnson, B. S. "Working with Impotence," *The Spectator,* Nov. 23, 1962, pp. 816, 818.
703*m*   Kermode, Frank. "Waiting for Godeau," *New Statesman,* LXIV (Nov. 2, 1962), 622.
703*n*   Lid, Richard N. *San Francisco Sunday Chronicle,* May 27, 1962, This World, p. 31.
703*o*   Rogers, W. G. *Saturday Review,* XLV (Feb. 17, 1962), 31.
703*p*   Sheridan-Smith, Alan. *London Magazine,* II (March, 1963), 72-73.
703*q*   Spender, Stephen. "What Is a Man's Life: A Joke or Something Sacred?" *New York Times Book Review,* Feb. 25, 1962, pp. 7, 32.
703*r*   Weightman, John. "Cogito ergo Sam," *The Observer,* Dec. 2, 1962, p. 26.

1962

704   COHN, Ruby. *Samuel Beckett: The Comic Gamut.* New Brunswick, N. J.: Rutgers University Press, 1962. 340 pp. [See **800.**]
       Contents:
       1. Portrait of the Artist as an Old Bum
       2. Early Elegance
       3. Murphy the Morph
       4. Watt Knott
       5. The First Burst into French
       6. A Trilogy of Novels
       7. Brief Fiction
       8. Comment c'est par le bout
       9. The Dramatic Shift to Waiting
       10. Endgame [see **1537**]
       11. Dramatic Contractions
       12. Samuel Beckett, Self-translator [see **1596**]
       13. A Comic Complex and a Complex Comic
       Appendix (contains "Whoroscope," "Text," "Ooftish," and a translation of Watt's antilanguage [see **5.3, 13.1, 26.1,** respectively])
       Notes
       Bibliography (pp. 328-340; contains a slightly inaccurate chronology of "Published Works of Samuel Beckett" and a "Checklist of Beckett Criticism." Bibliography reprinted in **901**; see also **3111**)

1962

704

A thorough study of Beckett as a comic writer who is seen as "a master of irony in the tradition of the great Irish writers." Analyzes all the works and the various comic devices, but the author states that "since almost the entire comic range is present in Beckett's work, a catalogue of his comic techniques can be compiled empirically, but the convenient and widely known classification of Bergson is usable as a springboard."

Reviews:

704a   Anonymous. *Times Literary Supplement,* Dec. 21, 1962, p. 988.
704b   _____. *Modern Fiction Studies,* VIII (Winter, 1962-63), 427-428.
704c   Federman, Raymond. *French Review,* XXXVIII (Feb., 1965), 577-579.
704d   Fletcher, John. *Bulletin de l'Université de Toulouse,* LXXII (Feb., 1963), 503-504.
704e   Friedman, Melvin J. *Comparative Literature,* XVI (Summer, 1964), 264-269.
704f   Griffin, Lloyd W. *Library Journal,* LXXXVII (Aug. 1, 1962), 2898.
704g   Guerard, Albert J. *Saturday Review,* XXXV (Oct. 6, 1962), 43.
704h   Hesla, David H. *Critique: Studies in Modern Fiction,* VI (Fall, 1963), 103-106.
704i   Reid, Alec. *Drama Survey,* III (Fall, 1963), 314-315.

705   HOFFMAN, Frederick J. *Samuel Beckett: The Language of Self.* Carbondale: Southern Illinois University Press, 1962. 177 pp. Reprinted by E. P. Dutton, New York, 1964. Paperback.

Contents:
1. Preface (by Harry T. Moore)
2. Introduction
3. The Underground Man: Background of the Modern Self
4. Literary Techniques and the Vanishing Self
5. Beyond Memory: Perspective in Modern Literature
6. The Elusive Ego: Beckett's M's [see **902**; also **1800**]
7. Being and Waiting: The Question of Godot
Bibliography (pp. 169-172)
Index

Half the book is devoted to an analysis of twentieth-century views of the self, with particular attention to the "underground man" in Russian literature. The chapters on Beckett provide an explanation of the style and the "new form of literary discourse" initiated in the major works of Beckett. One chapter is devoted to a discussion of Godot.

Reviews:

705a   Anonymous. *Times Literary Supplement,* Dec. 21, 1962, p. 988.
705b   Friedman, Melvin J. "Book Reviews," *Wisconsin Studies in Contemporary Literature,* III (Fall, 1962), 100-106.
705c   Griffin, Lloyd W. *Library Journal,* LXXXVII (May 15, 1962), 1905.

1962

705d   Harvey, J. R. *Cambridge Quarterly,* I (Autumn, 1966), 384-395 [see 1869].

705e   Hesla, David H. *Critique: Studies in Modern Fiction,* VI (Fall, 1963), 103-106.

705f   Knepler, Henry. *Modern Drama,* VI (May, 1963), 108.

1963

706   MARISSEL, André. *Samuel Beckett.* Paris: Éditions Universitaires, 1963. 123 pp.
Contents:
Beckett l'Irlandais
I. L'Œuvre du "Romancier"
   1. De l'anti-roman considéré comme un assassinat
   2. "Quelle galerie de crevés!"
   3. Un nœud de complexes [see **1748**]
II. L'Œuvre du Dramaturge
   1. La Farce du Sans-Dieu
   2. Humour de malheur, malheur de l'humour
Pour ou contre Beckett?
Chronologie (pp. 109-110)
Bibliographie (pp. 111-122; contains several errors)
   Œuvres de Samuel Beckett
   Principaux ouvrages à consulter sur Samuel Beckett
   Numéros Spéciaux de Revues
   Etudes et Articles consacrés à Beckett

First full-length study in French. Beckett's antinovels and plays are examined separately in an effort to draw the psychological and pathological portrait of what Marissel calls "ces déséquilibrés et ces moribonds" who rise from the "bas-fonds de l'esprit."

Reviews:
706a   Bertherat, Yves. *Esprit,* 324 (Jan., 1964), 146-147.
706b   Doms, André. *Marginales,* 95-96 (June, 1964), 100-101.
706c   Fletcher, John. *Bulletin de l'Université de Toulouse,* LXXIII (March, 1964), 738-739.
706d   François, Carlo. *French Review,* XXXVII (May, 1964), 694-695 (same review appears in *French Review,* XXXVIII [April, 1965], 710).
706e   Hubert, Renée Riese. *Esprit Créateur,* IV (Fall, 1964), 176-177.
706f   Miguel, André. *Nouvelle Revue Française,* 134 (Feb., 1964), 332-333.

1964

707   COE, Richard N. *Beckett.* Edinburgh and London: Oliver and Boyd, 1964. 118 pp. Reprinted by Grove Press, New York, 1964, under the title *Samuel Beckett.*

1964

707   *Contents:*
1. The Art of Failure
2. Baroque Rationalism
3. Words and Numbers
4. The Long Sonata of the Dead
5. The Right Kind of Silence
6. A Little Heap of Millet
Bibliography (pp. 111-118; contains several errors)

Concentrates mainly on the fiction. A bold and often convincing attempt to interpret Beckett's meaning in the light of religion and philosophy, incidentally clearing up several problems and obscurities. Points out some relationship between Beckett's work and various intellectual traditions such as Cartesianism, positivism, Buddhism, and existentialism.

Reviews:

707a   Anonymous. *Choice,* II (Oct., 1965), 488.
707b   _____. *Times Literary Supplement,* Dec. 17, 1964, p. 1146.
707c   Fletcher, John. *Durham University Journal,* LVIII (March, 1966), 113-114.
707d   Harvey, J. R. *Cambridge Quarterly,* I (Autumn 1966), 384-395 [see 1869].
707e   Mansell Jones, P. *French Studies,* XIX (July, 1965), 320-322.
707f   Ohmann, Richard. *Wisconsin Studies in Contemporary Literature,* VI (Autumn, 1965), 372-375.
707g   Wall, Stephen. *Essays in Criticism,* XVI (April, 1966), 245-252 [see 2888].
707h   Whittington-Egan, Richard. *Books and Bookmen,* X (Jan., 1965), 34.

708   FLETCHER, John. *The Novels of Samuel Beckett.* London: Chatto and Windus, 1964. 256 pp. Reissued by Barnes and Noble, New York.

Contents:
Preface and Acknowledgments
Part One: The Hero as Citizen
1. Belacqua
2. Murphy
Part Two: The Hero as Outcast
3. Watt
4. The First French Heroes
I. The Hero of the *Nouvelles*
II. Mercier and Camier
5. Molloy and Moran
6. Malone
Part Three: The Hero as Voice
7. The Unnamable
8. The Last Heroes
Conclusion: The Voice Continues

1964

708   Bibliography: Works of Samuel Beckett and Select Criticism (pp.
           234-251) [see 3118]
               A. Published Works of Samuel Beckett
                   I. English Works
                       Translations into French of the English Works
                   II. French Works
                       Translations into English of the French Works
                   III. Translations by Beckett, and Miscellaneous
               B. Known Unpublished Works of Samuel Beckett
               C. Sources of Biographical Information
               D. Select List of Criticism
                   I. Books
                   II. Articles
               E. Some Background Materials
           Index Nominum
           Index Rerum
           (The bibliography of Samuel Beckett's works was translated into
           German and reprinted in **716**.)

All the works of fiction are examined chronologically starting with the unpublished, unfinished novel *Dream of Fair to Middling Women* (1932) (**611**)
and ending with the more recent novel *Comment c'est* (1961) (**268**). Detailed and exact synopses of each work reveal the progressive disintegration
of plot and characters. The interplay between novels is carefully analyzed,
and interesting pages are devoted to Beckett's bilingualism.
           Reviews:
708a   Anonymous. *Times Literary Supplement,* Sept. 3, 1964, p. 808.
708b   Bates, R. *Canadian Forum,* XLV (Aug., 1965), 118.
708c   Burgess, Anthony. *The Guardian,* July 24, 1964, p. 9.
708d   Chambers, Ross. *Nation,* Nov. 28, 1964.
708e   Coe, Richard N. *The Bulletin,* Jan. 9, 1965, p. 37.
708f   Cruickshank, John. *Durham University Journal,* LVIII (Dec., 1965),
              53.
708g   Donoghue, Denis. *New Statesman,* LXVIII (Oct. 2, 1964), 498, 500.
708h   Dupont, V. "Samuel Beckett: Une thèse, un livre," *Bulletin de
              l'Université de Toulouse,* LXXIV (Jan., 1965), 330-337; reprinted
              in *Caliban: Annales publiées par la Faculté des Lettres et Sciences
              Humaines,* 2 (April, 1965), 159-166.
708i   Federman, Raymond. *Esprit Créateur,* V (Summer, 1965), 117-118.
708j   Harvey, J. R. *Cambridge Quarterly,* I (Autumn, 1966), 384-395
              [see **1869**].
708k   Johnson, B. S. *The Spectator,* Aug. 28, 1964, p. 280.
708l   Mansell Jones, P. *French Studies,* XIX (July, 1965), 320-322.
708m   Ohmann, Richard. *Wisconsin Studies in Contemporary Literature,*
              VI (Autumn, 1965), 372-375.
708n   Wall, Stephen. *Essays in Criticism,* XVI (April, 1966), 245-252 [see
              2888].

1964

709   JACOBSEN, Josephine, and William R. MUELLER. *The Testament of Samuel Beckett.* New York: Hill and Wang, 1964. 178 pp. Reprinted by Faber and Faber, London, 1966.

Contents:

Preface

Glossary of Abbreviations

Introduction

    1. The Murmur in the Mud

The Technique

    2. The Dimension of Poetry [see **1736**]

    3. The Epistemology: A Preliminary to Understanding

    4. The Comic Mode

The Vision

    5. The Human Condition

    6. The Quest

Conclusion

    7. The Enormous Time

A Partial Bibliography of Samuel Beckett's Works (p. 175)

A Selective Bibliography of Works on Samuel Beckett (pp. 177-178)

All Beckett's creations are discussed as a homogeneous mass reducing these to a "Poetic Dimension." Beckett is "primarily a poet" who expresses his sensibility in three poetic modes: poetry of joy, poetry of disparity, and poetry of intimation.

Reviews:

709*a*   Elman, Richard M. "Beckett's Testament," *Commonweal,* LXXX (June 26, 1964), 416-418.

709*b*   Federman, Raymond. *French Review,* XXXVIII (Feb., 1965), 579-580.

709*c*   Harvey, J. R. *Cambridge Quarterly,* I (Autumn, 1966), 384-395 [see 1869].

709*d*   Ohmann, Richard. *Wisconsin Studies in Contemporary Literature,* VI (Autumn, 1965), 372-375.

709*e*   Pryce-Jones, Alan. *New York Herald Tribune,* Feb. 29, 1964, p. 13.

709*f*   Segesta, J. *Library Journal,* LXXXIX (Feb. 15, 1964), 868.

709*g*   Smalley, W. *Quarterly Journal of Speech,* LI (Feb., 1965), 96.

709*h*   Sutherland, D. *New Leader,* XLVII (May 11, 1964), 12.

709*i*   Wall, Stephen. *Essays in Criticism,* XVI (April, 1966), 245-252 [see 2888].

710   TINDALL, William York. *Samuel Beckett.* New York and London: Columbia University Press, 1964. 48 pp. Columbia Essays on Modern Writers, no. 4.

1964

710 *Contents:*
Samuel Beckett (text, *passim,* contains quotes from some unpublished letters of Samuel Beckett to Jacob Schwartz and W. Y. Tindall)
Selected Bibliography (pp. 46-48)

Pamphlet consists of a single essay which plays up the humor of Beckett's strange works, a humor that "makes horror bearable," but also "intensifies what it guarantees relief from." Beckett's works are considered enigmas which seem to resist, by design, symbolic or systematic interpretation.

Reviews:
710a Anonymous. *Choice,* I (Feb., 1965), 592.
710b _____. *Library Journal,* XC (March 15, 1965), 1568.
710c Davison, P. *Modern Language Review,* LX (Oct., 1965), 610.
710d Harrison, Keith. *The Spectator,* Feb. 26, 1965, p. 273.
710e Ohmann, Richard. *Wisconsin Studies in Contemporary Literature,* VI (Autumn, 1965), 372-375.
710f Wall, Stephen. *Essays in Criticism,* XVI (April, 1966), 245-252 [see **2888**].

1965

711 ESSLIN, Martin, ed. *Samuel Beckett: A Collection of Critical Essays.* Englewood Cliffs, N. J.: Prentice-Hall, 1965. 182 pp.
Contents:
ESSLIN, Martin. Introduction, pp. 1-15.
BECKETT, Samuel, and Georges DUTHUIT. "Three Dialogues," pp. 16-22. Reprinted from *Transition 49* [see **7.2, 31.2**].
FLETCHER, John. "The Private Pain and the Whey of Words: A Survey of Beckett's Verse," pp. 23-32. Text of a lecture delivered at Durham University, England, Nov., 1964.
NADEAU, Maurice. "Samuel Beckett: Humor and the Void," pp. 33-36. Original title, "Samuel Beckett, l'humour et le néant," trans. Barbara Bray from *Littérature présente* [see **1000**]; essay originally published in **1301**.
LEVENTHAL, A. J. "The Beckett Hero," pp. 37-51. Text of a lecture delivered at Trinity College, Dublin, June, 1963. Reprinted in French in *Lettres Nouvelles,* and in English in *Critique: Studies in Modern Fiction* [see **1805**].
KENNER, Hugh. "The Cartesian Centaur," pp. 52-61. Originally a chapter of **703**.
HOEFER, Jacqueline. *"Watt,"* pp. 62-76. Reprinted from **900**.
MAYOUX, Jean-Jacques. "Samuel Beckett and Universal Parody," pp. 77-91. Original title, "Samuel Beckett et l'univers parodique," trans. Barbara Bray from *Vivants Piliers* [see **1021**].
WELLERSHOFF, Dieter. "Failure of an Attempt at De-Mythologization: Samuel Beckett's Novels," pp. 92-107. Originally a chap-

1965

711   ter from *Der Gleichgültige: Versuche über Hemingway, Camus, Benn und Beckett,* trans. Martin Esslin [see **1066** and **1765**].

ROBBE-GRILLET, Alain. "Samuel Beckett, or 'Presence' in the Theatre," pp. 108-116. Original title, "Samuel Beckett ou la présence sur la scène," trans. Barbara Bray from *Pour un nouveau roman* [see **1062**].

METMAN, Eva. "Reflections on Samuel Beckett's Plays," pp. 117-139. Reprinted from **1561**.

ANDERS, Günther. "Being without Time: On Beckett's Play *Waiting for Godot,*" pp. 140-151. Original title, "Sein ohne Zeit: zu Becketts Stück *En attendant Godot,*" in *Die Antiquiertheit des Menschen* [see **1002**].

CHAMBERS, Ross. "Beckett's Brinkmanship," pp. 152-168. Reprinted from **1714**.

COHN, Ruby. "Philosophical Fragments in the Works of Samuel Beckett," pp. 169-177. Reprinted from **1780**.

"Chronology of Important Dates," pp. 178-179
"Notes on the Editor and Authors," p. 180
"Selected Bibliography," pp. 181-182.

A useful collection of essays, many translated from foreign languages and thus presenting a good panorama of international criticism. Esslin's is a characteristically honest and helpful introduction to the work of Beckett and to the articles he has selected, most of which have been published before and therefore are commented on in chap. 10.

Reviews:

711a   Driver, Tom F. "Apostle of Failure," *New York Times Book Review,* Jan. 23, 1966, pp. 4, 22.

711b   Moore, Harry T. *St. Louis Post Dispatch,* Jan. 18, 1966.

712   FEDERMAN, Raymond. *Journey to Chaos: Samuel Beckett's Early Fiction.* Berkeley and Los Angeles: University of California Press, 1965. 243 pp. Reissued by Cambridge University Press, London, 1966.
Contents:
Preface
Introduction
    1. The Fiction of Mud
Social Reality: Lethargy, Doubt, and Insanity
    2. Belacqua and the Inferno of Society [see **1786**]
    3. Murphy's Search for an Asylum
    4. Watt's Mental Breakdown
Fictional Absurdity: Exile and Alienation
    5. The Pseudocouple Mercier-Camier
    6. The Expulsion

1965

712   Appendix (contains summaries of *Dream of Fair to Middling Women*
           and *More Pricks Than Kicks*)
           Bibliography (pp. 215-235 [contains "A Chronology of Beckett's
           Works" and "A Selected Bibliography of Beckett Criticism"] [see
           3117])
           Index

Traces in Beckett's early fiction, much of it out of print or unpublished, the
sources of the "paradoxical creative system which progressively draws toward
the formulation of a new reality as it negates common realities." This new
reality is "fictional absurdity." Federman proceeds to ask how the painful
"failure" *How It Is* came to be written, and in so doing devotes a particularly
valuable chapter to *Watt*.

           Reviews:

712*a*   Anonymous. *Choice,* II (Jan., 1966), 776.
712*b*   _____. *Times Literary Supplement,* May 5, 1966, p. 388.
712*c*   B., C. *Berkeley Daily Gazette,* Dec. 3, 1965.
712*d*   Brée, Germaine. *Modern Language Quarterly,* XXVII (June, 1966),
           235-237.
712*e*   Driver, Tom F. "Apostle of Failure." *New York Times Book Review,*
           Jan. 23, 1966, pp. 4, 22.
712*f*   Fletcher, John. *Durham University Journal,* LVIII (March, 1966),
           113-114.
712*g*   Friedman, Melvin J. *French Review,* XXXIX (April, 1966), 817-
           818.
712*h*   Hamilton, Iain. "Wets, Drys, and Sharps." *Illustrated London News,*
           Feb. 12, 1966, pp. 36-37.
712*i*   Harvey, J. R. *Cambridge Quarterly,* I (Autumn, 1966), 384-395 [see
           1869].
712*j*   Hedges, Elaine. *Wisconsin Studies in Contemporary Literature,* VII
           (Summer, 1966), 231-232.
712*k*   Kern, Edith. *Esprit Créateur,* VII (Summer, 1967), 152-155.
712*l*   Moore, Harry T. *St. Louis Post Dispatch,* Jan. 18, 1966.
712*m*   Strauss, Walter. *Modern Language Journal,* L (Nov., 1966), 505-506.

713   SCOTT, Nathan A. *Samuel Beckett.* London: Bowes and Bowes,
           1965. 141 pp.

           Contents:
           Chapters I to X (no chapter headings)
           Biographical Note (pp. 131-134)
           A Selected Bibliography (pp. 135-141; contains a few errors)

Beckett's works are considered occasions for flights from or approaches to
"empirical surfaces" which never detain the author. Beckett is related to the
French literary tradition from Baudelaire to Robbe-Grillet. Beckett's philosophy is shown as related to Heidegger, Wittgenstein, and Tillich. Some effort
is also made to interpret the symbolism in Beckett's work.

1965

Reviews:

713*a*   Anonymous. *Times Educational Supplement,* Feb. 5, 1965, p. 320.
713*b*   ————. *Times Literary Supplement,* March 25, 1965, p. 236.
713*c*   Chambers, Ross. *The Australian,* May 22, 1965, p. 8.
713*d*   Davison, P. *Modern Language Review,* LX (Oct., 1965), 610.
713*e*   Harrison, Keith. *The Spectator,* Feb. 26, 1965, p. 273.
713*f*   Harvey, J. R. *Cambridge Quarterly,* I (Autumn, 1966), 384-395 [see
          1869].
713*g*   Mansell Jones, P. *French Studies,* XIX (July, 1965), 320-322.
713*h*   Tindall, William Y. *Romanic Review,* LVI (Dec., 1965), 318.
713*i*   Wall, Stephen. *Essays in Criticism,* XVI (April, 1966), 245-252 [see
          2888].
713*j*   Woodcock, G. *New Leader,* XLVIII (June 7, 1965), 23.

1966

714   DUCKWORTH, Colin, ed. *En attendant Godot,* by Samuel Beckett,
       ed. Colin Duckworth, with a Foreword by Harold Hobson. Lon-
       don: George G. Harrap and Co., 1966. cxxxv + 101 pp [see
       259.31].

Contents:
Introduction
1. Samuel Beckett: A Man and His Mind
2. What are Beckett's Works 'About'?
3. *Godot:* Genesis and Composition [see **1864**]
4. Approaches to *Godot*
5. *Godot:* Structure and Style
6. Symbolism and Characterization
7. *Godot:* Constant or Variable?
8. Conclusion
Bibliography
En attendant Godot
     Act 1
     Act 2
Notes

A scholarly edition of the text of *Godot.* The long introductory essay of more
than 100 pages not only discusses sources of the play in Beckett's earlier works,
but through a close examination of the manuscript of *Godot* throws much light
on the final version. Of particular interest is the rapport Mr. Duckworth
establishes between *Godot* and Beckett's jettisoned first French novel *Mercier
et Camier* (a rapport also discussed in **1846**). The notes should prove helpful
to the student of the text.

Review:

714*a*   Fletcher, John. *Modern Language Review,* LXIV (Jan., 1969), 34-38.

1966

715   JANVIER, Ludovic. *Pour Samuel Beckett.* Paris: Éditions de
        Minuit, 1966. 291 pp.

        Contents:

        Description d'un trajet
            seuil
            du voyage manqué à la chambre mère
            naître et parler
            le temps à deux
            l'écho
            le souffle
            être vu se dire

        Les Cercles de l'humour
            l'écriture
            les jeux de mots
            les autres
            les occupations de l'être
            quel rire?

        L'A Venir des mots
            une vie par éclairs
            note
            combinaison et liberté: le bilinguisme
            les Nouvelles
            deux écrivains au travail
            départ des mots, mots du départ
            mieux que du temps de la faconde
            le souffle et la tension
            silence, à venir, musique
            dire

        Trois notes
            Beckett et autres
            'M'
            chapeau — père — opération gigogne

The second full-length study in French on Beckett and a much more ambitious
effort than **706** to assess all of Beckett's works because it includes the more
recent prose pieces and plays. The book is written in an impressionistic manner. The best pages are devoted to "Les Cercles de l'humour." A bibliography
and index would have been useful.

        Reviews:

715   JANVIER, Ludovic. *Pour Samuel Beckett.* Paris: Éditions de
715*b*   Federman, Raymond. *Novel: A Forum on Fiction,* II, 2 (Winter,
        1969), 191-192.

715*c*   Fletcher, John. *Modern Language Review,* LXIV (Jan., 1969), 34-38.

715*d*   Jean, Raymond. *Nouvel Observateur,* April 13-19, 1966, p. 49.

1966

716   MAYOUX, Jean-Jacques, and John FLETCHER. *Jean-Jacques Mayoux über Beckett mit einer Bibliographie von John Fletcher.* Frankfort on the Main: Suhrkamp, 1966. 147 pp.

Contents:

Über Beckett
    Beckett und die Grenzen des Ausdrucks
    'Wie es ist' [see **2518**]
    Das Theater Samuel Becketts [see **1406**]
    Samuel Beckett und das parodistische Universum [see **1021**]
Bibliographie (pp. 121-143) [see **3120**]
    Veröffentlichte Werke
    Bekannte unveröffentlichte Werke
    Quellen zur Biographie
Bibliographische Notiz

The essays by J.-J. Mayoux all appeared earlier and are commented on in chap. 10, "Articles Devoted to Samuel Beckett." Fletcher's bibliography was revised and brought up to date from his book [see **708**]. Mayoux's essays were translated from the French by Ursula Dreysse and Britta Titel, Fletcher's bibliography from the English by Rolf Dornbacher.

717   MÉLÈSE, Pierre. *Samuel Beckett.* Paris: Pierre Seghers, 1966. 192 pp.

Contents:

Préambule
Qui êtes-vous, Samuel Beckett?
    Biographie
    Des poèmes aux romans
    Des romans au théâtre
L'œuvre
    I.   *En attendant Godot*
    II. *Fin de Partie*
    III. *La dernière Bande*
    IV. *Oh!* [sic] *les beaux jours*
    V. *Comédie*
    VI. *Va-et-Vient*
    VII. Œuvres radiophoniques
        Tous ceux qui tombent
        From and [sic] *abandoned work*
        Cendres
        Paroles et Musique
        Cascando
        Dis Joe
    VIII. *Actes sans paroles*
        Acte sans paroles I
        Acte sans paroles II

1966

717   IX. Conclusion
          Documents
          Témoignages
              Quatre Metteurs en scène:
                  Roger Blin
                  Jean-Marie Serreau
                  Alan Schneider
                  Alan Simpson
              Deux Interprètes:
                  Madeleine Renaud
                  Lucien Raimbourg
              Un Collaborateur: Marcel Mihalovici
          Panorama critique
          Samuel Beckett et son Temps
          Tableau des Premières Représentations
          Bibliographie (pp. 188-190)
          Illustrations:
              Couverture: Beckett (photo by Lipnitzki)
              Portrait de Beckett, par Avigdor Arikha (p. 6)
              En attendant Godot (p. 32)
              Fin de partie (pp. 32, 64)
              Acte sans paroles I (p. 64)
              La dernière bande (p. 96)
              Oh les beaux jours (p. 96)
              Comédie (p. 128)
              Beckett pendant le tournage de *Comédie* (p. 128)
              Page manuscrite de *Comédie* (p. 134)

The second volume of a collection, "Théâtre de tous les Temps," prepared under the direction of Rose-Marie Moudouès and Pierre Lherminier. The first volume was devoted to Ionesco. Similar in format to the series "Poètes d'Aujourd'hui," this volume concentrates mainly on Beckett's theater. The critical judgments are superficial, but the book is rich in details and information about the plays, the performances, and those who were involved in staging the plays.

1967

718   FLETCHER, John. *Samuel Beckett's Art.* London: Chatto and
          Windus, 1967. 154 pp. Reissued by Barnes and Noble, New York.
          Contents:
          Foreword
          1. The Form and the Content
          2. Beckett as Critic
          3. The Art of the Poet
          4. The Art of the Dramatist
          5. Beckett and the Fictional Tradition

1967

718   6. Samuel Beckett's French
      7. Some Sources and Influences:
          i. The Debt to Dante
          ii. Beckett and the Philosophers
      8. The Morbid Dread of Sphinxes
      Appendix: Chronology of Samuel Beckett's Works, 1929-1966 (pp. 147-149)
      Index

Fletcher's second book on Beckett, but this time he directs his attention toward the method rather than the message of his subject. Parts of this book first appeared in somewhat different form: chap. 2 in **1847**, chap. 4 in **904**, chap. 5 in **1842**, chap. 7 in **1843** and **1844**, and chap. 8 in **1845**.

Reviews:

718a   Green, Martin. *The Guardian,* June 30, 1967, p. 7.
718b   Heppenstall, Rayner. *Daily Telegraph,* Aug. 10, 1967, p. 19.
718c   P[ayne], M[ervyn]. *Eastern Daily Press,* July 17, 1967, p. 4.
718d   Ricks, Christopher. *The Listener,* LXXVIII (Aug. 3, 1967), 148-149.
718e   Sprague, Clair. *New York Times Book Review,* Nov. 7, 1967, p. 67.
718f   Wilson, Angus. *The Observer,* July 16, 1967, p. 20.

719   *Beckett at 60* (A Festschrift). London: Calder and Boyars, 1967. 99 pp. [See **2889**.]
      Contents:
      CALDER, John. Introduction, pp. 1-4.
                PART I. Reminiscences
      LEVENTHAL, A. J. "The Thirties," pp. 7-13.
      JOLAS, Maria. "A Bloomlein for Sam," pp. 14-16.
      LINDON, Jérôme. "First Meeting with Samuel Beckett," pp. 17-19 (contains a letter from Samuel Beckett to Lindon, publisher of Beckett's French works, dated 10.IV.51, thanking him for the interest he is taking in his work).
      MIHALOVICI, Marcel. "My Collaboration with Samuel Beckett," pp. 20-22.
      MACGOWRAN, Jack. "Working with Samuel Beckett," pp. 23-24.
      HOBSON, Harold. "The First Night of *Waiting for Godot*," pp. 25-28.
      FLETCHER, John. "In Search of Beckett," pp. 29-33.
      SCHNEIDER, Alan. "Waiting for Beckett," pp. 34-52 [see **1464**, **3084**].
            PART II. Critical Examinations
      ESSLIN, Martin. "Samuel Beckett's Poems," pp. 55-60.
      KENNER, Hugh. "Progress Report, 1962-65," pp. 61-77.
                PART III. Tributes
      RENAUD, Madeleine. "Beckett the Magnificant," pp. 81-83.
      PINGET, Robert. "My Dear Sam," pp. 84-85.
      PINTER, Harold. "Beckett," p. 86.
      MONTEITH, Charles. "A Personal Note," p. 87.

1967

719   ARRABAL, Fernando. "In Connection with Samuel Beckett," p. 88.
STAIB, Philippe. "A Propos Samuel Beckett," pp. 89-90.
HIGGINS, Aidan. "Tribute," pp. 91-92.
HUTCHINSON, Mary. "All the Livelong Way," pp. 93-95.
SIMPSON, Alan. "Samuel Beckett," pp. 96-97.
HERBERT, Jocelyn. "A Letter," p. 98.
DEVINE, George. "Last Tribute," p. 99.
Illustrations:
Sketch of Samuel Beckett by Arikha (frontispiece)
Samuel Beckett at his mother's knee (f.p. 24 [see **3065**])
Photograph of Samuel Beckett 1951 (f.p. 25)
Samuel Beckett at Rehearsal (f.p. 40)
The view from Samuel Beckett's house (f.p. 41)

NOTE: *The following books appeared after our manuscript went to press. We cannot furnish detailed information at this late date, but we are grateful to the University of California Press for permitting us to list the titles.*

1967

720   CALDER, John, ed. *A Samuel Beckett Reader.* London: Calder and Boyars, 1967. 192 pp. [See **16.032.**]
721   COHN, Ruby, ed. *Casebook on Waiting for Godot.* New York: Grove Press, 1967. 192 pp.
722   HASSAN, Ihab. *The Literature of Silence: Henry Miller and Samuel Beckett.* New York: Alfred A. Knopf, 1967. 225 pp.
723   MÆRLI, Terje. *Samuel Beckett: en artikkelsamling.* Olso: Universitetsforlaget, 1967.
724   OLIVA, Renato. *Samuel Beckett, prima del silenzio.* Milan: U. Mursia, "Civiltà Letteraria del Novecento," 1967.
725   TAGLIAFERRI, Aldo. *Beckett e l'iperdeterminazione letteraria.* Milan: Feltrinelli, 1967. 165 pp.

1968

726   HARRISON, Robert. *Samuel Beckett's Murphy: A Critical Excursion.* Athens: University of Georgia Press, 1968. 99 pp.
727   HAYMAN, Ronald. *Samuel Beckett.* London: Heinemann, 1968. 80 pp.
728   ONIMUS, Jean. *Beckett.* Paris: Desclée de Brouwer, 1968. 187 pp.
729   REID, Alec. *All I Can Manage, More Than I Could: An Approach to the Plays of Samuel Beckett.* Dublin: The Dolmen Press, 1968. 94 pp.

1969

730   JANVIER, Ludovic. *Beckett par lui-même.* Paris: Éditions du Seuil, 1969. 190 pp.
731   BERNAL, Olga. *Samuel Beckett: Langage et fiction.* Paris: Gallimard, 1969.

6.

Dissertations and Theses on Samuel Beckett

Doctoral Dissertations Devoted Entirely to Samuel Beckett

1960

800   COHN, Ruby. "Samuel Beckett: The Comic Gamut." Unpublished Ph.D. dissertation. Washington University, St. Louis, 1960. 271 pp. [See **704**.] Listed in *Dissertation Abstracts,* XXI (March, 1961), 2711-2712.

1961

801   RADKE, Judith J. "Doubt and the Disintegration of Form in the French Novels and Drama of Samuel Beckett." Unpublished **Ph.D.** dissertation. University of Colorado, Boulder, 1961. 276 **pp.** Listed in *Dissertation Abstracts,* XXII (March, 1962), 3205-3206.

1963

802   FEDERMAN, Raymond. "Samuel Beckett's Early Novels: From Social Reality to Fictional Absurdity." Unpublished Ph.D. dissertation. University of California, Los Angeles, 1963. 315 **pp.** Listed in *Dissertation Abstracts,* XXIV (Nov., 1963), 2030.

1964

803   FLETCHER, John. "Techniques et méthodes littéraires dans l'œuvre de Samuel Beckett." Unpublished Ph.D. dissertation (**Third Cycle**). Faculté des Lettres et Sciences Humaines, **University of** Toulouse, 1964. 277 pp.

804   HESLA, David II. "The Shape of Chaos: An Interpretation of the Art of Samuel Beckett." Unpublished Ph.D. dissertation. University of Chicago, Evanston, 1964. 323 pp. Not abstracted in *Dissertation Abstracts.*

1965

805   KLAWITTER, Robert Louis. "Being and Time in Samuel Beckett's
       Novels." Unpublished Ph.D. dissertation. Yale University, New
       Haven, 1965. 404 pp. Listed in *Dissertation Abstracts*, XXVI
       (June, 1966), 7320.

806   WEBB, Eugene. "Samuel Beckett, Novelist: A Study of His Trilogy."
       Unpublished Ph.D. dissertation. Columbia University, New York,
       1965. 221 pp. Not listed in *Dissertation Abstracts*.

1966

807   HAMPTON, Charles Christy. "The Human Situation in the Plays
       of Samuel Beckett: A Study in Stratagems of Inaction." Unpub-
       lished Ph.D. dissertation. Stanford University, Stanford, Calif.,
       1966. 224 pp. Listed in *Dissertation Abstracts*, XXVII (July-
       Aug., 1966), 206A.

808   MOORJANI, A. "Intersubjectivity in the Works of Samuel Beckett."
       Ph.D. dissertation in progress at Johns Hopkins University, Balti-
       more, Md. Announced in "Dissertations in Progress," *French Re-
       view*, XLI (Oct., 1967), 134.

809   SAGE, Victor. "Structure and Paradox in the Novels of Samuel
       Beckett." Ph.D. dissertation in progress at the University of East
       Anglia, Norwich, England. Information communicated in a
       letter to us.

810   SOLOMON, Philip H. "The Imagery of Samuel Beckett: Linguistic
       Analysis of *Molloy*." Ph.D. dissertation in progress at the Univer-
       sity of Wisconsin, Madison. Announced in "Dissertations in
       Progress," *French Review*, XLI (Oct., 1967), 133.

Doctoral Dissertations Devoted
in Part to Samuel Beckett

1962

850   MARKUS, Thomas B. "The Concept of Communion in the Modern
       French Theater." Unpublished Ph.D. dissertation. Tulane Uni-
       versity, New Orleans, 1962. 318 pp. Listed in *Dissertation Ab-
       stracts*, XXIII (May-June, 1963), 4460-4461.

1964

851   GREENBERG, Alvin D. "The Novel of Disintegration: A Study of
       a World View in Contemporary Fiction" (Céline, Beckett, Robbe-
       Grillet, West, Algren, Bellow, Malamud, Ellison). Unpublished
       Ph.D. dissertation, Washington University, St. Louis, 1964. 295
       pp. Listed in *Dissertation Abstracts*, XXV (March, 1965), 5278.

1964

852   WELSBACHER, Richard C. "Four Projections of Absurd Existence
       in the Modern Drama" (Sartre, Camus, Beckett, and Ionesco).
       Unpublished Ph.D. dissertation. Ohio State University, Columbus,
       1964. 211 pp. Listed in *Dissertation Abstracts,* XXV (June,
       1965), 7423-7424.

1965

853   FRISCH, Jack E. "Ironic Theatre: Technique of Irony in the
       Plays of Samuel Beckett, Eugène Ionesco, Harold Pinter, and
       Jean Genet." Unpublished Ph.D. dissertation. University of
       Wisconsin, Madison, 1965. 260 pp. Listed in *Dissertation Ab-
       stracts,* XXV (April, 1965), 6114-6115.

854   SHORT, Robert S. "The Political History of the Surrealist Move-
       ment in France, 1918-1940." Unpublished D.Phil. dissertation.
       University of Sussex, England, 1965. (See p. 338 for details of
       an interview between Beckett and Short concerning the 1932
       surrealist issue of *This Quarter.*) [See **488.102**, Note.]

Theses and Diploma Essays
Devoted to Samuel Beckett

1957

855   STOTTLAR, James. "Samuel Beckett: An Introduction and an
       Interpretation." Unpublished M.A. thesis. Columbia University,
       New York, 1957. 128 pp.

1958

856   LAUFER, Pearl B. "The Shape of Samuel Beckett's Plays." Un-
       published M.A. thesis. Ohio State University, Columbus, 1958.

1961

857   O'BRIEN, Carol B. "The Plays of Samuel Beckett." Unpublished
       M.A. thesis. University of Dublin, Trinity College, Dublin, 1961.
       113 pp.

858   STACK, Joanna. "Molloy in Moran and Moran in Molloy." Un-
       published thesis in partial fulfillment of B.A. requirements. Ben-
       nington College, Bennington, Vt., Jan. 1961.

859   FLETCHER, John. "The Decaying Hero: A Study in Evolution in
       the Fiction of Samuel Beckett." Mémoire pour le diplôme d'études
       supérieures (Anglais). Faculté des Lettres et Sciences Humaines,
       University of Toulouse, June 1961. 222 pp.

1963

860   LUX, John M. "Mind over Matter: A Study of Mobility, Mental
       Activity, and Cartesian Parody in the Novels of Samuel Beckett."
       Unpublished M.A. thesis. Ohio State University, Columbus, 1963.

1964

861   FOTHERGILL, Robert A. "The Retrospective Hypothesis: A Study
       of the Pursuit of Identity in Samuel Beckett's Trilogy." Unpub-
       lished M.A. thesis. McMaster University, Hamilton, Ont., 1964.
       70 pp.

862   MAYHEW, Anne Lovitt. "The Use of Ritual in the Theatre of the
       Absurd: A Study of Beckett, Pinter, Genet." Unpublished M.A.
       thesis. University of British Columbia, Vancouver, 1964. 113 pp.

863   MICHAYLOV, Yury. "Le Théâtre de Samuel Beckett." Unpub-
       lished M.A. thesis. New York University, New York, 1964. 53 pp.

1965

864   DAVIS, Robin J. "A Bibliography of Samuel Beckett." Unpublished
       thesis submitted in partial requirement for the Diploma in Li-
       brarianship. University of London, England, Aug., 1965. 170 pp.
       [See **3112**.]

1966

865   ENSINK, Joan L. "Samuel Beckett: An Annotated Bibliography of
       Criticism, 1934-1965." Unpublished M.A. thesis. Columbia Uni-
       versity, New York, 1966. 205 pp. [See **3114**.]

866   THIEL, André. "La Condition tragique chez Samuel Beckett et
       son expression théâtrale." Licence en Philologie Romane. Uni-
       versity of Brussels, Belgium, 1966.

7.

Special Issues of Journals Devoted to Samuel Beckett

1959

900   *Perspective,* XI (Autumn, 1959), 119-196 (ed. Ruby Cohn).
Contents:
COHN, Ruby. "Preliminary Observations," pp. 119-131.
KENNER, Hugh. "The Cartesian Centaur," pp. 132-141 [see **703**].
MAYOUX, Jean-Jacques. "The Theatre of Samuel Beckett," pp. 142-155. Translated from the French "Le Théâtre de Samuel Beckett" in **1406**.
MINTZ, Samuel I. "Beckett's *Murphy:* A 'Cartesian' Novel," pp. 156-165.
HOEFER, Jacqueline. *"Watt,"* pp. 166-182 [see **711**].
KERN, Edith. "Moran-Molloy: The Hero as Author," pp. 183-193.
COHN, Ruby. "A Checklist of Beckett Criticism," pp. 193-196 [see **3110**].

For comments on these essays see **1486**, **1499**, **1508**, **1513**, **1497**, and **1501**.

Review:
900a   Dieckmann, Liselotte. *Comparative Literature,* XII (Spring, 1960), 175-176.

1963

901   *Cahiers de la Compagnie Madeleine Renaud–Jean-Louis Barrault,* 44 (Oct., 1963), 6-77. Reissued Nov., 1966.
Contents:
COE, Richard N. "Le Dieu de Samuel Beckett," pp. 6-36 [see **1716**]. Trans. Claude Clergé from the original "God and Samuel Beckett" in **1835**.
CHAMBERS, Ross. "Beckett, homme des situations limites," pp. 37-62. Trans. Claude Clergé from the original "Beckett's Brinkmanship" in **1714** [see also **711**].

1963

901 NADEAU, Maurice. "Le Chemin de la parole au silence," pp. 63-66. Reprinted in **1060**.

MAGNY, Olivier de. "Samuel Beckett et la farce métaphysique," pp. 67-72 [see **1745**].

COHN, Ruby. "Bibliographie des études critiques sur l'œuvre de Samuel Beckett," pp. 73-77. Trans. from **704**.

Photo of Beckett facing page 65.

The rest of this issue contains material on the theater unrelated to Beckett.

1964

902 *Revue des Lettres Modernes (Samuel Beckett: Configuration Critique, no. 8)*, 100 (1964), 1-184 (ed. Melvin J. Friedman).
Contents:
FRIEDMAN, Melvin J. Preface, pp. 9-21.

HOFFMAN, Frederick J. "L'Insaisissable moi: Les 'M' de Beckett," pp. 23-53. Previously published in **705**.

MORRISSETTE, Bruce. "Les Idées de Robbe-Grillet sur Beckett," pp. 55-67.

KERN, Edith. "Samuel Beckett et les poches de Lemuel Gulliver," pp. 69-81.

BRÉE, Germaine. "L'Étrange monde des 'Grands Articulés,'" pp. 83-97.

LAMONT, Rosette. "La Farce métaphysique de Samuel Beckett," pp. 99-116. Rev. and trans. from **1504**.

CHAMPIGNY, Robert. "Les Aventures de la première personne," pp. 117-130.

HAYMAN, David. "Molloy à la recherche de l'absurde," pp. 131-151. An earlier version of this essay appeared in **1051**.

HARVEY, Lawrence E. "Samuel Beckett: Initiation du poète," pp. 153-168.

BRYER, Jackson R. "Critique de Samuel Beckett," pp. 169-184 [see **3122**]. Selected bibliography, contains a few errors.

Essays written originally in English translated by Paul Rozenberg. For comments on the above see **1790**, **1800**, **1813**, **1801**, **1771**, **1803**, **1776**, **1799**, **1798**, and **1773**, respectively.

Reviews:

902a Federman, Raymond. *Modern Language Journal,* L (April, 1966), 241-242.

902b Lamotte, Frédéric. *Mercure de France,* 1217 (March, 1965), 565-566.

1965

903 *Esprit (Notre Théâtre: Théâtre Moderne et Public Populaire)*, 338 (May, 1965), 801-1040.

The issue is devoted almost entirely to the theater, particularly in France, and Beckett is mentioned throughout and discussed in several of the essays,

1965

903

especially in Jean-Marie Domenach's article, "Résurrection de la tragédie" [see **1839**].

1966

904   *Modern Drama,* IX (Dec., 1966), 237-346 (ed. Ruby Cohn).
Contents:

OVERVIEWS

COHN, Ruby. "Acting for Beckett," p. 237 [see **1861**].

MAYOUX, Jean-Jacques. "Beckett and Expressionism," pp. 238-241 [see **1875**]. An excerpt from a longer study, "Beckett and the Paths of Expressionism," written in French but published only in German. Trans. from the French by Ruby Cohn.

FLETCHER, John. "Action and Play in Beckett's Theater," pp. 242-250 [see **1867**]. Reprinted in an extended version in **718**.

ISER, Wolfgang. "Samuel Beckett's Dramatic Language," pp. 251-259 [see **1871**]. A slightly abridged version of an article that appeared in German in **1612**; trans. Ruby Cohn.

KERN, Edith. "Beckett and the Spirit of the Commedia Dell'Arte," pp. 260-267 [see **1873**].

GODOTOLOGY

SCHECHNER, Richard. "There's Lots of Time in *Godot*," pp. 268-276 [see **1878**].

MIHALYI, Gábor. "Beckett's *Godot* and the Myth of Alienation," pp. 277-282 [see **1876**]. Also published in *New Hungarian Quarterly,* 24 (Winter, 1966).

DUBOIS, Jacques. "Beckett and Ionesco: The Tragic Awareness of Pascal and the Ironic Awareness of Flaubert," pp. 283-291; trans. Ruby Cohn [see **1863**].

BROOKS, Curtis M. "The Mythic Pattern in *Waiting for Godot*," pp. 292-299 [see **1860**].

FRIEDMAN, Melvin J. "Crritic!" [*sic*], pp. 300-308 [see **1868**].

ATKINS, Anselm. "A Note on the Structure of Lucky's Speech," p. 309 [see **1858**].

SINGULARS

SHEEDY, John J. "The Comic Apocalypse of King Hamm," pp. 310-318 [see **1879**].

COHN, Ruby. "The Beginning of *Endgame*," pp. 319-323 [see **1862**].

ALPAUGH, David J. "The Symbolic Structure of Samuel Beckett's *All That Fall*," pp. 324-332 [see **1857**].

OBERG, Arthur K. *"Krapp's Last Tape* and the Proustian Vision," pp. 333-338 [see **1877**].

HUBERT, Renée Riese. "Beckett's *Play* Between Poetry and Performance," pp. 339-346 [see **1870**].

1967

905   *Livres de France*, XVIII (Jan., 1967), 1-27.
          Contents:
          BENMUSSA, Simone. "Samuel Beckett," pp. 2, 25.
          JANVIER, Ludovic. "Beckett et ses fables," pp. 4-13.
          MAYOUX, Jean-Jacques. "Samuel Beckett homme de théâtre," pp.
          14-21.
          MAZARS, Pierre, and Marcel LASSEAUX. "A propos de *Comédie*"
          (the film version), p. 22.
          BECKETT, Samuel. "Dans le cylindre" (prose text), pp. 23-24
          [see **277**].
          "Essai de Bibliographie," pp. 25-27.

This special issue of *Livres de France* devoted in part to Samuel Beckett reached
us in time for entry in this section but too late for listing each item in appro-
priate chapters.

8.
Books Devoted in Part to Samuel Beckett

1952

1000 NADEAU, Maurice. *Littérature présente.* Paris: Corrêa, 1952. "Samuel Beckett, l'humour et le néant," pp. 274-279. Reprinted from **1301**; see also **711**.

Discussion of *Molloy.* The three zones of Murphy's mind may be a key or "un moyen d'approche" to the understanding of later works. Beckett is a builder of ruins who saps the strength of his creation as he builds it.

1955

1001 ROUSSEAUX, André. *Littérature du vingtième siècle.* Paris: Albin-Michel, 1955. "L'Homme désintégré de Samuel Beckett," pp. 105-113.

The chapter on Beckett was written in 1952 after the publication of *Malone meurt,* but before *En attendant Godot, L'Innommable,* and other very important Beckett works. Therefore, this is a very partial and narrow discussion, one that denies Beckett any originality.

1956

1002 ANDERS, Günther. *Die Antiquiertheit des Menschen: Über die Seele im Zeitalter der zweiten industriellen Revolution.* Munich: C. H. Beck, 1956. "Sein ohne Zeit, zu Beckett's Stück *En attendant Godot,*" pp. 213-231. Reprinted from **1324**; see also **711**.

Waiting for Godot is a negative parable which presents not nihilistic men but the inability of men to be nihilists. The characters remain, therefore they are waiting for something. The mere act of waiting demonstrates God's existence *ex absentia.*

1003 BENTLEY, Eric. *What Is Theatre? A Query in Chronicle Form.* Boston: Beacon Press, 1956. "Undramatic Theatricality," pp. 148-158; Beckett, pp. 127, 230-231.

1956

1003

Discussion of *Waiting for Godot*. "Beckett's point of view seems pretty close to that of Anouilh or Sartre. *Waiting for Godot* is a play that one of them ought to have written. It is the quintessence of existentialism in the popular, and most relevant, sense of the term." Points out that Balzac also wrote a play where a certain Godeau never appears.

1004   HOBSON, Harold. *International Theatre Annual*, no. 1. London: John Calder, 1956. "Samuel Beckett, Dramatist of the Year," pp. 153-155.

Beckett's most faithful and devoted champion among British theater critics here has some interesting things to say about the symmetry of the structure of *Waiting for Godot*.

1005   POULET, Robert. *La Lanterne magique*. Paris: Nouvelles Éditions Debresse, 1956. "Samuel Beckett," pp. 236-242.

Discusses *Molloy* and *Malone meurt* as long interior monologues that derive from Joyce's systematic "écholalie," from Kafka's mythical delirium, and from the pathetic incoherence of the surrealists.

1958

1006   ALLSOP, Kenneth. *The Angry Decade: A Survey of the Cultural Revolt of the Nineteen-Fifties*. London: Peter Owen, 1958. Beckett, pp. 37-42 and *passim*.

Beckett is seen as one of "the last Mohicans" of the lost generation of the thirties, and as such is denied a place among the avant-garde writers of the fifties.

1007   BOISDEFFRE, Pierre de. *Une histoire vivante de la littérature d'aujourd'hui, 1938-1958*. Paris: Le Livre Contemporain, 1958. "Samuel Beckett ou l'au-delà" (novels), pp. 299-300; "L'Anti-théâtre total: Samuel Beckett ou la mort de l'homme" (theater), pp. 678-680; Beckett also *passim*.

   Idem, 1939-1959. 2d ed. Paris: Le Livre Contemporain, 1959. Novels, as above, pp. 303-304; theater, as above, pp. 682-684; Beckett *passim*.

   Idem. 3d ed. 1960. Reprint of 2d ed.

   Idem, 1939-1961. 4th ed. Paris: Librairie Académique Perrin, 1962. Novels, as above, pp. 303-304; theater, as above, pp. 708-710; Beckett *passim*.

   Idem, 1939-1964. 5th ed. Revised and brought up to date as of March 15, 1964. Novels, as above, pp. 363-364; theater, as above, pp. 768-770; Beckett *passim*.

A useful reference book, with an introduction and four main sections: novel, poetry, theatre, ideas; and a general bibliography. Boisdeffre is not always kind to Beckett, however, nor does he always grasp the complexity of Beckett's work.

1008   CLURMAN, Harold. *Lies Like Truth: Theatre Reviews and Essays*. New York: Macmillan, 1958. "Samuel Beckett," pp. 220-222,

1958

1008   224-225; see also pp. 9-10, 17, 169. Reprinted by Grove Press,
            New York and London (Evergreen Books), 1960.
Waiting for Godot is a "poetic harlequinade—tragicomic as the traditional
commedia dell'arte usually was: full of horseplay, high spirit, cruelty and a
great wistfulness." *Endgame* is "less attractive" than *Godot* because it uses
"more concrete and colorful symbols."

1009   GROSSVOGEL, David I. *The Self-Conscious Stage in Modern
            French Drama.* New York: Columbia University Press, 1958.
            Beckett, pp. 16, 324-334, 360. Reprinted as *Twentieth Century
            French Drama* (New York: Columbia University Press, 1961).
            Paperback.
Discusses the Chaplinesque aspects of *Godot,* a play that represents the "en-
during drama of man attempting to reclaim his incomplete being and the
gnawing frustration that is the particular idiom of these times." *Fin de partie*
is less successful because the "author's craft is less apparent" and because
"he makes use of grosser symbols."

1010   HUDSON, Derek, ed. *English Critical Essays: Twentieth Century.*
            2d ser. London: Oxford University Press, 1958. "*Waiting for
            Godot,*" by G. S. Fraser, pp. 324-332; originally a review of the
            play published anonymously under the title "They Also Serve"
            in **2073**.
Even at his most nihilistic, Beckett is "certainly one of T. S. Eliot's 'Christian
blasphemers' " in his peculiarly bitter and ambiguous use of Christian material.

1011   MAURIAC, Claude. *L'Alittérature contemporaine.* Paris: Albin-
            Michel, 1958. "Samuel Beckett," pp. 77-92. [See **1369**.] Trans.
            Samuel I. Stone as *The New Literature* (New York: George
            Braziller, 1959), pp. 75-90.
A general discussion of Beckett's major works. *Murphy* seems to contain, in
more accessible form, all the essential ideas to be developed in Beckett's
subsequent works. Each new Beckett creation pushes further the ultimate
boundary set in the preceding work.

1012   SCOTT, Nathan A., Jr. *Modern Literature and the Religious Fron-
            tier.* New York: Harper, 1958. Beckett, pp. 84-90, 102.
Beckett is not an existentialist because the existentialists have found a new
"gospel to preach . . . the gospel of the absurd" and in naming the source
of man's perplexities as the absurd, they have gained access "to a sense of
transcension over it, at least to the extent of finding life bearable once again,
upon the basis of a reinstatement of a kind of Stoic humanism." Beckett, on
the contrary, who preaches "waiting" in an age that is primarily "an age of
vigil" is therefore a Christian writer.

1959

1013   BEIGBEDER, Marc. *Le Théâtre en France depuis la Libération.*
            Paris: Bordas, 1959. Beckett, pp. 142-144 and *passim.*
Beckett's originality does not go any further than that of Joyce, Pirandello,
Camus, or even Anouilh and Salacrou.

1959

1014   BLANCHOT, Maurice. *Le Livre à venir*. Paris: Gallimard, 1959.
Beckett, *passim*, and "Où maintenant? Qui maintenant?" pp. 256-
264; reprinted from **1309**; trans. Richard Howard as "Where
Now? Who Now?" in **1481**; reprinted in **1071**.

Brilliant and perceptive essay comparing Beckett and Genet, and concentrating
on *L'Innommable*. Beckett's novels form "une expérience sans issue" which
rejects the weak resources that allow this experience to go on, even though
from book to book it seeks ultimate purity. Whoever writes these books does
not do it for the pleasure of writing beautiful books, nor because compelled
by inspiration, nor because he has important things to say, nor because it is
his task. Writing becomes a means of escaping the movement that forces the
writer to write.

1015   KESTING, Marianne. *Das epische Theater: Zur Struktur des
modernen Dramas*. Stuttgart: W. Kohlammer, 1959. Beckett, pp.
131-135.

1016   MAILER, Norman. *Advertisements for Myself*. New York: G. P.
Putnam's Sons, 1959. "A Public Notice on *Waiting for Godot*,"
pp. 320-325; originally published under the title "Reflections on
Waiting for Godot," in **1367**. Reissued by Signet Books, New
York, 1960, Beckett pp. 289-294; and by André Deutsch, London,
1961, Beckett pp. 262-272.

Waiting for Godot is a play about impotence rather than an ode to it. Vladimir
and Estragon (Didi and Gogo) are male and female homosexuals. Consciously
or unconsciously Beckett is restating in this play the moral and sexual basis
of Christianity which was lost with Christ, that is to say that "one finds life
by kissing the feet of the poor, by giving oneself to the most debased corners
of the most degraded." A rather flippant and unconvincing argument.

1017   REXROTH, Kenneth. *Bird in the Bush: Obvious Essays*. New
York: New Directions, 1959. "Samuel Beckett and the Importance of Waiting," pp. 75-85; originally published in the *Nation*,
April 14, 1956 (Dec. 7, 1957, incorrectly given in the book's
acknowledgments) [see **1376**].

Beckett is significant because he has stated the final word to date on the
long indictment of industrial and commercial civilization which began with
Blake, Sade, Hölderlin, and continued with Céline and Miller.

1960

1018   FOWLIE, Wallace. *Dionysus in Paris: A Guide to Contemporary
French Theatre*. New York: Meridian Books, 1960. "Beckett,"
pp. 210-217, and *passim*. Reissued by Victor Gollancz, London,
1960 [see **1490**].

A somewhat superficial discussion of *En attendant Godot* and *Fin de partie*.
The utter simplicity of *Godot* places it in the classical tradition of French
theater. "Its close adherence to the three unities is a clue to the play's
dramaturgy." In Beckett's art the elements of time and of reason are rejected

1960

1018

so that the playwright will be free to exploit the impotency of man. *Godot* is interpreted in the light of religious symbols.

1019 GASSNER, John. *Theatre at the Crossroads: Plays and Playwrights of the Mid-Century American Stage.* New York: Holt, Rinehart and Winston, 1960. "Beckett: *Waiting for Godot,*" pp. 252-256; "Beckett's *Endgame* and Symbolism," pp. 256-261 [see **2074**].

All the "tohu and bohu" about the ambiguity and profoundity of *Godot* must be kept in its proper perspective. A plea should be made for the truth about this "beautiful, symbolist play": that is, that there is "nothing painfully or exhilaratingly ambiguous about it."

1020 LUMLEY, Frederick. *Trends in Twentieth-Century Drama: A Survey since Ibsen and Shaw.* Rev. ed. Fair Lawn, N.J.: Essential Books, 1960. Beckett, pp. 5, 137, 179; "School for Pessimism: Samuel Beckett and Eugène Ionesco," pp. 141-146.

Contemporary pessimism is a result of the political situation in Europe, reinforced by the consequences of the peace of World War II. Samuel Beckett's theater unites all the moods of the time, the existentialist refusal, the search for and despair of religious salvation, and the blinding and merciless accusation of farce. Ionesco is entirely unlike Beckett, but together they may be said to be the exponent of antitheater.

1021 MAYOUX, Jean-Jacques. *Vivants piliers: Le Roman anglo-saxon et les symboles.* Paris: Julliard, 1960. "Samuel Beckett et l'univers parodique," pp. 271-291. This chapter, trans. Barbara Bray, appears under the title "Samuel Beckett and Universal Parody" in **711**; see also **716, 1560,** and **2466**.

One of the best introductions to Beckett's world, haunted by guilt and the fear of mysterious tyrants, the horror of the flesh and the anguish of identity. Links Beckett firmly with Ireland and Swift.

1022 PINGAUD, Bernard, ed. *Ecrivains d'aujourd'hui, 1940-1960: Dictionnaire anthologique et critique.* Paris: Grasset, 1960. "Samuel Beckett," by Robert Abirached, pp. 93-98; short extracts from *Molloy* and *L'Innommable,* pp. 93-100 [see **257.001, 260.03,** respectively]; Beckett, *passim* (photo of Beckett as frontispiece).

Useful reference volume with general information about the author and his essential ideas.

1023 ZELTNER-NEUKOMM, Gerda. *Das Wagnis des französischen Gegenwartsromans: die neue Welterfahrung in der Literatur.* Hamburg: Rowohlt, 1960. "Die lyrische Burleske," pp. 139-152.

1961

1024 ADORNO, Theodor W. *Noten zur Literatur, II.* Frankfort on the Main: Suhrkamp, 1961. "Versuch, das Endspiel zu verstehen," pp. 188-236 (about *Endgame*).

1025 ESSLIN, Martin. *The Theatre of the Absurd.* Garden City, N.Y.: Doubleday, 1961. "Samuel Beckett: The Search for the Self,"

1961

1025   pp. 1-46; Beckett, *passim*. Reprinted in London: Eyre and Spottis-
             woode, 1962, pp. 22-64 and *passim;* trans. into French as *Le
             Théâtre de l'absurde* (Paris: Buchet-Chastel, 1963); trans. into
             German as *Das Theater des Absurden* (Frankfort on the Main:
             Athenaeum, 1964) (contains a list of German translations of
             Beckett's works). [See also **1544**.]

The most thorough study on contemporary theater. Rich in information about
Beckett as a playwright and about the making of his plays. Probing discussions
of *Waiting for Godot* and *Endgame*. Situates Beckett in the center of the
Theater of the Absurd. [See **2554**, **2564**, and **2632** for reviews of this book.]

1026   GREGORY, Horace. *The Dying Gladiators and Other Essays*. New
             York: Grove Press; London: Evergreen Books, 1961. "The Dying
             Gladiators of Samuel Beckett," pp. 165-176; reprinted from **1362**.

Beckett is discussed essentially as a poet, and even his "prose comes from the
same imaginative fount that his early poems do." One should avoid, therefore,
reading immediate "social consciousness" into Beckett's writings; his concerns
are with the conflicts of flesh and spirit, of mind and soul.

1027   GUICHARNAUD, Jacques, in collaboration with June BECKEL-
             MAN. *Modern French Theatre from Giraudoux to Beckett*. New
             Haven: Yale University Press, 1961. "Existence on Stage: Samuel
             Beckett," pp. 193-220; Beckett, *passim;* reprinted in **1071**.

Undoubtedly one of the most perceptive and exhaustive analyses of *Waiting
for Godot*. Beckett's other plays are also discussed. "In Beckett's theatre,
man is again put face to face with himself. After the successive demystifica-
tions represented by the works of post-war playwrights, Beckett has tried the
supreme demystification. . . . His works cannot be called existentialist, although
they can be explained through the use of existentialist categories. His is a
theatre of existence which, in itself, is outside any one school of thought."

1028   HEPPENSTALL, Rayner. *The Fourfold Tradition*. London: Barrie
             and Rockcliff; Norfolk: New Directions, 1961. Beckett, pp. 254-
             265 and *passim*. [See also **3082**.]

Interesting discussion of Beckett's bilingualism, *Proust*, and so on, with a biographical summary of Beckett based on the "Profile" published in *The Observer*, Nov. 9, 1958.

1029   MONNIER, Adrienne. *Dernières gazettes et écrits divers*. Paris:
             Mercure de France, 1961. Beckett, pp. 15-20 [see **3063**].

Comments on *En attendant Godot,* leading to recollections of Beckett in Joyce's
circle in the thirties, with useful details on the translation of *Anna Livia Plurabelle*.

1030   TYNAN, Kenneth. *Curtains*. London: Longmans; New York:
             Atheneum, 1961. Selections from drama criticism and related
             writings. "*Waiting for Godot,*" pp. 101-103; "*Krapp's Last Tape
             and Endgame,*" pp. 225-228; "*Godot,*" p. 272; "*Fin de partie
             and Acte sans paroles,*" pp. 401-403; Beckett, *passim*. Selections
             published under the title *Tynan on Theatre* (Harmondsworth:

1961

1030   Penguin Books, 1964) ; *"Waiting for Godot,"* pp. 36-38; *"Krapp's Last Tape* and *Endgame,"* pp. 79-82; Beckett, *passim.*

Tynan, the leading British theater critic, has not always been fair to Beckett (or the avant-garde theater), as is shown in the parody he wrote of *Krapp's Last Tape* and *Endgame,* but he is always incisive and worth reading [see **2552** for a review of this book].

1031   ZAMORA, Juan Guerrero. *Historia del Theatro Contemporáneo.* Barcelona: Juan Flors, 1961. 3 vols. "Samuel Beckett," I, 281-299 and *passim;* II, III, *passim.*

En attendant Godot, Fin de partie, and *Tous ceux qui tombent* are discussed in detail in Vol. I. Also gives information about the Spanish version and presentation of *Godot.*

1962

1032   ALBÉRÈS, René Marill. *Histoire du roman moderne.* Paris: Albin-Michel, 1962. Beckett, pp. 372-374.

Compares the fiction of Maurice Blanchot with that of Beckett. Blanchot chooses deliberately "l'antilogique" as does Beckett for whom "le conte noir et illogique prend presque déjà une intention symbolique."

1033   BLOCK, Haskell M., and Robert G. SHEDD, eds. *Masters of Modern Drama.* New York: Random House, 1962. *Endgame* (in its entirety), pp. 1104-1117 [see **376.03**]; an introductory essay, "Samuel Beckett," pp. 1102-1103, double col.; and *passim* allusions to Beckett in "General Introduction," pp. 3-9.

The concise essay on Beckett written by the editors serves as an introduction to *Endgame* but also offers a very well-informed discussion of Beckett's theater as a whole. Although Beckett in his probing of existential mysteries finds "no evidence of systems operating in the universe, all his plays are constructed according to a system of antitheses in which either/or dichotomies are transformed into both/and unities."

1034   BOISDEFFRE, Pierre de, ed. *Dictionnaire de littérature contemporaine.* Paris: Éditions Universitaires, 1962; 2d ed., 1963. "Samuel Beckett," pp. 180-186 (section signed P. B.).

A useful volume with dictionary-style entries summarizing French critical attitudes toward Beckett, but not immune from the superficiality inherent in this form of writing.

1035   ――――. *Où va le roman?* Paris: Del Duca, 1962. "Samuel Beckett et la fin de la littérature," pp. 269-280; Beckett, pp. 285-293. [See **1586**.]

A negative approach to the new novel in France, but not without admiration for Beckett's originality. The author seems to feel that when a literary genre touches perfection, it also approaches its own death. The means and techniques of such a genre limit rather than facilitate the possibilities of renewal.

1036   BROWN, John Russell, and Bernard HARRIS, eds. *Contemporary Theatre.* London: Edward Arnold, 1962. Beckett, pp. 127-136, 155-163, 180-182, and *passim.*

1962

1036

In this collection of essays Beckett is mentioned throughout, but is discussed in more detail by R. D. Smith in his essay "Back to the Text" (pp. 117-138), alongside Simpson, Whiting, Pinter, Ionesco, and Chekhov. H. A. Smith in his essay "Dipsychus among the Shadows" (pp. 139-163) also devotes interesting pages to Beckett and particularly to *Godot* as he considers the shaping influence of romantic and existentialist ideas on contemporary theater.

1037   CRUICKSHANK, John, ed. *The Novelist as Philosopher: Studies in French Fiction 1935-1960*. London: Oxford University Press, 1962. "Samuel Beckett," by Martin Esslin, pp. 128-146; Beckett, *passim*.

Esslin's essay is a penetrating overall discussion of Beckett's fiction full of insights into the evolution of the works. It emphasizes that Beckett's literary production is "entirely *sui generis,* unclassifiable, disturbing, funny, cruel, and inspiring." Beckett can take his place next to Kafka and Joyce as one of the most profound and most significant novelists of our time. [See **2576**, **2618**, and **2630** for reviews of this book.]

1038   GASCOIGNE, Bamber. *Twentieth-Century Drama*. London: Hutchinson, 1962; 2d ed., 1963. Beckett, pp. 51-52, 54, 71, 80-81, 86-87, 184-188, 206-207.

A general reader's introduction to the whole field of twentieth-century drama, with reliable and appreciative comments on Beckett.

1039   GIRARD, Marcel. *Guide illustré de la littérature française moderne de 1918 à nos jours*. Rev. ed. Paris: Pierre Seghers, 1962. Beckett, pp. 145, 271-272, 295.

A useful though limited guide to twentieth-century French authors who are presented in two groups: "La génération de 1920" and "La génération de 1940." One is not certain, however, in which of these two categories Beckett falls.

1040   GROSSVOGEL, David I. *Four Playwrights and a Postscript: Brecht, Ionesco, Beckett, Genet*. Ithaca, N.Y.: Cornell University Press, 1962. "Samuel Beckett: The Difficulty of Dying," pp. 85-131; see also pp. xi-xviii, 177-179, and *passim*. Reissued as a paperback under the title *The Blasphemers: The Theater of Brecht, Ionesco, Beckett, Genet* (Ithaca: Cornell University Press, 1965).

A serious analysis of Beckett's major plays, somewhat marred by a heavy academic style. "If *Godot* represents the pastoral stage of Beckett's dramatic imagery, *Endgame* might be termed his drawing-room play." After *Godot*— "equipoise on the brink of that beyond which there is no longer drama"— Beckett could move neither back nor forward, "short of turning his stage people into indifferent objects." Interesting pages are also devoted to *Krapp's Last Tape, Embers,* and *All That Fall,* plays often neglected by critics.

1041   KARL, Frederick R. *The Contemporary English Novel*. New York: Farrar, Straus and Cudahy, 1962. Beckett, pp. 3, 6, 8, 9, 10, 12, 13, 18, 19-39, 111, 150, 184, 185, 190, 212; "Waiting for Beckett: Quest and Re-Quest," pp. 19-39, was reprinted from **1614**. Re-

1962

1041   issued in England under the title *A Reader's Guide to the Con-
             temporary English Novel* (London: Thames and Hudson, 1963)
             [see **1059**].
Beckett's vision springs from a world of "post-war hopelessness," and of
"cosmic despair."

1042   KENNER, Hugh. *Flaubert, Joyce and Beckett: The Stoic Comedians.*
             Boston: Beacon Press, 1962; London: W. H. Allen, 1964. "Sam-
             uel Beckett: Comedian of the Impasse," pp. 67-107.
With his usual brilliance of style and pointed observations, Kenner writes a
witty essay on the certainty, or the "uncertainty," of how Beckett writes his
books. "Clearly we are at the farthest possible remove from the omniscient
narrator who has so much of our fiction in his trust." Beckett takes up the
novel at the point to which James Joyce had brought it: the route to an
impasse. Yet, he can discard piece after piece and still hold our attention
with each new book. That is why the dead end of Beckett is so fecund a
beginning.

1043   KERMODE, Frank. *Puzzles and Epiphanies: Essays and Reviews,
             1958-1961.* Introduction by William Phillips. New York: Chil-
             mark Press; London: Routledge and Kegan Paul, 1962. "Beckett,
             Snow, and Pure Poverty," pp. 155-163; reprinted from **1559**.
In this comparison with Snow, who is "a great deal easier and more pleasant
to read" than Beckett, the Irish expatriate seems to be an old-fashioned writer
who certainly belonged to the primitivist and decadent avant-garde of 1932.
Beckett writes in a "spirit of integral pessimism," though occasionally his
work acquires a visionary quality. [See **2582** and **2621** for reviews of this book.]

1044   KOTT, Jan. *Shakespeare notre contemporain.* Trans. from the
             Polish by Anna Posner. Paris: Julliard, 1962. "Le *Roi Lear,*
             autrement dit *Fin de partie,*" pp. 115-158; this essay also appeared
             in **1687**. Trans. into English by Boleslaw Taborski under the title
             Shakespeare Our Contemporary, with a preface by Peter Brook
             (London: Methuen; New York: Doubleday, 1964). "*King Lear
             or Endgame,*" pp. 101-137; also appeared in English in **1802**.
Kott points out the contemporaneity of *King Lear* in the light of modern dramatic philosophy. He shows the relationship of the medieval morality play
with Shakespeare and the contemporary theater and illustrates how misunderstood the first two were by romantic and naturalist audiences. Comparing
action and dialogue in *Lear* with *Endgame, Godot,* and *Act Without Words,*
he points out that, in fact, Beckett simply repeats after Shakespeare: ". . . we
came crying hither. | When we are born, we cry that we are come. | To this
great stage of fools." Thus, he shows how the grotesque is more cruel than
tragedy.

1045   LE SAGE, Laurent. *The French New Novel: An Introduction and
             a Sampler.* University Park, Pa.: Pennsylvania State University
             Press, 1962. "Samuel Beckett," with excerpts from *Molloy* and
             Malone Dies, pp. 46-57; see also "Introduction to the New Novel,"
             pp. 1-44; Beckett, *passim.*

1962

1045

The introduction traces the history of the so-called "école du nouveau roman," and tries to define the school as a whole, but it appears that Beckett does not really fit in this movement. "As a novelist, Beckett stands as a living link between the young French authors and the foreign master James Joyce, whom they all revere. Beckett's ghostly and grisly fictions . . . anticipate the sort of writing the new generation advocates."

1046   LEWIS, Allan. *The Contemporary Theatre: The Significant Play-wrights of Our Time.* New York: Crown, 1962. Beckett, pp. 6, 144, 259, 260, 266-267, 270, 276, 277; "The Theatre of the 'Absurd'—Beckett, Ionesco, Genêt [*sic*]," pp. 259-281 (on *Waiting for Godot,* pp. 261-265).

The passage devoted to *Godot* is not an analysis of the play, but a mere synopsis of little critical value. Mr. Lewis feels that neither Beckett nor Ionesco can sustain a full-length drama. *Endgame* and even *Godot* grow wearisome, for "doubt and emptiness are not drama, but an exercise in acted symbols."

1047   MERCIER, Vivian. *The Irish Comic Tradition.* London: Oxford University Press, 1962. Beckett, pp. 74-77 and *passim.*

Like Mercier's seminal article on "Samuel Beckett and the Sheela-na-gig" [see **1622**], this book links Beckett to the great tradition of the comic grotesque in Irish and Anglo-Irish literature, and especially to its most famous representative, Swift.

1048   PRONKO, Leonard C. *Avant-Garde: The Experimental Theater in France.* Berkeley and Los Angeles: University of California Press; London: Cambridge University Press, 1962. "Samuel Beckett," pp. 22-58 and *passim.* Trans. into French by Marie-Jeanne Lefèvre under the title *Théâtre d'avant-garde: Beckett, Ionesco et le théâtre expérimental en France* (Paris: Éditions Denoël, 1963).

The chapter on Beckett, like the rest of the book, is written as a general introduction for the layman, and therefore without any pretensions of profundity. The interpretations of the plays, however, are intelligent and useful for the student who is curious to discover the avant-garde theater. [See **2679**, **2716**, and **2769** for reviews of this book.]

1049   SIMPSON, Alan. *Beckett and Behan, and a Theatre in Dublin.* London: Routledge and Kegan Paul, 1962. "Samuel Beckett," pp. 62-97; "Producing Beckett and Behan," pp. 98-137; Beckett, *passim.* [See **3064**.]

Mr. Simpson, founder of the Pike Theatre in Dublin, describes his personal relationship with Beckett and Behan and how he produced the first Irish performances of *The Quare Fellow* and *Waiting for Godot.* This is not a complete and accurate pair of biographies, but as a book of reminiscences it offers interesting insights into the lives of the two writers who are linked together not only because they are both Irish, but above all because they

1962
1049
perpetuate in their work the rebellion of all great Irish writers against the
stifling Puritanism of Ireland.
1050 STYAN, J. L. *The Dark Comedy: The Development of Modern
Comic Tragedy.* London: Cambridge University Press, 1962.
"Beckett, Ionesco and Others," pp. 226-238; Beckett, *passim.*
"The work of the Irishman Samuel Beckett and the Rumanian Eugène Ionesco
for the French theatre lies in direct line from that of Pirandello and Anouilh."
Both authors are in search of a new language, "a new *poésie de théâtre,*"
which will express the striking ambivalences of feeling of the postwar years.
1051 SUTHERLAND, William O. S., ed. *Six Contemporary Novels: Six
Introductory Essays in Modern Fiction.* Austin, Texas: Humanities Research Center, University of Texas Department of English,
1962. "Quest for Meaninglessness: The Boundless Poverty of
Molloy," by David Hayman, pp. 90-112. A revised version of
this essay trans. into French by Paul Rozenberg under the title
"Molloy à la recherche de l'absurde" appears in **902.**
Beckett is indebted to both Dante and Freud for the conception and the
construction of his trilogy (*Molloy* is the Inferno, *Malone Dies,* the Purgatory,
The Unnamable, the Paradise) and for the implications of psychoanalysis
(Molloy and his mother are the libido/id, Moran is the superego, Jacques
Moran, Jr., is the ego).
1052 SYPHER, Wylie. *Loss of the Self in Modern Literature and Art.*
New York: Random House, 1962. "The Anonymous Self: A
Defensive Humanism," pp. 147-165; Beckett, *passim.*
The "romantic-liberal" tradition of the nineteenth century created an idea
of the self which contemporary man has not only rejected but destroyed.
Samuel Beckett's work exemplifies the artist's quest to "extinguish the self,"
in the tradition of *Le Neveu de Rameau,* Dostoevski, Gide, Kafka, and in the
"romantic nihilism" of Nietzsche. The Beckett hero has an existence, but no
identity.
1053 WILSON, Colin. *The Strength to Dream: Literature and the Imagination.* London: Victor Gollancz; Boston: Houghton Mifflin,
1962. Beckett, pp. 87-90 and *passim.*
A predictably superficial dismissal of Beckett's work based on the context of
chap. 3 entitled "The Implications of Total Pessimism." Wilson claims that
Beckett has gone too far in his representation of "human boredom and misery."
1054 WOLF, Daniel, and Edwin FANCHER, eds. *The Village Voice
Reader: A Mixed Bag from the Greenwich Village Newspaper.*
Garden City, N.Y.: Doubleday, 1962; reprinted by Grove Press,
New York, 1963. Beckett, pp. 67-84, 180-186 (in the Doubleday
ed.); pp. 57-74, 163 169 (in the Grove Press ed.). Collection of
reviews, essays, and letters from the *Village Voice* which contains:
Pp. 67-84 (Doubleday), in section entitled "Drama Sequence I,"
a group of pieces on *Waiting for Godot:*

1962

1054   FERTIG, Howard. *"Waiting for Godot,"* pp. 67-69 [see **2072**].
          A review of the published text.

          TALLMER, Jerry. "Godot on Broadway," pp. 69-72 [see **2111**].
          A review of the original Broadway production.

          BERGHOF, Herbert. "Letters to the Editor," pp. 72-73. A letter
          from *Godot's* director attacking Tallmer's review.

          ROSSET, Barney. "A Note," p. 73. A letter from the editor of
          Grove Press, praising Tallmer's review.

          TALLMER, Jerry. *"Godot:* Still Waiting," pp. 73-76 [see **2225**].
          A review article attacking Brooks Atkinson's review [see **2056**].

          MAILER, Norman. "The Hip and the Square," pp. 76-77 [see
          1367]. A discussion of *Godot* by Mailer who states that even
          though he has not seen or read the play the mere title sug-
          gests to him a play about impotence.

          SCOTT, Bernard E. "The Press of Freedom: Waiting for God,"
          pp. 79-84. An essay on the theme of waiting inspired by
          Godot.

          ANONYMOUS. "Godot, Go Home," p. 84. A graffito observed
          by a *Village Voice* correspondent in the New York subway.

          Pp. 180-186 (Doubleday), in section entitled "Drama Sequence
          II," pieces on *Endgame:*

          TALLMER, Jerry. "Beckett's *Endgame,"* pp. 180-182 [see **2314**].
          A review of the New York production of the play.

          "Beckett's Letters on *Endgame,"* pp. 182-186 [see **36.1**]. Extracts
          from Beckett's correspondence with director Alan Schneider
          which retrace in the form of a chronicle "the development of
          Endgame from its origins 'in the Marne mud' to its realization
          on Commerce Street [at the Cherry Lane Theater] and else-
          where"; the first of the fourteen letters is dated Dec. 27, 1955,
          and the last, March 4, 1958.

1963

1055   ABEL, Lionel. *Metatheater: A New View of Dramatic Form.* New
          York: Hill and Wang, 1963. "Beckett and Metatheater," pp. 83-
          85; "Samuel Beckett and James Joyce in *Endgame,"* pp. 134-
          140; see also "The Theater and the 'Absurd,' " pp. 140-146. The
          chapter "Samuel Beckett and James Joyce in *Endgame"* was
          originally published under the title "Joyce the Father, Beckett
          the Son" in **1476**.

Metatheater considers the world a stage and life a dream. Beckett's plays
conform to the kind of dramatic form Mr. Abel designates as metatheater
because "what makes them so special is that life in these plays has been
theatricalized, not by any attitudes taken by the characters, not by any tricks
of dramaturgy, and not by the author's intent to demonstrate any proposition
about the world, but by the mere passage of time, that drastic fact of ordinary
life."

1963

1056   ARMSTRONG, William A., ed. *Experimental Drama*. London: G. Bell and Sons, 1963. "Godot and His Children: The Theater of Samuel Beckett and Harold Pinter," by Martin Esslin, pp. 128-146.

Esslin argues that *Waiting for Godot* is best read as a "poetic image" and not as a story: "this type of play is essentially lyrical." He also examines most of Beckett's plays and some by Pinter, who has been influenced by Beckett.

1057   CORVIN, Michel. *Le Théâtre nouveau en France*. Paris: Presses Universitaires de France, 1963. Beckett, pp. 67-72 and *passim*.

A brief but excellent survey of the "new theatre," stressing technical aspects (decor and direction) usually neglected in other surveys. The section on Beckett emphasizes circus and music-hall techniques, and the importance of language.

1058   GLICKSBERG, Charles I. *The Self in Modern Literature*. University Park, Pa.: Pennsylvania State University Press, 1963. "*Waiting for Godot* and *Endgame*," pp. 117-121; "The Lost Self in Beckett's Fiction," pp. 121-133; Beckett, *passim*. The section on Beckett's fiction is reprinted from an earlier article entitled "Samuel Beckett's World of Fiction," in **1672**.

A superficial discussion of Beckett's plays and fiction. *Endgame,* like *Waiting for Godot,* "communicates Beckett's metaphysical vision of despair, his version of the hopelessness of the human condition. . . . Beckett's fiction draws the portrait of the modern nihilistic self, alienated, solipsistically inarticulate, drowned in existential absurdity and despair. . . ."

1059   KARL, Frederick R. *A Reader's Guide to the Contemporary English Novel*. London: Thames and Hudson, 1963. [Same as **1041**.]

1060   NADEAU, Maurice. *Le Roman français depuis la guerre*. Paris: Gallimard, 1963. "Samuel Beckett," pp. 155-159; this section on Beckett also published in **901**, under the title "Le Chemin de la parole au silence."

In this survey of French novelists since World War II, Beckett's experimentation in the novel "marque l'aboutissement du procès fait à la littérature, au langage, à la parole." All that is left for Beckett is to stop writing or to repeat himself.

1061   PINGAUD, Bernard. *Molloy* and *L'Expulsé*. Paris: Union générale d'Éditions, 1963. "Beckett le précurseur," pp. 287-311 [see **257.2**].
        The essay by Pingaud also appeared in **1756**, under the title "*Molloy* douze ans après."
        This edition of *Molloy* and *L'Expulsé* also contains "Le Dossier de Presse de *Molloy*," as follows:
        1. NADEAU, Maurice. "En avant vers nulle part," pp. 257-263. Reprinted from **1954**.
        2. BLANZAT, Jean. "Un livre-événement," pp. 264-265. Reprinted from **1938**.
        3. PICON, Gaëtan. "L'Impossible néant," pp. 266-270. Reprinted from **1955**.

1963

1061   4. GADENNE, Paul. "Genet dépassé?" pp. 271-274. Reprinted
            from **1949**.
         5. KANTERS, Robert. "Un chef-d'œuvre préfabriqué," pp. 275-
            277. Reprinted from **1950**.
         6. ASTRE, G. Albert. "L'Humanisme de la pourriture," pp. 279-
            281. Reprinted from **1936**.
         7. POUILLON, Jean. "Une morale de la conscience absolue,"
            pp. 283-286. Reprinted from **1303**.

1062   ROBBE-GRILLET, Alain. *Pour un nouveau roman.* Paris: Éditions
         de Minuit, 1963. "Samuel Beckett ou la présence sur la scène,"
         pp. 95-107; Beckett, *passim*. [See also **1632**.] Reprinted by Galli-
         mard, Paris, 1964. [For an English version of this essay see **711**.]

A pertinent discussion of *En attendant Godot* and *Fin de partie* in which
Robbe-Grillet emphasizes the continuity of certain fundamental aspects of
Beckett's theater and fiction. Robbe-Grillet also finds some parallels between
his own literary doctrine which tends toward "la non-signification," and that
of Beckett.

1063   RUSSELL, L., ed. *Encore: The Sunday Times Book.* London:
         Michael Joseph, 1963. "Godot and After," by Harold Hobson,
         pp. 315-318.

In this review written in 1955 [see **2029** and **2030**], Hobson states that Beckett's
meaning in *Godot* is based on the assumption that humanity (which the characters represent) "dawdles . . . its life away . . . waiting for some divine
event" that never comes.

1064   SEIPEL, Hildegard. *Untersuchungen zum experimentellen Theater
         von Beckett und Ionesco.* Bonn: Romanisches Seminar der Uni-
         versität Bonn, 1963. Beckett, pp. 178-254, 272-279, and Bibli-
         ography, pp. 289-291.

1065   SHANK, Theodore J., ed. *A Digest of 500 Plays.* New York: Crowell-
         Collier Press; London: Collier-Macmillan, 1963. Beckett, pp. 201-
         203.

Plot outlines of *Waiting for Godot, Endgame,* and *Happy Days* are furnished
with useful information for potential directors about characters, sets, and cos-
tumes. Also gives amount of royalty.

1066   WELLERSHOFF, Dieter. *Der Gleichgültige: Versuche über Hem-
         ingway, Camus, Benn und Beckett.* Cologne and Berlin: Keipen-
         heuer and Witsch, 1963. Beckett, pp. 97-127. [For an English
         translation of the essay on Beckett see **711**.]

In Beckett's novels literature becomes "an infinite circle in which the desperate
determination to come to an end is identical with the determination not to
give up." The strength of Beckett's work is in the way the paradox is kept
up, until ultimately one can see that Beckett himself is caught up in the
"hopeless demonstration." A very interesting discussion of Beckett's fiction
which emphasizes the theme of failure.

1963

1067 WEST, Paul. *The Modern Novel.* London: Hutchinson University Library, 1963 (rev. ed., 1965). 2 vols. Beckett, I, 197-200 and *passim;* II, *passim.*

Vol. I of this study is a survey of the modern novel in France and England (Vol. II deals with the United States and other countries). Beckett is obsessed with the "flux of identity" and with the difference between "man's romantic dreams and the very little that life needs in order to sustain itself."

1964

1068 BLAU, Herbert. *The Impossible Theater: A Manifesto.* New York: Macmillan; London: Collier-Macmillan, 1964. Beckett, pp. 228-251, in "Counterforce II: Notes from the Underground," and *passim.*

While relating how he directed *Waiting for Godot* and *Endgame* as director of the San Francisco Actors' Workshop, Blau makes some revealing statements about Beckett's theater. "Beckett begins where Chekhov leaves off." He did not invent despair, neither does he rest in it. Salvation is a "fifty-fifty chance" in his theater.

1069 FREEDMAN, Morris, ed. *Essays in the Modern Drama.* Boston: D. C. Heath, 1964. Beckett, *passim.* Beckett is discussed in several of the essays reprinted in this collection. See particularly:

POPKIN, Henry. "Williams, Osborne or Beckett," pp. 235-242. Reprinted from **1567.**

ESSLIN, Martin. "The Theatre of the Absurd," pp. 320-334. Reprinted from **1544.**

HOOKER, Ward. "Irony and Absurdity in the Avant-Garde Theatre," pp. 335-348. Reprinted from **1555.**

BROWN, John Russell. "Mr. Pinter's Shakespeare," pp. 352-366. Reprinted from **1711.**

1070 HARWARD, T. B., ed. *European Patterns.* Dublin: Dolmen Press, 1964. Contains a review of *Krapp's Last Tape* by Alec Reid, pp. 38-43; also a biographical note on Samuel Beckett, p. 92.

A good, sympathetic, Irishman's view of *Krapp's Last Tape.*

1071 KOSTELANETZ, Richard, ed. *On Contemporary Literature: An Anthology of Critical Essays on the Major Movements and Writers of Contemporary Literature.* New York: Avon Books, 1964.

Four essays on Samuel Beckett:

REXROTH, Kenneth. "The Point is Irrelevance," pp. 244-248. Reprinted and abridged from **1017**; see also **1376.**

BLANCHOT, Maurice. "Where Now? Who Now?" pp. 249-254. Reprinted and abridged from **1481.**

FEDERMAN, Raymond. "Beckett and the Fiction of Mud," pp. 255-261. A revised and extended version appears in **1841.**

GUICHARNAUD, Jacques. "Existence on Stage," pp. 262-285. Reprinted from **1027.**

1964

1071   KOSTELANETZ, Richard. "Contemporary Literature," (intro-
            duction), pp. xv-xxvii (Beckett, *passim*).

1072   PEYRE, Henri. *Contemporary French Literature: A Critical An-
            thology.* New York: Evanston, and London: Harper and Row,
            1964. Samuel Beckett, pp. 316-336. Contains a short introduc-
            tory essay (pp. 316-323), "Biographical Note" (pp. 319-320),
            and excerpts from *En attendant Godot* (pp. 323-330) and from
            Fin de partie (pp. 330-336) [see **259.011, 265.32**].
Offers a useful summary of Beckett's career for undergraduates. Lists five
reasons why Beckett's plays may be labeled "theater of the absurd" or "antitheater."

1073   PRITCHETT, V. S. *The Living Novel and Later Appreciations.*
            New York: Random House, 1964. "An Irish Oblomov," pp.
            315-320. Reprinted from **1568**. Essay also appears in *The Work-
            ing Novelist* (London: Chatto and Windus, 1965), pp. 25-29.
At a time when the emphasis is on youth and achievement, Beckett, "the
grammarian of solitude," writes about old age, loneliness, and decrepitude.
In so doing, he arouses "our deepest repressed guilt and fears," and his
"verbose books are like long, ironical, stinging footnotes in small print to
some theme not formulated."

1074   SURER, Paul. *Le Théâtre français contemporain.* Paris: Société
            d'Édition d'Enseignement Supérieur, 1964. "Samuel Beckett," pp.
            435-449 and *passim* (photograph of Beckett, p. 435).
A survey of Beckett's plays which emphasizes the unconventional dramatic
construction and the dehumanization of the characters. Beckett's originality
resides in his subtle sense of ambiguity.

1075   WEISS, Samuel I., ed. *Drama in the Modern World: Plays and
            Essays.* Boston: D. C. Heath, 1964. Contains *All That Fall* [see
            34.21] with introductory note (pp. 487-502), and two short essays:
            WALKER, Roy. "Shagreen Shamrock," pp. 503-504. Reprinted
            from **1420**.
            DRIVER, Tom F. "Beckett by the Madeleine," pp. 505-508.
            Reprinted from **1599**.

1076   WELLWARTH, George E. *The Theater of Protest and Paradox:
            Developments in the Avant-Garde Drama.* New York: New York
            University Press, 1964; London: MacGibbon and Kee, 1965.
            "Samuel Beckett: Life in the Void," pp. 37-51 (reprinted from
            1644); Beckett, *passim;* "Selected Bibliography," pp. 298-299.
A negative judgment of Beckett who "decries existence on earth, makes disgust and loathing the earmarks of man's condition, and calls all attempts at
knowledge, reason, faith, love, and even power illusory and futile." There
are no "hidden symbolic implications" in Beckett's works. He is simply what
he appears to be: a "stark, uncompromising pessimist" overwhelmed by the
deterministic philosophy akin to Conrad's. [See **2863** for a review of this book.]

1965

1077   CHIARI, Joseph. *Landmarks of Contemporary Drama*. London:
Herbert Jenkins, 1965. Beckett, pp. 68-80 and *passim*.
Mostly a discussion of *Waiting for Godot*. Beckett's other plays merely repeat,
emphasize, and continue what is stated in *Godot:* the condition of absurdity.
The fundamental difference, however, between the concept of the absurd
of Ionesco and company and that of Beckett (which is also that of Pascal
and Kierkegaard) is that the world of Beckett is absurd and meaningless only
because of the absence of Godot. Ionesco's world is "just plain incoherent."
1078   COHN, Ruby, and Lily PARKER, eds. *Monologues de Minuit*.
New York: Macmillan, 1965. Contains *La Dernière Bande* [see
147.5] with an introductory essay (pp. 11-26), and *Textes pour
rien IV, VIII, XIII* (pp. 117-132) [see **263.04**]; see also "Introduction" pp. 1-9: Beckett, *passim*.
A collection of fiction and drama pieces selected from publications of Les
Éditions de Minuit. Useful reader for undergraduates. The short introductory
essays in English furnish concise interpretations of the Beckett pieces.
1079   GIRODIAS, Maurice. *The Olympia Reader: Selections from the
Traveller's Companion Series*. New York: Grove Press, 1965.
Contains a passage from *Watt* [see **32.05**], pp. 213-220; and
"Samuel Beckett," by Richard Seaver, pp. 220-225.
The piece by Richard Seaver relates how the editors of *Merlin* formed the
Olympia Press with Girodias and published as their first venture Beckett's
last English novel, *Watt*.
1080   MACNEICE, Louis. *Varieties of Parable*. London: Cambridge University Press, 1965. Beckett, pp. 4, 5, 13, 14, 16, 24, 26, 28,
60, 119-129, 140-143.
In this series of lectures (Clark Lectures delivered in Cambridge in the spring
of 1963) on the "Varieties of Parable," Beckett is discussed as an extreme
of parable writer.
1081   ROY, Claude. *L'Amour du théâtre*. Paris: Gallimard, 1965. "Sur
Samuel Beckett," pp. 158-165. [See **1824**.]
A praiseful discussion of Beckett who is considered one of the leading authors
of our time. Beckett's essay on Proust is one of the "chefs-d'œuvre de la prose
morale" which defines Beckett's own world.
1082   UPDIKE, John. *Assorted Prose*. New York: Alfred A. Knopf;
London: André Deutsch, 1965. "How How It Is Was," pp. 214-
218. Originally published in **2838**.
This piece on *How It Is* mockingly parodies the style of the novel.

1966

1083   CRONIN, Anthony. *A Question of Modernity*. London: Secker and
Warburg, 1966. "Molloy Becomes Unnamable," pp. 97-110.
An interesting chapter on Beckett whose work is seen as "a denial, a protest
against the temptation to falsify experience to which we are continually
subjected or subject ourselves, the assumption of extraneous and more pic-
turesque personality which are congenial in the human animal."

1966

1084   SERREAU, Geneviève. *Histoire du "Nouveau Théâtre."* Paris:
Gallimard, 1966. Beckett, pp. 83-116 and *passim.*

A sound, intelligent, and enthusiastic chronological study of Beckett's plays
by the wife of leading French director Jean-Marie Serreau. Mrs. Serreau was
connected with the first production of *En attendant Godot* at the Théâtre
Babylone and is secretary of *Les Lettres Nouvelles.* Her conclusion on Beckett
is that his entire work illustrates the Shakespearean dictum: "All the world's
a stage" with the corollary that the stage in turn is a world to itself.

9.

Selected Books
with Brief References to
Samuel Beckett

1941

1100 GORMAN, Herbert. *James Joyce: A Definite Biography*. London: John Lane; New York: Rinehart, 1941. Beckett, pp. 295, 346. [See **3056**.]

1945

1101 MacGREEVY, Thomas. *Jack B. Yeats: An Appreciation and an Interpretation*. Dublin: Victor Waddington Publications, 1945 (work written in 1938). Allusion to Beckett, pp. 14-15.

1946

1102 GUGGENHEIM, Marguerite. *Out of This Century: The Informal Memoirs of Peggy Guggenheim*. New York: Dial Press, 1946. Pp. 194-242 (Beckett, *passim*). Refers to Beckett as "Oblomov"; photograph of Beckett taken in 1938 f.p. 278. [See also **3057**.]

1947

1103 TINDALL, William York. *Forces in Modern British Literature, 1885-1946*. New York: Alfred A. Knopf, 1947. Allusion to *More Pricks Than Kicks* and *Murphy,* p. 296n; Beckett, pp. 339n, 350n. [See also *Forces in Modern British Literature, 1885-1956* (New York: Vintage Books, 1956), pp. 197n, 224n, 228n.]

1954

1104 MURDOCH, Iris. *Under the Net*. London: Chatto and Windus, 1954. Novel. Allusion to *Murphy,* p. 16.

1955

1105   PEYRE, Henri. *The Contemporary French Novel*. New York: Oxford University Press, 1955. Beckett, pp. 282, 303, 307-308.

1956

1106   FECHTER, Paul. *Das europäische Drama: Geist und Kultur im Spiegel des Theaters*. Mannheim: Bibliographisches Institut, 1956. 3 vols. Beckett, III, 395 f.

1107   GOTH, Maja. *Franz Kafka et les lettres françaises, 1928-1955*. Paris: José Corti, 1956. Beckett, pp. 120-122, 255.

1108   HAYMAN, David. *Joyce et Mallarmé*. Paris: Cahiers des Lettres Modernes, 1956. 2 vols. Beckett, I, 16n, 19, 53n, 71n, 125n, 159n.

1109   LUMLEY, Frederick, ed. *Theatre in Review*. Edinburgh: Richard Paterson 1956. Beckett, p. 13.

1110   MAGALANER, Marvin, and Richard M. KAIN. *James Joyce: The Man, the Work, the Reputation*. London: John Calder, 1957 (copyright 1956). Beckett, pp. 247, 262, 296, 341n.

1111   MELCHINGER, Siegfried. *Theater der Gegenwart*. Frankfort on the Main and Hamburg: Fischer-Bücherei, 1956. Beckett, pp. 129, 135, 202 f.

1112   SZONDI, Peter. *Theorie des modernen Dramas*. Frankfort on the Main: Suhrkamp, 1956. Beckett, p. 76.

1957

1113   BRÉE, Germaine, and Margaret GUITON. *An Age of Fiction: The French Novel from Gide to Camus*. New Brunswick, N.J.: Rutgers University Press, 1957. Beckett, pp. 236, 237, 240; see also rev. 2d ed. published under the title *The French Novel from Gide to Camus* (New York: Harcourt, Brace and World, 1962). Beckett, pp. 237-239.

1114   FOWLIE, Wallace. *A Guide to Contemporary French Literature from Valéry to Sartre*. New York: Meridian Books, 1957. Beckett, pp. 132, 225.

1115   GILBERT, Stuart. *Letters of James Joyce*. London: Faber and Faber, 1957. Beckett, pp. 280-281, 283; also allusion to Beckett's acrostic poem on Joyce's name, p. 323. [See **3058**.]

1116   HUTCHINS, Patricia. *James Joyce's World*. London: Methuen, 1957. Beckett, pp. 168-169, 207; facsimile of a lettercard from Beckett to Joyce, p. 169. [See **3059**.]

1117   MELCHINGER, Siegfried. *Drama zwischen Shaw und Brecht*. Bremen: Schünemann, 1957. Beckett, pp. 62, 164-165, 304, 306; see also rev. ed., 1961, pp. 191-192 and *passim*.

1118   WILSON, Colin. *Religion and the Rebel*. London: Victor Gollancz; Cambridge, Mass.: Riverside Press, 1957. Beckett, p. 50.

1958

1119 CHIARI, Joseph. *The Contemporary French Theatre: The Flight from Naturalism.* London: Rockliff; New York: Macmillan, 1958. P. 226 (on *Godot*).

1120 HENNECKE, Hans. *Kritik: Gesammelte Essays zur modernen Literatur.* Gütersloh: Bertelsmann, 1958. Beckett, p. 104.

1121 JACQUOT, Jean, ed. *Le Théâtre moderne: Hommes et tendances.* Paris: Centre National de la Recherche Scientifique, 1958. Beckett, pp. 44, 52-55, 85, 225, 233.

1122 LUKÁCS, Georg. *Wider den missverstandenen Realismus.* Hamburg: Claassen, 1958 (original title, *Die Gegenwartsbedeutung des kritischen Realismus*). Beckett, *passim.* Trans. into French by Maurice de Gandillac as *La Signification présente du réalisme critique* (Paris: Gallimard, 1960). Beckett, pp. 44, 56, 57, 84, 93, 99, 128, 129, 143, 145, 164. Trans. into English by John and Necke Manden as *The Meaning of Contemporary Realism* (London: Merlin Press, 1963). Beckett, pp. 26, 31-32, 66-67.

1123 MARCEL, Gabriel. *Théâtre et religion.* Lyon: Vitte, 1958. Beckett, pp. 51-52.

1124 QUENEAU, Raymond, ed. *Encyclopédie de la Pléiade; Histoire des littératures, III.* Paris: Gallimard, 1958. "Samuel Beckett," pp. 1358-1359.

1959

1125 ATHERTON, James S. *The Books at the Wake: A Study of Literary Allusions in James Joyce's 'Finnegans Wake.'* London: Faber and Faber, 1959. Beckett, pp. 15, 29, 49, 73, 191; Joyce and "Bethicket," p. 16. For "Bethicket," pun on Beckett's name, see *Finnegans Wake*, p. 112, ll. 5, 6. [See also 3060.]

1126 BALAKIAN, Anna. *Surrealism: The Road to the Absolute.* New York: Noonday Press, 1959. Beckett, pp. 195 f.

1127 CHARBONNIER, Georges. *Essai sur Antonin Artaud.* Paris: Pierre Seghers, 1959. Beckett, pp. 20, 171, 188, 198.

1128 ELLMANN, Richard. *James Joyce.* New York: Oxford University Press, 1959. Beckett, *passim* (see index). [See also 14 and 3061.] French trans. published by Gallimard, Paris, 1962.

1129 STEPHENS, Frances. *Theatre World Annual,* no. 10 (June 1, 1958- May 31, 1959). London: Barrie and Rockliff, 1959. *Endgame* and *Krapp's Last Tape,* p. 72; Beckett, pp. 14, 23, 25.

1960

1130 BRÉE, Germaine, ed. *Great French Short Stories.* Introduction by Germaine Brée. New York: Dell, 1960. Contains "Stories and Texts for Nothing, III" [see 381] (pp. 313-317), and "Samuel Beckett," a brief introductory note (p. 311).

1960

1131   COHEN, J. M., and M. J. COHEN, eds. *The Penguin Dictionary of Quotations.* Harmondsworth, Middlesex: Penguin Books, 1960. Contains a quote from *All That Fall* and one from *Waiting for Godot,* p. 26.

1132   GUGGENHEIM, Marguerite. *Confessions of an Art Addict.* London: André Deutsch; New York: Macmillan, 1960. Beckett, pp. 48-61 (*passim*). [See also **3062**.]

1133   HOGAN, Robert. *The Experiments of Sean O'Casey.* New York: St. Martin's Press, 1960. Beckett, pp. 9, 132, 179.

1134   KITCHIN, Laurence. *Mid-Century Drama.* London: Faber and Faber, 1960; see also 2d ed., 1962. Beckett, *passim.*

1135   KRAUSE, David. *Sean O'Casey: The Man and His Work.* London: MacGibbon and Kee, 1960. Beckett, pp. 51, 52, 212, 217, 218, 221.

1136   LAING, Ronald D. *The Divided Self: A Study of Sanity and Madness.* London: Tavistock Publications, 1960. Beckett, *passim.*

1137   LANGNER, Lawrence. *The Play's the Thing.* New York: G. P. Putnam's Sons, 1960. Beckett, p. 37.

1138   LEVIN, Harry. *James Joyce: A Critical Introduction.* Rev. and augmented ed. Norfolk, Conn.: New Directions, 1960. Beckett, p. 241.

1139   OLLES, Helmut. *Lexikon der Weltliteratur im 20. Jahrhundert.* Vol. I. Freiburg: Herder, 1960. Beckett, pp. 136-138 [see **1566**].

1140   PICON, Gaëtan. *Panorama de la nouvelle littérature française.* Rev. ed. Paris: Gallimard, 1960. Samuel Beckett, pp. 157-159, 164, 246, 247, 295, 301.

1141   ROWE, Kenneth T. *A Theater in Your Head.* New York: Funk and Wagnalls, 1960. Beckett, pp. 93, 144, 217, 242-243, 438.

1142   STYAN, J. L. *The Elements of Drama.* London: Cambridge University Press, 1960. *Waiting for Godot,* pp. 48, 255; *All That Fall,* p. 287.

1143   WHITTICK, Arnold. *Symbols, Signs and Their Meaning.* London: Leonard Hill, 1960. *Waiting for Godot,* pp. 372-374.

1961

1144   BOOTH, Wayne C. *The Rhetoric of Fiction.* Chicago and London: University of Chicago Press, 1961. Beckett, pp. 159n, 286 n. 8, 287, 433.

1145   BORCHARDT, George, ed. *New French Writing.* New York: Grove Press, 1961. "Trends in the Contemporary French Novel," by Henri Peyre, pp. 73-87 (Beckett, *passim*).

1146   BROMBERT, Victor. *The Intellectual Hero: Studies in the French Novel 1880-1955.* Philadelphia and New York: Lippincott, 1961; London: Faber and Faber, 1962. Beckett, pp. 209-210.

1961

1147 COE, Richard N. *Ionesco.* London and Edinburgh: Oliver and Boyd, 1961. Beckett, pp. 42-43, 53, 113. Reprinted by Grove Press, New York, 1961.

1148 EMPSON, William. *Milton's God.* London: Chatto and Windus, 1961. Beckett, p. 263.

1149 FRANZEN, Erich. *Formen des modernen Dramas: Von der Illusionsbühne zum Antitheater.* Munich: C. H. Beck, 1961. Beckett, *passim.*

1150 GAYE, Freda, ed. *Who's Who in the Theatre.* London: Putnam and Sons, 1961. Beckett, p. 237.

1151 GINESTIER, Paul. *Le Théâtre contemporain dans le monde: Essai de critique esthétique.* Paris: Presses Universitaires de France, 1961. Beckett, p. 13.

1152 GREBANIER, Bernard. *Playwriting.* New York: Thomas Y. Crowell, 1961. Beckett, pp. 138, 182.

1153 HASSAN, Ihab. *Radical Innocence: Studies in the Contemporary American Novel.* Princeton, N.J.: Princeton University Press, 1961. Beckett, pp. 27 f.; *The Unnamable,* p. 194.

1154 MAROWITZ, Charles. *The Method as Means: An Acting Survey.* London: Herbert Jenkins, 1961. Beckett, pp. 47, 112, 144-152 (*passim*). Reissued under the title *Stanislavsky and the Method* (New York: Citadel Press, 1964).

1155 MENNEMEIER, Franz Norbert. *Das moderne Drama des Auslandes.* Düsseldorf: Bagel, 1961. Beckett, pp. 304-318 *passim.*

1156 MIGNON, Paul-Louis, ed. *Les Entretiens d'Helsinski ou les tendances du théâtre d'avant-garde dans le monde.* Paris: Michel Brient, 1961. Beckett, *passim.*

1157 MOURGUE, Gérard. *Dieu dans la littérature d'aujourd'hui.* Paris: Éditions France Empire, 1961. Beckett, *passim.*

1158 REBELLO, Luiz Francisco. *Imagens do Théatro Contemporâneo.* Lisbon: Ediçôes Ática, 1961. Beckett, pp. 10, 23, 154, 158, 161, 162, 163, 224, 225, 226.

1159 STEINER, George. *The Death of Tragedy.* New York: Alfred A. Knopf, 1961. Beckett, pp. 349-350.

1160 VELLINGSHAUSEN, Albert Schulze. *Theaterkritik.* Hanover, 1961. Collected theater reviews. *Warten auf Godot* and *Endspiel,* pp. 200-204.

1962

1161 ALBÉRÈS, René Marill. *Histoire du roman moderne.* Paris: Albin-Michel, 1962. Beckett, pp. 372-374 (*Comment c'est*).

1162 BARJON, Louis, S.J. *De Baudelaire à Mauriac: L'inquiétude contemporaine.* Tournai, Belgium: Casterman, 1962. "Le Monde de la 'décomposition': Nouveau-théâtre et Nouveau-roman," pp. 281-300 (Beckett, *passim*). [See also **1579.**]

1962

1163 BROWN, Andrew. *Drama*. New York: Arc Books, 1962. *Waiting for Godot*, p. 35.

1164 CLURMAN, Harold, ed. *Seven Plays of the Modern Theater*. New York: Grove Press, 1962. Contains the text of *Waiting for Godot* [see **373.004**], pp. 1-83; see also introduction by Harold Clurman, pp. vii-xii (Beckett, *passim*).

1165 DENNIS, Nigel. *Dramatic Essays*. London: Weidenfeld and Nicolson, 1962. Beckett, *passim*.

1166 HAMILTON, C. D., ed. *Encore: The Sunday Times Book*. London: Michael Joseph, 1962. Beckett, *passim*.

1167 HARDWICK, Elizabeth. *A View of My Own: Essays in Literature and Society*. New York: Farrar, Straus and Cudahy, 1962. Beckett, p. 201 (*Endgame*).

1168 IONESCO, Eugène. *Notes et contre-notes*. Paris: Gallimard, 1962. Beckett, p. 114 and *passim*. [See also **1394**.]

1169 KESTING, Marianne. *Panorama des zeitgenössischen Theaters*. Munich: Piper, 1962. Beckett, *passim*.

1170 NORTH, Robert J. *Myth in the Modern French Theatre*. Keele, Staffordshire: University of Keele [1962]. An inaugural lecture by R. J. North delivered at the University of Keele, November 7, 1962. Beckett, *passim*.

1171 ONIMUS, Jean. *Face au monde actuel*. Paris: Desclée de Brouwer, 1962. Beckett, *passim*. See especially "L'Homme égaré," pp. 77-86, essay reprinted from **1337**.

1172 PINGET, Robert. *L'Inquisitoire*. Paris: Éditions de Minuit, 1962. Novel. Probable allusions to Sam and Suzanne Beckett and Jérôme Lindon, p. 80.

1173 PRICE, Julia S. *The Off-Broadway Theatre*. New York: Scarecrow Press, 1962. Beckett, pp. 160, 183, 190, 230, 243, 249.

1174 SIMON, Karl Günter. *Avant-Garde Theater aus Frankreich: Modern oder Mode*. Berlin: Rembrandt, 1962. Beckett, *passim*.

1175 SOUTHERN, Richard. *The Seven Ages of Theatre*. London: Faber and Faber, 1962. Beckett, p. 288.

1176 TAYLOR, John Russell. *Anger and After: A Guide to the New British Drama*. London: Methuen, 1962; 2d ed., Penguin Books, Harmondsworth, Middlesex, 1963. Beckett, pp. 13, 34, 104, 255-256, 272, 323. Reprinted by Penguin Books, Baltimore, Md., 1963.

1963

1177 ALBÉRÈS, René Marill. *L'Aventure intellectuelle du XXe siècle*. 3d ed., rev. and augmented. Paris: Albin-Michel, 1963. Beckett, pp. 310, 312, 358, 359.

1178 BEAUVOIR, Simone de. *La Force des choses*. Paris: Gallimard, 1963. *En attendant Godot*, p. 320; Beckett, pp. 649-650.

1963

1179   BLOCH-MICHEL, Jean. *Le Présent de l'indicatif: Essai sur le nouveau roman.* Paris: Gallimard, 1963. Beckett, pp. 128-131 and *passim*. [See **1585**.]

1180   BROWN, John Mason. *Dramatis Personae: A Retrospective Show.* New York: Viking Press, 1963. Beckett, pp. 536, 538.

1181   BURTON, Ernest James. *The Student's Guide to British Theatre and Drama.* London: Herbert Jenkins, 1963. Beckett, p. 162.

1182   CHAMPIGNY, Robert. *Le Genre romanesque.* Monte Carlo: Éditions Regain, 1963. Beckett, *passim*.

1183   COX, C. B. *The Free Spirit.* London: Oxford University Press, 1963. Beckett, pp. 135, 165.

1184   DUSSANE, Béatrix. *J'étais dans la salle.* Paris: Mercure de France, 1963. (Contains eyewitness accounts of Beckett and other premieres.) See pp. 30, 31, 185-188 (*Godot*), 192, 200. [See **2477**.]

1185   EISENREICH, Herbert. *Reaktionen: Essays zur Literatur.* Gütersloh: Sigbert Mohn, 1963. Beckett, *passim*.

1186   COWASJEE, Saros. *Sean O'Casey: The Man behind the Plays.* Edinburgh and London: Oliver and Boyd, 1963; New York: St. Martin's Press, 1964. Beckett, pp. 231, 233.

1187   FORD, Boris. *The Modern Age: The Pelican Guide to English Literature.* Vol. VII. Harmondsworth, Middlesex, and Baltimore, Md.: Penguin Books, 1963; rev. ed., 1964. Beckett, pp. 96, 204-205, 210, 501, 527-528.

1188   GRIGSON, Geoffrey, ed. *The Concise Encyclopedia of Modern World Literature.* London: Hutchinson; New York: Hawthorn Books, 1963. Beckett, pp. 14, 23, 28, 47-48, 59 (photograph), 214, 251, 319, 372, 402.

1189   HEPPENSTALL, Rayner. *The Intellectual Part.* London: Barrie and Rockliff, 1963. Beckett, pp. 177-178 (brief account of Beckett attending a rehearsal of *Endgame* in London).

1190   KERR, Walter. *The Theater in Spite of Itself.* New York: Simon and Schuster, 1963. "The Ambiguity of the Theater of the Absurd," pp. 189-211 (Beckett, *passim*).

1191   KILLINGER, John. *The Failure of Theology in Modern Literature.* New York: Abingdon Press, 1963. Beckett, pp. 13, 57; *Waiting for Godot*, pp. 215-217.

1192   LALOU, René. *Le Roman français depuis 1900.* 9th ed. Paris: Presses Universitaires de France, 1963. Beckett, p. 122.

1193   LANGNAS, Isaac, and Jacob S. LIST. *Concise Dictionary of Literature.* New York: Philosophical Library, 1963. Beckett, p. 49.

1194   LEVIN, Harry. *The Gates of Horn: A Study of Five French Realists.* New York: Oxford University Press, 1963. Beckett, pp. 407, 451.

1195   McMAHON, Joseph H. *The Imagination of Jean Genet.* New Haven and London: Yale University Press; Paris: Presses Universitaires de France, 1963. Beckett, p. 137; *En attendant Godot*, pp. 9, 199; *Fin de partie*, p. 9.

1963

1196 MOORE, Dick. *Opportunity in Acting.* New York: Universal Publishing and Distributing, 1963. Beckett, p. 37 and *passim.*

1197 MORRISSETTE, Bruce. *Les Romans de Robbe-Grillet.* Paris: Éditions de Minuit, 1963. Beckett, pp. 22, 53 n. 4, 132.

1198 SEAVER, Richard, Terry SOUTHERN, and Alexander TROCCHI, eds. *Writers in Revolt: An Anthology.* New York: Frederick Fell, 1963. Samuel Beckett, pp. 348-349 (a short introduction), and *The End,* pp. 350-366 (a translation of Beckett's *La Fin,* a short story trans. from the French by Richard Seaver in collaboration with the author [see **372.11**]).

1199 VALENCY, Maurice. *The Flower and the Castle: An Introduction to Modern Drama.* New York: Macmillan; London: Collier-Macmillan, 1963. Beckett, pp. 9, 349.

1964

1200 ADAMOV, Arthur. *Ici et maintenant.* Paris: Gallimard, 1964. Beckett, *passim.*

1201 AYLEN, Léo. *Greek Tragedy and the Modern World.* London: Methuen, 1964. Beckett, *passim.*

1202 BAECQUE, André de. *Le Théâtre d'aujourd'hui: Clefs du temps présent.* Paris: Pierre Seghers, 1964. "Le Purgatoire d'*En attendant Godot,*" pp. 103-104; Beckett, *passim.*

1203 BARRÈRE, Jean-Bertrand. *La Cure d'amaigrissement du roman.* Paris: Albin-Michel, 1964. Beckett, p. 103.

1204 BARTHES, Roland. *Essais critiques.* Paris: Éditions du Seuil, 1964. Beckett, *passim.*

1205 BEEBE, Maurice. *Ivory Towers and Sacred Founts: The Artist as Hero in Fiction from Goethe to Joyce.* New York: New York University Press, 1964. Beckett, p. 299.

1206 BENTLEY, Eric. *The Life of the Drama.* New York: Atheneum, 1964. *Waiting for Godot,* pp. 99-101; Beckett, pp. 130, 320, 345, 348-351.

1207 BERNAL, Olga. *Alain Robbe-Grillet: Le Roman de l'absence.* Paris: Gallimard, 1964. Beckett, pp. 18, 25 n. 2, 70, 91, 161-162, 192, 245, 251.

1208 BONHEIM, Helmut. *Joyce's Benefictions.* Berkeley and Los Angeles: University of California Press, 1964. Beckett, pp. 16, 133.

1209 BRUSTEIN, Robert. *The Theatre of Revolt: An Approach to the Modern Drama.* Boston and Toronto: Little, Brown, 1964; London: Methuen, 1965. Beckett, pp. 27, 30-32, 316, 376-377; *Happy Days,* p. 29; *Waiting for Godot,* pp. 28-30, 163n.

1210 CHAIGNE, Louis. *Les Lettres contemporaines.* Vol. X. Paris: Del Duca, 1964. Beckett, pp. 594, 600.

1211 FANIZZA, Franco. *Letteratura come Filosofia.* Firenze: La Nuova Italia Editrice, 1964. Beckett, *passim.*

1964

1212 FLETCHER, Angus. *Allegory: The Theory of a Symbolic Mode.* Ithaca, N.Y.: Cornell University Press, 1964. Beckett, pp. 4, 355n.

1213 GASSNER, John, and Ralph G. ALLEN. *Theatre and Drama in the Making.* Boston: Houghton Mifflin, 1964. Beckett, pp. 813, 815, 994.

1214 HAEDENS, Kléber. *Paradoxe sur le roman.* Rev. ed. Paris: Bernard Grasset, 1964. Beckett, *passim.*

1215 HARVEY, John. *Anouilh: A Study in Theatrics.* New Haven and London: Yale University Press, 1964. Beckett, pp. x, xi, 150, 157.

1216 HARWARD, T. B., ed. *European Patterns.* Dublin: Dolmen Press, 1964. Review of *Krapp's Last Tape,* by Alec Reid, pp. 38-43; biographical note on Beckett, p. 92.

1217 HOFFMAN, Frederick J. *The Mortal No: Death and the Modern Imagination.* Princeton, N.J.: Princeton University Press, 1964. Beckett, pp. 25, 267; quotes from *Endgame* and *The Unnamable,* pp. 463-464; *Waiting for Godot,* pp. 437, 480, 484.

1218 HOLBROOK, David. *The Quest for Love.* London: Methuen, 1964. Beckett, pp. 40, 41.

1219 JANVIER, Ludovic. *Une Parole exigeante: Le Nouveau roman.* Paris: Éditions de Minuit, 1964. Beckett, pp. 9, 38, 89.

1220 MELCHINGER, Siegfried. *The Concise Encyclopedia of Modern Drama.* Trans. George Wellwarth. Ed. Henry Popkin. New York: Horizon Press, 1964. Foreword by Eric Bentley: "Drama from Ibsen to Beckett," pp. 11-15; Samuel Beckett, p. 169.

1221 MERCIER, Vivian, ed. *Great Irish Short Stories.* Introduction by Vivian Mercier. New York: Dell, 1964. *Dante and the Lobster* [see **16.031**], pp. 297-308; Samuel Beckett (a brief introductory note), pp. 296-297.

1222 SCHNEIDER, Marcel. *La Littérature fantastique en France.* Paris: Arthème Fayard, 1964. "Fantastique poétique: Ionesco-Beckett," pp. 397-402.

1223 SELZ, Jean. *Le Dire et le faire óu les chemins de la création.* Paris: Mercure de France, 1964. "L'Homme finissant de Samuel Beckett," pp. 134-137. Reprinted from **1415.**

1224 STOLTZFUS, Ben F. *Alain Robbe-Grillet and the New French Novel.* Preface by Harry T. Moore. Carbondale: Southern Illinois University Press, 1964. Beckett, *passim.*

1225 VOLTZ, Pierre. *La Comédie.* Paris: Armand Colin, 1964. Beckett, pp. 185-187, 454; also contains extract from end of Act I of *En attendant Godot,* pp. 439-445 [see **259.012**].

1226 WEALES, Gerald. *A Play and Its Parts.* New York: Basic Books, 1964. Beckett, pp. 24-25, 67, 80-81, 154.

1965

1227   BARRAULT, Jean-Louis, and Simone BENMUSSA. *Odéon Théâtre de France*. Paris: Éditions du Temps, 1965. Beckett, *passim*. Book of photographs.

1228   BOISDEFFRE, Pierre de, ed. *Une Anthologie vivante de la littérature d'aujourd'hui*. Paris: Librairie Académique Perrin, 1965. See "Aspects du Théâtre Contemporain—L'Anti-Théâtre" (Beckett, p. 708) with extract from *En attendant Godot*, pp. 709-711.

1229   BOGARD, Travis, and William I. OLIVER, eds. *Modern Drama: Essays in Criticism*. New York: Oxford University Press, 1965. Beckett, *passim* (see esp. "Between Absurdity and the Playwright," by W. I. Oliver, pp. 3-19 [see **1755**]).

1230   BRUSTEIN, Robert. *Seasons of Discontent: Dramatic Opinions 1959-1965*. New York: Simon Schuster, 1965; London: Jonathan Cape, 1966. Beckett, pp. 24, 26-28, "Déjà Vu," 53-56 [see **1589**], 60, 61, 92, 103, 182-183, 184, 197, 202, 203, 279, 285.

1231   CLARK, Barrett H., ed. *European Theories of the Drama: An Anthology of Dramatic Theory and Criticism from Aristotle to the Present Day*. Rev. ed. A series of selected texts, with commentaries, biographies, and bibliographies by Barrett H. Clark. Rev. Henry Popkin. New York: Crown Publishers, 1965. Beckett, pp. 351, 397, 405, 406, 407.

1232   ESSLIN, Martin, ed. *Absurd Drama*. Harmondsworth, Middlesex: Penguin Books, 1965. Introduction by Martin Esslin, pp. 7-23 (Beckett, *passim*).

1233   FLANNER, Janet [*pseud*. Genêt]. *Paris Journal, 1944-1965*. Ed. William Shawn. New York: Atheneum, 1965. Beckett, pp. 197-198. [See **2491**.]

1234   FREUND, Gisèle, and V. B. CARLETON. *James Joyce in Paris: His Final Years*. Preface by Simone de Beauvoir. New York: Harcourt, Brace and World, 1965. Beckett, p. 56, with photograph.

1235   KENNER, Hugh, ed. *Studies in Change: A Book of the Short Story*. Englewood Cliffs, N.J.: Prentice-Hall, 1965. Contains a passage from *Molloy* entitled "Stones" [see **374.04**] (pp. 200-204), and a brief introductory note (p. 200); Beckett also *passim* in introduction (pp. v-xiv).

1236   ROUDIEZ, Leon S. *Michel Butor*. New York and London: Columbia University Press, 1965. Beckett, *passim*.

1237   SARTRE, Jean-Paul. *Les Troyennes,* by Euripides, adapted by Jean-Paul Sartre. Paris: Gallimard, 1965. Beckett, *passim* in "Introduction" (pp. 2-8) by Jean-Paul Sartre.

1238   SCOTT, Nathan A., ed. *Man in the Modern Theatre*. Richmond, Va.: John Knox, 1965. Beckett, *passim*.

1239   STYAN, J. L. *The Dramatic Experience: A Guide to the Reading of Plays*. London: Cambridge University Press, 1965. *Waiting for Godot*, pp. 78, 90, 94, 104; *All That Fall*, p. 118.

1965

1240   THOMAS, Hugh. *The Spanish Civil War.* 2d ed., rev. Harmonds-
        worth, Middlesex: Penguin Books, 1965. Beckett, p. 291 n. 3.

1241   WEISSMAN, Philip. *Creativity in the Theater: A Psychoanalytic
        Study.* New York and London: Basic Books, 1965. Beckett, pp.
        250-251, 253n.

1242   WILSON, Colin. *Beyond the Outsider: The Philosophy of the Future.*
        Boston: Houghton Mifflin, 1965. Beckett, pp. 25, 27, 28, 32, 43,
        145, 147, 150, 222-223.

1243   WYLIE, Laurence. *Village in the Vaucluse: An Account of Life in
        a French Village.* New York: Harper and Row, 1965. Beckett,
        p. ix.

The village discussed in this book happens to be the one where Beckett lived
and worked during the German occupation of France.

1966

1244   KITCHIN, Laurence. *Drama in the Sixties: Form and Interpreta-
        tion.* London: Faber and Faber, 1966. Beckett, *passim.*

1245   MATTHEWS, Honor. *The Primal Curse: The Myth of Cain and
        Abel in the Theatre.* London: Chatto and Windus, 1966. Beckett,
        passim.

1246   SMITH, Eunice Clark, and John K. SAVACOOL. *Voix du siècle 2.*
        New York: Harcourt, Brace and World, 1966. Contains *La
        Dernière Bande* [see **147.6**] (pp. 113-124), and "Samuel Beckett,"
        a brief introductory note (pp. 112-113).

1247   SONTAG, Susan. *Against Interpretation and Other Essays.* New
        York: Farrar, Straus and Giroux, 1966. Beckett, *passim.*

1248   TAYLOR, John Russell. *The Penguin Dictionary of the Theatre.*
        Harmondsworth, Middlesex: Penguin Books, 1966. Beckett,
        passim.

1249   WILLIAMS, Raymond. *Modern Tragedy.* London: Chatto and
        Windus, 1966. Beckett, pp. 153-155.

10.

Articles Devoted to Samuel Beckett

1951

1300   BATAILLE, Georges. "Le Silence de Molloy," *Critique*, VII (May 15, 1951), 387-396.
Even though written as a review of *Molloy*, this article can be considered as the first full-length one on Beckett. What the novel exposes is not reality, but reality in a pure state. The obvious influence of Joyce on Beckett does not necessarily furnish the key to the latter's work.

1301   NADEAU, Maurice. "Samuel Beckett, l'humour et le néant," *Mercure de France*, CCCXII (Aug., 1951), 693-697. Reprinted in **1000**; see also **711**.

1302   PINGAUD, Bernard. "*Molloy*," *Esprit*, XIX (Sept., 1951), 423-425.
A review of *Molloy* which gains critical importance in the light of the article Pingaud wrote in 1963 entitled "*Molloy* douze ans après" [see **1756**].

1303   POUILLON, Jean. "*Molloy*," *Temps Modernes*, VII (July, 1951), 184-186. Reprinted in **1061**.
Essentially a review, quite unfavorable, of the novel. Pouillon considers the novel a failure, an insult to man's intelligence.

1952

1304   NADEAU, Maurice. "Samuel Beckett, ou le droit au silence," *Temps Modernes*, VII (Jan., 1952), 1273-1282 [see also **1372**].
In this discussion of *L'Expulsé, Molloy, Malone meurt,* and *L'Innommable*, Nadeau compares Beckett to Kafka, but in Beckett "la négation triomphante s'installe à l'intérieur de l'œuvre même et la dissout dans un brouillard d'insignifiance à mesure qu'elle se crée. . . ."

1305   SEAVER, Richard. "Samuel Beckett: An Introduction," *Merlin*, I (Autumn, 1952), 73-79.
One of the first general introductions to Beckett's work, but limited in scope because several of the published works after 1952 were not available to Mr. Seaver. Nevertheless, he tries to show how from *Murphy* to *Malone Dies*

1952

1305

there is "a movement away from the world of the body toward the world of the mind." Also points out how unfortunate it is that Beckett's literary reputation is invariably linked with that of Joyce.

1953

1306   ANOUILH, Jean. "Godot ou le sketch des *Pensées* de Pascal traité par les Fratellini," *Arts-Spectacles*, 400 (Feb. 27-March 5, 1953), 1.

According to Anouilh, this play "is as important as the first production of Pirandello in Paris by Pitoeff in 1923."

1307   AUDIBERTI, Jacques. "Au Babylone et au Lancry, deux coups heureux sur le damier du théâtre," *Arts-Spectacles*, 394 (Jan. 16-22, 1953), 3.

On *Godot* and a play by Ugo Betti.

1308   BELMONT, Georges. "Un classicisme retrouvé," *Table Ronde*, 62 (Feb., 1953), 171-174.

In discussing *En attendant Godot*, Belmont states that it is a classical play because "les trois unités y sont—on ne dira pas: observées—mais impitoyablement présentes." He also claims that in the past decade (1943-1953), only Sartre's *Huis clos* and *Les Mouches* have brought such "nouveauté" to the theater.

1309   BLANCHOT, Maurice. "Où maintenant? Qui maintenant?" *Nouvelle Revue Française*, II (Oct., 1953), 678-686. Reprinted in **1014**. An English version of this essay appears in **1071, 1481**.

1310   BRENNER, Jacques. "L'Avant-garde au théâtre s'est reformée," *Arts-Spectacles*, 414 (June 5-11, 1953), 3.

1311   BROUSSE, Jacques. "Theater in Paris," *The European*, 10 (Dec., 1953), 39-43.

Beckett in *Godot* shows himself to be the "foremost spokesman of contemporary nihilism." The play's originality is extraordinary, but its philosophy is "despairing, like three out of four contemporary works." Some comparison is made between Beckett and Claudel.

1312   DORT, Bernard. "*En attendant Godot*, pièce de Samuel Beckett," *Temps Modernes*, VIII (May, 1953), 1842-1845.

The essential fact about Beckett's play is that it refuses all interpretation, even though everyone tries to find in it what they put in it. "Il est à craindre que, refusant toute action, inscrivant sa pièce dans un mythe en trompe-l'œil, Beckett ne l'ait dangereusement réduite et que, loin de nous faire découvrir l'insignifiance comme la plus profonde assise de toute vie, il n'ait acculé ses héros et son œuvre à une sorte d'insignifiance."

1313   GRENIER, Jean. "Samuel Beckett, un monument singulier," *Arts-Spectacles*, 418 (July 3-9, 1953), 5-6.

1314   GRÖNDAHL, Henry G. "Fransk Teater," *Nya Argus*, 11 (June 1, 1953), 172-174.

1953

1315   HARTLEY, Anthony. "Samuel Beckett," *The Spectator*, Oct. 23,
            1953, pp. 458-459.
Deals especially with *Watt*. Beckett's early work is full of "cranky, difficult
talent" which develops in the trilogy into a "taut, poetic style, purged of the
Irishry and conceited wit" of *Murphy* and *Watt*.

1316   LEVENTHAL, A. J. "Nought into Zero," *Irish Times*, Dec. 24, 1953.

1317   MAUROC, Daniel. "The New French Literary Avant-garde," *Points*,
            17 (Autumn, 1953), 47.

1318   NADEAU, Maurice. "La 'Dernière' Tentative de Samuel Beckett,"
            Lettres Nouvelles, I (Sept., 1953), 860-864.

1319   POLAC, M. "Controverse autour de *Godot*," *Arts-Spectacles*, 400
            (Feb. 27-March 5, 1953), 3.

1320   ROBBE-GRILLET, Alain. "Samuel Beckett, auteur dramatique,"
            Critique, IX (Feb., 1953), 108-114.
Robbe-Grillet has been a fervent supporter of Beckett since the early 50's.
In this article on *Godot*, he sees the play as "un aboutissement." Everything
in it happens as though it was meant to force man's thinking backward. It is
this element of regression which marks the whole of Beckett's work.

1321   RYAN, Sebastian. "Samuel Beckett," *Icarus*, III (Nov., 1953), 79-86.
A general introduction to Beckett's work stating that, though Beckett has been
acclaimed in France as a creative artist of major importance, the French critics
"are somewhat at a loss for an interpretation of his work." In order to understand Beckett one must consider him primarily as an Irish artist and a product
of the Irish environment.

1322   SALACROU, Armand. "Ce n'est pas un accident mais une réussite,"
            Arts-Spectacles, 400 (Feb. 27-March 5, 1953), 1.
On *Godot*.

1323   SIMON, Alfred. "Samuel Beckett et les rendez-vous manqués,"
            Esprit, XXI (April, 1953), 595-598.
In this review of *Godot* and *Philippe et Jonas* by Irwin Shaw, Simon favors
the latter and states that "fidèle à l'homme dans son pessimisme, Samuel
Becket [*sic*] tend à provoquer la fission de la banalité quotidienne; irrespirable
dès qu'elle révèle l'exil de l'homme et le manque de ponctualité de Godot."
For the impossible victory of contemporary literature, Beckett substitutes impossible failure.

1954

1324   ANDERS, Günther. "Sein ohne Zeit, zu Becketts Stück *En attendant
            Godot*," *Neue Schweizer Rundschau*, 9 (Jan., 1954). Reprinted
            in **1002**; see also **711**.

1325   BEIGBEDER, Marc. "Le Théâtre à l'âge métaphysique," *L'Age
            Nouveau*, IX (Jan., 1954), 30-41.

1326   BJURSTRÖM, C. G. "Samuel Beckett," *Bonniers Litterära Magasin*,
            XXIII (Jan., 1954), 27-33.

1327   CASPARI, C.-H. "Zu Samuel Becketts Theater," *Atoll*, 1 (1954), 24.

1954

1328   DELFOSSE, Guy. "Aspects du théâtre d'aujourd'hui: (II). L'Impasse de l'hermétisme," *Aspects,* I (Dec., 1954), 45-48.
On Ghelderode, Vilar, Genet, Beckett.

1329   FRANZEN, Erich. "Einführung zu Becketts *Molloy,*" *Merkur,* VIII (March, 1954), 239-241 (with extracts from *Molloy* in German, pp. 241-257).
Serves as an introduction to two extracts from *Molloy* in the German translation of Erich Franzen.

1330   HOGAN, Thomas. "The Reversed Metamorphosis," *Irish Writing,* 26 (March, 1954), 54-62.
Beckett is a deliberately ambiguous writer, and "to seek meanings, to find what Mr. Beckett's work is all about, is a risky and hazardous enterprise which, one can feel sure, will not lack intrepid Americans to undertake, in the future." Beckett seems to feel that the artist cannot effect a change and so should not desire to do so in his work.

1331   HORST, Karl A. "*Molloy* oder die Psychologie des Clowns," *Merkur,* VIII (Oct., 1954), 983-987.
In this intriguing discussion of *Godot* and *Molloy,* both viewed as pantomimes dealing with a "missing person," Horst asks whether or not it is necessary for the "missing person" to appear in order to fill the void of the situation as with the ghost of Hamlet's father.

1332   KENNEBECK, Edwin. "The Moment of Cosmic Ennui," *Commonweal,* LXI (Dec. 31, 1954), 365-366.
In this review of *Waiting for Godot,* the author sees the play as an almost textureless "tragicomedy" whose language seldom exploits style, metaphor, connotation, though when these appear they count for a great deal.

1333   KERN, Edith. "Drama Stripped for Inaction: Beckett's *Godot,*" *Yale French Studies,* 14 (Winter, 1954-55), 41-47.
The first scholarly article on Beckett to appear in the United States. Miss Kern emphasizes that "it is Beckett's genius to have found the simple word, the absurdly comical situation to express his thoughts on man's place in the universe." In this "play-without-action" he manages to convey the paradox of the condition of man, whose intellect makes him aware of the universe's slighting of reason and makes him long for a state where reason shall be conferred upon this universe: "a paradise of beauty and order, created by a a saviour."

1334   LEVENTHAL, A. J. "Mr. Beckett's *En attendant Godot,*" *Dublin Magazine,* XXX (April-June, 1954), 11-16.
Dr. Leventhal has been a faithful interpreter of Beckett's work. In this piece on *Godot* he states that "the critic who comes to this play with prefabricated theories will be shocked into accepting a new form." *Waiting for Godot* "belongs to no school; it will make one."

1335   MICHA, René. "Une nouvelle littérature allégorique," *Nouvelle Revue Française,* III (April, 1954), 696-706 (Beckett, *passim*).
Gracq, Daumal, Buzatti, Devaulx, Borges, Blanchot, Beckett, and others are discussed in this article as novelists having something in common: they are

1954
1335
all concerned with the relationship of man and the world, and they are allegorical storytellers.
1336 MONTGOMERY, Niall. "No Symbols Where None Intended," *New World Writing,* 5 (April, 1954), 324-337.
One of the earlier pieces to reveal interesting and valuable information about Beckett's early literary career. Mr. Montgomery states that he will "respectfully examine Beckett's writing . . . first, in the light giving of nationality and religion, second, in the light of personality, third, in terms of supposed mythical obsessions (Oedipus). . . . Polite reference will be made to Mr. Beckett's independence of certain literary influences proposed for him (Joyce, Dante, Kafka), and finally, and with deference, attention will be directed to the general and specific qualities of his languages, his feelings for fun, hats, sex, etc."; see **3076**; reprinted in *Arna,* n.v. (1962), 36-49 [one annual issue] with extract from *How It Is* [see **384.03**].
1337 ONIMUS, Jean. "L'Homme égaré: Notes sur le sentiment d'égarement dans la littérature actuelle," *Études,* CCLXXXIII (Dec., 1954), 320-329 (Beckett, *passim*). Reprinted in **1171**.
1338 SCHNEIDER, Pierre. "Play and Display," *The Listener,* LI (Jan. 28, 1954), 174-176 (Beckett, *passim*).
A commentary on the contemporary French theater. "Our stage must turn resolutely away from escapist display and assume the destitute and perplexed condition which today is the one really common lot." Along these lines, Beckett gives us "the most important dramatic work of the past few seasons" with his *En attendant Godot.*

1955
1339 ANONYMOUS. "Foreign Origins: Expatriate Writers in Paris," *Times Literary Supplement,* May 27, 1955, p. x (Beckett, *passim*).
Beckett is the most significant writer of the group, about whom it is "trivial to make moral judgments. His world has been dominated by the concentration . . . camps, the abduction by night; his days filled with the sight of human beings destroyed by society." He speaks out of the horror "without rhetoric or complaint."
1340 A[RON], S[uzanne]. "Balzac a-t-il inspiré *En attendant Godot?*" *Figaro Littéraire,* Sept. 17, 1955, p. 12.
The first article to point out a possible connection between Balzac's play, *Mercadet,* and *Godot.* For further details on this question see **1659** and **1757**.
1341 CHAUCER, Daniel. "*Waiting for Godot,*" *Shenandoah,* VI (Spring, 1955), 80-82.
This "small classic of modern drama" is a kind of calculated banality with considerable expressive power. It is actually a representation of Beckett's theory of history as a cyclical process, and, through his essay on this subject ("Vico and Joyce"), one may arrive at possible interpretations of *Godot.*
1342 DHOMME, Sylvain. "Des auteurs à l'avant-garde du théâtre," *Cahiers de la Compagnie Madeleine Renaud—Jean-Louis Barrault,* III, no. 13 (1955), 112-118 (Beckett, *passim*).

1955

1343   HARTLEY, Anthony. "Theatre," *The Spectator,* Aug. 12, 1955,
            p. 222.
Waiting for Godot is a "skillful and powerful *tour de force,*" in which the
"basic minimum of human life, something that is not changed one jot by
such trifles as jealousy or anger or lust, is excellently depicted." The play
may be superficially pessimistic, but actually it establishes the hopeful premise
that human communication on some level is possible, and that "Godot may
come."

1344   HARTUNG, R. "Samuel Beckett, die Nacht der Welt," *Eckart,*
            XXXIV (April-June, 1955), 243-246.

1345   HOPE-WALLACE, Philip. "Samuel Beckett," *Time and Tide,*
            XXXVI (Aug. 13, 1955), 1045.

1346   MANNES, Marya. "A Seat in the Stalls," *The Reporter,* XIII (Oct.
            20, 1955), 42-43.
It would be interesting to find out if the opinion of the critic is the same
today as in 1955 when she wrote of *Godot:* "I doubt whether I have ever
seen a worse play. Those intellectual friends who found the play good, did
so out of the necessity of embracing obscurity, pretense, ugliness and negation
as protective covering for their own confusions."

1347   MERCIER, Vivian. "Beckett and the Search for Self," *New Re-
            public,* CXXXIII (Sept. 19, 1955), 20-21.
Each of Beckett's fictional heroes is in the respective process of finding, deny-
ing, or annihilating his "self," an activity that may represent Beckett's own
lack of assimilation as an Anglo-Irishman: "From the 'seedy solipsist' Murphy,
who constantly struggles to enjoy his self, to Watt, who is altogether without
personality, to Molloy-Moran in an id-ego conflict, to Malone, who dislikes
his self and tries to invent a new one on the eve of his ceasing to be, to the
Unnamable, whose self is unwilling even to be born, and who may represent
life at the center of the closed world of the schizophrenic."

1348   ⸺. "A Pyrrhonian Eclogue," *Hudson Review,* VII (Winter,
            1955), 620-624.
Beckett has, in *Godot,* "patiently" and "mockingly" turned man's search for
God into "a vaudeville act," in the tradition of Irish humorists from Swift to
Joyce.

1349   ⸺. "Godot, Molloy et Cie," *New Statesman and Nation,* L
            (Dec. 3, 1955), 754-755 [see also **2085**].
Beckett, taking the proscribed course of other Anglo-Irishmen (Yeats, Shaw,
Wilde), is looking for a "self" in his five novels, and, especially in *Molloy,*
he has "explored the nature of the self and the means by which a self is
found, preserved, and annihilated."

1350   RATTIGAN, Terence. "Aunt Edna Waits for Godot," *New States-
            man and Nation,* L (Oct. 15, 1955), 468-470.
An imaginary conversation between Mr. Rattigan and his Aunt Edna, who
represents several generations (during the course of their talk) of "middlebrow theatre-goers." The implication is that *Godot*'s value is boosted by the

1955

1350

"poverty of the London season," therefore the play is a "good, hearty meal for hungry theatre-lovers."

1351 WORSLEY, T. C. "Cactus Land," *New Statesman and Nation,* L (Aug. 13, 1955), 184-185.

Waiting for Godot is a sad, but not dreary, play with a comic surface. It reduces humanity "to the lowest common level . . . mere existence, undisturbed by even the round of petty business which fills our days." The play leaves behind a "compelling, easing and puzzling image."

1956

1352 ANOUILH, Jean. "Du chapitre des chaises," *Figaro Littéraire,* April 23, 1956, p. 1.

On Ionesco and Beckett.

1353 BARRETT, William. "Real Love Abides," *New York Times Book Review,* Sept. 16, 1956, p. 5.

Malone Dies is an important and powerful novel in which Beckett attempts, like some modern painters, to empty the canvas "of all recognizable forms" yet keep a visually exciting surface. He succeeds in getting across a "really larger portion of life than most of us are willing to admit to ourselves. . . . Behind all his mournful blasphemies . . . there is real love" for man.

1354 BECKETT, Jeremy. *"Waiting for Godot,"* Meanjin, XV, no. 2 (1956), 216-218.

The play is probably the easiest of Beckett's works to understand. It is "boredom dramatized" with affinities in its tone and dialogue to certain Christian and existential problems. Vladimir and Estragon are "actually one person in the uneasy equilibrium of 'Who am I?' and 'Do I exist?' "

1355 BENTLEY, Eric. "The Talent of Samuel Beckett," *New Republic,* CXXXIV (May 14, 1956), 20-21.

This "undramatic" but highly theatrical play (*Godot*) has provided food for critical dissension and shown a schism in American criticism between "nonintellectual pro-intellectualism and non-intellectual anti-intellectualism." Beckett has been able to define the existentialist point of view more sharply than those who are more famously associated with it (Sartre), and he has found for its expression a vehicle of a sort that people have been recommending without following their own recommendations.

1356 BOLLNOW, Otto F. "Samuel Beckett," *Antares,* IV (March, 1956), 31-36; IV (April, 1956), 36-38; IV (June, 1956), 42-43.

1357 BONNEFOI, Geneviève. "Textes pour rien?" *Lettres Nouvelles,* 36 (March, 1956), 424-430.

One of the few articles devoted to *Nouvelles et Textes pour rien.* These texts are important in the evolution of Beckett's work and "permettent . . . d'en dégager les thèmes essentiels."

1358 CAMARGO, J. "A reforma do teatro pela 'geraçao espontanea,' " *Dionysos,* V, no. 4 (1956), 28-36.

1359 CARR, Bill. "Samuel Beckett," *Delta,* 9 (Summer, 1956), 17-20.

1956

1360 DAVIN, Dan. "Mr. Beckett's Everymen," *Irish Writing,* 34 (Spring, 1956), 36-39.
The attempt of the artist to stand aside and "pare his nails" has taken a curious turn in Beckett's writing. In it, "objectivity betrays itself" and we can see that in his progress from the representation of a "relative diversity of characters" (as in Dickens) he reaches toward a "single character spawning diversities" (*The Unnamable*). Beckett is not "paring indifferent fingernails. He is chewing them, and in the centre of the book."

1361 GOLD, Herbert. "Beckett: Style and Desire," *The Nation,* CLXXXIII (Nov. 10, 1956), 397-399.
The theme of estrangement in Beckett's novels, *Mulloy* [*sic*] and *Malone Dies,* is suggested by the author's own exile from Ireland and the English language. Beckett's ultimate meaning must be synthesized with the style in which he presents it: "the philosophy is almost pure nihilism but the author's joy in coming to adequate expression of his feelings is communicated to us as pleasure in creativity, in life."

1362 GREGORY, Horace. "Beckett's Dying Gladiators," *Commonweal,* LXV (Oct. 26, 1956), 88-92. Reprinted in **1026**; see also **1495**.

1363 JOHNSTON, Denis. "Waiting with Beckett," *Irish Writing,* 34 (Spring, 1956), 23-28.
A somewhat sarcastic view of Beckett. "Don't examine this comb for any of Joyce's dandruff. While Joyce is a master of formlessness, Beckett has a sense of shape that makes each step in his play as inevitable as Anglican Morning Prayer." Beckett is "no simple arithmetician." He is "too clever to have fashioned anything that can be solved by means of a crib."

1364 LEVY, Alan. "The Long Wait for Godot," *Theatre Arts,* XL (Aug., 1956), 33-35, 96 [see **373.001**].
Serves as an introduction to the reprinted complete text of *Waiting for Godot* (pp. 36-61), describes briefly the story of its production in Miami and on Broadway, and quotes various critical reactions to the play. Among these is Beckett's (most unlikely) comment on audience reaction: "If they don't understand it, the hell with them."

1365 LOY, J. Robert. " 'Things' in Recent French Literature," *PMLA,* LXXI (March, 1956), 27-41 (Beckett, *passim;* see esp. p. 33).
In the recent trend, things, rather than people and ideas, become the literary subject. In Beckett specifically, there is "complete absence of human action and motivation." Generally, this experimentation has a revitalizing effect on a tired literature.

1366 MAGNY, Olivier de. "Samuel Beckett ou Job abandonné," *Monde Nouveau/Paru,* XI (Feb., 1956), 92-99.

1367 MAILER, Norman. "Reflections on *Waiting for Godot,*" *Village Voice,* May 2 and 7, 1956. Reprinted in **1016**; see also **1054**.

1368 MARCABRU, Pierre. "*En attendant Godot* au Théâtre Hébertot," *Arts-Spectacles,* 573 (June 20-26, 1956), 3.

1956

1369   MAURIAC, Claude. "Samuel Beckett," *Preuves,* 61 (March, 1956),
        71-76. A slightly different version of the article was reprinted
        in **1011.**

1370   MERCIER, Vivian. "The Uneventful Event," *Irish Times,* Feb.
        18, 1956, p. 6.

On *Godot.*

1371   MULLER, André. "Techniques de l'avant-garde," *Théâtre Populaire,*
        18 (May, 1956), 21-29 (Beckett, *passim*).

1372   NADEAU, Maurice. "Samuel Beckett oder das Recht auf Schwei-
        gen," *Texte und Zeichen,* 6 (1956). German translation of **1304.**

1373   PARIS, Jean. "The Clock Struck Twenty-nine," *The Reporter,* XV
        (Oct. 4, 1956), 39-40 (Beckett, *passim*).

A new conception of theater is being developed in France, the "three French
Hamlets," Beckett, Ionesco, and Adamov, at the forefront. The drama is
moving gradually away from "nihilistic pessimism," toward greater "affirma-
tion," and will probably return to the tragic genre eventually.

1374   RAINOIRD, Manuel. *"En attendant Godot,"* Monde Nouveau/Paru,
        XI (Aug.-Sept., 1956), 115-117.

1375   REDA, J. "N'attendons plus Godot," *Marginales,* Dec. 8, 1956,
        pp. 50-51, 63-64.

1376   REXROTH, Kenneth. "The Point Is Irrelevance," *The Nation,*
        CLXXXII (April 14, 1956), 325-328. Reprinted in **1017.**

Although Samuel Beckett has been around for a good many years, *Waiting
for Godot* "catapulted him into an international reputation."

1377   SHENKER, Israel. "Moody Man of Letters," *New York Times,*
        May 6, 1956, sec. 2, pp. x, 1, 3.

One of the first reports of an interview with Samuel Beckett. Reveals interesting comments by Beckett on life, art, and his own work. Beckett discusses
"with pained hesitation, but . . . with brilliance" his early life and appren-
ticeship with Joyce, his self-imposed exile to France, the writing of the trilogy
and *Godot.* He comments on Kafka and Joyce as technicians, the absence of
"system" from his own work, and "what to do when you find nothing to
say." [See also **3080.**]

1957

1378   BARRETT, William. "Samuel Beckett's World in Waiting: The
        Works of Beckett Hold Clues for an Intriguing Riddle," *Satur-
        day Review of Literature,* XL (June 8, 1957), 15-16. Part II of
        a two-part introduction to Beckett [see **1381**].

Western Europe has been "at the brink of the abyss where Beckett exists, and
the United States has not." This accounts for the very popular reception the
author has received in Europe, and the very "tepid" one he faces in the
United States. His artistic affinities, however, lie with another American
author, Nathanael West.

1957

1379   BELMONT, Georges. "Lettre de Londres: Avec *Fin de partie*
        Beckett a atteint la perfection classique," *Arts-Spectacles,* 614
        (April 10-16, 1957), 1-2.

1380   BERTRAND, Joseph. "De Bertolt Brecht à Jean Anouilh," *Revue
        Générale Belge,* XCIII (Jan. 15, 1957), 153-158 (Beckett, *passim*).

1381   BRIGGS, Ray. "Samuel Beckett's World in Waiting: The Life of
        an Enigmatic New Idol of the Avant-Garde of Two Continents,"
        Saturday Review of Literature, XL (June 8, 1957), 14. Part I
        of a two-part introduction to Beckett [see **1378**].

Serves as a brief survey of Beckett's critical reputation. His work is seen as
inspiring alternations of "rapture and ridicule." So enigmatic does the author
intend it, only the "boldest critics" are inspired to interpretation.

1382   CHAPSAL, Madeleine. "Un célèbre inconnu: Samuel Beckett,"
        L'Express, Feb. 8, 1957, pp. 1 (photo), 26-27.

1383   CHRISTIE, Erling. "Det absurde Drama: Tanker omkring Samuel
        Becketts *Waiting for Godot,*" *Samtiden,* LXVI, no. 9 (1957),
        578-584.

1384   CODIGNOLA, Luciano. "Il teatro della guerra fredda. 3. Samuel
        Beckett," *Tempo Presente,* II, no. 1 (1957), 53-56.

1385   COLE, Connelly. "A Note on *Waiting for Godot,*" *Icarus,* VII (Jan.,
        1957), 25-27.

The underlying conceptions of *Godot* are very clear and present no difficulties: "The loneliness of man's estate and the bitter-sweet-pea nature of the
flowers he husbands there, plucking from time to time to decorate the mind's
interior with madness."

1386   DORT, Bernard. "Sur une avant-garde: Adamov et quelques autres,"
        Théâtre d'Aujourd'hui, 3 (Sept.-Oct., 1957), 13-16.

1387   DREYFUS, Dina. "Vraies et fausses énigmes," *Mercure de France,*
        CCCXXXI (Oct., 1957), 268-285 (Beckett, esp. pp. 276-285).

A very interesting article which raises important questions on the nature of
fiction. There are two ways of understanding Beckett's novels: one, the most
common, is to deal with them as symbolic works; the second is to approach
them simply as novels, thus asking "what is a novel? what is a novelist?" In
other words, what are the conditions ("non esthétique mais ontologique") of
the novel?

1388   ENZENSBERGER, Hans M. "Die Dramaturgie der Entfremdung,"
        Merkur, XI (March, 1957), 231-237 (Beckett, esp. pp. 234-237).

Discusses particularly the impact of Artaud's *Irrationalismus* on Adamov,
Ionesco, and Beckett.

1389   FIEDLER, Leslie. "Search for Peace in a World Lost," *New York
        Times Book Review,* April 14, 1957, p. 27 [see **2202**].

Making the "schizophrenic his model and hero," Beckett, "most old-fashioned
of writers," revitalizes the techniques of stream of consciousness and dislocated
memory to reach the depths where the "real no longer matters." *Murphy* is
perhaps the funniest but the "least poetic of Beckett's 'denuded' novels."

1957

1390   GIRARD, René. "Où va le roman?" *French Review,* XXX (Jan., 1957), 201-206 (Beckett, *passim*).

At a certain point in their stylistic evolution some novelists feel the need to bury either the novelist they were or the writer they have become. One cannot go much further than Beckett in *L'Innommable* in this kind of *ascèse.* "La lecture de l'œuvre doit nous conduire au paroxysme d'impuissance et d'effarement dont l'Innomable [*sic*] fait précisement l'expérience, seule authentique aux yeux de son auteur."

1391   GRAY, Ronald. "*Waiting for Godot:* A Christian Interpretation," *The Listener,* LVII (Jan. 24, 1957), 160-161. The article gave rise to a number of letters to the editor; see **2168, 2178, 2180, 2219, 2236.** [See also **3002.**]

The play is structured around imagery of Christianity which develops the theme in the form of several questions: "Why was one thief saved? Was he in fact saved? Which of us is saved and which is damned?" Vladimir and Estragon represent the "spiritual, yet vindictive few" who stand around and wait, "frightened at the thought that Godot may come after all." They show an unchristian complacency, a lack of faith, an unrepentant blindness.

1392   HANSEN-LÖVE, Friedrich. "Samuel Beckett oder die Einübung ins Nichts," *Hochland,* L (Oct., 1957), 36-46.

1393   HEIDICKE, M. "Die Versöhnung mit dem Nichts," *Theater der Zeit,* 2 (1957), 24-26.

1394   IONESCO, Eugène. "There Is No Avant-Garde Theater," trans. Richard Howard, *Evergreen Review,* I, no. 4 (1957), 101-105 (Beckett, *passim*). The original French version of this essay was published in **1168.**

The expression "avant-garde theater" is confusing largely because of the various prejudices around these words. Perhaps the "absurdity" of this theater is absurd only as a matter of definition. Beckett's *Endgame,* "a dramatic work called avant-garde, is much closer to the lamentation of Job, the tragedies of Sophocles and Shakespeare, than our shoddy '*théâtre engagé*' and our contemporary commercial theater."

1395   JESSUP, Bertram. "About Beckett, Godot and Others," *Northwest Review,* I (Spring, 1957), 25-30.

1396   LEE, Warren. "The Bitter Pill of Samuel Beckett," *Chicago Review,* X (Winter, 1957), 77-87.

Beckett's books have been the victims of "critical bungling" in this country because American criticism is largely in the hands of the "wealthy man," who seeks only the "ornamental value" of literature, and not the "anxious man," who seeks its meaning. The theme of *Molloy* is a further development of the theme of *Godot:* the "waiting" becomes the "journey." The journey or quest of Molloy-Moran results in a "disintegration of meaning" for the protagonists, just as the act of waiting turns meaning into meaningless for the tramps.

1397   Le HARDOUIN, Maria. "L'Anti-héros, ou 'Richard n'aime plus Richard,'" *Synthèses,* XII (Dec., 1957), 398-405.

1957

1398   LEVENTHAL, A. J. "Close of Play: Reflections on Samuel Beckett's New Work for the French Theater," *Dublin Magazine,* XXXII (April-June, 1957), 18-22.

Endgame, a hopeless, utterly despairing "look upon the face of God," is a profound experience which, "however painful, is still preferable to the vapid reiterations of tried and tiring formulae."

1399   ————. "Samuel Beckett: Poet and Pessimist," *The Listener,* LVII (May 9, 1957), 746-747 [see **3006**].

Beckett "shares the notion of the futility of the arts" in making any statement. Poetry was for him, as it was for Valéry, an "exercise, rather than a communication," and it is only in the novels and the plays that he allows himself to express his view of "the pitiful state of man."

1400   LOGUE, Christopher. "For Those Still Standing," *New Statesman,* LIV (Sept. 14, 1957), 325.

All That Fall is "radio triumphant." Mrs. Rooney, "a frowsty old bitch, loose in the hilts," is drawn with a greatness characteristic of Beckett's artistry, which creates the "stale dignity of the world" inhabited by "ten-foot tall cretins," laughable, filthy, but "whose squalor has awful magnificence." Beckett and Brecht may well be western Europe's only two great playwrights.

1401   LÜBREN, R. "Realismus in modernen Drama," *Theater und Zeit,* V, no. 6 (1957).

1402   MACKWORTH, Cecily. "French Writing Today: Les Coupables," *Twentieth Century,* CLXI (May, 1957), 459-468 (Beckett, *passim;* see esp. p. 463).

"Any new current in France's literary life is sure to be congealed . . . into a 'school,' and 'Anti-literature' already has its practitioners, its theoreticians . . . and even a Prix de *l'anti-littérature.*" All the novelists who adhere to it go much further than Camus in their determination to eliminate any kind of characterization from their work. "The heroes of Beckett's *Molloy* and *Mallone meurt* [*sic*] have few of the recognizable attributes that Camus still allowed his Mersault [*sic*] to possess."

1403   MARCABRU, Pierre. "Décomposition des êtres et du langage," *Arts-Spectacles,* 618 (May 8-14, 1957), 2.

On *Fin de partie.*

1404   MARCEL, Gabriel. "Atomisation du théâtre," *Nouvelles Littéraires,* June 20, 1957, p. 10.

Having been asked by his readers to give his opinion of Beckett's new play, *Fin de partie,* Marcel is sorry to say, though he does not want to hurt the author's feelings, that he spent a most painful evening watching this play. Such a play can be justified only if it is a parable proposing a certain image of man's destiny. In this case, the extreme is such that one cannot identify with the play.

1405   MAULNIER, Thierry. "De Beckett à Bernanos," *Revue de Paris,* LXIV (June, 1957), 139-142.

On *Fin de partie.*

1957

1406   MAYOUX, Jean-Jacques. "Le Théâtre de Samuel Beckett," *Études Anglaises,* X (Oct.-Dec., 1957), 350-366 [see **716, 900,** and **1508**].

Perhaps one of the best articles on Beckett's theater. According to Jean-Jacques Mayoux, Beckett follows Epictetus' philosophy of theater: " 'Remember you are an actor in a drama.' " He seeks to create a "theatrical reality," artistic truth, where "absolute truth is an illusion." His characters are not "tramps, but men to whom the master has assigned the role of tramps."

1407   MERCIER, Vivian. "Savage Humour," *Commonweal,* LXVI (May 17, 1957), 188, 190.

In this review of *Murphy, Proust,* and some Beckett poems published in the first issue of *Evergreen Review,* Mercier states that in the process of hindsight, critics will be looking in *Murphy* and *Proust* for the seeds of Beckett's later work, and as a result, both older books will be misjudged. Though there are "certain passages" in *Proust* which do presage themes in the later works, on the whole, the book is badly written. *Murphy* is, contrary to popular opinion, "a philosophic rather than a satiric novel." As for the poems, they are "bad" though they may have been "fashionable" when they were written in 1935.

1408   MIDDLETON, Christopher. "Randnotizen zu den Romanen von Samuel Beckett," *Akzente,* IV (Oct., 1957), 407-412.

A general discussion of Beckett's novels from *Murphy* to *L'Innommable.* Beckett's world is a paradox—it is a world standing on the edge between an unbearably breakable outer appearance and an unexplainable darkened inner zone.

1409   NADEAU, Maurice. "Beckett: La Tragédie transposée en farce," *Avant-Scène,* 156 (Aug., 1957), 4-6. Originally published as a review of *Fin de partie* in **2206**, it is used here as a preface to the text of the play [see **265.1**].

1410   NORÈS, Dominique. "La Condition humaine selon Beckett," *Théâtre d'Aujourd'hui,* 3 (Sept.-Oct., 1957), 9-12.

1411   PETRIC, V. "Drama i Antidrama," *Knjizevnost,* 3 (1957).
Discussion of *En attendant Godot.*

1412   PRONKO, Leonard C. "Beckett, Ionesco, Schehadé: The Avant-Garde Theatre," *Modern Language Forum,* XLII (Dec., 1957), 118-123.

Although Beckett's writing "is marked by a stark pessimism, a discouraged and gloomy outlook" on life which should provide tedious and "monstrous" theater, this is not the case. His plays are "strikingly theatrically effective."

1413   ROUSSELOT, Jean. "Deux nouvelles œuvres de Beckett," *France-Asie,* 14 (1957), 67-69.

A discussion of *Fin de partie* and *Acte sans paroles I.*

1414   SASTRE, Alfonso. "Siete notas sobre *Esperando a Godot,*" *Primer Acto,* 1 (April, 1957), 46-52.

1957

1415   SELZ, Jean. "L'Homme finissant de Samuel Beckett," *Lettres Nou-
            velles,* V (July-Aug., 1957), 120-123. Reprinted in **1223**.

Man and his end is the unique theme of Beckett's work. "L'herbe ne pousse
plus depuis longtemps sur la terre où vivent les héros de Samuel Beckett."
Dispossessed of everything, except the faculty of speech, the Beckettian heroes
are reduced to the extreme possibility of existence: "Je suis en mots, je suis
fait de mots."

1416   TOUCHARD, Pierre-Aimé. "Un théâtre nouveau," *Avant-Scène,*
            156 (Aug., 1957), 1-2.

1417   VAHANIAN, Gabriel. "The Empty Cradle," *Theology Today,* XIII
            (Jan. 4, 1957), 521-526.

In setting out to show "how anachronistic Christianity has become," Beckett
has used the "more authentic and existential language of Christianity" and
woven its "images and symbols and legends into the texture" of *Waiting for
Godot.*

1418   VANNIER, Jean. "Samuel Beckett: *Fin de partie*," *Théâtre Popu-
            laire,* 25 (July, 1957), 68-72.

1419   VIGÉE, Claude. "Les Artistes de la faim," *Comparative Literature,*
            IX (Spring, 1957), 97-117 (Beckett, *passim*).

Mainly a discussion of Kafka and the decline of the novel. "Dans les romans
de Beckett on ne trouve plus trace de cet activisme forcené dont Spengler et
Malraux, hier encore, nous offraient le douteux exemple. . . . Les personnages
de Beckett et de Kafka parachèvent en eux-mêmes la destruction lente de
l'être que leur prépara tout le romantisme européen."

1420   WALKER, Roy. "Shagreen Shamrock," *The Listener,* LVII (Jan.
            24, 1957), 167-168 [see **1075**].

1421   ―――――. "In the Rut," *The Listener,* LVIII (Dec. 19, 1957), 1047-
            1048.

On *Molloy* and *From an Abandoned Work* readings, on the BBC Third Programme.

1422   WORSLEY, T. C. "Minority Culture," *New Statesman and Nation,*
            LIII (Jan. 26, 1957), 97-98.

Mr. Worsley complains about the poverty of the London theater, and argues
that the situation of the playwright is as "despairing" as that of the novelist
and the poet, even though the playwright reaches directly for an audience.
In the case of Beckett, whose plays are particularly directed to a "minority
culture," he has very little chance of ever becoming popular.

1423   ZÉRAFFA, Michel. "Le Théâtre: Beckett, Schehadé, Shakespeare,"
            Europe, XXXV (Dec., 1957), 159-162.

1958

1424   ANONYMOUS. "Godot Gets Around," *Theatre Arts,* XLII (July,
            1958), 73-74.

About the success of *Waiting for Godot* at San Quentin prison, where the
"identification of Godot himself seemed somewhat easier for San Quentin
audience than for the average group."

1958

1425 _____. "Paradise of Indignity," *Times Literary Supplement,* March
          28, 1958, p. 168.
The novels of Beckett are more like poems than novels. They are "lyrical,
contemplative, and discursive," and are sustained by the tension developed
between objects and emotions, rather than by the narrative or by "plausible
concatenations." Mainly a discussion of *Malone Dies* and *From an Abandoned
Work.*

1426 ANGELI, Siro. "Il teatro di prosa," *Studi Romani,* VI (Sept.-Oct.,
          1958), 608-611.
On *Fin de partie.*

1427 BACHMANN, Claus-Henning. "Die Hoffnung am Strick: Notizen
          zu Beckett und Béjart," *Antares,* VI (May, 1958), 207-210.

1428 _____. "Worte sind durch ihren Sinn vereist," *Die Anregung,* X,
          no. 13 (1958), 263-264.
Notes on Beckett and other writers.

1429 BARBOUR, Thomas. "Beckett and Ionesco," *Hudson Review,* XI
          (Summer, 1958), 271-277.
A comparison of the two authors. Barbour points out, however, that the frequent coupling of these two playwrights is misleading and puts both of them
at a disadvantage. Ionesco is "not an egghead," not at all philosophic, but
purely "theatrical." Beckett is all these things, and "superior" in all of them.

1430 BOWLES, Patrick. "How Samuel Beckett Sees the Universe," *The
          Listener,* LIX (June 19, 1958), 1011-1012 [see **3007**].
As the cotranslator with Beckett himself of *Molloy,* Bowles is well qualified to
discuss this novel. He sees it as the first novel in which Beckett reveals
clearly his own "vision of the Universe," and in it, he is "preparing himself
to abandon literary writing" and move on to a structureless universe of
"natural rhythms."

1431 BRIEN, Alan. "Waiting for Beckett," *The Spectator,* Nov. 7, 1958,
          p. 609.
In this review-article of *Krapp's Last Tape* and *Endgame,* art is discussed as
the "last illusion, and Beckett seeks to destroy even that by creating deliberately
inartistic works of art. . . . He is a literary suicide desperate to die alone."

1432 BROOKE-ROSE, Christine. "Samuel Beckett and the Anti-Novel,"
          London Magazine, V (Dec., 1958), 38-46.
Beckett belongs to the timeless tradition of "anti-novelists" whose ranks
number also Cervantes, Sterne, Gide, and Wilder. The genre may be defined
by the following characteristics: it "eludes period and is bound by no 'style,' "
it is both romantic and classical—"anti-formally fantastic and rigidly formal,"
it questions, with its self-mocking, form-conscious technique, the "realness of
reality. . . . Every anti-novel is an attempt to challenge some false reality."

1433 CALENDOLI, Giovanni. "Il giuoco di Beckett al margine dell'er-
          metismo," *Fiera Letteraria,* XIII (Sept. 21, 1958), 1.

1434 CAMI, B. "Lawrence Durrell, Samuel Beckett," *Vlaamse Gids,* XLII
          (Oct., 1958), 635-637.

1958

1435   CAVANAGH, Maura. "Waiting for God," *Audience,* V (Summer, 1958), 94-114.

A play parodying all of Beckett's work. Its two main characters are Sebastian Wickett and the Devil, whom Wickett does not know how to exorcise. An example of the dialogue: "Given the existence of a God qua mysterium tremendum who am the sine qua qua qua alpha and omega without end, who are we to say, that she is not a raspberry soufflé?"

1436   CHIAROMONTE, Nicola. "Beckett e la fine del mondo," *Il Mondo,* Sept. 16, 1958, p. 14.

1437   CIMATTI, Pietro. "Beckett uomo zero," *Fiera Letteraria,* XIII (Jan. 19, 1958), 2, 4, 7.

1438   CURTIS, Anthony. "Mood of the Month: IV," *London Magazine,* V (May, 1958), 60-65.

Endgame is one of the most serious and courageous dramatic experiments of our time. It has the astonishing concentration (the fantastic compliment that Beckett pays to an audience's reaction and quickness), the trusting economy and density, of his whole approach to the theater. Beckett's work has in general attempted to universalize Beckett's personal vision of modern man in decay.

1439   DAVIE, Donald. "Kinds of Comedy," *Spectrum,* II (Winter, 1958), 25-31.

The drama of *All That Fall* is "all in the language." It is about the concern with the dignity or the decrepitude of language, which is, after all, a "concern for the dignity or decrepitude of man." Beckett is here applying Joycean "perceptions of parody" not to the word, as Joyce did, but to the sentence.

1440   DEMING, Barbara. "John Osborne's War against the Philistines," *Hudson Review.* XI (Autumn, 1958), 411-419 (see esp. pp. 416-417).

Includes a comparison of *Endgame* and Osborne's *The Entertainer.* The two plays are alike in setting ("a domestic Hell"), and in tone; there is, however, more "affection" in Osborne's play, and more "insight" in Beckett's. The effort of *Endgame* is clearly to sharpen in us the sense of a familiar plight.

1441   DOBRÉE, Bonamy. "The London Theater, 1957: The Melting Pot," *Sewanee Review,* LXVI (Winter, 1958), 146-160 (Beckett, esp. **pp. 149-152).**

"Abundant and diverse material" is provided by this season's new plays as to how a play should be written. "Do you begin with an idea, for which you invent a symbol . . . or do you work from living beings . . . whose movements and passions become a symbol?" These are the basic questions asked and answered by contemporary dramatists. In *Endgame,* the author works around the first question and the play, as a result, "resolves itself into an elaborate game of 'hunt the symbol.' "

1442   DRIVER, Tom F. "Out in Left Field," *Christian Century,* LXXV (March 5, 1958), 282-283.

Though not so good a play as *Godot, Endgame* is not without its points. At the deepest level, the meaning is "horrifying, but the playwright manages to keep the surface of it interesting, comic, and even sentimental."

1958

1443   ETTO, E., and L. EHRLICH. "Keine Versöhnung mit dem Nichts," *Theater der Zeit,* III (1958), 31-34.

1444   FOWLIE, Wallace. "Fallen out of the World," *New York Herald Tribune Book Week,* Nov. 23, 1958, p. 4.

On *The Unnamable.*

1445   GASSNER, John. "Broadway in Review," *Educational Theatre Journal,* X (May, 1958), 122-131.

Beckett's *Endgame* is discussed among other plays: Gibson's *Two for the Seesaw,* Osborne's *The Entertainer,* Williams' *Something Unspoken* and *Suddenly Last Summer.* "*Endgame* is possessed of an integrity, a singleness of tone, a tenacity of purpose that is not 'left-bankish' for all its negativisim and Existentialist nausea."

1446   GELB, Philip. "Strictly Controversial: Most Playwrights are Fascists," *Tulane Drama Review,* III (Oct., 1958), 58-60 (Beckett, *passim*).

Gelb is complaining not because most dramatists "are fascists" — after all "it's a free country" — but because there are too many "randomly resentful plays." Dürrenmatt, Beckett, Anouilh, Aymé, Osborne, and others are writing primarily from a "sense of grievance . . . out of the psychology of resentment . . . to express emotions, not to achieve results."

1447   GRANSDEN, K. W. "The Dustman Cometh," *Encounter,* XI (July, 1958), 84-86.

According to Gransden, in this discussion of *Watt, Malone Dies,* and *Endgame,* man, as far as Beckett is concerned, is "absolutely and wretchedly innocent," condemned to his spiritually arrested "cell," at the "fag-end of human effort." His characters are "like men in a pub telling a very long shaggy-dog story," which, though funny, draws no laughs.

1448   HAMBRO, Carl. " 'Abstrakt roman'?" *Vinduet,* XII, no. 4 (1958), 285-293.

1449   HICKS, Granville. "Beckett's World," *Saturday Review of Literature,* XLI (Oct. 4, 1958), 14.

On Beckett's trilogy. All three novels, *Molloy, Malone Dies,* and *The Unnamable,* are dominated by "images of decay. . . . Never, I think, have the Anglo-Saxon monosyllables been used so effectively for the evocation of disgust."

1450   HAYMAN, David. [Introduction to an extract from *The Unnamable*], *Texas Quarterly,* I (Spring, 1958), 127-128 [see **377.002**].

1451   HOPE-WALLACE, Philip. "Theatre," *Time and Tide,* XXXIX (Nov. 8, 1958), 1344-1345.

On *End Game* [*sic*].

1452   KENNER, Hugh. "Samuel Beckett vs. Fiction," *National Review,* VI (Oct. 11, 1958), 248-249.

Because of a quirk of history, the "great Irish nihilists . . . have been the persistent reformers of fiction." Closely following this tradition, Beckett "has the true radical's grasp of how, in his own time, the art he would practise is situated," and "out of a simple perception of what the novel is," he

1958

1452

succeeds in being "the most accomplished master of the English prose sentence now living."

1453 ———. "The Beckett Landscape," *Spectrum*, II, no. 1 (Winter, 1958), 8-24.

This and the preceding piece are Hugh Kenner's first studies in a series of essays which led to his 1961 book, *Samuel Beckett: A Critical Study* [see **703**], the first important full-length study of Beckett. In this article Kenner sets the tone and the theme of his critical approach. Beckett's bizarre characters and themes resemble the uniquely comicotragic repertoire of the circus clown, while his novel settings "bear a moral resemblance to . . . the circus, where virtuosity is the principle of life." For Beckett, however, it is the mental virtuosity of memory that is all important, as he is convinced that novels "aren't lived but written out of the head."

1454 LEBESQUE, Morvan. "Le Théâtre aux enfers: Artaud, Beckett et quelques autres," *Cahiers de la Compagnie Madeleine Renaud–Jean-Louis Barrault*, 22-23 (May, 1958), 191-196.

In this special issue, "Artaud et le théâtre de notre temps," Mr. Lebesque's essay makes a rapprochement between Artaud and Beckett, and declares: "Je rougirais d'écrire une étude sur Artaud que je n'ai pas connu et sur Beckett que nul ne peut encore 'expliquer' valablement, à mon avis. Je ne crois pourtant pas m'éloigner d'une vérité à venir en affirmant que tous deux sont les représentants les plus authentiques du Théâtre aux Enfers." He concludes, however, by stating that Artaud is an intrepid traveler whereas Beckett still hesitates on the threshold of "Hell."

1455 McCOY, Charles. "*Waiting for Godot:* A Biblical Approach," *Florida Review*, 2 (Spring, 1958), 63-72. Reprinted in **1505**.

1456 MAGNY, Olivier de. "Panorama d'une nouvelle littérature romanesque," and "Voici dix romanciers," *Esprit*, XXVI (July-Aug., 1958), 3-53 (Beckett, *passim;* see esp. pp. 3-17, 36-39).

1457 MICHA, René. "Le Nouveau Roman," *L'Arc*, 4 (Autumn, 1958) (Beckett, p. 49).

1458 NICOLETTI, G. "Théâtre d'aujourd'hui: Ionesco et Beckett," *Biennale di Venezia*, VIII, no. 30 (1958), 33-37.

1459 NOON, William T. "Modern Literature and the Sense of Time," *Thought*, XXXIII (Winter, 1958-1959), 571-604 (Beckett, *passim*).

Bergson, Proust, Vico, Joyce, Beckett, and others are discussed in this well-documented article. Basically, Noon states that time and history are the two most distinctively characteristic literary themes of this century. "Can a man hope today to salvage his identity, to say nothing of his human dignity, from what T. S. Eliot has called this 'drifting wreckage' of time?" Beckett does not have the consciousness of a Joyce or a Proust about time; for him the dismissal of time (of society and all its institutions) is the starting point of the creative process.

1958

1460 PEARSON, Gabriel. "The Monologue of Samuel Beckett," *The Spectator,* April 11, 1958, p. 466.

On *Malone Dies* and *Watt.* "Beckett, of course, is a religious writer concerned with existence stripped of its trappings in time and place." The "boringness" of Beckett's work can be explained, partly by his "expatriate's condition," partly by his "outmoded modernism," and partly by his "unawareness of the reader."

1461 PICCHI, Mario. "Samuel Beckett: Introduzione," *Fiera Letteraria,* XIII (June 29, 1958), 7.

1462 _____. "Beckett: *Malone muore,*" *Fiera Letteraria,* XIII (Nov. 30, 1958), 2.

1463 ROSENBERG, Marvin. "A Metaphor for Dramatic Form," *Journal of Aesthetics and Art Criticism,* XVII (Dec., 1958), 174-180 (Beckett, *passim*).

Waiting for Godot is a good example of a "purely contextual drama, a theater image of a mental state." The play ends exactly where it began, though there are bits of movement within it, because it is a story not of the life of its characters but of a condition of living, and that is timeless.

1464 SCHNEIDER, Alan. "Waiting for Beckett: A Personal Chronicle," *Chelsea Review,* 2 (Autumn, 1958), 3-20 [see **719** and **3084**].

A personal and moving account of Schneider's friendship with Beckett. Schneider comments on the production problems of Beckett's plays: explaining meaning to the actors, the necessity of emphasizing local situation. He sees Beckett's characters as "individual personalities operating in a given set of circumstances," even if the circumstances are as irregular as two truncated figures in ash cans. "They are not to be considered as abstractions or symbols, or as representing anything other than themselves."

1465 SCHUMACH, Murray. "Why They Wait for Godot," *New York Times Magazine,* Sept. 21, 1958, pp. 36, 38, 41.

A general review of critical response to *Godot* from professional critics, the cast, producer, and director, and overheard audience comments. This article also quotes a letter from Beckett to the producer: "It is gratifying to learn that the bulk of your audience was made up of young people. I must, after all, be less dead than I thought."

1466 SIMON, Alfred. "Le Théâtre est-il mortel?" *Esprit,* XXVI (Jan., 1958), 1-19 (Beckett, *passim;* see esp. "L'Avant-garde," p. 17).

An interesting and well-documented discussion of the crisis of contemporary French theater. "Chez Ionesco et Becket [*sic*] la scène est toujours le cul-de-sac de l'attente, le bout d'une route sans issue partie de l'existence humaine."

1467 SPENDER, Stephen. "Lifelong Suffocation," *New York Times Book Review,* Oct. 12, 1958, p. 5.

In reviewing *The Unnamable,* Spender claims that one of the "dozen or so writers whom those concerned with modern man in search of his soul should read is Beckett." In this novel, he pursues the theme of the "search for self." The theme is analogous to Yeats's "identity of opposites," and in pursuing it, Beckett turns "frustration into its opposite: the theme of the lifelong ordeal

1958

1467

of suffocation, which cannot stop. He has discovered the other side of negativism, the strange joy of the man who lives in a darkened cave and watches the images of life outside reflected dancing on the wall."

1468   STONIER, G. W. "Waiting for What-Not," *New Statesman*, LV (March 15, 1958), 342-343.

Watt is a "splendid comedy in the murk." It exhibits Beckett's "great gift for clowning," combining "lucid comedy with maddeningly impassable stretches of prose." In *Malone Dies* "the obsessive and reiterative itch has been eliminated, but there is less comedy."

1469   THIÉBAUT, Marcel. "Le 'Nouveau Roman,' " *Revue de Paris*, LXV (Oct., 1958), 140-155 (Beckett, esp. pp. 140-148).

1470   TINDALL, William York. "Beckett's Bums," *Critique: Studies in Modern Fiction*, II (Spring-Summer, 1958), 3-15. Reprinted privately as a brochure (70 copies) by Shenval Press, London, 1960.

All Beckett's characters are splittings off of *L'Innommable*—all outsiders who through impotence, ignorance, or disintegration have become insiders. The plays and novels compose a single vision, the unidentifiable seeking identity, the indefinable seeking definition. Beckett's controlling principle seems to be monotonous, repetitious with variation, a technique where tedium itself becomes a functional stylistic and thematic element. The trilogy [*Molloy, Malone Dies, The Unnamable*] is in a sense "a portrait of the artist as an old man."

1471   WALKER, Roy. "Samuel Beckett's Double Bill: Love, Chess and Death," *Twentieth Century*, CLXIV (Dec., 1958), 533-544.

On *Endgame* and *Krapp's Last Tape*. "Those who hold, with Hamlet, that the purpose of playing is to show man his own nature and the very age and body of the time his form and pressure . . . may have to recognize Beckett's scathing satires on the sin and instability of man as among the greatest plays yet to appear on the modern stage."

1472   WANDERSCHECK, H. "Die Pariser Theateravantgardisten," *Maske und Kothurn*, IV (1958), 1-14.

1473   WORSLEY, T. C. "Private Worlds and Public," *New Statesman*, LVI (Nov. 8, 1958), 630.

In this review of *Endgame* and *Krapp's Last Tape*, Beckett is compared to Hauptmann, but Worsley concludes by saying, "What a relief to step into the lucidity of Hauptmann after the inverted explorations of the seamier side of Mr. Beckett's nasty unconscious!"

1959

1474   ANONYMOUS. "The Anti-Novel in France," *Times Literary Supplement*, Feb. 13, 1959, p. 82.

Beckett is one of the "group," whose fiction is a reaction, similar to that of the Beat generation in the United States, to a "world which has become too complicated . . . with problems of money and power." A tendency toward literary "anarchism" is characteristic of this group of novelists.

1959

1475   ABBEY, Edward. *"Watt," New Mexico Quarterly,* XXIX (Autumn, 1959), 381-383.

In *Watt,* as in others of Beckett's novels, the specialty seems to be "lunatic rationalism, grotesque suffering, and comic misery." These dominant themes represent another expression of the "malady which has troubled Western literature for the last 200 years—the Great Christian Hangover." For those still suffering from this hangover, *Watt* may provide some entertainment and consolation.

1476   ABEL, Lionel. "Joyce the Father, Beckett the Son," *New Leader,* XLII (Dec. 14, 1959), 26-27. Reprinted in **1055**.

Godot and *Endgame* may be interpreted as dramatizations of Beckett's relationship with Joyce. Figures of superiority (Hamm, Pozzo) represent Beckett's idealization and fear of Joyce; figures of subservience (Clov, Lucky) are Beckett himself in relation to the "Master." All Beckett's novels are "flights from Joyce, perhaps towards Kafka." In the light of more recent criticism which, rightly so, underplays the Joyce influence on Beckett, this type of argument is less and less convincing.

1477   BAJINI, Sandro. "Samuel Beckett o l'emblema totale," *Il Verri,* III (April, 1959), 70-88.

1478   BARR, Donald. "One Man's Universe," *New York Times Book Review,* June 21, 1959, pp. 4, 26.

Watt is an "exquisitely boring" novel which shows Mr. Beckett's universe to be filled with "cruelty, yet empty of purpose, deformed, yet ultimately formless."

1479   BARRETT, William. "How I Understand Less and Less Every Year," *Columbia University Forum,* II (Winter, 1959), 44-48.

Beckett's philosophic conclusion to the problems posed in his writing is reached in *The Unnamable:* "language exists in order to make silence possible, just as, in turn, language is possible only through its vast environing silence." With the aid of a "traditional and orthodox imagination," Beckett, in the trilogy, attacks the eternal subjects of "human art and thought, the passage of time, and the incomprehensible and questionable identity of the self."

1480   BIRMINGHAM, William. *"The Unnamable," Crosscurrents,* IX (Winter, 1959), 74.

This novel is a fine example of "unwholesome theory . . . superbly communicated." Beckett's work is a *"summa* of lyrical objections, woven around the single vision of an existence that can only be endured."

1481   BLANCHOT, Maurice. "Where Now? Who Now?" *Evergreen Review,* II (Winter, 1959), 222-229. Trans. by Richard Howard of the article that first appeared in **1309**.

1482   BOISDEFFRE, Pierre de. "Un nouveau roman français," *Études,* CCCI (April, 1959), 70-79.

1483   BRICK, Allan. "The Madman in His Cell: Joyce, Beckett, Nabokov, and the Stereotypes," *Massachusetts Review,* I (Oct., 1959), 40-55.

Interesting parallels are drawn between the work of these three writers. All three deal with the "imprisonment of the public mind by mass culture."

1959

1483

Each author tries in his own way to come to terms with "stereotyped reality." Joyce creates a Bloom who, aware of being "manipulated," becomes in turn a manipulator." Nabokov, on the other hand, writing in the full tradition of American idealism as well as of English social analysis, succeeds with Humbert Humbert, in "frontally assaulting" stereotyped reality and mass culture. Beckett writes from the standpoint that perhaps "man himself doesn't exist," much less the stereotyped reality around him.

1484   COHN, Ruby. "The Comedy of Samuel Beckett: 'Something Old, Something New' . . . ," *Yale French Studies*, 23 (Summer, 1959), 11-17.

Ruby Cohn has written extensively on Beckett. This is her first article. Particularly interested by the comic gamut [see **704**] of Beckett's work, she points out that he avails himself of the full tradition of comic domains, from Aristotle, through Bergson to the present-day genre. His wit exploits "situation, language and character," comedy of manners, "cosmological comedy," *l'humour noir*. But Beckett also creates a "unique philosophical genre, the epistemological comedy."

1485   _____. "Still Novel," *Yale French Studies*, 24 (Fall, 1959), 48-53 [erroneously dated as 23 (Summer, 1959)].

The novels of the trilogy are traditional in the sense that their movement depends on the "quest" motif, symbolic quests that they may be. There is a double and parallel "quest" going on throughout the trilogy: that of an individual finding a "distinctive identity," and that of a writer finding his fiction. Beckett's heroes are not "rationalists," but "romantics," and as such are "always prey to their quests."

1486   _____. "Preliminary Observations," *Perspective*, XI (Autumn, 1959), 119-131 [see **900**]. Also in this issue (pp. 193-196) "A Checklist of Beckett Criticism," compiled by Ruby Cohn, this being the first attempt at a Beckett bibliography [see **3110**].

Serves as an introduction to the special Samuel Beckett issue of *Perspective*. Ruby Cohn emphasizes that all of Beckett's work, from the poems and smaller pieces published early in the 30's to the later plays and novels, shows evidence of a single developing train of thought, which, though expressed by different voices—the "itinerant 'I' " of the early poems to the (variously named or unnamed narrator) creators of the later work—develops toward the premise that the "quest for identity and a distinctive language" can only drive man to an impasse from which he can never be extricated.

1487   CORRIGAN, Robert W. "The Image of Man in the Contemporary Theatre," *Forum*, III (Spring, 1959), 46-55 (Beckett, *passim*).

1488   DREWS, Wolfgang. "Die grossen Unsichtbaren: VII, Godot," *Theater der Zeit*, VI (Feb., 1959), 107-109.

1489   EASTMAN, Richard M. "The Strategy of Samuel Beckett's *Endgame*," *Modern Drama*, II (May, 1959), 36-44.

Although it is stultifying to dismiss this play as an unanalyzable allegory, since it is based on Beckett's belief that the "isolation of individuality precludes

1959

1489

communication in terms of conventional surface," still the spectator must
make an effort to understand. The setting's indefiniteness suggests that the
play deals with "man and his situation," though it also suggests a chess game
and the "theater reality" (the play as play).

1490 FOWLIE, Wallace. "The New French Theater: Artaud, Beckett,
Genet, Ionesco," *Sewanee Review,* LXVII (Autumn, 1959), 643-
657 (see esp. pp. 648-651). Reprinted in a slightly different form
in **1018.**

Despite its conglomeration of effects and technique. *Godot* is "far from being
a pastiche." It possesses an "utter simplicity" in the classical French tradition.
Endgame is a metaphysical treatment of the "problem of solitude" and of
"the approach of the end."

1491 FRIEDMAN, Melvin J. "The Achievement of Samuel Beckett,"
Books Abroad, XXXIII (Summer, 1959), 278-281.

A general introduction to Beckett's work, including some biographical data,
and a discussion of the differences of his French work from his English.

1492 GERARD, Martin. "Is Your Novel Really Necessary?" *X: A Quarterly Review,* I (Nov., 1959), 46-52 (Beckett, *passim*).

"When we look at those prose-writers who have tried to solve this problem
(on the one hand, silence: on the other, lies) of giving truth its being, of
bringing it into existence through the medium of a fiction which should not
be fictitious, we find that one and all are distinguished from the novelists
of a spurious invention by the possession of a language which can, like the
language of poets, comprehend and render interesting in the actual inscape
of being: Melville, Joyce, Beckett, Proust, for example."

1493 GIRAUD, Raymond. "Unrevolt among the Unwriters in France
Today," *Yale French Studies,* 24 (Fall, 1959), 11-17 [erroneously
dated 23 (Summer, 1959)].

Compares Sartre, Camus, Malraux to Beckett, Butor, Robbe-Grillet, but also
attempts to explain the complexity of the modern novel in relation to a simpli-
fied tradition of the novel. "The objectivity of Robbe-Grillet, the interminable
unanswered questionings of Beckett's characters . . . all these are curiously
suggestive of Flaubert's refusal to 'conclude,' the futile inquiries of Bouvard
and Pécuchet, the pessimistic 'Buddhism' of Schopenhauer and of Leconte de
Lisle and, of course, the aestheticism of *l'art pour l'art,* in which passion for
art responds to the despair of life."

1494 GORELICK, Mordecai. "An Epic Theatre Catechism," *Tulane
Drama Review,* IV (Sept., 1959), 90-95 (Beckett, *passim*).

Mostly a discussion of the misused and misunderstood notion of "epic theater"
as conceived by Brecht. Mr. Gorelick asks: "Are plays like Samuel Beckett's
Waiting for Godot epic?" And he answers: "This notion is naïve. Epic is
opposed to naturalistic writing and the picture-frame, peep-box, proscenium-
frame stage; the supposition is, therefore, that all non-naturalistic plays are
epic. But in fact epic opposes all plays, whether naturalistic or not, which
fail to create living characters, plausible motivations, or rational dilemmas."

1959

1495   GREGORY, Horace. "Prose and Poetry of Samuel Beckett," *Commonweal*, LXXI (Oct. 30, 1959), 162-163. An abridged restatement of an article that appeared in **1362**.

1496   HAMILTON, Kenneth. "Boon or Thorn? Joyce Cary and Samuel Beckett on Human Life," *Dalhousie Review*, XXXVIII (Winter, 1959), 433-442.

By comparing the trilogies of the two authors, Hamilton comes to the conclusion that Cary is an "optimist" and Beckett a "pessimist" in their respective observations on the value of human existence. Cary's mode of "traditional realism" sustains a character, Gulley Jimson, who resembles Beckett's Molloy in his "independent indifference to fate and fortune which makes them appear as having nothing yet possessing all things."

1497   HOEFER, Jacqueline. *"Watt," Perspective*, XI (Autumn, 1959), 166-182 [see **900**]. Reprinted in **711**.

One of the most quoted articles on *Watt*. Miss Hoefer is the first to have pointed out the possible parallel between Wittgenstein's logical positivism and *Watt*'s "philosophical satire." The subject of the novel is the significance of system, and its ultimate "uselessness" when confronted with that which eludes rational analysis. Watt is a "peculiarly modern hero . . . seeking with . . . modern weapons to comprehend that which is beyond human comprehension."

1498   INGHAM, Patricia. "The Renaissance of Hell," *The Listener*, LXII (Sept. 3, 1959), 349-351 (Beckett, *passim*).

Anouilh, Cocteau, Williams, and Beckett are sharing in the revival and modernization of the Orpheus myth, in which Hell is given a contemporary "domestic" setting. In *Endgame*, Hell is characterized as "other people, and the pattern of our shared misery . . . the inescapableness of the sharing."

1499   KENNER, Hugh. "The Cartesian Centaur," *Perspective*, XI (Autumn, 1959), 132-141 [see **900**]. Reprinted in **703**; see also **711**.

In the image of Beckett's man riding a bicycle—an image that occurs throughout his earlier work—three philosophic ideals are united: the Greek centaur, which combined the "noblest functions of rational and animal being," Newtonian equilibrium—man and machine mingled "in conjoint stasis, each indispensable to the other's support"—and a resolution of the Cartesian mind-body schism, troubling philosophers for three centuries. Beckett symbolizes mankind's weaning from the Cartesian process backward in the trilogy.

1500   ———. "The Absurdity of Fiction," *The Griffin*, VIII (Nov., 1959), 13-16.

In this discussion of the trilogy, Kenner emphasizes that "Samuel Beckett is a comic writer: not a clown, nor even a specialist in ludicrous situations, but a man who has discovered comedy in the very movements of the human mind." Beckett's fiction has a "spiral form," it closes in on a "pursuit for identity which the novelist shares with every 20th-century citizen: have we made this queer culture . . . or has it made us?"

1501   KERN, Edith. "Moran-Molloy: The Hero as Author," *Perspective*, XI (Autumn, 1959), 183-193 [see **900**].

1959

1501

Moran is an "author consciously engaged in literary creation . . . his *raison d'être.*" On one level of interpretation, he is on an artistic quest to fully create his character, Molloy; on another level, Moran is engaged in a search for Yeats's "other self." On the level of artistic creation, Moran's journey is from the "Apollonian microcosmic" world of "individual existence, reason, beauty, and will to the Dionysian macrocosmic" world of the "eternal, the universal, the immaterial, and the mythical."

1502 _____. "Samuel Beckett, Dionysian Poet," *Descant,* III (Winter, 1959), 33-36.

Beckett's novel *Molloy* blends the myth of the hero in two aspects: the protagonist seeks his opposite, or other self, and the hero searches for his mother-bride, in whom he finds both death and new life. This blending evokes the Nietzschean conception of the Apollonian and Dionysian elements in Greek poetry.

1503 LA CAPRIA, Raffaele. "Il 'nuovo romanzo' sta aspettando Godot?" *Tempo Presente,* IV (April, 1959), 283-289.

1504 LAMONT, Rosette C. "The Metaphysical Farce: Beckett and Ionesco," *French Review,* XXXII (Feb., 1959), 319-328 [see **902**, **1803**].

To reflect postwar nihilism ("the sickness of the void which the existentialists call 'nausea' ") a new form of theater was needed. The new genre was created by Beckett and Ionesco: "the metaphysical farce." It is an "anti-play, comic drama, a tragic farce, a pseudo drama . . . a twentieth century morality play which does not preach."

1505 McCOY, Charles. *"Waiting for Godot:* A Biblical Appraisal," *Religion in Life,* XXVIII (Fall, 1959), 595-603. Originally published in **1455**.

1506 McDONNELL, Thomas A. *"The Unnamable,"* *The Critic,* XVII (April-May, 1959), 49-50.

"It is not Samuel Beckett's . . . English that is impenetrable. On the contrary, it is overwhelmingly lucid." It is rather the motive that "compelled its writing in the first place." The question that arises after "attempting" to read *The Unnamable* is this: is Beckett "one of the first authentic searchers for the human soul in modern fiction," or has he "succeeded in amassing the most insidious structure . . . of solipsism ever put down on paper?"

1507 MARCABRU, Pierre. "Le Théâtre étranger de langue française: Ionesco, Beckett, Adamov, Schehadé," *Signes du Temps,* I (Aug.-Sept., 1959), 32-33.

1508 MAYOUX, Jean-Jacques. "The Theater of Samuel Beckett," *Perspective,* XI (Autumn, 1959), 142-155 [see **900**]. Trans. and reprinted from **1406**.

1509 MERCIER, Vivian. "The Mathematical Limit," *The Nation,* CLXXXVIII (Feb. 14, 1959), 144-145.

This ingenious discussion of Beckett's fiction shows to what extent it can inspire the imagination of the critic. By means of converting the discussion

1959

1509

of Beckett's novels into mathematical terminology (*"Malone Dies* could probably be represented as a parabolic curve from nothingness back to nothingness," or "Watt's career might be represented graphically as the curve of a
function which diminishes until it approaches zero and then gradually in-
creases"), one can see that Beckett "seems to be trying to define the limit of
the novel and . . . of existence itself."

1510   ———. "The Arrival of the Anti-Novel," *Commonweal,* LXX
        (May 8, 1959), 149-151 (see esp. p. 151).

A general discussion of the "new novel" in France. Mr. Mercier points out,
however, that "the new writers have succeeded best in the novel's negation
of itself. Beckett's trilogy is from one point of view a treatise on the impossibility of writing a novel, and one which parodies many familiar types of novel."

1511   ———. "How To Read *Endgame,*" *The Griffin,* VIII (June,
        1959), 10-14.

Endgame is "unquestionably a play about the end of the world," in which
Beckett is trying to create a new dramatic genre out of a combination of a
"purposefully aborted tragedy," with "tragic monsters" replacing "tragic
heroes," and a "willfully aborted comedy," in which the laughs are all of a
"mirthless" variety. Whereas *Godot* is a "despairing study of hope," *Endgame*
is a "despairing study of despair."

1512   MILLER, Karl. "Beckett's Voices," *Encounter,* XIII (Sept., 1959),
        59-61.

On *All That Fall* and *Embers.* Radio is a good medium for Beckett's expression because "broadcasting protects his lack of interest in character and drama
as they are normally understood." These plays are, however, "technically weak
and repetitive, and their obscurity points to a writer who is consumed with
certain feelings and who hasn't the means of control which art is supposed
to need."

1513   MINTZ, Samuel I. "Beckett's *Murphy:* A 'Cartesian' Novel," *Per-
        spective,* XI (Autumn, 1959), 156-165 [see **900**].

One of the few, and no doubt one of the best, articles devoted to *Murphy.*
This "funny, Geulincxian novel" is a completely successful novel of ideas. It
parodies the philosopher Geulincx, who reworked Descartes's theories of mind
and body and announced the dictum: "The parts of the body are God's
puppets; but the human mind is free." Murphy's life is a series of events
designed to carry him from the "macrocosmos" within to the "microcosmos"
of the mind.

1514   MONTICELLI, R. de. "L'Ultima avanguardia," *Il Sipario,* 164
        (1959), 38-44.

1515   PICCHI, Mario. "Lettera romana: Conclusione su Beckett," *Fiera
        Letteraria,* XIV (Jan. 4, 1959), 6.

1516   POLITZER, Heinz. "The Egghead Waits for Godot," *Christian
        Scholar,* XLII (March, 1959), 46-50.

Waiting for Godot was written by "the extreme egghead and Irishman, Samuel
Beckett, who was a friend of the founding father of modern literature, the

1959

1516

still more extreme egghead and Irishman, James Joyce." The play "abounds in veiled and direct references to Christology; it is one of the few experimental dramas in which Christ has won out over Oedipus as well as Priapus and Narcissus."

1517   PULLINI, Giorgio, and Renato CASAROTTO. "Da Patroni Griffi a Beckett, a Venezia," *Letterature Moderne,* IX (May-June, 1959), 366-376.

1518   RAES, Hugo. "Samuel Beckett im Amerika," *Vlaamse Gids,* XLIII (July, 1959), 495-496.

On *The Unnamable.*

1519   RODGER, Ian. "Perishing on the Shore," *The Listener,* LXII (July 2, 1959), 35-36.

On *Embers:* "it had the familiar trade marks of our greatest living obscurantist." Henry contemplates his life's omissions, his "sin of incapacity."

1520   STRAUSS, Walter A. "Dante's Belacqua and Beckett's Tramps," *Comparative Literature,* XI (Summer, 1959), 250-261.

One of the first articles to examine Beckett's debt to Dante. Beckett can be studied as a contemporary commentator on the "spiritual dilemma of expectancy." He uses, as Dante used, the image of Belacqua waiting in the foetal position to enter purgatory. This image depicts for Beckett the "self in the process of disintegration." In this sense, Beckett can be called the "poet of vegetation," his *Godot* the "blissful fiction of our Belacqua imagination."

1521   UNTERECKER, John. "Notes on Off-Broadway Theater," *Evergreen Review,* II (Spring, 1959), 152-163 (Beckett, *passim*).

"As everyone who has ever attended a play knows, the paying customers fall into two very clearly opposed camps: in one camp, the bored audience in search of distraction ('I don't go to the theater to think; I go to be entertained') . . . in the other camp, an eager (often grim) audience in search of elemental truth ('I don't go to the theater to be amused; I go to be confronted with Reality')." *Endgame,* Beckett's "funny, grim account of the species man's terrible anguish of survival in a post-Darwinian meaningless world, belongs to the audience who wants to be confronted with reality."

1522   _____. "Samuel Beckett's No-Man's-Land," *New Leader,* XLII (May 18, 1959), 24-25.

Beckett provides for his readers only "syntactical patterns without any assigned values," realizing that the order that man is compelled to construct upon the "jumble of reality . . . is a fake order," and that man, being rational, must recognize the "illusory nature of living."

1523   VERKEIN, Lea. "Wachten met Beckett," *Vlaamse Gids,* XLIII (Dec., 1959), 842-845.

On *Fin de partie.*

1524   VOGEL, M. "Endstation Beckett, Ionesco, und was weiter?" *Theater der Zeit,* VI (May, 1959).

1525   WILSON, Colin. "Existential Criticism," *Chicago Review,* XIII (Summer, 1959), 152-181 (Beckett, *passim*).

1959

1525

Existentialism attempts to philosophize with no reference to a priori intellectual concepts, except for the value judgment concerned with inner reality. Existential criticism is based upon this philosophical position. The existential critic can therefore dismiss Beckett's pessimism as arrested metaphysical growth, and find a more authentic vision in D. H. Lawrence, though his mysticism cannot be taken at face value, and see T. S. Eliot's world rejection as an inability to get a kick out of living.

1960

1526   ANONYMOUS. "On the Margin," *X: A Quarterly Review*, I (March, 1960), 158-160 (Beckett, *passim*).

This piece about experimental writing states that "the term experimental writing, as applied say to Beckett, is in any case meaningless. Any experiment is something that is torn up or remains in a drawer. *Molloy* is not an experiment but a rip-roaring success."

1527   ABIRACHED, Robert. "Carnet de théâtre." *Études*, CCCV (June, 1960), 404-407.

1528   BENITEZ-CLAROS, Rafael. "Teatro europeo del existencialismo al antiteatro," *Revista de la Universidad de Madrid*, IX, no. 33 (1960), 235-254.

1529   BLAU, Herbert. "Meanwhile, Follow the Bright Angels," *Tulane Drama Review*, V (Sept., 1960), 89-101 (see esp. pp. 90-91).

This articulate statement of purpose in the American theater came about as a result of Blau's observations of the European theater scene. He met with Beckett in Paris and talked about his work and plans. "What enlivened and disturbed him most was my remark about the language of his dramas. I said that by writing in French he was evading some part of himself (pause). He said yes, there were a few things about himself he didn't like, that French had the right 'weakening' effect." Beckett's choice of language "accounts for the stringent clarity . . . of his plays, and for their limits, for the English language, like French politics, has an impulse toward anarchy, a stretch of accident and evocation that he could not allow himself."

1530   BRUSTEIN, Robert. "Krapp and a Little Claptrap," *New Republic*, CXLIII (Feb. 22, 1960), 21-22.

Krapp's Last Tape is a brief and beautiful work of art, Beckett's "best dramatic poem about the Old Age of the world." Flawless in form, as *Godot* and *Endgame* were not, the play presents the "perfect realization of Beckett's idea of human isolation."

1531   CHADWICK, C. "*Waiting for Godot:* A Logical Approach," *Symposium*, XIV (Winter, 1960), 252-257.

An "anti-Christian" play built around the image of a "cruel God" (in the person of Pozzo), a "tyrant and a slave-driver," who is indifferent to man's suffering, and is not worthy of "awe and respect." Pozzo (God) exhibits his "callous sense of fun" by playing blind in the second act.

1960

1532 CHAMPIGNY, Robert. "Interprétation de *En attendant Godot,*" *PMLA,* LXXV (June, 1960), 329-331.

The play is examined from three different points of view: from a mythological perspective ("le couple Pozzo-Lucky se place dans la perspective d'un mythe sociologique, le couple Vladimir-Estragon dans la perspective d'un mythe théologique") ; in function of its theatrical language ("les personnages existent par la parole . . . par le jeu scénique") ; as an "anti-Cartesian" meditation, that is to say in existentialist terms.

1533 CIMATTI, Pietro. "L'Ironia di Beckett," *Fiera Letteraria,* XV (March 6, 1960), 1-2.

1534 CLOSS, August. "Formprobleme und Möglichkeiten zur Gestaltung der Tragödie in der Gegenwart," *Stil- und Formprobleme,* V (1960), 483-491.

Compares the poetic drama of Eliot, Fry, and Beckett.

1535 CLURMAN, Harold. "Theater," *The Nation,* CXC (Feb. 13, 1960), 153-154.

Krapp's Last Tape is a "study of loneliness" with a thread of "sentimentality running through its dismal fabric." It is only a "marginal sketch in the body" of Beckett's more ambitious work.

1536 CMARADA, Geraldine. "*Malone Dies:* A Round of Consciousness," *Symposium,* XIV (Autumn, 1960), 199-212.

The novel is a "case history" of an "absurd man" in an atheistic, existential world, the victim of a vicious system that denies him hope, self-respect, and real knowledge. "Beckett has seized the existential devil, and freed it of mere theoretical value by displaying its fiendish operation in the soul of Malone." The novel is a "philosophic satire," in which the "perverted sense of freedom" existentialism gives is mocked.

1537 COHN, Ruby. "*Endgame:* The Gospel According to Sad Sam Beckett," *Accent,* XX (Autumn, 1960), 223-234. Reprinted in **704**.

Endgame is a "bitterly ironic version of creation and resurrection." Just as "waiting" summarizes the action in *Godot,* the constant repetition of the word "finished" gives this play its predominant movement. "The dramatic action presents the death of the stock props of Western civilization—family cohesion, filial devotion, parental and connubial love, faith in God, empirical knowledge, and artistic creation." Biblical symbolism predominates, from the obvious device of the naming of the characters, to the very special parody of the Gospel according to St. John (" 'In the beginning, was the Word' ").

1538 _____. "Waiting Is All," *Modern Drama,* III (Sept., 1960), 162-167.

In a subtle building and then destruction of the symmetry and repetition, Beckett gives the "impression of stasis" in *Godot.* At the same time, the tension developed between the building and destruction creates the "dramatic movement" of the play.

1960

1539   ———. "A Note on Beckett, Dante, and Geulincx," *Comparative Literature*, XII (Winter, 1960), 93-94.
A brief refutation of Walter Strauss's contention that Beckett's heroes are "vegetative" [see **1520**]. Ruby Cohn answers that, to the contrary, they "are fighting with a fierceness unparalleled in metaphysical art." She also discusses sources in Beckett's work, and calls it "a happy-hunting-ground for comparatists."

1540   COLEMAN, John. "Under the Jar," *The Spectator*, April 8, 1960, p. 516.
On the trilogy. The world of Beckett is characterized by its "extraordinary emotional poverty." It is peopled by heroes who are "senile, impotent, maimed, given to prurience, blasphemy, and amnesia; as devalued as the 'little portable things in wood and stone' that they hoard." The author seems to relish their torment.

1541   CRAIG, H. A. L. "Poetry in the Theater," *New Statesman*, LX (Nov. 12, 1960), 734, 736.
Beckett, alone, of all contemporary poetic playwrights, "has the language, invention, and the unremitting discipline to sustain poetry for the length of a play."

1542   DRIVER, Tom F. "Rebuke to Nihilism," *Christian Century*, LXXVII (March 2, 1960), 256-257.
Krapp's Last Tape is "the best theater now visible in New York." The quality of human love shining in all Beckett's plays instills in them the "hope" that is "evidence that true art is always a rebuke to nihilism."

1543   EASTMAN, Richard M. "The Open Parable: Demonstration and Definition," *College English*, XXII (Oct., 1960), 15-18 (Beckett, *passim*).
The "open parable" is a small genre of modern narrative brought to high intensity by such writers as Kafka and Beckett. The authors of such parables usually enforce a "logical refusal to explain intention." *Molloy* and *Endgame* are fine examples of the "open parable."

1544   ESSLIN, Martin. "The Theatre of the Absurd," *Tulane Drama Review*, IV (May, 1960), 3-15 [see **1069**].
Esslin is largely responsible for the popularity of the expression "theatre of the absurd." The definition he gives in this article was subsequently expanded in **1025**. The plays of Beckett, Adamov, and Ionesco have been successful, though the audience "could not understand what they meant." One explanation invokes the values of pure theater and of abstract stagecraft; a more complete explanation is that these plays meet some of the "deepest needs and unexpressed yearnings of their audience." The plays reveal the "irrationality of the human condition and the illusion of its apparently logical structure," by attempting to externalize and project outward what is happening in the deeper recesses of the mind.

1545   ———. "The Absurdity of the Absurd," *Kenyon Review*, XXII (Fall, 1960), 670-673.
A "correction" of Ward Hooker's faulty definition of "absurd" in **1555**. Esslin

1960

1545

points out that in French the term absurd does not mean "funny" or "ironical," but "contrary to reason," purposeless, meaningless. The absurdity of the French avant-garde dramatists thus does not spring from their use of irony. It springs from the subject matter of their plays, "the absurdity of the human condition." Laughter, in this case, is not caused by perception of the ironical situation, but by the "release within the audience of their own repressed feelings of frustration."

1546   FANIZZA, Franco. "La Parola e il silenzio nel *Innommable* di Samuel Beckett," *Aut Aut*, 60 (Nov., 1960), 380-391.

1547   FRIEDMAN, Melvin J. "The Creative Writer as Polyglot: Valéry Larbaud and Samuel Beckett," *Transactions of the Wisconsin Academy of Sciences, Arts and Letters*, XLIX (1960), 229-236.

Among the twentieth-century writers who have felt the need to express themselves in more than one language, Larbaud and Beckett stand out—each an accomplished representative of a different kind of polyglot. Larbaud uses his "cosmopolitan" knowledge of languages as a literary device; he translates texts. Beckett is a writer who is "ambidextrously" suited to change languages "when he feels aesthetically disposed," and his "profound immersion" in either French or English causes his "literary personality" to change as he changes his language. He creates a new "genuinely original version" of the text he translates.

1548   _____. "The Novels of Samuel Beckett: An Amalgam of Joyce and Proust," *Comparative Literature*, XII (Winter, 1960), 47-58.

Beckett's early English novels are influenced by Joyce primarily, and the trilogy by Proust, although echoes of both authors are discerned throughout all stages of Beckett's work. One could read Beckett's critical essays on both Proust and Joyce as "program notes to the finished trilogy." He is indebted to Joyce for a strong sense of "spatial awareness," a concentration on "things," on the "purely physical," and for the generous portions of "Irish wit" which spice his novels. Proust gave him a sense of "temporal awareness," introspection, and the "psycho-literary device" of involuntary memory.

1549   _____. "Samuel Beckett and the *Nouveau Roman*," *Wisconsin Studies in Contemporary Literature*, I (Spring-Summer, 1960), 22-36 [see **1789**].

Beckett deserves to be considered with the contemporary French school of "antinovelists," rather than with England's "angry young men." Whereas the English school concentrates on social themes, the French "chosistes" are concerned with experiment in form, with the structure of the novel. Beckett follows also the tradition of Dostoevski and Kafka who tried to isolate man and study his relationship with his "self," and although Beckett's novels "proceed with the unhurried pace of leisurely essays," his characters are almost invariably grotesques, on the verge of insanity, and both psychologically and physically inept.

1550   FRYE, Northrop. "The Nightmare Life in Death," *Hudson Review*, XIII (Autumn, 1960), 442-449.

1960

1550

On the trilogy. Beckett's work has a "mythic" rather than an "allegorical" quality. It moves simultaneously in the areas of psychology, society, and religion, "interconnecting them, and the all-inclusiveness gives his work a wide appeal and stimulates diversified criticism."

1551   GERARD, Martin. "Molloy Becomes Unnamable," *X: A Quarterly Review*, I (Oct., 1960), 314-319.

The trilogy, criticized for its formlessness, indeed has a form, a form in "anagogical relationship to the meaning"; and the meaning may be expressed as an act of faith in literary creation, which, while questioning the ability of an artist to "speak directly to the truth," still asserts his need to arrive at it, even though the only means at his disposal are "fiction" and "lies."

1552   GRILLO, Giuseppe. "Samuel Beckett fra anti-teatro e anti-romanzo," *Idea*, XVI (Oct., 1960), 698-700.

1553   HARVEY, Lawrence E. "Art and the Existential in *En attendant Godot*," *PMLA*, LXXV (March, 1960), 137-146.

Godot is a work of art, primarily, and its function as such is the function of all art: to destroy the conventional world and re-create a "deeper level of reality," in this case, an existential reality. Beckett accomplishes this "erosion" by means of wordplay, the symbolic replacement of "chronometric time" with existential time (watch tick becomes heartbeat), the replacement of circular imagery, which represents the Judeo-Christian concept of eternity, with linear imagery—the existential "fearful descending line that ends in the grave."

1554   HATCH, Robert. "Laughter at Your Own Risk," *Horizon*, III (Sept., 1960), 112-116.

Krapp's Last Tape is the portrayal of the death of an artist, which is perhaps Beckett himself. Beckett, however, is certainly not any more "despairing" than Sophocles or Heine; his "fables" may deal with "dire experiences" but they do not depress. "There is a poetic virility to his people, an assumption of equality with juggernaut, that gives off the exciting smell of human pride."

1555   HOOKER, Ward. "Irony and Absurdity in the Avant-Garde Theatre," *Kenyon Review*, XXII (Summer, 1960), 436-454 [see 1069].

Dramatic irony in the theater may be defined as speech or action whose meaning is more fully or differently understood by the audience than by the player. In the drama of Marivaux and his contemporaries, the irony is "fully understood" by the audience. Moving closer to the present through the work of Giraudoux, Anouilh, and Ionesco, the irony gets progressively more subtle and abstract, until finally, with Beckett's plays, it reaches the point of total obscurity, "humorous ambiguity," and "absurdity." The absurdity of Beckett and contemporary playwrights writing in the same vein is essentially rooted in the "funny," the "non-serious." For a reply to this argument, see **1545**.

1556   HOROVITZ, Michael. "Notes on 3 Novels by Samuel Beckett," *Tomorrow*, 4 (1960), 57-59.

On the trilogy.

1960

1557   HUGHES, Daniel J. "Reality and the Hero: *Lolita* and *Henderson the Rain King*," *Modern Fiction Studies*, VI (Winter, 1960-1961), 345-364 (see esp. pp. 345-346) [see **2501**].

Nabokov's *Lolita* and Bellow's *Henderson the Rain King* start with a comic version of reality and end with the discovery of a reality the hero thought to be only a dreamworld. By this quest for reality, the "withdrawal from objects into an isolate self" which Beckett offers in his experimental writing is overcome.

1558   KENNER, Hugh. "Samuel Beckett: The Rational Domain," *Forum*, III (Summer, 1960), 39-47.

"It is Descartes who leads the Western mind to the place where realistic fiction, its accuracy checked by many particular experiments, becomes a focal mode of art." Along with Descartes, it is Geulincx, who, by the "ceremonious resignation of his prose," and his doctrine of the " 'body-tight' " mental world, most influences Beckett.

1559   KERMODE, Frank. "Beckett, Snow, and Pure Poverty," *Encounter*, XV (July, 1960), 73-77. Reprinted in **1043**.

1560   MAYOUX, Jean-Jacques. "Samuel Beckett et l'univers parodique," *Lettres Nouvelles*, VIII (Aug., 1960), 271-291 [see **711**, **716**, **1021**].

1561   METMAN, Eva. "Reflections on Samuel Beckett's Plays," *Journal of Analytical Psychology*, V (Jan., 1960), 41-63. Reprinted in **711**.

A most revealing article which, however, calls for a refutation. Beckett's plays illustrate the desire of the contemporary existentialist thinker to "rouse man from his anonymous collective existence" and to insist upon the "importance of an 'authentic' individual life." The tensions in Beckett's work have their roots in the contemporary struggle between the existing "collective pseudo-ego" and the as yet unconscious desire in mankind for an "unborn true ego."

1562   MILLER, J. Hillis. "The Anonymous Walkers," *The Nation*, CXC (April 23, 1960), 351-354.

Mainly a discussion of the French "nouveau roman" and its place in contemporary fiction. "The revelation of the frightening neutrality of inanimate objects" is one of the most "unsettling effects" of the *nouveau roman*. The tragedy of Beckett's novels "is the inability of the mind to free itself of all content, and thus free itself from itself."

1563   MOORE, John R. "A Farewell to Something," *Tulane Drama Review*, V (Sept., 1960), 49-60.

Although definitely an avant-garde play, *Waiting for Godot* "nevertheless retains all the seediness of a down-at-the-heel realism," with the emphasis on the "little things of life," such as the problems of "buttoning one's fly." The play represents the "eternal circle of existence" and ends where it begins, in "comic impasse, not in tragic resolution."

1564   MORSE, J. Mitchell. "The Uses of Obscenity," *New World Writing*, 17 (1960), 246-256 (Beckett, esp. pp. 249-250).

1960

1565 NORÈS, Dominique. "Un théâtre de la mémoire et de l'oubli," *Lettres Nouvelles,* VIII (June, 1960), 146-148.
Compares Pinget's *Lettre morte* and Beckett's *La Dernière Bande.* "Si le souvenir garantit le héros de Pinget de la solitude totale, ceux de Beckett, eux, y sont faits: chacun n'a-t-il pas toujours été seul?"

1566 OLLES, Helmut. "Samuel Beckett," *Welt und Wort,* XV (June, 1960), 173-174. Reprinted in **1139**.

1567 POPKIN, Henry. "Williams, Osborne, or Beckett?" *New York Times Magazine,* Nov. 13, 1960, pp. 32-33, 119-121. Reprinted in **1069**.
The three playwrights represent three different emphases in modern drama, in turn illustrating the differing "psychologies" of their countries. The American theater "serves up untidy neuroses, usually garnished with pat solutions"; Britain's new "social drama . . . slays the dragons of poverty, prejudice, and war"; and the French playwrights concern themselves with the "endless conversations on the timeless issues" their literary ancestors presented. Beckett belongs to the well-established tradition of French literature, to "an old inheritance of ironic and meditative pessimism."

1568 PRITCHETT, V. S. "An Irish Oblomov," *New Statesman,* LIX (April 2, 1960), 489. Reprinted in **1073**.

1569 REPS, Albert. "*Warten auf Godot:* Zum gleichnamigen Werk von Samuel Beckett," *Die Drei: Zeitschrift für Anthroposophie und Dreigliederung,* 6 (Nov.-Dec., 1960), 300-319 [see **269**].

1570 THIBAUDEAU, Jean. "Un théâtre de romanciers," *Critique,* XVI (Aug.-Sept., 1960), 686-692.
Discusses the problems of adapting a novel into a play as is the case with Pinget's novel, *Le Fiston,* into the play *Lettre morte.* Beckett's plays seem to be mere adaptations of his novels, and, in fact, Pinget is more successful in his adaptation than Beckett.

1571 THOORENS, L. "Deux pièces de Beckett," *Revue Générale Belge,* XCVI (April, 1960), 152-154.
On *La Dernière Bande* and *Cendres.*

1572 VALENCY, Maurice. "Flight into Lunacy," *Theatre Arts,* XLIV (Aug., 1960), 8-9, 68-69 (Beckett, *passim*).
Ubu Roi introduced an "era of *merde*" to the theater, "an era in which every sort and shade of *merde* has been promoted, without shame, without discrimination, all the way from 'Merde in the Rue Morgue' to 'Merde in the Cathedral.'" Of course, some of the avant-garde playwrights have produced masterpieces, but Beckett falls into the other category, that of the "didactic, pseudoallegorical, insolvent" drama, of which after seeing, one says, "'Was this trip necessary?'" *Waiting for Godot* is a "long, futile, and unbearably repetitious business, and that is the point. . . . But the fact that the author is determined to rub our noses in it indicates a hostile attitude which it is difficult not to reciprocate."

1573 VIATTE, Auguste. "La Littérature dans l'impasse," *Revue de l'Université Laval,* XV (Nov., 1960), 254-259 (Beckett, *passim*).

1961

1574   ANONYMOUS. "Waves in a Teacup: French Novelists and Their Spheres," *Times Literary Supplement*, Oct. 13, 1961, pp. 712-713 (Beckett, *passim*).

Beckett belongs to the group of writers who, "willingly or unwillingly," can be labeled "New French Novelists," or given other labels that are "excellent slogans, but wonderfully misty."

1575   ABIRACHED, Robert. "Carnet de théâtre," *Études*, CCCX (July-Aug., 1961), 131-134.

Discusses Beckett's *En attendant Godot* at the Odéon-Théâtre de France.

1576   AUBARÈDE, Gabriel d'. "En attendant . . . Beckett," *Nouvelles Littéraires*, Feb. 16, 1961, pp. 1, 7 [see also **3087**]. Trans. Christopher Waters and reprinted in *Trace*, 42 (Summer, 1961), 156-158, under the title "Waiting for Beckett."

The record of an interview with Beckett, in which he discusses, among other things, the impulses that make him write. He states that he never reads philosophers, denies any debt to the existentialists, and ends by saying: "I'm no intellectual. All I am is feeling. *Malloy* [*sic*] and the others came to me the day I became aware of my own folly."

1577   BACHMANN, Claus-Henning. "Französische Stücke in Deutschland," *Theater der Zeit*, VIII (March, 1961), 130-132.

1578   BAJINI, Sandro. "*Comment c'est*," *Il Verri*, V (April, 1961), 100-102.

1579   BARJON, Louis. "Une littérature de 'décomposition'?" *Études*, CCCXI (Oct., 1961), 45-60 [see **1162**].

1580   BARTHES, Roland. "Le théâtre français d'avant-garde," *Français dans le Monde*, 2 (June-July, 1961), 10-15.

1581   BELMONT, Georges. "Samuel Beckett—l'honneur d'être homme," *Arts*, 821 (May 10-16, 1961), 14 (portrait).

Belmont talks about his thirty-year acquaintance with Beckett.

1582   BIALOS, Anne. "Samuel Beckett," *Studies in Literature*, I (Spring, 1961), unpaginated.

1583   BLANZAT, Jean. "Les Romans de Samuel Beckett," *Figaro Littéraire*, May 13, 1961, p. 2.

1584   BLAU, Herbert. "The Popular, the Absurd, and the *Entente Cordiale*," *Tulane Drama Review*, V (March, 1961), 119-151 (Beckett, *passim*).

Blau discusses contemporary trends in French and German drama, making brief references to Beckett. He quotes French actor-director Roger Blin, who refused the role of Krapp in the French version of *Krapp's Last Tape*: "I am weary . . . of the Absurd. It makes me feel ancient."

1585   BLOCH-MICHEL, Jean. "Nouveau roman et culture des masses," *Preuves*, 121 (March, 1961), 17-28 (Beckett, p. 24). Reprinted in **1179**.

The traditional language of the novel is reason. Therefore, it suffices to use an irrational language to strike down the traditional form of literature. It is Beckett, in particular, who has taken charge of this assault against reason in

1961

1585

his long, endless, interior monologues: "Il y a chez lui une rupture entre le langage, sa syntaxe et la raison."

1586   BOISDEFFRE, Pierre de. "Où va le roman?" *Table Ronde*, 164 (Sept., 1961), 15-27. Reprinted in **1035**.

1587   BOYLE, Kevin. "*Molloy:* Icon of the Negative," *Westwind*, V (Fall, 1961), unpaginated.

This brilliant analysis of *Molloy* written by an undergraduate and published in *Westwind*, a student magazine, points out how "upon entering the fictional world of Samuel Beckett's *Molloy*, one is aware of its rational limitations." The novel is compared to Faulkner's *The Sound and the Fury*, and to Sartre's *Nausea*. "Beckett's distortive technique is analogous to that of the modern painter. However, the truly creative painter distorts the common static perspective to construct a more cogent reality from its dynamic parts. Sartre succeeds in a similar manner in his novel *Nausea*. . . . In *Molloy* there is no recognizable reality to sustain the distortion. The twisted fable is not a creation: it does not go beyond the destructive."

1588   BRICK, Allan. "A Note on Perception and Communication in Beckett's *Endgame*," *Modern Drama*, IV (May, 1961), 20-22.

The play is an illustration of man's unsuccessful and successful attempts to assure his individual existence. Hamm and Clov may represent either two individual persons, in the respective roles of Master and Servant, or "one dual self," enacting the conflicts of "self-destruction."

1589   BRUSTEIN, Robert. "An Evening of *Déjà-vu*," *New Republic*, CXLV (Oct. 2, 1961), 45-46. Reprinted in **1230**.

Happy Days is "the least" of Beckett's dramatic efforts, mainly because it repeats what Beckett has already better expressed in his great works. He has "fallen into self-imitation," a practice that unhappily results in mechanical action and predictability.

1590   BUTLER, Michael. "Anatomy of Despair," *Encore*, VIII (May-June, 1961), 17-24.

"To consider *Waiting for Godot* anything else but an expression of pessimistic resignation is to willfully misread the play." Its theme is the "impossibility of communication between human beings," and between man and God.

1591   CALENDOLI, Giovanni. "Personaggi atomizzati nel teatro di Beckett," *Fiera Letteraria*, XVI (Oct. 1, 1961), 1-2.

1592   CHAPSAL, Madeleine. "Le Jeune Roman," *L'Express*, Jan. 12, 1961, p. 31.

1593   CLURMAN, Harold. "Theater," *The Nation*, CXCIII (Oct. 7, 1961), 234-235.

Happy Days is a "poem of despair and forbearance and optimism." Behind its irony lies a "repressed tenderness" which serves to refute the notion that Beckett, "the poet of a morally stagnant society," is all pessimist.

1961

1594   CODIGNOLA, Luciano. "Il Grigio di Beckett," *Il Mondo,* June 13, 1961, p. 14.
Beckett's texts depict increasing lack of communication in a world dedicated to communication's instruments, physical poverty in an age nourished on myths of physical health and affluence, human bondage in a time when men are probing outer space. His writings have been thought to be for the sophisticated few . . . but they strike a blow at the hypocrisy of mass culture.

1595   COHN, Ruby. "*Watt* in the Light of *The Castle,*" *Comparative Literature,* XIII (Spring, 1961), 154-166.
Though Beckett insists that he was not influenced by Kafka, their works do bear certain resemblances. Both authors have "given contemporary relevance to the myth of the questing hero," and both have written novels in which "the failure of the quest results from the human limitations of the hero." *The Castle* and *Watt* are basically alike in their presentations of "absurd universes, which ironically reflect the absurdity of ours."

1596   _____. "Samuel Beckett Self-Translator," *PMLA,* LXXVI (Dec., 1961), 613-621. Reprinted in **704**.
There are certain prominent differences in Beckett's English versions of his French novels. The English translations are generally "bleaker" and more ironic in tone than their "more colloquial," more "comical" French equivalents. This perhaps owes to the passage of time that elapsed between original conception and translation, and indicates that Beckett is inclining toward deeper pessimism.

1597   CORRIGAN, Robert W. "The Theatre in Search of a Fix," *Tulane Drama Review,* V (June, 1961), 21-35.
Comments on the ways in which new playwrights, Beckett, Ionesco, Adamov, Genet, Ghelderode, are revitalizing the theater. Their plays are efforts to "fix" the theater, by expressing the "senselessness and irrationality of all human actions."

1598   DAMIENS, Claude. "Regards sur le 'théâtre nouveau': Beckett, Ionesco, Genet, Duras, Adamov," *Paris-Théâtre,* XIV (1961), 12-13.

1599   DRIVER, Tom. "Beckett by the Madeleine," *Columbia University Forum,* IV (Summer, 1961), 21-25 [see **1075, 3088**].
Record of an interview with Beckett in Paris, in which he discusses "meaning" in his work, his philosophy, his views on religion. Driver makes a strong plea for the positive elements in Beckett's drama and fiction. He also claims, in this much quoted interview, that Beckett's writing seems "permeated with love for human beings" and with a kind of humor irreconcilable with the despair and nihilism he is known for. He quotes Beckett as saying: "to say 'perhaps' as the plays do, is not to say 'no.'" Although the world Beckett sees is a "mess . . . a buzzing confusion," a form can be put to it, as exemplified in his own work: "To find a form that accommodates the mess, that is the task of the artist now."

1961

1600   _____. "Unsweet Song," *Christian Century,* LXXVIII (Oct. 11, 1961), 1208-1209.

Happy Days "never gets off the ground." It is primarily "a sardonic statement about marriage—a mid-century version of, say, the *Kreutzer Sonata.* As such, it is terribly heavy-handed."

1601   DUMUR, Guy. "Le Nouveau Roman," *France-Observateur,* March 9, 1961, pp. 15-17 (Beckett, *passim*).

1602   FINDLATER, Richard, ed. *Twentieth Century,* CLXIX (Feb., 1961), 162-163, 176, 180, 183.

A special issue devoted to the theater, particularly in England. Beckett is discussed briefly in several places; see particularly "Pinter and the Absurd," by Martin Esslin, pp. 176-185.

1603   FITCH, Brian T. "Narrateur et narration dans la trilogie romanesque de Samuel Beckett: *Molloy, Malone meurt, L'Innommable,*" *Bulletin des Jeunes Romanistes,* 3 (May, 1961), 13-20.

1604   FLOOD, Ethelbert. "A Reading of Beckett's *Godot,*" *Culture,* XXII (Sept., 1961), 257-262.

It is irrelevant to query "who is Godot?" and "will a presence eventually cancel" the tramps' waiting? Godot is "merely a dramatic device" used by Beckett to keep the play moving. The play "issues from the postulatory atheism of Nietzsche . . . a sobering coda to the exultant rhapsody of a superman philosophy." It proves Berdyaev's statement that "man cannot exist where there is no God."

1605   FOURNIER, Edith. "Pour que la boue me soit contée . . . ," *Critique,* XVII (May, 1961), 412-418.

In *Comment c'est,* Beckett invites us to make an exploration of the self, a difficult journey in darkness, in the mud of our inner world. But the novel is built on a double symbol: "Ce long cheminement est tout à la fois une quête de soi-même et une quête d'autrui."

1606   GILMAN, Richard. "The Stage: Beckett's *Happy Days,*" *Commonweal,* LXXV (Oct. 13, 1961), 69-70.

The play is Beckett's furthest move in "the direction of absolute stillness," in which language and "antilanguage" are juxtaposed to present an effective drama which reaches us despite the fact that it abandons "most of the traditional means of dramatic communication."

1607   GLICKSBERG, Charles I. "Forms of Madness in Literature," *Arizona Quarterly,* XVII (Spring, 1961), 42-53 (Beckett, *passim*).

Many modern writers are afflicted with a metaphysical, not clinical, madness. This madness is revealed in their quest for meaning in a world that seems to be meaningless. The revolt against the absurd meaninglessness of oblivion may be a powerful creative force in writers such as Camus and Beckett.

1608   GOUHIER, Henri. "Le Théâtre," *Table Ronde,* 159 (March, 1961), 179; 163 (July-Aug., 1961), 145-149; 164 (Sept., 1961), 151.

Several allusions are made to Beckett in these three different issues. See particularly no. 163 for a discussion of the revival of *Godot* at the Odéon-Théâtre de France.

1961

1609 GRESSET, Michel. "Le 'parce que' chez Faulkner et le 'donc' chez Beckett," *Lettres Nouvelles,* IX (Nov., 1961), 124-138.
This profound study of the repeated use of two terms, one by Faulkner and one by Beckett, opens new vistas on the work of these two authors. "Le parce que de Faulkner et le donc de Beckett sont, à des degrés différents. . . . les signes d'une vision de la nudité de l'être dans le monde dont la plus belle réussite de l'homme est d'avoir chassé l'humain." Faulkner's use of "because" is a sign or a symbol of a quest for innocence; Beckett's use of "therefore" is a parody of Cartesian method in the sense that he states: "J'écris donc je suis."

1610 GRILLANDI, Massimo. "Samuel Beckett," *Italia che Scrive,* XLIV (July-Aug., 1961), 147-148.

1611 HESSE, Eva. "Die Welt des Samuel Beckett: Versuch einer Koordinierung," *Akzente,* VIII (June, 1961), 244-266.

1612 ISER, Wolfgang. "Samuel Becketts dramatische Sprache," *Germanisch-Romanische Monatsschrift,* XI (Oct., 1961), 451-467 [see **904** and **1871** for English versions].

1613 JOLLY, L. "Il relatore decadente," *Europa Letteraria,* II (June-Aug., 1961), 167-168.

1614 KARL, Frederick R. "Waiting for Beckett: Quest and Re-Quest," *Sewanee Review,* LXIX (Autumn, 1961), 661-676. Reprinted in **1041** and **1059**.

1615 KENNER, Hugh. "Voices in the Night," *Spectrum,* V (Spring, 1961), 3-20.
On Beckett's radio plays and *Comment c'est.* Radio drama "asserts its nature" in *All That Fall* and *Embers,* "just as radio proves to be the perfect medium for Beckett's primary concern: the relationship between words, silence, and existence." Beckett's theme is Proust's, the impossibility of communication between humans, a theme that can be traced to the replacement of humanistic dialogue by meditative philosophy. *Comment c'est* is Beckett's most extreme statement of this theme.

1616 KRÄMER-BADONI, Rudolf. "Die Annihilierung des Nihilismus, ein Versuch über Samuel Beckett," *Forum,* VIII (April, 1961), 148-152.

1617 LANCELOTTI, Mario A. "Observaciones sobre Molloy," *Sur,* 273 (Nov.-Dec., 1961), 50-52.

1618 LEES, F. N. "Samuel Beckett," *Memoirs and Proceedings of the Manchester Literary and Philosophical Society,* Session 1961-62, CIV (1962), 1-14.
Originally a lecture delivered on December 13, 1961, to the Manchester Literary and Philosophical Society, this piece discusses primarily *Watt* and *Molloy* with allusions to other Beckett works in an effort to elucidate Beckett's philosophical position. Mr. Lees concludes that from Beckett's work "arises a very simple old-fashioned message—the message of Charity (in its fullest sense) to the aging, the incapacitated, the baffled, the oppressed—and, most truly of all, perhaps, to struggling and scrupulous minds like Beckett's own, haunted by such visions."

1961

1619   LENNON, Peter. "Samuel Beckett's Month," *Manchester Guardian
           Weekly,* June 8, 1961, p. 14; see also *Manchester Guardian,* June
           2, 1961, p. 11.

"May 1961 is likely to go down in history as the month in which Beckett
received the final accolades of popular, critical, and academic acclaim. While
a revival of *Waiting for Godot* was being prepared in England, an international
group of publishers awarded Beckett, jointly with Borgès, a $10,000 interna-
tional prize—and now here he is received under the dome of the Théâtre de
France in Paris."

1620   MARMORI, Giancarlo. "Il fango di Beckett," *Il Mondo,* March 21,
           1961, p. 15.

On *Comment c'est.*

1621   MATTHEWS, John H. "Nathalie Sarraute: An Approach to the
           Novel," *Modern Fiction Studies,* VI (Winter, 1960-61), 337-344
           (Beckett, pp. 338, 341).

Essay based on Ortega y Gasset's questioning of "the novel's ability to survive."
Sarraute's "era of suspicion" explains the "curiously equivocal, almost amor-
phous central characters" of Beckett's novels.

1622   MERCIER, Vivian. "Samuel Beckett and the Sheela-na-gig," *Ken-
           yon Review,* XXIII (Spring, 1961), 299-324 [see **1047**].

Beckett's writing shows influences from traditional Irish folklore and its
emphasis on the "macabre" and the "grotesque," which, for the purposes of
this study, may be defined as a terror of death (macabre), and a dread of
the mysteries of reproduction or sex (grotesque). Laughter, in each case,
results as a mechanism of defense against the reader's concern with both
death and sex. The Sheela-na-gig is a distorted female figure appearing on
early Irish structures such as bridges and buildings, whose breasts and sex
organs are exaggerated and misshapen, as is the verbal portrait Beckett offers
the reader of the *hag-amours* in his novels. Beckett, along with Swift, Shaw,
Joyce, Yeats, and Synge, utilizes fully this tradition of the grotesque and the
macabre in his humor.

1623   MURDOCH, Iris. "Against Dryness," *Encounter,* XVI (Jan., 1961),
           16-20 (Beckett, p. 19).

Most modern English novels indeed are not *written.* "One feels they could
slip into some other medium without much loss. It takes a foreigner like
Nabokov or an Irishman like Beckett to animate prose language into an
imaginative stuff in its own right."

1624   PARIS, Jean. "L'engagement d'aujourd'hui," *Liberté,* III (Nov.,
           1961), 683-690 (Beckett, *passim*).

1625   PERNIOLA, Mario. "Beckett e la scritura esistenziale: commento
           a *L'Innominabile,*" *Tempo Presente,* VI (Sept.-Oct., 1961), 727-
           733.

1626   PERRIN, Michel. "La Monnaie de la pièce . . . de Samuel Beckett,"
           Nouvelles Littéraires, March 2, 1961, p. 2.

A parody of *Comment c'est.*

1961

1627 PORTAL, Georges. "Pour l'amour de Dieu," *Écrits de Paris*, 195 (July-Aug., 1961), 139-146.

On the revival of *En attendant Godot* at the Odéon-Théâtre de France.

1628 PUMPHREY, Arthur. "A.P. at the Theater," *Theatre Arts*, XLV (Nov., 1961), 57-58.

The action of *Happy Days* bears a "strong similarity to music, that is, it cannot be broken down into a series of logical propositions; it is an evocation of feeling, set, as music is set, into some kind of mathematical framework, and aimed squarely at the solar plexus." The play creates a mood that "encompasses hilarious laughter and a lump in the throat at the same time."

1629 RAZUM, Hannes. "Theater of the Absurd," *World Theater*, X, no. 4 (1961), 37-43 (Beckett, *passim*).

A discussion of the theater in contemporary Germany, and the influence of the "absurd dramatists" (Camus, Beckett, and Ionesco) on young German playwrights.

1630 RINDAUER, Gerhart. "Endspiel und neuer Anfang," *Forum*, VIII (Nov., 1961), 412-413.

1631 ROBBE-GRILLET, Alain. "The Case for the New Novel," *New Statesman*, LXI (Feb. 17, 1961), 261, 264.

1632 ————. "Nouveau Roman, Homme nouveau," *Revue de Paris*, 9 (Sept., 1961), 115-121 (Beckett, p. 117). Reprinted in **1062**.

1633 ROMULUS, Hans. "Beckett Positiv," *Theater Heute*, II (April, 1961), 8-9.

1634 SAUREL, Renée. "En attendant un nouveau théâtre," *Temps Modernes*, XVII (July, 1961), 180-183.

En attendant Godot at the Odéon-Théâtre de France.

1635 SIMON, Alfred. "Paris et la vocation populaire du théâtre," *Esprit*, XXIX (Dec., 1961), 939-941.

En attendant Godot at the Odéon-Théâtre de France.

1636 SIMON, John. "A Theater Chronicle," *Hudson Review*, XIV (Winter, 1961), 586-592 (Beckett, *passim*).

Happy Days shows an "Aeschylean Beckett, its unfortunate heroine, who stands for the human condition, immobilized and talking."

1637 TALLMER, Jerry. "The Magic Box," *Evergreen Review*, V (July-Aug., 1961), 117-122.

The recent television production of *Godot* was "an abortion, an abomination, a bomb." If the play is "anything, it is a drama, not of anger, but of compassion, and, I persist in thinking, of hope." On TV, however, there was "no hope, just haste. Hasty squirrels in a lunatic squirrel-cage."

1638 TEYSSÈDRE, Bernard. "Réalisme critique et avant-garde," *Lettres Nouvelles*, IX (July, 1961), 144-154 (Beckett, esp. p. 150).

1639 THOMAS, Henri. "Le Théâtre dans l'œuvre de T. S. Eliot," *Nouvelle Revue Française*, IX (Jan., 1961), 30-40 (Beckett, p. 35).

1640 TOUCHARD, Pierre-Aimé. "Le Théâtre de Samuel Beckett," *Revue de Paris*, LXVIII (Feb., 1961), 73-87.

Beckett's *En attendant Godot* intensified by an attitude of the absurd, arising

1961

1640
out of the despair created by Hiroshima, presents the spectacle of men who lack hope enough to believe and force enough to despair in the coming of Godot.

1641   VEDRÈS, Nicole. "La Baleine des Invalides," *Mercure de France,* CCCXLI (April, 1961), 687-688.
Quotes from Gabriel d'Aubarède's interview with Beckett [see **1576**].

1642   VERKEIN, Lea. "Samuel Beckett: een Classicus van de avant-garde?" *Vlaamse Gids,* XLV (Jan., 1961), 62-63.

1643   VIATTE, Auguste. "Le 'Nouveau Roman,' " *Revue de l'Université Laval,* XVI (Oct., 1961), 122-128.

1644   WELLWARTH, George E. "Life in the Void: Samuel Beckett," *University of Kansas City Review,* XXVIII (Oct., 1961), 25-33. Reprinted in **1076**.

1645   WENTZ, John C. "The Second MLA Conference on Modern Drama," *Modern Drama,* III (Feb., 1961), 335-338.
The secretary's report on the conference, mentioning several papers read which discussed Beckett.

1646   WILCOCK, J. Rodolfo. "Nulla da fare," *Il Mondo,* Oct. 17, 1961, p. 14.

1647   WILLIAMS, Raymond. "Hope Deferred," *New Statesman,* LXI (May 19, 1961), 802.
About the Irish production of *Waiting for Godot.* It is a "morality play," but about "uncertainty" rather than "faith." In it, Beckett shows the "deadlock" between good and evil rather than their resolution.

1648   ――――. "New English Drama," *Twentieth Century,* CLXX (Autumn, 1961), 169-180 (Beckett, esp. pp. 177-178).

1649   WORMS, Jeannine. "Poésie et roman, compassion et beauté," *Mercure de France,* CCCXLIII (Dec., 1961), 650-656 (Beckett, *passim*).

1650   YERLÈS, Pierre. "Le Théâtre de Samuel Beckett," *Revue Nouvelle,* XXXIII (April 15, 1961), 401-407.
Like Ionesco, Vauthier, and others, Beckett is faithful to a particular logic of demystification. He destroys space and time. His "miracle" is that he creates a theater of the pure word as distinct from a theater of action and spectacle.

1651   ZÉRAFFA, Michel. "Reprises importantes," *Europe,* XXXIX (July-Aug., 1961), 351-352.
On *En attendant Godot* at the Odéon-Théâtre de France.

1962

1652   ANONYMOUS. "The Core of the Onion," *Times Literary Supplement,* Dec. 21, 1962, p. 988.
Meaning in Beckett's world is "merely an appearance of order which man imposes upon his experience to make it tolerable." Hence, even art imposes its order on "a vision of ultimate incoherence." In *Comment c'est,* Beckett has succeeded in substituting "metaphoric approximation" for words.

1962

1653   ALVAREZ, A. "Audience of Captives," *New Statesman,* LXIII
             (June 1, 1962), 798-799.
On *Waiting for Godot.*

1654   ASHMORE, Jerome. "Philosophical Aspects of *Godot," Symposium,*
             XVI (Winter, 1962), 296-306.
The play illustrates the "inadequacy of man" at every level of his existence:
"speech, sensual experience, knowledge, imagination, and his creation of
institutions." Beckett makes living "a colossal cockery" in which man's
activity is shown to be a "series of aimless antics."

1655   ASHWORTH, Arthur. "New Theatre: Ionesco, Beckett, Pinter,"
             Southerly, XXII, no. 3 (1962), 145-154.
In the drama of the absurd, the plots are "scarcely existent" as in Beckett, or
unrealistic and fantastic as in Ionesco. Characters act in unmotivated and
inexplicable ways so that "personal identity is blurred."

1656   BLANCHOT, Maurice. "Samuel Beckett," *Merkur,* XVI (Feb.,
             1962), 143-150. Trans. of the chapter on Beckett in **1014.**

1657   BLAU, Herbert. "Windlasses and Assays of Bias," *Encore,* IX (Sept.-
             Oct., 1962), 24-40 (photograph of Beckett on cover).
Polonius' desire to find out direction by indirection can serve as a technique for
examining the drama of art as a whole in Beckett. In *Endgame,* for example,
the absolute is cracked so that the futility of existence can be revealed. The
indirection of Yeats and Genet may be too easily dismissed as simply cryptic
or perverse. But these men and others like them take a chance of being
misunderstood by seeing the "terribly sane" in the "consummately lunatic."

1658   BRAY, J. J. "The Ham Funeral," *Meanjin,* XXI (March, 1962),
             32-34.
First produced in 1961, White's play, *The Ham Funeral,* dates from 1947 and
anticipates some of the techniques later used by Fry, Beckett, Ionesco, and
Pinter.

1659   BUTLER, Harry L. "Balzac and Godeau, Beckett and Godot: A
             Curious Parallel," *Romance Notes,* III (Spring, 1962), 13-17.
Balzac's *Mercadet* and Beckett's *Waiting for Godot* are significantly similar in
the respect that the movement of each play is around an absent person (Godeau
and Godot) who, if he were to arrive, would solve the problems of the other
characters. For further remarks on this parallel see **1723.**

1660   CHAMBERS, Ross. "Samuel Beckett and the Padded Cell," *Meanjin,*
             XXI (Dec., 1962), 451-462.
It is in *Murphy*'s "padded cell" (of self) that the essence of the trilogy—the
timeless, spaceless "little world," the "mote in the dark of absolute freedom"—
is conceived. This "bottom-most point of bliss" is the goal toward which
strive Molloy-Moran, Malone, and the Unnamable. Their respective journeys
in time, space, and consciousness form the structural thread of the trilogy.

1661   COFFEY, Brian. "Memory's Murphy Maker: Some Notes on Samuel
             Beckett," *Threshold,* 17 (1962), 28-36.
The author of this article, a personal friend of Beckett, has written down, in
the form of journal notes, some impressions of the man and his work. He

1962
1661

finds Beckett's work in general dominated by a strong sense of "ritual," which in the stories becomes man's habits. Beckett the poet supersedes both the philosopher and the storyteller.

1662   COHN, Ruby. "The World of Harold Pinter," *Tulane Drama Review*, VI (March, 1962), 55-68 (Beckett, *passim*).

1663   _____. "*Comment c'est:* de quoi rire," *French Review*, XXXV (May, 1962), 563-569.

An interesting attempt to elucidate *Comment c'est* as to both form and content. Objects and names are given possible sources, many of them of biblical origin.

1664   _____. "Plays and Players in the Plays of Samuel Beckett," *Yale French Studies*, 29 (Spring-Summer, 1962), 43-48.

Using variations on the old metaphor of *theatrum mundi*, where man performs for an eternal spectator, Beckett creates a new, semicynical drama, in which the characters are all "performing artists" who are acting in a play that is obviously a "play." Man the actor no longer believes in the play: only a spectator can force the show to go on. And to this end, Beckett seems to suggest, the actor may have to invent his audience.

1665   COLMANT, Guy. "La Recherche de l'absolu," *Revue Nouvelle*, XXXIV (Sept. 15, 1962), 235-239.

A comparison of Péguy, Bernanos, and Beckett.

1666   DONOGHUE, Denis. "The Play of Words," *The Listener*, 1737 (July 12, 1962), 55-57 (Beckett's theater, *passim*). [See also Editorial, *ibid.*, p. 48; and letters to the editor in **2592, 2612,** and **2617**; see also **3013**.]

The modern dramatist does not believe in dialogue, or "the turning of one person to another in full acknowledgment." As a result, the modern play has become the apotheosis of Yeats's "beautiful sterile form." In the theater of Beckett only words and monologue remain to represent the isolation of man in his search for self.

1667   DUKORE, Bernard. "Gogo, Didi, and the Absent Godot," *Drama Survey*, I (Winter, 1962), 301-307 [see **1719, 1750**].

The predominant symbolism in *Waiting for Godot* is Freudian. Even the names of the characters have Freudian implications: Gogo is "ego-ego," Didi is "id-id," and Godot represents the "superego." The theme of the play is "the futility of human existence when man pins his hopes on a force outside of himself."

1668   FASANO, Giancarlo. "Samuel Beckett," *Belfagor*, XVII, no. 4 (1962), 432-457.

A general introduction to Beckett's fiction.

1669   FLETCHER, David. "Molloy for Prime Minister," *Left-Wing*, n.v. (Nov., 1962), 22-24.

Despite its title, attempts to analyze *Molloy* on lines familiar to readers of Kenner's book, using as a starting point the fact that Molloy is a writer working alone in a room.

1962

1670   FLETCHER, John. "Samuel Beckett et Jonathan Swift: Vers une étude comparée," *Littératures X: Annales publiées par la Faculté des Lettres de Toulouse,* XI, no. 1 (1962), 81-117.

Beckett criticism has not failed to note striking similarities between Beckett and Swift; their lives have something in common, their works show an analogous evolution, and they share much the same literary myths and obsessions, especially a horror of the body and of sex that is fundamental to the Irish temperament. Moreover, their literary methods have much in common, especially their use of irony as a wide-ranging device; both use their fictional creatures as masks.

1671   FRIEDMAN, Melvin J. "The Neglect of Time: France's Novel of the Fifties," *Books Abroad,* XXXVI (Spring, 1962), 125-130 (Beckett, *passim*).

In this discussion of the experimental novelists (Robbe-Grillet, Butor, Sarraute) of the fifties, Beckett is aligned with the "chosistes" because of their indifference to "time-space" considerations.

1672   GLICKSBERG, Charles I. "Samuel Beckett's World of Fiction," *Arizona Quarterly,* XVIII (Spring, 1962), 32-47. Reprinted in **1058**.

Beckett makes no pretense of telling a story. His novels are formless, of "unrelieved pessimism shot through with elements of sacrilegious irony," his unheroic heroes move "will-less" in an "anesthesia of indifference," from futile birth to ever-imminent death.

1673   _____. "The Lost Self in Modern Literature," *The Personalist,* XLIII (Autumn, 1962), 527-538 (Beckett, esp. pp. 535-537) [see also **1058**].

1674   GUICHARNAUD, Jacques. "The 'R' Effect," *Esprit Créateur,* II (Winter, 1962), 159-165.

Discusses new directions in the French theater. Quotes from Beckett's plays.

1675   HAMILTON, Carol. "Portrait in Old Age: The Image of Man in Beckett's Trilogy," *Western Humanities Review,* XVI (Spring, 1962), 157-165.

In his fiction, Beckett employs the common novelistic metaphor of the journey from youth to old age, but in the trilogy he portrays the end of the journey. Life is seen through the fading eyes of age rather than the bright eyes of youth. The journey symbolizes the return, in extreme age, to the "primal non-conceptual understanding" of a child, in which the "mind no longer commands," and the experience of the world is not "inchoate sensation, but is understood through form alone." At the end of the three novels, the author moves closer to a fusion of "inner and outer reality."

1676   HAMILTON, Kenneth. "Negative Salvation in Samuel Beckett," *Queen's Quarterly,* LXIX (Spring, 1962), 102-111.

The very action of writing, even though he preaches in his work a "negative salvation," shows that Beckett is not wholly the pessimist he would seem to be. His characters are of two sorts: those who are "slaves to the illusion of Christian salvation" and are attached to "outer reality," and those who possess

1962

1676

a "self-contained indifference," who are self-sufficient and self-determining, and who, like Molloy, are ruthless and intolerant toward all "that interferes with their freedom of unmotivated choice."

1677   HOPPER, Stanley R. "Irony, the Pathos of the Middle," *Crosscurrents,* XII (Winter, 1962), 31-40 (Beckett, *passim*).

Discusses Camus, Ionesco, Beckett. Modern drama occupies a "middle" ground, somewhere between tragedy and comedy, characterizations like Prufrock and Krapp being "ironic equivocations of sophisticated insecurity."

1678   HUBERT, Renée Riese. "The Couple and the Performance in Samuel Beckett's Plays," *Esprit Créateur,* II (Winter, 1962), 175-180.

Beckett's theater focuses on complementary-couple relationships, symbolizing the ultimate couple—illusion and reality. This coupling depends primarily on "theatrical" tricks, such as dialogue, costuming, a rope linking two characters, the twin ash cans, and various roles ascribed to the actors ("mother and father, master and servant"). *Endgame* best portrays this ultimate coupling of theater and reality, which are "clad in endless greyness, yet still subjected to erosion," and "need the support of each other to maintain their shadow-like existence."

1679   HUGHES, Catherine. "Beckett's World: Wherein God Is Continually Silent," *The Critic,* XX (April-May, 1962), 40-42.

Beckett's study of Proust, almost a literary credo with its recognition of man's failure to communicate and connect, anticipates the themes that recur in his plays. Beckett, a "deeply concerned poet of the theater, a compassionate participant in humanity's day-by-day defeat and revitalization," seems far from sure that men are without God. Thus, despite its "integral pessimism," his work does "rise above a mere plethora of despair": the bums continue to wait for Godot, a boy is seen on the horizon, Winnie proclaims herself happy.

1680   _____. "Beckett and the Game of Life," *Catholic World,* CXCV (June, 1962), 163-168.

Waiting for Godot obscures all but a handful of other works in the theater of the fifties.

1681   KAUFMAN, R. J. "On the Newness of the New Drama," *Tulane Drama Review,* VI (June, 1962), 94-106 (Beckett, *passim*).

The new drama is deeply moralistic and hopeful rather than amoral and defeatist. Its masters "practice a well-centered though unorthodox moral art. They are at work rehabilitating the imaginative habits of a generation made dull by an over-formalized existence."

1682   KENNER, Hugh. "Art in a Closed Field," *Virginia Quarterly Review,* XXXVIII (Summer, 1962), 597-613 (Beckett, *passim*).

General number theory with its "closed field" helps us to make critical discoveries because poets and novelists of the last hundred years stumbled onto applications of the field. The field is a discovery device for Joyce, Lewis Carroll, but especially in the diction of William Carlos Williams, Eliot, Whitman, and Pound. Even Beckett, in *Watt,* uses the "catechism of the 17th

1962

1682

episode of *Ulysses* in elaborate permutations deriving from them a number of true propositions."

1683   KERN, Edith. "Beckett's Knight of Infinite Resignation," *Yale French Studies,* 29 (Spring-Summer, 1962), 49-56.

Happy Days attempts a dramatization of the "bodilessness and motionlessness" of Beckett's novelistic characters. Winnie appears as a "stage-rendering of Heidegger's 'here and now' of being, helplessly thrown into time and place and humanness, and surrounded by the implements that belong to the everyday existence of man."

1684   KESTING, Marianne. "Das Romanwerk Samuel Becketts," *Neue Deutsche Hefte,* IX (March-April, 1962), 97-109.

1685   _____. "Experimentelles Theater," *Hochland,* LV (Oct., 1962), 36-50.

Compares Adamov, Ionesco, and Beckett.

1686   KEY-ÅBERG, Sandro. "Om absurdismen," *Ord Och Bild,* LXXI, no. 2 (1962), 119-126.

On Ionesco and Beckett.

1687   KOTT, Jan. "Le *Roi Lear* autrement dit *Fin de partie,*" *Temps Modernes,* XVIII (July, 1962), 48-77 [see also **1044, 1802**].

1688   LAPPALAINEN, Armas. "Under Becketts presenning," *Ord Och Bild,* LXXI, no. 5 (1962), 439-442.

1689   MACÉ, Nicole. "Iakttagernes tid," *Samtiden,* LXXI, no. 2 (1962), 161-170.

1690   MACKSEY, Richard. "The Artist in the Labyrinth: Design or *Dasein,*" *Modern Language Notes,* LXXVII (May, 1962), 239-256 (Beckett, *passim*).

1691   MAYERSBERG, Paul. "The Shared Dream," *The Listener,* LXVIII (Sept. 27, 1962), 473-475 (allusions to Beckett's novels).

1692   MICHA, René. "L'Homme indistinct," *Nouvelle Revue Française,* X (Feb., 1962), 306-321 (Beckett, esp. p. 306).

1693   MORSE, Mitchell J. "The Contemplative Life According to Samuel Beckett," *Hudson Review,* XV (Winter, 1962-63), 512-524.

All Beckett's novels are related "with a unity that is not formal but metaphysical, a matter not of related plots but of recurrent symbols." His heroes all prefer the contemplative to the active life. They are all "gods," from Murphy who is a "Messiah" for Cooper and Celia, to the Unnamable who is "Satan" as well as a "lonely God," inventing others to play with. Beckett's protagonists suffer from "cosmopsis," or "seeing everything whole." This shared trait leaves them unfit for "mortality."

1694   NOON, William T. "God and Man in Twentieth-Century Fiction," *Thought,* XXXVII (1962), 35-36 (Beckett, *passim*).

Discusses Kafka, Joyce, D. H. Lawrence, Beckett, and others.

1695   OATES, J. C. "The Trilogy of Samuel Beckett," *Renascence,* XIV (Spring, 1962), 160-165.

1962
1696   PRITCHETT, V. S. "Saints and Rogues," *The Listener*, LXVIII
        (Dec. 6, 1962), 957-959 (Beckett, *passim*).
1697   RADKE, Judith. "The Theater of Samuel Beckett: 'Une durée à
        animer,' " *Yale French Studies*, 29 (Spring-Summer, 1962), 57-64.
Waiting for Godot is a drama of "existential despair" which parodies verbal
and physical activity, and whose action is meant to represent "all the days
in the lives of the personages . . . and of the audience." The characters of the
play "passively endure" their uncertain existence, neither knowing nor hoping
to determine the purpose.
1698   REID, Alec. "Beckett and the Drama of Unknowing," *Drama Sur-
        vey*, II (Fall, 1962), 130-138.
Beckett cannot be interpreted in allegorical or symbolic terms since he tries to
avoid definition. Nothing happens or can happen in his plays, and the reason
is that "Beckett is seeking to portray the state of non-knowing," with the
anger, frustration, violence, and madness it begets in us.
1699   RICKELS, Milton. "Existential Themes in Beckett's *Unnamable*,"
        Criticism, IV (Spring, 1962), 134-147.
Beckett's novels can be classified "existential," after Heidegger, Kierkegaard,
Ortega y Gasset, Sartre, and Camus, whose philosophies share the concept
of man's existence being "solitary, suffering, and anxious," and who believe
that what man seeks is a "form" for his experience in a meaningless universe.
The novel is a metaphor of how being knows itself. Words are "the only
instrument" for self-knowledge. In *The Unnamable* the self "exists in language, in words, and the creature is aware that he gets these from others.
Because the words are borrowed, they are false from the beginning."
1700   SCOTT, Nathan A. "The Recent Journey into the Zone Zero: The
        Example of Beckett and his Despair of Literature," *Centennial Re-
        view of Arts and Sciences*, VI (Spring, 1962), 144-181.
Largely a discussion of the tradition of contemporary French existential literature, whose central themes reflect the "precariousness of existence and the
remoteness of meaning in the time of the absent God," a concern that manifests
itself in the distrust of the literary enterprise. Beckett is the "most impressive"
representative of this "new nihilism." His work forces the reader to regard
as natural and expectable, an "absurd . . . maleficent . . . irrational . . .
grotesque and hopeless universe."
1701   VIA, D. O., Jr. "*Waiting for Godot* and Man's Search for Com-
        munity," *Journal of Bible and Religion*, n.v. (Jan., 1962), 32-37.
1702   WEALES, Gerald. "The Language of *Endgame*," *Tulane Drama
        Review*, VI (June, 1962), 107-117.
Producing *Endgame* gave insight into the play's sources of power. Although
the characters in this play are interesting, in that Beckett has not clothed them
in "abstract covering," but allowed them to be individuals and members of a
"family," it is the use of language that is the most important point of discussion. Beckett exploits fully such linguistic devices as "cliché," vaudevillian
verbal play, "gaggery," and the insistence upon the literal meaning of words,
which results in either comedy or "pain." His verbal connections from one line
to the next "may be a little oblique, but they are . . . there."

1963

1703   ANONYMOUS. "Forty-Eight Playwrights in Apartheid Protest,"
          Times of London, June 26, 1963, p. 12*d.*
Beckett is among the forty-eight British playwrights who have withdrawn
their work from "any theatre anywhere which discriminates against coloured
people."

1704   _____. "Busy Theatre Life in Warsaw," *Times of London,* Aug.
          12, 1963, p. 12.
Describes the vitality of the theater world in Warsaw, commenting that the
Poles staged Beckett's *Godot* before the English did. Beckett has an extraordi-
nary influence on young Polish dramatists.

1705   ALLEY, J. N. "Proust and Art: The Anglo-American Critical View,"
          Revue de Littérature Comparée, XXXVII (July-Sept., 1963),
          410-430 (Beckett, *passim*).
Discusses Beckett's study of Proust.

1706   ANGUS, William. "Modern Theatre Reflects the Times," *Queen's
          Quarterly,* LXX (Summer, 1963), 255-263.
Beckett, Pinter, Simpson, and others are discussed. The theater holds "the
mirror up to nature, reflecting the times," even when these times appear to
be absurd, as they do nowadays, and as they do in Beckett's plays.

1707   ASTRE, G. Albert. "Notes," *Critique,* XIX (Nov., 1963), 1020-
          1021.
Beckett is shamed by the sordid in man, fascinated by the absurd.

1708   BLANCHOT, Maurice. "A Rose Is a Rose . . . ," *Nouvelle Revue
          Française,* XI (July, 1963), 86-93 (Beckett mentioned).

1709   BRÉCHON, Robert. "Le Confort intellectuel," *Français dans le
          Monde,* 17 (June, 1963), 6-7 (Beckett, *passim*).

1710   BRÉE, Germaine. "Beckett's Abstractors of Quintessence," *French
          Review,* XXXVI (May, 1963), 567-576.
Beckett is discussed in the light of Rabelais and Leibniz. But, although the
methods of Beckett's satire can be compared with those of Rabelais, the
effect is quite different. Whereas Rabelais's "intellectual bum" is a scholastic,
a "good giant" presenting an essentially reassuring vision of the world, Beckett's
"metaphysical bum," particularly Watt, eager to "foist meaning upon the
meaningless," is actually a "clown forever uncommitted, a sum unfinished,
no abstractor of quintessence as he would like to be." *Watt* and the world
of "pre-established arbitrary" are created as a direct parody of Leibniz' "pre-
established harmony," a direct "refutation of Leibniz' 'best possible of worlds.' "

1711   BROWN, John Russell. "Mr. Pinter's Shakespeare," *Critical Quarter-
          ly,* V (Autumn, 1963), 251-265 [see **1069**].
Primarily a discussion of Pinter, based on the premise that contemporary drama
has come a long way from the old methods of exposition, development, and
conclusion, and suggesting that "it is more accurate to say that exposition has
become development and conclusion as well." Beckett is referred to several
times in the article.

1963

1712   _____. "Mr. Beckett's Shakespeare," *Critical Quarterly,* V (Winter,
              1963), 310-326.
In a vein similar to that of the preceding article, this is an interesting attempt
to relate problems of Shakespeare criticism to problems of interpretation of
Waiting for Godot. The pattern of conflicting symbols and issues presented
in Beckett's *Godot* suggests a similar pattern to be found in Shakespeare's plays.

1713   CASTELLANO, José. "Lo trágico en Beckett y Unamuno: Una
              coyuntura en el teatro europeo del siglo XX," *Punta Europa,*
              n.v. (Oct., 1963), 75-97.

1714   CHAMBERS, Ross. "Beckett's Brinkmanship," *AUMLA,* 19 (May,
              1963), 57-75 [for a French version see **901**].
Deals with Beckett's "experience of time." "The process of abstraction is
never complete, we can never reach the centre itself, and even death may
not end our search for it." Whereas in Proust's world, emancipation from
time is possible through both memory and artistic creation, Beckett denies the
possibility of such freedom.

1715   CHIAROMONTE, Nicola. "Da Chechov a Beckett," *Il Mondo,*
              April 30, 1963, p. 21.

1716   COE, Richard N. "Le Dieu de Samuel Beckett," *Cahiers de la
              Compagnie Madeleine Renaud–Jean-Louis Barrault,* 44 (Oct.,
              1963), 6-36 [see **901**: for original English version see **1835**].
Man discovered pity—God invented death. Beckett's God, "Dieu du mal, de
la mort et de la torture," hypocritically "n'a que le mot de 'pitié' à la bouche."
In spite of an error of interpretation over *Molloy* and *The Unnamable,* this
is an ingenious and often impressive attempt at interpreting Beckett's symbolism
of God.

1717   DENNIS, Nigel. "No View from the Toolshed," *Encounter,* XX
              (Jan., 1963), 37-39.
In discussing *Happy Days,* Dennis states that a "large new dimension" has
been added to "human emptiness by the introduction of a woman to the
Beckett ménage." The play must be viewed in a comic and not serious frame
of mind, although in the last analysis it is the humorist "who suffers most at
Mr. Beckett's hands, because the humorist is always seeing . . . whole jokes
that are only really half-jokes."

1718   _____. "Burying Beckett Alive," *Show,* III (Nov., 1963), 46,
              54-55.
With the same negative attitude toward Beckett's work as in the preceding
article, and still discussing *Happy Days,* Dennis this time attacks the author
rather than the work. He finds in Beckett a total lack of humanity.

1719   DUKORE, Bernard. "Controversy: A Non-interpretation of *Godot,*"
              Drama Survey, III (May, 1963), 117-119.
An answer to a refutation by Thomas B. Markus (see **1750**) of an article by
Dukore in **1667**. Markus rejects the "concept of definite interpretations while
offering such an interpretation. . . . Neither the critic nor the director . . .
should avoid the responsibility of attempting a specific interpretation."

1963

1720 DUPREY, Richard A. "The Battle for the American Stage," *Catholic World*, CXCVII (July, 1963), 246-251.

Today's theater is tired of realism. It needs intellectual, spiritual, and emotional stimulus. The "epic" theater (Brecht, Bolt, Chayefsky) tells man his shortcomings—as did Aristophanes—that he may amend his ways. Avant-garde writers (Ionesco, Beckett, Albee, Genet), also known as the theater of the absurd, show existence to be meaningless without God, purpose, order, or ideals. Although these writers excel in symbols, understatement, and surprise, they lack communicativeness.

1721 FITCH, Brian T. "Bardamu dans sa nuit à lui," *Bulletin des Jeunes Romanistes*, 8 (Dec., 1963), 31-36.

A comparison of Céline and Beckett.

1722 FLETCHER, David. "The Language of *Godot*," *Sixty-One*, n.v. (May, 1963), unpaginated.

1723 FLETCHER, John. "Balzac and Beckett Revisited," *French Review*, XXXVII (Oct., 1963), 78-80.

In part a comment on an article by S. A. Rhodes in **1757**. Fletcher asks if the analogy of waiting in Beckett and Balzac is merely coincidental. More likely, Balzac made a distinct and conscious impression on Beckett, especially Balzac's *Le Faiseur*, of which *Godot* seems a definite paraphrase.

1724 FRENCH, Judith A. "The Destruction of Action," *Kerygma*, III (Spring, 1963), 9-12 (Beckett, *passim*).

Action is fundamental to drama, but not all action is dramatic. The action upon which drama is based must be found in the psychic states of a man's soul, in his endless search for absolutes. The problem with such characters as Estragon and Vladimir in *Godot* is that they fail to make any moral decision. The dramatist's duty is "to embody the actions within the soul of modern man."

1725 FRIEDMAN, Melvin J. "A Note on Leibniz and Samuel Beckett," *Romance Notes*, IV (Spring, 1963), 93-96.

Beckett has used Leibniz as he did Descartes and Geulincx, to offer a genial pastiche in literary terms of a philosophical system. The Molloy-Moran relationship can be compared with the complementary-couple structure in *La Monadologie*, in which the couple is the soul and the body, or the "agent and the messenger." Beckett also borrowed from Leibniz the concept of God as architect and monarch of the universe (Youdi, in *Molloy*).

1726 FRISCH, Jack E. "*Endgame*: A Play as Poem," *Drama Survey*, III (Oct., 1963), 257-263.

Endgame is "a poem to be performed in the theater." Its action is a poetic action, the stress lying on the notion of "silence" as a "space around a word." The interplays of silence and word, silence and rhythm, silence and mime create "ambiguity" and establish "holes in the universe of the poem, holes through which we can and must face ourselves in relation to that universe."

1727 GELLERT, Roger. "Catch 62," *New Statesman*, LXV (Jan. 4, 1963), 24-25 (Beckett, *passim*).

This summary of the year-in-theater in London makes brief mention of *Happy Days* as a "notable foreign import."

1963

1728   GOLDBERG, Gerald Jay. "The Search for the Artist in Some Recent
           British Fiction," *South Atlantic Quarterly*, LXIII (Summer,
           1963), 387-401.
Beckett's trilogy is discussed as being typical of much recent British fiction in
which the search for man through art is evidenced by the choice of the artist-
hero. Durrell's *Alexandria Quartet*, Golding's *Free Fall*, Murdoch's *Under
the Net* are novels given as examples.

1729   GOUHIER, Henri. "Le Théâtre a horreur du vide," *Table Ronde*,
           182 (March, 1963), 120-124 (Beckett, *passim*).

1730   GRAY, Wallace. "The Uses of Incongruity," *Educational Theatre
           Journal*, XV (Dec., 1963), 343-347 (Beckett, *passim*).
The outstanding technique of such writers as Albee, Beckett, Ionesco, and
Pinter, writers for the so-called theatre of the absurd, is the functional use
of incongruity as both a source of humor and an integral part of the meaning
of their plays.

1731   GRESSET, Michel. "Création et cruauté chez Beckett," *Tel Quel*,
           15 (Autumn, 1963), 58-65.
An effort is made to determine whether or not the so-called cruelty in Beckett's
works is not a form of sadism. Gresset sees this sadism particularly in "les
rapports . . . entre parents et enfants," that is to say, particularly in *Molloy*
and *Fin de partie*. He concludes by saying that "l'image du père est devenue
la clé de voûte de l'univers de Beckett."

1732   HABICHT, Werner. "Theater der Sprache: Bermerkungen zu eini-
           gen englischen Dramen der Gegenwart," *Neueren Sprachen*, 7
           (July, 1963), 302-313 (Beckett, *passim*).
Even more than Ionesco or Beckett, young British playwrights use conscious
disintegration of language to dramatize the difficulty or impossibility of
human contact in the modern world. Simpson, Pinter, and Wesker are given
as examples.

1733   HAFLEY, James. "The Human Image in Contemporary Art,"
           Kerygma, III (Summer, 1963), 25-34 (Beckett, *passim*).
Abstract expressionism in art which imagines man as engaged in an extra-
intellectual, concrete quest for identity is related to the theater of the absurd
(Beckett, Albee, Pinter, and others), and the novel of the "nouvelle vague,"
which have in common themes of quest and question.

1734   HALLDÉN, Ruth, Ingemar HEDENIUS, and Sandro KEY-ÅBERG.
           "Ett samtal om Samuel Beckett," *Ord Och Bild*, LXXII (1963),
           93-104.

1735   HESLA, David H. "The Shape of Chaos: A Reading of Beckett's
           Watt," *Critique: Studies in Modern Fiction*, VI (Spring, 1963),
           85-105.
Watt is a perfect example of the task of the artist according to Beckett: " 'to
find a form to accommodate the mess.' " With an ironic twist in this novel
the hero, Watt, is able to find a form to shield himself from the "mess," even
though he cannot "accommodate it."

1963

1736   JACOBSEN, Josephine, and William R. MUELLER. "Beckett as
            Poet," *Prairie Schooner,* XXXVII (Fall, 1963), 196-216. Re-
            printed in **709.**

Beckett is "primarily a poet" whose work is constructed around three kinds of
"poetic sensibility." The first is the "poetry of observation" which results
in an intensification of "passionate fidelity" to the "thing" described. The
second is the "poetry of disparity" (antipoetry), his most characteristic mode,
which "relapses continually into chaos"; it is a world of "demented logic . . .
swelled to giant proportions." The third kind of poetry accounts for the
metaphysical in Beckett's world; it is "poetry of intimation." Its chief
characteristic is the sense of advent, of something larger, more significant,
more revealing, than is exactly stated.

1737   KITCHIN, Laurence. "The Cage and the Scream," *The Listener,*
            LXIX (Jan. 24, 1963), 157-159 (Beckett, *passim*). [See **3016.**]

1738   _____. "The Wide Stage: On Epic Drama," *The Listener,* LXIX
            (April 11, 1963), 631-633.

1739   LAMBERT, J. W. "Plays in Performance," *Drama,* 68 (Spring,
            1963), 20-27.

Happy Days is discussed along with other recent British works for the theater.
This play is "worth doing" as a monologue, or in radio production. It should
not be theatricalized. "To clutter the proceedings with laborious symbolism,
by having the heroine buried, first up to the waist, then up to the chin, was
only to distract attention from what she was saying."

1740   LANZA, Giuseppe. "Brecht e Beckett al Festival di Venezia,"
            Osservatore Politico Letterario, IX (Nov., 1963), 59-64.

1741   LITTLEJOHN, David. "The Anti-Realists," *Daedalus,* XCII
            (Spring, 1963), 250-264 (Beckett, *passim*).

The chief characteristic of antirealism in the novel is "a radical and willful
distortion of the nature of real experience, a distortion commonly made in
the manner of dreams or other manifestations of subconscious experience."
Beckett has the most valid claim to classic stature among the antirealists today.

1742   MACRON, Michèle. " 'Oh les Beaux Jours' de Samuel Beckett,"
            Signes du Temps, 3 (Dec., 1963), 46.

1743   MAGNAN, Jean-Marie. "Jalons: I. Samuel Beckett ou les chaînes
            et relais du néant. II. Alain Robbe-Grillet ou le labyrinthe du
            voyeur," *Cahiers du Sud,* L (April-May, 1963), 73-80.

1744   MAGNY, Olivier de. "Écriture de l'impossible," *Lettres Nouvelles,*
            XXXII (Feb., 1963), 125-138.

1745   _____. "Samuel Beckett et la farce métaphysique," *Cahiers de la
            Compagnie Madeleine Renaud–Jean-Louis Barrault,* 44 (Oct.,
            1963), 67-72 [see **901**].

The theater of Beckett presents these paradoxes: "un bien de nulle part; des
personnages qui ne sont personne; une action qui se dérobe en l'attente de ce
qui n'arrive pas, ou bien en la démonstration inlassablement répétée, mais
toujours implicite, qu'il n'y a pas d'action possible."

1963

1746   MANDEL, Oscar. "Artists without Masters," *Virginia Quarterly Review*, XXXIX (Summer, 1963), 401-419 (Beckett, *passim*).
Discusses Camus, Montherlant, Sarraute, Sartre, Mallarmé, Beckett.

1747   MARINELLO, Leone J. "Samuel Beckett's *Waiting for Godot*," *Drama Critique*, VI (Spring, 1963), 75-81.
The play is "a modern classic affirming man's dignity and nobility and ultimate salvation." It is true that "Beckett shows man to be cruel and absurd" but his ultimate portrayal is one of man being capable of exercising the moral virtues of faith, hope, and charity.

1748   MARISSEL, André. "L'Univers de Samuel Beckett: un nœud de complexes," *Esprit*, XXXI (Sept., 1963), 240-255. Reprinted in **706**.
The main emphasis in this article is on sexuality (homosexuality, masturbation, near impotence) in Beckett's heroes. Discusses the father image in Beckett's work, and suggests a possible neurosis of Beckett in relation to his own father.

1749   ———. "Molloy, Macmann, Malone et tant d'autres," *Marginales*, XVIII (Dec., 1963), 16-24. Extract reprinted from **706**.

1750   MARKUS, Thomas B. "Bernard Dukore and *Waiting for Godot*," *Drama Survey*, II (Feb., 1963), 360-363.
A refutation of an article by Dukore (**1667**; for Dukore's reply see **1719**). According to Markus, Dukore's critical method is basically faulty because of its implication that one can "tie up" various themes of the play *Godot* in a neat "Freudian parcel," admitting of no other interpretations.

1751   MOLE, Jack. "What To Do with the Body," *The Listener*, LXX (Sept. 5, 1963), 339-340 (Beckett, *passim*).
Contemporary man has "exorcized his phantom soul" and discovered his "body," and the question now facing artists and philosophers is: "How can this individual, sensuous, active . . . mortal thing that is *me* achieve its full destiny?"

1752   MORSE, J. Mitchell. "The Choreography of the New Novel," *Hudson Review*, XVI (Autumn, 1963), 396-419.
The "new novelists," those who are experimenting with new techniques, have taken at least three directions in France. The two most important are directed to English letters; "Brancusi's Way" seeks a radical psychology and much of the external world; "Joyce's Way" followed by Robbe-Grillet and Butor produces more interesting novels in which a complexity of structure matches a complexity of thought. The third direction is taken by Beckett, the most original of the new novelists. Unfortunately many have imitated Beckett (like Pinget) who would have done better to follow their own originality.

1753   NADEAU, Maurice. "Le Chemin de la parole au silence," *Cahiers de la Compagnie Madeleine Renaud–Jean-Louis Barrault*, 44 (Oct., 1963), 63-66 [see **901, 1060**].

1754   NORÈS, Dominique. "Situation du jeune théâtre," *Lettres Nouvelles*, XXXII (Feb., 1963), 213-224 (Beckett, *passim*).

1963

1755   OLIVER, William I. "Between Absurdity and the Playwright,"
        Educational Theatre Journal, XV (Oct., 1963), 224-235 (Beckett,
        passim). Reprinted in **1229**.

1756   PINGAUD, Bernard. "*Molloy* douze ans après," *Temps Modernes*,
        XVIII (Jan., 1963), 1283-1300. Reprinted under the title "Beck-
        ett le précurseur" in **1061** [see also **257.2**].

A major attempt to reassess the "nouveau roman," pointing out not only the
permanent artistic quality of *Molloy*, but that it was the first important new
novel to appear in France after the war. Pingaud speaks of a kind of classicism
of the new novel.

1757   RHODES, S. A. "From Godeau to Godot," *French Review*, XXXVI
        (Jan., 1963), 260-265.

There is a "coincidental analogy in the theme of 'waiting' between Balzac's
Mercadet and Beckett's *Godot*. The themes of both plays are identical, although
the first is a 19th-century social satire in a realistic setting, and the second is
a 20th-century mystery play." Mr. Rhodes naïvely thought that he was the
first to point out this parallel; he was corrected by Bruce Morrissette in *idem*,
4 (Feb., 1963), 351, who stated that it was Martin Esslin who first made
the parallel, and subsequently Eric Bentley. Rhodes apologized to both Bentley
and Esslin; further comments on this question were furnished by John Fletcher
[see **1723**].

1758   ROY, Claude. "L'Utilité de ne pas tout comprendre," *Nouvelle Re-
        vue Française*, XI (April, 1963), 703-709 (Beckett mentioned).

1759   SAUREL, Renée. "Dieux contumax, le vicaire complice," *Temps
        Modernes*, XIX (Dec., 1963), 1137-1144 (Beckett, *passim*).

1760   SÉNART, Philippe. "La Fin de l'homme," *Table Ronde*, 182
        (March, 1963), 113-119 (Beckett, *passim*).

1761   SIMON, Alfred. "Le Degré zéro du tragique," *Esprit*, XXXI (Dec.,
        1963), 905-909.

With *Oh les beaux jours* Samuel Beckett's case "ne cesse de s'aggraver." In
Fin de partie, the character of the last monologue could still remember a
beautiful line from Baudelaire, and tried to extract from it a remnant of
meaning. But in *Oh les beaux jours*, Beckett "a l'art très sûr de faire prendre
les lanternes pour des vessies, qui est le comble de la mystification, et son
tragique propre. Il se sert du style ordurier, des poncifs et des clichés comme
de pièges."

1762   TOYNBEE, Philip. "Art and Catastrophe," *The Observer*, May 19,
        1963, p. 23.

The article is "an attack on the assumption that artists living in an anarchic
age must produce anarchic art," which seems at present to be the conven-
tion. Beckett, and his alliance with the "anti-art, anti-life" philosophy of the
atomic age, is one of the many artists Toynbee is "trying to deprecate."

1763   VIATTE, Auguste. "Panorama des lettres françaises," *Revue de
        l'Université Laval*, XVIII (Dec., 1963), 327-332 (Beckett men-
        tioned).

1963

1764   WARHAFT, Sidney. "Threne and Theme in *Watt*," *Wisconsin Studies in Contemporary Literature*, IV (Autumn, 1963), 261-278.
An interesting interpretation of *Watt*. The protagonist's "threne" in the ditch is a clue to the meaning of the entire novel. The threne is his "lament for his dimly-realized entanglement with uncertain reality." It is not an entirely hopeless situation though, for the "dirge" progresses from the key of B minor and ends on a "dominant chord," and however Watt may suffer the "grotesque fate" of all mankind, he can at least weep and "stumble" through "barren lands."

1765   WELLERSHOFF, Dieter. "Gescheiterte Entmythologisierung: Zu den Romanen Samuel Becketts," *Merkur*, XVII (1963), 528-546.

1766   WENDT, Ernst. "Spiel in Urnen: Die Aufführung des Monats, Becketts neues Stück *Spiel* in Ulm," *Theater Heute*, IV (July, 1963), 6-10.

1964

1767   ABIRACHED, Robert. "La Voix tragique de Samuel Beckett," *Études*, CCCXX (Jan., 1964), 85-88.

1768   ————. "Sur le roman moderne en France," *Français dans le Monde*, 29 (Dec., 1964), 6-9 (Beckett, *passim*).
On Beckett, Robbe-Grillet, Pinget, Sarraute, Simon, Duras, Butor.

1769   ARNOLD, Bruce. "Samuel Beckett," *The Dubliner*, III (Summer, 1964), 6-16 [see **606**].
In this general introduction to Beckett an interesting reference is made to Beckett's cross-examination in the Gogarty libel case. Mr. Arnold quotes from a paper Beckett allegedly read to the Dublin University Modern Language Society in the "late twenties" on "Le Convergisme," an imaginary movement founded in Paris cafés by a decadent poet.

1770   BENEDETTI, Robert. "Metanaturalism: The Metaphorical Use of Environment in the Modern Theatre," *Chicago Review*, XVII, nos. 2-3 (1964), 24-32 (Beckett, *passim*).

1771   BRÉE, Germaine. "L'Étrange monde des 'Grands Articulés,' " *Revue des Lettres Modernes. Samuel Beckett: Configuration Critique, no. 8*, 100 (1964), 83-97 [see **902**].
Aside from Beckett's debt to Dante, Milton is discussed as a possible influence. In this panoramic view of Beckett's work, an interesting distinction is made about "l'œuvre romanesque de Beckett [qui] se scinde en trois parties séparées par deux 'pauses.' "

1772   ————, and Eugénia ZIMMERMAN. "Contemporary French Criticism," *Comparative Literature Studies*, I, no. 3 (1964), 175-196 (Beckett, *passim*).
Mainly a discussion of critical trends in France today; several allusions are made to Beckett and his place in contemporary literature.

1773   BRYER, Jack R. "Critique de Samuel Beckett" (Sélection Bibliographique), *Revue des Lettres Modernes. Samuel Beckett: Configuration Critique, no. 8*, 100 (1964), 169-184 [see **902, 3122**].

1964

1774   BÜCHLER, Franz. "Notizen zum Werk Samuel Becketts," *Neue Rundschau,* LXXV, no. 3 (1964), 482-487.

1775   CATTAUI, Georges. "Proust et les lettres anglo-américaines," *Table Ronde,* 192 (Jan., 1964), 36-47 (Beckett and Proust, esp. pp. 46-47).

1776   CHAMPIGNY, Robert. "Les Aventures de la première personne," *Revue des Lettres Modernes. Samuel Beckett: Configuration Critique, no. 8,* 100 (1964), 117-130 [see **902**].
A discussion of *L'Innommable* based on philosophic and semantic methods. Deals particularly with the use of monologue, and Beckett's fascination to choose M and W as initials for his characters. Champigny concludes by saying that "Il faut bien voir que, ainsi conçue, la première personne ne représente ni un individu, ni une classe d'individus (les moi), ni une qualité: elle représente une totalité."

1777   CHIAROMONTE, Nicola. "La predica di Beckett," *Il Mondo,* May 26, 1964, p. 17.

1778   CLURMAN, Harold. "The Idea of the Theater: A Conversation with Digby R. Diehl," *Transatlantic Review,* 16 (Summer, 1964), 17-24.
On Beckett and Ionesco.

1779   COHEN, Robert S. "Parallels and the Possibility of Influence between Simon Weil's *Waiting for God* and Samuel Beckett's *Waiting for Godot,*" *Modern Drama,* VI (Feb., 1964), 425-436.
Godot can be read as a "dramatic companion-piece" to Simone Weil's philosophical treatise, without, however, the postulation of faith. Both situations are set upon the site of the crucifixion where, in Simone Weil's belief, man is farthest from God. Salvation is possible only through great affliction. But if Simone Weil believes in the eventual coming of God, Beckett gives no answer.

1780   COHN, Ruby. "Philosophical Fragments in the Works of Samuel Beckett," *Criticism,* VI (Winter, 1964), 33-43. Reprinted in **711**.
Though both Beckett and his characters deny it, the content of Beckett's work is made up of affiliations with philosophical systems, "the old philosophical questions" which can be systematically pointed out. His allusion to and parody of Descartes, Geulincz, Malebranche and the Occasionalist doctrine, Wittgenstein, Heidegger, and Sartre, as well as lesser figures in these spokesmen's respective schools, exhibit Beckett's erudition as well as his art.

1781   CUNARD, Nancy. "The Hours Press: Retrospect, Catalogue, Commentary," *Book Collector,* XIII (Winter, 1964), 488-496 [see **5**, Note].
A brief history of the Press, including a catalogue of publications. The first printing of **5** (*Whoroscope,* the poem that won a cash prize in a contest sponsored by Miss Cunard and her Press) is described: "This long poem was Samuel Beckett's first separately published work. Neither Aldington nor myself knew his name."

1782   CURTIS, Jean-Louis. "La Voix qui babille dans le désert," *Cahiers des Saisons,* 36 (Winter, 1964), 105-106.

1964

1783   DAVIS, Robin. "Radio and Samuel Beckett," *Prompt,* 5 (1964), 46-51.

The medium of radio has given Beckett the opportunity for experimentation between his creations of the major works. Of the four radio plays he has written, *All That Fall* is the "least successful." *Cascando* is a radio version, in a sense, of Beckett's masterpiece, *How It Is.* Both works use the same elements of "little syntax, short phrases, and images uttered in a low, panting voice" creating the impression of a slow, continuous but extremely difficult progression.

1784   EASTMAN, Richard M. "Samuel Beckett and *Happy Days,*" *Modern Drama,* VI (Feb., 1964), 417-424.

In this play Beckett continues his previous comments on "entropy" (or the "running down from energy to exhaustion"), and on the void that operates as a "charged vacuum."

1785   EWART, Gavin. "*Play* by Samuel Beckett," *London Magazine,* IV (May, 1964), 95-96.

1786   FEDERMAN, Raymond. "Beckett's Belacqua and the Inferno of Society," *Arizona Quarterly,* XX (Summer, 1964), 231-241 [see 712].

Although the indications of Beckett's later themes can be found in the stories of *More Pricks Than Kicks,* the hero Belacqua Shuah, a "neurotic pedant," is a different character from the later "French derelicts." Belacqua lives entirely in the present, temporal world of "physical and social impositions," and, though he resents and "thumbs his nose" at the world, "he never achieves the fictional freedom which Beckett grants his later heroes—the freedom of controlling their own minds and actions, however absurd and meaningless these might be." Belacqua is truly caught, as was his namesake in Dante's *Comedy,* in a "purgatorial existence."

1787   FLETCHER, John. "Beckett et Proust," *Caliban: Annales Publiées par la Faculté des Lettres de Toulouse,* 1 (Jan., 1964), 89-100.

In discussing Beckett's study of Proust, Fletcher points out not only the originality of Beckett's critical point of view, even though "l'interprétation beckettienne de Proust paraît de temps à autre assez curieuse, pour ne pas dire erronée," but more important he shows that "l'admiration évidente que Beckett porte à Proust doit avoir ses origines dans certaines affinités existant entre la pensée des deux écrivains."

1788   _____. "Beckett's Verse: Influences and Parallels," *French Review,* XXXVII (Jan., 1964), 320-331.

Though not quite "poetry," Beckett's verse deserves "sympathetic consideration," rather than the neglect from which it suffers. He writes in the French tradition (and when he is writing in French itself, he does a better job of it than Eliot did in that language) of Rimbaud, Apollinaire, Jouve, Aragon, and Tzara, and the corresponding influences of symbolism and surrealism are evident both in his English and French verse.

1964

1789   FRIEDMAN, Melvin J. "Les Romans de Samuel Beckett et la tradition du grotesque," *Revue des Lettres Modernes* (*Un Nouveau Roman? Recherches et tradition*), ed. J. H. Matthews, 94-99 (1964), 31-50. Originally published in English in **1549**.

1790   _____. "Préface," *Revue des Lettres Modernes. Samuel Beckett: Configuration Critique*, no. 8, 100 (1964), 9-21 [see **902**].
In this special issue devoted to Beckett, Friedman not only edits the texts but in his preface introduces the work of each contributor and attempts to give a summary of critical attitudes toward Beckett's work.

1791   FURBANK, P. N. "Beckett's Purgatory," *Encounter,* XXII (June, 1964), 69-70, 72.
Discussion of the trilogy and of *Comment c'est.* Beckett may have found his style through the influence of Dante, Joyce, Valéry, Urquhart, and Maeterlinck, but in his latest four novels he truly comes into his own. They are "not about anything except the rights and wrongs of writing at all."

1792   GOUHIER, Henri. "Boulevard et avant-garde," *Table Ronde,* 192 (Jan., 1964), 122-128.
A comparison of the techniques of theatrics in Beckett and Roussin.

1793   GROSS, John. "Amazing Reductions," *Encounter,* XXIII (Sept., 1964), 50-52.
On *Endgame.*

1794   GUIDACCI, Margherita. "A proposito delle 'poesie' di Samuel Beckett," *Fiera Letteraria,* XIX (Oct. 25, 1964), 6.

1795   GURMÉNDEZ, Carlos. "Mendigos metafisicos, Beckett o la desesperación," *Indice de Artes y Letras,* XVII, no. 181 (1964), 19-20.

1796   HAMBRO, Carl. "Samuel Becketts 'romantrilogi,' " *Vinduet,* XVIII, no. 1 (1964), 9-14.

1797   HARRIS, Wendell V. "Style and the Twentieth-Century Novel," *Western Humanities Review,* XVIII (Spring, 1964), 127-140 (Beckett, *passim*).

1798   HARVEY, Lawrence E. "Samuel Beckett: Initiation du poète," *Revue des Lettres Modernes. Samuel Beckett: Configuration Critique,* no. 8, 100 (1964), 153-167 [see **902**].
In this study of Beckett's poetry, particularly of *Echo's Bones and Other Precipitates,* the poems are explained with the help of certain biographical events of Beckett's "inner" life. Harvey states that "le point de départ du poème se trouve aussi dans la vie intérieure du poète, c'est-à-dire dans ses souvenirs littéraires, aussi vivants, aussi réels pour lui que les êtres et les événements du monde extérieur."

1799   HAYMAN, David. "Molloy à la recherche de l'absurde," *Revue des Lettres Modernes. Samuel Beckett: Configuration Critique, no. 8,* 100 (1964), 131-151 [see **902**]. A slightly different version in English appears in **1051**.

1964

1800   HOFFMAN, Frederick J. "L'Insaisissable Moi: Les 'M' de Beckett,"
            *Revue des Lettres Modernes. Samuel Beckett: Configuration
            Critique, no. 8,* 100 (1964), 23-53 [see **902**]. Originally chap. vi
            of **705**, English title "The Elusive Ego: Beckett's M's."

1801   KERN, Edith. "Samuel Beckett et les poches de Lemuel Gulliver,"
            *Revue des Lettres Modernes. Samuel Beckett: Configuration Cri-
            tique, no. 8,* 100 (1964), 69-81 [see **902**].

A brilliant essay that attempts to characterize two kinds of literary climates:
the rational and organized world of the eighteenth century, and the disabused
universe full of absurd objects of the twentieth. More than just a study of
Beckett's debt to Swift, this essay reveals how two different temperaments tackle
a similar subject to reach similar conclusions.

1802   KOTT, Jan. *"King Lear* or *Endgame," Evergreen Review,* 33 (Aug.-
            Sept., 1964), 53-65 [see **1044, 1687**].

1803   LAMONT, Rosette. "La Farce métaphysique de Samuel Beckett,"
            *Revue des Lettres Modernes. Samuel Beckett: Configuration Cri-
            tique, no. 8,* 100 (1964), 99-116 [see **902**].

Basically the same ideas are expressed here as in **1504**, under the title "The
Metaphysical Farce: Beckett and Ionesco."

1804   LEECH, Clifford. "When Writing Becomes Absurd," *Colorado Quar-
            terly,* XIII (Summer, 1964), 6-24 (Beckett, *passim*).

All serious writing may be seen as absurd in that it suggests not only a norm
for man's affairs and for the cosmos but also the absurdity of forgetting how
fragile that norm is. From Marlowe's *Tamburlaine* to Beckett's *Waiting for
Godot,* man is seen either as magnificent and absurd or as comical and absurd
in his conflict with human irrationality.

1805   LEVENTHAL, A. J. "The Beckett Hero," *Critique: Studies in
            Modern Fiction,* VII (Winter, 1964-65), 18-35. Reprinted in
            711. For a French version of this article, entitled "Le Héros de
            Beckett," see also *Lettres Nouvelles,* XII (June, 1964), 32-52.

To get a complete understanding of Beckett's work it is necessary to show
that the "germ of his characters" lies in the "melancholy brood" of Dante's
Divine Comedy, and more specifically in the Belacqua fetal image that origi-
nates in *L'Inferno* and reappears throughout Beckett's novels and plays.

1806   LEWIS, Allan. "The Fun and Games in Edward Albee," *Educational
            Theatre Journal,* XVI (March, 1964), 29-39 (Beckett, *passim*).

Albee's work echoes Ionesco, Beckett, Strindberg, and particularly Genet.

1807   LEWIS, John. "Samuel Beckett and the Decline of Western Civiliza-
            tion," *Marxism Today,* VIII (Dec., 1964), 381-384.

1808   LEYBURN, Ellen D. "Comedy and Tragedy Transposed," *Yale
            Review,* LIII (June, 1964), 553-562 (Beckett, *passim*).

Discusses Ionesco, Beckett, and Camus.

1809   LYONS, Charles R. "Beckett's *Endgame:* An Anti-Myth of Cre-
            ation," *Modern Drama,* VII (Sept., 1964), 204-209.

The play is an "ironic reversal of the Biblical account of creation . . . and a
return to the void." With this work Beckett seems to be asserting that

1964

1809
external reality does not exist any more than do the "earth" and the "sea"
outside the windows. What he posits in its place is an "abstract" reality.

1810   MAROWITZ, Charles. *"Play," Encore,* XI (May-June, 1964), 48-52.

1811   MAZUCCO, Roberto. "Crisi e morte del personnaggio," *Il Ponte,* XX
(May, 1964), 632-641.
On Beckett and Robbe-Grillet.

1812   MITTENZWEI, Werner. "Endspiele der Absurden. Zum Problem
des Figurenaufbaus," *Sinn und Form,* XVI, no. 5 (1964), 733-751.
Deals with Beckett, Ionesco, Arrabal, Schehadé.

1813   MORRISSETTE, Bruce. "Les Idées de Robbe-Grillet sur Beckett,"
*Revue des Lettres Modernes. Samuel Beckett: Configuration Cri-
tique, no. 8,* 100 (1964), 55-67 [see **902**].

1814   MORSE, J. Mitchell. "The Ideal Core of the Onion: Samuel Beckett's Criticism," *French Review,* XXXVIII (Oct., 1964), 23-29.
One of the few articles to deal with Beckett's critical writings, pointing out
that Beckett's criticism not only contains the core of the meaning of the rest
of his work, it is also "a form of self-expression, an exposition of his intellectual
conceptions, an intellectualization of his passions, a form of poetry."

1815   NORÈS, Dominique. "Une nouvelle voix dans le théâtre de Beckett,"
Lettres Nouvelles, XI (Feb.-March, 1964), 165-171.
On the production in Paris of *Oh les beaux jours.*

1816   PALLAVICINI, Roberto. "Aspetti della drammaturgia contempo-
ranea," *Aut Aut,* 81 (May, 1964), 68-78 (Beckett, *passim*).

1817   PEAKE, Charles. *"Waiting for Godot* and the Conventions of the
Drama," *Prompt,* 4 (1964), 19-23.
Beckett's form "negates all the traditional conventions in order to present the
comic absurdity of man's endeavours to reduce experience to sense and order."
He employs the devices of music-hall knockabout to articulate a vision of
ultimate human tragedy.

1818   PEVEL, Henri. "Résonances mallarméennes du nouveau roman,"
Médiations, 7 (Spring, 1964), 95-113.
Deals with Robbe-Grillet, Simon, Ricardou, and Beckett.

1819   PIERSTORFF, Erik. "Fra det absurde til absurdismen," *Vinduet,*
XVIII, no. 1 (1964), 60-67.
Deals with Camus, Ionesco, and Beckett.

1820   PRONKO, Leonard C. "Modes and Means of the Avant-Garde
Theater," *Bucknell Review,* XII (May, 1964), 46-56 (Beckett,
passim).
On Ionesco, Beckett, and Rimbaud.

1821   RECHTIEN, John, S. M. "Time and Eternity Meet in the Present,"
Texas Studies in Literature and Language, VI (Spring, 1964),
5-21.
The two couples in *Waiting for Godot,* Vladimir-Estragon and Pozzo-Lucky,
represent, respectively, eternity and time. Their complementary-couple rela-

1964

1821

tionship typifies the tension within each man between the religious and the scientific "myths," and the audience can truly experience catharsis, because this tension is universal.

1822   RICKS, Christopher. "The Roots of Samuel Beckett," *The Listener,* LXXII (Dec. 17, 1964), 963-964, 980 [see **3021**].

"Easily the most important of Beckett's predecessors are Swift and Dante, and what they have in common is that each created an unforgettable picture of man's longing for extinction." Beckett, who actually calls one of his decrepit characters a Struldbrug in his first book, has devoted his life to rewriting—with obsessional intensity and ingenuity—the nightmares of Swift.

1823   ROMANÒ, Angelo. "Le 'Poesie inglese' di Samuel Beckett," *Fiera Letteraria,* XIX (Oct. 11, 1964), 4.

1824   ROY, Claude. "Samuel Beckett," *Nouvelle Revue Française,* XII (Nov., 1964), 885-890. Reprinted in **1081**.

1825   SENNEFF, Susan Field. "Song and Music in Samuel Beckett's *Watt,*" *Modern Fiction Studies,* XI (Summer, 1964), 137-149.

The meaning of *Watt* can be found in the "perfectly consistent" musical addenda to the book. The "ditch song" previews Watt's stay in the house of Mr. Knott, the "random rhythmic variations in the song anticipate the randomly arranged series" and permutations of the stay at Knott's establishment. The "frog song," which provides a humorous interlude of noise, represents the nonsensical, comic-ridiculousness of the whole novel. This very ingenious study written by an undergraduate shows to what extent one can carry the interpretation of a Beckett novel.

1826   SPENDER, Stephen. "With Lukács in Budapest," *Encounter,* XXIII (Dec., 1964), 53-57 (Beckett, especially p. 56).

In this report of an interview of Lukács by Spender, Beckett is mentioned several times.

1827   TRUSSLER, Simon. "*Happy Days:* Two Productions and a Text," *Prompt,* 4 (1964), 23-25.

Discusses two different productions of the play in England, one at the Royal Court Theatre, the other at Stratford East. Both productions are unfavorably judged by Trussler.

1828   VERDOT, Guy. "Recherche de Beckett chez ceux qui l'ont découvert les premiers," *Paris-Théâtre,* 206 (1964), 24-27.

Talks about Roger Blin and Beckett's theater.

1829   WENDLER, Herbert W. "Graveyard Humanism," *Southwest Review,* XLIX (Winter, 1964), 44-52.

1830   WILSON, Robert N. "Samuel Beckett: The Social Psychology of Emptiness," *Journal of Social Issues,* XX (Jan., 1964), 62-70.

Beckett, in the tradition of Swift, Voltaire, and Shaw, "loves human beings utterly," and is angry at man, not "for being as he is, but for his failing to be what he might be, his forfeit of glorious possibility." His plays describe

1964

1830
a life that has become "desocialized," in which his characters "are adult fore-
runners of the savage boys in Golding's *Lord of the Flies.*"
1831   YNDURAIN, Francesco. "Para la estética de 'Nouveau roman,' "
           Revista de Ideas Estéticas, XXII (April-May-June, 1964), 109-
           122.
On Beckett, Butor, Robbe-Grillet, Sarraute.

1965

1832   BROOK, Peter. *"Endgame* as *King Lear* or How To Stop Worrying
           and Love Beckett," *Encore,* XII (Jan.-Feb., 1965), 8-12.
In this interesting analysis of audience reaction to Beckett's themes, Director
Brook states that "Beckett's plays are like armoured cars or zombies. . . .
You can snipe at them, you can throw custard pies at them; they continue
serenely on their way. . . . They are critic-proof."
1833   BROWN, John Russell. "Dialogue in Pinter and Others," *Critical
           Quarterly,* VII (Autumn, 1965), 225-243 (Beckett, *passim*).
1834   CLURMAN, Harold. *"Happy Days,"* *The Nation,* 201 (Oct. 18,
           1965), 258-259.
1835   COE, Richard N. "God and Samuel Beckett," *Meanjin,* XXIV,
           no. 1 (1965), 66-85 [see **901**].
1836   COHN, Ruby. "The Plays of Yeats through Beckett Coloured
           Glasses," *Threshold,* 19 (Autumn, 1965), 41-47.
1837   _____. "The Absurdly Absurd: Avatars of Godot," *Comparative
           Literature Studies,* II, no. 2 (1965), 233-240.
On Beckett, Pinter, and others.
1838   _____. "Tempest in an Endgame," *Symposium,* XIX (Winter,
           1965), 328-334.
An attempt to establish some connection between Shakespeare's *The Tempest*
and Beckett's *Endgame.*
1839   DOMENACH, Jean-Marie. "Résurrection de la tragédie," *Esprit,*
           338 (May, 1965), 995-1015 (Beckett, *passim*) [see **903**].
In this discussion of modern tragedy, Domenach makes interesting comments
on Beckett, particularly *Oh les beaux jours.*
1840   DUKORE, Bernard. "Beckett's Play, *Play,"* *Educational Theatre
           Journal,* XVII (1965), 19-23.
1841   FEDERMAN, Raymond. *"How It Is* with Beckett's Fiction," *French
           Review,* XXXVIII (Feb., 1965), 459-468 [see **1071**].
A novel such as *Comment c'est* which lies in "the realm of uncertainty," which
discloses the secret of its creation as it progresses, which exposes its own shortcomings, imperfections, and failure, cannot be created without some antecedent.
Therefore, "to grasp Beckett's vision in *Comment c'est,* to accept this novel
without brushing it aside as a mere literary hoax . . . it is necessary to return
to the beginning of his creations."

1965

1842   FLETCHER, John. "Beckett and the Fictional Tradition," *Caliban:*
Annales Publiées par la Faculté des Lettres et Sciences Humaines
de Toulouse, n.s., I, no. 1 (1965), 147-158.

Taking his lead from a statement by Christine Brooke-Rose in **1432**, that
Beckett's novels were not unworthy scions of a family that boasted such
illustrious members as *Don Quixote, Le Roman bourgeois, Tristram Shandy,*
and *Jacques le fataliste,* Fletcher views Beckett's fiction "in the tradition of
the ironical novel of the seventeenth and eighteenth centuries" [see **718**].

1843   _____. "Samuel Beckett and the Philosophers," *Comparative Liter-*
ature, XVII (Winter, 1965), 43-56.

Because of the lack of "adequate" exploration of the philosophical influences
in the work of Beckett, and despite the fact that Beckett claims no "philosophy," it seems necessary to outline the major influences from the pre-Socratics
(Pythagoras, Heraclitus, Democritus, and Empedocles, whose suicide "im-
pressed" Beckett) through the medieval Christian philosophers (St. Augustine,
Guillaume de Champeaux, Bruno) to Descartes. Then also there are Geulincx,
and traces of Spinoza, Malebranche, Locke, Berkeley, and Leibniz [see **718**].

1844   _____. "Beckett's Debt to Dante," *Nottingham French Studies,* IV,
no. 1 (1965), 41-52.

Despite some useful material already published on the subject (see esp. **1520,**
1539, 1786), this article brings new insight to the question of Beckett's debt
to Dante [see **718**].

1845   _____. "Samuel Beckett; or, the Morbid Dread of Sphinxes," *New*
Durham, n.v. (June, 1965), 5-9.

Discussing the staging of *Waiting for Godot,* Fletcher states that Beckett "ac-
quired overnight a reputation for obscurity that has dogged him ever since,"
but he is an essentially simple writer, uttering a "magnificent cry of revolt
against the sentence passed on mankind, to die on a dying planet" [see **718**].

1846   _____. "Sur un roman inédit de Samuel Beckett," *Littératures XII:*
Annales publiées par la Faculté des Lettres et Sciences Humaines
de Toulouse, n.s., I (Nov., 1965), 139-152.

A useful analysis of Beckett's unpublished first French novel, *Mercier et Camier,*
of which an excerpt is given with the article, pp. 153-154 [see **273**].

1847   _____. "Samuel Beckett as Critic," *The Listener,* LXXIV (Nov.
25, 1965), 862-863 [see **3024**].

Fletcher turns his attention here to that much neglected part of Beckett's
work, his critical writing: his essay on Joyce, his study of Proust, and the
various essays he wrote on painting [see **718**].

1848   FRANCIS, Richard Lee. "Beckett's Metaphysical Tragicomedy,"
Modern Drama, VIII (Dec., 1965), 259-267.

An attempt to reinterpret *Waiting for Godot,* but without bringing much that
is new in the understanding of the play.

1849   HARVEY, Lawrence E. "Samuel Beckett on Life, Art, and Criticism," *Modern Language Notes,* LXXX (Dec., 1965), 545-562
[see **612**].

1965

1849

Through a close examination of Beckett's critical writings on the painting of Geer and Bram van Velde, and quoting from some unpublished documents, Harvey draws some interesting conclusions about Beckett's attitude toward life, art, and the artist. Beckett himself is described as an artist whose "isolation . . . and . . . unintellectual pursuits militate against 'communication' with his audience."

1850 HURLEY, Paul J. "France and America: Versions of the Absurd," *College English,* XXVI (1965), 634-640.

Discussion and comparison of Albee, Kopit, Gelber, Ionesco, and Beckett.

1851 LAMONT, Rosette. "Death and Tragi-comedy: Three Plays of the New Theater," *Massachusetts Review,* VI (Winter, 1965), 381-402.

The contemporary mode of tragicomedy is rooted in the contemplation of one's own death. The mode allows us, in this age of anxiety, to defeat our ghosts with paroxysms of laughter. A good example of this "self-conscious death" is found in *Happy Days,* in which Winnie, a "narcissistic middlebrow," is paralyzed by "the ever-tightening girdle of the earthly grave which will swallow all."

1852 ROSI, Luca. "Beckett e il teatro dell'assurdo," *Cenobio,* XIV (1965), 23-27.

1853 SCHECHNER, Richard. "TDR Comment: Theatre Criticism," *Tulane Drama Review,* IX (Spring, 1965), 13-24 (Beckett, *passim*).

1854 SCHNEIDER, Alan. "Reality Is Not Enough," *Tulane Drama Review,* IX (Spring, 1965), 118-152.

Record of an interview with Alan Schneider by Richard Schechner (editor of *TDR*). Schneider discusses his philosophy of theater with regard to the interpretation and direction of certain plays, including those of Beckett. Some interesting comments are made on how Beckett's *Film* was produced and filmed with Buster Keaton.

1855 VOLD, Jan Erik. "Samuel Becketts romaner," *Samtiden,* LXXIV (1965), 441-447.

1856 WILDER, Amos N. "Mortality and Contemporary Literature," *Harvard Theological Review,* LVIII (Jan., 1965), 1-20 (Beckett, *passim*).

1966

1857 ALPAUGH, David J. "The Symbolic Structure of Samuel Beckett's *All That Fall,*" *Modern Drama,* IX (Dec., 1966), 324-332 [see **904**].

One of the few pieces that deal specifically with *All That Fall* as a radio play. "Taking advantage of the listener's blindness, Beckett makes a metaphor of the radio play form itself."

1966

1858   ATKINS, Anselm. "A Note on the Structure of Lucky's Speech," *Modern Drama,* IX (Dec., 1966), 309 [see **904**].
Lucky's speech in *Waiting for Godot* is examined as a "carefully wrought poetic structure."

1859   BERSANI, Leo. "No Exit for Beckett," *Partisan Review,* XXXIII (Spring, 1966), 261-267.
Brushing aside the work of many critics who have attempted to elucidate the meaning of Beckett's fiction through various approaches (symbol interpretations, explications of names, philosophic sources, and so on), Bersani prefers to see in Beckett a writer who is "far less interested in, say, Occasionalist philosophy than in the anus, unadorned and admirably unsublimated."

1860   BROOKS, Curtis M. "The Mythic Pattern in *Waiting for Godot,*" *Modern Drama,* IX (Dec., 1966), 292-299 [see **904**].
An interesting interpretation of *Godot* by a graduate student, this being his first published article. "The setting of *Godot* is at the center of the world, since two preeminent symbols of the center are used in the play: the tree of life and the difficult road."

1861   COHN, Ruby. "Acting for Beckett," *Modern Drama,* IX (Dec., 1966), 237 [see **904**].
A brief note on Beckett's activities in the theater which serves as an introduction to this special issue of *Modern Drama* edited by Ruby Cohn.

1862   _____. "The Beginning of *Endgame,*" *Modern Drama,* IX (Dec., 1966), 319-323 [see **904**].
Some interesting facts about the play and Beckett's creative process are revealed in this study of earlier drafts of *Endgame.*

1863   DUBOIS, Jacques. "Beckett and Ionesco: The Tragic Awareness of Pascal and the Ironic Awareness of Flaubert," *Modern Drama,* IX (Dec., 1966), 283-291 [see **904**].
An effort, not totally successful, at comparing "the structural similarity of *Godot* and *The Chairs* to the dissimilarity of their sociological vision."

1864   DUCKWORTH, Colin. "The Making of *Godot,*" *Theatre Research,* VII, no. 3 (1966), 123-145. Reprinted in **714** [see also **259**, Note].
A scholarly study of the "making of *Godot*" based on an examination of the original manuscript and in the light of earlier Beckett works.

1865   FEDERMAN, Raymond. "*Film,*" *Film Quarterly,* XX (Winter, 1966-67), 46-51.
An analysis of *Film,* Beckett's first experiment with the cinema. Beckett's approach to this medium is discussed in the light of his work in ficton and drama.

1866   FLETCHER, John. "Roger Blin at Work," *Modern Drama,* VIII (Feb., 1966), 403-408.
An eyewitness at the rehearsals in Toulouse of *Godot* staged for the "fourth or fifth time" by Blin, Fletcher gives penetrating insights into the director's work and his understanding of the play.

1867   _____. "Action and Play in Beckett's Theater," *Modern Drama,* IX (Dec., 1966), 242-250 [see **904**]. Reprinted in an extended version in **718**, under the chapter heading "The Art of the Dramatist."

1966

1868 FRIEDMAN, Melvin J. "Crritic!" [*sic*], *Modern Drama*, IX (Dec., 1966), 300-308 [see **904**].

A survey of critical controversies around *Godot,* showing, not without irony, the numerous contradictory interpretations that have been formulated around the play.

1869 HARVEY, J. R. "La Vieille Voix Faible: Writers on Beckett," *Cambridge Quarterly,* I (Autumn, 1966), 384-395 [see **703j**, **705d**, **707d**, **708j**, **709c**, **712i**, **713f**].

Basically a review article of seven recent books on Beckett.

1870 HUBERT, Renée Riese. "Beckett's *Play* between Poetry and Performance," *Modern Drama,* IX (Dec., 1966), 339-346 [see **904**].

A view of *Play* by a poet with emphasis on the fact that "the characters' mobility and the impact of natural lights tend to decrease" as one examines Beckett's plays in chronological order.

1871 ISER, Wolfgang. "Samuel Beckett's Dramatic Language," *Modern Drama,* IX (Dec., 1966), 251-259 [see **904**]. Originally published in German in **1612**.

One of the few attempts at analyzing Beckett's language. *Godot* and *Endgame* are discussed specifically here, in an effort to show that "language is no longer directed toward depicting given situations, for the transformation of words into stimuli sets up chains of association, the links and development of which cannot be grasped."

1872 JANVIER, Ludovic. "Réduire à la parole," *Cahiers de la Compagnie Madeleine Renaud–Jean-Louis Barrault,* 53 (Feb., 1966), 42-48.

All of Beckett's damned creatures desire the Hell in which they exist; they wish it "comme un repos enfin gagné." Every means is used to lead the characters to this infernal condition, and in the end all that is left is speech: "La voix qui fut dehors est dedans, la mutilation a forcé à l'expression, la fixité a fait que le personnage est totalement personne dans le moindre de ses silences."

1873 KERN, Edith. "Beckett and the Spirit of the Commedia Dell'Arte," *Modern Drama,* IX (Dec., 1966), 260-267 [see **904**].

Though Beckett utilizes none of the commedia's most obvious features, what seems to justify this classification are the traces of the very spirit of the commedia dell'arte that are to be observed in his plays: "its *lazzi,* that is, its stage business; something of its attitude towards language; and above all, its preference for grotesque stylization at the total expense of verisimilitude and probability."

1874 MAYOUX, Jean-Jacques. "Beckett et l'humour," *Cahiers de la Compagnie Madeleine Renaud–Jean-Louis Barrault,* 53 (Feb., 1966), 33-41.

With his usual perspicacity, Mayoux examines various aspects of Beckett's humor, and emphasizes that this humor is primarily Irish in the tradition of Swift, Sterne, and Joyce.

1966

1875 ⸺⸺. "Beckett and Expressionism," *Modern Drama,* IX (Dec., 1966), 238-241 [see **904**].

It is among northern peoples that imaginative creation has most often taken the expressionist path. But northern expressionism is often heavy-handed, whereas Beckett's Irish expressionism almost always has the charm of humor to temper it and occasionally to cancel it in the wink of an eye.

1876 MIHALYI, Gábor. "Beckett's *Godot* and the Myth of Alienation," *Modern Drama,* IX (Dec., 1966), 277-282 [see **904**]. Also published in *New Hungarian Quarterly,* 24 (Winter, 1966), unpaginated.

The theater of the absurd is intent on exposing myths that are now empty of validity, untrue, devoid of substance. In *Godot,* Beckett repudiates the Christian myth of redemption; but he also attacks the myths of enlightenment, progress, nature, and love.

1877 OBERG, Arthur K. *"Krapp's Last Tape* and the Proustian Vision," *Modern Drama,* IX (Dec., 1966), 333-338 [see **904**].

Beckett's understanding of the Proustian voluntary and involuntary memory allows him in *Krapp's Last Tape* to present a dramatic study of the changing and changeless self.

1878 SCHECHNER, Richard. "There's Lots of Time in *Godot,*" *Modern Drama,* IX (Dec., 1966), 268-276 [see **904**].

Much has been said of the element of time in *Godot,* but Schechner goes much further here than anyone has attempted to go. He shows that there are "two time rhythms in *Godot:* one of the play and one of the stage."

1879 SHEEDY, John J. "The Comic Apocalypse of King Hamm," *Modern Drama,* IX (Dec., 1966), 310-318 [see **904**].

An interesting juxtaposition of comic and apocalyptic aspects of *Endgame* is revealed here. The fusion of these two elements can be observed in the play's smallest parts, sometimes simply in a pun or a gesture of the characters.

1880 TAGLIAFERRI, Aldo. "Il concreto e l'astratto in Beckett," *Il Verri,* 20 (1966), 29-54.

11.

Selection of Reviews, Notes, Allusions, and Miscellaneous Items

1930

1900   ANONYMOUS. *T.C.D.: A College Miscellany,* XXXVI (March **6,** 1930), 137.
Reference to *Che Sciagura* [see **3**].

1931

1901   ANONYMOUS. *T.C.D.: A College Miscellany,* XXXVII (Feb. **26,** 1931), 116 [see **8,** Note].
Review of *Le Kid* [see **609**].

1902   _____. *The Listener,* V (March 25, 1931), Supplement, p. xv.
Review of *Proust.*

1903   _____. *Times Literary Supplement,* April 2, 1931, p. 274.
Review of *Proust.*

1904   _____. *T.C.D.: A College Miscellany,* XXXVII (June 4, 1931), 185.
Reference to *The Possessed* [see **8**].

1905   DOBRÉE, Bonamy. *The Spectator,* April 18, 1931, pp. 641-642.
Review of *Proust.*

1906   F[LINT], F. S. *The Criterion,* X (July, 1931), 792.
Review of *Proust.*

1907   MacCARTHY, Desmond. *Sunday Times,* May 24, 1931, p. 6.
Review of *Proust.*

1908   M[ANDY], W. J. K. *T.C.D.: A College Miscellany,* XXXVII (May 28, 1931), 177.
Review of *Proust.*

1934

1909   ANONYMOUS. *Irish Times,* June 23, 1934, p. 5.
Review of *More Pricks Than Kicks.*

1910   ————. *Times Literary Supplement,* July 26, 1934, p. 526.
Review of *More Pricks Than Kicks.*

1911   CALDER-MARSHALL, Arthur. *The Spectator,* June 1, 1934, p.
        863.
Review of *More Pricks Than Kicks.*

1912   GOULD, Gerald. *The Observer,* June 10, 1934, p. 6.
Review of *More Pricks Than Kicks.*

1913   H., N. *Dublin Magazine,* IX (July-Sept., 1934), 84-85.
Review of *More Pricks Than Kicks.*

1914   MUIR, Edwin. *The Listener,* XII (July 4, 1934), 42.
Review of *More Pricks Than Kicks.*

1915   QUENNELL, Peter. *New Statesman,* VII (May 26, 1934), 802.
Review of *More Pricks Than Kicks.*

1916   WATSON, Francis. *The Bookman,* LXXXVI (July, 1934), 219-220.
Review of *More Pricks Than Kicks.*

1936

1917   ANONYMOUS. *Dublin Magazine,* XI (April-June, 1936), 78.
Review of *Echo's Bones and Other Precipitates.*

1918   ————. *Times Literary Supplement,* Dec. 12, 1936, p. 1037.
Note on *Our Exagmination Round His Factification for Incamination of
Work in Progress,* including a reference to Beckett as one of the contributors.

1919   M., C. *Irish Times,* July 25, 1936, p. 7, col. 1.
Review of the latest issue of *Transition,* including a reference to the poems
from *Echo's Bones and Other Precipitates* reprinted in that issue [see **22.01**].

1938

1920   ANONYMOUS. *Times Literary Supplement,* March 12, 1938, p.
        172, col. 1. (Condensed version published in the Spring Books
        issue, March 26, 1938, p. 220, cols. 1 and 2, under the general
        heading of "A Selection of Novels Political and Social.")
Review of *Murphy.*

1921   MUIR, Edwin. *The Listener,* XIX (March 16, 1938), 597.
Review of *Murphy.*

1922   O'BRIEN, Kate. *The Spectator,* March 25, 1938, p. 546.
Review of *Murphy.*

1938

1923 POWELL, Dilys. *Sunday Times,* March 13, 1938, p. 8.
Review of *Murphy.*

1924 SWINNERTON, Frank. *The Observer,* March 20, 1938, p. 6.
Review of *Murphy.*

1925 THOMAS, Dylan. *New English Weekly,* XII (March 17, 1938),
454-455.
Review of *Murphy.*

1939

1926 ANONYMOUS. *Dublin Magazine,* XIV (April-June, 1939), 98.
Review of *Murphy.*

1946

1927 ANONYMOUS. *Irish Times,* June 27, 1946, p. 5, col. 1.
Letter about *Saint-Lo 1945* [*sic*] by Samuel Beckett.

1928 LOVE, Oscar. *Irish Times,* July 4, 1946, p. 5, col. 1.
Letter about *Saint-Lo 1945* [*sic*] by Samuel Beckett.

1929 WHITE, H. O. *Irish Times,* July 3, 1946, p. 5, col. 6.
Letter about *Saint-Lo 1945* [*sic*] by Samuel Beckett, written by a professor at
Trinity College, Dublin.

1950

1930 DUTHUIT, Georges. "Sartre's Last Class," *Transition Fifty,* 6 (Oct.,
[1950]), 90.
Reference to Beckett.

1951

1931 ANONYMOUS. *La Cité,* April 24, 1951.
Review of *Molloy* (original French text).

1932 ———. *Liens,* June 1, 1951.
Review of *Molloy* (original French text).

1933 ———. *Revue de la Pensée Française,* X (Oct., 1951), 61-63.
Review of *Molloy* (original French text).

1934 ———. *Combat,* Oct. 11, 1951.
Review of *Malone meurt.*

1935 ALBERT-HESSE, Jean. "Fierté, patience et solitude," *Franc-Tireur,*
Nov. 17, 1951.
Review of *Malone meurt.*

1951

1936   ASTRE, G. Albert. "L'Humanisme de la pourriture," *Action*, May
        7-13, 1951 [see **1061**].
Review of *Molloy* (original French text).

1937   BÉRARD, J. *Bel-Abbès Journal*, April 6, 1951.
Review of *Molloy* (original French text).

1938   BLANZAT, Jean. *Figaro Littéraire*, April 14, 1951, p. 9 [see **1061**].
Review of *Molloy* (original French text).

1939   BRENNER, Jacques. *L'Observateur*, June 28, 1951.
Review of *Molloy* (original French text).

1940   CARROUGES, Michel. *Monde Nouveau/Paru*, VII, no. 50 (1951),
        64.
Review of *Molloy* (original French text).

1941   CHAMBURE, Guy de. *Gazette des Lettres*, VII (July 15, 1951), 119.
Review of *Molloy* (original French text).

1942   CHARBONNIER, Georges. *La Nef*, VIII (June-July, 1951), 250-
        251.
Review of *Molloy* (original French text).

1943   DALMAS, André. "De la critique géométrique à la critique de
        finesse," *Tribune des Nations*, Oct. 19, 1951.
Review of *Molloy* (original French text).

1944   DEBIDOUR, V.-H. *Bulletin des Lettres*, XIII (June 15, 1951), 232-
        233.
Review of *Molloy* (original French text).

1945   DUMUR, Guy. "Écrivains étrangers de langue française," *Médecine
        de France*, 23 (1951), 43-45.
Includes Beckett among foreign writers using French.

1946   DUVIGNAUD, Jean. "Monsieur Teste gâteux," *Combat*, Dec. 20,
        1951.
Review of *Malone meurt*.

1947   ELSEN, Claude. "Une épopée du non-sens," *Table Ronde*, 42 (June,
        1951), 135-139.
Review of *Molloy* (original French text).

1948   FOUCHET, Max-Pol. "Une Chronique de la décomposition,"
        Carrefour, April 24, 1951, p. 8.
Review of *Molloy* (original French text).

1949   GADENNE, Paul. "Faut-il 'savonner' l'humanité?" *Cahiers du Sud*,
        XXXIII, no. 307 (1951), 511-518 [see **1061**].
Review of *Molloy* (original French text).

1951

1950   KANTERS, Robert. "Autant en emporte le vent," *Age Nouveau,* 62 (June, 1951), 68-70 [see **1061**].
Review of *Molloy* (original French text).

1951   LALOU, René. "Le Livre de la semaine," *Nouvelles Littéraires,* Nov. 8, 1951, p. 6.
Review of *Malone meurt.*

1952   LECOMTE, Marcel. *Synthèses,* VI (Aug., 1951), 428-429.
Review of *Molloy* (original French text).

1953   MARCHAND, Jean-Jacques. *Le Rassemblement,* June 8-14, 1951.
Review of *Molloy* (original French text).

1954   NADEAU, Maurice. 1. "Samuel Beckett, ou: En avant vers nulle part," *Combat,* April 12, 1951 [see **1061**].
2. *Samedi-Soir,* Dec. 15-21, 1951.
Reviews of *Molloy* (original French text).

1955   PICON, Gaëtan. 1. "Héritier de Joyce, l'Irlandais Samuel Beckett a choisi la langue française," *Le Rouge et le Noir,* May 12, 1951.
2. *Samedi-Soir,* May 12-18, 1951 [see **1061**].
Reviews of *Molloy* (original French text).

1956   ROUSSELOT, Jean. *Nouvelles Littéraires,* April 19, 1951; same text also in *Libre Poitou,* May 23, 1951.
Review of *Molloy* (original French text).

1957   SLOCOMBE, G. *New York Herald Tribune* (European edition), May 3, 1951.
Review of *Molloy* (original French text).

1952

1958   GREGORY, C. *L'Observateur,* Jan. 10, 1952.
Review of *Malone meurt.*

1959   LEMARCHAND, Jacques. *Le Figaro,* Dec. 14, 1952.
Information on *En attendant Godot.*

1960   MAGNY, Claude-Edmonde. *Preuves,* 2 (Feb., 1952), 43-44.
Review of *Malone meurt.*

1961   MARCHAND, Jean-Jacques. *Le Rassemblement,* Jan. 25-31, 1952.
Review of *Malone meurt.*

1962   MAZARS, Pierre. *Table Ronde,* 53 (May, 1952), 148-149.

Review of *Malone meurt.*

1963   NADEAU, Maurice. *Mercure de France,* CCCVIX (March, 1952), 503-504.
Review of *Malone meurt.*

1952

1964   ROUSSEAUX, André. "Le Journal d'un cadavre," *Figaro Littéraire,*
             Jan. 5, 1952, p. 2.
Review of *Malone meurt.*

1953

1965   ANONYMOUS. *Bulletin Critique du Livre Français,* VIII (1953),
             69.
Review of *En attendant Godot* (published text).

1966   _____. "Samuel Beckett est enfin joué," *Figaro Littéraire,* **Jan.** 10,
             1953, p. 1 (with photograph of the first production).
Note on *En attendant Godot.*

1967   _____. *Paris-Casablanca,* Feb. 20, 1953.
Review of *En attendant Godot* (first production).

1968   _____. *L'Express,* July 4, 1953.
Review of *L'Innommable.*

1969   _____. *Nouvelles Littéraires,* July 23, 1953.
Review of *L'Innommable.*

1970   _____. *Der Spiegel,* 38 (Sept. 16, 1953), 42.
Review of *En attendant Godot* (on tour in Germany).

1971   _____. *Die Zeit,* Sept. 17, 1953.
Review of *En attendant Godot* (on tour in Germany).

1972   _____. *Kölner S.-A.,* Nov. 3, 1953.
Review of *En attendant Godot* (on tour).

1973   _____. "Der Mensch findet nicht statt," *Basler Nachrichten,* Nov.
             30, 1953.
Review of *En attendant Godot* (on tour).

1974   _____. *Corriere della Sera,* Dec. 1, 1953.
Review of *En attendant Godot* (on tour).

1975   _____. *L'Italia,* Dec. 1, 1953.
Review of *En attendant Godot* (on tour).

1976   _____. *Il Popolo,* Dec. 1, 1953.
Review of *En attendant Godot* (on tour).

1977   ANEX, Georges. "Samuel Beckett, ou la vie inusable," *Gazette de
             Lausanne,* Jan. 23, 1953.
On *En attendant Godot.*

1978   BECKMANN, H. *Rheinischer Merkur,* Nov. 27, 1953.
Review of *En attendant Godot* (on tour).

1953

1979   BONNEFOI, Geneviève. "La Quête de l'impossible identité,"
L'Observateur, Sept. 17, 1953.
Review of L'Innommable.

1980   BOSQUET, Alain. "Deux portraits du néant," Combat, July 16, 1953.
Review of L'Innommable.

1981   BRON, J. Semeur Vaudois, Sept. 26, 1953.
Review of En attendant Godot (on tour).

1982   CAPRON, Marcelle. Combat, Jan. 8, 1953.
Review of En attendant Godot (first production).

1983   CHONEZ, Claudine. L'Observateur, Jan. 8, 1953.
Review of En attendant Godot (first production).

1984   CLÉMENT, Danièle. "Samuel Beckett," Terre Humaine, 42 (June-
July, 1953), 29.
Brief discussion of Beckett and his work.

1985   DALMAS, André. Tribune des Nations, Feb. 6, 1953.
Review of En attendant Godot (first production).

1986   DAVID, A. L'Information, Jan. 17, 1953.
Review of En attendant Godot (first production).

1987   ELLMAR, Paul. "Warten und hoffen," Die Zeit, Feb. 12, 1953.
Review of En attendant Godot.

1988   ESTANG, Luc. "Cendres," La Croix, Feb. 22-23, 1953.
Review of En attendant Godot (first production).

1989   GILLES, W. Morgen, Nov. 26, 1953.
Review of En attendant Godot (on tour).

1990   GORDEAUX, P. France-Soir, Jan. 10, 1953.
Review of En attendant Godot (first production).

1991   GRENIER, Jean. Disque Vert, I (July-Aug., 1953), 81-86.
Review of En attendant Godot.

1992   GÜNTHER, Gerhard. Sonntagsblatt, March 1, 1953.
Review of En attendant Godot (first production).

1993   JEENER, J.-B. Le Figaro, Jan. 10-11, 1953, p. 6.
Review of En attendant Godot (first production).

1994   JOSBIN, Raoul. Études, 150 (July-Aug., 1953), 77-83. **Reprinted**
in English in **2087**.
Review of En attendant Godot.

1995   JOTTERAND, F. Gazette de Lausanne, Jan. 31, 1953.
Review of En attendant Godot (first production).

1953

1996   JOUHEAUD, J.-H. *L'Informateur Critique,* Jan. 23, 1953, pp. 11-13.
Review of *En attendant Godot* (first production).

1997   KEMP, Robert. *Le Monde,* Jan. 14, 1953, p. 9.
Review of *En attendant Godot* (first production).

1998   LANDOLFI, Tommaso. "Il Caso Beckett," *Il Mondo,* Nov. 10, 1953.
Review of *L'Innommable.*

1999   LEMARCHAND, Jacques. *Figaro Littéraire,* Jan. 17, 1953, p. 10.
Review of *En attendant Godot* (first production).

2000   LOBET, M. *Revue Générale Belge,* Aug. 15, 1953.
Review of *L'Innommable.*

2001   MARCEL, Gabriel. *Nouvelles Littéraires,* Jan. 15, 1953.
Review of *En attendant Godot* (first production).

2002   MARCHAND, Jean-Jacques. *Le Rassemblement,* Oct. 1-7, 1953.
Review of *L'Innommable.*

2003   MAULNIER, Thierry. *Revue de Paris,* LX (Feb., 1953), 136-137.
Review of *En attendant Godot* (first production).

2004   MONTIJO, Edwin. *"Warten auf Godot,"* *Kurier,* Sept. 9, 1953.
Review of *En attendant Godot.*

2005   RYAN, Desmond. "Letter from Paris," *Time and Tide,* March 21,
1953.
Note on *En attendant Godot.*

2006   SAUREL, Renée. "Deux pièces drôles et cruelles sur la vie à l'envers,"
Lettres Françaises, XI (Jan. 15-22, 1953), 6.
Review of *En attendant Godot.*

2007   SAUVAGE, Marcel. *"l'Innommable,"* *Pour Tous,* Dec. 15, 1953.
Review of *L'Innommable.*

2008   SCHLOZER, G., Pasteur. "L'Homme en attente," *Semeur Vaudois,*
Sept. 26, 1953.
Review of *En attendant Godot.*

2009   SEAVER, Richard. *Nimbus,* II (Autumn, 1953), 61-62.
Review of *Watt.*

2010   SÖDERBERG, Lasse. "Skaftlös dolk utan blad," *Expressen,* May 18,
1953.
Review of *En attendant Godot.*

2011   VERDOT, Guy. *"En attendant Godot,"* *Franc-Tireur,* Jan. 8, 1953.
Review of first production.

2012   ZEGEL, Sylvain. *Libération,* Jan. 7, 1953.
Review of *En attendant Godot* (first production).

1953

2013   ZELTNER-NEUKOMM, Gerda. *Neue Zürcher Zeitung,* X (March
            10, 1953), 3.
Review of *En attendant Godot* (first production).

1954

2014   ANONYMOUS. *Carrefour,* April 28, 1954.
Translation of report in *New York Times Book Review* of Dublin court case
dialogue between Beckett and counsel.

2015   BROCK-SULZER, Elisabeth. *"Warten auf Godot," Die Tat,* Jan.
            29, Feb. 28, 1954, p. 2.
Review of *En attendant Godot.*

2016   WEBER, Werner. "Variationen über das Warten," *Neue Zürcher
            Zeitung,* XIII (March 13, 1954), 3.
On the theme of waiting in *En attendant Godot.*

2017   WIJKERSLOOTH, R. de. "Nieuw Idool van Parijs," *Elseviers
            Weekblad,* Feb. 20, 1954.
About Beckett as a playwright.

1955

2018   ANONYMOUS. *The Times,* Sept. 13, 1955, p. 12.
Review of *Waiting for Godot* (London production).

2019   _____. "Muck-Raker: Talented Writer Turns Agony into Sheer
            Mud," *Mexico News Weekly,* Dec. 4, 1955.
On *Molloy.*

2020   AHOLAS, J. "Voimaton älgmystö," *Parnasso,* 2 (1955).
Review of *Waiting for Godot.*

2021   BARISSE, Rita. "Books and Bookmen Abroad: Paris," *Books and
            Bookmen,* I (Dec., 1955), 56.
Mentions Beckett writing and living in Paris.

2022   BARKER, R. *Plays and Players,* II (Sept., 1955), 18-19.
Review of *Waiting for Godot* (London production).

2023   BOEHMER, Bob. "His Exercise in Language," *Journal Northwest
            Living Magazine,* Sept. 18, 1955.
Review of *Molloy.*

2024   BOSQUET, Alain. "Le Monde déliquescent de Samuel Beckett,"
            Combat, Jan. 13, 1955. Reprinted in *Presse-Tunis,* Jan. 29, 1955.
About Beckett's fiction.

2025   _____. "Samuel Beckett ou l'écriture abstraite," *Combat,* Dec. 29,
            1955.

1955

2026   BRYANT, Joe. "Joycean Theme is Dismal," *Fort Lauderdale News and Sentinel,* Oct. 23, 1955.
On *Molloy.*

2027   CHAPSAL, Madeleine. *L'Express,* Dec. 24-25, 1955.
Review of *Nouvelles et Textes pour rien.*

2028   FRANK, Nino. "Scherzi di Beckett," *Il Mondo,* Oct. 4, 1955, p. 10.
On Beckett in general.

2029   HOBSON, Harold. "Tomorrow," *Sunday Times,* Aug. 7, 1955, p. 11.
Review of *Waiting for Godot* (London production).

2030   _____. "Samuel Beckett," *Sunday Times,* Aug. 14, 1955, p. 11.
Review of *Waiting for Godot* (London production).

2031   LALOU, René. *Nouvelles Littéraires,* Dec. 22, 1955.
Review of *Nouvelles et Textes pour rien.*

2032   LOVELL, Florence. "Literary Event, But Too Avant," *Bridgeport Sunday Post,* Sept. 25, 1955.
On *Molloy.*

2033   MAURIAC, Claude. "Beckett l'obscur," *Le Figaro,* Dec. 14, 1955, p. 17.
Review of *Nouvelles et Textes pour rien.*

2034   POS, W. Ph. "Beckett's *En attendant Godot,*" *Kroniek van Kunst en Kultuur,* XV (1955), 54-56.
On the production of the play.

2035   POULET, Robert. "L'Œuvre de Samuel Beckett," *Rivarol,* Jan. 6, 1955.
On Beckett's work in general.

2036   TOYNBEE, Philip. "Going Nowhere," *The Observer,* Dec. 18, 1955, p. 11.
Review of *Molloy* (English translation).

2037   TREWIN, J. C. "Waiting and Waiting," *Illustrated London News,* CCXXVII (Oct. 1, 1955), 582.
Review of *Waiting for Godot* (London production).

2038   TYNAN, Kenneth. "New Writing," *The Observer,* Aug. 7, 1955, p. 11.
Review of *Waiting for Godot* (London production).

1956

2039   ANONYMOUS. "*Waiting for Godot* in New York," *The Times,* Jan. 6, 1956, p. 3a.
On New York production.

1956

2040 _____. *Evening Standard,* Jan. 19, 1956.
Discussion of drama award, mentions Beckett.

2041 _____. [*pseud.* Thespis]. *English,* XI (Spring, 1956), 18.
Review of *Waiting for Godot* (London production).

2042 _____. 'Puzzling about Godot," *Times Literary Supplement,* April
      13, 1956, p. 221.
Review of *Waiting for Godot;* discusses particularly the name Godot.

2043 _____. "Baffling but Fun," *Newsweek,* XLVII (April 30, 1956),
      76.
Review of *Waiting for Godot* (New York production).

2044 _____. "New Play in Manhattan," *Time,* LXVII (April 30, 1956),
      55.
Review of *Waiting for Godot* (New York production).

2045 _____. "Lahr in the Middle of a Riddle," *Life,* XL (May 7, 1956),
      155-156, 158.
Review of *Waiting for Godot* (New York production).

2046 _____. *Cyprus Mail,* May 10, 1956.
Review of *Waiting for Godot.*

2047 _____. "Myerberg's Mystery," *New Yorker,* XXXII (May 19,
      1956), 25-26.
Interview with Michael Myerberg, director of the New York production of
Waiting for Godot.

2048 _____. *Theatre Arts,* XL (June, 1956), 18.
Review of *Waiting for Godot* (New York production).

2049 _____. "Variaties op het liefdesthema," *Nieuwe Rotterdamse
      Courant,* Aug. 4, 1956.
On *Waiting for Godot.*

2050 _____. *Newsweek,* XLVIII (Sept. 24, 1956), 102.
Comment on the Columbia recording of *Waiting for Godot.*

2051 _____. "Molten Gloom," *Time,* LXVIII (Oct. 15, 1956), 118
      (with photograph of Beckett).
Review of *Malone Dies.*

2052 _____. *The Reporter,* XV (Oct. 4, 1956), 48.
Review of *Malone Dies.*

2053 _____. *Chicago Books on Trial,* XV (Nov., 1956), 138.
Review of *Waiting for Godot.*

2054 _____. "Anti," *New York Times,* Dec. 9, 1956.
On *Waiting for Godot.*

1956

2055 ———. *The Times,* Dec. 20, 1956, p. 2*f*.
News item on Beckett and *All That Fall.*

2056 ATKINSON, Brooks. *New York Times,* April 20, 1956 [see **1054,** **2225**].
Review of *Waiting for Godot.*

2057 BAGBY, Philip H. *Times Literary Supplement,* March 23, 1956, p. 181.
Letter to the Editor on *Waiting for Godot.*

2058 BERGER, John. *Daily Worker,* March 22, 1956, p. 2.
Review of *Waiting for Godot* (published text).

2059 BERTRAM, Anthony. "*Waiting for Godot:* Qui Quaerit Invenit," *The Tablet,* CCVII (Feb. 25, 1956), 179-180.

2060 BLANCHOT, Maurice. "La Douleur du dialogue," *Nouvelle Revue Française,* IV (March, 1956), 492-503.
Mentions Beckett.

2061 BREIT, Harvey. "In and Out of Books," *New York Times Book Review,* Dec. 9, 1956, p. 8.
On Beckett and the contemporary theater.

2062 BRUUN, Erik. "Saa kom Godot da endelig," *Information,* April 20, 1956.
On *Waiting for Godot.*

2063 CARTER, Thomas H. "Recent Fiction," *Shenandoah,* VII (Summer, 1956), 53-54.
Review of *Molloy* included.

2064 CLURMAN, Harold. *The Nation,* CLXXXII (May 5, 1956), 387, 390.
Review of *Waiting for Godot* (New York production).

2065 COOKE, Richard P. "Cosmic Prank," *Wall Street Journal,* April 23, 1956.
Review of *Waiting for Godot.*

2066 CRIST, Judith. "*Waiting for Godot,*" *New York Herald Tribune,* April 15, 1956.
Review of the New York production.

2067 DONNELLY, Tom. "So 'Malone Dies'—Or Does He Really?" *World-Telegram and Sun,* Oct. 1, 1956.

2068 DUDAR, Helen. "The Lady Who Wouldn't Wait for Godot," *New York Post,* May 16, 1956.
On *Waiting for Godot.*

1956

2069   DUVIGNAUD, Jean. *Gazette de Lausanne,* July 1, 1956.
Review of *En attendant Godot* (Théâtre Hébertot production).

2070   EMPSON, William. *Times Literary Supplement,* March 30, 1956,
p. 195.
Letter to the Editor on *Waiting for Godot.*

2071   EVANS, Fallon. *"Malone Dies," Chicago Books on Trial,* XV (Nov.,
1956), 137.
Review of *Malone Dies.*

2072   FERTIG, Howard. *Village Voice,* Aug. 29, 1956 [see **1054**].
Reviews of *Molloy* (English translation) and of *Waiting for Godot.*

2073   [FRASER, G. S.] "They Also Serve," *Times Literary Supplement,*
Feb. 10, 1956, p. 84. Reprinted in **1010**.
Review of *Waiting for Godot* (published text).

2074   GASSNER, John. *Educational Theatre Journal,* VIII (Oct., 1956),
217-225 [see **1019**].
Review of *Waiting for Godot.*

2075   GAUTIER, Jean-Jacques. *Le Figaro,* June 15, 1956, p. 10.
Review of *En attendant Godot* (Théâtre Hébertot production).

2076   GELB, A. *New York Times,* April 15, 1956.
Review of *Waiting for Godot* (New York production).

2077   GIBBS, Wolcott. "Enough Is Enough Is Enough," *New Yorker,*
XXXII (May 5, 1956), 89-90.
Review of *Waiting for Godot* (New York production).

2078   GINGRAS, Angele de T. *"Molloy," Oswego County Weeklies,* Nov.
3, 1956.
Review of the English translation.

2079   GREGORY, Horace. "After Godot, Waiting for Death," *New York
Post,* Sept. 16, 1956.
Review of *Malone Dies.*

2080   HAGESTAD, William. "Gad Books!" *Student Voice,* Jan. 10, 1956.
Includes review of *Molloy.*

2081   HAYES, Richard. "Nothing," *Commonweal,* LXIV (May 25, 1956),
203.
Review of *Waiting for Godot* (New York production).

2082   HEWES, Henry. "Mankind in the Merdecluse," *Saturday Review
of Literature,* XXXIX (May 5, 1956), 32.
Review of *Waiting for Godot* (New York production).

1956

2083   ――――. "No Longer in Love with Amy," *Saturday Review of Litera-
           ture,* XXXIX (May 19, 1956), 46.
Note in emendation of preceding item.

2084   HOBSON, Harold. *Sunday Times,* July 15, 1956, p. 4.
Review of *En attendant Godot* (Théâtre Hébertot production).

2085   HUTCHINSON, Mary. *New Statesman,* LI (Jan. 21, 1956), 74.
Letter to the Editor on *Molloy* in answer to **1349**.

2086   IGOE, William J. "London Letter," *America,* XCV (June 9, 1956),
           265-266.
Includes comments on *Waiting for Godot.*

2087   JOSBIN, Raoul. *"Waiting for Godot,"* *Crosscurrents,* VI (Summer,
           1956), 204-207. Reprinted from **1994**; trans. J. E. Cunneen.

2088   KAPADIA, B. "Beckett's *Waiting for Godot*," *Theatre Unit Bulletin,*
           IV, no. 9 (1956).
Review of the play.

2089   KAVANAGH, P. "Some Reflections on *Waiting for Godot,*" *Irish
           Times,* Jan. 28, 1956, p. 8.

2090   KELLER, Keith. "Irsk Galskab i Aarhus," *Berlingske Tidende,*
           April 20, 1956.

2091   KERR, Walter. *New York Herald Tribune,* April 29, 1956.
Review of *Waiting for Godot* (New York production).

2092   L[EMARCHAND], J[acques]. *Figaro Littéraire,* June 30, 1956, p. 12.
Review of *En attendant Godot* (Théâtre Hébertot production).

2093   LERNER, Max. *New York Post,* April 25, 1956.
Review of *Waiting for Godot* (New York production).

2094   LEVENTHAL, A. J. *Dublin Magazine,* XXXI (Jan.-March, 1956),
           52-53.
Review of *Waiting for Godot* (Dublin and London productions).

2095   LEWIS, Theophilus. *America,* XCV (May 12, 1956), 182.
Review of *Waiting for Godot* (New York production).

2096   MacMANUS, Francis. "An Irish Wonder," *Irish Press,* June 23, 1956.
About Beckett.

2097   MARCEL, Gabriel. *Nouvelles Littéraires,* June 28, 1956, p. 8.
Review of *En attendant Godot* (Théâtre Hébertot production).

2098   MAURIAC, Claude. "Samuel Beckett," *Figaro Littéraire,* August 11,
           1956, p. 2.
On Beckett and *En attendant Godot.*

1956

2099   MIERS, Virgil. "The Little Theatre *Godot:* Think It Out or Just Look," *Dallas Times Herald,* Dec. 14, 1956.
On *Waiting for Godot.*

2100   MOGIN, Jean. *Le Soir,* April 4, 1956.
Review of *Nouvelles et Textes pour rien.*

2101   O., J. "Samuel Beckett Indicts Modern Life," *Newhaven Journal Courier,* Oct. 6, 1956.
On *Waiting for Godot.*

2102   OESTERREICHER, Arthur. "Waiting for Youdi," *New Leader,* XXXIX (Nov. 6, 1956), 19.
Review of *Molloy* (English translation).

2103   O'MEARA, John J. *Times Literary Supplement,* April 6, 1956, p. 207.
Letter to the Editor on *Waiting for Godot.*

2104   PASCAL, Jérôme. *Tribune des Nations,* July 6, 1956.
Review of *En attendant Godot* (Théâtre Hébertot production).

2105   PAULDING, Gouverneur. "Samuel Beckett's New Tale," *New York Herald Tribune Book Week,* Sept. 16, 1956, p. 5.
Review of *Malone Dies.*

2106   ROBINSON, Mrs. A. M. *"Molloy," Columbia Record,* May 25, 1956.
Comments on *Molloy.*

2107   ROGERS, W. G. *"Malone Dies," Associated Press,* Sept. 17, 1956.
Review of *Malone Dies.*

2108   _____. "A Major Experiment: His Fading Mind Flashes Memories," *Miami News,* Sept. 23, 1956.
Review of *Malone Dies.*

2109   STONE, Harriet. "Beckett's Molloy Must Like His Play *Waiting for Godot,*" *People's World,* Aug. 8, 1956.
On *Molloy* and *Waiting for Godot.*

2110   STONE, Jerome. "Man in the Shadow," *Saturday Review of Literature,* XXXIX (Oct. 27, 1956), 25.
Review of *Malone Dies.*

2111   TALLMER, Jerry. *Village Voice,* April 25, 1956 [see **1054**].
Review of *Waiting for Godot* (New York production).

2112   TAVERNIER, René. "Le Nouveau Mal du siècle," *Le Progrès,* Jan. 21, 1956.
On Beckett in general.

1956

2113   TOMPKINS, J. M. S. *Times Literary Supplement,* Feb. 24, 1956, p. 117.
Letter to the Editor on *Waiting for Godot.*

2114   TREWIN, J. C. "Thick and Clear," *Birmingham Post,* May 2, 1956.
On *Waiting for Godot.*

2115   Van RENSSELAER, Euphenia. *Catholic World,* CLXXXII (June, 1956), 227-228.
Review of *Waiting for Godot* (New York production).

2116   VENAISSIN, Gabriel. "La France, pays tempéré," *Combat,* Feb. 9, 1956.
Mentions Beckett.

2117   VIVIER, M. de. "A propos de Beckett," *Le Thyrse,* LVIII, no. 9 (1956), 359-360.
About Beckett and his work in general.

2118   W., A. H. "Poet-Playwright's Inspired Dialogue," *Winnipeg Tribune,* June 23, 1956.
On *Waiting for Godot.*

2119   WALSH, J. S. *Times Literary Supplement,* March 9, 1956, p. 149.
Letter to the Editor on *Waiting for Godot.*

2120   WATKINS, R. F. "Long Monologues Tell Story of Despair," *Democrat Chronicle,* June 24, 1956.
Review of *Molloy.*

2121   WILSON, Katharine M. *Times Literary Supplement,* March 2, 1956, p. 133.
Letter to the Editor on *Waiting for Godot.*

2122   ZELTNER-NEUKOMM, Gerda. *Neue Zürcher Zeitung,* XXIX (Jan. 20, 29, 1956), 6.
Review of *Nouvelles et Textes pour rien.*

1957

2123   ANONYMOUS. "A Successor to *Waiting for Godot,*" *The Times,* Jan. 14, 1957, p. 4.
Review of *All That Fall* (BBC broadcast).

2124   _____. *Daily Worker,* Jan. 22, 1957.
Review of *All That Fall* (BBC broadcast).

2125   _____. *Times Educational Supplement,* Jan. 25, 1957.
Review of *All That Fall* (BBC broadcast).

2126   _____. *De Tijd,* March 2, 1957.
News item on *Fin de partie.*

1957

2127 _____. "Beckett jouera à Londres le pièce refusée à Paris," *Arts*,
        March 6, 1957.
News item on *Fin de partie*.

2128 _____. *The Times*, March 13, 1957, p. 3*b*.
News item on Beckett and *Fin de partie*.

2129 _____. "Hurry, Godot, Hurry," *Time*, LXIX (March 18, 1957),
        108.
Review of *Murphy* (American edition).

2130 _____. [*pseud*. Pendennis]. "Table Talk: Waiting for Beckett,"
        The Observer, March 31, 1957, p. 11.
Review of *Fin de partie* in London.

2131 _____. *Theatre Arts*, XLI (April, 1957), 16.
Review of Negro production of *Waiting for Godot* on Broadway.

2132 _____. *The Times*, April 1, 1957, p. 3.
News item on Beckett and *Fin de partie*.

2133 _____. *The Times*, April 4, 1957, p. 3.
Review of *Fin de partie* in London (first production).

2134 _____. "London Letter," *Irish Times*, April 5. 1957, p. 5.
Reference to *Fin de partie* and *Acte sans paroles*.

2135 _____. [i.e. general authorship, including Jean Duvignaud].
        Tworczosc, April 7, 1957.
Studies on contemporary French culture, including Beckett.

2136 _____. "Ash-Can School of Drama," *Life*, XLII (April 22, 1957),
        143.
Review of *Endgame*.

2137 _____. "Fin de parti [*sic*] (d'après la nouvelle pièce de Samuel
        Beckett)," *Canard Enchaîné*, April 30, 1957.
A mocking review of *Fin de partie*.

2138 _____. "Billet de Londres: Samuel Beckett, Jean Genet et John
        Osborne," *Beaux-Arts*, May 3, 1957.
About plays by the three authors in London.

2139 _____. *The Times*, May 15, 1957, p. 3*b*.
News item on Beckett and *Fin de partie* in Paris.

2140 _____. "Das Leben im Mülleimer," *Der Spiegel*, 15 (April 10,
        1957), 55-56.
Review of *Fin de partie*.

2141 _____. *Synthèses*, XI (June, 1957), 97-99.
Review of *Fin de partie*.

1957

2142 _____. "The Train Stops," *Times Literary Supplement,* Sept. 6,
                 1957, p. 528.
Review of *All That Fall* (published text).

2143 _____. 1. "The Play's the Thing," 2. "Memos of a First-Nighter,"
                 3. "San Francisco Group Leaves S. Q. Audience Waiting for
                 Godot," *San Quentin News,* Nov. 28, 1957, pp. 1, 3.
These three pieces in the San Quentin Prison newspaper are fascinating com-
ments by the inmates in the form of reviews of the production of *Waiting for
Godot* by the San Francisco Actors' Workshop at the prison. For comments
on the production of the same play by the inmates' own theater group see
San Quentin News, Feb. 15, 1962, pp. 1, 3.

2144 _____. *British Book News,* 208 (Dec., 1957), 752.
Review of *All That Fall* (published text).

2145 ALTER, André. *"En attendant Godot* n'était pas une impasse—
                 Beckett le prouve dans sa seconde pièce," *Figaro Littéraire,* Jan.
                 12, 1957, pp. 1, 4.
Review of *Fin de partie.*

2146 ATKINSON, Brooks. "Godot Is Back," *New York Times,* Jan. 22,
                 1957.
Review of Negro production of *Waiting for Godot.*

2147 [BERNARD, Marc.] *Nouvelles Littéraires,* May 9, 1957, p. 10.
Review of *Fin de partie* in Paris.

2148 BERTAL, Fernand. *Rives d'Azur,* June 3, 1957.
Review of *Fin de partie.*

2149 BLANQUET, M. *France-Soir,* May 3, 1957.
Review of *Fin de partie* in Paris.

2150 BÖKEMKAMP, Werner. *Frankfurter Allgemeine Zeitung,* March
                 7, 1957.
On *Fin de partie.*

2151 BOSQUET, Alain. *Combat,* Feb. 21, 1957, p. 7.
Review of *Fin de partie* (published text).

2152 BOURGET-PAILLERON, Robert. *Revue des Deux Mondes,* 10
                 (May 15, 1957), 347-348.
Review of *Fin de partie* in Paris.

2153 CAPRON, Marcelle. *Combat,* May 2, 1957, p. 2.
Review of *Fin de partie* in Paris.

2154 CHAPMAN, John. *"Godot* Given Second Chance," *New York Daily
                 News,* Jan. 22, 1957.
Review of Negro production of *Waiting for Godot.*

1957

2155   CHURCH, Richard. *Truth,* Jan. 25, 1957.
Review of *All That Fall* (BBC broadcast).

2156   CLARKE, Austin. "Why the 12:30 Was Late," *Irish Times,* Sept. 7, 1957, p. 8.
Review of *All That Fall.*

2157   COLEMAN, Robert. *"Godot* Gives Back All That You Give to It," *New York Mirror,* Jan. 22, 1957.
On *Waiting for Godot.*

2158   DALMAS, André. *Tribune des Nations,* Dec. 20, 1957.
Review of *Tous ceux qui tombent* (published text).

2159   DAVIE, Donald. "Samuel Beckett's Dublin," *Irish Times,* March 23, 1957, p. 6.
A poem of four stanzas, twenty lines.

2160   De DURE, Ivan. *"En attendant Godot," Journal d'Anvers,* Jan. 18, 1957.

2161   DONNELLY, Tom. "I'll Buy Half-a-Loaf of *Godot," World Telegram and Sun,* Jan. 22, 1957.
On *Waiting for Godot.*

2162   DUMOULIN, J.-C. *Tribune des Nations,* Aug. 23, 1957.
Review of *Fin de partie.*

2163   DUVIGNAUD, Jean. *Gazette de Lausanne,* May 4, 1957.
Review of *Fin de partie.*

2164   FERRIS, Paul. "Waiting for Rooney," *The Observer,* Jan. 20, 1957, p. 11.
Review of *All That Fall* (BBC broadcast).

2165   GAUTIER, Jean-Jacques. *Le Figaro,* May 3, 1957, p. 16.
Review of *Fin de partie* in Paris.

2166   GERHORE, Pietro. "Uomini di Teatro," *Roma-Napoli,* Aug. 31, 1957.
On Beckett's theater in general.

2167   GONNET, Hubert. "Fin de Beckett?" *Lettres Françaises,* May 9-15, 1957, p. 5.
Review of *Fin de partie* in Paris.

2168   GRAY, Ronald. *The Listener,* LVII (Feb. 7, 1957), 235 [see **1391**].
Letter to the Editor on *Waiting for Godot.*

2169   GREENE, Henry. "Shaggy Dog Story With Irish Music," *Chicago Tribune,* April 28, 1957.
Review of *Murphy.*

1957

2170   GUSTAFSON, Ingemar. "Den ändlösa Monologen," *Aftonbladet*,
         Feb. 4, 1957.
On *Molloy*.

2171   HAWTREY, Freda. *The Listener*, LVII (Jan. 31, 1957), 197.
Letter to the Editor on *All That Fall*.

2172   HÉBERTOT, Jacques. *Artaban*, I (June 7, 1957).
Review of *Fin de partie*.

2173   HENDERSON, Robin S. "Beckett Country," *The Spectator*, Oct. 4,
         1957.
Letter in verse on *All That Fall*.

2174   HEWES, Henry. "Crawling between Dark and Light," *Saturday Review of Literature*, XL (Feb. 9, 1957), 25.
Review of Negro production of *Waiting for Godot*.

2175   HOBSON, Harold. *Sunday Times*, Jan. 20, 1957.
Review of *All That Fall* (BBC broadcast).

2176   ————. *Sunday Times*, Feb. 17, 1957, p. 17.
Review of *Fin de partie* (published text).

2177   ————. "Samuel Beckett's New Play," *Sunday Times*, April 7, 1957.
Review of *Fin de partie* (London production).

2178   HOUFE, E. A. S. *The Listener*, LVII (Jan. 31, 1957), 197 [see **1391**].
Letter to the Editor on *Waiting for Godot*.

2179   HUGHSON, Kenneth. *Socialist Leader*, Jan. 26, 1957.
Review of *All That Fall*.

2180   HUTCHINSON, Mary. *The Listener*, LVII (Feb. 7, 1957), 235
         [see **1391**].
Letter to the Editor on *Waiting for Godot*.

2181   JEBB, Julian. "The Arrival of Godot," *The Tablet*, CCIX (Jan. 19,
         1957), 56.
Review of *All That Fall* (BBC broadcast).

2182   KANTERS, Robert. "En attendant la fin . . . ," *L'Express*, May 10,
         1957.
Review of *Fin de partie* in Paris.

2183   KEMP, Robert. "La Pièce la plus noire," *Le Soir*, March 7, 1957.
Review of *Fin de partie*.

2184   KEMPTON, Murray. "End of a Wait," *New York Post*, Jan. 22,
         1957.
On *Waiting for Godot*.

2185   KOSKI. "Fin början på spelets slut," *Aftonbladet*, Oct. 16, 1957.

1957

2186   L., S. "Godot braucht nicht zu kommen," *Frankfurter Allgemeine Zeitung,* Oct. 3, 1957.
Review of *Fin de partie.*

2187   LANZMANN, Jacques. *Lettres Françaises,* May 9-15, 1957, p. 5.
Review of *Fin de partie.*

2188   LEBESQUE, Morvan. "En attendant le néant," *Carrefour,* May 15, 1957.
Review of *Fin de partie* in Paris.

2189   LEMARCHAND, Jacques. *Figaro Littéraire,* May 11, 1957, p. 14.
Review of *Fin de partie* in Paris.

2190   _____. *Nouvelle Revue Française,* IX (June, 1957), 1085-1089.
Review of *Fin de partie.*

2191   _____. *Bühnen der Stadt Köln: Programmheft,* 4 (1957-1958), 7.
Review of *Fin de partie.*

2192   LERMINIER, Georges. *Parisien Libéré,* May 3, 1957.
Review of *Fin de partie* in Paris.

2193   LEVENTHAL, A. J. *Dublin Magazine,* XXXII (Oct.-Dec., 1957), 42-43.
Review of *All That Fall* (published text).

2194   LOMBARD, S. "Billet de Londres," *Beaux-Arts,* April 5, 1957.
Note on *Fin de partie* (London production).

2195   LOW, Ian. *"All That Fall,"* News Chronicle, Jan. 25, 1957.

2196   LUFT, Friedrich. "Wieder das gleiche Grauen, die gleiche Leere," *Die Welt,* 229 (1957), 7.
Review of *Fin de partie.*

2197   M., D. *"All That Fall,"* Belfast News Letter, Oct. 26, 1957.

2198   McCLAIN, John. *"Waiting for Godot* Play Revival," *New York Journal-American,* Jan. 22, 1957.
On Negro production.

2199   McWHINNIE, Donald. *"All That Fall,"* Radio Times, CXXXIV (Jan. 11, 1957), 4.
The producer's introduction to the radio broadcast.

2200   MAURIAC, Claude. "La Nouvelle Pièce de Samuel Beckett," *Le Figaro,* Feb. 27, 1957, p. 15.
Review of *Fin de partie* (published text).

2201   MELVIN, Edwin F. *"Waiting for Godot* Arrives," *Christian Science Monitor,* Jan. 11, 1957.
On Negro production.

1957

2202   MERCIER, Vivian. *New York Times Book Review,* May 12, 1957, p. 20.
Letter to the Editor correcting inaccurate information in **1389**.

2203   MONKS, Julia. *"All That Fall,"* Irish Press, Jan. 21, 1957.
Review of published text.

2204   MURRAY, David. *Dalhousie Review,* XXXVII (Spring, 1957), 104, 106.
Review of *Murphy* and *Malone Dies.*

2205   NACHTSHEIM, Hans. *"En attendant Godot* in Diskussionen von 'modernes Drama,' " *Provinz,* 7-8 (1957).

2206   NADEAU, Maurice. *France-Observateur,* Feb. 28, 1957. Reprinted in **1409**.
Review of *Fin de partie* (published text).

2207   NEPVEU-DEGAS, Jean. *France-Observateur,* May 9, 1957.
Review of *Fin de partie* in Paris.

2208   O'BRIEN, Conor. "One-Way Journey," *The Tablet,* CCX (Oct. 19, 1957), 340-341.
Review of *All That Fall* (published text).

2209   OLDEN, G. A. *Irish Times,* Jan. 18, 1957.
Review of *All That Fall* (BBC broadcast).

2210   PEEREBOMM, J. J. "Onze correspondent meldt Parijs," *Litterair Paspoort,* XII (Feb., 1957), 42-43.
On *Fin de partie* and other plays in Paris.

2211   ROBINSON, Robert. *Sunday Times,* Jan. 20, 1957.
Review of *All That Fall* (BBC broadcast).

2212   ROGERS, W. G. *Uniontown Herald,* March 15, 1957.
Review of *Malone Dies.*

2213   ROSE, Richard. "Different If Not Better," *St. Louis Post Dispatch,* April 6, 1957.
Review of *Malone Dies.*

2214   RYAN, Desmond. *"Fin de partie,"* Time and Tide, March 2, 1957.
Review of published text.

2215   S[ARRAUTE], C[laude]. "Au Studio des Champs-Élysées Samuel Beckett et Roger Blin disputent une *Fin de partie,"* Le Monde, April 27, 1957, p. 12.

2216   SAUREL, Renée. *L'Information,* May 4, 1957.
Review of *Fin de partie* in Paris.

1957

2217   SCHOTT, Webster. "Samuel Beckett Stirs Readers and Critics with
            His New Approach," *Kansas City Star,* Feb. 9, 1957.
On *Malone Dies.*

2218   SCHWARTZ, Alvin. *American Scholar,* XXVI (Spring, 1957), 26.
Review of *Malone Dies.*

2219   SCHWARTZ, D. J. *The Listener,* LVII (Jan. 31, 1957), 197 [see
            1391].
Letter to the Editor on *Waiting for Godot.*

2220   SEED, D. *Isis,* Nov. 20, 1957.
Review of *All That Fall* (published text).

2221   SPIRAUX, Alain. *"Fin de partie,"* Combat, April 26, 1957.
Review of the play in Paris.

2222   _____. *"Fin de partie* de Samuel Beckett suscite des polémiques,"
            Combat, May 10, 1957.

2223   STRACHEY, Julia. "Beckett Country," *The Spectator,* Sept. 20,
            1957, p. 373.
Review of *All That Fall* (published text).

2224   T., J. "Sur l'antenne de la BBC, rentrée de Samuel Beckett," *Le
            Figaro,* Feb. 5, 1957, p. 13.
Review of *All That Fall* (BBC broadcast).

2225   TALLMER, Jerry. *"Godot:* Still Waiting," *Village Voice,* Jan. 30,
            1957 [see **1054, 2056**].
Review of *Waiting for Godot.*

2226   TERRY, Walter. *"Waiting for Godot,"* New York Herald Tribune,
            Jan. 22, 1957.
Review of the play in New York.

2227   TRACY, Honor. "Where the Voices Rattle On," *New Republic,*
            LXXXVI (May 6, 1957), 19.
Review of *Murphy.*

2228   TREWIN, J. C. "The End Crowns All," *Illustrated London News,*
            CCXXX (April 20, 1957), 652.
Review of *Fin de partie* (London production).

2229   TRILLING, Ossia. "Teaterbomber över London," *Göteborgs-
            Posten,* April 26, 1957.
Review of *Fin de partie.*

2230   TROCH, E. *"Fin de partie,"* De Standaard, April 6, 1957.
Review of the London production.

1957

2231   TYNAN, Kenneth. "A Philosophy of Despair," *The Observer*, April
             7, 1957, p. 15.
Review of *Fin de partie* (London production).

2232   VALOGNE, Catherine. "L'Insaisissable Samuel Beckett," *Tribune de
             Lausanne*, April 21, 1957.
Review of *Fin de partie* (London production).

2233   VEDRÈS, Nicole. "En attendant Beckett," *Mercure de France*,
             CCCXXX (May, 1957), 134-136.
Review of *Fin de partie*.

2233A   VELLINGSHAUSEN, Albert Schulze. "Beckett, Humanist und
             Gewissensforscher," *Frankfurter Allgemeine Zeitung*, Nov. 29,
             1957, p. 10.
Review of *Fin de partie*.

2234   VERDOT, Guy. *Franc-Tireur*, May 3, 1957.
Review of *Fin de partie* in Paris.

2235   VOGLER, Lewis. "Beckett's Sordid Novel Spouts Fine Language,"
             This World, March 31, 1957.
Review of *Murphy*.

2236   WACE, Michael. *The Listener*, LVII (Feb. 14, 1957), 275 [see **1391**].
Letter to the Editor on *All That Fall*.

2237   WALKER, Roy. "Judge Not . . . ," *The Listener*, LVII (May 9,
             1957), 767-768.
Review of *Fin de partie* (BBC broadcast of studio performance of first production).

2238   _____. "Music and Word-Music," *New Statesman*, LIV (Dec. 28,
             1957), 87.
On a BBC reading of some excerpts of Beckett's prose.

2239   WATTS, Richard, Jr. "Two on the Aisle: A Revival of *Waiting for
             Godot*," *New York Post*, Jan. 22, 1957.

2240   WIJKERSLOOTH, R. de. "Beckett wordt nog granwer," *Elseviers
             Weekblad*, March 16, 1957.
Review of *Fin de partie*.

2241   _____. "Na . . . Wachten op Godot . . . Het eind van het lied,"
             Haagsche Courant, March 23, 1957.
On *Waiting for Godot*.

2242   YEISER, Frederick. "Books Reviewed: Two by Beckett," *Cincinnati
             Enquirer*, March 13, 1957.
Reviews of *Molloy* and *Malone Dies*.

1957

2243 _____. *Cincinnati Enquirer,* April 28, 1957.
Review of *Murphy.*

2244 ZELTNER-NEUKOMM, Gerda. *Neue Zürcher Zeitung,* XXX
(April 1, 1957), 2.
Review of *Fin de partie.*

2245 ZIVI, Georg. "Becketts *Endspiel* bei Barlog," *Berliner Morgenpost,*
Oct. 2, 1957.
Review of *Fin de partie.*

1958

2246 ANONYMOUS. "Beckett's *Endgame,*" *The Day: Jewish Journal,*
Feb. 2, 1958.
Review of *Endgame.*

2247 _____. *The Times,* Feb. 10, 1958, p. 3*b*.
News item on Beckett (*Endgame* refused British licence).

2248 _____. *The Times,* Feb. 19, 1958, p. 4*c*.
News item on Beckett (Dublin Drama Festival postponement).

2249 _____. *Christian Century,* LXXVIII (March 5, 1958), 282.
Review of *Endgame* (New York production).

2250 _____. *Theatre Arts,* XLII (April, 1958), 26.
Review of *Endgame* (New York production).

2251 _____. "Slow Motion," *Times Literary Supplement,* April 25, 1958,
p. 225.
Article on the relationship between the theater of Beckett and Ionesco and the
"new novel."

2252 _____. *British Book News,* 213 (May, 1958), 344.
Review of *Malone Dies.*

2253 _____. "*Endgame,*" *Irish Independent,* May 24, 1958.
Review of the play.

2254 _____. "*Fin de partie,*" *Nieuwe Rotterdamse Courant,* June 23,
1958.
Review of the play.

2255 _____. *British Book News,* 216 (Aug., 1958), 547.
Review of *Endgame* and *Act Without Words.*

2256 _____. "Cocteau e Beckett al teatro dei Satiri," *Il Tempo,* Sept.
9, 1958.

2257 _____. *Time,* LXXII (Oct. 13, 1958), 107.
Review of *The Unnamable* (American edition).

1958

2258   ———. *The Times,* Oct. 29, 1958, p. 3.
Review of *Endgame* and *Krapp's Last Tape* (London productions).

2259   ———. "Unfinished Design," *Times Literary Supplement,* Dec. 26,
        1958, p. 752.
Review of *From an Abandoned Work* (British edition).

2260   ALLSOP, Kenneth. "Beckett Comes Back to Death Valley," *Daily
        Mail,* March 8, 1958.
Review of *Watt* and *Malone Dies* (British editions).

2261   ALWES, Betty. *"The Unnamable:* Anal But Not Banal," *Gazette of
        the Arts in Louisville,* Nov. 5, 1958.
Review of *The Unnamable.*

2262   ANDERSON, Stan. *"Endgame," Cleveland Press,* May 24, 1958.
Review of the play.

2263   ASIS, V. Fernandez. *"Final de partida," Pueblo,* June 11, 1958.
Review of *Fin de partie.*

2264   ATKINSON, Brooks. *New York Times,* Jan. 29, 1958, p. 32.
Review of *Endgame* (New York production).

2265   ———. "Abstract Drama," *New York Times,* Feb. 16, 1958, sec. 2,
        p. 1.
More by Atkinson on *Endgame.*

2266   BELMONT, Hollis. *"Endgame* Is a Puzzler," *Town and Village,* Feb.
        14, 1958.
Review of *Endgame.*

2267   BOSQUET, Alain. "Samuel Beckett," *Programm des Schlosspark-
        Theater, Berlin,* 65 (1957-58).
On *Fin de partie.*

2268   CAIN, Alex. *The Tablet,* CCXII (Nov. 8, 1958), 408.
Reviews of *Endgame* and *Krapp's Last Tape* (London productions).

2269   CHAPMAN, John. "Beckett's *Endgame* Is Off-Broadway and Out
        of One Reviewer's Mind," *Daily News,* Jan. 29, 1958.

2270   COE, Richard L. "Theatre Lobby Offers *Godot," Washington Post
        and Times Herald,* April 16, 1958.
On *Waiting for Godot.*

2271   D., F. W. "Samuel Beckett," *Oxford Times,* May 16, 1958.
On Beckett and his theater.

2272   DASH, Thomas R. *"Endgame," Virginia Pilot,* Feb. 9, 1958.
Review of the play.

1958

2273   DE SENA, Jorge. "Duas Peças Inglesas Recentes," *Diário Popular,*
        May 15, 1958.
On *Endgame* and *Krapp's Last Tape.*

2274   DUBOIS, Pierre H. "Beckett gaat tot de kern in *Fin de partie,*" *Het
        Vaderland,* June 23, 1958.
Review of *Fin de partie.*

2275   DUMMETT, A. *Oxford Magazine,* Jan. 30, 1958.
Review of *All That Fall.*

2276   DUMUR, Guy. "Le Droit de la poésie," *Arts-Spectacles,* 4 (Dec.,
        1958), 3-5.
Mentions Beckett.

2277   ELLIS, Edward. "Beckett Drama Here for Third Time," *New York
        World Telegram,* Aug. 6, 1958.
On *Endgame.*

2278   FERNANDEZ-SANTOS, Angel. *"Fin de partida,"* *Indice de Artes
        y Letras,* n.v. (July, 1958).

2279   FINDLATER, Richard. *"Endgame* and *Krapp's Last Tape,"* *Sunday
        Dispatch,* Nov. 2, 1958.

2280   FRATELLI, Arnaldo. "Beckett e Cocteau al Teatro dei Satiri," *Paese
        Sera,* Sept. 9, 1958.
Compares Beckett and Cocteau.

2281   GARLAND, Patrick. "Sam Agonistes," *Cherwell,* Nov. 26, 1958.
Review of *From an Abandoned Work.*

2282   GLEASON, Gene. *"Waiting for Godot* Given in a Revival at the
        York," *New York Herald Tribune,* Aug. 6, 1958.

2283   GOMPERTS, H. A. *"Fin de partie* in Rotterdam," *Het Parool,*
        June 23, 1958.
Review of the play.

2284   GONZALEZ, N. "Estreno de *Final de partida* de Beckett," *Madrid,*
        June 11, 1958.
Review of *Fin de partie.*

2285   GUSTAFSON, Ingemar. "Det eviga schackpartiet," *Aftonbladet,*
        Feb. 3, 1958.
Review of *Fin de partie.*

2286   "Slutspel i Göteborg," *Aftonbladet,* April 17, 1958.
On *Fin de partie.*

2287   HATCH, Robert. *The Nation,* CLXXXVI (Feb. 15, 1958), 145-146.
Review of *Endgame* (New York production).

1958

2288   HEWES, Henry. *Saturday Review of Literature,* XLI (Feb. 15, 1958), 28.
Review of *Endgame* (New York production).

2289   HOBSON, Harold. "Annus Mirabilis," *Sunday Times,* Feb. 9, 1958.
Review of *Endgame.*

2290   ———. "The Arts and Other Things," *Christian Science Monitor,* March 5, 1958.
Review of *Endgame.*

2291   HORN, Effi. *Münchner Merkur,* Sept. 29, 1958.
Review of *Endgame.*

2292   HOYT, Harlowe R. "*Endgame* Expected To Stir Controversy," *Cleveland Plain Dealer,* May 11, 1958.

2293   HUDSON, Joe. "*Endgame,*" *Cleveland News,* May 23, 1958.
Review of the play.

2294   IRVING, Jules. "Europe Never Asked 'Why Godot?' " *San Francisco Chronicle,* Oct. 19, 1958.
On *Waiting for Godot.*

2295   JEFFERY, Sydney. "Beckett Ends the Game," *Liverpool Daily Post,* May 14, 1958.
On *Endgame.*

2296   KENNEDY, Maurice. "Delights," *Irish Times,* May 3, 1958.
Review of *Endgame.*

2297   KERR, Walter. *New York Herald Tribune,* Jan. 29, 1958.
Review of *Endgame* (New York production).

2298   LAMBERT, J. W. *Sunday Times,* Nov. 2, 1958.
Reviews of *Endgame* and *Krapp's Last Tape* (London productions).

2299   LESLIE, Mary. "*Act Without Words,*" *Steamboat Pilot,* Aug. 17, 1958.

2300   MAVOR, Ronald. *The Scotsman,* May 9, 1958, in section "Drama Review."
On *Endgame.*

2301   MINDLIN, Moir. "Nonentity Identity," *Jerusalem Post,* May 18, 1958.
On *Molloy,* and Beckett in general.

2302   MYERS, Sim. "Waiting Game," *Times Picayune,* Jan. 15, 1958.
On *Waiting for Godot.*

2303   ———. "Beckett Play Opens at Attic," *Times Picayune,* Jan. 17, 1958.
Review of *Waiting for Godot.*

1958

2304   PEDROSA, V. "Beckett," *Jornal do Brasil,* Jan. 26, 1958.
On Beckett in general with particular mention of *Endgame.*

2305   PINETTE, G. *Books Abroad,* XXXII (Winter, 1958), 21.
Review of *Fin de partie* (published text).

2306   _____. *Books Abroad,* XXXII (Autumn, 1958), 384.
Review of *Tous ceux qui tombent* (published text).

2307   PREGO, Adolfo. *"Fin de partida,"* *Informaciones,* June 11, 1958.
Review of the play.

2308   R., P. "Mensen als verwelkte planten in Beckett's *Fin de partie,"*
Haagsche Courant, June 23, 1958.
Review of *Fin de partie.*

2309   RICE, Cyrus F. "Why the Fuss over *Godot?*" *Milwaukee Sentinel,*
Aug. 3, 1958.
On *Waiting for Godot.*

2310   S., B. "Zelfmoord van het rationalisme: Beckett's *Fin de partie* in
het Holland Festival," *Algemeen Handelsblad,* June 23, 1958.

2311   SCHOTT, Webster. "Some Dare Break with Tradition," *Kansas
City Star,* Nov. 15, 1958.
On Beckett and *Endgame.*

2312   SHERMAN, Thomas B. *St. Louis Post Dispatch,* Feb. 23, 1958.
Review of *Waiting for Godot.*

2313   TALLMER, Jerry. *Village Voice,* Jan. 1, 1958.
Review of *All That Fall.*

2314   _____. *Village Voice,* Feb. 5, 1958 [see **1054**].
Review of *Endgame* (New York production).

2315   _____. *"Endgame,"* *Village Voice,* April 2, 1958.
More on *Endgame.*

2316   TORRENTE. *"Final de Partida,"* *Arriba,* June 12, 1958.
Review of *Fin de partie.*

2317   TOYNBEE, Philip. "A New Vanguard," *The Observer,* May 4, 1958,
p. 16.
Review of *Endgame* (British edition).

2318   TYNAN, Kenneth. *The Observer,* Feb. 9, 1958, p. 13.
Note on censorship of *Endgame.*

2319   _____. "Slamm's Last Knock," *The Observer,* Nov. 2, 1958, p. 19.
Parody-reviews of *Endgame* and *Krapp's Last Tape* (London productions).

2320   VICE. "Il Giveo è finito," *L'Unità,* Sept. 9, 1958.
On Beckett in general.

1958

2321   VON PHUL, Ruth. "Four Names and Unnamable," *San Antonio Express and News,* Nov. 30, 1958.
Review of *Endgame.*

2322   WALD, Richard C. "Samuel Beckett Is No Gag," *New York Herald Tribune,* Jan. 26, 1958.
Review of *Endgame* (New York production).

2323   WALKER, Roy. "End Game [*sic*]," *The Listener,* LIX (June 26, 1958), 1071-1072.
Review of *Endgame.*

2324   WATTS, Richard, Jr. "San Francisco's *Waiting for Godot,*" *New York Post,* Aug. 6, 1958.
Review of the play.

2325   WILSON, Cecil. "The Play London Saw in French Is Banned in English," *Daily Mail,* Feb. 10, 1958.
About *Endgame.*

2326   ZINNES, Harriet. *Books Abroad,* XXXII (Spring, 1958), 132.
Review of *Murphy.*

1959

2327   ANONYMOUS. "*Warten auf Godot* zur Düsseldorfer Aufführung," *Blätter der Gesellschaft für Christliche Kultur,* 1 (1959), 12-14.
On *Waiting for Godot.*

2328   _____. *The Times,* Jan. 8, 1959, p. 5*e.*
News item on Beckett and *The Unnamable.*

2329   _____. *The Times,* Jan. 19, 1959, p. 9*e.*
News item on Beckett (*The Unnamable* on BBC Third Programme).

2330   _____. *The Times,* Feb. 26, 1959, p. 12*d.*
News item on Beckett receiving Dublin honorary degree.

2331   _____. *Düsseldorfer Nachrichten,* March 9, 1959.
Review of *Waiting for Godot.*

2332   _____. *Frankfurter Allgemeine Zeitung,* March 12, 1959.
Review of *Waiting for Godot.*

2333   _____. "Beckett: Das Leben ein Tonband," *Der Spiegel,* 19 (May 6, 1959), 51-52.
Review of *Krapp's Last Tape.*

2334   _____. "Waiting for Oblivion," *Time,* LXXIII (June 1, 1959), 90-91.
Review of *Watt* (American edition).

1959

2335   _____. *The Times,* June 25, 1959, p. 5.
Review of *Embers* (BBC production).

2336   _____. *The Times,* July 3, 1959, p. 9*d*.
News item on Beckett (Doctor, Honoris Causa, Trinity College, Dublin).

2337   _____. "Beckett-Hörspiel: Warten auf Nichts," *Der Spiegel,* 28
          (July 8, 1959), 56-57.
Review of *Endgame.*

2338   _____. *Christian Century,* LXXVI (July 22, 1959), 854.
Review of *Watt* (American edition).

2339   _____. *The Times,* Sept. 15, 1959, p. 14*b*.
News item on Beckett (*Embers,* Italia Prize).

2340   APOTHÉLOZ, Charles. *Nô,* 1 (Feb., 1959), 1-2.
Review of *Fin de partie.*

2341   ATKINSON, Brooks. *Venture,* III, no. 3 (1959), 69-70.
Review of *Watt* (American edition).

2342   BARO, Gene. "Beckett's Dark Vision and Sardonic Wit," *New York
          Herald Tribune Book Week,* July 5, 1959.
Review of *Watt* (American edition).

2343   BRÜES, Otto. "Wie die Nacht blind wird und welkt," *Der Mittag,*
          March 9, 1959.
Review of *Waiting for Godot.*

2344   CARTER, Boyd. *Prairie Schooner,* XXXIII (Winter, 1959-1960),
          355-361.
Review of *Anthology of Mexican Poetry.*

2345   CHIAROMONTE, Nicola. "E adesso aspettiamo Godot," *Il Sipario,*
          155 (1959), 11-12.
On *Waiting for Godot.*

2346   COOLEY, Franklin. *"The Unnamable,"* *Richmond Times-Dispatch,*
          Jan. 18, 1959.
Review of American edition.

2347   DUNOYER, Jean-Marie. "Un Cas unique: Samuel Beckett; un
          chef-d'œuvre du jeune roman: *Molloy,*" *Liens,* XIII (Oct., 1959),
          6-7.
Review of *Molloy.*

2348   ENGBERG, Harald. "Saa længe der er liv er der intet haab,"
          Politiken, Feb. 28, 1959

2349   FERNEZ, Michel. *Le Phare,* March 22, 1959.
Review of *La Dernière Bande.*

1959

2350 FERRIS, Paul. *The Observer,* Jan. 25, 1959, p. 16.
Review of *The Unnamable* (extract read on BBC Third Programme).

2351 ———. *The Observer,* June 28, 1959, p. 18.
Review of *Embers* (BBC production).

2352 HIRSCH, W. "Wir warten auf Godot," *Theater der Stadt Bonn,* 8
(1959-60).
Program notes for *Waiting for Godot.*

2353 HÜBNER, Paul. *Rheinische Post,* March 9, 1959.
Review of *Waiting for Godot.*

2354 HUGH-JONES. "Books I Am Reading," *The Tatler,* Jan. 14, 1959.
Review of *From an Abandoned Work.*

2355 KRAGH-JACOBSEN, Svend. "Dommedagsvision," *Berlingske
Tidende,* Feb. 23, 1959.
On *Waiting for Godot.*

2356 LARA, Carlos. "Le Bon Élève Arrabal," *Lettres Françaises,* Jan. 8,
1959, p. 5.
Shows Arrabal's debt to Beckett.

2357 MARTIN, Burke. *"Act Without Words," London Free Press,* March
12, 1959.

2358 MILLS, Ralph J., Jr. "Samuel Beckett's Man," *Christian Century,*
LXXVI (Dec. 30, 1959), 1524-1525.
Review of the trilogy (*Molloy, Malone Dies, The Unnamable*).

2359 NERVA, Sergio. *"Final de Partida," España de Tánger,* June 22,
1959.
Review of *Fin de partie.*

2360 NEUKIRCHEN, Alfons. "Poesie am Rande des Abgrunds," *Düsseldorfer Nachrichten,* March 9, 1959.

2361 OLDEN, G. A. "New Beckett Play," *Irish Times,* July 2, 1959, p. 8.
On *Embers.*

2362 SCHMIDT, Dr. Hannes. "Viel Einsicht-Wenig Trost," *Neue Rhein-
Zeitung,* March 9, 1959.

2363 SCHUYLER, James. *Evergreen Review,* II (Winter, 1959), 221.
Review of *Anthology of Mexican Poetry.*

2364 SCHWARZENFELD, G. "Samuel Beckett: Ende der Partie,"
Volksbühnen-Spiegel, V, no. 4 (1959).
Review of *Fin de partie.*

2365 STANDISH, Myles. *"Endgame," St. Louis Post Dispatch,* Jan. 7,
1959.
Review of the play.

1959

2366   SUTER, G. "Kleinmeister des Zerfalls," *Weltwoche,* 1323 (1959), 5.
On Beckett in general.

2367   ULIBARRÍ, S. R. *New Mexico Quarterly,* XXIX (Autumn, 1959),
355-356.
Review of *Anthology of Mexican Poetry.*

2368   V[ELLINGSHAUSEN], A[lbert] S[chulze]. "Beckett als Passionsspiel,"
Frankfurter Allgemeine Zeitung, March 12, 1959.
On *Waiting for Godot.*

2369   XIRAY, Ramon. "Existentialist Beckett Exploits Nihilistic View,"
Mexico News Weekly, May 3, 1959.
Review of *Watt.*

1960

2370   ANONYMOUS. *Bulletin du Livre Français,* XV (1960), 409.
Review of *La Dernière Bande, suivi de Cendres* (French text).

2371   _____. "The Dying of the Light," *Times Literary Supplement,* Jan.
8, 1960, p. 20.
Review of *Krapp's Last Tape* and *Embers* (published text, British edition).

2372   _____. *New Yorker,* XXXV (Jan. 23, 1960), 75.
Review of *Krapp's Last Tape* (New York production).

2373   _____. *The Times,* Jan. 26, 1960, p. 12.
News item on Beckett and *Act Without Words II.*

2374   _____. *The Nation,* CLXC (Feb. 13, 1960), 153.
Review of *Krapp's Last Tape* (New York production).

2375   _____. *British Book News,* 235 (March, 1960), 201.
Review of *Krapp's Last Tape* (published text, British edition).

2376   _____. *Theatre Arts,* XLII (April, 1960), 26.
Review of *Endgame.*

2377   _____. *Punch,* April 6, 1960, p. 495.
Review of the trilogy (*Molloy, Malone Dies, The Unnamable*), British edition.

2378   _____. *The Times,* April 28, 1960, p. 6.
News item on Beckett and *Waiting for Godot.*

2379   _____. *British Book News,* 238 (June, 1960), 438.
Review of the trilogy (*Molloy, Malone Dies, The Unnamable*).

2380   _____. "Prince of Darkness," *Times Literary Supplement,* June 17,
1960, p. 381.
Review of the trilogy (*Molloy, Malone Dies, The Unnamable*), British edition.

1960

2381   _____. "The Virtue of Endurance," *High Point Enterprise,* July
           10, 1960.
Reviews of *Endgame* and *Act Without Words.*

2382   _____. *The Times,* Aug. 25, 1960, p. 12.
News item on Beckett and *The Old Tune.*

2383   ATKINSON, Brooks. "Village Vagrants," *New York Times,* Jan. 31,
           1960, p. 1.
Mentions Beckett.

2384   C., J. "Mimodrama de S. Beckett en el Larranaga," *La Nacion,* Dec.
           7, 1960.
Review of *Act Without Words.*

2385   CAMBON, G. *Poetry,* XCV (March, 1960), 379-381.
Review of *Anthology of Mexican Poetry.*

2386   CARMONA, Dario. "Drama móvil vibró 24 horas," *Ercilla,* Sept.
           21, 1960.
Review of *En attendant Godot.*

2387   DENNIS, Nigel. "Optical Delusions," *Encounter,* XV (July, 1960),
           63-66.
On Beckett, Pinter, and Ionesco.

2388   DUSSANE, [Béatrix]. *"La Dernière Bande,"* *Mercure de France,*
           CCCXXXIX (June, 1960), 317-319.
Review of the published text.

2389   FEDERMAN, Raymond. *Books Abroad,* XXXIV (Autumn, 1960),
           361.
Review of *La Dernière Bande, suivi de Cendres* (French text).

2390   FEIED, Frederick. *San Francisco Sunday Chronicle,* June 5, 1960,
           p. 23.
Review of the trilogy (*Molloy, Malone Dies, The Unnamable*), American
edition.

2391   FERRIS, Paul. "Beckett Embalmed," *The Observer,* April 1, 1960,
           p. 22.
On *Waiting for Godot* (BBC broadcast).

2392   FRANKESTEIN, Alfred. *New York Herald Tribune,* Oct. 2, 1960,
           p. 10.
Review of *Bram van Velde* (American edition).

2393   FUCHS, Michel. "The Modern French Novel," *Cambridge Opin-
           ion,* 21 (June, 1960).
Mentions Beckett, *passim.*

2394   GAVOTY, André. *Revue des Deux Mondes,* 8 (April 15, 1960), 738.
Review of *La Dernière Bande* (Paris production).

1960

2395   GISSELBRECHT, André. *Théâtre Populaire,* 37 (First trimester, 1960), 120.
Reviews of *La Dernière Bande* and *Cendres.*

2396   GREGORY, Horace. "Portrait of the Irish as James Joyce," *Evergreen Review,* IV (Jan.-Feb., 1960), 186 ff.
Reference to Beckett in this review of Richard Ellman's biography of Joyce.

2397   GRÖZINGER, Wolfgang. "Das Ende der grossen Zyklen," *Hochland,* LII (April, 1960), 377.
Reveiw of *The Unnamable.*

2398   HEPPENSTALL, Rayner. *The Observer,* April 10, 1960, p. 20.
Review of the trilogy (*Molloy, Malone Dies, The Unnamable*), British edition.

2399   HEWES, Henry. "It's Not All Bananas," *Saturday Review of Literature,* XLIII (Jan. 30, 1960), 28.
Review of *Krapp's Last Tape* (New York production).

2400   KANTERS, Robert. *L'Express,* March 31, 1960.
Review of *La Dernière Bande* (Paris production).

2401   KIESEL, Frédéric. *La Métropole,* April 16-17, 1960.
Review of *La Dernière Bande.*

2402   KNIPP, Christopher. "Last Tapes and Endgames," *Amherst Student,* Sept. 22, 1960.
On *Krapp's Last Tape.*

2403   LeGRAND, Albert. *Queen's Quarterly,* LXVI (Winter, 1960), 694.
Review of *Proust.*

2404   LEMAR, Yves. "Beckett retrouve la langue anglaise," *Arts,* Jan. 20, 1960.
Review of *La Dernière Bande.*

2405   LUCCIONI, Gennie. *Esprit,* XXVIII (May, 1960), 913-915.
Review of *La Dernière Bande* and *Cendres.*

2406   M., V. "L'Innominabile," *Il Reporter,* March 1, 1960.
Review of *L'Innommable.*

2407   MALCOLM, Donald. *New Yorker,* XXXV (Jan. 23, 1960), 75.
Review of *Krapp's Last Tape* (New York production).

2408   MARCEL, Gabriel. *Nouvelles Littéraires,* April 7, 1960, p. 10.
Review of *La Dernière Bande.*

2409   MARMORI, Giancarlo. "Beckett con magnetofono alla ricerca del tempo perduto," *Il Giorno,* Feb. 16, 1960.
Review of *La Dernière Bande.*

1960

2410 MAURIAC, Claude. "Samuel Beckett est aussi un poète," *Le Figaro,* Feb. 3, 1960, p. 14.
Review of *La Dernière Bande* and *Cendres.*

2411 POIROT-DELPECH, Bertrand. *Le Monde,* March 9, 1960.
Review of *La Dernière Bande* (Paris production).

2412 RICHARDSON, Ralph. *Sunday Times,* July 10, 1960.
Extract from *Memoirs* discussing a projected first British production of *Waiting for Godot.*

2413 SARRAUTE, Claude. *France-Observateur,* March 15, 1960.
Review of *La Dernière Bande* (Paris production).

2414 SAUREL, Renée. *L'Information,* March 15, 1960.
Review of *La Dernière Bande* (Paris production).

2415 SIRABELLA, R. "Recentissime su Beckett," *Europa Letteraria,* 2 (March, 1960), 199-201.
On Beckett in general.

2416 T., V. "Acto sin Palabras," *Clarín,* Dec. 28, 1960.
Review of *Acte sans paroles I.*

2417 VERDOT, Guy. "Beckett continue d'attendre Godot," *Figaro Littéraire,* March 12, 1960, p. 3.
Review of *La Dernière Bande.*

2418 VICARI, Giambattista. "Lo strano monologo di un 'arrabbiato,' " *Incom,* March 3, 1960.
Review of *La Dernière Bande.*

2419 WHITING, John. *London Magazine,* VII (May, 1960), 87.
Review of *Krapp's Last Tape* and *Embers.*

2420 ZELTNER-NEUKOMM, Gerda. *Neue Zürcher Zeitung,* Feb. 25, 1960, p. 6.
Review of *La Dernière Bande.*

2421 ZINNES, Harriet. *Books Abroad,* XXXIV (Autumn, 1960), 401-402.
Review of *The Unnamable.*

1961

2422 ANONYMOUS. *Bulletin Critique du Livre Français,* XVI (1961), 188. Reprinted in English in *Recent French Books,* II (1961), 8-9.
Review of *Comment c'est.*

2423 _____. *Hudson Review,* XIV (Winter, 1961), 589.
Review of *Happy Days.*

2424 _____. "Band-Bariton," *Der Spiegel,* 12 (March 8, 1961), 79-80.
About the opera based on *Krapp's Last Tape.*

1961

2425   _____. *Journal Musical Français,* April 6, 1961.
Note on the opera *Krapp, ou la dernière bande* by Marcel Mihalovici, based
on the play by Beckett.

2426   _____. "Life in the Mud," *Times Literary Supplement,* April 7,
          1961, p. 213.
Review of *Comment c'est.*

2427   _____. *The Times,* April 10, 1961, p. 3.
News item on Beckett and the United States performance of *Krapp's Last Tape.*

2428   _____. "Un Nouveau Nobel?" *L'Express,* May 4, 1961, p. 38.
News item on the Prix International des Éditeurs.

2429   _____. "The Long Wait," *Times Literary Supplement,* May 5,
          1961, p. 277.
About the BBC Third Programme feature on Beckett and the first London
production of *Waiting for Godot.*

2430   _____. *Canard Enchaîné,* May 10, 1961, p. 5.
Review of *En attendant Godot* at the Odéon-Théâtre de France.

2431   _____. *The Times,* May 12, 1961, p. 19.
News item on Beckett and *Endgame.*

2432   _____. *The Times,* May 16, 1961, p. 17.
Item on Beckett and *Waiting for Godot.*

2433   _____. *The Times,* May 26, 1961, p. 18.
News item on Beckett.

2434   _____. *The Times,* May 31, 1961, p. 17.
News item on Beckett and *Krapp's Last Tape* as opera.

2435   _____. "Se estrenó una pieza de Samuel Beckett," *La Nacion,*
          June 4, 1961.

2436   _____. "End Game" [*sic*], *Sunday Times,* June 18, 1961, p. 13.
About Beckett at a cricket match with Harold Hobson [see **3086**].

2437   _____. *The Times,* June 27, 1961, p. 7.
News item on Beckett and *Waiting for Godot* televised.

2438   _____ [*pseud.* Atticus]. "Oh My Hobson and My Beckett," *Sunday
          Times,* July 2, 1961, p. 13.
About Beckett at a cricket match with Harold Hobson [see **3086**].

2439   _____. *The Times,* July 7, 1961, p. 18.
News item on Beckett and *Krapp's Last Tape* as opera.

2440   _____. *The Times,* Sept. 19, 1961.
News item on Beckett and New York production of *Happy Days.*

1961

2441   _____. "*Happy Days* Has Two Characters," *The Villager,* Sept. 21,
          1961.

2442   _____. "Beckett's Study of an Incurable Optimist," *The Times,*
          Sept. 25, 1961.
Review of *Happy Days* (New York production).

2443   _____. "Winnie's Wake," *Time,* LXXVIII (Sept. 29, 1961), 48, 74.
Review of *Happy Days.*

2444   _____. *Radio Times,* Oct. 5, 1961.
Notice of BBC broadcast entitled *New Comment* on the works of Beckett,
Oct. 11, 1961 [see **3012**].

2445   _____. *Theatre Arts,* XLV (Nov., 1961), 57-58.
Review of *Happy Days.*

2446   _____. *The Times,* Nov. 17, 1961, p. 7.
News item on Beckett and plans for *Happy Days* in London.

2447   _____. *The Times,* Dec. 21, 1961, p. 3.
News item on Beckett and *Waiting for Godot.*

2448   _____. "Anatomy of the Absurd," *Time,* LXXVII (Dec. 22, 1961),
          36.
About Martin Esslin's notion of the theater of the absurd and Beckett.

2449   ADAM, Georges. "Débat fiévreux au Prix International des Éditeurs:
          Comment Beckett et Borgès se sont partagé le premier Prix In-
          ternational des Éditeurs," *Figaro Littéraire,* May 13, 1961, pp.
          1 ff.

2450   ALBÉRÈS, R.-M. "De Job à Lafcadio," *Nouvelles Littéraires,* March
          2, 1961, pp. 2-3.
Review of *Comment c'est.*

2451   ALTER, André. *Témoignage Chrétien,* May 12, 1961.
Review of *En attendant Godot* at the Odéon-Théâtre de France.

2452   ALVAREZ, A. "Poet Waiting for Pegasus," *The Observer,* Dec. 31,
          1961, p. 21.
Review of *Poems in English.*

2453   ANEX, Georges. *Gazette de Lausanne,* Jan. 21-22, 1961.
Review of *En attendant Godot.*

2454   BALLIET, Whitney. *New Yorker,* XXXVII (April 1, 1961), 100.
Review of *The Old Tune* by Pinget translated by Beckett.

2455   BOSQUET, Alain. "Une Litanie de Samuel Beckett," *Combat,* Jan.
          19, 1961, p. 7.
Review of *Comment c'est.*

1961

2456   BOURGET-PAILLERON, Robert. "*En attendant Godot* au Théâtre de France," *Revue des Deux Mondes*, 11 (June 1, 1961), 541-543.

2457   BRAY, Barbara. *The Observer*, May 28, 1961, p. 23.
Item on Prix International des Éditeurs.

2458   BRENNER, Jacques. *Paris-Normandie*, Jan. 20, 1961.
Review of *Comment c'est*.

2459   BUTOR, Michel. "Derrière *Les Paravents*," *L'Express*, Feb. 16, 1961, p. 29.
On Beckett and Genet.

2460   CAMILUCCI, Marcello. "Samuel Beckett: Le ceneri del romanzo," *Il Popolo*, March 7, 1961.
Review of *Comment c'est*.

2461   CAMPROUX, Charles. "La Langue et le style," *Lettres Françaises*, May 11, 1961, p. 5.
Review of *Comment c'est*.

2462   CARDUNER, Jean. "L'année littéraire 1959-1960," *French Review*, XXXIV (Jan., 1961), 239-240.
References to Beckett.

2463   CARMODY, Jay. *Evening Star*, April 5, 1961.
Review of *Krapp's Last Tape*.

2464   CHAPMAN, John. "Beckett Reads Beautifully," *Sunday News*, Oct. 1, 1961.
Review of *Happy Days*.

2465   COE, Richard L. "Beckett Tops Trio at Arena," *Washington Post and Times Herald*, April 6, 1961.
Review of *Krapp's Last Tape*.

2466   COHN, Ruby. *Minnesota Review*, I (Summer, 1961), 510-514.
Review of *1021*.

2467   COLEMAN, Robert. "*Happy Days* — Just a Rocky Gabfest," *New York Mirror*, Sept. 18, 1961.
Review of *Happy Days*.

2468   DALMAS, André. "L'Humeur des lettres," *Tribune des Nations*, Jan. 20, 1961.
Review of *Comment c'est*.

2469   DAVID, Louis. *Le Provençal*, March 26, 1961.
Review of *Comment c'est*.

2470   DAVIS, James. "Beckett's *Happy Days* Is Strangely Holding," *Washington Daily News*, Sept. 18, 1961.
Review of the New York production.

1961

2471   DE ROOS, Elisabeth. "Een Modderige Klaagzang," *Het Parool,*
        March 25, 1961.
Review of *Comment c'est.*

2472   DONNELLY, Tom. "Ghosts on File," *Washington Daily News,* April
        12, 1961.
Review of *Krapp's Last Tape.*

2473   DORT, Bernard. "*Le Gardien* par Harold Pinter," *Théâtre Populaire,*
        41 (First trimester, 1961), 122-124.
Reference to Beckett.

2474   DUMOULIN, J.-C. "*En attendant Godot* à l'Odéon-Théâtre de
        France," *Libération,* May 10, 1961, p. 5.

2475   D[UMUR], G[uy]. *France-Observateur,* Feb. 16, 1961.
Review of *Comment c'est.*

2476   _____. "Les Métamorphoses du théâtre d'avant-garde," *Théâtre
        Populaire,* 42 (Second trimester, 1961), 100-106, with a photo-
        graph.
Reference to Beckett.

2477   DUSSANE, [Béatrix]. "*En attendant Godot* au Théâtre de France,"
        Mercure de France, CCCXLII (July, 1961), 496-498 [see also
        1184].

2478   EDINGA, H. *Elseviers Weekblad,* March 18, 1961.
Review of *Comment c'est.*

2479   ERIKSSON, Göran O. *Stockholms Tidningen,* Oct. 26, 1961.
Review of *Comment c'est.*

2480   ERVAL, François. *L'Express,* May 11, 1961, pp. 33-34.
Item on Prix International des Éditeurs.

2481   ESSLIN, Martin. "Samuel Beckett: *Waiting for Godot,*" *From the
        Fifties,* n.v. (1961), 65-67.
BBC publication to accompany 1961-62 Sound Radio Drama series.

2482   ESTANG, Luc. "Les Romans de la semaine," *Figaro Littéraire,* Feb.
        18, 1961, p. 15.
Review of *Comment c'est.*

2483   FABRE, Eugène. "Beckett ou l'art de la décomposition," *Journal de
        Genève,* Feb. 6, 1961.
Review of *Comment c'est.*

2484   FABRE, Pierre. "Beckett et Borgès: Le Prix International des
        Éditeurs revient à des auteurs difficiles," *Carrefour,* 870 (May 17,
        1961), 25.

1961

2485   FAVARELLI, Max. "*En attendant Godot* n'effarouche plus personne," *Paris-Presse,* May 9, 1961.
Review of *En attendant Godot* at the Odéon-Théâtre de France.

2486   FEDERMAN, Raymond. *French Review,* XXXIV (May, 1961), 594-595.
Review of *Comment c'est.*

2487   _____. *Books Abroad,* XXXV (Autumn, 1961), 337.
Review of *Comment c'est.*

2488   FLETCHER, John. "Actualités," *Lettres Nouvelles,* IX, n.s. (April, 1961), 169-171.
Review of *Comment c'est.*

2489   GALEY, Matthieu. *Arts,* 806 (Jan. 25-31, 1961), 4.
Review of *Comment c'est.*

2490   GASSNER, John. "Broadway in Review," *Educational Theatre Journal,* XIII (Dec., 1961), 289-296.
Review of *Happy Days.*

2491   GENÊT, *pseud.* [i.e., Janet Flanner]. "Letter from Paris," *New Yorker,* XXXVII (March 4, 1961), 95-100. Reprinted in **1233**.
Beckett, *passim,* especially on *Comment c'est.*

2492   GUISSARD, Lucien. *La Croix,* Feb. 20, 1961.
Review of *Comment c'est.*

2493   HAHN, K. J. "Samuel Beckett: Eindpunt van de Zelfvervreemding," *De Linnie,* May 13, 1961.
Review of *Comment c'est.*

2494   HALLIER, Jean-Édern. "*Comment c'est* de Samuel Beckett," *Cahiers de la République,* n.v. (April, 1961), 86-87.

2495   HASTINGS, Ronald. "*Godot* Less Amusing: Newly Assessed at Stratford East," *Daily Telegraph,* May 16, 1961.
Review of *Waiting for Godot* revival.

2496   HECHT, Howard B. "In Hope of Godot," *Humanities,* XII (Fall, 1961), 47-49.
On *Waiting for Godot.*

2497   HELMÈS, Jean. "*Comment c'est:* Le Voyage au bout de la boue," *Démocratie 61,* Feb. 23, 1961.

2498   HEWES, Henry. "Speak Your Wait," *Saturday Review of Literature,* XLIV (Oct. 7, 1961), 38.
Review of *Happy Days.*

2499   HOBSON, Harold. "Another Way Up Everest," *Sunday Times,* May 21, 1961.
Waiting for Godot at Stratford East.

1961

2500   _____. "Conversations with Gielgud," *Sunday Times,* Sept. 24,
        1961, Magazine, pp. 25-26.
About Beckett *inter alia.*

2501   HUGHES, Daniel J. "Reality and the Hero," *Modern Fiction Studies,*
        VI (Winter, 1960-61), 345-346 [see **1557**].
On Beckett, *passim.*

2502   JOLY, G. *L'Aurore,* May 9, 1961.
Review of *En attendant Godot.*

2503   JUIN, Hubert. "Prix International des Éditeurs," *Lettres Françaises,*
        May 11, 1961.
On Beckett and Borges.

2504   KANTERS, Robert. *"En attendant Godot* au Théâtre de France,"
        L'Express, May 11, 1961, p. 49.

2505   _____. *"En attendant Godot* au Théâtre de France," *L'Express,*
        May 25, 1961, p. 45.

2506   _____. *Revue de Paris,* 12 (Dec., 1961), 154.
Note on a paper entitled "Le Monologue intérieur dans *La Princesse de Clèves,*"
by Marie-Jeanne Durry, published in *La Littérature narrative de l'imagination*
(Paris: Presses Universitaires de France, 1961). Kanters makes several allusions to Beckett and in particular to *La Dernière Bande.*

2507   KERR, Walter. *"Happy Days,"* New York Herald Tribune, Sept. 18,
        1961.
Review of the play.

2508   KUTZKEY, John. *"Waiting for Godot* Difficult To Interpret,"
        Sienna News, Nov. 17, 1961.

2509   LAWS, Frederick. *The Listener,* LXVI (Dec. 28, 1961), 1135, with
        photograph.
Reference to the televising of *Waiting for Godot* by the BBC.

2510   LEMARCHAND, Jacques. *"En attendant Godot* au Théâtre de
        l'Odéon," *Figaro Littéraire,* May 13, 1961, p. 16.

2511   LUCCIONI, Gennie. *Esprit,* XXIX (April, 1961), 710-713.
Review of *Comment c'est.*

2512   LUNDKVIST, Artur. "Ansiktet i Dyn," *Stockholms Tidningen,* June
        5, 1961.
Review of *Comment c'est.*

2513   MacNEICE, Louis. *"Godot* on TV," *New Statesman,* LXII (July 7,
        1961), 27-28.
BBC-TV production of *Waiting for Godot.*

2514   MALONEY, Alta. "Charles Playhouse," *Boston Traveler,* May 10,
        1961.
Review of *Krapp's Last Tape.*

1961

2515   MARCABRU, Pierre. *Arts,* 821 (May 10-16, 1961), 14.
Review of *En attendant Godot* at the Odéon-Théâtre de France.

2516   MAROWITZ, Charles. "Heroes and Un-Heroes," *Drama,* n.v.
(Spring, 1961), 39-43.
On Beckett, *passim.*

2517   MAURIAC, Claude. "L'Héroïque Lecteur de Beckett," *Le Figaro,*
Feb. 1, 1961.
Review of *Comment c'est.*

2518   MAYOUX, Jean-Jacques. *Mercure de France,* CCCXLII (June,
1961), 293-297 [see **716**].
Review of *Comment c'est.*

2519   MENDIA, José Antonio. "Algo asi como una voz," *La Prensa,* May
28, 1961.
Review of *Comment c'est.*

2520   MIHALOVICI, Marcel. "Beckett a collaboré à la musique de
Krapp," *Figaro Littéraire,* July 1, 1961.
About the opera based on *Krapp's Last Tape.*

2521   MITGANG, Herbert. "Waiting for Beckett—and His *Happy Days*
Première," *New York Times,* Sept. 17, 1961, sec. 2, pp. 1, 3.
Review of New York production.

2522   NADEAU, Maurice. *L'Express,* Jan. 26, 1961, pp. 25-26.
Review of *Comment c'est.*

2523   NADEL, Norman. "Beckett's *Happy Days,*" *New York World Telegram,* Sept. 18, 1961.
Review of New York production.

2524   O'CONNOR, Jim. "*Happy Days* Aren't," *New York Journal-
American,* Sept. 18, 1961.
Review of New York production.

2525   OLIVER, Edith. "Off-Broadway," *New Yorker,* XXXVII (Sept. 30,
1961), 119.
Review of *Happy Days.*

2526   OLIVIER, Claude. "Musée Godot," *Lettres Françaises,* May 11,
1961.
On the revival of *En attendant Godot* at the Odéon-Théâtre de France.

2527   P., J. J. "Beckett als Vorheen," *Nieuwe Rotterdamse Courant,* March
30, 1961.

2528   PASO, Alfonso. "La Tragicomedia," *ABC,* May 30, 1961.
On Beckett's theater in general.

1961

2528A PIATIER, Jacqueline. *"Comment c'est:* un halètement dans la boue," *Le Monde,* Nov. 2, 1961, p. 9.
Review of *Comment c'est.*

2529 PILER, Jack. "An Irish 'Godot' of Merit," *Daily Herald,* May 16, 1961.
About an Irish production of *Waiting for Godot.*

2530 PILLEY, Michael. *"Waiting for Godot* Evokes Superlatives," *Times-Union,* Nov. 11, 1961.
Review of the play.

2531 POIROT-DELPECH, Bertrand. *Le Monde,* May 9, 1961.
Review of *En attendant Godot* at the Odéon-Théâtre de France.

2532 PORQUEROL, Élisabeth. "Blaise Cendrars," *Nouvelle Revue Française,* IX (March, 1961), 517-519.
Contains several allusions to Beckett.

2533 RICHARDSON, Joanna. "Waiting for What?" *The Listener,* LXV (April 20, 1961), 716.
Review of a BBC program on Beckett [see **3011**].

2534 ROSNAY, Jean-Pierre. "Rencontre avec Jérôme Lindon, premier éditeur du 'nouveau roman,'" *Combat,* Jan. 19, 1961, p. 7.
Mentions Beckett.

2535 ROULET, Alfred. "Comment c'est? Pas de réponse," *Tribune de Genève,* Feb. 7, 1961.
Review of *Comment c'est.*

2536 SÉNART, Philippe. *"Comment c'est:* Parler de soi afin de pouvoir se taire," *Combat,* Jan. 19, 1961, p. 7.

2537 SMITH, Michael. *Village Voice,* Sept. 21, 1961, p. 9.
Review of *Krapp's Last Tape* at East End Theater, New York, directed by Alan Schneider and starring Donald Davis as Krapp.

2538 TALLMER, Jerry. *Village Voice,* Sept. 21, 1961, pp. 9-10.
Review of *Happy Days.*

2539 TAUBMAN, Howard. "Reason To Live," *New York Times,* Oct. 1, 1961.
Review of *Happy Days.*

2540 THIBAUDEAU, Jean. *Temps Modernes,* XVI (April, 1961), 1384-1392.
Review of *Comment c'est.*

2541 TOYNBEE, Philip. "Literature at the End of Its Tether," *The Observer,* Feb. 26, 1961, p. 31.
Review of *Comment c'est.*

1961

2542   V., C. *Tribune de Lausanne*, May 14, 1961, p. 5.
Review of *En attendant Godot* at the Odéon-Théâtre de France.

2543   VANCE, Vera L. "Proust's Guermantes as Birds," *French Review*, XXXV (Oct., 1961), 3-10 (Beckett, p. 3).
Mentions Beckett and quotes from *Proust*.

2544   VAN GEELEN, Jan. "Nieuw Werk van Léautaud, Beckett en Mauriac," *De Groene Amsterdammer*, Aug. 9, 1961.
Review of *Comment c'est* with other new books.

2545   _____. "Hoe Het Is," *Algemeen Handelsblad*, Sept. 2, 1961.
Review of *Comment c'est*.

2546   VELLINGSHAUSEN, Albert Schulze. "Ein Requiem der 'Glücklichen Tage,' " *Frankfurter Allgemeine Zeitung*, Nov. 8, 1961.
Review of *Happy Days*.

2547   VERDOT, Guy. "*Godot* à l'Odéon," *École Libératrice*, May 26, 1961.
Review of *En attendant Godot* at the Odéon-Théâtre de France.

2548   WATTS, Richard, Jr. "The Wasteland of Samuel Beckett," *New York Post*, Sept. 18, 1961.
On *Happy Days*.

2549   _____. "Two on the Aisle," *New York Post*, Oct. 1, 1961.
Review of *Happy Days*.

2550   ZELTNER-NEUKOMM, Gerda. "Das Inferno Samuel Becketts," *Neue Zürcher Zeitung*, XXXIV (Feb. 23, 1961), 8.
Review of *Comment c'est*.

1962

2551   ANONYMOUS. *The Times*, Jan. 5, 1962, p. 11.
News item on Beckett's theater in Romania.

2552   _____. "A Hunger for the Theater," *Times Literary Supplement*, Jan. 26, 1962, p. 54.
Review of **1030**, Beckett *passim*.

2553   _____. "From the Fifties," *Radio Times*, Feb. 1, 1962, pp. 18, 24.
Note on *Waiting for Godot*, broadcast by the BBC Home Service, Feb. 5, 1962.

2554   _____. "Sense of the Absurd," *Newsweek*, LIX (Feb. 26, 1962), 79.
Review of *Endgame* and of **1025**.

2555   _____. "Twelve Cheers for Joyce," *Times Literary Supplement*, April 6, 1962, p. 234.
Review of *Our Exagmination Round His Factification for Incamination of Work in Progress* (British reissue).

1962

2556 _____. "Notes on Broadcasting," *The Times*, April 21, 1962.
Reference to *Waiting for Godot*.

2557 _____. "Gaudy and Inane?" *Times Literary Supplement*, May 25,
    1962, p. 374.
Review of *Poems in English*.

2558 _____. *Radio Times*, June 7, 1962.
Note on broadcast of *Endgame* by the BBC Third Programme, May 22 and
    June 15, 1962.

2559 _____. *The Times*, June 7, 1962.
Reference to *Act Without Words II*.

2560 _____. *British Book News*, 263 (July, 1962), 514.
Review of *Our Exagmination Round His Factification for Incamination of
Work in Progress* (British reissue).

2561 _____. "Silent Study of Tramps," *The Times*, July 3, 1962, p. 15.
Review of *Act Without Words [II]*.

2562 _____. "French Dramatist's New View of Life," *The Times*, July
    3, 1962, p. 15.
On Adamov with allusions to Beckett.

2563 _____. *"End of Day," The Times*, July 31, 1962.
News item on Dublin Festival including Jack MacGowran's selections from
Beckett, *End of Day*.

2564 _____. "Dreams of Reason," *Times Literary Supplement*, Aug. 3,
    1962, p. 556.
Review of **1025**.

2565 _____. *The Times*, Sept. 4, 1962, p. 7g.
News item on filming of *Waiting for Godot* and *Act Without Words*.

2566 _____. *Virginia Quarterly Review*, XXXVIII (Autumn, 1962),
    cxviii.
Review of *Our Exagmination Round His Factification for Incamination of
Work in Progress*.

2567 _____. *British Book News*, 266 (Oct., 1962), 737-738.
Review of *Happy Days*.

2568 _____. *The Times*, Oct. 18, 1962.
Review of Jack MacGowran's selections from Beckett, *End of Day*, performed
at the New Arts Theatre in London.

2569 _____. *The Times*, Oct. 20, 1962.
News item on *Happy Days*.

2570 _____. *The Observer*, Oct. 21, 1962, p. 28.
Review of Jack MacGowran's selections from Beckett, *End of Day*, performed
at the New Arts Theatre in London.

1962

2571   _____. *The Times,* Nov. 1, 1962, p. 8e.
News item on Beckett's radio play *Words and Music.*

2572   _____. "One-Sided Dialogue by Half-Buried Wife," *The Times,*
          Nov. 2, 3, 1962.
Review of *Happy Days* at Royal Court Theatre, London.

2573   _____. *The Times,* Nov. 17, 1962.
Review of *Words and Music* (BBC Third Programme production).

2574   _____. "Tar Parti för Människan," *Dagens Nyheter,* Dec. 6, 1962.
Review of *Happy Days.*

2575   ADAMOV, Arthur. *The Observer,* July 1, 1962, Weekend Review,
          p. 21.
Interview by Carl Wildman, with mention of Beckett.

2576   ALBÉRÈS, R.-M. *Table Ronde,* 178 (Nov., 1962), 112-114.
Review of 1037.

2577   ANDERSON, Jack. "Workshop in Fantasy by Beckett," *Oakland
          Tribune,* Sept. 1, 1962.
Review of *Happy Days.*

2578   BAKEWELL, Michael. *Radio Times,* May 17, 1962, p. 26.
Note on broadcast production of *Endgame.*

2579   _____. *Radio Times,* Nov. 8, 1962, p. 31.
Note on *Words and Music* (BBC broadcast on Third Programme, Nov. 13 and
Dec. 7, 1962).

2580   BARILLI, Renato. "Samuel Beckett, *Molloy,*" *Convivium,* XXX
          (Jan.-Feb., 1962), 125.
Review of *Molloy.*

2581   BARTHOLOMEW, Rati. "Theatre: Three One-Act Plays,"
          Thought, XIV (Feb. 10, 1962), 18.
On Beckett and Ionesco.

2582   BAYLEY, John. *The Spectator,* May 18, 1962, pp. 660-661.
Review of 1043, with a comparison of Beckett and C. P. Snow.

2583   BERGONZI, Bernard. "Early Beckett," *The Guardian,* Feb. 9, 1962,
          p. 7. Reprinted in *Manchester Guardian Weekly,* Feb. 15, 1962,
          under the title "Explorers of Paralysis."
Review of *Poems in English.*

2584   BRANDSTRUP, Ole. "Den Bunke har Talent," *Berlingske Aften-
          avis,* May 10, 1962.
Review of *Happy Days.*

1962

2585   BROADBENT, J. B. *The Spectator,* April 6, 1962, pp. 453-454.
Review of *Poems in English* and *Our Exagmination Round His Factification for Incamination of Work in Progress.*

2586   BROOK, Peter. "*Happy Days* and *Marienbad,*" *Encore,* IX (Jan.-Feb., 1962), 34-38.
Review of *Happy Days* and *Marienbad.*

2587   BURGESS, Anthony. *The Observer,* Dec. 30, 1962, p. 11.
Item on the publication of *Malone Dies* in paperback by Penguin Books.

2588   CAIN, Alex. "Far Lower Than the Angels," *The Tablet,* CCXVI (Nov. 10, 1962), 1082-1083.
Review of *Happy Days.*

2589   CHAMBERS, Ross. "The Other," *Nation,* 103 (Sept. 22, 1962), 22-23.
Review of *Happy Days.*

2590   CHOUPAUT, Y.-M. "Samuel Beckett choisit la langue française," *Paris-Normandie,* March 6, 1962.
On Beckett's French in general.

2591   CLARKE, Austin. "Three Irish Poets," *Irish Times,* Feb. 3, 1962, p. 8.
Review of *Poems in English.*

2592   CRANE, Muriel. *The Listener,* LXVIII (July 19, 1962), 103-104.
Letter to the Editor on **1666**.

2593   DAVIE, Donald. "Nightingales, Anangke," *New Statesman,* LXIII (Jan. 5, 1962), 20-21.
Review of *Poems in English.*

2594   _____. *New Statesman,* LXIII (Jan. 12, 1962), 43.
Letter to the Editor on **2593** and **2627**.

2595   DOUBROVSKY, Serge. *Nouvelle Revue Française,* X (Dec., 1962), 1100.
Review of *Maître-Objet* by Alain Bosquet (Paris: Gallimard, 1962) making a comparison with Beckett.

2596   DUNCAN, Ronald. "An Intimate Portrait of Lord Harewood," *Sunday Times,* Sept. 2, 1962, p. 26.
Mention of *Waiting for Godot.*

2597   EICHELBAUM, Stanley. "A Weird Joyride with Samuel Beckett: Workshop's *Happy Days,*" *San Francisco Examiner,* Sept. 18, 1962.
Review of *Happy Days.*

2598   ESSLIN, Martin. "Forget the Dustbins," *Plays and Players,* X (Nov., 1962), 32-33.

1962

Short article presenting Beckett's *Happy Days.*

2599   FAGERSTRÖM, Allan. "En röst i öknen," *Aftonbladet,* Dec. 6, 1962.
Review of *Happy Days.*

2600   FERRIS, Paul. *The Observer,* Nov. 18, 1962, p. 29.
Review of *Words and Music* (BBC production).

2601   FURBANK, P. N. *The Listener,* LXVII (Feb. 8, 1962), 265.
Review of *Poems in English.*

2602   GASCOIGNE, Bamber. "From the Head," *The Spectator,* July 27,
        1962, p. 115.
Review of *Act Without Words [II].*

2603   _____. "Dying of the Light," *The Spectator,* Nov. 9, 1962, pp.
        715, 717.
Review of *Happy Days.*

2604   GELLERT, Roger. "Long Pause for Gallantry," *New Statesman,*
        LXIV (Nov. 9, 1962), 679.
Review of *Happy Days.*

2605   HARRIE, Ivar. "Slutet i Sandhögen," *Expressen,* Dec. 6, 1962.
Review of *Happy Days.*

2606   HOBSON, Harold. "Lunch with Iris Murdoch," *Sunday Times,*
        March 11, 1962, p. 28.
Murphy mentioned.

2607   _____. *Sunday Times,* Oct. 21, 1962, p. 27.
Review of Jack MacGowran's selections from Beckett, *End of Day,* performed
at the New Arts Theatre in London.

2608   _____. "The Really Happy Woman," *Sunday Times,* Nov. 4, 1962,
        p. 41.
Review of *Happy Days* at the Royal Court Theatre in London.

2609   HOPE-WALLACE, Philip. *The Guardian,* Nov. 2, 1962, p. 6.
Review of *Happy Days.*

2610   JOHNSON, Bryan S. "Saying Is Inventing," *The Spectator,* July 20,
        1962, p. 92.
Review of *Happy Days.*

2611   _____. "Key to Beckett—Who Doesn't Give a Damn," *Scene,* 7
        (Oct. 25, 1962).
On *Happy Days.*

2612   KITCHIN, Laurence. *The Listener,* LXVIII (July 19, 1962), 103-
        104.
Letter to the Editor on **1666.**

1962

2613   KNICKERBOCKER, Paine. "Acting Triumph at the Encore," *San Francisco Chronicle,* Sept. 18, 1962.
Review of *Happy Days.*

2614   KRUTCH, Joseph Wood. "What I Learned about Existentialism," *Saturday Review of Literature,* XLV (April 21, 1962), 10-12.
Beckett mentioned.

2615   LE CLECH'H, Guy. "Sur une scène de Londres Beckett crée sa 'première' femme et l'enterre aussitôt," *Figaro Littéraire,* Nov. 17, 1962, p. 20.
Review of *Happy Days* in London.

2616   MACK, Dave. "Show-Biz Audience Applaud Local Première, *Waiting for Godot,*" *San Quentin News,* Feb. 15, 1962, pp. 1, 3.
Review of production of *Waiting for Godot* by the drama group of San Quentin Prison.

2617   MAY, F. *The Listener,* LXVIII (July 26, 1962), 140-141.
Letter to the Editor on **1666**.

2618   NOTT, Kathleen. *The Observer,* Sept. 30, 1962, p. 28.
Review of **1037**, Beckett *passim.*

2619   O'TOOLE, Peter. "After Lawrence-Oscar Bill Baal Sam Godot Me," *Scene,* 14 (Dec. 12, 1962), 6-9.
Interview by Tom Stoppard.

2620   PINTER, Harold. "Pinter between the Lines," *Sunday Times,* March 4, 1962, p. 25.
Pinter quoting from *The Unnamable.*

2621   PRITCHETT, V. S. *New Statesman,* LXIII (May 11, 1962), 679-680.
Review of **1043**, with a comparison of Beckett and C. P. Snow.

2622   RODGER, Ian. "A Cleaned Picture," *The Listener,* LXVII (Feb. 15, 1962), 313-314.
Review of BBC Home Service broadcast of *Waiting for Godot,* Feb. 5, 1962.

2623   SCHONBERG, Knud. "I morgen blever værre end i dag," *Ekstrabladet,* May 10, 1962.
Review of *Happy Days.*

2624   SÉNART, Philippe. "Jalons pour le nouveau roman," *Table Ronde,* 169 (Feb., 1962), 107.
Mentions Beckett.

2625   SHUTTLEWORTH, Martin. "Ultimate Causes," *The Listener,* LXVIII (Nov. 22, 1962), 883-884.
Review of *Words and Music* (BBC production).

1962

2626   SPEEGLE, Paul. *"Happy Days* Tour de Force," *San Francisco News Call Bulletin,* Sept. 17, 1962.
Review of *Happy Days.*

2627   STARKIE, Enid. "The Answer Is a Sunset," *New Statesman,* LXIII (Jan. 12, 1962), 43.
Letter to the Editor on **2593** [see also **2594**].

2628   STOPPARD, Tom. "Crying Till You Laugh," *Scene,* 7 (Oct. 25, 1962), 19.
About selections from Beckett, *End of Day.*

2629   TOYNBEE, Philip. *The Observer,* Feb. 18, 1962, p. 28.
Review of *Auto-da-Fe* by Elias Canetti, with a reference to Beckett.

2630   TURNELL, Martin. *The Listener,* LXVIII (Aug. 30, 1962), 326.
Review of **1037**.

2631   TURNILL, Oscar. *Sunday Times,* Nov. 18, 1962.
Review of *Words and Music* (BBC production).

2632   TYNAN, Kenneth. *The Observer,* June 3, 1962, p. 27.
Review of **1025**.

2633   _____. "Intimations of Mortality," *The Observer,* Oct. 28, 1962, p. 29.
Review of *Happy Days.*

2634   WARDLE, Irving. *The Observer,* July 15, 1962, p. 20.
Review of *Act Without Words II.*

1963

2635   ANONYMOUS. "Beckett n'a pas dit un mot," *Paris-Presse,* Jan. 27-28, 1963.
Review of *Tous ceux qui tombent* on French television.

2636   _____. "The Arts," *The Times,* Feb. 11, 1963.
Allusion to *Waiting for Godot.*

2637   _____. *The Times,* March 16, 1963.
News item on Beckett's projected collaboration on a film with Ionesco.

2638   _____. "Londres: Jusqu'au cou," *L'Express,* March 21, 1963, p. 23.
Review of *Oh les beaux jours.*

2639   _____. "One-Act Triangle," *The Observer,* March 24, 1963.
About *Play* performed in Ulm.

2640   _____. "Lyckans dar på Folkan," *Göteborgs Handels-och Sjöfarts-Tidningen,* April 3, 1963.
Review of *Play.*

1963

2641 _____. "University Play Withdrawn," *The Times,* April 18, 1963.
About *Waiting for Godot.*

2642 _____. "Au Caire, remous suscités par Beckett," *Observateur du Moyen-Orient et de l'Afrique,* May 3, 1963.
About *Oh les beaux jours.*

2643 _____. "Warum denn leben?" *Der Bund,* May 17, 1963.
Review of *Happy Days.*

2644 _____. "Glückliche Tage," *Neue Berner Nachrichten,* May 18, 1963.
Review of *Happy Days.*

2645 _____. *Nation Française,* May 29, 1963.
Review of *Oh les beaux jours.*

2646 _____. "Mme. Renaud To Act in Beckett Play," *The Times,* June 7, 1963.
About *Happy Days.*

2647 _____. "Voices from Limbo," *The Times,* June 24, 1963.
Review of *Play* performed in Ulm.

2648 _____. "Beckett and the Theater of the Concrete," *Time,* LXXXI (June 28, 1963), 48 ff.
Review of *Play* performed in Ulm.

2649 _____. "Problems That Confront the New Abbey Theatre," *Irish Digest,* LXXVIII (Oct., 1963), 79-82.
Allusions to Beckett.

2650 _____. "Dublin Festival," *Times Educational Supplement,* Oct. 11, 1963, p. 481.
Allusion to *Waiting for Godot* and *Happy Days.*

2651 _____. "Belfast Evening with Beckett," *The Times,* Nov. 7, 1963.
About performance of *Endgame.*

2652 _____. *Sunday Times,* Nov. 10, 1963.
Item on BBC-TV production of *Krapp's Last Tape,* Nov. 13, 1963.

2653 _____. "Films from the Avant-Garde," *The Times,* Nov. 13, 1963.
News item about projected film by Beckett and Ionesco [see **2637**].

2654 _____. *The Observer,* Nov. 17, 1963, p. 22.
Item on Jupiter Books reprint of *Murphy* and *Watt.*

2655 _____. "Irish Lilt Suits Beckett Play," *The Times,* Dec. 10, 1963.
About *Happy Days.*

2656 A[LTER], A[ndré]. "Une Vieille Femme obèse va chercher son mari," *Télérama,* Jan. 20, 1963.
Review of *Tous ceux qui tombent.*

1963

2657   _____. "Becket et le refus de Dieu," *Témoignage Chrétien,* March 29, 1963.
On Beckett's theater in general.

2658   B., J. *"Fin de partie,"* *Écho de Lyon,* May 17, 1963.

2659   B.-S., H. "Glückliche Tage," *Neue Berner Zeitung,* May 18-19, 1963.
Review of *Happy Days.*

2660   B[ÉJEAN], G[eorges]. *"En attendant Godot* par la Comédie des Alpes," *Témoignage Chrétien,* May 10, 1963.
Review of *En attendant Godot.*

2661   BERNADELLI, Francesco. *"Oh les beaux jours,"* *La Stampa,* Sept. 29, 1963.
Review of the play.

2662   BOLL, David. "Questing for Godot," *Books and Bookmen,* VIII (May, 1963), 45-46.
On Beckett's fiction.

2663   BONNIER, Henry. "Une Littérature épuisée," *Dépêche du Midi,* Oct. 29, 1963, p. 5.
On *Molloy* reissue.

2664   BOUVIER, Émile. "L'Anti-Théâtre," *Midi Libre,* Feb. 20, 1963.
On Beckett's theater in general.

2665   BRAY, Barbara. "The New Beckett," *The Observer,* June 16, 1963, p. 29.
About *Play* performed in Ulm.

2666   BRENDEMÜHL, Rudolf. "Becketts *Spiel,"* *Nacht-Depesche,* Nov. 19, 1963.
Review of *Play.*

2667   BROCKBANK, J. P. *The Observer,* Oct. 13, 1963, p. 29.
Letter to the Editor concerning Beckett on York University syllabus.

2668   BURKE, Herbert. *Library Journal,* LXXXVIII (June 1, 1963), 2257.
Review of *Poems in English.*

2669   CALDER, John. *Times Literary Supplement,* Nov. 21, 1963, p. 947.
Letter to the Editor concerning Beckett's influence on Burroughs.

2670   CÉZAN, Claude. "Madeleine Renaud présente *Oh les beaux jours,"* *Nouvelles Littéraires,* Oct. 24, 1963, p. 12.
Review of the play.

2671   DAMERINI, Gino. *"Oh les beaux jours,"* *Gazzettino Venezia,* Sept. 29, 1963.
Review of the play.

1963

2672 DE FOLEY, Maria Isabel Butler. *"Happy Days," ABC,* Oct. 27, 1963.
Review of the play.

2673 DELEHANTY, James. "Books," *Kilkenny Magazine,* n.v. (Spring,
1963), 71-73.
Review of *Happy Days.*

2674 DE MONTICELLI, Roberto. *"Oh les beaux jours," Il Giorno,* Sept.
29, 1963.
Review of the play.

2675 DENNIS, Nigel. "No View from the Toolshed," *Encounter,* XX
(Jan., 1963), 37-39.
Review of *Happy Days.*

2676 DÉON, M. *Nouvelles Littéraires,* Nov. 7, 1963, p. 12.
Note on *Oh les beaux jours.*

2677 DUMUR, Guy. "L'Avant-Garde entre dans l'histoire," *France-
Observateur,* Nov. 7, 1963, p. 14.
About Esslin's definition of the theater of the absurd [see **1025**].

2678 ERIKSSON, Göran O. "Erinringar ur Gyttjan," *Stockholms Tidningen,* Oct. 26, 1963.
Review of *How It Is.*

2679 ESSLIN, Martin. *The Listener,* LXIX (March 28, 1963), 567.
Review of **1048**.

2680 FEHLING, Dora. "Buntes und bleiches Frauen," *Telegraf,* Nov. 19,
1963.
Review of *Play.*

2681 F[INNEGAN], J. J. "Marie Kean's Winnie Is Unforgettable," *Evening Herald,* Oct. 2, 1963.
Review of *Happy Days.*

2682 FLETCHER, John. *Bulletin de l'Université de Toulouse,* LXXII
(April, 1963), 714-715.
Review of *Molloy* reissue.

2683 ———. *Bulletin de l'Université de Toulouse,* LXXIII (Nov., 1963),
268.
Review of *Oh les beaux jours* (published text).

2684 FROISSART, André. "Encres noirs," *Le Figaro,* Oct. 21, 1963, p. 21.
About *Oh les beaux jours.*

2685 GAUTIER, Jean-Jacques. *Le Figaro,* Oct. 30, 1963, p. 20.
Review of *Oh les beaux jours.*

2686 GRACK, Günther. "Menschen ohne Antlitz," *Der Tagesspiegel,* Nov.
19, 1963.
Review of *Play.*

1963

2687   GRAHAM, P. *The Observer*, Oct. 6, 1963, p. 27.
Item on Beckett's film collaboration with Ionesco.

2688   GUILLEMINAULT, G. *L'Aurore*, Oct. 31, 1963, p. 12.
Review of *Oh les beaux jours*.

2689   GUNPERTZ, Kenneth. "End of Madman or World? Laugh It Up
        at T. G. *Endgame*," *Ka Leo O Hawaii*, Jan. 15, 1963.
Review of *Endgame*.

2690   HAHN, Pierre. "Roger Blin: 'J'ai dû attendre trois ans pour monter
        En attendant Godot,'" *Paris-Théâtre*, XVI, no. 201 (1963), 22.
Interview with Blin, director of the original French production of *En attendant
Godot*.

2691   HANSINGVAR, Hanson. "Vilket irriterande Stycke!" *Stockholms
        Tidningen*, April 3, 1963.
Review of *Happy Days*.

2692   HEDLUND, Magnus. "*Comment c'est*," *Ny Tid*, Nov. 7, 1963.
Review of the novel.

2693   HJERTÉN, Hanserik. "Beckett i Välfärdssamhället," *Dagens Ny-
        heter*, April 16, 1963.
Review of *Happy Days*.

2694   HOBSON, Harold. "The Hidden Persuaders," *Sunday Times*, Jan.
        20, 1963, p. 39.
Mentions Beckett.

2695   _____. "Not Good Enough for M. Gautier," *Sunday Times*, April
        28, 1963.
A critique of Gautier's reviewing of Beckett.

2696   _____. *Sunday Times*, Aug. 25, 1963, p. 26.
Review of *Waiting for Godot* (Cambridge University production).

2697   HOLMQVIST, Bengt. "Frågor Kring Samuel Beckett," *Dagens
        Nyheter*, April 1, 1963.

2698   HOPE-WALLACE, Philip. "*Happy Days*," *The Guardian*, Dec. 10,
        1963.
Review of the play.

2699   JEENER, J.-B. "Beckett est joué aussi en javanais," *Télé-Magazine*,
        Jan. 20, 1963.

2700   JOHNSON, B. S. "A Master Stylist," *The Spectator*, Dec. 13, 1963,
        p. 800.
Reviews of *Murphy* and *Watt* reissues.

2701   KANTERS, Robert. "La Reine grise: Les deux pieds dans la tombe
        . . . et le reste," *L'Express*, Nov. 7, 1963, pp. 34-35.
Review of *Oh les beaux jours*.

1963

2702   KIELY, Benedict. *"Happy Days* with Refrains That Tear the Heart," *Irish Press,* Oct. 1, 1963.
Review of the play.

2703   KIENZL, Florian. "Absurd und absurd ist zweierlei," *Kurier,* Nov. 18, 1963.
Review of *Play.*

2704   KLEBERG, Lars. "Beckett och Rösterina," *Dagens Nyheter,* Dec. 23, 1963.
Reviews of *Words and Music* and *Cascando.*

2705   LECKIUS, Ingemar. *"Comment c'est,"* *Aftonbladet,* Oct. 13, 1963.
Review of the novel.

2706   LEMARCHAND, Jacques. *"Oh les beaux jours,"* *Figaro Littéraire,* Nov. 7-13, 1963, p. 22.
Review of the play.

2707   LINDE, Ebbe. "En rik och skonlös pjäs," *Dagens Nyheter,* April 3, 1963.
Review of *Happy Days.*

2708   LINDON, Jérôme. "Le Nouveau Roman aux Éditions de Minuit, 1951-1963," *Arts,* 923 (July 3-9, 1963), 4.
With reference to the novels of Beckett published by Lindon.

2709   LLOVET, Enrique. "Dias Felices," *ABC,* March 21, 1963.
Review of *Happy Days.*

2710   McALEER, John J. *Books Abroad,* XXXVII (Winter, 1963), 79.
Review of *Oh les beaux jours* (published text).

2711   MAROWITZ, Charles. "A View from the Gods," *Encore,* X (Jan.-Feb., 1963), 6-7.
Review of *Happy Days.*

2712   MAULNIER, Thierry. "Claudel et Beckett," *Revue de Paris,* LXX (Dec., 1963), 124-127.
Review of *Oh les beaux jours* with a comparison of Beckett and Claudel.

2713   MAURIAC, François. *Figaro Littéraire,* Feb. 2, 1963, p. 17.
Review of ORTF-TV production of *Tous ceux qui tombent.*

2714   _____. "Bloc-Notes," *Figaro Littéraire,* Nov. 7-13, 1963, p. 24.
About *Oh les beaux jours.*

2715   MAYER, Phil. "Thinking Man's Play," *Saturday Star Bulletin,* Jan. 12, 1963.
Review of *Endgame.*

1963

2716   MIGUEL, André. *Nouvelle Revue Française,* XI (May 1, 1963), 934-935.
Review of **1048.**

2717   PAGET, Jean. *Combat,* Oct. 31, 1963, p. 10.
Review of *Oh les beaux jours.*

2718   PIATIER, Jacqueline. "Maurice Nadeau explore le roman français," *Le Monde,* Dec. 7, 1963.
Beckett mentioned.

2719   PLAISANT, Michèle-S. "Littérature contemporaine: *Happy Days,*" *Langues Modernes,* LVII (Jan.-Feb., 1963).
Review of *Happy Days.*

2720   POIROT-DELPECH, Bertrand. *"Fin de partie,"* Le Monde, June 18, 1963, p. 15.
Review of the play.

2721   _____. *Le Monde,* Oct. 31, 1963, p. 14. Reprinted in *Le Monde Hebdomadaire,* Oct. 31-Nov. 6, 1963, p. 11.
Review of *Oh les beaux jours.*

2722   PROSPERI, Giorgio. *"Oh les beaux jours,"* Il Tempo, Sept. 29, 1963.
Review of the play.

2723   RADICE, Raul. *"Oh les beaux jours,"* Corriere della Sera, Sept. 29, 1963.
Review of the play.

2724   REID, Alec. "Samuel Beckett," *Irish Times,* March 20, 1963.
On Beckett in general.

2725   _____. "Beckett Play at Ebland," *Irish Times,* Oct. 1, 1963.
Review of *Happy Days.*

2726   RICHARDSON, Maurice. *The Observer,* Nov. 17, 1963, p. 23.
Review of BBC-TV production of *Krapp's Last Tape,* Nov. 13, 1963.

2727   RIFBJERG, Klaus. "Hver dag nok i sin glæde," *Politiken,* May 10, 1963.
Review of *Happy Days.*

2728   RUMLER, Fritz. "Drei arme Seelen im Fegefeuer," *Donau Zeitung,* June 18, 1963.
Review of *Play* performed in Ulm.

2729   RUSHE, Desmond. "Beckett Absurd and Inexplicable as Ever," *Irish Independent,* Oct. 2, 1963.
Review of *Happy Days.*

2730   SAINER, Arthur. "Hurrah for the Bridge," *Village Voice,* Sept. 19, 1963.
Beckett, *passim.*

1963

2731   SANDIER, Gilles. "Le Génie c'est ça," *Arts,* 935 (Nov. 6-12, 1963),
           1, 8.
Review of *Oh les beaux jours.*

2732   SARRAUTE, Claude. "Venise a eu la primeur de la nouvelle pièce
           de Beckett," *Le Monde,* Oct. 26, 1963, p. 15.
On *Oh les beaux jours.*

2733   _____. *France-Observateur,* Nov. 7, 1963, p. 13.
Review of *Oh les beaux jours* at the Odéon-Théâtre de France.

2734   SCHOTT, Webster. "Existentialist But Hardly Necessary," *Kansas
           City Star,* March 24, 1963.
Review of *Poems in English.*

2735   SHARE, Bernard. "Sam Beckett dans le métro," *Irish Times,* Dec.
           28, 1963.
On *Murphy* and *Watt.*

2736   SHORTER, Eric. "The Right Laughter for Beckett," *Daily Tele-
           graph,* Dec. 10, 1963.
Review of *Happy Days.*

2737   _____. "A Taste of Theater in Paris," *Daily Telegraph,* Dec. 20,
           1963, p. 7.
Review of *Oh les beaux jours.*

2738   SICLIER, Jacques. *"Tous ceux qui tombent* de Samuel Beckett,"
           Le Monde, Jan. 26, 1963.
Review of the ORTF-TV production.

2739   SIMON, Alfred. *Esprit,* XXXI (March, 1963), 440-441.
Review of the ORTF-TV production of *Tous ceux qui tombent.*

2740   _____. *Esprit,* XXXI (Sept., 1963), 282-283.
On Beckett and Jan Kott.

2741   SMITH, Richard F. "Far-Out Drama Handled Well by University
           Cast," *Honolulu Advertiser,* Jan. 12, 1963.
On *Waiting for Godot.*

2742   SOJCHER, Jacques. "Samuel Beckett ou l'innommable nommé,"
           Schismes, 2 (1963).
On Beckett's fiction.

2743   STEPANCHER, Stephen. *New York Herald Tribune,* Aug. 11, 1963,
           p. 6.
Review of *Poems in English.*

2744   TAYLOR, John Russell. *The Listener,* LXX (Nov. 21, 1963), 855.
Review of BBC-TV production of *Krapp's Last Tape,* Nov. 13, 1963.

1963

2745 TILLIER, Maurice. "Mais qui est donc l'étrange, l'envoûtant M. Beckett?" *Figaro Littéraire*, Nov. 14-20, 1963, p. 21.
Interview with Madeleine Renaud and Roger Blin.

2746 TREVISANI, Giulio. *"Oh les beaux jours,"* L'Unità, Sept. 29, 1963.
Review of the play.

2747 TRIOLET, Elsa. *Lettres Françaises*, Nov. 7-13, 1963, pp. 1, 8.
Review of *Oh les beaux jours* at the Odéon-Théâtre de France.

2748 WALDBERG, Michel. "Samuel Beckett ou l'abîme du désespoir," *Paraboles*, 93 (March-April, 1963), 6.
Review of *Oh les beaux jours*.

1964

2749 ANONYMOUS. "Beckett Plus Pinter," *New Yorker Staats-Zeitung und Herold*, Jan. 10, 1964.
Review of *Play*.

2750 ———. "Pas de Trois—Twice," *Time*, LXXXIII (Jan. 17, 1964), 64.
Review of *Play*.

2751 ———. *Commonweal*, LXXIX (Jan. 24, 1964), 484-485.
Review of *Play*.

2752 ———. "A Vote for the Little World," *Times Literary Supplement*, Jan. 30, 1964, p. 81.
On *Murphy* and *Watt*.

2753 ———. "Producer of Difficult Playwrights," *The Times*, Feb. 4, 1964, p. 14.
News item on Alan Schneider.

2754 ——— [*pseud.* Outsider]. *The Observer*, Feb. 9, 1964, p. 29.
Item on projected film of *Oh les beaux jours*.

2755 ———. *Sud-Ouest*, Feb. 11, 1964.
Review of *Fin de partie* (Toulouse production).

2756 ———. "Off-Broadway Resorts to Readings as Well as Plays," *The Times*, Feb. 20, 1964.
About *Play*.

2757 ———. "Incroyable: L'homme qui rit, c'est . . . Samuel Beckett!" *Figaro Littéraire*, Feb. 27-March 4, 1964, p. 2.
Caption to photograph of Beckett in company of *Endgame* cast in Paris.

2758 ———. "Waiting for the Dark," *Times Literary Supplement*, April 9, 1964, p. 292.
Review of *Play*.

1964

2759 ———. *The Times,* May 7, 1964, p. 18*b*.
Review of *How It Is* (British edition).

2760 ———. "Death and Resurrection," *Times Educational Supplement,*
May 15, 1964, p. 1340.
Review of *Play*.

2761 ———. "Les Dernières Représentaticns de *En attendant Godot*
vont mener Le Grenier de Toulouse d'Auch à Montpellier et à
Decazeville," *Dépêche du Midi,* May 20, 1964, p. 14.
Item on Roger Blin's production, with photograph of Beckett.

2762 ———. "Pim Pem Bom et al ad inf," *Times Literary Supplement,*
May 21, 1964, p. 429.
Review of *How It Is*.

2763 ———. *British Book News,* 287 (July, 1964), 523 and 541-542,
respectively.
Reviews of *Play* and *How It Is* (British editions).

2764 ———. "American Clowns with a Weakness for Beckett," *The
Times,* Aug. 1, 1964, p. 10*a*.
About Bert Lahr acting in *Waiting for Godot,* and Buster Keaton in *Film*.

2765 ———. "Beckett," *New Yorker,* XL (Aug. 8, 1964), 22-23.
Item on Beckett's visit in New York to set of *Film*.

2766 ———. "L'Homme en question" (p. 2), "L'Auteur de *En attendant
Godot:* Samuel Beckett" (p. 3), "*En attendant Godot,* analyse de
la pièce (p. 4), "Une Interview du metteur-en-scène, Roger Blin"
(p. 5), "Le Théâtre de l'absurde" (p. 7), *Grenier de Toulouse,* 3
(Dec., 1964), on pages indicated, with photographic illustrations.
Series of brief articles about the revival of *En attendant Godot* in Toulouse.

2767 ———. "Work Gave Theater New Language," *The Times,* Dec.
31, 1964, p. 4.
Waiting for Godot at the Royal Court Theatre in London.

2768 ———. "Year's Best Books," *The Times,* Dec. 31, 1964, p. 13.
A note on **708**.

2769 ALLEN, Louis. *Prompt,* 4 (1964), 29-31.
Review of **1048**.

2770 BARO, Gene. "Where Is the Where, Why Is Why," *New York Times
Book Review,* March 22, 1964, p. 5.
Review of *How It Is*.

2771 BARRAULT, Jean-Louis. "*Oh les beaux jours,*" *Avant-Scène,* 313
(June 15, 1964), 9.
About the production of the play at the Odéon-Théâtre de France.

1964

2772   BROOKE-ROSE, Christine. "Patterns in the Mud," *Sunday Times,*
          May 3, 1964.
Review of *How It Is.*

2773   BRUSTEIN, Robert. "Mid-Season's Gleanings," *New Republic,* CL
          (Feb. 1 ,1964), 28, 30.
Review of *Play.*

2774   BRYDEN, Ronald. "Absurds," *New Statesman,* LXVII (April 17,
          1964), 616.
Review of *Play.*

2775   CLURMAN, Harold. *The Nation,* CXCVIII (Jan. 27, 1964), 106-
          108.
Review of *Play.*

2776   COOKE, Richard P. "Beckett and Pinter," *Wall Street Journal,* Jan.
          7, 1964.
Review of *Play.*

2777   CRUTTWELL, Patrick. "Fiction Chronicle," *Hudson Review,* XVII
          (Summer, 1964), 303-311.
Review of *How It Is* among other recent novels.

2778   DARLINGTON, W. A. "*Godot* Gets Many Curtains," *Daily Tele-
          graph,* Dec. 31, 1964. Reprinted *idem,* Jan. 1, 1965.
Review of *Waiting for Godot* at the Royal Court Theatre in London.

2779   DONOGHUE, Denis. "And Me If It's Me," *The Guardian,* May 1,
          1964, p. 11.
Review of *How It Is.*

2780   DUCHENE, Anne. "Da Capo," *The Guardian,* May 1, 1964, p. 11.
On *Play,* and two short pieces for radio, and *Endgame* and *Act Without Words.*

2781   FLETCHER, John. *Langues Modernes,* LVIII (March-April, 1964),
          111-112, 183-184.
Review of Howard Moss, *The Magic Lantern of Marcel Proust* (London,
1963), with comments on Beckett's *Proust.*

2782   FROIS, Étienne. "*Oh les beaux jours,*" *Français dans le Monde,* 24
          (April-May, 1964), 25.
Review of the play.

2783   FURBANK, P. N. "A New Work by Beckett," *The Listener,* LXXII
          (Oct. 15, 1964), 604.
About *Cascando.*

2784   GASCOIGNE, Bamber. "How Far Can Beckett Go?" *The Observer,*
          April 12, 1964, p. 24.
Review of *Play.*

1964

2785   GENÊT, *pseud*. [i.e., Janet Flanner]. "Letter from Paris," *New Yorker*, XL (Feb. 22, 1964), 102-104.
Review of *Oh les beaux jours*.

2786   GLAUBER, R. H. *Christian Century*, LXXXI (April 8, 1964), 461.
Review of *How It Is*.

2787   GOTTFRIED, Martin. "*Play*," *Women's Wear Daily*, Jan. 7, 1964.
Review of *Play*.

2788   GOUHIER, Henri. "Boulevard et avant-garde," *Table Ronde*, 192 (Jan., 1964), 122-128.
Review of *Oh les beaux jours*.

2788A   GRESSET, Michel. *Mercure de France*, 1209-1210 (July-Aug., 1964), 546-547.
Review of *Comédie* (published text in *Les Lettres Nouvelles*).

2789   GRIFFIN, L. W. *Library Journal*, LXXXIX (May 1, 1964), 1964.
Review of *How It Is*.

2790   HEWES, Henry. "Intramural Sport," *Saturday Review of Literature*, XXVII (Jan. 25, 1964), 25.
Review of *Play*.

2791   HOBSON, Harold. "The Second Time Round," *Sunday Times*, April 12, 1964.
About *Play*.

2792   HOLMSTROM, John. "Come On!" *New Statesman*, LXVIII (Oct. 16, 1964), 588-589.
Review of *Cascando*.

2793   HOPE-WALLACE, Philip. *The Guardian*, Dec. 31, 1964, 7.
Review of *Waiting for Godot* at the Royal Court Theatre in London.

2794   JENNY, Urs. "Ungluck mit Urnen," *Süddeutsche Zeitung*, May 15, 1964, p. 29.
Review of *Play*.

2795   JOHNSON, B. S. "Exploration," *The Spectator*, June 26, 1964, p. 858.
Reviews of *How It Is, Play, Words and Music,* and *Cascando*.

2796   JOST, Edward F. *America*, CX (Feb. 29, 1964), 291.
Review of *How It Is*.

2797   KANTERS, Robert. "Le Péché de vivre," *L'Express*, June 18, 1964.
Review of *Comédie*.

2798   KERMODE, Frank. *New York Review of Books*, II (March 19, 1964), 9.
Review of *How It Is*.

1964

2799   KERR, Walter. *"Play," New York Herald Tribune,* Jan. 6, 1964.
Review of *Play.*

2800   KITCHIN, Laurence. "Samuel Beckett's *Play," The Listener,* LXXI
            (April 30, 1964), 718-719.
Review of *Play.*

2801   KRETZMER, Herbert. "The Three Faces of Beckett's Contempt,"
            Daily Express, April 8, 1964.
Review of *Play.*

2802   LAMBERT, J. W. "Splendour and Severity," *Sunday Times,* July
            12, 1964.
About *Endgame.*

2803   LEMARCHAND, Jacques. *Figaro Littéraire,* July 2-8, 1964, p. 24.
Review of *Comédie.*

2804   LENNON, Peter. "Beckett's *Endgame* in Paris," *The Guardian,* Feb.
            21, 1964, p. 11.

2805   _____. "Buster Beckett," *The Guardian,* July 25, 1964, p. 6.
Comments on Beckett and Ionesco and projected film collaboration.

2806   LEVIN, Bernard. "I Admit It, Mr. Hobson Was Right," *Daily Mail,*
            Dec. 31, 1964, p. 10.
About *Waiting for Godot* at the Royal Court Theatre in London.

2807   LUKÁCS, Georg. "Literature and Creative Marxism," *Manchester
            Guardian,* April 9, 1964, p. 8.
About Beckett and Proust (*passim*).

2808   MALCOLM, Derek. "The Day the Malt Fused," *The Guardian,* Dec.
            30, 1964, p. 7 [see **33**, Note].
Interview with Jack MacGowran, with photograph of Beckett with Mac-
Gowran.

2809   MARCEL, Gabriel. *Nouvelles Littéraires,* July 9, 1964, p. 12.
Review of *Comédie.*

2810   McCLAIN, John. "Two Plays: Abstract But Clear," *New York
            Journal-American,* Jan. 6, 1964.
Review of *Play.*

2811   NIGHTINGALE, Benedict. *"Endgame* at the Aldwych," *The Guard-
            ian,* July 11, 1964, p. 7.
About revival of *Endgame.*

2812   OLIVER, Edith. "Off-Broadway," *New Yorker,* XL (Jan. 11, 1964),
            112.
About *Play.*

1964

2813   PAGET, Jean. "Estival 64," *Combat,* June 29, 1964.
Review of *Comédie.*

2814   PALATSKY, Gene. "Cherry Lane Pair Incisive," *Newark Evening News,* Jan. 6, 1964.
Review of *Play.*

2815   PIATIER, Jacqueline. "Jean-Paul Sartre s'explique sur *Les Mots,*" *Le Monde,* April 18, 1964, p. 13.
Mentions Beckett and Robbe-Grillet.

2816   PIERRE, Henri. "Première à Londres de *Play,* de Samuel Beckett," *Le Monde,* April 9, 1964, p. 13.
Review of *Play.*

2817   PIERRET, Marc. "Du théâtre anti-roman," *France-Observateur,* June 18, 1964, p. 17.
Review of *Comédie.*

2818   POIROT-DELPECH, Bertrand. "Expérience d'été," *Le Monde,* June 13, 1964, p. 14.
Review of *Comédie.*

2819   POPKIN, Henry. *Vogue,* CXLIII (Feb. 15, 1964), 22.
Review of *Play.*

2820   PRITCHETT, V. S. "No Quaqua," *New Statesman,* LXVII (May 1, 1964), 683.
Review of *How It Is.*

2821   PRYCE-JONES, David. "Classics and Commercials," *The Spectator,* April 17, 1964, pp. 516, 518.
Review of *Play.*

2822   RICKS, Christopher. "Beckett and the Lobster," *New Statesman,* LXVII (Feb. 14, 1964), 254-255.
On *Murphy* and *Watt.*

2823   _____. "Congress Achieved," *New Statesman,* LXVII (April 17, 1964), 604-605.
On *Molloy.*

2824   ROGOFF, Gordon. "Following Beckett," *New Leader,* XLVII (Jan. 20, 1964), 29-30.
Review of *Play.*

2825   ROQUEBERT, Michel. "Au carrefour des arts," *Dépêche du Midi,* Jan. 31, Feb. 1, 3, 4, 6, 1964.
About *Fin de partie* in Toulouse.

2826   ROSS, Maggie. *The Listener,* LXXI (Jan. 23, 1964), 165.
Reviews of *Murphy* and *Watt.*

1964

2827   SANDIER, Gilles. "J.-M. Serreau retrouvé," *Arts,* 967 (June 17-23, 1964), 7.
Review of *Comédie* as directed by J.-M. Serreau.

2828   SAUREL, Renée. "Des Nourrissons pervers au théâtre viril," *Temps Modernes,* XX (July, 1964), 175-176.
Review of *Comédie.*

2829   SHARKEY, John J. "poemsequence for sam beckett" [*sic*], *Times Literary Supplement,* Aug. 6, 1964, p. 706.
Poem.

2830   SIMON, John. *Book Week,* March 8, 1964, p. 5.
Review of *How It Is.*

2831   ――――――. "Theater Chronicle," *Hudson Review,* XVII (Summer, 1964), 233-242.
Mentions Beckett.

2832   ――――――. "Theater Chronicle," *Hudson Review,* XVII (Autumn, 1964), 421-430.
Mentions Beckett.

2833   SMITH, Michael. *"Play," Village Voice,* Jan. 9, 1964.
Review of *Play.*

2834   STAMBUSKY, Alan A. "Continuing Trends in U.S. College and University Play Selection, 1962-1963," *Educational Theatre Journal,* XVI (May, 1964), 160-166.
Beckett college performances: statistics and tables.

2835   TAUBMAN, Howard. *New York Times,* Jan. 6, 1964, p. 6.
Review of *Play.*

2836   THOMPSON, Howard. "Buster Keaton in Beckett's First Film," *New York Times,* July 21, 1964, p. 26.
About *Film.*

2837   TOUCHARD, Pierre-Aimé. "La Civilisation des bidons perdus," *Le Monde,* Dec. 1, 1964, pp. 1, 12.
Reflections on *Comédie.*

2838   UPDIKE, John. "How How It Is Was," *New Yorker,* XL (Dec. 19, 1964), 165-166. Reprinted in **1082**.
Parody review of *How It Is.*

2839   VICKY, *pseud. New Statesman,* LXVIII (July 31, 1964), 139.
Political cartoon based on *Endgame.*

2840   WALKER, Roy. *Times Literary Supplement,* April 16, 1964, p. 311.
Letter to the Editor on *Play.*

1964

2841   WATTS, Richard, Jr. "The News of Pinter and Beckett," *New York Post,* Jan. 6, 1964.
About *Play.*
2842   WEIGHTMAN, John. "The Paris Scene: Yes Yes . . . and Ye Ye," *The Observer,* Jan. 26, 1964, p. 24.
Happy Days mentioned.
2843   _____. "Talking Heads," *The Observer,* May 3, 1964, p. 27.
Reviews of *How It Is* and *Play.*
2844   WILSHER, Peter. "Compulsive Subtlety," *Sunday Times,* Oct. 11, 1964.
Review of *Cascando.*

1965

2845   ANONYMOUS. "Argument: Laughter and Cheers," *New Statesman,* LXIX (April 2, 1965), 541.
On Beckett in London's West End, attacking a remark by Frederick Laws [see **2861** and **2862**].

2846   _____. "U.S. Joyceans to Tour Writer's Paris Haunts," *New York Times,* June 16, 1965, p. 49, col. 2.
Refers to Beckett.

2847   _____. "Beckett et Ionesco en dessins animés au Festival d'Annecy," *Le Monde,* June 16, 1965, p. 14 [see **265.21** and **2867**].

2848   _____. *Times Educational Supplement (Scotland),* Oct. 29, 1965, p. 888.
Review of Beckett readings at Traverse Theatre, Edinburgh [see **503**, Note].

2849   _____. "Beckett on Proust," *Times Literary Supplement,* Dec. 30, 1965, p. 1208 [see **7**, Note].
Reviews of *Proust* and *Three Dialogues.*

2850   ALLEN, Paul. "Unfair to Trinity," *New Statesman,* LXIX (Feb. 5, 1965), 198.
Letter to the Editor in reply to **2852**.

2851   B[OSQUET], A[lain]. "Dix petites pages de Beckett," *Le Monde,* Oct. 30, 1965, p. 12.
Review of *Imagination morte imaginez.*

2852   BRYDEN, Ronald. "Second Non-Coming," *New Statesman,* LXIX (Jan. 8, 1965), 50-51.
Review of *Waiting for Godot* at the Royal Court Theatre in London.

2853   C., C. [Cyril Connolly?] "Short List," *Sunday Times,* Dec. 12, 1965.
Reviews of *Proust* and *Three Dialogues.*

2854   DURANT, Jack D. *Studies in Short Fiction,* II (Spring, 1965), 299-301.
Review of *How It Is.*

1965

2855   FLETCHER, John. *Comparative Literature Studies,* II, no. 1 (1965), 87-89.
Review of Maurice Beebe, *Ivory Towers and Sacred Founts* (New York, 1964), reference to *Malone Dies.*

2856   _____. *Journal of General Education,* XVII (Oct., 1965), 246-248.
Review of Leon Edel, *The Modern Psychological Novel* (New York, 1964), Beckett *passim.*

2857   FURLONG, Monica. "TV," *Daily Mail,* Feb. 24, 25, 1965, p. 3.
About BBC-TV "Monitor" program *Beginning to End.*

2858   GILLIATT, Penelope. "Growing Up with Godot," *The Observer,* Jan. 3, 1965, p. 23.
Review of *Waiting for Godot* at the Royal Court Theatre in London.

2859   HOBSON, Harold. "With a Frightened Lustre," *Sunday Times,* Jan. 17, 1965, p. 43.
Review of *Waiting for Godot* at the Royal Court Theatre in London.

2860   JOUFFROY, Alain. "Une Clé pour Beckett," *L'Express,* Dec. 6-12, 1965, p. 127.
Review of *Imagination morte imaginez.*

2861   LAWS, Frederick. *The Listener,* LXXIII (March 4, 1965), 347.
Review of *Beginning to End* (BBC-TV production).

2862   _____. "Becketteer," *New Statesman,* LXIX (April 9, 1965), 571.
Letter to the Editor in reply to **2845**, asserting incorrectly that he "reviewed a book of [Beckett's] in your pages in 1934."

2863   MORTIMER, John. "Avant-Garde Drama," *New Statesman,* LXIX (Jan. 22, 1965), 120-121.
Review of **1076**.

2864   POWELL, Dilys. "Hard Cheese on Jerry Lewis," *Sunday Times,* Nov. 21, 1965.
About *Film.*

2865   RATCLIFFE, Michael. "Flesh and Bone," *Sunday Times,* Jan. 3, 1965.
Review of *Waiting for Godot* at the Royal Court Theatre in London.

2866   _____. "The Collaborators," *Sunday Times,* Feb. 28, 1965.
About Beckett rehearsing *Beginning to End.*

2867   ZAND, Nicole. "Le Festival du film d'animation: Succès français à Annecy," *Le Monde,* June 24, 1965, p. 14 [see **265.21**].

1966

2868   ANONYMOUS. "Quand Beckett tourne *Comédie*," *Arts,* Jan. 19-25, 1966, p. 29.
Photo story of the filming of *Comédie*.

2869   _____. *Times Literary Supplement,* March 10, 1966, p. 202.
Review of Richard Aldington symposium [see **44**].

2870   _____. "The Essential Q." *Times Literary Supplement,* June 30, 1966, p. 570.
Review of *Imagination Dead Imagine* and **709**.

2871   ABIRACHED, Robert. "Images d'enfer," *Nouvel Observateur,* 70 (March 16-22, 1966), 40.
Review of *Comédie* and *Va et vient*.

2872   BABY, Yvonne. *Le Monde,* Aug. 30, 1966, p. 10.
Review of *Comédie* (film version) at Venice Festival.

2873   C[RAWFORD], S[tanley]. "The Great Buster," *Film,* 44 (Winter, 1965-66), 23-24.
Review of *Film*.

2874   CURTISS, Thomas Quinn. "Beckett: He Never Complains, Never Explains," *New York Times,* Feb. 27, 1966, sec. 10, p. 13.
Review of *Play* as film.

2875   EDSTRÖM, Mauritz. "Ansiktet pa Väggen," *Ord Och Bild,* LXXV (1966), 19-24.
Review of *Film*.

2876   ELROD, Norman. *"Come and Go,"* *Schauspielgruppe Dr. Elrod,* Nov. 1966. 13 pp.
Program.

2877   HEPPENSTALL, Rayner. *The Listener,* LXXVI (Oct. 20, 1966), 579-580.
Review of **1233**, Beckett mentioned.

2878   HOBSON, Harold. *Sunday Times,* Jan. 9, 1966, p. 23.
Reviews of student productions of *Endgame* and *Act Without Words* [*I*].

2879   JEAN, Raymond. "M le coincé," *Nouvel Observateur,* 74 (April 13-19, 1966), 49.
Review of *Comédie et actes divers*.

2880   JOUFFROY, Alain. "Un Cri dans la nuit," *L'Express,* Feb. 21-27, 1966, pp. 70-71.
Review of *Comédie et actes divers*.

2881   KANTERS, Robert. "Anthologie de la nouvelle avant-garde," *L'Express,* March 14-20, 1966, p. 64.
About *Comédie* and *Va et vient*.

1966

2882   KOTT, Jan. "A Note on Beckett's Realism," *Tulane Drama Review,* X, no. 3 (1966), 156-159; trans. Boleslaw Taborski.
On Beckett's theater in general.

2883   LEMARCHAND, Jacques. "Spectacle Beckett, Pinget, Ionesco à l'Odéon," *Figaro Littéraire,* March 17, 1966, p. 14.
About *Comédie* and *Va et vient.*

2884   POWELL, Dilys. "Vindicating Venice," *Sunday Times,* Sept. 4, 1966.
About *Comédie* (film version).

2885   REID, Alec. "Samuel Beckett at 60," *Manchester Guardian Weekly,* April 21, 1966, p. 12.
A short biographical sketch of Beckett.

2886   RICKS, Christopher. "Beckett's Bizarre Text," *Sunday Times,* Feb. 20, 1966, p. 31.
Review of *Imagination Dead Imagine.*

2887   TREWIN, J. C. *The Listener,* LXXVI (July 21, 1966), 103.
Review of *Eh Joe* (BBC-TV production).

2888   WALL, Stephen. *Essays in Criticism,* XVI (April, 1966), 245-252.
Review of *How It Is;* see also **707g, 708n, 709i, 710f,** and **713i.**

2889   WILLIAMS, Vivian Craddock. "Samuel Beckett's 'Birthday Book' . . . Commemorating the Gap between New Writing and Old Readers," *Daily Telegraph Weekend Magazine,* 81 (April 15, 1966), 15.
On forthcoming Calder and Boyars publication [see **719**].

12.

Criticism of Samuel Beckett on the BBC, 1955-1965

We are grateful to M. J. Tulloch, Office of the Director of External Broadcasting, the BBC, for the list of programs devoted to criticism and discussion of Samuel Beckett. The abbreviations HS, TP, and Net 3 refer to Home Service, Third Programme, and Network 3, respectively. The name of the program is italicized.

1955

3000   LAMBERT, J. W. *"Waiting for Godot," The Critics* (HS), Aug. 21, 1955.
Theater review.

1956

3001   MILNE, Lennox. *"Waiting for Godot," Arts Review* (HS), Aug. 1, 1956.
Theater review.

1957

3002   GRAY, Ronald. *"Waiting for Godot," The Critics* (TP), Jan. 9, 1957 [see **1391**].
A Christian interpretation of the play.

3003   BUDBERG, Marie. *"All That Fall," The Critics* (HS), Jan. 20, 1957.
Review of the radio broadcast.

3004   FRASER, G. S. *"All That Fall," Comment* (TP), Jan. 24, 1957.
Broadcast review.

3005   WHITEMAN, H. J. *"Fin de partie"* and *"Acte sans paroles," Comment* (TP), April 4, 1957.
Theater review.

3006   LEVENTHAL, A. J. "Samuel Beckett: Poet and Pessimist" (TP), April 30, 1957 [see **1399**].

1958

3007   BOWLES, Patrick. "A Master Work of Disillusion" (TP), June 15,
            1958 [see **1430**].

Patrick Bowles spent eighteen months working with Beckett translating *Molloy*,
and he suggests it marks the turning point in Beckett's writing.

1959

3008   MILLER, Karl. *"Embers"* and *"All That Fall,"* Comment (TP),
            June 25, 1959.

Broadcast review.

3009   GILLETT, Eric. *"An Anthology of Mexican Poetry,"* World of
            Books (Net 3), July 16, 1959. Trans. Beckett.

Review.

1961

3010   BRAY, Barbara. *"Comment c'est,"* Comment (TP), Feb. 2, 1961.

Review.

3011   BULL, Peter. *"Waiting for Godot,"* Comment (TP), April 14, 1961.

Documentary on the play.

3012   BRAY, Barbara (novels), Patrick MAGEE (plays), Martin ESSLIN
            (plays), Karl MILLER (plays), Ossia TRILLING. *"Happy
            Days,"* New Comment (TP), Oct. 11, 1961.

Discussion.

1962

3013   DONOGHUE, Denis. "The Play of Words" (TP), June 30, 1962 [see
            1666].

Denis Donoghue argues that dramatists such as Beckett have come close to
refining their work out of existence by their concentration on purely verbal
events to the exclusion of dramatic situation and real dialogue.

3014   GASCOIGNE, Bamber. *"Happy Days,"* The Critics (HS), Nov. 18,
            1962.

Review.

3015   BRAY, Barbara. *"Words and Music,"* The Critics (HS), Dec. 9, 1962.

Broadcast review.

1963

3016   KITCHIN, Laurence. "Compressionism: The Cage and the Scream"
            (TP), Jan. 8, 1963 [see **1737**].

An attempt to isolate and trace the history of a crucial twentieth-century trend
in the theater from Strindberg to Beckett.

1963

3017 MacNIECE, Louis, and Jack MacGOWRAN. *New Comment* (TP), July 11, 1963.
Discussion about Beckett's work from the actor's viewpoint.

1964

3018 HOBSON, Harold. *"Play," The Critics* (HS), April 19, 1964.
Theater review.

3019 BRAY, Barbara. *"Endgame," New Comment* (TP), June 2, 1964.
Barbara Bray talks to Jack MacGowran and Patrick Magee who were working with Beckett on the Paris production of *Endgame*.

3020 LAMBERT, J. W. *"Endgame," The Critics* (HS), July 19, 1964.
Review.

3021 RICKS, Christopher. "The Roots of Samuel Beckett" (TP), Nov. 18, 1964 [see **1822**].
Discussion of the plays and novels of Beckett in relation to their literary ancestors.

1965

3022 RHODE, Eric. *"Waiting for Godot," New Comment* (TP), Jan. 6, 1965.
Review.

3023 LAMBERT, J. W. *"Waiting for Godot," The Critics* (HS), Jan. 10, 1965.
Review.

3024 FLETCHER, John. "Beckett as Critic" (TP), Oct. 2, 1965 [see **1847**].
Beckett's criticism helps us to view his work in a fresh light.

13.

Sources of
Biographical Information

Standard Works of Reference,
Journals, and Yearbooks

3050   *The Public Schools Yearbook.* London, 1924-1928. Rubric "Portora Royal School."
Information about Samuel Beckett's school and university career.

3051   *Dublin University Calendar.* Dublin, 1924-1933, 1959-1960.
Information about Beckett's courses and academic progress, and later about his honorary degree.

3052   *TCD: A College Miscellany.* Dublin, 1924-1932.
The files of *TCD,* the newspaper of the students at Trinity College, Dublin, contain several minor items of information about Beckett's activities in sports and other spheres, especially under the following dates: Nov. 13, 1924, p. 29; Feb. 26, 1925, pp. 115, 116; March 12, 1925, p. 137; May 28, 1925, p. 166; June 18, 1925, p. 197; Feb. 25, 1926, p. 102; June 3, 1926, pp. 163, 168; May 19, 1927, p. 232; Feb. 12, 1931, pp. 86, 87; Feb. 4, 1932, p. 74.

3053A   *Trinity College Record Volume.* Dublin and London, 1951. Pp. 99, 282, 357, 363.

3053B   *Catalogue of Graduates of the University of Dublin.* Vol. V (1917-1931). Dublin, 1931. P. 7. Vol. VI (1931-1952). Dublin, 1952. P. 9.
Information about Samuel Beckett's university career.

3054   *Thom's Directory, Ireland.* Dublin, 1960. Vol. I: *Dublin, City and County,* pp. 105, 489, 911, 930.
Information about the Becketts' family firm and residences.

3055A   *Who's Who in France.* Paris, 1959   .

3055B   *International Who's Who.* London, 1960——.
Standard biographical entries on Samuel Beckett.

Books

1941

3056   GORMAN, Herbert. *James Joyce: A Definitive Biography*. London: John Lane, The Bodley Head, 1941. Pp. 295, 346. [See **1100**.]

1946

3057   GUGGENHEIM, Marguerite ("Peggy"). *Out of This Century: The Informal Memoirs of Peggy Guggenheim*. New York: Dial Press, 1946. Pp. 194-242, with photograph of Samuel Beckett with Bram van Velde (*ca.* 1938), f.p. 278. [See also **30**, **492C**, Note, **1102**.]

1957

3058   GILBERT, Stuart. *Letters of James Joyce*. London: Faber and Faber, 1957. Pp. 280-281, 283, 323. [See **1115**.]

3059   HUTCHINS, Patricia. *James Joyce's World*. London: Methuen, 1957. Pp. 168-169, 207. [See **35**, **1116**.]

1959

3060   ATHERTON, James S. *The Books at the Wake*. London: Faber and Faber, 1959. P. 16. [See **1125**.]

3061   ELLMANN, Richard. *James Joyce*. New York: Oxford University Press, 1959; French trans., Paris: Gallimard, 1962. [See **14**, **1128**.]

1960

3062   GUGGENHEIM, Marguerite ("Peggy"). *Confessions of an Art Addict*. New York: Macmillan; London: André Deutsch, 1960. Pp. 48-61. A revised version of **1102**, **3057**, giving impressions of Beckett in 1938.

1961

3063   MONNIER, Adrienne. *Dernières gazettes et écrits divers*. Paris: Mercure de France, 1961. Pp. 15-20. [See **486**, Note, and **1029**.]

1962

3064   SIMPSON, Alan. *Beckett and Behan, and a Theatre in Dublin*. London: Routledge and Kegan Paul, 1962. Pp. 62-97, 98-137. [See **1049**.]

1964

3065   GLENAVY, Lady Beatrice. *Today We Will Only Gossip*. London: Constable, 1964. Pp. 48, 178-179, with photograph of Samuel Beckett as a young child kneeling at his mother's knee, f.p. 160. Information on the Dublin background of Beckett's childhood and the Gogarty case [see **3071**].

1964

3066 O'CONNOR, Ulick. *Oliver St. John Gogarty: A Poet and His Times.* London: Jonathan Cape, 1964. Pp. 280 ff.
The Gogarty libel action [see **3071**].

1966

3067 FOOT, M. R. D. *S. O. E. in France: An Account of the Work of the British Special Operations Executive in France, 1940-1944.* London: Her Majesty's Stationery Office, 1966. Pp. 319-320.
Samuel Beckett's Resistance association with the agent Armel Guerne.

Articles

1933

3068 ANONYMOUS. "Wills and Bequests," *The Times,* Nov. 3, 1933, p. 7.
"Other latest wills include the following: BECKETT, Mr. William Frank [the author's father], of Dublin, quantity surveyor (personal estate in England and Ireland): Gross value £42,395."

1936

3069 ANONYMOUS. "Notes on Contributors," *Transition,* 24 (June, 1936), 5.
Includes Samuel Beckett.

1937

3070A ANONYMOUS. "Poet Accused of 'Venomous and Vile' Libels" and "These Names Make News: Hickey in Dublin," *Daily Express,* Nov. 23, 1937, pp. 5 and 6, respectively.

3070B _____. "£900 Verdict Against Poet," *Daily Express,* Nov. 24, 1937, p. 7.

Mentions of Samuel Beckett in connection with the Gogarty libel action. The case was also reported in the London *Daily Mail* of the same dates, but without reference to Samuel Beckett [see **3071**].

3071 _____. *Irish Times,* Nov. 23, 1937, p. 5, cols. 4 and 5; and Nov. 24, 1937, p. 5, cols. 3, 5, and 6.

Full report of the action for libel brought by Henry Morris Sinclair, whose late twin brother had married Samuel Beckett's aunt, against Dr. Oliver St. John Gogarty in respect of two passages in *As I Was Going Down Sackville Street;* report includes cross-examination of Samuel Beckett as plaintiff's witness by Mr. J. M. FitzGerald KC (for Gogarty) and summing-up from the judge.

3072 _____. *The Times,* May 14, 1937, p. 14*d*; June 8, 1937, p. 18*a*; June 21, 1937, p. 10*e*; Nov. 23, 1937, p. 16*c*; Nov. 24, 1937, p. 16*e*; Nov. 30, 1937, p. 4*f*.
Information on the Gogarty case [see **3071**].

1938

3073   ANONYMOUS. *The Times,* Jan. 8, 11, 1938 (3d and 4th eds. only),
            pp. 9*b* and 11*f*, respectively.
News item on the stabbing of Samuel Beckett in Paris.

1948

3074   ANONYMOUS. "Notes about Contributors," *Transition Forty-Eight,*
            2 ([June], 1948), 146-147. Condensed version reprinted in *Books
            Abroad,* XXIII (Summer, 1949), 247-248, under the title "Why
            Samuel Beckett Writes in French."

1953

3075   BLIN, Roger, Adrienne MONNIER, and J. THOMAS. *Arts-
            Spectacles,* 418 (July 3-9, 1953), 5.
Three personal impressions of Samuel Beckett by friends.

1954

3076   MONTGOMERY, Niall. "No Symbols Where None Intended,"
            New World Writing, 5 (1954), 324-337 [see **1336**].

1956

3077   ANONYMOUS. "The Man Himself," *Trinity News,* III (June 7,
            1956), 5 [see also **33**].
Samuel Beckett, biographical note.

3078   _____. "Portrait Gallery: Samuel Beckett," *Irish Times,* Aug. 18,
            1956, p. 8.

3079   JOYCE, James. *Mercure de France,* CCCXXVI (Jan., 1956), 123-
            124.
Letter in French to Adrienne Monnier, mentioning Samuel Beckett and his
address (6, rue des Favorites), and *Murphy.* The letter, dated March 28, 1940,
from St.-Gérand-le-Puy, asks Mlle. Monnier if Maurice Denhof has published
recently in *Mercure de France* a review of *Murphy* and *At Swim Two Birds,*
both admired by Joyce. Denhof's article never appeared in the journal.

3080   SHENKER, Israel. "Moody Man of Letters," *New York Times,* May
            6, 1956, sec. 2, pp. x, 1, and 3 [see **1377**].
Interview with Samuel Beckett.

1957

3081   KONSTANTINOVIĆ, R. *Nin,* Aug. 18, 1957.
Interview with Samuel Beckett.

1958

3082 ANONYMOUS. "Profile: Messenger of Gloom," *The Observer,* Nov. 9, 1958.

This profile of Samuel Beckett was substantially reproduced by Rayner Heppenstall in **1028**.

3083 SAY, A. de. "Roussillon," *L'Arc,* 2 (Spring, 1958), 83.

Samuel Beckett in the Vaucluse, 1943.

3084 SCHNEIDER, Alan. "Waiting for Beckett: A Personal Chronicle," *Chelsea Review,* 2 (Autumn, 1958), 3-20 [see also **36, 1464**].

1959

3085 ANONYMOUS. "Honorary Degrees Conferred by Dublin University . . . Samuel Barclay Beckett, Litt. D," *Irish Times,* July 3, 1959, p. 6, col. 4, with photograph of Samuel Beckett in academic dress, p. 1.

Translation of Latin Oration by Public Orator, Dr. W. B. Stanford, F. T. C. D.

1961

3086 ANONYMOUS [*pseud.* Atticus]. *Sunday Times,* June 18, 1961, p. 13, and July 2, 1961, p. 13 [see **2436, 2438**].

Samuel Beckett at a cricket match with Harold Hobson.

3087 AUBARÈDE, Gabriel d'. "En attendant . . . Beckett," *Nouvelles Littéraires,* Feb. 16, 1961, pp. 1, 7. Engl. trans. in **1576**.

Interview with Samuel Beckett.

3088 DRIVER, Tom F. "Beckett by the Madeleine," *Columbia University Forum,* IV (Summer, 1961), 21-25 [see **1599**].

Interview with Samuel Beckett.

3089 WALDBERG, Patrick. "Adrienne Monnier," *Critique,* 164 (Jan., 1961), 15.

Reference to Beckett.

1962

3090 MAROWITZ, Charles. "A Quick Walk Away from Samuel Beckett," *Village Voice,* VII (March 1, 1962), 1, 13. Reprinted in *Encore,* IX (March-April, 1962), 43-45.

Interview with Samuel Beckett.

1963

3091 HANOTEAU, Guillaume. "Samuel Beckett: Écrivain génial ou maître de l'ennui?" *Paris-Match,* 762 (Nov. 16, 1963), 111 ff.

A biographical piece marred by errors of fact.

1964

3092   MIGNON, Paul-Louis. "Le Théâtre de A jusqu'à Z: Samuel Beckett," *L'Avant-Scène du Théâtre*, 313 (June 15, 1964), 8 [see also **148.2, 149.1**].

Interview and biographical notes.

3093   SIGAL, Clancy. "Is This the Person To Murder Me?" *Sunday Times (Color Magazine)*, March 1, 1964, pp. 17-22.

Account of Beckett at *Endgame* rehearsals.

Background Information

1945

3094   ANONYMOUS. *Irish Times*, April 30, 1945, p. 1.
News item about the Irish Red Cross Hospital about to be set up at Saint-Lô, in which Beckett later worked.

1946

3095   ANONYMOUS. "The Irish Red Cross Hospital at Saint-Lo [*sic*], by Our Paris Correspondent," *Irish Times*, Aug. 21, 1946, p. 4.

14.
Principal
Bibliographical Sources

✓ 3100 *Abstracts of English Studies.* Boulder, Colo.: An Official Publication of the National Council of Teachers of English.

3101 *Annual Bibliography of English Language and Literature.* London: Cambridge University Press (Modern Humanities Research Association).

3102 *Bibliographie der Deutschen Zeitschriftenliteratur.* Osnabrück: Felix Dietrich.

3103 *Bibliographie der Fremdsprachigen Zeitschriftenliteratur.* Osnabrück: Felix Dietrich.

3104 *British Museum General Catalogue of Printed Books.* London: Trustees of the British Museum.

✓ 3105 *Book Review Digest.* New York: H. W. Wilson.

3106 *Bulletin critique du livre français.* Paris: Association pour la diffusion la pensée française.

3107 *Carpenter Masters' Essays.* New York: Butler Library, Columbia University.

3108 *Catholic Periodical Index.* Haverford, Pa.: Catholic Library Association.

3109 Clipping files of the New York Public Library. New York: Drama Department, Lincoln Center Branch.

3110 COHN, Ruby. "Checklist of Samuel Beckett Criticism," *Perspective*, XI (Autumn, 1959), 193-196 [see **900**].

3111 ———. *Samuel Beckett: The Comic Gamut.* New Brunswick, N.J.: Rutgers University Press, 1962. Pp. 328-340. [See **704**.]

3112 DAVIS, Robin J. "A Bibliography of Samuel Beckett." Unpublished thesis submitted in partial requirement for the Diploma in Librarianship. University of London, Aug. 1965. 170 pp. [See **864**.]

3113   *Dissertation Abstracts.* Ann Arbor, Mich.: University Microfilms, Inc. [See index *s.v.* "Samuel Beckett."]

3114   ENSINK, Joan L. "Samuel Beckett: An Annotated Bibliography of Criticism, 1934-1965." Unpublished M.A. thesis. Columbia University, New York, 1966. 205 pp. [See **865**.]

✓ 3115   *Essay and General Literature Index.* New York: H. W. Wilson.

3116   *Études anglaises.* Paris: Didier. [See section "Revue des Revues" in every issue.]

3117   FEDERMAN, Raymond. *Journey to Chaos: Samuel Beckett's Early Fiction.* Berkeley and Los Angeles: University of California Press, 1965. Pp. 217-235. [See **712**.]

3118   FLETCHER, John. *The Novels of Samuel Beckett.* London: Chatto and Windus, 1964. Pp. 234-251. [See **708**.]

3119   _____. *Principales études consacrées à Samuel Beckett* (Extrait du catalogue). Paris: Éditions de Minuit, Jan., 1966.

3120   _____. Bibliography in *Jean-Jacques Mayoux über Beckett.* Frankfort on the Main: Suhrkamp, 1966. Pp. 123-143. [See **716**.]

3121   *French VII Bibliography: Critical and Biographical References for the Study of Contemporary French Literature.* New York: A Joint Publication of the French VII Section (Modern Language Association of America) and of the French Institute. General ed.: Douglas W. Alden.

3122   FRIEDMAN, Melvin J., ed. *Revue des Lettres Modernes, Samuel Beckett: Configuration Critique, no. 8,* 100 (1964), 169-184. Compiled by Jackson R. Bryer. [See **902, 1773**.]

✓ 3123   *Index to Book Reviews in the Humanities.* Williamston, Mich.: Phillip Thomson.

3124   *Index to Little Magazines.* Ed. Eugene P. Sheehy and Kenneth A. Lohf. Denver: Alan Swallow, 1948-1959.

3125   *Index Translationum.* International Bibliography of Translations, n.s. Paris: Unesco.

3126   *International Index to Periodicals* (after 1964 retitled *Social Sciences and Humanities Index*). New York: H. W. Wilson.

3127   KLAPP, Otto. *Bibliographie der Französischen Literaturwissenschaft.* Frankfort on the Main: Vittorio Klostermann.

✓ 3128   *MLA International Index.* Modern Language Association of America. New York: Kraus Reprint.

3129   *National Union Catalogue, Author List.* Washington, D.C.: Library of Congress.

3130   *New York Times Index.* New York: New York Times.

3131   *PMLA Annual Bibliography.* Menasha, Wisc.: George Banta.

3132   *Polska Bibliographia Literacka.* Warsaw and Lodz: Panstwowe Wydawnictwo Naukowe (State Scientific Publishing House), 1956-1959.

3133   *Reader's Guide to Periodical Literature.* New York: H. W. Wilson.

3134   *Revue d'Histoire du Théâtre.* Paris: Centre National de la Recherche Scientifique.

3135   *Subject Index to Periodicals* (after 1960 retitled *British Humanities Index*). London: Library Association.

3136   *Times (London) Official Index.* London: The Times Publishing Company.

3137   *Times (London) Literary Supplement (Yearly Index).* London: The Times Publishing Company.

3138   WEBB, Eugene. "Critical Writing on Samuel Beckett: A Bibliography," *West Coast Review* (Simon Fraser University, Burnaby, B. C.), I (Spring, 1966), 56-70.

3139   WENNING, Henry W. *Modern Authors* (catalog no. 5). New Haven, Conn.: Henry W. Wenning, Rare Books, n.d. 68 pp.

3140   *Year's Work in English Studies.* Oxford: English Association, Oxford University Press.

3141   *The Year's Work in Modern Language Studies.* Cambridge, England: Cambridge University Press (Modern Humanities Research Association).

Appendixes

Appendix I

Selection of Rare Items at
Ohio State University Library, Columbus,
and Manuscripts and Marked Proofs
at University of Texas Library, Austin

34   *All That Fall.* Ams* with extensive A revs and inscription to Jake Schwartz dated 1957 January. [51 pp.] 1956 September. Bound. [Tex.]
       ———. TccmsS with one T rev and A emends. 1956 (Paris). Bound. [Tex.]
       ———. Mimeo (32 pp.). 1957. BBC entry for the Italia Prize. Paralleled text in French (*Tous ceux qui tombent*). In spiral booklet. [34 cm. One of 60 H.C. Autographed by the author. In both Ohio State University Library and University of Texas Library.]

501   *Anthology of Mexican Poetry.* Tccms with A emends and A note S. 1950. [Tex.]

613   *Bosquets de Bondy, Les.* AmsS with A revs and A note [2 bound notebooks]. *Ca.* 1945. "One of first writings in French . . . unpublished, jettisoned." [Tex.]

263B   *Calmant, Le.* Ams with A revs and A note S [45 pp.]. 1946 Dec. 23 [started]. "Figures in Nouvelles et Textes pour rien." Boxed. [Tex.]

148   *Cendres.* Tms with A revs and A note [14 pp.]. N.d. Boxed. [Tex.]

268   *Comment c'est.* Ams with A revs and A note S [6 exercise books]. 1959-1960. Included with this: 3 successive Tmss with A revs. Boxed. [Tex.]

147   *Dernière Bande, La.* Tccms with A emends and A note [9 pp.]. N.d. Boxed. [Tex.]

38   *Embers.* Tccms with A emends and A note [10 pp.]. N.d. Boxed. [Tex.]
       ———. Mimeo (13 pp.). 1959. BBC entry for the Italia Prize. Paralleled text in French (*Cendres*). In spiral booklet. [34 cm. One of 60 H.C. Autographed by the author. Both Ohio and Tex.]

259   *En attendant Godot.* Ams with A emends [150 pp.]. N.d. Original French MS. Boxed. [Tex.]

254   *L'Expulsé.* AmsS with A revs and A note [1 bound notebook]. 1946 October 6-14. Boxed. [Tex.]

265A   *Fin de partie.* MS plus 3 TSS of successive versions and TS of *Endgame*. [Ohio.]

33   *From an Abandoned Work.* Ams with A emends and signed inscription to Jake Schwartz. "1954 or 1955." Boxed. [Tex.]

---

*Abbreviations taken from library catalogue cards, as received by compiler.

39   *Happy Days.* MS (dated October 1960–May 1961) and 4 successive TSS with many autograph corrections. [Ohio.]

384   *How It Is.* MS (2 notebooks) plus first TS and corrected proofs for John Calder (dated London March 1964) and Grove Press (dated February 1964). [Ohio.]

260   *L'Innommable.* Ams with A revs and A note S [2 bound notebooks]. 1949-1950. "Original MS." Boxed. [Tex.]

37   *Krapp's Last Tape.* Four successive Tmss with A revs and A inscriptions to Jake Schwartz (various pagings). 1958. Boxed. [Tex.]
        ———— and **38** *Embers.* Page proofs with numerous corrections (36 pp.). 1959. Inscribed to Jake Schwartz 1960 Feb. Boxed. [Tex.]

375   *Malone Dies.* TccmsS with A emends and A note (159 pp.). 1956. Boxed. [Tex.]

258   *Malone meurt.* AmsS with A revs and A note S [2 bound notebooks, 1 containing part of **32** *Watt*]. 1947-1948. Original title: "L'Absent." Boxed. [Tex.].

257   *Molloy.* Ams with A emends [388 pp.]. 1947. Bound in four notebooks. [Tex.]

25   *Murphy.* TccmsS with A emends and A note [192 pp.]. 1936 June 26 [completed]. Bound and boxed. [Tex.]

614   *Premier Amour.* Ams with extensive A revs and A note S [38 pp.]. 1946 Oct. 28–Nov. 12. "Unpublished—jettisoned." Boxed. [Tex.]

263D-R *Textes pour rien.* Ams with A revs and A notes S [2 spiral notebooks]. 1950-1952. Also some unpublished material, **617**. [Tex.]

377   *Unnamable, The.* AmsS with A emends and deletions and A notes, one signed [3 bound notebooks]. 1957-1958. "This is the original Ms of my translation of L'Innommable." Boxed. [Tex.]
        ————. Composite T and Tccms with A revs and A note [146 pp.]. 1958 June (finished). "1st revision up to page 25." [Tex.]

373   *Waiting for Godot.* AmS with A emends [163 pp. in 2 notebooks]. N.d. Boxed. [Tex.]

32   *Watt.* AmsS with A revs and A note [6 bound notebooks, 1 containing part of **258** *Malone meurt*]. 1940-1945. Boxed. [Tex.]
        ————. Composite T and Tccms/inc with A revs and A note S. N.d. Boxed. [Tex.]

5   *Whoroscope.* Ams with A revs and A note S [5 pp. on 3 leaves]. 1930. "Original Ms of my first published poem." On verso last page: unpublished sonnet. Boxed. [Tex.]

NOTE. We understand from Mrs. Lois Friedberg-Dobry that Box I, Folder 5, of the Morton Dauwen Zabel Papers, deposited in the Department of Special Collections, University of Chicago Library, contains author's TS copies of **9D** (titled "Moly"), **22B**, **22E**, and **22N** (variants), the whole bearing the date Nov. 1, 1934.

Appendix II

Variants in the Works of Samuel Beckett, with Special Reference to *Bing*

In Part One we frequently had occasion to draw attention to the existence of variants in Samuel Beckett's works. This was especially true, for example, in the case of the *Nouvelles* (**252.1, 254.1, 372.1**); indeed, more entries are noted to have variants than not. It was neither feasible nor necessary to detail the exact nature and extent of the variants: not feasible because of the space required; and unnecessary because the variants can be seen by interested scholars in reasonably accessible published texts. Nevertheless this bibliography would be incomplete without an example of the kind of variants that occur in Beckett's writings. We are therefore profoundly grateful to Mr. Beckett for his generosity in making available to us all ten typescript drafts of the recent text *Bing*, covering its complex and changing development from first conception to final copy dispatched to the printer. We reproduce them below in their entirety, followed by Mr. Beckett's own English translation of the definitive French text, *Ping*. Typescript matter in the original is printed here in normal roman characters; manuscript additions are printed in italics. Matter struck through is enclosed within square brackets, and, where this is illegible, a series of x's gives some guidance as to the extent of the erasure. Illegible autograph additions are indicated by a series of periods, and autograph corrections of mere typing errors are usually ignored.

For permission to print both the preliminary drafts and the final versions we offer grateful thanks to Samuel Beckett, to Jérôme Lindon of the Éditions de Minuit, Paris, to Calder and Boyars, Ltd., London, and to Grove Press, Inc., New York. *These texts, both published and hitherto unpublished, are fully protected by copyright with the aforementioned publishers.*

Text 1.

[Largeur un mètre. Profondeur un mètre. Hauteur deux mètres. Angles droits. Quatre murs cardinaux. Un mètre carré de sol plat. Même chose plafond. Mesures approximatives comme toutes à venir. Pas d'ouvertures. Grand éclairage. Tout est blanc.] Pas d'ombre. [Des périodes de noir. Grande chaleur. Des périodes de froid. Deux niches centre est et ouest. Une échelle blanche d'un mètre. Tout est caoutchouc. Sous les coups sans céder sonne à peine. Quelques traces noires. Un corps nu d'un mètre. Petite tête lisse. Jambes courtes même par rapport. Tronc cylindrique long par rapport. Pas de poils. Petits bras pendants. Membre glabre. Brèves demi-érections spontanées. Tout petits pieds tournés vers l'extérieur. Très droit et blanc. Longues immobilités. Seuls les yeux et encore. Déplacements très soudains et rapides. Tout à coup de nouveau immobile ailleurs. Certains insectes des étangs.] Toujours même pose. Petites [jambes serrées. Pieds à angle droit. Petits bras pendouillants. Mains à l'échelle ouvertes creux en avant. Très droit. Petite tête droite bien dans l'axe. Cille presque pas.] Si peu de savoir. Si peu à savoir. [Un mètre sur un mètre sur deux mètres. Grande chaleur. Périodes de grand froid. Grande lumière.

Périodes de noir. Non liées. Chaleur lumière. Chaleur noir. Froid lumière. Froid noir. Chaleur lumière et noir. Froid lumière et noir. Lumière chaleur et froid. Noir chaleur et froid. Changements foudroyants. Paf noir. Paf éblouissement. Paf fournaise et glace. Yeux bleu de glaire. Presque blancs. Voient tout. Très écartés. Enorme éventail. Certains insectes. Depuis toujours pour toujours douleurs sourdes partout. Fidèle indémêlable harmonie. Petite tête lisse et ronde. Blancheur d'os. Plus blanc que les six faces. Dedans silence. Brefs murmures de loin en loin.

Tous

xxxxxxxxxxxx Toujours les mêmes. Ils sont sus. Il manque un échelon. Par terre dans un coin. Blanc sur blanc invisible. Le troisième celui du milieu. Pas repérable. Rien xx de repérable. Petit vide à mi-montée. Echelle blanche invisible. Position sue. Dressée contre le mur sous l'une ou l'autre niche. Niches blanches invisibles. Position sue centre est et ouest. Chaque millimètre carré jette son rayon. D'un autre blanc le corps à peine. Tout entier su dehors et dedans. xxxxxxxxxxxxxxxxxxxxxxxxxxxxxx xxxxxxxxxxxxxxxxxxxxxxxxxxx Immobilités. Pas un frémissement. A peine les yeux. Paf ailleurs. xxxxxxxxxxxxxxxxxxxxxxxxxxxxxxx Vers d'autres traces.]

$4 \times 2 + 2 \times 1$
10 mètres carrés
originellement
1o traces [à la création] noires
pâlies diversement jusqu'au
gris pâle presque blanc
ou effacées

[Doodle]

Text 2.

Grande lumière. Un corps nu d'un mètre. Un mètre carré de sol plat. Tout [est]
                                                ne   *pas.*
caoutchouc. Sous les coups sans céder   sonne   [à peine.] Petite tête lisse. Angles droits. Une échelle blanche d'un mètre. Périodes de noir. Largeur un mètre. Pas d'ouvertures. Petites jambes serrées. Grande chaleur. Depuis toujours pour toujours douleurs sourdes partout indémêlable concert. Profondeur un mètre. Hauteur
                                          boule
deux mètres. Périodes de froid. Petite tête [ronde]. Quatre murs cardinaux.
        lisse
Tronc cylindrique [sans poils]. Tout [est] blanc. Un mètre carré de plafond plat. Longues immobilités. Seuls les yeux *à peine*. Périodes de grand froid. Traces *gris pâle à presque blanc.*
        [noires].   Petits bras pendouillants. Périodes de noir. Un échelon par terre invisible blanc sur blanc. Dix mille millimètres carrés. Plus. Chacun jette son rayon. Petits pieds à angle droit. Chaleur lumière. Chaleur noir. Froid lumière. Froid noir. Chaleur lumière et [froid.] noir. Froid lumière et noir. Lumière chaleur
                                        foudroyants
et froid. Noir chaleur et froid. Déplacements [brusques]. Soudain immobile[s]
                                                                Hop
ailleurs. Certains insectes [des étangs]. Un mètre sur un mètre sur deux mètres. [Paf]
        Hop   *Hop*
noir. [Paf] éblouissement. [Paf] fournaise et glace. Très droit. Blancheur d'os plus blanc que les six faces. Deux niches centre est et ouest. Yeux bleu de glaire presque
        près des tempes. Champ énorme.
blancs [. Voient tout. Enorme éventail.] Certains insectes. Echelle blanche invisible. Position sue. Niches blanches invisibles. Position sue centre est et ouest. Petite tête

droite bien dans l'axe. Dedans silence. Rares brefs murmures toujours les mêmes
    fouillis gris pâle   *du*
tous sus. Traces [noires].   Petites jambes collées comme cousues [depuis le]
cul [jusqu'] aux talons joints à angle droit. Un mètre carré de sol plat. Immobilités.
           Hop
Pas un frémissement. A peine les yeux. [Paf] ailleurs. Vers d'autres traces.

Text 3.

                       Partout
Grande lumière. Un corps nu d'un mètre. Un mètre carré de sol plat. [Tout]
            aucun son
caoutchouc. Sous les coups sans céder [ne sonne pas]. Petite tête lisse. Angles droits
partout. Une échelle blanche d'un mètre. Période[s] de noir. Largeur un mètre. [Pas
d'ouvertures.] Petites jambes serrées. Grande chaleur. Depuis toujours pour toujours
douleurs sourdes partout indémêlable concert. Profondeur un mètre. Hauteur deux
mètres. Périodes de froid. Petite tête boule. Quatre murs cardinaux. Tronc cylindrique lisse. [Tout] blanc *partout.* Un mètre carré de plafond plat. Longues
immobilités. Seuls les yeux à peine. Périodes de grand froid. Traces gris pâle à
presque blanc. Petits bras pendouillants. Périodes de noir. Un échelon par terre
invisible blanc. Dix mille millimètres carrés *lumineux.* Plus. [Chacun jette son rayon.]
Petits pieds à angle droit. *Systèmes indépendants.* Chaleur lumière. Chaleur noir.
Froid lumière. Froid noir. Chaleur lumière et [froid] noir. Froid lumière et noir.
Lumière chaleur et froid. Noir chaleur et froid. Déplacements foudroyants. Soudain
immobile ailleurs. Certains insectes. Toujours même pose. Un mètre sur un mètre
sur deux mètres. Hop noir. Hop éblouissement. Hop fournaise et glace. Très droit.
Blancheur d'os plus blanc que les six faces. Deux niches centre est et ouest. Yeux
bleu de glaire presque blanc près des tempes. Champ énorme. Certains insectes.
Echelle blanche invisible. Position sue. Niches blanches invisibles. Position sue centre
est et ouest. Petite tête droite bien dans l'axe. Dedans silence. Rares brefs murmures
toujours les mêmes tous sus. Traces fouillis gris pâle. Petites jambes collées comme
cousues du cul aux talons joints à angle droit. Un mètre carré de sol plat. Immobilités.
Pas un frémissement. A peine les yeux. Hop ailleurs. Vers d'autres traces. Respiration inaudible. Pas d'ombre. Traces seules inachevées noires jadis pâlies pâlissant
gris pâle presque blanc sur blanc ou effacées. Niches sur mesure trente centimètres
de diamètre un mètre de profondeur. Nez deux trous blanc sur blanc invisibles.
Traces fouillis gris pâle à presque blanc sur blanc de signes insignifiants en partie
effacés sous forme de lacunes. Grande chaleur. Un mètre sur un mètre sur deux
mètres. Niches blanches invisibles. Niches reliées par un tunnel même calibre trente
centimètres dans l'épaisseur des murs. Oreilles deux trous blanc sur blanc invisibles.
      Partout   *sans céder aucun son.*
Périodes de noir. [Tout] caoutchouc. Sous les coups [ne cède ni ne sonne.] Traces
éclaboussures larges à peine comme la main humaine comme lorsqu'un petit oeuf
     Pas de demi-tour
s'écrase.   [Corps]   dans niche fourreau [impossible se retourner]. Bref murmure
de loin en loin que peut-être une issue. *Bouche mince commissure blanche invisible
comme cousue.* Périodes de grand froid. Grande lumière. Traces cinq en tout un par
  vers le coin   *vers le centre*
mur [dans un coin] plus un au plafond [dans un coin]. Petits pieds à angle droit
visibles plus blancs que le sol. Petit visage à la bouche d'une niche visible par différence
de blanc. Bref murmure de loin en loin que peut-être pas seul. Corps nu d'un mètre.
  Blanc
[Blancheur] d'os plus blanc[he] que les six faces. Passage d'une niche à l'autre par le

nord par un tunnel horizontal ellipsoïdal cylindrique même calibre trente centimètres quatre mètres de parcours. Ensemble du corps visible blanc d'os plus blanc que les six faces. Yeux seuls inachevés bleu pâle jadis pâlis presque blancs. Petite* mains *Tunnel[s] blanc[s] [même chose]* pendouillantes entrouvertes creux en avant. [Niches et tunnels comme le reste lumière et noir chaleur et froid.] Immobilités. Pas un frémissement. Seuls les yeux à peine seuls inachevés bleu de glaire pâlissant. *Tunnels lumière et noir chaleur et froid pareils.* Hop l'échelon à la main et paf toute volée mur sol tête sans colère sans bruit très bref. Hop de nouveau immobile lâché l'échelon sans bruit qui fuseau roule un instant sans bruit invisible. A la bouche de la niche d'entrée seuls les pieds talons en haut joint à angle droit seule possibilité. Douleurs aigues mal senties xxxxxxxx xxxxxxxx partout. [*Corps visible dans Petit corps visible dans les tunnels par différence de blanc*] *Dans le tunnel petit corps visible blanc d'os plus blanc que les parois.*

Text 4.

Grande lumière. Un corps nu d'un mètre. Un mètre carré de sol plat. Caoutchouc partout. Sous les coups sans céder aucun son.† Petite tête lisse. Angles droits partout. Une échelle blanche d'un mètre. Periodes de noir. Largeur un mètre. Petites jambes serrées. Grande chaleur. Depuis toujours xxxxx pour toujours douleurs sourdes partout indémêlable concert. Profondeur un mètre. Hauteur deux mètres. Périodes de froid. Petite tête boule. Quatre murs cardinaux. Tronc cylindrique lisse. Blanc partout. Un mètre carré de plafond plat. Longues immobilités. Seuls les yeux à peine. Périodes de grand froid. Traces gris pâle à presque blanc. Petits bras pendouillants. Périodes de noir. Un échelon par terre invisible blanc sur blanc. Dix mille millmètres carrés aveuglants. Plus. Petits pieds à angle droit. Chaleur lumière. Chaleur noir. Froid lumière. Froid noir. Chaleur lumière et noir. Froid lumière et noir. Lumière chaleur et froid. Noir chaleur et froid. Déplacements foudroyants. Soudain immobile ailleurs. Certains insectes. Toujours même pose. Un mètre sur un mètre sur deux mètres. Changements foudroyants. Hop noir. Hop éblouissement. Hop fournaise et glace. Toujours même pose. Très droit. Blancheur d'os plus blanc que les six faces. Deux niches centre faces est et ouest. Yeux près des tempes bleu de xxxxxx glaire presque blanc. Vaste champ. Certains insectes. Echelle blanche invisible. Position sue sous l'une ou l'autre niche. Niches blanches invisibles. Position sue centre est et ouest. Petite tête droite bien dans l'axe. Dedans silence. Rares brefs murmures toujours les mêmes tous sus. Traces fouillis gris pâle. Petites jambes collées comme cousues du cul aux talons joints à angle droit. Un mètre carré de sol plat. Immobilités. Pas un frémissement. Seuls les yeux à peine. Hop ailleurs. Vers d'autres traces. Respiration inaudible. Pas d'ombre. Noires jadis traces seules inachevées pâlies pâlissant gris pâle presque blanc sur blanc ou xxxx effacées. Niches sur mesure trente centimètres de diamètre un mètre de profondeur. Nez invisible deux trous blanc sur blanc. Traces fouillis gris pâle à presque blanc sur blanc de signes insignifiants en partie effacés sous forme de lacunes. Grande chaleur. Un mètre sur un mètre sur deux mètres. Niches blanches invisibles. Niches reliées par un tunnel même calibre trente centimètres dans l'épaisseur des murs. Oreilles deux trous blanc sur blanc invisibles. Périodes de noir. Cautchouc partout. Sous les coups sans céder aucun son. Traces éclaboussures larges comme la main comme lorsqu'un petit xxxxxxx oeuf s'écrase. Dans les niches fourreaux pas de demi-tour. Bref murmure de loin en loin que peut-être une issue. Bouche mince commissure blanche invisible comme cousue.

---

*Sic.

†These last two sentences underscored with wavy line in original.

Périodes de grand froid. Grande lumière. Traces cinq en tout un par mur vers l'angle plus un au plafond vers le centre. Petits pieds à angle droit visibles plus blancs que le sol. Petit visage à xxxx la bouche d'une niche visible par différence de blanc. xxxxx Bref murmure de loin en loin que peut-être pas seul. Corps d'un mètre blanc d'os plus blanc que les six faces. Passage d'une niche à l'autre *par le nord* par un tunnel horizontal ellipsoïdal cylindrique même calibre trente centimètres quatre mètres de parcours. Ensemble du corps visible blanc d'os plus blanc que les six faces. Bleu pâle jadis yeux seuls inachevés pâlis presque blancs. Petites mains pendouillantes entrouvertes creux en avant. Immobilités. Pas un frémissement. Seuls les yeux à peine seuls inachevés bleu de glaire pâlissant. Tunnel blanc lumière et noir chaleur et froid. Hop l'échelon à la main et paf toute volée sol mur tête sans colère sans bruit très bref. Hop de nouveau immobile lâché l'échelon sans bruit qui fuseau roule un instant sans bruit invisible. A la bouche d'entrée seuls les pieds talons en haut joints à angle droit seule possibilité. Douleurs aigues mal senties partout. Dans le tunnel petit corps visible blanc d'os plus blanc que les parois. A la bouche d'entrée petites plantes visibles talons en haut joints à angle droit par différence de blanc. Bref murmure de loin en loin que peut-être pas seul. Bref murmure de loin en loin que peut-être une issue. Bing* murmure. Bing long silence. Traces avec yeux seules inachevées aux quatre murs vers les quatre angles. Si entrée xxx par la bouche est tête à la bouche ouest à la suite du tunnel seule possibilité. Petites jambes collées comme cousues du cul aux talons joints à angle droit. Petits bras pendouillants mains entrouvertes creux en avant. Bing murmure de loin en loin que peut-être une nature. Petite tête boule bien dans l'axe yeux droit devant.

Text 5.

d'

Tout su. Grande lumière *blanche*. Un corps nu blanc [taille] un mètre. Un mètre
Angles invisibles
carré de sol blanc. Chiffres ronds. [Angles droits. Largeur un mètre.] Jambes serrées. Chaleur de serre. Pas de douleur. [Profondeur un mètre. Hauteur deux mètres. Ni poils ni cheveux.] Quatre murs [cardinaux] blancs *1 m. sur 2.* Un mètre carré de
Fixités.
plafond blanc. [Longues [*I*]immobilités] Seuls les yeux à peine. [Traces gris pâle
[*millions*]
presque blanc] [Dix mille] millimètres *dix millions* carrés rayonnants. *Traces gris pâle presque blanc.* [Bras pendants] [m]Mains *pendues* entrouvertes creux en avant.
Talons   *Soudainetés.*   *fixe*
[Pieds] joints à angle droit. [Déplacements soudains.] Soudain [immobile] ailleurs.
Pose unique
[Toujours] [même pose] [*toujours*.] [Un mètre sur un mètre sur deux mètres.] Six faces blanches *rayonnantes*. Un corps *nu* blanc d'un mètre. Chaleur de serre. Pas d'ombre. Pas de douleur. Corps blanc *1 mètre* invisible blanc sur blanc. Seuls près
haute
des tempes les yeux bleu pâle presque blanc. Tête *boule* bien [droite] bien dans l'axe
fixe
yeux [droit] devant. Dedans silence. Rares brefs murmures tous sus. Traces fouillis gris pâle. Jambes collées comme cousues du cul aux talons joints à angle droit. [Pas de memoire.] Un mètre carré de sol blanc. Chaleur de serre. [Pas de sueur.]
Fixités.
[Immobilités.] Seuls les yeux à peine. Hop ailleurs. Vers d'autres traces. Pas d'ombre. Traces seules inachevées jadis noires gris pâle presque blanc sur blanc ou effacées.

---

*First occurrence.

Nez invisible* deux trous blanc sur blanc. Murs blancs *rayonnants* un mètre sur deux.
sans sens
Traces fouillis gris pâle presque blanc sur blanc de signes [insignifiants] en partie
effacés sous forme de lacunes. Oreilles deux trous blanc sur blanc invisibles.* Bref
murmure de loin en loin que peut-être une issue. Bouche mince commissure blanche
comme cousue invisible. Traces fouillis gris pâle quatre en tout un par mur. Pieds joints
à angle droit blanc sur blanc invisibles. Yeux seuls inachevés bleus jadis pâlis presque
blancs. Bref murmure de loin en loin *avec brève image* que peut-être pas seul. Corps
t
nu d'un mètre blanc sur blanc invisible. Tou[s] su enfin. *Grande lumière blanche.* Pas
de douleur. [Pas de mémoire.] Rares brefs murmures toujours les mêmes tous sus.
ues   *Fixités.*
Mains pend[antes] entrouvertes creux en avant. [Immobilités.] A peine les yeux bleus
fixe
jadis pâlis presque blancs. Hop [immobiles] ailleurs. Bref murmure de loin en loin
que peut-être une issue. Bing murmure[.] [B]*bing* silence. [Bras pendants] [m]*M*ains
haute
pendues entrouvertes creux en avant. Tête sans traits bien [droite] bien dans l'axe
fixe   [*Dix millions de*]
yeux [droit] devant. [Dix mille] millimètres *dix millions moins les traces* carrés [moins
les traces] rayonnants. Bing bref murmure de loin en loin avec brève image que
peut-être une nature. Ca† de mémoire de loin en loin. Chaque mur sa trace [éclabous-
sure] sous le centre hauteur d'yeux [comme lorsqu'un petit oeuf s'écrase.] [F]*f*ouillis
sans sens
gris pâle presque blanc sur blanc de signes [insignifiants.] *Pas d'ombre. Invisibles*
rencontres des faces. Bref murmure de loin en loin que peut-être un sens. Ca† de
fixe
mémoire de loin en loin. Hop [immobiles] ailleurs. [Bras pendants] [m]*M*ains *pendues*
entrouvertes creux en avant. Jambes collées comme cousues[.] [P]*p*ieds joints à angle
Silence dedans.
droit. Tête *boule bien haute* bien dans l'axe yeux fixe devant. [Dedans silence.]
près
Corps nu [d'] un mètre blanc sur blanc invisible. Seuls [les yeux] [vers] des tempes
les yeux seuls inachevés bleu pâle presque blanc sur blanc seule couleur. Pas de
clins. *Pas de cils.* Longues fermetures. [Pas de cils.] Paupières blanches invisibles.
Grande lumière blanche
Hop *paupières* deux points bleu pâle presque blanc. Tout su enfin.   [Dit enfin.]
Brefs murmures *bing* de loin en loin seuls inachevés. [Que] [p]*P*eut-être pas seul
avec xxxxxxx *image.* [Que] [p]*P*eut-être une issue. [Que] [p]*P*eut-être un sens.
[Que] [p]*P*eut-être une nature avec [brève] image. Une deux secondes temps sidéral.
Ca† de mémoire de loin en loin. Six faces [rayonnantes] blanches [*rayonnants*
millimètres] *dix millions de millimètres moins les traces carrés rayonnants.*
Chaleur de serre
[Grande chaleur]. Pas xx de douleur. Pas d'ombre. [Un mètre sur un mètre sur deux
mètres.] Corps nu [d']un mètre fixe debout [même] pose *unique* blanc sur blanc
invisible *coeur souffle inaudible.* Seuls les yeux bleus jadis pâlis [pâlissants] presque
Fixités.
blanc*s* seule couleur seuls inachevés. [Immobilités.] Hop fixe ailleurs. Autour du

---

*Preceding word struck out and "stet" written above it.
†*Sic.*

centre. Le long des murs. Dans les angles. Tous les degrés du tour sur place.
sinon su que non.
Invisibles rencontres des faces. Un seul plan blanc à l'infini[. Mais tout su.] Instants
de regard. Instants d'écoute. Une [*sur de*] deux secondes[. D]*de* loin en loin *temps*
faces blanches.
sidéral. Hop traces [et blancheur] Hop silence. Ca* de sens de loin en loin. De
bing
loin en loin [temps sidéral] brefs murmures une seconde deux secondes seuls inachevés
toujours les mêmes tous sus. Bouche *mince* [blanche] commissure *blanche* comme
cousue invisible. Tête boule *diamètre* quinze centimètres.† [de diamètre.] Tronc
cylindre quarante-cinq du cul ou cou. Jambes collées comme cousues quarante-cinq
du cul aux talons joints à angle droit blanc sur blanc invisibles. Un mètre chiffre
rond rose *à peine* jadis blanchi invisible tout su dedans dehors [rose] [carné jadis].
Bing peut-être une nature une seconde deux secondes avec image même temps un peu
moins ciel bleu et blanc. Hop hop le long des murs seul plan à l'infini sinon su que
non. [Immobilités.] [Toujours immobile là depuis toujours pour toujours là ou hop
fixe immobile ailleurs] *Fixe là de tout temps là où hop fixe ailleurs* sinon su que non.
Pieds joints à angle droit blanc sur blanc invisibles hop ailleurs aucun son. Plafond
blanc un mètre carré jamais vu bing peut-être une issue peut-être par là une seconde
deux secondes *sans image.* Sol blanc un mètre carré jamais vu bing peut-être une
issue peut-être par là *sans image sans douleur* même temps bing [long] silence. Traces
seules inachevées noires jadis gris pâle presque blanc fouillis de signes sans sens ou
toujours les mêmes
effacés quatre en tout un par mur sous le centre hauteur d'yeux [tous pareils]. Bing
peut-être pas seul une seconde deux secondes *avec image* ça de mémoire *de loin en*
loin sans [douleur bing silence] douleur bing silence. Ongles achevés par terre tombés
roses [encore] à peine blanchis invisibles. Cheveux par terre tombés blancs invisibles
achevés. Cicatrices invisibles pas plus blanches que les chairs blessées roses *à peine*
jadis. [*mm. 10 millions Dix millions carrés rayonnants*] Millimètres dix mill[e]*ion*
carrés rayonnants moins les traces éclaboussures gris pâle [comme la main fouillis]
[de sig] presque blanc[*s*] signes sans sens avec lacunes. *Bing* Image une seconde deux
secondes bleu et blanc [le temps d'un flocon] au vent. Boule blanche unie nez oreille
trous blancs invisibles bouche mince commissure blanche invisible. Seuls les yeux
bleus jadis pâlis presque blancs près des tempes deux points bleu pâle presque blanc
rien
seule couleur seuls inachevés. Hop paupières plus [rien] seules les traces *fouillis* gris
de   *gris pâle presque blancs*
[pâle presque blanc petits nuages de] signes sans sens   [ou effacés].   Hop
paupières deux points bleu pâle presque blanc près des tempes seuls inachevés. *Tout*
   Clarté blanche   *millions* [*carrés*]
su [Grande lumière] [six] faces *blanches* rayonnantes millimètres dix [mille] rayonnants
moins les traces chaleur de serre. [Angles invisibles droits invisibles quatre murs un
mètre sur deux plan *blanc* à] *Murs blancs rayonnants angles invisibles un seul plan blanc*
jusqu'à l'infini l'infini sinon su que non. [chacun sa trace.] Tout blanc achevé rayonnant moins les yeux bleus jadis pâlis bleu pâle presque blanc et les traces noires
jadis pâli*es* gris pâle presque blanc sur blanc. Instants d'écoute de loin en loin [une
seconde deux secondes] ça de sens inachevé une seconde deux secondes temps espaces
infinis coeur souffle inaudibles bing silence. Bing peut-être une nature une seconde
deux secondes avec image *même temps un peu moins* toujours la même bleu et blanc
[du ciel] [même temps un peu moins] [temps d'une effiloche] au vent. Instants de

---

*Sic.
†Period is a manuscript addition.

regard une seconde deux secondes traces fouillis gris pâle sans sens faces blanches
achevées ça de sens de loin en loin en loin hop néant blanc. [Fixed Fixe droit] Fixe
droit un mètre blanc nu chiffre rond jambes collées comme cousues pieds joints à
angle droit mains pendues entrouvertes creux en avant. Boule blanche unie invisible .
                                haute
moins les yeux bien [droite] bien dans l'axe yeux points bleu pâle presque blanc près
des tempes fixe devant silence dedans. Hop [même pose] ailleurs là où aussitôt
  de tout temps
[depuis toujours] [sinon su que non.] sinon su que non. Bing peut-être pas seul une
seconde deux secondes avec image même temps un peu moins oeil noir et blanc mi-clos
                                        fixe devant
longs cils implorant ça de mémoire de loin en loin. Hop [tout contre] une trace gris
pâle presque blanc [bing peut-être un sens] hop paupières deux points bleu pâle
presque blanc bing peut-être un sens une seconde deux secondes sans image bing
silence. Temps temps futurs tout su tout achevé [pas peu à peu hop achevé.] pas peu
à peu hop achevé. Hop six faces blanches rayonnantes sans traces millimètres un
million[s] carrés rayonnants. Yeux bleus jadis bleu pâle presque blanc près des
tempes hop blancs achevés. Hop fixe *ailleurs dernier* [dernier ailleurs] là où de tout
temps sinon su que non. Jambes *collées* comme cousues du cul aux [pieds aux] talons
joints à angles droit. Tronc cylindre bien droit mains pendues entrouvertes creux en
avant. Tête boule bien haute bien dans l'axe yeux blancs invisibles fixe devant. Un
mètre invisible chiffre rond nu blanc rose *à peine* jadis tout su dedans dehors achevé.
Plafond blanc jamais vu millimètre[s] un million carrés rayonnants murmure bing
jadis une seconde deux secondes peut-être une issue *sans image* peut-être par là
sol blanc jamais vu. Peut-être un sens *sans image* bing jadis une nature une seconde
deux secondes avec image sans douleur même temps un peu moins bleu *et* blanc
au vent. Quatre murs sans traces angles [*droits*] invisibles un seul plan blanc *à l'inifini*
sinon su que non [jusqu'] [à l'infini]. *Grande lumière blanche tout su six faces blanches*
xxxxxxxx *millimètres dix millions carrés rayonnants chaleur de serre souffle inaudibles.*
Boule blanche unie bien haute bien dans l'axe yeux blancs fixe devant vieux bing
murmure dernier peut-être pas seul une seconde deux secondes avec image même
temps un peu moins oeil embu noir et blanc mi-clos long cils implorant bing silence
hop achevé.

Text 6.

        Grande lumière.
Tout su. [Clarté blanche.] [Un] corps nu blanc [d']un mètre. [Pose unique.]
                               collées   *Grande chaleur*
[Un mètre carré] [de] sol blanc *un mètre carré*. Jambes [serrées]. [Chaleur de serre].
Pas de douleur. Quatre murs blancs un mètre sur deux. *plafond blanc* Un mètre
carré [de] [plafond blanc]. Fixités. Seuls les yeux à peine. Millimètres dix millions
carrés rayonnants. Traces gris pâle presque blanc. [Pose unique.] Mains pendues
entrouvertes creux en avant. Talons joints à angle droit. Hop fixe ailleurs. Six
faces blanches rayonnantes. Corps nu blanc [d']un mètre. Chaleur de serre. Pas
de douleur. Pas d'ombre. [Corps blanc invisible Corps nu blanc invisible] Corps nu
blanc un mètre invisible blanc sur blanc. [Seuls] [p]Près de*s* tempes *seuls* les yeux bleu
pâle presque blanc*s*. Tête boule bien haute bien dans l'axe yeux fixe devant. [Dedans]
silence *dedans*. Rares brefs murmures tous sus. Traces fouillis gris pâle presque
blancs. Jambes collées comme cousues du cul aux talons joints à angle droit. Un
mètre carré de sol blanc. Pas de douleur. Chaleur de serre. Fixités. Seuls les yeux
à peine. Hop fixe ailleurs. [Vers d'autres traces.] Pas d'ombre. Noires jadis traces
seules inachevées gris pâle presque [blanc sur] blanc[s]. Nez invisible deux trous
blancs. Murs blancs rayonnants un mètre sur deux. Traces fouillis gris pâle presque

blanc de signes sans sens. Oreilles invisibles deux trous blancs. Bref murmure de
loin en loin sans image que peut-être une issue. Bouche mince commissure blanche
comme cousue invisible. Murs blancs rayonnants chacun sa trace fouillis gris [blanc]
pâle presque blanc. [Bref murmure de loin en loin avec brève image que peut-être
pas seul. Corps nu un mètre blanc sur blanc invisible.] Pieds joints à angle droit
blancs invisibles. Bleus jadis yeux seuls inachevés pâlis presque blancs. Bref murmure
de loin en loin avec brève image que peut-être pas seul. Corps nu un mètre blanc sur
blanc invisible. Tout su [enfin]. [Clarté blanche.] Pas de douleur. *Clarté blanche.*
Rares brefs murmures toujours les mêmes tous sus. Mains pendues entrouvertes creux
en avant. Fixités. Bleus jadis seuls les yeux pâlis presque blancs. Hop fixe ailleurs.
Bref murmure de loin en loin une seconde deux secondes sans image que peut-être
une issue. Bing murmure bing silence. Tête boule bien haute bien dans l'axe yeux fixe
devant. Millimètres dix millions moins les traces carrés rayonnants. Mains pendues
entrouvertes creux en avant. Bing bref murmure de loin en loin avec brève image que
peut-être une nature. Ca* de mémoire de loin en loin. Chaque mur sa trace sous
le centre hauteur d'yeux fouillis gris pâle presque blanc de signes sans sens. Pas
d'ombre. Invisibles rencontres des faces. Bref murmure de loin en loin sans image
que peut-être un sens. Ca* de mémoire de loin en loin. Hop fixe ailleurs. Mains
pendues entrouvertes creux en avant. Jambes collées comme cousues pieds joints à
angle droit. Tête boule bien haute bien dans l'axe yeux fixe [devant.] devant silence
dedans. Corps nu blanc un mètre blanc sur blanc invisible. Près des tempes seuls
les yeux seuls inachevés bleu pâle presque blancs seule couleur. Pas de clins. Pas
de cils. Longues fermetures. Paupières blanches invisibles. Hop paupières deux
points bleu pâle presque blancs. Tout su enfin. Clarté blanche. Brefs murmures
bing de loin en loin seuls inachevés. Peut-être pas seul avec image. Une issue. Un
sens. Une nature avec image. Une deux secondes temps sidéral. Ca* de mémoire de
loin en loin. Six faces blanches rayonnantes millimètres dix millions moins les traces
carrés rayonnants. Pas de douleur. Pas d'ombre. Corps nu blanc un mètre fixe
debout pose unique [blanc sur blanc invisible coeur souffle inaudibles.] coeur souffle
inaudibles blanc sur blanc invisible. Bleus jadis seuls les yeux pâlis presque blancs
seule couleur seuls inachevés. Hop fixe ailleurs. Autour du centre. Le long des
murs. Dans les angles. Tous les degrés du tour sur place. Invisibles rencontres des
faces. Un seul plan blanc à l'infini sinon su que non. Instants de regard. Instants
d'écoute. Une deux secondes de loin en loin temps sidéral. Hop traces faces blanches.
Hop [silence] même silence. Ca* de sens de loin en loin. De loin en loin bing brefs
murmures avec et sans image une seconde deux secondes toujours les mêmes tous
sus. Bouche fil blanc comme cousu invisible. Tête boule diamètre quinze. Tronc
cylindre quarante-cinq du cul au cou. Jambes collées comme cousues quarante-cinq
du cul aux talons joints à angle droit. Rose à peine jadis un mètre chiffre rond
blanchi invisible tout su [dedans dehors] dehors dedans. Bing peut-être une nature
une seconde deux secondes avec image même temps un peu moins bleu et blanc au
vent. Hop hop le long des murs seul plan blanc à l'infini sinon su que non. Fixe là
d'éternité là où hop fixe ailleurs sinon su que non. Pieds blancs invisibles talons
joints à angle droit hop ailleurs aucun son. Plafond blanc un mètre carré jamais vu
bing peut-être une issue peut-être par là une seconde deux secondes sans image.
Sol blanc un mètre carré jamais vu bing peut-être une issue peut-être par là sans
image sans douleur bing silence. Noires jadis traces seules inachevées [gris pâle
presque] fouillis de signes sans sens gris pâle presque blancs quatre en tout toujours
les mêmes. Bing peut-être pas seul une seconde deux secondes avec image même temps

---

*Sic.

presque jamais

une* peu moins ça de mémoire [de loin en loin] sans douleur bing silence. Tombés roses à peine ongles achevés par terre blanchis invisibles. Cheveux par terre tombés blanc*s* invisibles achevés. Cicatrices invisibles pas plus blanches que les chairs blessées roses à peine jadis. Millimètres carrés rayonnants dix millions moins les traces fouillis de signes sans sens gris pâle presque blancs quatre en tout toujours les mêmes. Bing image une seconde deux secondes bleu et blanc au vent. Tête boule bien haute bien dans l'axe quatre trous blancs invisibles bouche fil blanc invisible achevée. Bleus jadis seuls les yeux pâlis presque blancs près des tempes deux points bleu pâle presque blancs seule couleur seuls inachevés. Hop paupières plus rien seules les traces fouillis de signes sans sens gris pâle presque blancs. Hop paupières deux points bleu pâle presque blancs près des tempes seules inachevés. Clarté blanche faces blanches rayonnantes millimètres dix millions carré*s* rayonnants moins les traces chaleur de serre. Murs blancs rayonnants angles invisibles un seul plan blanc jusqu'à l'infini sinon su que non. Instants d'écoute de loin en loin ça de sens inachevé une deux secondes deux secondes temps espaces infinis coeur souffle inaudibles bing silence. Bing peut-être une nature une seconde deux secondes avec image même temps un peu moins toujours la même bleu et blanc au vent. Instants de regard [de loin en loin] une seconde deux secondes traces fouillis gris pâle sans sens faces blanches achevées ça de sens de loin en loin hop néant blanc. Fixe droit un mètre blanc nu chiffre rond jambes collées comme cousues pieds joints à angle droit mains pendues entrouvertes creux en avant. Boule unie invisibles moins les yeux bien haute bien dans l'axe deux points bleu pâle presque blancs près des tempes fixe devant silence dedans. Hop ailleurs là où aussitôt d'éternité sinon su que non. Bing peut-être pas

moins . . . . . .†

seul une seconde deux secondes avec image même temps un peu [noir] oeil [noir] et blanc mi-clos longs cils implorant ça de mémorie de loin en loin *sans douleur presque jamais*. [Hop paupières deux points bleu pâle presque blancs bing peut-être un sens une seconde deux secondes sans image bing silence. Temps temps futurs tout su tout [*achevé*]

achevés pas peu à peu hop achevé.] Hop six faces blanches rayonnantes sans traces millimètres dix millions carrés rayonnants. Bleus jadis yeux bleu pâle presque blanc près des tempes hop blancs achevés. Hop fixe ailleurs dernier là où d'éternité sinon su que non. Jambes collées comme cousues [du cul aux] talons joints [à] angle droit.

bien dans l'axe   *face*

Tronc cylindre fixe droit mains pendues [entr]ouvertes creux [en avant]. Tête boule

face

bien haute bien dans l'axe yeux blancs invisibles fixe [devant]. Un mètre [invisible chiffre rond] nu blanc *donné* rose à peine [jadis] tout su dehors dedans achevé. Plafond blanc jamais vu millimètres un million[s] [carrés] carrés rayonnants murmure [bing] jadis une seconde deux secondes *sans douleur presque jamais* peut-être [une issue sans image peut-être] par là sol blanc jamais vu. Peut-être un sens sans image *jadis* bing jadis une nature une seconde deux secondes avec image sans douleur même temps un peu moins bleu et blanc au vent *ça de mémoire plus jamais*. Murs blancs rayonnants sans traces [angles invisibles un] seul plan blanc [jusqu']à l'infini sinon su que

grande lumière grande chaleur   *aucun son*   *Tête boule*

non. Tout blanc tout su   [chaleur de serre coeur]   souffle [inaudibles]. [Boule blanche]

face

bien haute bien dans l'axe yeux blancs fixe [devant] vieux bing murmure dernier peut-

---

*Sic.

†Periods represent illegible autograph additions, as explained in the introductory note.

être pas seul une seconde *sans douleur* deux secondes avec image [*sans douleur*] même temps un peu moins oeil embu noir et blanc mi-clos long cils implorant bing silence hop achevé.

Text 7.

Tout su. Grande lumière. Corps nu blanc un mètre. Jambes collées comme cousues.
nulle.
Sol blanc un mètre carré. Grande chaleur. Ombre [neant.] Plafond blanc un mètre
nulle
carré. Douleur [neant]. Quatre murs blancs un mètre sur deux. Corps nu blanc fixe [pas un frémissement]. Seuls les yeux à peine. Millimètres dix millions carrés rayonnants. Traces fouillis gris pâle presque blanc. Mains pendues ouvertes creux face. Talons joints angle droit. Hop fixe ailleurs. Six faces blanches rayonnantes. Ombre
nulle   *nulle*
[néant]. Grande chaleur. Grande lumière. Tout su. Douleur [néant]. Corps nu blanc un mètre invisible blanc sur blanc. Seuls les yeux à peine bleu pâle presque blanc. Tête boule bien haute bien dans l'axe yeux fixe face silence dedans. Brefs murmures presque jamais tous sus.* Traces fouillis signe*s* sans sens gris pâle presque blanc. Jambes collées comme cousues talons joints angle droit. Sol blanc un mètre
[*nulle*]   ....
carré rayonnant. [Douleur néant.] [Grande chaleur. Pas un frémissement. Seuls les
....   [*nulle*]
yeux à piene. Hop fixe ailleurs. Ombre néant.] Traces seules inachevées données noires [pâlies] gris pâle presque blanc sur blanc. Murs blancs rayonnants un mètre
....
sur deux. Traces fouillis signes sans sens gris pâle presque blanc. *Corps nu blanc fixe un m. hop fixe ailleurs.* Pieds blancs invisibles talons joints angle droit. Yeux seuls inachevés donnés bleus pâlis bleu pâle presque blanc. Bref murmure *à peine* presque jamais peut-être pas seul. Donné rose à peine corps nu blanc fixe un mètre blanc
[*nulle*] *Lumière chaleur silence*
sur blanc invisible. [Tout su. Douleur néant.   Grande lumière.   Brefs] murmures presque jamais toujours les mêmes tous sus. Mains blanches invisibles pendues ouvertes creux face. [Hop fixe ailleurs.] *Corps nu blanc fixe un mètre hop fixe ailleurs.* Seuls
                 ....
les yeux à peine donnés bleus pâlis   bleu pâle presque blanc fixe face. [Bref] murmure *à peine* presque jamais une seconde deux secondes peut-être une issue. Bing murmure bing silence. Tête boule bien haute [bien dans l'axe] yeux pâles fixe face silence dedans. [Millimètres dix millior., carrés
[*Traces au moins.*]
rayonnants moins les traces.] [Mains pendues ouvertes creux face.] Bing murmure *à peine* presque jamais une seconde deux secondes avec image peut-être une nature. Ca† de mémoire presque jamais. Murs blancs rayonnants chacun sa trace donnée noire
s   [*nulle*]
pâli[e] fouillis gris signes sans sens gris pâle presque blanc sur blanc. [Ombre néant.] Invisibles rencontres des faces. Bing murmure presque jamais peut-être un sens ça de mémoire presque jamais. Hop fixe ailleurs. Mains pendues ouvertes creux face.
p
Jambes collées comme cousue[s] [m]ieds blancs invisibles talons joints angle[s] droit.

---

*This sentence underscored with wavy line in original; vertical line also down left-hand margin from beginning to this point.
†*Sic.*

Tête boule bien haute [bien dans l'axe] yeux *bleu* pâle[s] presque blanc fixe face silence dedans. Hop fixe ailleurs. Seuls les yeux seuls inachevés donnés bleus pâlis deux points bleu pâle presque blanc seule couleur fixe face. Tout su. Grande lumière. Bing murmure presque jamais une deux seconde[s] temps sidéral ça de mémoire presque [jamais] jamais. [Peut-être pas seul avec image. Une issue. Un sens.] Une nature avec image. Faces blanches rayonnantes millimètres dix millions carrés *traces en moins.*
rayonnants [moins les traces.] Corps nu blanc un mètre fixe droit coeur souffle *sans son. Corps nu blanc. blanc*.........
[aucun son blanc sur blanc invisible] Seuls les yeux donnés bleus [pâlis] bleu pâle presque blanc seule couleur seuls inachevés. Invisibles rencontres des face*s*. [s]*S*eul plan *rayonnant* blanc à l'infini sinon su que non. Bouche fil blanc comme cousue invisible. Bing murmures presque jamais une seconde [deux secondes] toujours les mêmes tous sus. Donné rose à peine corps blanc nu fixe un mètre invisible tout su dehors dedans. Bing peut-être une nature une seconde [deux secondes] avec image
                                        Plafond
même temps un peu moins bleu et blanc au vent.   [Sol]   blanc un mètre carré
                                    une seconde
jamais vu bing peut-être par là une issue [sans image sans douleur] bing silence. Traces seules inachevées données noires fouillis gris signes sans sens gris pâle presque blanc toujours les mêmes. Bing peut-être pas seul une seconde [deux secondes] avec image même temps un peu moins sans douleur ça de mémoire presque jamais bing silence.
                                        blancs
Tombés roses à peine ongles achevés [par terre blanchis] invisibles. Cheveux [par terre] tombés blancs ça [et là] invisibles achevés. Cicatrices invisibles même blanc que les chairs blessées roses à peine jadis. Bing image presque jamais une seconde [deux secondes] temps espaces infinis bleu et blanc au vent. Tête boule bien haute [bien dans l'axe] nez oreille trous blancs invisibles bouche fil blanc comme cousue invisible achevée. Seuls les yeux donnés bleus pâlis presque blancs fixe face bleu pâle presque blanc seule couleur seuls inachevés. [Faces blanches rayonnantes millimètres dix millions
                                traces en moins
carrés rayonnants moins les traces grande chaleur.] *Lumière chaleur murs* [Murs] blancs rayonnants seul plan blanc à l'infini sinon su que non. Ecoute *à peine* presque jamais
                            sans   *Signe sans sens*
une seconde [deux secondes] coeur souffle [aucun] son hop silence. [Fouillis] *gris* [gris] pâle deux points bleu pâle presque blanc bing peut-être un sens presque jamais une seconde [deux secondes] bing silence. Une nature presque jamais une seconde deux secondes avec image même temps un peu moins toujours la même bleu et blanc au vent. Regard presque jamais une seconde deux secondes fouillis gris signes sans sens gris pâle presque blanc murs blancs [rayonnants] hop vide blanc. Blanc nu un mètre fixe droit jambes collées comme cousues talons joints angle droit mains pendues ouvertes creux face. Tête boule bien [droit bien dans l'axe] haute [bien dans l'axe] yeux points bleu pâle presque blanc fixe face silence dedans. Hop ailleurs là où aussitôt de tout temps sinon su que non. Bing peut-être pas seul une seconde [deux secondes] avec image même temps un peu moins oeil noir et blanc mi-clos longs cils implorant ça de mémoire presque jamais. Au loin temps éclair tout blanc achevé tout jadis hop éclair murs blancs sans traces yeux dernière couleur hop blancs achevés. Dernier ailleurs hop fixe jambes collées comme cousues talons joints angle droit mains pendues ouvertes creux face tête boule bien haute [bien dans l'axe] yeux blancs invisibles fixe face achevés [là où de tout temps sinon su que non.] Donné rose à peine un mètre invisible nu blanc tout su dedans dehors achevé. Plafond blanc jamais vu millimètres un million[s] carrés rayonnants bing jadis presque jamais une seconde [deux seconde*s*] sol blanc jamais vu peut-être par là. Bing jadis peut-être

un sens [sans image] une nature une seconde [deux secondes] presque jamais bleu et blanc au vent ça de mémoire plus jamais. Murs blancs rayonnants sans traces seul plan rayonnant blanc à l'infini sinon su que non. Tout blanc tout su grande chaleur

sans

grande lumière coeur souffle [aucun] son. Tête boule bien haute bien dans l'axe yeux blancs fixe face vieux bing murmure dernier peut-être pas seul une seconde [deux secondes] oeil embu noir et blanc mi-clos longs cils implorant bing silence hop achevé.

Text 8.

Tout su tout blanc corps nu blanc un mètre jambes collées comme cousues. Lumière chaleur sol blanc un mètre [jamais vu.] carré jamais vu. Murs blancs un mètre sur deux plafond blanc un mètre carré jamais vu. Corps nu blanc fixe seuls les yeux à peine. Traces fouillis gris pâle presque blanc sur blanc. Mains blanches pendues ouvertes creux face talons joints angle droit. Lumière chaleur faces blanches rayonnantes. Corps nu blanc fixe un mètre hop fixe ailleurs. Traces fouillis signes sans sens gris pâle presque blanc. Corps nu blanc fixe invisible blanc sur blanc. Seuls les yeux à peine bleu pâle presque blanc. Tête boule bien haute yeux bleu pâle presque blanc fixe face silence dedans. Brefs murmures à peine presque jamais tous sus. Traces fouillis signes sans sens gris pâle presque blanc. Jambes collées comme cousues talons joints angle droit. [Sol blanc plafond blanc un mètre carré rayonnants jamais vus.] Traces seules inachevées données noires gris pâle presque blanc sur blanc. Murs blancs rayonnants un mètre sur deux. Traces fouillis signes sans sens gris pâle presque blanc. Corps nu blanc fixe un mètre hop fixe ailleurs. Pieds blancs invisibles talons joints angle droit. Yeux seuls inachevés donnés bleus bleu pâle presque blanc. Murmure à peine presque jamais une seconde peut-être pas seul. Donné rose à peine corps nu blanc fixe un mètre blanc sur blanc invisible. Lumière silence murmures à peine presque jamais toujours les mêmes tous sus. Mains blanches invisibles pendues ouvertes creux face. Corps nu blanc fixe un mètre hop fixe ailleurs. Seuls les yeux à peine bleu pâle presque blanc fixe face. Murmure à peine presque jamais une seconde peut-être une issue. [Bing murmure bing silence.] Tête boule bien haute yeux bleu pâle presque blanc [fixe face silence dedans] *bing murmure bing silence.* Bouche *fine* commissure blanche comme cousue invisible. [Bing murmure à peine presque jamais une seconde avec image peut-être une nature. Ca*] de mémoire presque jamais. Murs blancs chacun sa trace [fouillis gris] signes sans sens gris pâle presque blanc [sur blanc]. Invisibles rencontres des faces. Bing murmure à peine presque jamais une seconde peut-être un sens ça de mémoire presque jamais. Pieds blancs invisibles talons joints angle droit hop ailleurs sans son. Mains pendues ouvertes creux face jambes collées comme cousues. Tête boule bien haute yeux bleu pâle presque blanc fixe face silence dedans. Hop [fixe] ailleurs là où de tout temps sinon su que non. Seuls les yeux seuls inachevés donnés bleus deux trous bleu pâle presque blanc seule

tout blanc

couleur fixe face. Tout su [lumière chaleur] faces blanches rayonnantes bing murmure

espaces infinis

à peine presque jamais une seconde temps   [sidéral]   ça de mémoire presque jamais. Corps nu blanc un mètre fixe hop fixe ailleurs blanc sur blanc invisible coeur souffle sans son. Seuls les yeux donnés bleus bleu pâle presque blanc fixe face seule couleur seuls inachevés. Invisibles rencontres des faces seule face rayonnante blanche à l'infini sinon su que non. Nez oreilles trous blancs bouche fil blanc comme cousue invisible. Bing murmures à peine presque jamais une seconde toujours les mêmes tous

---

*Sic.

sus. Donné rose à peine corps blanc nu fixe un mètre invisible tout su dehors dedans.
Bing peut-être une nature une seconde avec image même temps un peu moins bleu
et blanc au vent. Plafond blanc rayonnant un mètre carré jamais vu bing peut-être
par là une issue une seconde bing silence. Traces seules inachevées données noires
[gris pâle presque blanc] fouillis gris signes sans sens gris pâle presque blanc toujours
les mêmes. Bing peut-être pas seul une seconde avec image toujours la même [une
seconde] même temps un peu moins ça de mémoire presque jamais bing silence.
Tombés roses à peine ongles blancs achevés. Longs cheveux tombés blancs invisibles
achevés. Invisibles cicatrices même blanc que les chairs blessées roses à peine jadis.
Bing image à peine presque jamais une seconde temps espaces infinis [image mouvante*]
bleu et blanc au vent. Tête boule bien haute nez oreilles trous blancs [invisibles]
bouche fil blanc comme cousue invisible achevée. Seuls les yeux donnés bleus fixe
face bleu pâle presque blanc seule couleur seuls inachevés. Lumière chaleur faces
blanches rayonnantes seule face rayonnante blanche à l'infini sinon su que non.
Ecoute à peine presque jamais une seconde coeur souffle sans son hop silence. Traces
fouillis gris pâle yeux trous bleu pâle presque blanc fixe face bing peut-être un sens
à peine presque jamais bing silence. Une nature à peine presque jamais une seconde
avec image même temps un peu moins toujours la même [mouvante] bleu et blanc
au vent. Regard à peine presque jamais une seconde fouillis gris signes sans sens gris
pâle presque blanc murs blancs rayonnants hop vide blanc. Blanc nu un mètre
fixe hop fixe ailleurs jambes collées comme cousues talons joints angle droit mains
pendues ouvertes creux face. Tête boule bien haute yeux trous bleu pâle presque
blanc fixe face silence dedans. Hop ailleurs là où de tout temps sinon su que non.
Bing peut-être pas seul une seconde avec image même temps un peu moins oeil noir
et blanc mi-clos longs cils implorant ça de mémoire presque jamais. Au loin temps
éclair tout blanc achevé tout jadis hop éclair murs blancs sans traces yeux [dernière
couleur] *couleur dernière* hop blancs achevés. Hop fixe dernier ailleurs jambes collées
comme cousues talons joints angle droit mains pendues ouvertes creux face tête boule
bien haute yeux blancs invisibles fixe face achevés. Donné rose à peine un mètre
invisible nu blanc tout su dehors dedans achevé. Plafond blanc jamais vu bing jadis
à peine presque jamais une seconde sol blanc jamais vu peut-être par là. Bing jadis
à peine peut-être un sens une nature une seconde presque jamais bleu et blanc au
vent ça de mémoire plus jamais. Murs blancs rayonnants sans traces seule face rayonnante blanche à l'infini sinon su que non. Lumière chaleur tout su tout blanc coeur
souffle sans son. Tête boule bien haute yeux blancs fixe face vieux bing murmure
dernier [à peine] peut-être pas seul[e] une seconde oeil embu noir et blanc mi-clos
long cils implorant[s] bing silence hop achevé.

Text 9.

Tout su tout blanc corps nu blanc un mètre jambes collées comme cousues. Lumière
chaleur sol blanc un mètre carré jamais vu. Murs blancs un mètre sur deux plafond
blanc un mètre carré jamais vu. Corps nu blanc seuls les yeux à peine. Traces
fouillis gris pâle presque blanc sur blanc. Mains pendues ouvertes creux faces talons
pieds blancs joints angle droit. Lumière chaleur faces blanches rayonnantes. Corps
nu blanc fixe hop fixe ailleurs. Traces fouillis signes sans sens gris pâle presque
blanc. Corps nu blanc fixe invisible blanc sur blanc. Seuls les yeux à peine bleu
pâle presque blanc. Tête boule bien haute yeux bleu pâle presque blanc fixe face
silence dedans. Brefs murmures à peine presque jamais tous sus. Traces fouillis signes
sans sens gris pâle presque blanc *sur blanc*. Jambes collées comme cousues talons joints

---

*This phrase underscored with wavy line and struck through.

angle droit. Traces seules inachevées données noires gris pâle presque blanc sur blanc. *Lumière chaleur.* Murs blancs rayonnants un mètre sur deux. Corps nu blanc fixe un mètre hop fixe ailleurs. Traces fouillis signes sans sens gris pâle presque blanc. Pieds blancs invisibles talons joints angle droit. Yeux seuls inachevés donnés bleus bleu pâle presque blanc. Murmure à peine presque jamais une seconde peut-être pas seul. Donné rose à peine corps nu blanc fixe un mètre blanc sur blanc invisible. Lumière chaleur murmures à peine presque jamais toujours les mêmes tous sus. Mains blanches invisibles pendues ouvertes creux face. Corps nu blanc [un mètre] fixe un mètre hop fixe ailleurs. Seuls les yeux à peine bleu pâle presque blanc fixe face. Murmure à peine presque jamais une seconde peut-être une issue. Tête boule bien haute yeux bleu pâle presque blanc bing murmure bing silence. Bouche [fine commissure] comme cousue *fil blanc* invisible. Bing peut-être une nature une seconde presque jamais ça de mémoire presque jamais. Murs blancs chacun sa trace fouillis signes sans sens gris pâle presque blanc. Lumière chaleur *tout su tout blanc* invisibles rencontres des faces. Bing murmure à peine presque jamais une seconde peut-être un sens ça de mémoire presque jamais. Pieds blancs invisibles talons joints angle droit hop ailleurs sans son. *Mains pendues ouvertes creux face jambes collées comme cousues.* [Jambes collées comme cousues talons joints angle droit.] Tête boule bien haute yeux bleu pâle presque blanc fixe face silence dedans. Hop ailleurs [là] où de tout temps sinon su que non. Seuls les yeux seuls inachevés donnés bleus trous bleu pâle presque blanc seule couleur fixe face. Tout su tout blanc faces blanches rayonnantes bing murmure à peine presque jamais une seconde temps espaces infinis ça de mémoire presque jamais. Corps nu blanc fixe un mètre hop fixe ailleurs blanc sur blanc invisible coeur souffle sans son. Seuls les yeux donnés bleus bleu pâle presque blanc fixe face seule couleur seuls inachevés. Invisibles rencontres des faces *une* seule face [rayonnante] blanche à l'infini sinon su que non. Nez oreilles trous blancs bouche fil blanc comme cousue invisible. Bing murmures à peine presque jamais une seconde toujours les mêmes tous sus. Donné rose à peine corps nu blanc fixe [un mètre] invisible tout su dehors dedans. Bing peut-être une nature une seconde avec image même temps un peu moins bleu et blanc au vent. Plafond blanc rayonnant un mètre carré jamais vu bing peut-être par là une issue une seconde bing silence. Traces seules inachevées données noires fouillis gris signes sans sens gris pâle presque blanc toujours les mêmes. Bing peut-être pas seul une seconde avec image toujours la même même temps un peu moins ça de mémoire presque jamais bing silence. Tombés roses à peine ongles blancs achevés. Longs cheveux tombés blancs invisibles achevés. Invisibles

Bing

cicatrices même blanc que les chairs blessées roses à peine jadis. [Temps] image à peine presque jamais une seconde temps espaces infinis bleu et blanc au vent. Tête boule bien haute nez oreilles trous blancs bouche fil blanc comme cousue invisible achevée. Seuls les yeux donnés bleus fixe face bleu pâle presque blanc seule couleur seuls inachevés. Lumière chaleur faces blanches rayonnantes *une* seule face [rayonnante] blanche à l'infini sinon su que non. [Ecoute à peine presque jamais une seconde coeur souffle sans son hop silence.] Une nature à peine presque jamais une seconde avec image même temps un peu moins toujours la même bleu et blanc au vent. Traces fouillis gris pâle yeux trous bleu pâle presque blanc fixe face bing peut-être un sens à peine presque jamais bing silence. [Regard à peine presque jamais une seconde fouillis gris signes sans sens gris pâle presque blanc murs blancs rayonnants hop vide blanc.] Blanc nu un[e] mètre fixe hop fixe ailleurs sans son jambes collées comme cousues talons joints angle droit mains pendues ouvertes creux face. Tête boule bien haute yeux trous bleu pâle presque blanc fixe face silence dedans[. H]*h*op ailleurs [là] où de tout temps sinon su que non. Bing peut-être pas seul [avec image] une seconde avec image même temps un peu moins oeil noir et blanc mi-clos longs cils implorant ça de mémoire presque jamais. Au loin temps éclair tout blanc achevé tout jadis hop éclair murs blancs rayonnants sans traces yeux couleur dernière hop blancs achevés. Hop fixe dernier ailleurs jambes collées comme cousues talons joints angle droit mains pendues ouvertes creux face tête boule bien haute yeux blancs invisibles fixe face achevés. Donné rose à peine un mètre invisible nu blanc tout su dehors dedans achevé. Plafond blanc jamais vu bing jadis à peine presque jamais une seconde sol blanc jamais vu peut-être par là. Bing jadis à peine peut-être un sens une nature une seconde presque jamais bleu et blanc au vent ça de mémoire plus jamais. [Murs blancs rayonnants sans traces seule face rayonnante blanche] *Faces blanches sans traces une seule rayonnante blanche* à l'infini sinon su que non. Lumière chaleur tout su tout blanc coeur souffle sans son. Tête boule bien haute yeux blancs fixe face vieux bing murmure dernier peut-être pas seul une seconde oeil embu noir et blanc mi-clos longs cils implorant bing silence hop achevé.

Text 10 and final.

BING
By
Samuel Beckett

Tout su tout blanc corps nu blanc un mètre jambes collées comme cousues. Lumière chaleur sol blanc un mètre carré jamais vu. Murs blancs un mètre sur deux plafond blanc un mètre carré jamais vu. Corps nu blanc fixe seuls les yeux à peine. Traces fouillis gris pâle presque blanc sur blanc. Mains pendues ouvertes creux face pieds blancs talons joints angle droit. Lumière chaleur faces blanches rayonnantes. Corps nu blanc fixe hop fixe ailleurs. Traces fouillis signes sans sens gris pâle presque blanc. Corps nu blanc fixe invisible blanc sur blanc. Seuls les yeux à peine bleu pâle presque blanc. Tête boule bien haute yeux bleu pâle presque blanc fixe face silence dedans. Brefs murmures à peine presque jamais tous sus. Traces fouillis signes sans sens gris pâle presque blanc sur blanc. Jambes collées comme cousues talons joints angle droit. Traces seules inachevées données noires gris pâle presque blanc sur blanc. Lumière chaleur murs blancs rayonnants un mètre sur deux. Corps nu blanc fixe un mètre hop fixe ailleurs. Traces fouillis signes sans sens gris pâle presque blanc. Pieds blancs invisibles talons joints angle droit. Yeux seuls inachevés donnés bleus bleu pâle presque blanc. Murmure à peine presque jamais une seconde peut-être pas seul. Donné rose à peine corps nu blanc fixe un mètre blanc sur blanc invisible. Lumière chaleur murmures à peine presque jamais toujours les mêmes tous sus. Mains blanches invisibles pendues ouvertes creux face. Corps nu blanc fixe un mètre hop fixe ailleurs. Seuls les yeux à peine bleu pâle presque blanc fixe face. Murmure à peine presque jamais une seconde peut-être une issue. Tête boule bien haute yeux bleu pâle presque blanc bing murmure bing silence. Bouche comme cousue fil blanc invisible. Bing peut-être une nature une seconde presque jamais ça de mémoire presque jamais. Murs blancs chacun sa trace fouillis signes sans sens gris pâle presque blanc. Lumière chaleur tout su tout blanc invisibles rencontres des faces. Bing murmure à peine presque jamais une seconde peut-être un sens ça de mémoire presque jamais. Pieds blancs invisibles talons joints angle droit hop ailleurs sans son. Mains pendues ouvertes creux face jambes collées comme cousues. Tête boule bien haute yeux bleu pâle presque blanc fixe face silence dedans. Hop ailleurs où de tout temps sinon su que non. Seuls les yeux inachevés donnés bleus trous bleu pâle presque blanc seule couleur fixe face. Tout su tout blanc faces blanches rayonnantes *sidéral* bing murmure à peine presque jamais une seconde temps [espaces infinis] ça de mémoire presque jamais. Corps nu blanc fixe un mètre hop fixe ailleurs blanc sur blanc invisible cœur souffle sans son. Seuls les yeux donnés bleus bleu pâle presque

blanc fixe face seule couleur seuls inachevés. Invisibles rencontres des faces une seule
rayonnante
[face] blanche à l'infini sinon su que non. Nez oreilles trous blancs bouche fil
blanc comme cousue invisible. Bing murmures à peine presque jamais une seconde
toujours les mêmes tous sus. Donné rose à peine corps nu blanc fixe invisible tout
su dehors dedans. Bing peut-être une nature une seconde avec image même temps
un peu moins bleu et blanc au vent. Plafond blanc rayonnant un mètre carré jamais
vu bing peut-être par là une issue une seconde bing silence. Traces seules inachevées
données noires fouillis gris signes sans sens gris pâle presque blanc toujours les mêmes.
Bing peut-être pas seul une seconde avec image toujours la même même temps un
peu moins ça de mémoire presque jamais bing silence. Tombés roses à peine ongles
blancs achevés. Longs cheveux tombés blancs invisibles achevés. Invisibles cicatrices
même blanc que les chairs blessées roses à peine jadis. Bing image à peine presque
sidéral
jamais une seconde temps [espaces infinis] bleu et blanc au vent. Tête boule bien
haute nez oreilles trous blancs bouche fil blanc comme cousue invisible achevée.
Seuls les yeux donnés bleus fixe face bleu pâle presque blanc seule couleur seuls
rayonnante
inachevés. Lumière chaleur faces blanches rayonnantes une seule [face] blanche
à l'infini sinon su que non. Une nature à peine presque jamais une seconde avec
image même temps un peu moins toujours la même bleu et blanc au vent. Traces
fouillis gris pâle yeux trous bleu pâle presque blanc fixe face bing peut-être un sens
à peine presque jamais bing silence. Blanc nu un mètre fixe hop fixe ailleurs sans
son jambes collées comme cousues talons joints angle droit mains pendues ouvertes
creux face. Tête boule bien haute yeux trous bleu pâle presque blanc fixe face
silence dedans hop ailleurs où de tout temps sinon su que non. Bing peut-être pas
seul une seconde avec image même temps un peu moins oeil noir et blanc mi-clos
suppliant
long cils [implorant] ça de mémoire presque jamais. Au loin temps éclair tout blanc
achevé tout jadis hop éclair murs blancs rayonnants sans traces yeux couleur dernière
hop blancs achevés. Hop fixe dernier ailleurs jambes collées comme cousues talons joints
angle droit mains pendues ouvertes creux face tête boule bien haute yeux blancs
invisibles fixe face achevés. Donné rose à peine un mètre invisible nu blanc tout su
dehors dedans achevé. Plafond blanc jamais vu bing jadis à peine presque jamais
une seconde sol blanc jamais vu peut-être par là. Bing jadis à peine peut-être un
sens une nature une seconde presque jamais bleu et blanc au vent ça de mémoire
plus jamais. Faces blanches sans traces une seule rayonnante blanche à l'infini sinon
su que non. Lumière chaleur tout su tout blanc cœur souffle sans son. Tête boule
bien haute yeux blancs fixe face vieux bing murmure dernier peut-être pas seul
suppliant
une seconde oeil embu noir et blanc mi-clos longs cils [implorant] bing silence hop
achevé.

PING

All known all white bare white body fixed one yard legs joined like sewn. Light heat
white floor one square yard never seen. White walls one yard by two white ceiling
one square yard never seen. Bare white body fixed only the eyes only just. Traces
blurs light grey almost white on white. Hands hanging palms front white feet heels
together right angle. Light heat white planes shining white bare white body fixed
ping fixed elsewhere. Traces blurs signs no meaning light grey almost white. Bare
white body fixed white on white invisible. Only the eyes only just light blue almost
white. Head haught eyes light blue almost white silence within. Brief murmurs only
just almost never all known. Traces blurs signs no meaning light grey almost white. Legs

joined like sewn heels together right angle. Traces alone unover given black light grey almost white on white. Light heat white walls shining white one yard by two. Bare white body fixed one yard ping fixed elsewhere. Traces blurs signs no meaning light grey almost white. White feet toes joined like sewn heels together right angle invisible. Eyes alone unover given blue light blue almost white. Murmur only just almost never one second perhaps not alone. Given rose only just bare white body fixed one yard white on white invisible. All white all known murmurs only just almost never always the same all known. Light heat hands hanging palms front white on white invisible. Bare white body fixed ping fixed elsewhere. Only the eyes only just light blue almost white fixed front. Ping murmur only just almost never one second perhaps a way out. Head haught eyes light blue almost white fixed front ping murmur ping silence. Eyes holes light blue almost white mouth white seam like sewn invisible. Ping murmur perhaps a nature one second almost never that much memory almost never. White walls each its trace grey blur signs no meaning light grey almost white. Light heat all known all white planes meeting invisible. Ping murmur only just almost never one second perhaps a meaning that much memory almost never. White feet toes joined like sewn heels together right angle ping elsewhere no sound. Hands hanging palms front legs joined like sewn. Head haught eyes holes light blue almost white fixed front silence within. Ping elsewhere always there but that known not. Eyes holes light blue alone unover given blue light blue almost white only colour fixed front. All white all known white planes shining white ping murmur only just almost never one second light time that much memory almost never. Bare white body fixed one yard ping fixed elsewhere white on white invisible heart breath no sound. Only the eyes given blue light blue almost white fixed front only colour alone unover. Planes meeting invisible one only shining white infinite but that known not. Nose ears white holes mouth white seam like sewn invisible. Ping murmurs only just almost never one second always the same all known. Given rose only just bare white body fixed one yard invisible all known without within. Ping perhaps a nature one second with image same time a little less blue and white in the wind. White ceiling shining white one square yard never seen ping perhaps way out there one second ping silence. Traces alone unover given black grey blurs signs no meaning light grey almost white always the same. Ping perhaps not alone one second with image always the same same time a little less that much memory almost never ping silence. Given rose only just nails fallen white over. Long hair fallen white invisible over. White scars invisible same white as flesh torn of old given rose only just. Ping image only just almost never one second light time blue and white in the wind. Head haught nose ears white holes mouth white seam like sewn invisible over. Only the eyes given blue fixed front light blue almost white only colour alone unover. Light heat white planes shining white one only shining white infinite but that known not. Ping a nature only just almost never one second with image same time a little less blue and white in the wind. Traces blurs light grey eyes holes light blue almost white fixed front ping a meaning only just almost never ping silence. Bare white one yard fixed ping fixed elsewhere no sound legs joined like sewn heels together right angle hands hanging palms front. Head haught eyes holes light blue almost white fixed front silence within. Ping elsewhere always there but that known not. Ping perhaps not alone one second with image same time a little less dim eye black and white half closed long lashes imploring that much memory almost never. Afar flash of time all white all over all of old ping flash white walls shining white no trace eyes holes light blue almost white last colour ping white over. Ping fixed last elsewhere legs joined like sewn heels together right angle hands hanging palms front head haught eyes white invisible fixed front over. Given rose only just one yard invisible bare white all known without within over. White ceiling never seen ping of old only just almost never one second light time white floor never seen ping of old perhaps there. Ping of old only just perhaps a meaning a nature one second almost never blue and white in the wind that much memory henceforth never. White planes no trace shining white one only shining white infinite but that known not. Light heat all known all white heart breath no sound. Head haught eyes white fixed front old ping last murmur one second perhaps not alone eye unlustrous black and white half closed long lashes imploring ping silence ping over.

(Translated from the French by the author)

Appendix III

Appendix IV

Periodicals and Newspapers
in Which Works of Samuel Beckett
and Criticism of His Work
Have Appeared

Periodicals

Accent (Urbana, Ill.)
Action (New York)
L'Age Nouveau (Paris)
Akzente (Munich)
America (New York)
American Scholar (New York)
Annales Publiées par la Faculté des Lettres de Toulouse, Littératures (Toulouse)
Die Anregung (Munich)
Antares (Baden-Baden, Germany)
L'Arc (Aix-en-Provence, France)
Archiv für das Studium der Neueren Sprachen (Brunswick, Germany)
Arizona Quarterly (Tucson, Ariz.)
Arna (Sydney, Australia)
Artaban (Paris)
Arts-Spectacles (became *Arts*) (Paris)
Aspects (Brussels)
Atoll (Freiburg im Breisgau, Germany)
Audience (Cambridge, Mass.)
AUMLA (*Journal of the Australasian Language and Literature Association*) (Christchurch, New Zealand)
Aut Aut (Milan)
L'Avant-Scène (*L'Avant-Scène/Fémina Théâtre* became *L'Avant-Scène du Théâtre*; now *L'Avant-Scène*) (Paris)

Belfagor (Florence)
Biennale di Venezia (Venice)
Blätter der Gesellschaft für Christliche Kultur (Düsseldorf)
Bonniers Litterära Magasin (Stockholm)
Book Collector (London)
The Bookman (London)

Books Abroad (Oklahoma University, Norman, Okla.)
Books and Bookmen (London)
Bookweek (Chicago)
British Book News (London)
Bucknell Review (Lewisburg, Pa.)
Bühnen der Stadt Köln: Programmheft (Cologne)
Bulletin Critique du Livre Français (Paris)
Bulletin de l'Université de Toulouse (Toulouse)
Bulletin des Jeunes Romanistes (Strasbourg, France)
Bulletin des Lettres (Lyon)

Cahiers d'Art (Paris)
Les Cahiers d'Art—Documents (Geneva)
Cahiers de la Compagnie Madeleine Renaud–Jean-Louis Barrault (Paris)
Cahiers des Saisons (Paris)
Cahiers du Sud (Marseille)
Caliban: Annales Publiées par la Faculté des Lettres et Sciences Humaines (Toulouse)
Cambridge Opinion (Cambridge, Engl.)
Cambridge Quarterly (Cambridge, Engl.)
Canadian Forum (Toronto, Ont.)
Catholic World (New York)
Cenobio (Lugano, Switzerland)
Centennial Review of Arts and Sciences (Michigan State University, East Lansing, Mich.)
Chelsea Review (New York)
Chicago Books on Trial (Chicago)
Chicago Review (University of Chicago, Chicago)
Choice (New York)

Christian Century (now *Cosmopolitan*)
  (Chicago)
Christian Scholar (New York and
  Somerville, N. J.)
College English (Chicago)
Colorado Quarterly (Boulder, Colo.)
Columbia University Forum (New York)
Commonweal (New York)
Comparative Literature (University of
  Oregon, Eugene, Ore.)
Comparative Literature Studies (formerly
  College Park, Md.; now University of
  Illinois, Urbana, Ill.)
Contempo (Chapel Hill, N.C.)
Convivium (Turin)
The Criterion (London)
The Critic (London)
Critical Quarterly (London)
Criticism (Wayne State University,
  Detroit, Mich.)
Critique (Paris)
Critique: Studies in Modern Fiction
  (Minneapolis, Minn.)
Crosscurrents (New York)
Cue (New York)
Culture (Quebec)

Daedalus (American Academy of Arts
  and Sciences, Cambridge, Mass.)
Dalhousie Review (Halifax, Nova
  Scotia)
Delta (Cambridge, England)
Derrière le Miroir (Galerie Maeght,
  Paris)
Descant (Texas Christian University,
  Fort Worth, Tex.)
Dionysos (Rio de Janeiro)
Le Disque Vert (Paris and Brussels)
Dissertation Abstracts (Ann Arbor, Mich.)
Drama (London)
Drama Critique (Lancaster, N. Y.)
Drama Survey (Minneapolis, Minn.)
*Die Drei: Zeitschrift für Anthroposophie
  und Dreigliederung* (Stuttgart)
Dublin Magazine (Dublin)
Durham University Journal (Durham,
  England)

Eckart (Witten, Germany)
Écrits de Paris (Paris)
Educational Theatre Journal (Ann Arbor,
  Mich.)
Encore (London)

Encounter (London)
English (London)
Envoy (Dublin)
Esprit (Paris)
L'Esprit Créateur (Minneapolis, Minn.)
Essays in Criticism (Oxford)
Études (Paris)
Études Anglaises (Paris)
L'Europa Letteraria (Rome)
Europe (Paris)
The European (London)
Evergreen Review (New York)

La Fiera Letteraria (Rome)
Film (Woking, England)
Film Quarterly (University of Cali-
  fornia, Berkeley, Calif.)
Florida Review (Tallahassee, Fla.)
Fontaine (Paris)
Forum (Texas University, Houston, Tex.)
Forum (Vienna)
Le Français dans le Monde (Paris)
French Review (New York)
French Studies (Oxford)
From the Fifties (BBC, London)

La Gazette des Lettres (Paris)
Germanisch-Romanische Monatsschrift
  (Heidelberg)
The Griffin (New York)

Harvard Theological Review (Cam-
  bridge, Mass.)
Hochland (Munich)
Horizon (London)
Hudson Review (New York)
Humanities (Humanities Association of
  Canada) (University of Western
  Ontario, London, Ont.)

Icarus (Dublin University, Dublin)
Idea (Rome)
Illustrated London News (London)
Indice de Artes y Letras (Madrid)
Irish Digest (Dublin)
Irish Writing (Cork, Ireland)
L'Italia che Scrive (Rome)

Journal of Aesthetics and Art Criticism
  (New York)
Journal of Analytical Psychology
  (London)

Journal of Bible and Religion (Wolcott, N. Y.)
Journal of General Education (University of Chicago, Chicago)
Journal of Social Issues (New York)

Kenyon Review (Gambier, Ohio)
Kerygma (Göttingen)
Kilkenny Magazine (Dublin)
Knjizevnost (Belgrade, Yugoslavia)
Kroniek van Kunst en Kultuur (Amsterdam)

Les Langues Modernes (Paris)
Left-Wing (Leeds, England)
Letterature Moderne (Bologna)
Lettres Françaises (Paris)
Les Lettres Nouvelles (Paris)
Liberté (Montreal)
Library Journal (New York)
Life (Chicago)
The Listener (London)
Literatur Kompassen Stockholms Tidnigen (Stockholm)
Litterair Paspoort (Amsterdam)
Livres de France (Paris)
London Bulletin (formerly *London Gallery Bulletin*) (London)
London Magazine (London)
L'VII [i.e., *Le Sept*] (Brussels)

Marginales (Brussels)
Marxism Today (London)
Maske und Kothurn (Cologne)
Massachusetts Review (Amherst, Mass.)
Meanjin (Melbourne, Australia)
Médecine de France (Paris)
Médiations (Paris)
Memoirs and Proceedings of the Manchester Literary and Philosophical Society (Manchester, England)
Mercure de France (Paris)
Merkur (Stuttgart)
Merlin (*Merlin: The Paris Quarterly*) (Paris)
Minnesota Review (Minneapolis, Minn.)
Modern Drama (University of Kansas, Lawrence, Kan.)
Modern Fiction Studies (Department of English, Purdue University, Lafayette, Ind.)
Modern Language Forum (Los Angeles)
Modern Language Journal (New York)

Modern Language Notes (Baltimore, Md.)
Modern Language Quarterly (Seattle, Wash.)
Modern Language Review (Cambridge, England)
Monde Nouveau/Paru (Paris)
Nation (Sydney, Australia)
The Nation (New York)
National Review (New York)
La Nef (Paris)
Neue Deutsche Hefte (Gütersloh, Germany)
Die Neue Rundschau (Berlin)
Neue Schweizer Rundschau (Zurich)
Neue Zürcher Zeitung (Zurich)
Neueren Sprachen (Marburg)
New Departures (South Hinksey [near Oxford], England)
New Durham (Durham University, Durham, England)
New English Weekly (London)
New Hungarian Quarterly (Budapest)
New Leader (New York)
New Mexico Quarterly (Albuquerque, N.M.)
New Republic (New York)
The New Review (Paris)
New Statesman (London)
New Statesman and Nation (London)
Newsweek (Dayton, Ohio)
New World Writing (New York)
New Yorker (New York)
New York Review of Books (New York)
Nimbus (Bolivia)
Nô (Fleurier, Switzerland)
Northwestern Review (renamed *United States Review*) (Chicago, Ill.)
Northwest Review (Winnipeg)
Nottingham French Studies (Nottingham, England)
Nouvelle Revue Française (formerly *Nouvelle Nouvelle Revue Française*) (Paris)
Le Nouvel Observateur (Paris)
Novel: Forum on Fiction (Brown University, Providence, R.I.)
Nya Argus (Helsinki, Finland)

Ord Och Bild (Stockholm)
L'Osservatore Politico Letterario (Rome and Milan)
Paraboles (Paris)
Paris-Match (Paris)

Paris-Théâtre (Paris)
Parnasso (Helsinki, Finland)
Partisan Review (New York)
The Personalist (University of Southern
  California, Los Angeles, Calif.)
Perspective (Washington University,
  St. Louis, Mo.)
Plays and Players (London)
PMLA (*Publications of the Modern
  Language Association of America*)
  (New York)
Poetry (Chicago)
Poetry Ireland (Cork, Ireland)
Points (Paris)
Il Ponte (Rome)
Prairie Schooner (Lincoln, Neb.)
Preuves (Paris)
Primer Acto (Madrid)
Programm des Schlosspark-Theater
  (Berlin)
Prompt (University College Dramatic
  Association, London)
Provinz (Frankfort on the Main)

Quarterly Journal of Speech (Chicago)
Queen's Quarterly (Kingston, Ont.)
La Quinzaine Littéraire (Paris)

Radio Times (London)
Recent French Books (New York)
Religion in Life (New York)
Renascence (St. Mary-of-the-Woods, Ind.)
The Reporter (New York)
Revista de la Universidad de Madrid
  (Madrid)
Revista de Ideas Estéticas (Madrid)
La Revue de la Pensée Française (Paris)
Revue de Littérature Comparée (Paris)
La Revue de l'Université Laval (Quebec)
La Revue de Paris (Paris)
Revue des Deux Mondes (Paris)
La Revue des Lettres Modernes (Paris)
Revue Générale Belge (Brussels)
La Revue Nouvelle (Paris)
Romance Notes (University of North
  Carolina, Chapel Hill, N.C.)
Romanic Review (Columbia University,
  New York)

Samtiden (Bergen and Oslo, Norway)
Saturday Review of Literature (New
  York)
Scene (London)

Schauspielgruppe Dr. Elrod (Sanatorium
  Bellevue, Kreuzlingen, Switzerland)
Schismes (Brussels)
Sewanee Review (Sewanee, Tenn.)
Shenandoah (Luray, Va.)
Show (New York)
Signes du Temps (Paris)
Sinn und Form (Potsdam, Germany)
Il Sipario (Milan)
Sixty-One (Leeds, England)
Soutes (*Soutes: Revue de Culture
  Révolutionnaire Internationale*) (Paris)
South Atlantic Quarterly (Durham, N.C.)
Southerly (Sydney, Australia)
Southwest Review (Austin and Dallas,
  Tex.)
Spectrum (Goleta, Calif.)
Der Spiegel (Hanover)
Stand (Leeds, England)
Studies in Literature (Brooklyn College,
  Broolyn, N.Y.)
Studies in Short Fiction (Newberry, S.C.)
Studi Romani (Rome)
Sur (Buenos Aires)
Symposium (Syracuse University, Syra-
  cuse, N.Y.)
Synthèses (Brussels)

La Table Ronde (Paris)
The Tablet (London)
T.C.D.: A College Miscellany (Trinity
  College, Dublin)
The Teacher (now *Current Education*)
  (Philadelphia, Pa.)
Tel Quel (Paris)
Tempo Presente (Madrid)
Les Temps Modernes (Paris)
Terre Humaine (Paris)
Texas Quarterly (Austin, Tex.)
*Texas Studies in Literature and Lan-
  guage* (Austin, Tex.)
Texte und Zeichen (Berlin)
Theater der Stadt Bonn (Bonn)
Theater der Zeit (Berlin)
Theater Heute (Hanover)
Théâtre d'Aujourd'hui (Paris)
Theatre Arts (New York)
Théâtre Populaire (Paris)
Theatre Research (Florence, later
  London)
Theatre Unit Bulletin (Bombay)
Theology Today (Princeton, N.J.)
This Quarter (Paris)

Threshold (Belfast, Ireland)
Thought (Delhi)
Thought (Fordham University, N.Y.)
Le Thyrse (Brussels)
Time (New York)
Time and Tide (London)
Tomorrow (Oxford)
Transactions of the Wisconsin Academy of Sciences, Arts and Letters (Madison, Wisc.)
Transatlantic Review (Rome, N.Y.)
Transition (Paris)
Transition: A Quarterly Review (The Hague)
Transition: Tenth Anniversary (Neuilly-sur-Seine, France)
Trinity News (Dublin)
Tulane Drama Review (New Orleans, La.)
Twentieth Century (London)

University of Kansas City Review (Kansas City, Mo.)

Venture (New York)
Il Verri (Milan)
Verve (Paris)
Vinduet (Oslo, Norway)
Virginia Quarterly Review (University of Virginia, Charlottesville, Va.)
De Vlaamse Gids (Antwerp)
Vogue (New York)
Volksbühnen-Spiegel (Berlin)

Weekend Telegraph Magazine (London)
Die Welt (Vienna)
Welt und Wort (Tübingen)
Weltwoche (Zurich)
Western Humanities Review (University of Utah, Salt Lake City, Utah)
Westwind (formerly *Chimera*) (University of California, Los Angeles)
Wisconsin Studies in Contemporary Literature (University of Wisconsin, Madison, Wisc.)
World Theater (Brussels)

X: A Quarterly Review (London)

Yale French Studies (New Haven, Conn.)
Yale Review (New Haven, Conn.)

Newspapers

ABC (Madrid)
Action (Paris)
Aftonbladet (Stockholm)
Algemeen Handelsblad (Amsterdam)
Amherst Student (Amherst, Mass.)
Arriba (Madrid)
Associated Press (i.e., *AP World*) (New York)
L'Aurore (Paris)
The Australian (Canberra, Australia)

Basler Nachrichten (Basel)
Beaux-Arts (Brussels)
Bel-Abbès Journal (Bel-Abbès, Algeria)
Belfast News Letter (Belfast, Ireland)
Berkeley Daily Gazette (Berkeley, Calif.)
Berliner Morgenpost (Berlin)
Berlingske Aftenavis (Copenhagen)
Berlingske Tidende (Copenhagen)
Birmingham Post (Birmingham, Engl.)
Boston Traveler (Boston, Mass.)
Bridgeport Sunday Post (Bridgeport, Conn.)
The Bulletin (Sydney, Australia)
Der Bund (Bern)

Cahiers de la République (Paris)
Le Canard Enchaîné (Paris)
Carrefour (Paris)
Cherwell (Oxford)
Chicago Tribune (Chicago, Ill.)
Christian Science Monitor (Boston, Mass.)
Cincinnati Enquirer (Cincinnati, Ohio)
La Cité (Brussels)
Clarín (Buenos Aires)
Cleveland News (Cleveland, Ohio)
Cleveland Plain Dealer (Cleveland, Ohio)
Cleveland Press (Cleveland, Ohio)
Columbia Record (Columbia, S.C).
Combat (Paris)
Corriere della Sera (Milan)
La Croix (Paris)
Cyprus Mail (Nicosia, Cyprus)

Dagens Nyheter (Stockholm)
Daily Express (London)
Daily Herald (London)
Daily Mail (London)
Daily Telegraph (London)
Daily Worker (New York)

Dallas Times Herald (Dallas, Tex.)
The Day: Jewish Journal (New York)
Democrat Chronicle (Rochester, N.Y.)
Démocratie 61 (Paris)
La Dépêche du Midi (Toulouse)
Diário Popular (Lisbon, Portugal)
Donau Zeitung (Dillingen)
Düsseldorfer Nachrichten (Düsseldorf)

Eastern Daily Press (Norwich, England)
L'Écho de Lyon (Lyons)
L'École Libératrice (Paris)
Ekstrabladet (Copenhagen)
Elseviers Weekblad (Amsterdam)
Ercilla (Santiago de Chile)
España de Tánger (Tangier)
Evening Herald (Dublin)
Evening Standard (London)
Evening Star (Washington, D.C.)
L'Express (Paris)
Expressen (Stockholm)

Le Figaro (Paris)
Le Figaro Littéraire (Paris)
Fort Lauderdale News and Sentinel (Fort
    Lauderdale, Fla.)
France-Asie (Saigon)
France-Observateur (Paris)
France-Soir (Paris)
Franc-Tireur (Paris)
Frankfurter Allgemeine Zeitung (Frank-
    fort on the Main)

Gazette de Lausanne (Lausanne)
Gazette of the Arts in Louisville (Louis-
    ville, Ky.)
Il Gazzettino Venezia (Venice)
Il Giorno (Milan)
*Göteborgs Handels-och Sjöfarts-
    Tidningen* (Göteborg, Sweden)
Göteborgs-Posten (Göteborg, Sweden)
Grenier de Toulouse (Toulouse)
De Groene Amsterdammer (Amsterdam)
The Guardian (London)

Haagsche Courant (The Hague)
Het Parool (Amsterdam)
Het Vaderland (The Hague)
High Point Enterprise (High Point, N.C.)
Honolulu Advertiser (Honolulu)

Incom (Rome)
Informaciones (Buenos Aires)

L'Informateur Critique (Paris)
Information (Holland)
L'Information (Paris)
Irish Independent (Dublin)
Irish Press (Dublin)
Irish Times (Dublin)
Isis (Oxford)
L'Italia (Milan)

Jerusalem Post (Jerusalem)
Jornal do Brasil (Rio de Janeiro)
Journal d'Anvers (Antwerp)
Journal de Genève (Geneva)
Journal Musical Français (Paris)
Journal Northwest Living Magazine

Ka Leo O Hawaii (Honolulu)
Kansas City Star (Kansas City, Kan.)
Kölner S.-A. (Cologne)
Kurier (Berlin)

Libération (Paris)
La Libre Belgique (Brussels)
Le Libre Poitou (Poitiers, France)
Liens (Monte Carlo)
De Linnie (Amsterdam)
Liverpool Daily Post (Liverpool,
    England)
London Free Press (London)

Madrid (Madrid)
Manchester Guardian (Manchester,
    England), later *The Guardian*
    (London) [see above]
Manchester Guardian Weekly (Man-
    chester, England)
La Métropole (Antwerp)
México News Weekly (México, D.F.)
Miami News (Miami, Fla.)
Midi Libre (Montpellier, France)
Milwaukee Sentinel (Milwaukee, Wisc.)
Der Mittag (Düsseldorf)
Le Monde (Paris)
Le Monde Hebdomadaire (Paris)
Il Mondo (Rome)
Morgen (Berlin)
Münchner Merkur (Munich)

Nacht-Depesche (Berlin)
La Nación (Buenos Aires)
La Nation Française (Paris)
Neue Berner Nachrichten (Bern)
Neue Rhein-Zeitung (Aachen, Germany)

Newark Evening News (Newark, N.J.)
Newhaven Journal Courier (New Haven, Conn.)
News Chronicle (London)
New York Daily News (New York)
New Yorker Staats-Zeitung und Herold (New York)
New York Herald Tribune (New York)
New York Herald Tribune (European edition) (Paris)
New York Herald Tribune Book Week (New York)
New York Journal-American (New York)
New York Mirror (New York)
New York Post (New York)
New York Times (New York)
New York Times Book Review (New York)
New York Times Magazine (New York)
Nieuwe Rotterdamse Courant (Rotterdam)
Nin (Belgrade)
Les Nouvelles Littéraires (Paris)
Ny Tid (Göteborg, Sweden)

Oakland Tribune (Oakland, Calif.)
L'Observateur (Paris)
L'Observateur du Moyen-Orient et de l'Afrique (Paris and Cairo)
The Observer (London)
Oswego County Weeklies (Oswego, N.Y.)
Oxford Magazine (Oxford)
Oxford Times (Oxford)

Paese Sera (Rome)
Paris-Casablanca (Paris and Casablanca)
Le Parisien Libéré (Paris)
Paris-Normandie (Rouen)
Paris-Presse (Paris)
People's World (San Francisco)
Le Phare (Brussels)
Politiken (Copenhagen)
Il Popolo (Rome and Milan)
Pour Tous (Lausanne)
La Prensa (Buenos Aires)
La Presse-Tunisie (Tunis)
Le Progrès (Lyon)
Le Provençal (Marseille)
Pueblo (Madrid)
Punch (London)

Le Rassemblement (Rennes, France)
Il Reporter (Rome)

Rheinische Post (Düsseldorf)
Rheinischer Merkur (Cologne)
Richmond Times-Dispatch (Richmond, Va.)
Rivarol (Paris)
Rives d'azur (Monte Carlo)
Roma-Napoli (Rome and Napoli)
Le Rouge et Le Noir (Marseille)

St. Louis Post Dispatch (St. Louis, Mo.)
Samedi Soir (Paris)
San Antonio Express and News (San Antonio, Tex.)
San Francisco Chronicle (San Francisco)
San Francisco Examiner (San Francisco)
San Francisco News Call Bulletin (San Francisco)
San Francisco Sunday Chronicle (San Francisco)
San Quentin News (San Quentin Prison, Calif.)
Saturday Star Bulletin (Honolulu)
The Scotsman (Edinburgh)
Semeur Vaudois (Lausanne)
Sienna News (Loudonville, N.Y.)
Socialist Leader (London)
Le Soir (Brussels)
Sonntagsblatt (Hamburg)
The Spectator (London)
La Stampa (Turin)
De Standaard (Brussels)
Steamboat Pilot
Stockholms Tidningen (Stockholm)
Student Voice (Atlanta, Ga.)
Süddeutsche Zeitung (Munich)
Sud-Ouest (Bordeaux, Toulouse ed.)
Sunday Dispatch (London)
Sunday News (New York)
Sunday Times (London)

Der Tagesspiegel (Berlin)
Die Tat (Zurich)
The Tatler (London)
Telegraf (Berlin)
Télé-magazine (Paris)
Télérama (Paris)
Témoignage Chrétien (Paris)
Il Tempo (Milan and Rome)
This World (New York)
De Tijd (Amsterdam)
Times Educational Supplement (London)
Times Literary Supplement (London)
The Times (London)

Times Picayune (New Orleans, La.)
Times-Union (Albany, N.Y.)
Town and Village (New York)
Tribune de Genève (Geneva)
Tribune de Lausanne (Lausanne)
Tribune des Nations (Paris)
Truth (Sydney, Australia)
Tworczosc (Warsaw, Poland)

Uniontown Herald (Uniontown, Pa.)
L'Unità (Milan)

The Villager (New York)

The Village Voice (New York)
Virginian Pilot (Norfolk, Va.)

Wall Street Journal (New York)
Washington Daily News (Washington, D.C.)
Washington Post and Times Herald (Washington, D.C.)
Winnipeg Tribune (Winnipeg, Canada)
Women's Wear Daily (New York)
World Telegram and Sun (New York)

Die Zeit (Hamburg)

Index

Index

This index refers to items by number and comprises five sections:

1. *Names:* Lists all persons (authors, translators, directors, actors, illustrators, photographers, etc.) mentioned in this bibliography who have written on or have been connected with Beckett and his works, or have been discussed in connection with his works.
2. *Samuel Beckett's Works:* Lists all references to individual works; main entry or entries are in boldface.
3. *Samuel Beckett:* Lists all references to items in Part II devoted to Beckett's life, his works in general, his theater, fiction, poetry, criticism, and various other aspects of his literary activities.
4. *Periodicals and Collections:* Lists those mentioned in Part I in which Beckett's works have appeared.
5. *Publishers and Printers:* Lists those connected with Beckett's works as listed in Part I.

1. NAMES

Abbey, Edward, **1475**
Abel, Lionel, 1055, **1476**
Abirached, Robert, 1022, 1527, 1575, 1767, 1768, 2871
Acton, Harold, 6
Adam, Georges, 2449
Adamov, Arthur, 1200, 1373, 1388, 1507, 1544, 1597, 1598, 1685, 2562, 2575
Adet, Georges, 265
Adorno, Theodor W., 1024
Aholas, J., 2020
Albee, Edward, 1720, 1730, 1733, 1806, 1850
Albérès, René Marill, 1032, 1161, 1177, 2450, 2576
Albert-Hesse, Jean, 1935
Aldington, Richard, 5, 5 n., 6, 7 n., 44, 2869

Allen, Louis, 2769
Allen, Paul, 2850
Allen, Ralph G., 1213
Alley, J. N., 1705
Allsop, Kenneth, 1006, 2260
Alpaugh, David J., 904, 1857
Alter, André, 2145, 2451, 2656, 2657
Alvarez, A., 1653, 2452
Alwes, Betty, 2261
Anders, Günther, 711, 1002, 1324
Anderson, Jack, 2577
Anderson, Stan, 2262
Anex, Georges, 1977, 2453
Angeli, Siro, 1426
Angus, William, 1706
Anouilh, Jean, 1003, 1013, 1050, 1215, 1306, 1353, 1446, 1498, 1555

2. SAMUEL BECKETT'S WORKS

3. SAMUEL BECKETT

Balzac, Honoré de, and Beckett, 1003, 1340, 1659, 1723, 1757

Bibliographical references, 716, 864, 865, 900, 902, 1486, 1773, 3100-3141

Biographical data, 703, 719, 730, 1028, 1049, 1070, 1072, 1102, 1132, 1243, 1336, 1377, 1463, 1486, 1491, 1576, 1581, 1599, 1641, 1781, 2014, 2159, 2332, 2337, 2885, 2889, 3050-3095

Criticism, Beckett's, 1814, 1847, 1849, 3024

Dante, Alighieri, and Beckett, 712, 718, 1051, 1336, 1520, 1539, 1771, 1786, 1791, 1805, 1822, 1844. *See also* Dante, Alighieri, in section 1 of index

Descartes, René, and Beckett, 703, 711 (Kenner), 712, 900 (Kenner, Mintz), 1499, 1513, 1558, 1725, 1780, 1843. *See also* Descartes, René, in section 1 of index

Fiction, Beckett's, in general, 707, 708, 712, 721, 722, 723, 724, 725, 802, 805, 806, 809, 851, 859, 860, 861, 1011, 1032, 1035, 1037, 1041, 1045, 1051, 1058, 1059, 1060, 1066, 1067, 1073, 1304, 1335, 1361, 1387, 1390, 1408, 1415, 1419, 1432, 1452, 1453, 1456, 1470, 1483, 1485, 1492, 1493, 1496, 1500, 1509, 1510, 1540, 1548, 1549, 1550, 1551, 1556, 1557, 1562, 1579, 1583, 1585, 1603, 1607, 1609, 1621, 1623, 1660, 1668, 1671, 1672, 1675, 1676, 1682, 1684, 1693, 1695, 1700, 1728, 1752, 1765, 1789, 1796, 1800, 1801, 1805, 1842, 1859, 1880, 2024, 2393, 2501, 2582, 2621, 2662, 2708, 2718, 2742

Humor in Beckett's works, 702, 704, 706, 711 (Nadeau), 800, 1047, 1622, 1874

Ionesco, Eugène, and Beckett, 852, 853, 1020, 1050, 1064, 1077, 1147, 1352, 1373, 1388, 1412, 1429, 1458, 1466, 1490, 1504, 1507, 1524, 1544, 1555, 1597, 1598, 1629, 1650, 1655, 1658, 1677, 1685, 1686, 1720, 1730, 1732, 1778, 1803, 1806, 1808, 1812, 1819, 1820, 1850, 1863, 2251, 2387, 2581, 2637, 2653, 2687, 2805, 2847. *See also* Ionesco, Eugène, in section 1 of index

Joyce, James, and Beckett, 1005, 1013, 1029, 1037, 1042, 1045, 1055, 1100, 1108, 1110, 1115, 1116, 1125, 1128, 1138, 1205, 1208, 1234, 1300, 1305,

1336, 1341, 1348, 1363, 1377, 1439, 1459, 1476, 1483, 1492, 1516, 1548, 1622, 1682, 1694, 1752, 1791, 1847, 1874, 2396, 2846. *See also* Joyce, James, in section 1 of index

Kafka, Franz, and Beckett, 1005, 1037, 1052, 1107, 1304, 1336, 1377, 1419, 1476, 1543, 1549, 1595, 1694. *See also* Kafka, Franz, in section 1 of index

Language, Beckett and, 700, 715, 731, 1028, 1547, 1596, 1612, 1871, 1872, 2590

Philosophy, Beckett and, 711 (Cohn), 718, 1406, 1497, 1539, 1710, 1725, 1780, 1843

Poetry, Beckett's, 709, 711 (Fletcher), 719 (Esslin), 902 (Harvey), 1407, 1788, 1794, 1798, 1823, 1917, 1919, 2452, 2557, 2583, 2585, 2591, 2593, 2594, 2595, 2601, 2627, 2668, 2734, 2743, 2829, 3006, 3009

Proust, Marcel, and Beckett, 700, 1028, 1081, 1407, 1459, 1492, 1548, 1615, 1705, 1714, 1775, 1787, 1847, 1877, 2543, 2781, 2807, 2849. *See also* Proust, Marcel, in section 1 of index

Shakespeare, William, and Beckett, 1044, 1084, 1331, 1394, 1397, 1471, 1687, 1711, 1712, 1802, 1832, 1838

Swift, Jonathan, and Beckett, 902 (Kern), 1021, 1047, 1348, 1622, 1670, 1801, 1822, 1830, 1874

Theater, Beckett's, in general, 701, 717, 729, 807, 850, 852, 853, 856, 857, 862, 863, 903, 904, 1008, 1009, 1013, 1015, 1018, 1019, 1020, 1025, 1027, 1030, 1031, 1033, 1036, 1038, 1044, 1046, 1048, 1049, 1050, 1055, 1056, 1057, 1058, 1064, 1065, 1068, 1069, 1074, 1075, 1076, 1077, 1081, 1084, 1160, 1310, 1325, 1327, 1328, 1338, 1342, 1352, 1358, 1371, 1373, 1384, 1401, 1406, 1412, 1422, 1446, 1454, 1494, 1504, 1508, 1529, 1534, 1544, 1545, 1555, 1561, 1567, 1597, 1602, 1629, 1650, 1655, 1664, 1677, 1678, 1685, 1697, 1698, 1720, 1724, 1730, 1745, 1803, 1804, 1812, 1828, 1852, 1854, 1861, 1867, 1873, 2017, 2040, 2061, 2138, 2166, 2248, 2251, 2256, 2271, 2276, 2387, 2448, 2459, 2473, 2476, 2516, 2527, 2528, 2551, 2562, 2575, 2581, 2592, 2619, 2649, 2657, 2664,

4. PERIODICALS AND COLLECTIONS

5. PUBLISHERS AND PRINTERS